SUSAN KAY

She has a spirit full of incantation.
SIMON RENARD

Crown Publishers, Inc.
New York

For my husband, who encouraged
me to complete this book

ACKNOWLEDGMENTS

I am indebted to Mrs Jane Barton for her meticulous typing
of my manuscript.

Manufactured in the United States of America

AUTHOR'S NOTE

When portraying characters and incidents based on recorded historical facts I have tried to be as accurate as possible, with one notable exception. Henry Ratcliffe and Thomas Ratcliffe, both Earls of Sussex, were actually father and son; but, for the purposes of dramatic cohesion, I have condensed the two into one character. Also, the reader will find Edward Seymour introduced on his first appearance in the text as the Earl of Hertford. This title did not actually become his until later in the reign of Henry VIII. Several major characters were elevated following Henry's death and it seemed inappropriate to alter the elder Seymour's title twice within such a relatively short space of narrative.

CONTENTS

England
in the Time of
Elizabeth I

NORTH SEA

Syderstone

Chartley
Avon
Kenilworth

Great Ouse
Little Ouse
Cam
Waveney

Framlingham

Woodstock
Ashridge

Stour
Ipswich

Hatfield
Cheshunt

Thames

Whitehall
Chelsea
Hanworth
Windsor
Richmond
Kew
Hampton
Court

Wanstead
Tower of London
Thames

Placentia
at Greenwich

Wolf Hall

Titchfield
Manor

ISLE OF
WIGHT

ENGLISH CHANNEL

FRANCE

0   10   20   30   40   50 MILES

PROLOGUE

He was only a small rat, but bolder than most, with a disproportionately long tail which curled behind him on the stone floor, losing itself in the half-gloom of a solitary candle's light.

The crumbs of bread and stale marchpane, which had first tempted him out into danger, were long since finished. But still he sat there furtively, listening to the rain which teemed down the rough glass windows and drummed into the dirty moat outside the fortress. Black eyes, like polished buttons, gleaming yet opaque, nose quivering with the pungent tang of human scent, he sat and watched a shadowy prey. Young and female, it would be sweet between his teeth if only he dared to bite. But he did not dare, not yet; he was uncertain.

Once, in a darker, deeper cell than this, he had eaten away the entire face of a young boy on death's helpless threshold. It had been enough to teach him that human flesh was better warm and void of decay; and now that dangerous craving inched him forward against the warning note of instinct. All his sharply defined senses told him that *this* victim was still dangerously alert. And yet there was an utter immobility which lulled him, drawing him ever closer in the faint, hungry hope that he might have been mistaken.

She sat on a low stone window-seat, wrapped in a cloak against the creeping cold and, like the solitary stone pillar that supported the roof, she might have been carved in that pose out of stone. She sat staring out of the window into the courtyard below, straining her eyes to see the yawning cavern that was the Tower's main gateway.

The gate was her lodestone. Night and day it drew her to the stone-hooded window, and there was a starkly simple reason for her obsession. She had not entered beneath that archway and had even less hope of leaving by it. Through Traitor's Gate she had come to this 'very narrow place', a grim fortress which had swallowed up so many lives—one of them, her mother's.

Her long legs were drawn up beneath her chin, and a crumpled sheet of red-gold hair fell like a curtain over the arms which clasped them. She was just twenty, and had been waiting here to die for so many days that there had begun to be hours when she even forgot about it. Tonight she was well beyond her native fear of consequences, past caring about a tomorrow she had less hope of seeing than most.

Within the deeper shadows of the semi-circular room, there was a movement and a sudden shriek which sent the little piece of vermin fleeing through the stinking rushes for sanctuary.

'Hell's teeth!' said a voice from the window-seat, strong and vibrant, yet curiously soft. 'What have you seen *now*, Markham?'

Isabella Markham drew her cloak more closely round her shoulders and replied defensively. 'A rat, madam. Close enough to have bitten Your Grace.'

The girl laughed. 'The only rats I fear walk on two legs.'

'Then you ought to fear them, madam,' insisted Markham severely. 'Father swears they carry the plague.'

'There are worse deaths,' said the girl, and was silent, thinking of one.

Markham snatched up the single candle and began to beat about in the dark corners of the room with a poker. There was an agitated savagery about her movements which suggested hysteria.

'When I find his hole I shall stop it up with rags. I won't have you shut up in this filthy God-forsaken place with that—that unspeakable creature.'

'For Christ's sake, Markham, it's only a *little* rat.' The girl's voice was still amused, but suggested a touch of impatience now. 'We have them bigger than that at Hampton Court and Greenwich.'

'It's not his size that troubles me,' muttered Markham grimly. 'It's the way he watched you. Madam, it was horrible—if you had seen him . . .'

'Oh, I've seen him, several times. Bold little devil, isn't he? If he survives the attention of your poker, I shall try my hand at taming him.'

Markham straightened up and looked round with the poker suspended in her hand. 'Tame him?' she echoed, stupid with disbelief, 'You can't tame a Tower rat—they're flea-bitten and vicious.'

'So are most men!' The girl smiled and stretched her cramped limbs. 'Shall I tame one of them instead? They too make diverting pets, you know.'

Markham laughed nervously. 'Wouldn't you rather have a dog, madam?'

'Ah no—too loyal! They present no challenge.' Behind the girl's steady eyes a shadow stirred, darkening them to the hue of gleaming wet pitch. 'My mother had a dog once. She used to make it jump through a burning hoop to prove its devotion to her, until she found my father did it better. He jumped through that hoop for over six years. When he finally got tired of performing for her amusement he killed her. And that's what makes men such interesting pets, Markham—you never know when they're going to turn and bite.'

Markham sank on to the stone seat beside her, chilled into silence. Between them the candle flared in a draught, sending ripples of light over the girl's angular face.

Strictly speaking it was not a beautiful face by conventional standards, but it was curiously arresting. Elizabeth Tudor was a labyrinth. She drew people, without conscious effort, into the maze of her own personality and abandoned them there, leaving them to find their own way out again—if they could. Most found they were unable to, many never even tried. And those few who succeeded were troubled by a vague sense of loss for the rest of their days. Isabella Markham, already safely in love with a young man languishing within these same walls, would be one of those few who held a lifeline to the outer world.

She looked up and found Elizabeth's eyes upon her.

'You're cold, Belle. Go and sit by the fire before it goes out.'

Markham resisted the narcotic of her presence, that instinctive automatic inclination to obey her without question.

'I'm not cold, truly, madam.' She hesitated. 'I'm curious.'

'Curious?' Elizabeth's eyes were suddenly veiled and wary.

'About tonight—about the man you're waiting for. Is he to be no more than a pet to you?'

'Pet, playmate, partner,' said Elizabeth slowly, turning the words around in her mind as a squirrel turns a nut. 'How shall I know until he comes?'

'He's not coming now,' said Markham darkly. 'I knew it would be prevented. And to take such a risk in the first place—oh, madam, it's *so* unlike you!'

'Is it?' Again that strange, maddening smile.

'You know it is! All these years you've been so careful, ever since—' She stopped and looked away, 'Ever since the Admiral.'

Elizabeth put one hand on Markham's shoulder and tilted her chin gently upwards.

'I can only die once, however many crimes are laid to my charge. I've lived a nun's life since I was fifteen and where has all that circumspection brought me? Only here to this prison cell. Don't you see, Belle, our fate is written in the stars, we can't alter it. And if I'm to go to my mother's death this spring, *careful* is not a word I wish to take with me.'

Markham said nothing. She was very close to tears. At length she rose, curtsied and went obediently to her seat at the hearth, leaving Elizabeth to rub the black glass where her breath had misted it, and stare out again towards the river.

The sand in the hour-glass swallowed up another hour and the rats chattered in the wainscoting; beyond the brooding fortress the east wind wailed peevishly like a spoilt and fretful child.

PART ONE

The Girl

'Affection? Affection is false!'
ELIZABETH

CHAPTER 1

Her path to the Tower wound back beyond her birth, to the chance meeting of a man and a woman more than a quarter of a century before that windswept April night of her imprisonment.

It was an uneventful meeting in itself, with nothing exchanged except the electric glance of a lusty man and the coyly inviting look of an ambitious girl; yet it changed the whole course of British history. It was the beginning of a cataclysmic love affair that rocked Europe and turned all England upside down, spawning in its wake a whole new Church, but only one living child: Elizabeth.

Rank and virility had accustomed the eighth Henry to the quick surrender of eager women, and when he misread that look of promise in the black eyes of Anne Boleyn he never envisaged anything less. He would conquer and walk away, and the world would no more be concerned with the fate of Anne than it had been with a score of pretty women who, at one time or another, had provided a few diverting hours in the royal bed.

Six years later he was still waiting for that satisfaction, waiting in the humiliation of the public gaze, with the world a scandalized witness of his insane pursuit. War and religious schism hung in the balance, because a wilful young woman had put the ultimate price on her favours, and a prince, mad with desire, had sworn to pay it.

For six years the Divorce dragged through foreign universities and papal courts, while Henry hacked at the legal shackles which bound him to his wife, the Emperor's aunt, Katherine of Aragon. And all that time Anne held him at bay, alternately enticing and repulsing, changing a confident easy-going man into a monster of poisonous self-doubt and paranoia, a man unable to distinguish friends from enemies, who swept aside all opposition with a merciless hand. Late in 1532 Anne staked her fate on a final desperate gamble and surrendered the citadel; by New Year she had laid her last card on the table and won the game: she was pregnant.

Henry was aghast, amazed, overjoyed; neatly trapped, like a rabbit in a snare, between his desire for compromise with Rome, and his pressing need for the son Anne swore she carried. So an unborn child tipped the balance and Rome lost the battle with Henry's conscience. Within three months a new independent Church of England had authorized the annulment of Henry's first marriage and presided over Anne's extravagant coronation in Westminster Abbey.

Four months to go, thought Anne, as she rode through the hostile crowds, and neither the Pope's impotent threats nor the moody muttering of this ragtag and bobtail crowd could make a scrap of difference to her new state. She was Queen of England and she would rule through Henry as she had done these past six years of her scheming; if he died, she would rule through the boy now kicking vigorously beneath her heart.

When Anne went into labour that hot, still seventh of September, there was silent anticipation all over the sprawling riverside palace of Placentia at Greenwich. Tension had everyone by the throat, for friends and enemies alike of the new Queen knew how much depended on the birth of a son, the final vindication of all the ugly and unprecedented events which had led up to the 'the Concubine's' present triumph.

It was just after three in the afternoon, when the heat was at its most oppressive, that they brought the news to Henry and for a moment he refused to believe it was true. After all the frustrations, the humiliations, the risks to his power and his eternal soul—another girl to take the place of Katherine's daughter, Mary, recently bastardized to make room for a new prince.

One by one the horrors he had dared to defy rose up to hit him like separate blows. Excommunication; war; rebellion—they were words to make any Christian monarch tremble, but he had risked it all and much more for the spurious promise of a clever woman who had not been quite so clever after all. Oh yes, he could hear it already, the tittering sniggers, the self-righteous satisfaction that would attend the announcement in European courts that 'God has entirely deserted this king'.

Blood pounded through his swollen veins and throbbed hot with the urge to take the whole world in his mighty hands and crush it like a ripe fruit. They were plucking at his sleeve, asking in timid voices if he would be pleased to look upon his new daughter. As he went blindly out of the room, only pride restrained him from having the brat thrown into the river; no one must know how keenly he felt this failure to justify his own behaviour.

Anne's room was still crowded with spectators, who backed out hastily when the King entered. The child lay on a cushion on the midwife's lap, naked, bawling and still caked with blood. He paused to examine her resentfully and found her as ugly as only an unwanted new-born child could be, yet perfectly formed, infuriatingly healthy. He remembered his sons by Katherine, miserable, mewling scraps of short-lived flesh that had torn his heart with anguish. There was nothing about this child to excite his concern or his pity, and he would have turned away without another glance when a tiny flailing hand closed about his thumb and smeared him with blood—Anne's blood.

He jerked his thumb free and was about to wipe it fastidiously on his sleeveless coat when he stopped and stared at it curiously. He ran his thumb across the palm of his other hand and watched the red streak grow long and thin.

Anne's blood!

Turning his vast bulk slowly, he looked at the only woman in the kingdom who had ever dared to make him look a fool.

That familiar piquant face was pale with exhaustion, but still haughty, even in defeated terror, still held high on that white neck. Such a little neck; odd how he had never seen before how easy it would be to break or sever it. One blow was all it would take—and then—freedom, a possession he had lost more than six years ago and never missed, till now.

He felt them watching him, the sharp-eyed biddies who had tended her through the birth, old doctor Butts standing with silent reproach by her bed —yes, he must move to greet her civilly and hide his thoughts. Not yet. Another year he would give her to rectify this grievous failure—and then he would see.

Bending to kiss her cold cheek, he realized that he no longer loved her. He was like a man awakening from a drugged dream to find reality chill in his hands. It was as though he looked no longer on her face, but on her soul, finding it unlovely and grasping, touched with evil.

For years his people had said she was a witch, ensnaring him with unnatural arts, and he had dismissed the allegation as the superstitious gossip of ignorant minds. Suddenly he saw how that allegation might be useful. Seduced into marriage by foul practices of witchcraft—why, he would be innocent of all those crimes he had committed for her sake. Twelve months—not a day longer: and for a moment he passionately hoped she *would* fail.

The new baby, dismissed by the Spanish Ambassador as 'the Little Bastard', was sent to the royal nursery at the old palace of Hatfield, there to live in royal estate, attended by Queen Katherine's bastardized daughter. Mary Tudor had suffered many humiliations since the day her father fell under the Concubine's influence, but this was the final degradation. The two years she spent at Hatfield, waiting in a menial capacity upon Elizabeth, were years of unimagined persecution which warped her generous nature for the rest of her days. 'I know of no other princess in England but myself,' she said on her arrival, and for that allegation, stubbornly maintained, was kept a virtual prisoner in a house governed by Anne's relatives. Stripped of her status, forced to take her meals in the Great Hall with the servants, forbidden the courtesy of a food taster, she lived in daily fear of poison and spent her only happy hours in the nursery.

Katherine of Aragon was dead, and had she dared, Anne would have seen to it that Mary Tudor followed her mother swiftly to the grave. But the birth of Elizabeth had diminished her hold upon the King; she could no longer use him to strike down her enemies, as she had earlier disposed of Cardinal Wolsey and others who stood in her path. A short while longer her influence wavered, like a dwindling candle flame in a strong draught, until the day she was delivered of a still-born son.

'You will get no more boys by me,' said Henry, ominously calm. 'I see God does not mean to give me male children.'

He turned on his heel abruptly, walked out of her room and out of her life, leaving her to the vultures.

Without the mantle of his protection she knew the days of her power were ended. She suspected divorce and feared annulment; but even in the depths of her despair she never once considered death.

Henry avoided her company; the court shunned her; Secretary Cromwell quietly gathered his evidence. She was aware of nothing but a hollow sense of insecurity as she played with Elizabeth and taught her to prattle a few words in the French which reminded her of happier days in a foreign court. Elizabeth, her only child, all that was left to her out of nine gaudy, worthless years. She would give up the crown and the jewels and the magnificent gowns; but she would not surrender the child who had cost her these things.

April at Greenwich and the pale sun shone invitingly down in the sheltered courtyard. Too cold to play out, thought Anne absently, watching Elizabeth hide from their attendants behind a pillar, and yet she had no heart to stop the game. She looked up at the palace, where the flash of sunlight on diamonds had caught her vacant gaze, and saw the King. It was days since he had spoken to her, and desperate for some gesture of acknowledgement from him, she lifted her hand and smiled boldly. Once, he would have sold his soul for that smile, but now there was no response. His heavy face was moody and preoccupied; he stared past her, almost without recognition, his sullen attention riveted upon the laughing child.

Anne knew a moment of wrenching fear. She remembered his subtle cruelty to Katherine, how he had sent her from the court and forbidden her all access to the Princess Mary. He meant to do the same to her. He would take Elizabeth in payment for the boy she had lost, peevish as a child denied a promised toy. And he would do it without a qualm of conscience unless—unless she could shame him here in public.

'Elizabeth, come here.'

Elizabeth's immediate response was to bunch up her sweeping skirts and run clumsily across the courtyard in the opposite direction.

Anne repressed the sudden urge to scream.

'Elizabeth!'

The child froze at her tone, along with every other person in the courtyard. The women clipped their chatter off dead and over near the gate a young man paused to stare at her.

Anne was white with tension; she dared not call again. Across the courtyard she met her child's eyes and saw in them the wilful, stubborn nature that could defeat her even now. She held her arms out in silence and waited an endless moment before her hands closed around her daughter.

Triumphantly she swung Elizabeth round and up on to her hip, carrying her beneath the window where the King still stood, looking down on them. The frown that touched his face made her want to laugh because she knew him so well, that sensitive conscience which craved public approval in everything he did.

'Wave to him,' she whispered urgently in the child's ear, knowing how petty and stupid it would make him look before spectators. 'Wave for *Maman.'*

Elizabeth waved vigorously. Now he would open the window and call them up; with everyone watching what else could he do? And once Anne got him alone she would know what to do, she would know what to say to him.

Her heart jerked violently as the King turned away without a word or gesture.

'Bastard!' she breathed into Elizabeth's hair. *'You bastard!'*

Slowly, wearily, trembling with rage and humiliation, Anne lowered her child to the gravel and stilled the little arm which continued to wave uncertainly at the empty window.

'Don't cry, precious,' she said softly, wiping away two hot smudgy tears with her thumbs. 'When he rots in hell you will be King and Queen both and the whole of England will wave to you.' She put both her hands on the child's thin shoulders and added darkly, 'Let no man take it from you!'

Elizabeth stared up at the palace, a bleak row of mullioned windows sprawling beneath a multitude of turrets.

'*Naughty* papa!' she announced sullenly; and that phrase, that intonation, so obviously borrowed from those worthy ladies who attended upon her, made Anne's eyes sting with sudden tears as she struggled a moment longer to regain composure, normality—sanity.

'The King didn't see us, that's all,' she began shakily.

Elizabeth stamped her foot angrily.

'Did see me,' she muttered mutinously, '*did see me!* See *Maman* too!'

Anne knelt and cupped Elizabeth's chin in her hand.

'If I could put a curse on him and all my enemies,' she whispered venomously, 'it would be just that—to look at you and see me!' She hesitated. 'Elizabeth—if *Maman* should go away you wouldn't forget her, would you?'

The child frowned, pouted, kicked at a stone. 'Don't want you to go 'way!'

'Not for long,' said Anne hastily. 'I shall go home to Hever perhaps—or back to France—whatever he chooses. If he wants a divorce I won't make difficulties. I learned from Katherine, you see—take what you can and go with dignity.'

She was silent a moment, vaguely aware that she should not be saying these things to the child, yet unable to help it, swallowed up in the panic-ridden sweep of her own thoughts.

The King of France is my friend, he could bring influence to bear on Henry. A few months and I could send for her . . . he'll be too busy with that Seymour sheep to care by then . . .

She looked down at the child, sum total of her life's achievement, her legacy to this worthless world.

'Whatever his terms, he shall not part us for ever,' she said softly. 'I swear it!'

Elizabeth was silent a moment, held by the strange, compelling urgency of her mother's gaze; but at length she wriggled free of Anne's embrace to say brightly, '*Maman* hide now.'

Anne glanced towards the palace. Maybe it was not too late even now, if she could only speak to him; show him just how reasonable she was prepared to be—

'Not now, precious, *Maman* is busy. Tomorrow.'

She planted an absent kiss on the upturned face and swept out of the courtyard, away from the pitying eyes of her women and the frightened glance of a very young man, whose only place in history would be to recall this day more than twenty years from now.

A cluster of women surrounded Elizabeth in Anne's wake; unnerved, agitated, mindless as a gaggle of geese, they hemmed her in a cage of silk and taffeta, until, struggling furiously, she won a chink of light between the smothering skirts.

Within that chink she framed the tiny image of a woman, all in black satin, slender and insubstantial, like a distant shadow. She stretched out her fingers to that image, no bigger than a doll, and they closed around nothing. Suffocated by the press of skirts, she kicked wildly at the nearest woman and that lady, mortally offended, moved sharply aside; she had a better view then.

On the steps the image paused, looked back once, and disappeared beneath the arched doorway. And that was her last conscious memory of her mother—a shadow in the April sun, forever flying beyond the reach of her frantic grasp.

On the first of May Anne was arrested and taken to the Tower, accused of adultery with five different men. Three of them were the King's close friends, one a low court musician, one her own brother. When she heard that last she knew the King was mad and lost all hope. At her trial she was found guilty; she had expected nothing less and looked for no reprieve. Then she was taken to Archbishop Cranmer and shown the annulment papers. Crazy with relief she signed them, signed away her own rights, signed away her child's legitimacy and her inheritance—what did it matter, after all, if she were only free to take Elizabeth and live abroad? Back in her cell she learned that she was still to die, her reward for that signature to be beheaded rather than burned, at the King's pleasure. She had betrayed Elizabeth for nothing—

On the 19th of May the sword of a French executioner severed her neck. The Tower cannon echoed along the river bank to where Henry waited on horseback, straining his ears to hear the first blast. Like a man let out of Hell, he turned his horse and led the hunt across country to Wolf Hall, where Jane Seymour waited, timid as a doe rabbit, to receive his wedding ring.

Deep in the Hertfordshire countryside, in a house shrouded by a pall of silence, Elizabeth's chatter frayed the raw nerves of her attendants. She had played most of the day in the privy garden in the hot May sunshine, and no one had called her in to her lessons or taken her to task over the rent in her gown. No one crossed her will at table or tried to make her go to bed at the usual hour, so that by the end of that momentous day, not a single tear had wet the cheeks of Anne's only child. But, though humoured on every side, she sensed the tense atmosphere and grew fretful and belligerent. She was only bribed between the sheets at last by the offer of her governess's comfit box, and even with that trophy safely stowed beneath her pillow, it seemed an endless time before she fell asleep.

Margaret Bryan was exhausted when she closed the nursery door and her first impulse was to go straight down to the Great Hall and take her ease with a tankard of ale. She went instead to the other side of the house, to the room where Henry's eldest daughter had sat alone all day, tasting the bitter-sweet flavour of revenge.

It was a small, shabby room, hardly fit for a maid, let alone a king's daughter, and it was in darkness when Lady Bryan entered it.

'Madam?'

Mary Tudor started up from a hearth stool. In the light of Bryan's candle her young face looked yellow, haggard, almost old.

'Is she asking for me?' The voice too was old, hollow with guilt.

'No, madam.' Bryan smiled tightly. 'I'd say you were the only thing she didn't demand tonight—a sweet, a story, a drink, the chamber pot, another drink—God forgive me, but it would have tried the patience of a saint. Still, she's sleeping now.'

Mary sagged visibly with relief and sank back on the stool.

'Then you don't think—you don't suppose she was aware of—anything?'

Bryan lifted her shoulders in a hesitant shrug.

'Who can say what she was aware of, madam? She's so sharp—that look of hers would see through lead.'

Mary bit her lip, but said nothing. Bryan glanced at her uneasily, put the candle down and went over to poke the fire vigorously. 'Madam,' she said after a moment, 'there are rumours in the Great Hall.'

Mary stiffened; her fingers crept automatically up to her crucifix as she announced with wooden defiance: 'The Princess of Wales does not concern herself with idle gossip.'

'If you persist in this stubborn attitude,' said Bryan wearily, 'the King's Grace will punish you further.'

'Oh no,' Mary shook her head, suddenly galvanized to life. 'Bryan, you don't know my father as I do. He was so good, so gentle and loving before the Concubine bewitched him. Now she's dead I *know* he will return to his senses and acknowledge me once more—his only legitimate child.'

Bryan was silent with pity for the mindless trust of a proud girl. In all this long bitter history of tangled emotion nothing remained more remarkable than Mary's unwavering affection for the man who had hounded her mother to the grave and broken her own health with years of steady persecution. But the news from London should open her eyes to the truth at last.

'It's better that you hear this from me,' began Bryan kindly. 'We have it on reliable authority that the King's marriage to Queen Anne was annulled with her written consent several days before the execution.'

'It's a lie!' shouted Mary. 'She would never consent—*never*. She was proud as Lucifer.'

Bryan's gaze was steady.

'Cranmer has the document in his keeping, madam. In due time it will be displayed at the King's pleasure.' And *this*, she added silently, is the man you defy, you stupid girl. Don't you know the danger you are in?

Mary stood up slowly. She was trembling with rage.

'Do you stand there, madam, and tell me to my face that my father is a *murderer?*'

Before Bryan could reply she swung away, talking to herself feverishly.

'If it was done, it was done without my father's knowledge. And what of it? Guilty or innocent of the charge, you know she deserved to die. I would he had burnt her at the stake like the witch and heretic she was! I would I had been there to see it!'

Shaken and chilled by the harsh hysteria in Mary's voice, Bryan curtsied briefly and left the room without another word. Useless to reason with anyone in the grip of such ugly emotion; and in that moment, when she had seen the girl look suddenly so like her father, Bryan resolved to keep her distance in future. The wretched fate of Mary Tudor was no concern of hers; she had been a fool to add to her responsibilities and take the risk of being seen by Anne's sharp-eyed, sharp-tongued aunt. Angry and depressed, she hurried away to seek a sympathetic ear in the Great Hall, leaving Mary alone with her black thoughts.

The room was absolutely still when she had gone. Mary stood where she had left her and clung to her rage for protection. The creeping silence pressed in upon her, stealing her courage, leaving her defenceless against a truth which rocked her reason. The Concubine had consented to annulment, admitted that her marriage was null and void and had never existed in the eyes of God.

So how could she be executed on the grounds of adultery?

Mary tried to blur the issue in her panic-ridden mind, but a stubborn streak of resolute honesty dragged before her eyes the unwelcome realization that Anne had been murdered. And she looked upon murder as the ultimate violation of body and soul.

'Murder,' said Katherine's gentle voice from some long-lost memory of her childhood, 'is always murder, and deserves the just retribution of God.'

Retribution! The word hummed fearfully in Mary's head, building terrible pictures out of the growing shadows. For suppose such a violation should leave the restless spirit of its victim at liberty in this world—and suppose that victim to be as cruelly vindictive in death as she had been in life—

The tortured fabrications of her guilty conscience sent her fleeing from the room. She ran down the Long Gallery until a stabbing stitch in her side made her stop to catch her breath and realize that she had no idea where she was running to. There was no one in this house she could turn to for comfort now that she had driven her only friend away in disgust, no one in this world who cared whether she lived or died—no one except a child not yet three, whose precious innocence excluded her from blood feuds and the savage rivalry of women. Elizabeth's nursery—home of the only warmth and light she had known in almost three years of darkness; she knew suddenly where she was going and what she would find when she got there. Peace of mind and the sweet, humdrum pattern of normality.

She got up unsteadily and continued more calmly down the gallery, hearing the soft rustle of straw beneath her feet which seemed to be the only sound in this strangely deserted house. There was no echo of laughter from the Great Hall to mock her unhappiness, no servant in sight to snub her by neglecting to curtsey or address her as 'my lady' instead of 'Your Highness'.

She entered Elizabeth's room with measured dignity, prepared to give a haughty nod of dismissal to the gossiping nursery-maids, but none was required; the room was empty. Mary checked in astonishment and felt a sudden prick of tears behind her eyes, for she knew from experience what this desertion signified. The King's heir must be guarded while she slept; the King's bastard required less stringent security.

But how heartless of them to leave her alone, tonight of all nights, just because she no longer mattered. Mary's face hardened with anger. *What if she had woken up and found herself alone for the first time in her life? I shall speak to Bryan tomorrow—*

But, for tonight, it was comforting to have some genuine excuse to stay.

At the far side of the room stood a miniature four-poster bed, a little green-curtained extravagance built on Anne's personal commission for the daughter she had dressed like an expensive doll. The spoilt child had a harem's wardrobe, but the King was not generous to relatives who lost his favour. That wardrobe would be outgrown in a few short months and what would become of Elizabeth's precocious vanity when the pretty things came no more?

Mary drew the curtains aside and smiled involuntarily. Always restless, even in sleep, Elizabeth had kicked off all her covers and lay face down on the mattress, holding a little doll dressed in black satin. The pillows were on the floor, in company with an empty comfit box, and the bed was covered with crumbled marchpane and half-eaten suckets.

Mary brushed the sheets and replaced the pillows, held her breath as the child stirred and turned over on to her back, breathed easy again as she lay still, tucked the coverlet around her. Stepping back to pull up a stool, her foot struck the comfit box and sent it spinning against the wainscoting. She bit her lip with vexation, bent to retrieve it, thought what a fool Bryan was, seeing the initials on the empty box, glanced back at the bed anxiously—and froze.

Two eyes were fixed upon her in an unwavering stare. She knew those eyes, midnight-black—she had seen them often enough before, set in a pale, clever oval beneath a crown of raven hair. In the childish innocence of her sister's face they had no conceivable right; and yet they belonged, so wonderfully, so horribly, that even in her moment of terror, Mary could not have sworn what filled her with such mindless horror.

As suddenly as they had opened, the heavy eyelids fell like shutters and the suffocating sense of hostility left Mary. She looked at the finely chiselled little face on the pillows and felt the numb, uncaring calm of total despair. She had been warned; in the depth of her superstitious nature, she accepted that warning with wretched resignation.

She left the room and walked blindly back to her own. The lonely walls held no terror for her now. Anne's vengeful soul did not hover there, nor in the dark winding corridors of any other palace.

It had found a better place to rest.

That same fateful May, Henry called his bastard son, the young Duke of Richmond, to his side, threw one arm around his shoulders and told him with emotional tears how narrowly he and his sister Mary had escaped 'from that woman who planned your deaths by poison'.

Two months later Richmond was dead, and Henry, mad with grief and terror, was screaming of witchcraft and curses. Elizabeth was cloistered at Hatfield and no one dared to mention her name in the King's presence, not even Secretary Cromwell, who received a pitiful letter from the child's governess, begging sufficient clothes to cover her decently.

For almost a year Elizabeth lived in a strangely altered world, a world which seemed reluctant to acknowledge her existence. Her skirts grew so short that she could see her ankles, the seams of her bodices split, the pretty little coifs sat so absurdly on the top of her head that she refused to wear them.

One hot August day she climbed into the window-seat in the Long Gallery, a puzzled but not unhappy little girl who thought it would be fun to hide from her attendants. For a long time no one missed her and a group of ladies gathered around the empty hearth with their embroidery and their wagging tongues.

'At least it was quick,' someone said morbidly, and in a moment the thing, which had never been openly discussed, was being chewed over with that restrained, ghoulish relish with which women discuss a tragedy that does not directly affect them.

'It's always clean and quick with a sword—should be, too, for what it cost to bring that executioner from France. £23.6s.8d.—that's fair pay for two minutes' work. *He* gave her the best of everything, even in death.'

Somebody sniffed and said sharply, 'Pity he didn't see fit to give her a coffin. Imagine her lying there all day in a pool of blood till one of her women found an arrow chest.'

'Yes—all those flies, it was such a hot day! I wonder where she was buried?'

There was a decent pause as they bent their heads and applied their needles diligently. Soon they turned their attention to the new Queen, Jane Seymour.

'What does he see in her?—such a plain, whey-faced little sheep.'

'At least she'll be faithful to him.'

'She'd better be! Christ's soul, *I* wouldn't share a bed with him to be Empress of the World.'

'Well, in my opinion, if the Lady Elizabeth had been a boy it would never have happened. A son for England is all he cares about now, and he'll get one sooner or later, if he has to murder a dozen wives in the process—'

Elizabeth sat very still, staring out of the window. An hour later, Lady Bryan, searching angrily, pulled back the hanging and found her there, quietly arranging the black satin skirts of her favourite doll. She looked like any normal three-year-old, absorbed in play, and the doll too was like any other, save for one small detail.

It was headless.

The painted, black-haired bauble lay at the foot of the window seat in an attitude which suggested that it had been thrown there. Bryan picked it up and turned to look uncertainly at her charge.

'It broke,' said Elizabeth flatly.

'Never mind.' Bryan was brisk, wrestling with a curious feeling of unease. 'Give it to me and we'll see if Mr Shelton can mend it for you.'

Elizabeth put the doll behind her back.

'I don't want Mr Shelton to mend it.'

She got down from the window and ran out of the gallery, and some inner instinct warned Bryan not to make an issue of the incident. Clearly, in spite of her strict instructions, tongues had been wagging carelessly. She made a mental note to dispose of the wretched doll as soon as the child was safely in bed, but when she came to look for it later that night, it was nowhere to be seen.

She considered questioning the maids, then thought better of it; it would only start a lot of morbidly exaggerated rumours. It was better to assume that Elizabeth, having lost interest, had dropped the miserable object and that one of the servants had quietly disposed of it. And if, by some chance, it should continue to hang about the house in a forgotten corner, what did it matter anyway?

It was only a doll, after all.

CHAPTER 2

The summer of 1537 seemed endless to Jane Seymour, dragging through the sultry days, heavy with the King's child, and heavier still with guilt. A shrinking presentiment of death was upon her; Anne's death and Anne's neglected child were like twin millstones round her thin neck, pulling her down into an abyss of languid despair.

'For Christ's sake, what ails you?' snapped Henry, and Jane turned her face away into the pillow.

'My lord—bring Elizabeth back to court and let me show kindness to her. I am afraid.'

Afraid for his unborn son, he knew it. And with Richmond's death still heavy on his heart he too was afraid, afraid of a shadow, a shadow in the sun.

He brought Elizabeth back to court, but he could not bear to touch her. He stalked his palace like a hunted fugitive, fleeing the dreadful trusting smile of a little girl, but Jane at least was at peace; and her son was born safely. They called him Edward.

The bells rang, the crowds surged around the palace, singing and stamping, roaring their delight. Henry roared too, but with rather less conviction, for he had been through this before. The bells, the crowds, the gorgeous christening—and two months later a tiny coffin laid to rest.

He woke at every sound, fearful to find them plucking at his arm with the dreadful news. *My lord—the little prince—*

That beautiful May day when the Tower cannon fired, he had believed that he rode along the river bank to total freedom. Now he knew that his haunted sleep would never be free of a jealous presence unless he accorded it some token of satisfaction. He could not, of course, legitimize Elizabeth without making himself a public laughing-stock in Europe, but he could grant her a certain measure of status.

He thought of the christening, traditionally a midnight ceremony and no place for small children. He would make his public gesture there.

And perhaps then he could close his eyes without seeing a bloody sword above the neck of his new-born son.

The Lady Elizabeth was to bear the Prince's christening robe to the font and be carried there, in formal procession, by no less a person than the Queen's eldest brother, Edward Seymour, Lord Hertford. The announcement produced tittering speculation about the court and stunned silence in the nursery.

Lady Bryan sat heavily down by a smoking fire and wondered why this must happen now, when only another week or so would have seen her safely installed in the Prince's nursery. Young Kat Champernowne, who had been so eager to take her place, should have borne this awful responsibility.

On the other side of the hearth a fat Welsh nursemaid caught her eye and smiled knowingly.

'Of course, madam, she might be ill.'

'She's never ill,' said Bryan glumly. 'Never.'

'She could be, if I doctored her milk. Oh, just a pinch, not enough to do her any real harm, but sufficient for the purpose if you follow my meaning, madam.'

Bryan looked up startled, scandalized—tempted. If the woman opposite had sprouted horns and a forked tail, she would not have been unduly surprised to see them.

A moment more she hesitated then stood up and marched to the door.

'Blanche Parry!' she announced primly. 'You're not fit to rock a peasant's cradle!'

'Suit yourself, madam,' muttered Blanche, when the door had closed, 'it's your funeral.'

Midnight on a cold October night and the corridors of the palace were red with torchlight.

Elizabeth, released at length from the attentions of her tirewomen, climbed on Lady Bryan's lap for inspection and the final adjustment of her coif.

'Am I beautiful?'

'Yes.'

Technically speaking Bryan supposed that was a lie, but doubted that anyone would ever notice. Certainly no man. If one as prejudiced as the Spanish Ambassador could call her 'very pretty' there was little hope for the rest.

'How beautiful?'

'Don't be vain!' said Bryan sharply.

Elizabeth was silent, fingering the folds of her new gown.

'Don't you love me any more?' she asked solemnly.

'What a question,' said Bryan, shocked and guilty with affection. 'Of course I love you. I love you very much.'

'Better than my new brother?'

Beneath the child's penetrating stare Bryan felt she had turned to glass, empty, transparent, brittle and heartless. So she knew! One of the maids must have told her, some silly gossiping hussy with nothing better to do.

Tears glimmered suddenly in Bryan's hard eyes. Such a difficult child in so many irritating ways and yet, if it were not for the honour and the status, nothing in the world would have parted her from her present post. Suddenly she pitied Kat Champernowne—young, inexperienced, unhardened, she wouldn't stand a chance. And when you were paid to take care of a child, the worst thing you could do was to give your heart—you never got it back intact.

Behind her the door opened. Someone announced, 'Lord Hertford, madam,' and Bryan started to her feet, tumbling Elizabeth from her lap in her confusion. As she sank into a hasty curtsey before the King's eldest brother-in-law, Bryan saw the haughty gentleman was not alone; his younger brother, Thomas Seymour, lounged just behind him in the doorway and gave her a rake's amused, appraising gaze. She blushed like a girl and lowered her eyes, remembering tales about him that, in modesty, she would have preferred to forget.

The two men, blood uncles to the little Prince, were as different as chalk and cheese. One, cold and cheerless as a crescent moon, the other, glowing like a noon-day sun; the sight of them standing side by side was charged with all the drama of a total eclipse. Cain and Abel, thought Bryan irrelevantly, and we all know how *that* finished—

'The Lady Elizabeth's Grace will accompany my lord at his immediate convenience.' She got quickly to her feet and put a hand on Elizabeth's shoulder, pressing her down into a curtsey.

The moment she had dreaded was at hand. Elizabeth, smiling obliquely at the younger man, held her fingers out formally to be escorted from the room like a court lady; and in that moment Hertford bent down without ceremony and picked her up.

The door closed and for the space of perhaps twenty seconds there was silence; then a familiar little voice shrilled into fury in the gallery beyond and Lady Bryan cringed and wished she had taken Parry's unethical advice.

'I don't want to be carried. I can walk—I can walk all by myself. Put me down, my lord. Put me *down!'*

'Cromwell told me the brat was a handful,' remarked Hertford sullenly over his shoulder. 'I had no idea he meant it quite so literally.' He broke off abruptly. 'She kicked me, did you see it? The mannerless little wretch actually kicked me!'

'I'm not surprised,' said his brother, smiling unpleasantly, 'she's the King's daughter, not a sack of vegetables. I'd kick you too if you held me like that.'

'I'm sure you would.' Hertford's glance was frigid with hostility. 'And enjoy it if I gave you so much as half a chance—isn't that so, dear brother?'

Tom patted his brother's hand with a maddening air of patronage.

'Claws in there, Ned, let's draw no blood on a family occasion. This is our day of triumph—remember?'

'What triumph is there for me, I'd like to know, playing nursemaid to the illegitimate child of a low-born strumpet? Everyone will laugh at me.'

'They wouldn't dare!' said Tom maliciously. Hertford marched on, impervious to sarcasm, his lean face longer than a mournful bloodhound's.

'As I said to the King at the time,' he muttered half to himself, 'it should have been you.'

The light-hearted mockery died out of the younger man's eyes, leaving them hard and unsmiling.

'Any particular reason why it should have been me?' The voice was deceptively calm and still suggested half-hearted banter.

'Well, naturally, being the youngest, you have less stature to lose. When you consider my position as the Prince's eldest uncle—'

'Christ's soul,' exploded his brother, 'the boy's no more your bloody nephew than he is mine.'

Edward's long stride halted abruptly.

'Just what exactly is that supposed to mean?'

'It means I'll not thank any man who chooses to forget it,' said Tom coldly. 'So take a little more care how you claim your first-born privileges, Ned, or you may find my brotherly fist in your fat ear!'

'Are you threatening me, you damned pup?' Edward's free hand shot out and caught Tom by the collar and for a moment they stood there quivering with rage, ready to knock each other down, as they had done so often in their boyhood at Wolf Hall.

Elizabeth shut her eyes instinctively and hid her face in the chrisom. It was enough to bring Tom to his senses, making him shrug off his brother's angry hand with a rueful laugh.

'Let it be! Not just now with the King waiting for us.' He glanced at Elizabeth with a wary smile. 'And not with his daughter taking it all in. Believe me, Ned, this one misses nothing! Sharp as a dagger aren't you, my pretty?'

Edward looked at Elizabeth too, half embarrassed as he let his arm drop limply back to his side, glad of the distraction.

'She's no damned business to be listening,' he said primly. 'It shows her want of breeding. Why the King wants the little bastard present has been beyond me from the start. I thought he couldn't bear the sight of her since Boleyn lost her head.'

Elizabeth's face stilled, suddenly empty, then the dark eyes blazed and she threw the chrisom on the floor and Edward dropped her at Tom's feet in his effort to catch the trailing yards of white satin. It was the second time in less than ten minutes that she had landed without ceremony on terra firma and she was suddenly more than ready to yell.

She looked up at Tom and saw him shake his head and lay a finger against his lips. He had a wicked laughing look that made her reserve the yell for future use. Sitting on the rushes, she searched in vain for the source of his amusement and saw nothing but Hertford frantically shaking out the robe beneath the orange glow of a wall torch further down the gallery.

'Who's a naughty girl then?' whispered Tom as he picked her up. She liked the admiring way he said that as though she had done something which gave him immense satisfaction and automatically her arms went about his neck in a quick, instinctive gesture of response.

'I don't like him,' she said. 'You may carry me instead.' The corners of his lips twitched beneath his fair moustache.

'I can't do that, poppet,' he said lightly, 'much as I'd like to.'

'But I want you to. I *want* it.'

Her lips trembled and stretched themselves into a thin querulous line; he knew an ominous sign when he saw one so close.

'Sweetheart,' he added hastily, 'the King wants me to carry the canopy over your little brother. And if I make the King angry—'

'He will chop off your head!'

The flat little statement made him blink in astonishment. He bit back an oath and managed to turn it into an uncomfortable cough instead.

'Well,' he said, struggling for nonchalance beneath her calm gaze, 'you wouldn't want that to happen to poor old Uncle Tom, would you?'

She touched his golden beard with a hesitant finger.

'No,' she murmured softly, 'I wouldn't like that at all. You have a nice head.'

'Then we'll do our best to keep it where it is, shall we—just for a little while longer?'

She nodded solemnly, and then pouted.

'Does that mean *he* has to carry me?'

'I'm afraid so. But if you're a good girl and give him no more trouble tonight I'll give you a gingerbread boy.'

Elizabeth looked across the gallery. *He* was coming back, folding the chrisom with all the precision of a laundrymaid. She put her head down on Tom's shoulder and twined her fingers in his hair.

'*Two* gingerbread boys?' she whispered.

He laughed and gave her a hearty shake.

'You shameless little minx. You really *are* just like—' He broke off unexpectedly. 'It's a bargain,' he continued, and was suddenly serious as he put her down.

Something, he could not have said what, had sent a chill jangling through every nerve in his body, making him for a moment inexplicably sad. They walked on down the gallery in silence and he was glad when they joined the crowds in the chapel.

Elizabeth, at the age of four, was seriously smitten with a puppy's blind adoration for 'Uncle Tom'.

The moment the christening was over and she was released from Hertford's odious guardianship, she bobbed through a sea of hose-clad legs and swaying skirts in Queen Jane's airless bedchamber, seeking the flamboyant garter which marked him in her memory.

At length she found him.

'I have to go to bed now,' she confided urgently. 'Will you bring my gingerbread boys tomorrow?'

'What an avaricious young lady you are!' he remarked, looking down on her from a smiling height. 'Remind me never to owe you any money.'

She looked at him anxiously, suddenly suspicious.

'You will come, won't you?'

'If I can remember the way.'

'*Elizabeth!*'

They both looked round with a start, and Tom swept a mocking bow to

Mary Tudor's unsmiling figure. Reluctantly Elizabeth bobbed a curtsey and went to take her sister's stiffly outstretched hand. The look she gave him over her shoulder, the oddest mix of trust and coquetry he had ever seen, was enough to decide him. He determined to find his way back to the nursery at the earliest convenient moment. He considered teasing Ned with his new conquest, but looking round saw, with a frown, that his brother was with the King. Henry's great voice boomed around the crowded chamber, trumpeting victory like a cockerel, and Hertford stood there, looking so smug, one might have thought he had borne the brat himself. It was insufferable the way Ned pushed himself forward, grabbing all the honours because of a few years' seniority! Automatically Tom began to elbow his way towards the Queen's bed. At some point in the night, between making his royal brother-in-law bellow with laughter and his own brother glare with jealous envy, he spared a glance for his sister and saw with a shock of horror that she looked half dead.

Less than a week later they buried her, and for a while both Seymours feared they might be burying their influence on the King with her. Slowly, in the months that followed, they began to realize that this was not the case. For once, a woman had been taken from Henry before he had had time to grow tired of her charms, a woman, moreover, who had martyred herself to give him the one thing he had wanted and lacked all these years—a legitimate son. He was maudlin and sentimental and enjoying a certain degree of reverent self-pity as he strolled one afternoon in his privy garden with the brothers of his late wife.

'Your sister was the only woman in this world I ever loved,' he said, and waited for the tactful words of condolence which bolstered his ego.

'The Lord giveth and the Lord taketh away, Your Majesty,' said Tom, and the sarcasm with which he said it took his brother's breath away like a blow in the crutch.

The King halted, examining the young man with eyes grown hard and shrewd with ruling. He had strolled in this same garden earlier with some pretty little nobody, whose name he had already forgotten, hanging on his arm and on his every word. His ministers were already combing Europe for a suitable bride. They were simple facts of life that no one else at court would ever dare to draw attention to, except this arrogant young devil who had as good as told him to his face that he made a remarkably merry widower. And slowly the corners of Henry's thin mouth curled into a smile of grudging admiration.

'God works in a mysterious way,' he remarked smoothly, eyeing Edward's lean white face with a certain satisfaction, watching him sweat discreetly beneath his collar, terrified that his fool of a brother had ruined all they had worked for. 'And as you say, Tom—as you so rightly say—who are we mere mortals to question *His* will?'

Edward Seymour's breath of relief was clearly audible, the glance he cast at his brother venomous as a snake's. Henry saw it and was amused. Divide and rule was a principle he took seriously. He put an amiable arm about the young man's shoulders and strode on between the two of them, strongly reminded of the way chained bandogs strained to savage each other. The aim of a good master was to keep them wanting to savage each other rather than the man who held them in their chains; and Henry was a good master; he knew all the tricks. While he lived there would be fair balance held between the ambitious dogs about his court who jostled for power; but he was no longer young and the Tudors were a short-lived, unhealthy stock. A festering sore was creeping steadily up one leg and the stench of it was beginning to permeate his rooms. The Seymours had taken the scent of his weakness, like the good bloodhounds they were. They padded after their master and looked to the future, to the possibility of a child upon the throne and a long period of minority. But only Tom followed the trail as far as the nursery door, and made a pleasure out of political necessity by courting the affection of Henry's son.

He had a chameleon quality which made him fit unobtrusively against any background. In foreign courts the suave diplomat; on high seas the respected captain; in the nursery the devoted uncle; in all of these roles he was genuinely at home, without any conscious effort. There was no need to feign affection for his royal nephew; he had an infinite capacity for light-hearted love. And among those many little loves which gathered about him, like a collection of semiprecious gems, there was Elizabeth, that amusing, lively, acquisitive little girl, whose greed for life reminded him so fondly of his own. 'What have you got for me?' said her eyes each time he appeared fresh from a voyage to foreign parts and the attitude never gave him offence, for he also asked that same silent question of everyone he met.

It was grand sport, this playing for power in virgin territory, a highly enjoyable mixture of business and pleasure. There were pleasant byways along the stony roads of ambition for those who were sharp enough to read the map.

Tom Seymour took many a profitable detour down them; and enjoyed the scenery.

Elizabeth was six when the King chose her next stepmother. He had been nearly three years without a wife, a merry widower, and he was reluctant to exchange his freedom for marriage with an insignificant German princess named Anne. Indeed, the name itself might have put an end to the negotiations before they started but for Cromwell's thick-skinned persistence. They needed the alliance with Cleves—and the woman was comely, said Cromwell slyly, one had only to look at Holbein's miniature, specially commissioned for the purpose, to see that.

Henry looked and was appeased, yet still his vague sense of unease remained. Another Anne! However fair the creature, how could he help but make unhappy comparisons? So, when he heard of Elizabeth's hot impatience to meet this new stepmother he was touched on the rawest of nerves.

'Tell her,' he snapped, turning on those who had thought to please him with news of the child's delight, 'that she had a mother so different from this woman she ought not to *wish* to see her.'

It fell to Mr Shelton, governor of the household, to deliver the King's unkind message to his daughter. He saw her eyes widen in hurt astonishment before she turned away slowly and climbed up into the window-seat to watch the rain teeming down the little leaded panes. She sat very straight and still with her back to him and though he knew she was crying he dared not go and take her on his lap. She was too old now for familiarity from a distantly related man-servant. Mr Shelton went out of the room, leaving her alone, and felt sadly that that was how he would always leave her now. He kicked the wall savagely when the door had closed behind him and wished it was his sovereign lord and master.

Yet when Anne of Cleves arrived in England Elizabeth was at court with her sister Mary to greet the lady after all. In decency Henry could not leave her out—it would look so pointed. And once he had set eyes on this new wife he decided rashly that he ought not to wish to see her himself. He went to his wedding squealing like a staked pig, 'What remedy, hey? None but to marry this fat Flanders mare!' and the look he gave Cromwell as he said it told that unfortunate man that he was not long for this world.

Anne of Cleves was a warm, compassionate, sensible woman. Everybody liked her, except the husband who flatly refused to share her bed, but then Henry had not been led to expect an amiable virgin sow. He was loud in his disappointment and already in love with his new wife's maid of honour, Katherine Howard. This time it took Archbishop Cranmer only five months to dissolve another unfortunate marriage for his master. Cromwell laid his head on the block for bungling the affair, and on the morning of that execution Henry married Anne Boleyn's little Howard cousin.

The fat Flanders mare had escaped to comfortable retirement at Richmond Palace, considerably happier to be known as the King's 'good sister'.

She had shown almost indecent relief at the annulment and had indeed made only one condition to it. She desired to see Elizabeth regularly because 'I would rather have been her mother than your Queen.'

Only a foreigner could have hoped to get away with such insolence, and Henry, not daring to endanger relations with Cleves any further, chose to turn the other cheek with astonishing restraint. Let her have Elizabeth! Let her have anything she wanted provided he gained his freedom without armed hostilities. So Elizabeth went often to visit 'Aunt Anne' and learnt sufficient cookery in the kitchens at Richmond under the tutelage of that extremely practical German lady to justify her later boast that should she be turned out of the realm in her petticoat, she would make her living anywhere in Europe.

When she was not at Richmond, she was at court, having her pert head turned by the attentions of Henry's Rose without Thorns, the reckless, penniless, wanton little Queen who welcomed her with open arms. At seven years old she had never been in such demand and she was ready to worship the lovely, laughing girl, just on eighteen, who made so much of her.

For a little over a year the court sunned itself in the warmth of Katherine Howard's youth, and it began to be said, with some reason, that the King was in his happy dotage at last. Whoever Katherine favoured found a place in the King's circle; whoever she loved was automatically admitted to his affection. And Katherine loved Elizabeth, her cousin's child, and made no secret of it. A place of honour at the royal table, a wardrobe fit for a princess and the attention of the father she had always adored—all this and more Elizabeth owed to the young stepmother who chose to make an especial friend of her. The reign of Katherine Howard was the high-water mark of Elizabeth's turbulent childhood, one unending party which, like her reckless little stepmother, she believed would never end—

Sunlight filled the deserted Long Gallery, winking on the massive stones that adorned the King's vast chest and fat fingers.

He was hot and short of breath to the point of tetchy irritation as he lumbered over the wooden floorboards like a clumsy baited bear, watching the two maddening figures darting further from his reach. He had no hope of catching them in the fair contest he had demanded as proof of his rejuvenated youth, and even as he thought it, he saw Elizabeth turn her head, met the cool considering glance and knew she knew it too.

A moment later she was sprawling full length in the dirty rushes. The little Queen exclaimed and began to run back, but Henry reached his daughter first, picking her up with the effortless movement of one hand, and brushing the clinging straw from her bodice with lingering fingers. There was an odd expression in his eyes as he turned her chin up and kissed her slowly and deliberately on the mouth.

Anne!

Elizabeth shivered. He released her.

'Are you hurt?' asked Katherine, touching her arm.

'She's not hurt,' said Henry strangely. 'She knows how to fall. She has been well taught.'

Beneath his compelling gaze, Elizabeth flushed and muttered something about catching her foot in her gown. But still the King smiled at her strangely, with mocking tenderness.

'Take care of that foot, Bess, it has discretion. Only find a tongue to match it and you'll be a politician.'

Katherine laughed lightly, a little tinkling note of affectionate indulgence, sweet and shallow, like herself.

'Ah, my lord, she speaks so well, better than I. What could possibly be amiss with her tongue?'

'That tongue,' said Henry shrewdly, 'is the tail that wags the dog, too long and too impudent by half. It would answer the Devil himself as pertly as it answers me—isn't that so, child?'

'Assuredly, sir.'

Elizabeth looked up; her eyes were black and hard, crazy with daring, no longer a child's. 'But then—some would say it was the same thing.'

She had gone too far.

Even ignorant, tactless little Katherine caught her breath as the King's eyes narrowed to slits and the veins bulged at his temples.

Do you mock me still, you devil's strumpet?

Her gaze wavered, crumpled, became a bewildered tearful amber stare. Henry saw it and softened.

Anne, you bitch, only you could use a child against me!

He reached out and touched his daughter's pale cheek.

'You should have been a boy,' he said softly. 'Why were you not a boy? *Why?*'

Elizabeth bowed her head guiltily and stared at his huge jewelled feet.

'You will be wasted,' he said resentfully and turned away.

The cruel sunlight etched a score of tiny lines in the sagging skin around his eyes and mouth. He felt old and petulant as the dead past rushed upon him and a dark murderous mood, inseparable product in him of any prolonged contact with Elizabeth, was growing steadily.

Wasted! Six years of his prime, his lovely glowing virile life, and nothing to show for it but a haunted conscience and this strange, frightening little girl.

Why in God's name hadn't the child died at birth, like her brother, and spared him the continual torment of a hideous memory? How narrowly he had got her born in wedlock, this love-child conceived in the triumph of Anne's artful capitulation. Her unborn promise had been the final spur that made him brave the break with Rome. For her sake he had taken on the world, torn down the English Church, chopped off the heads of loyal friends who could not stomach the change—More, Fisher, all good men—got himself excommunicated, everlastingly damned after death. For her sake he had lost his immortal soul, and though the mother had died for it, the child lived on to torture him, telling him with every movement of her body and every flicker of her bold, clever eyes, that she, not his pale puny son, was the heir he wanted.

But she was useless to him. Women were not fit to rule kingdoms. He had built his life around that simple axiom, murdered to justify his belief in it. If he questioned it now, he made a mockery of his whole existence. All he had done, he had done for England, to save this wilful little half isle from the hazardous rule of a woman. His greatest achievement, as man and monarch, must be the siring of Edward. He could not, would not see the seed of greatness in Elizabeth. He did not want to see it: the thought turned his brain.

She will never be Queen, he told his restless conscience. Edward will marry and sire many sons. And after Edward there is Mary. Should I replace her in the succession she will never rule. You waste your soul in vain, Anne. She will never be Queen. Your day is done—

Defiance eased his spirit and the grey mood lifted a little; he lowered himself stiffly into a chair and beckoned the living forward. They sat on cushions at his feet and he smiled at them smugly, for it gave him a perverted pleasure to see them together, Anne's cousin and Anne's child, both his, to use as he pleased.

He was doubly blessed in Katherine, his Rose without Thorns; she was his jewel of womanhood, lusty but pure. 'No other will but his' she had chosen as her motto, and every man at court knew what it meant. None had loved his Rose as he did and none would ever dare. By God, they knew the price!

Elizabeth leaned against his knee and her flaming hair spread like a silk cloak across his thigh. Beautiful hair! He liked to stroke and twine it round his fingers while he lolled sleepily in the great chair and his thoughts, like little imps, danced him back to Hever Castle, to the first wild days of his pursuit of Anne. He had never loved that way before and he never would again. No man would. Anne was a unique experience.

Whoso list to hunt, I know where is an hind,

Wyatt had written that of her, Thomas Wyatt her cousin, who had made no secret of his love for her. Bitter and public had been the rivalry between himself and the King for her favours, until at last Wyatt bowed to defeat, not through fear of Henry but because he saw at last he had nothing to offer Anne that could compete with a crown.

> Who list her hunt, I put him out of doubt,
> As well as I, may spend his time in vain;
> And graven with diamonds in letters plain
> There is written her fair neck round about,
> *'Noli me tangere,* for Caesar's I am,
> And wild for to hold, though I seem tame.'

Wyatt had relinquished her, written his famous poem of farewell, and Anne had shown it to Henry as proof of the man's integrity, to quiet his jealousy. But he had never been sure after that, never quite sure, whether she had come to him unsoiled as she swore. And he was jealous of Wyatt, jealous of all those stolen moments of her extreme youth, of every moment in her life which he had been unable to share. Jealous, jealous, murderously jealous. Sometimes, in painful moments of honesty, he wondered if that were not the reason he had insisted on her death, a grim determination, after she had agreed to all his terms, that no one else should enjoy her. He had wanted to kill her and only regretted that, in common decency, he could not wield the axe himself.

At the time of her arrest, he had sent Wyatt to the Tower, along with those five other men; it had seemed the perfect moment to be revenged for all those years of uncertainty and anguish. And he would have sent Wyatt to his death, along with the rest, if it were not for those wretched lines of verse.

'Noli me tangere, *for Caesar's I am—*'

No, he knew Wyatt had not committed adultery with her, no matter what they had done together before the marriage. He knew Wyatt too well, the stubborn courage which had made him challenge his monarch on man-to-man terms, the honest integrity which had made him keep his distance once he retired from the field of honour. He could not square Wyatt's death with his conscience and so the man had been released. Whenever he woke now from guilty, terrified dreams he could point to Wyatt's existence and assure himself that he was a just and honourable man who had killed his wife in good faith.

He still read those verses and others that Wyatt had written for Anne, all dominated by images of hunting and passionate entreaty to: *Forget not yet.*

Yet Anne had forgotten Wyatt, as she forgot young Harry Percy and many others, trivial, insignificant conquests along her road to power. She had loved none of them, loved no one at all except herself and her daughter; and even Elizabeth she had abandoned at the end. Katherine of Aragon had gone to her death refusing to sign annulment papers; Anne had hoped to save that precious little neck of hers. Yet she had gone laughing to the block and the knowledge troubled him, for what in this world or the next could have given her amusement at such a time? Sometimes when he looked at Elizabeth, he was afraid he knew the answer to that.

Wyatt's words still mocked him across the years. *Forget not yet.* For he could not forget, that was the bitter irony, he remembered every detail of his miserable enslavement to that witch. The tears he had shed for her, the abject grovelling letters he had written in desperation each time she flounced away from court to sulk at the endless delay of the Divorce.

'My heart and I surrender themselves into your hands—absence has placed distance between us, nevertheless fervour increases, at least on my part.'

Even now, four years after the axe had fallen, he was still a prisoner in a cage of memories and as his glance fell upon Elizabeth he knew why. Exchange those red-gold tresses for a raven crown and it might have been Anne kneeling at his feet, the same quick turn of her head, the same sudden spurt of mocking laughter. In certain moods or a certain light he could have sworn her amber eyes were black; and then he must dismiss her abruptly, wherever they were, whatever they were doing and it would be days, weeks—once even a whole year—before he could bear to look at her again.

But now there was Katherine to dam the flood of his destructive desire and channel it to safer waters. Under Katherine's gentle tuition he was learning to love his daughter as a child, and the nerve-jerking moments of conflicting hate and indecent interest came less often to shake his composure. His hand wandered from Elizabeth's bright head to Katherine's thigh, plump and soft beneath her stiff gown. He squeezed it with obscene gratitude, welcoming the healthy tide of desire rising steadily in his veins. Katherine cut him free from the shackles of past horrors—horrors of his own making, it was true, but none the less horrible for that. And it was always the same. An innocent hour with Elizabeth—then that sudden, savage need which Katherine so sweetly slaked, enabling him to emerge from his chamber at peace with the world, and at peace with Anne's child.

Hastily he sent Elizabeth away with a coin. For all his lechery he had a curious narrow-minded primness where the morality of the young was concerned. He desired to keep his younger daughter in the same state of cloistered innocence which had shrouded his eldest into her early teens. He would have died a thousand deaths rather than allow her to watch as he fondled Katherine.

Elizabeth curtsied and ran to the other end of the gallery, where her governess stood staring discreetly out of a window, feigning great indifference, but watching everything avidly from the corner of a roving eye.

'Your Grace's coif!' scolded the young woman, as they hurried away. 'How many times have I told you not to take it off?'

'The King took it off,' said Her Grace pertly, 'because Queen Katherine said my hair is like spun silk and too beautiful to stay hidden.'

The governess repressed a sigh of irritation. Privately she considered Queen Katherine to be an interfering little busybody who ought to know better than to make other people's jobs more difficult than they need be. It would take at least a week of coaxing to get a coif back on Elizabeth's head. All this spoiling, following hard on years of virtual neglect, was making the child quite insufferable.

'Look, Kat.' Elizabeth held out the palm of her hand to display the single gold coin. 'The King gave me this to buy ribbons. What will Jane say?'

'Now, madam,' said the governess severely, 'you're not to tease your cousin with it. The lord knows that poor child never receives anything from her parents except a beating.'

Elizabeth frowned. She was weary of considering the feelings of Lady Jane Grey and wished she would go home to Bradgate, where she belonged. But at least she could make her little brother Edward jealous—

'Just give that coin to me and don't be a little troublemaker,' said Kat, reading her expression accurately.

Elizabeth ducked out of her grasp and ran. Nothing in the world was going to deprive her of this singular triumph. She pushed open the door to the schoolroom and stopped, immediately aware from the discrete, childish hush which reigned, that intruders were present.

In front of the hearth an arrogantly handsome man stood with fine legs astride and hands clasped behind his back in the masterful stance favoured by the King himself. She knew him vaguely as Sir John Dudley, one of the up and coming men about the court, but the two sulky little boys, one dark and one fair, she had never seen before.

'. . . in addition to the inestimable honour of his Royal Highness's company,' continued the gentleman in the cold manner of one who considers himself rudely interrupted, 'you will both make acquaintance of the Lady Elizabeth's Grace.'

The slight, ironic emphasis on the final word was not wasted on the girl, or the flustered governess, who came forward with the missing head-dress and fastened it with mortified haste. The taller boy—the dark one—suppressed a snigger of amusement and received a sharp poke in the small of the back from his father.

'Manners, Robin! Bow to Her Grace—you also, Guildford.'

The two boys did as they were told and Elizabeth responded with the most perfunctory curtsey they had ever seen.

When Dudley had gone, Guildford went to sit in the window seat with Lady Jane Grey and the little Prince, whose timid smiles suggested friendly overtures. But neither Robin nor Elizabeth moved a muscle. In the centre of the room they stood and stared at each other, as wary and suspicious as two young cubs from alien packs. Instant antagonism and reluctant interest pulsed in the air between them

Sudden and violent, like sheet lightning, it lit the flame of a long, long candle, a candle that was to burn for nearly half a century.

CHAPTER 3

No one who knew John Dudley well had ever doubted he was a man who would go far, in spite of formidable obstacles in his path. And they were right, for by 1541 he had overcome most of them and was cutting a fine figure at court.

Men called him a traitor's son, but the insult was largely academic. His father, the hated tax collector of Henry VII, had been executed at the beginning of the present King's reign in a cheap bid for popular acclaim, and the bereaved son, a practical man, would have been the first to admit the astonishing success of the ploy. A man was a fool who made a personal affront out of pure political expediency. Whenever Henry, surveying a shrinking treasury with regret, sighed and made some wistful reference to Edmund Dudley's sound head for business, John Dudley neither winced nor felt anger at the memory of that sound head decorating the ramparts of London Bridge. There was no place for pride or sentiment in the serving of a Tudor prince.

Positively cordial relations now existed between King and courtier and Dudley was quick to milk Henry's guilty conscience, seizing the first opportunity to manoeuvre two of his sons into the company of the royal children.

The possibilities accruing from a politic cultivation of childhood acquaintance were endless and when Dudley closed that nursery door he did so with quiet satisfaction, convinced that he had made yet another shrewd move. But the first meeting was not a success and he knew it the moment the two boys sidled into his closet an hour later.

'May we go to the stables now, Father?' asked Robin stiffly.

Dudley turned in his chair, and Guildford leaned on his shoulder confidingly.

'We don't have to go back do we, Father? She doesn't like us.'

It was not necessary for a man as astute as Dudley to inquire who *she* might be.

'Surely the little Prince made you welcome?' he insisted irritably. He turned to Robin for confirmation and suddenly noticed a blazing, swollen patch on his forehead. Getting up to take a closer look he demanded to know how it came to be there.

'She hit him with a book,' piped Guildford solemnly, 'she hit him ever so hard.'

'What's that?' roared Dudley, glaring at them both. 'Is it true?'

Robin stared at the floor; his father shook him furiously.

'Is it true?'

'Yes, sir.'

Dudley pushed him away with a curse.

'My own son! God's blood, is it possible? Can't you be trusted out of my sight for five minutes?'

'She said I was a low-born Dudley,' Robin burst out hotly in defence. 'She said my grandfather was a traitor! She asked for it!'

'Asked for what?' inquired Dudley, ominously calm.

Robin was silent.

'What's a Little Bastard?' asked Guildford suddenly.

Dudley's hand suddenly shot out and cuffed Robin smartly across the ear.

'You oaf! You clod! You surely were not such a fool as to call her that!'

'It's only what everyone calls her,' muttered the boy, tenderly feeling his ear.

Dudley put his hands resolutely behind his back and strode to the window. It was perfectly true of course. Even the ambassadors called her that—but not to her face!

He imagined the scene. And suddenly, in spite of his annoyance, his lips began to curl beneath a trim moustache. He turned to look at his son.

'What did she hit you with?'

'A Bible, sir—I think.'

Dudley laughed shortly.

'Well—there are worse ways of spreading God's word, I suppose.' He came back and rubbed the boy's red ear with rough affection. 'So! The little lady made a lasting impression on you, hey? Will you retire from the field or live to fight another day?'

Robin lifted his head and shared his father's smile without resentment.

'If it please you, sir—I should like to fight.'

'That's what I thought.' Dudley put a hand on the boy's shoulder and walked him to the door. 'Take my advice and leave insults to the women, Robin, a sharp tongue is the only weapon they have. Get out the broadswords and show her what a low-born Dudley is made of. I fancy when the two of you are done with fighting you'll be the best of friends—'

Dudley was a remarkably clever man; when he made a calculated prediction of events it was usually shrewd and accurate. Within a month Robin was actively seeking her spiteful company. She was quick and abrasive and more full of mischief than any boy he knew. He was not ashamed to call her friend and as a mark of his respect, he admitted her to his secret retreat in the bushes at Hampton Court.

'It's not very big, is it?' she complained. They were sitting like two peas in a pod, with her gown billowing over his muddy boots.

'It's big enough,' he said sulkily. 'You didn't expect an anteroom, did you?'

She looked up at the central branch.

'Is that what holds it in place?'

'Yes—*don't do that!*'

She was swinging on the branch with all her weight and a second later the whole fragile structure collapsed on top of them.

'You mean rat!' he burst out. 'You've ruined it.'

'I didn't know that would happen,' she said innocently. 'I'm only a girl.'

Slightly mollified he sat down again, clearing a path in the debris first. After a moment she began to collect up the branches.

'I'm going to build a better one,' she announced. 'Are you going to help me?'

'No,' he said sullenly. 'Why should I?'

She gave him a push with her foot.

'Get out of my way then, you're sitting in the entrance.'

For the rest of the afternoon he sat and watched and jeered; when she had finished he was quietly amazed; it was more than half as big again. Flushed with triumph she came to stand beside him.

'It's good, isn't it?' she said modestly.

'It's all right, I suppose, for a first attempt. But it won't last. One gust of wind and the whole thing will fall to pieces.'

She smiled and said, 'We'll see.'

Buoyant as a cobweb, the thing stood there week after week, defying the laws of gravity and several storms. Years later, when he heard the accusations of 'no human agency' applied to the fantastic, fragile substance of her vast success, he remembered that secret place and how he had thought, It isn't possible. Tomorrow it's sure to be down.

They went there often, holding their breaths when Henry's courtiers passed to and from within a few feet of them, but they were never discovered, not even by Guildford Dudley who spent many wasted hours searching for them.

'Guess what!' said Robin, one cold October morning when they sat on his cloak because the grass was damp. 'John brought a kitchen maid to our bedroom last night. I saw him take her.'

Elizabeth frowned. 'Where did he take her?'

'On his bed of course. You don't suppose they did it on the floor like peasants, do you?'

There was a blank, bewildered look on her face and understanding burst upon him in a delightful thunderclap. So she didn't know everything, after all!

'Do you want me to tell you how a man takes a woman?' he inquired loftily.

'Thank you,' she said, stiff and defensive, 'I already know.'

He looked at her thoughtfully. 'I don't believe it,' he said slowly. 'You really don't know, do you? You don't know the first thing about it. You—ow!'

She had seized his little finger and bent it backwards.

'Tell me then, master high and mighty Dudley, who can't decline the simplest Latin noun—tell me what you know, if anything.'

He pulled his finger away and looked at her, suddenly sly.

'Knowledge is expensive,' he said. 'What's this piece worth to Your Grace?'

She considered a moment. 'I'll do your Latin translation tomorrow.'

'And the next day?'

'Oh, all right!' she said ungraciously. 'Now get on with it.'

When he had told her all she needed to know she gave him a derisive nudge.

'I don't believe you. Love isn't like that. Who would want to do anything so disgusting?'

'It's true,' he said angrily, 'every bit of it. Even kings and queens do it like that.'

She flushed to the roots of her hair.

'They don't! My father and Queen Katherine—they do *not.*' Suddenly, unexpectedly, she began to cry wildly. 'I hate you, Robin Dudley, I hate you. Go away!'

He went. They did not speak again for over a week, a long tense week during which the younger children, quick to sense the hostility between them, sided pointedly with Elizabeth, as experience had taught them it was wise to do. Even Guildford Dudley decamped to the enemy with the half-shamed explanation that he had never expected a princess to pinch so hard. It was Robin's first experience of royal disfavour, and he found it every bit as uncomfortable and humiliating as he was to find the real thing in later life. The only attention he received in the schoolroom was from their tutor, and that was more unwelcome than ever.

'I am a patient man, Master Robert,' said Dr Cox sanctimoniously, examining a dog-eared piece of Latin prose with distaste, 'but there is a point where unrequited patience and discipline cease to meet. Be pleased to accompany me into the next room at your earliest convenience.'

The children stared as Robin got up and sauntered with feigned nonchalance after the tutor, but only Elizabeth looked up from her work when he returned with clenched teeth. She watched him walk gingerly to the window-seat and lower himself with care on to a cushion. After a moment she slipped off the wooden bench and joined him.

'Did it hurt?'

He unclenched his teeth just sufficiently to say, 'No.'

'That's what I thought.' She went back to the table and fetched the sheet of parchment she had been working on. 'Here—you can copy it if you want.'

'Can I?' His strained face relaxed and lit up; he held out his hand and she withdrew the paper just beyond his reach, looking at him with a curious suppressed excitement.

She said very softly, 'It's not true, is it?'

There was a moment of silence while he looked from her face to the paper and shifted his throbbing body on the cushion.

'No,' he said at last, 'it's not true. I made it all up to annoy you.'

As he watched, the corners of her mouth curled slowly up into a smile of delight.

'Liar!' she said, and dropped the paper down beside him.

He never forgot the absurd incident, trivial as it seemed at the time, a child's quarrel in which she had had the last word after all. Years later, when her name had blazed a trail of flaming light across Europe, he would recall that moment when he first acknowledged her superior will.

Their friendship healed after its breach, as it would later heal time and time again, and life resumed its petty round of study and play, giving neither warning nor preparation for the tragedy which was less than a month away.

In November the tranquil Indian summer of the King's fifth marriage erupted, with a violence that devastated several lives.

The King was the first casualty. When Archbishop Cranmer pushed that piece of paper into his pudgy hand at morning service, he thought his head would burst with rage and grief. Others had loved his Rose, even as he had done. Names were before him, dates—oh God, they would pay for this.

Winter descended, like a curtain upon a stage, and the court, touched with frosty fears, huddled in small whispering groups to talk of the little Queen's crimes. In the forgotten nursery, a terrified silence reigned. Robin Dudley from the height of his superior knowledge had elucidated 'adultery and high treason' for the benefit of the youngest. There was nothing more to be said; they all knew what would happen now. Even so, no one was quite prepared for the screaming. Peal after peal of it went shivering through the gallery of Hampton Court, screams born of blind terror which splintered through the palace on the day Katherine Howard tried to reach Henry and beg for her life.

The unearthly cries shuddered across the schoolroom where Robin Dudley, staring at the Princess Elizabeth, saw a look he never wished to see again on the face of any human creature. Suddenly, the screams were mingled with the shouts and footsteps of guards. Katherine had almost reached the King in the Chapel when they took her and, still screaming, dragged her away.

She never saw the King again. There was no trial. An Act of Attainder was passed against her and on the 13th of February little Katherine Howard followed Anne Boleyn to the block.

When it was all over a great quiet spread over the palace, an air almost of desertion. Courtiers kept themselves to themselves, revels ground to a halt, corridors stood silent.

In the quiet of the countryside Katherine Champernowne watched her charge with increasing concern. For what seemed an unnatural length of time Elizabeth showed no outward sign of grief. And then the nightmares began and the childish roundness fell away from her cheeks. She was pale and sullen and aggressive, less readily affectionate than before and the spectacular tantrums of her early years returned.

'I can't deal with it any longer—she's quite beyond me!' sobbed the governess one evening, when a particularly irrational and violent outburst from her charge had reduced her to tears. 'I'm going to write to the King.'

Blanche Parry stared at her steadily in the firelight.

'I wouldn't do that if I were you, madam. She's the last person the King wants to be reminded of under the circumstances. He might have you removed from your post and then—God forgive me for saying this—I wouldn't trust that child alone in a room with a length of rope.'

Kat turned deathly pale. 'She's only eight!'

'She can tie a knot, can't she?—that's all it takes. She may not show it, but she's very fond of you, madam.'

'I'm fond of her,' admitted Kat, 'more than fond. But when she screams like that I'm damned if I know what to do.'

'Let her scream,' said Blanche wisely, 'until she learns how to cry.'

The clock in the schoolroom ticked steadily, for life continued and so did lessons. Katherine's death had left small impression on the Dudley boys and the little Prince was young enough to lose an unpleasant memory in the pressing urgency of daily concerns.

But Elizabeth harboured a strange obsession with the gallery that led to the Royal Chapel at Hampton Court. She faithfully collected the morbid snippets of conversation drifting around and embroidered tales that made the younger children wide-eyed with fear.

'The gallery's haunted!' she said with grim authority. 'That's why no one cares to walk there alone after dark.'

The silence which greeted this remark, profound and very satisfying, lasted roughly ten seconds, the time it took for Robin Dudley to retrieve a soggy pellet of paper from the inkwell with a ragged quill.

'Father says there's no such thing as ghosts,' he said derisively. 'And *I* wouldn't be afraid to go there after dark even if there were!'

Elizabeth closed her copy of Terence and returned her own quill to the central stand on the table.

'Tonight,' she said softly, 'we'll see just how brave you are.'

They stood in the silent gallery, huddled in their sable-trimmed night robes, with their cold feet tucked inside velvet house shoes and their huge shadows spreading over the panelled wall behind them.

'I don't like it here, Rob,' said Guildford Dudley in a tremulous whisper.

'Well, you would come,' snapped his brother, who didn't like it either, but was certainly not going to admit it. 'I told you not to.'

'Aren't you afraid we might see—*her*?'

'Nobody's ever seen her. They only say that you can hear her voice crying here at night.'

They both shivered, moved closer together, and were silent. At the far end of the gallery they could see the distant, bobbing light of a solitary candle. For a moment it paused by the door of the Chapel, where the Queen had been captured, then it came slowly, flickering and swaying, back towards them. In her long white nightgown, Elizabeth looked like a small ghost herself, with the light shimmering over her pale face and glinting on her red hair. Guildford clutched his brother's arm and was roughly shaken off.

'Don't be stupid, Gil.'

'I want to go back, Robin—I'm scared!'

'Cry-baby,' said Elizabeth sharply as she reached them. 'What did you bring him for?'

'I didn't bring him,' said Robin furiously, 'he followed me—he's always following someone, like a silly sheep.'

Guildford began to snivel softly into his furred sleeve. Elizabeth turned away impatiently to set down her candle and beside it the little doll she carried beneath her arm. After a moment she made the sign of the cross above the flame and began to speak softly in Latin. They could not catch what she said, but she looked so uncannily like a witch repeating the words of an incantation that Guildford began to sob in good earnest.

'I want to go back, I want to go back. Come with me, Robin.'

'I can't leave her here by herself,' said Robin sharply. 'She's only a girl. Look—take my candle and go back if you want to—but don't let the guards see you.'

Guildford fled silently down the corridor and after a moment Robin went over to her and touched her arm.

'What are you doing?' he asked uneasily. 'What did you say just then?'

She picked up the candle and looked at him through the dancing yellow flame.

'I said that I would never marry.'

He laughed outright. 'Why did you say that?'

Turning, she glanced once more down the empty gallery and shivered.

'Because I meant it.'

'Oh,' he said uncomfortably and picked up the doll, turning it over in surprise. 'Why do you play with this?' he asked slowly. 'It's broken!'

'It's not broken!' she said strangely and took it from him.

'Of course it is,' he insisted. 'It's got no—' The word died on his lips as he saw her face. As he watched she took the doll and the candle and began to walk away down the gallery.

He was forced to run after her, to avoid being left in the dark.

*   *   *

Months passed and the King, climbing out of a dark abyss of self-pity, began to search for a new wife. Foreign princesses were conspicuous by their sudden absence in the matrimonial stakes, and a number of women averted their eyes nervously whenever they felt the King's gaze heavy upon them. Among these anxious ladies was Lord Latimer's widow, Katherine Parr, who stared uneasily across the banqueting table to meet Tom Seymour's eyes and look hastily away once more. The King watched this interesting little side play and suddenly knew he had found what he was looking for. He admired his brother-in-law's taste in women and very soon was making his intentions clear, amused by the opportunity to get one up on Tom, that notorious ladies' man.

Unaware of the momentous decision her father had made, Elizabeth closed her book and went out to the stables with Robin, down the kitchen stairs and past the tennis court, hitching up her skirts among the dirty rushes. Beside a bale of hay lay a sleek bitch, suckling half a dozen greedy puppies.

'Caesar's litter,' said Robin proudly.

'Caesar *again!* Does he ever stop to eat?'

Robin grinned and they exchanged the furtive snigger of children with a little worldly knowledge.

'Mother says he ought to be castrated.'

'If I were your mother,' said Elizabeth wickedly, 'I'd castrate more than poor old Caesar. She's always pregnant.'

Robin laughed. 'Father says Dudleys will inherit the earth.'

'They certainly ought to—they breed like rabbits.' Elizabeth shuddered. 'It must be awful to have a baby every year.'

'It's nothing,' said Robin, cheerfully heartless. 'It's only like shelling peas. It's much worse for a horse. They let me watch Black Cherry foal the other day and the foal's head was stuck so far back that old Wilks had to get his whole arm inside and—'

'Be quiet!'

He turned to look at her in astonishment.

'Listen!' she said curtly.

Footsteps were crunching heavily across the courtyard and they exchanged a look of alarm. There would be trouble if they were caught together here, without her attendants.

'Over here!' said Robin and pulled her down behind the bale of hay.

The fat puppies waddled after them and the bitch growled as a tall man came quickly through the door. They recognized Tom Seymour at once from his golden beard and arrogant swagger, and Elizabeth, relaxing in the sudden knowledge that they had nothing to fear from him, would have stood up and shown herself in quick delight, but Robin held her back. Almost immediately there was another sound outside, the sound of frantic running footsteps and the swirl of a heavy train across the dried straw.

A woman dressed in unrelieved black burst suddenly into the barn and fell into the arms of the waiting man, laughing and crying in a wild panic, repeating over and over again, 'What can I do—oh God, what can I do?'

'Be quiet, be calm, Kate—my poor Kate. It can't be for long. The King is old—the King is often sick. Our time will come if you are wise and careful now.'

'*Wise!* As wise as Katherine Howard or Anne Boleyn? Oh, Tom, Tom, how can I bear it?'

'You must bear it, Kate, you must! If you refuse him now it will mean both our heads, for he knows about us—oh yes, he knows! There's nothing misses the old devil's eye! He told me this morning that I was to go to Flanders as his ambassador. He's clearing the stage, Kate—for your sake and mine I must go without a word of protest. And when he asks for your hand, as he will do any day now, you must say yes.'

'I won't, I *can't!* Oh, Tom, take me with you—we could go to France, to Germany, anywhere, we would be safe.'

Tom Seymour shook his great head and his voice was bitter.

'He spares neither man in his anger nor woman in his lust. We would be hunted down before we reached Dover. Marry him now with a brave heart and know that in a year or two he will be dead—he rots before our eyes with that leg. And when you're free you'll find me waiting—'

Savagely he closed her protesting mouth with his own and they clung together in an agonized moment of passion.

'Go now,' he said softly as they broke away from each other at last. 'You must not be missed. God keep you, God help you, Kate—my Kate.'

Crushed and apathetic she went to the door in silence and slipped away and after a few minutes he followed her. The barn was silent again except for the restless stamping of horses' hooves and the soft cooing of the pigeons who sat on the rafters.

Robin knelt up, picked the clinging straw from his apricot hose and whistled softly through clenched teeth.

'It looks,' he said calmly, 'as though Katherine Parr will shortly be your new stepmother.'

Elizabeth said nothing for so long that he looked round in surprise and found that she was crying. Two big tears had rolled down her white little face and she was staring at the puppy who had curled asleep on her velvet skirts.

He sat on the bale of hay, swinging his long legs and feeling oddly uncomfortable, as he would feel perhaps to find another boy crying at his side. A steadily increasing line of sisters inured him as a rule to girlish tears, but this furtive grief affected him like a premonition of tragedy. He felt a curious need to make her stop.

Hunting for a handkerchief, he discovered that as usual he hadn't got one. Instead he found the apple he had been saving for some appropriate moment of privacy. He polished it against his doublet, eyed its round rosiness with regret, and after a moment's hesitation he offered it to her.

She looked up, drew the long hanging sleeve of her dress across her nose in what he considered to be a most vulgar fashion and climbed up beside him on the bale of hay.

'I don't want it.' After a moment she remembered to thank him.

He began to eat it himself before she could change her mind; he was always hungry. But all the time he ate he was horribly aware of those silent tears rolling faster and faster. At last he said uncomfortably, 'I wish you wouldn't cry like that.'

'I'm not crying—there's something in my eye.'

He turned to look at her with open disbelief. 'What—both of them?'

She made no reply to his gross impertinence and refused to look at him. He finished the apple and threw the core away into the straw, supposing with rough sympathy that she wept for her last stepmother. Perhaps she was afraid the same thing would happen again.

'I expect,' he said, intending to be cheerful, 'that the King will just *divorce* this one when he's tired of her—then your uncle can have her after all.'

That did not appear to comfort her at all. She began to get off the bale in a monstrous hurry.

'He's Edward's uncle, not mine,' she sobbed, hunting furiously for the slipper she had lost in her hasty descent. 'And he won't marry her—he won't marry anyone except—' She broke off so abruptly that her mouth snapped shut like the spring of a trap. He heard no more of whom she expected Tom Seymour to marry and it was to be four years before malicious rumour supplied the missing name to his by then unwilling ears.

But for the time being he quickly forgot it.

So the King married Katherine Parr and Elizabeth's favourite step-uncle sailed away to sanctuary in Flanders. It was almost three years before he judged it safe to return to court, a court paralysed with fear and uncertainty under a sick tyrant's rule. He felt the oppressive atmosphere as soon as he arrived and his bold laugh rang through the whispering corridors like a breath of fresh air. 'He's back!' said the gay glances of all the unmarried girls at court; 'He's back!' said his brother's sombre stare with a flicker of dislike and distrust; 'He's back!' said the King's jaundiced eye as it roved over that bronzed figure, and remembered with envy how many years it was since he had looked like that.

The new Queen folded her hands in her lap and carefully averted her gaze, afraid to betray herself by looking at him too directly. It had been the longest three years of her life, full of alarms and fears which had aged her. Tom could see in that first moment that she was not the gay laughing widow she had been when the King first set eyes upon her. Poor Kate!

All around him Tom felt the nervous shifting glances of men who wondered how much longer they would keep their heads these days. And those few who did not fear the block, being spotless in their honour, were anxious lest their religious leanings should shortly lead them to the stake.

Heresy had been a delicate subject for Catholics and Protestants alike ever since the break with Rome. Too orthodox a Roman Catholic and you were a traitor; too vigorous a reformer and you were a heretic. Either way Henry had the majority of his courtiers in a cleft stick and fear pulsed through the palace like a tangible force. He could not bear the doctrinal controversy spreading through England, nor could he accept that he was largely responsible for its growth. To suit his personal convenience, he had pushed open the door to the Reformation one necessary chink; now he found himself unable to close it once more and he was equally savage in his reprisals to offenders on either side of the religious fence. All he had done was to remove papal authority from the land, along with iniquitous monasteries—he'd never had much time for monks and nuns anyway—and now this insufferable spiritual chaos! Had he not made the position clear, simple and unquestionably right? Who dared to raise the voice of dispute in England? He would root it out with axe and rope and fire. He was King; he was Pope; was he not, perhaps, even God? Paranoid with suspicion, the small eyes ran here and there seeking treason and heresy behind every face, while the little mortals around him trembled like autumn leaves in a fierce wind, torn between worship and hate for this ageing Zeus from whose hands had fallen so many thunderbolts.

It was a relief and a pleasure for Tom Seymour to escape at last to the apartments of the royal children, where at least a man did not need to watch his every look and word. He strode down the familiar corridors with a tiny monkey dressed in imitation of a courtier swaying on his shoulder and a host of childish foreign trinkets in his hands. They danced around him with undignified delight, swamping him with a wave of genuine affection which touched his broad but shallow heart.

'Get back, you little vultures! Never saw such a clutch of cupboard lovers in all my life! And that's God's truth.' He swung Edward over his shoulder and capered round the room until the little boy crowed with delight. It was strange just how much he had missed this ill-assorted collection of young creatures, the pale delicate little Prince, the grave-faced Grey sisters and the 'Little Bastard' herself.

His eyes fell at last on the boys who stood embarrassed and forgotten on the edge of the family circle. Who were those lads? Ah yes, he remembered now, two of Dudley's considerable brood—that fellow was like a tom cat! How many was it, twelve, thirteen? Could be more by now, of course. There was a man who'd bear watching, too smooth by half, always with an eye on the next rung of the ladder, not averse to rising on the backs of his own offspring, he'd be bound. What was behind the apparently innocuous presence of these two disturbingly handsome and well-grown lads? Two boys and a choice of three girls, the Lady Jane, the Lady Katherine—the Lady Elizabeth. God's blood, what a conniving devil! Was it possible the King couldn't see what Dudley was after?

He swung round with an unpleasant smile. He had his own designs on the royal children and Dudley could keep his long grasping fingers out of that pie. His hot glance fell suddenly on the Lady Elizabeth and with a shock he stared at her, as though seeing her for the first time. The pert child he had left behind three years ago was gone, and instead he saw a girl on the brink of womanhood, quite striking now with her bold colouring and slim figure, not exactly pretty, but handsome enough in a mysterious way. She had grown up behind his back. For the first time in three years he forgot the woman he had lost to the King and thought how very pleasant it might be to know another. She must be twelve by now, young for marriage it was true, but then she was always notoriously quick to learn and he was an able tutor, heh? Once he'd bent that fiery little will to his own, he'd have the warmest bed in Christendom and a powerful trump card to play if necessary in the next reign against his own brother.

But how best to go about it? Was it wise to suggest such a marriage to the King, who so lately had regarded him as a rival in the bedchamber? The mood of the court had not been wasted on him. He had seen at a glance that the King was more dangerously unpredictable than he had ever been. Better to wait a while before sticking his neck out in what might prove to be a distressingly literal fashion. He had waited three years—he could wait a little longer, wait and watch her grow into a woman. He'd always had the softest of spots for the wretch—courting her would be the best sport yet; and possibly the most profitable.

He looked up at the sound of a sudden skirmish, in time to see the little monkey, frightened by the attentions of so many strangers, bolt up the nearest tapestry, chattering with fear.

'Robin will get him down,' said Elizabeth's voice at his shoulder. 'Animals like him, did you know that? He can do anything with a horse.'

Tom watched the boy with hostility. He didn't like the warmth in her voice, or the boy's dark good looks. Good with horses—he knew what *that* led to more often than not.

'You like him, don't you,' he remarked, keeping the edge out of his voice with an effort.

She blushed. 'Oh—not particularly.'

Now he was thoroughly alarmed. It was the first time he had ever seen a blush on the cheeks of this brazen little madam.

'You know, of course, that his grandfather was a traitor.'

Her blush deepened to crimson. 'Not a *real* traitor,' she said hastily.

'He died on the block and I didn't hear anyone at the time complaining about it. I'm damned if I know what the sons of a low-born knave are doing here in the first place. I should have thought your father could provide you with better company.'

She had a guilty look which infuriated him. By God, he had not come home a day too soon by the look of things. He put his hands on her shoulders and tilted her chin upwards.

'Get your governess and I'll take you riding. I've got a new mare for you to try.'

As they walked to the door, Robin stepped across their path and offered the monkey with a gesture that suggested arrogance. The boy had an odd look on his face that might have been resentment.

'Don't forget your monkey, sir,' he said, and looked pointedly at Elizabeth as he said it.

Tom clapped him roughly on the shoulder.

'Oh, you'd better keep him, young man.' In his eyes was the hostility of like poles repelling. 'I fancy he'll be quite at home with your family. Haven't Dudleys been apes for more than three generations?'

Elizabeth laughed and put her hand on Tom's arm and Robin watched them walk away down the corridor together, the magnificent courtier and the half-grown girl, silhouetted against the bright sunlight. Humiliation, rage and jealousy filled him with the urgent desire to kick something.

For the rest of his life he would see, at intervals, those two bright mocking figures laughing at him as they walked together down an endless dark corridor in his mind.

*   *   *

Katherine Parr had lived on borrowed time for the best part of three years and all the signs now were that time was rapidly running out. Increasing ill-health worked on the King's moody temper, caused him to take out his catalogue of grievances against his wife and multiply them daily. Another barren wife! A wife moreover who would not see thirty again and sported opinions on religious reform. Barren *and* opinionated—what a miserable combination of faults!

He began to lend an ear to the tales of her enemies, Gardiner and Wriothesley, both working for her downfall. 'She succours heretics, Your Majesty—'

Interesting that, and possibly useful. He filed the knowledge for future reference. And soon the rumour was all over the court that the King smiled very warmly on the widowed Duchess of Suffolk.

'They're taking bets on the date of the wedding,' said Robin Dudley heartlessly, but Elizabeth did not smile; she had not smiled for a long time. She was stiff with tension, bracing herself against another tragedy, for this Queen too had been endlessly kind to her so that slowly, unwillingly, she had come to care. She was afraid to go into her stepmother's apartments and see Katherine's hunted face, that sick despair, that utter hopelessness.

The waiting was unbearable, a steady growth of choking tension until rumour said at last the most dreadful thing of all. The King had signed a warrant for the arrest and interrogation of Katherine Parr. There would shortly be a seventh wife.

The dreadful news felled Katherine to her bed with a hysterical fit that shook the palace. Elizabeth crept to the Queen's bedside but the dreadful staring eyes which greeted her bore no recognition and she was swept out of the room by a horde of panicking women. Robin found her wandering aimlessly in the garden, white and silent, like the sole survivor of some terrible disaster. They sat in silence on a stone bench and he tried in vain to make her smile. Presently she was sick. He took her to her governess, who thanked him curtly and shut the door in his face and he saw no more of her until the crisis was over.

'What the devil is that infernal noise?' glowered the King, listening with increasing irritation to the dreadful shrieks which echoed from the adjoining apartments. 'It sounds like an animal in a snare.'

The nervous doctor paused in the act of winding a bandage around the King's leg and met his master's shrewd gaze.

'Your Majesty, it is the Queen who cries.'

'The Queen, the Queen?' blustered Henry. 'What the devil ails the woman? Am I to have no rest in my sick-room?'

There was silence in the chamber. No one dared to meet his eyes. Henry sat back in his huge chair and glared at his attendants. What was this, eh? Did she know about the warrant—had some fool blabbed before he was quite ready to spring the trap?

Well, now he came to think about it perhaps he had been a shade too hasty. He was in a low state of health today and could have used a wife about him. She had gentle fingers had Kate, and a soothing manner—not much to excite a man's flagging interest it was true, but just at this moment his pain was of more significance to him than sexual desire. And Kate was a good nurse. Of course, she'd had the effrontery to question him on one or two religious issues and by God he was not about to be taught in his old age by a wife—but really, was it worth the upheaval to get rid of her? No doubt, after this fright, she'd be none too eager to question him again and the prospect of a grateful, repentant wife ministering to his cantankerous wants had a certain appeal. No need to put on any show for Kate, no need to woo and charm a selfish kitten like my lady Suffolk. He had himself conveyed to her bedside in the great wheeled chair that was now necessary whenever he wished to hoist his enormous bulk around the palace, and cleared up this stupid misunderstanding between them. And when Chancellor Wriothesley with forty halberdiers marched into his presence next morning to arrest the Queen he was most considerably put out. The unfortunate man was blasted thence by a royal bellow of rage and went away to inquire furiously how it was he had not been told that the King and Queen were 'perfect friends' once more.

Wriothesley complained bitterly to Bishop Gardiner, who shrugged and told him to bide his time. There would be other opportunities to rid themselves of Katherine Parr and her Lutheran leanings. Elizabeth, as she looked at her stepmother's pinched, grey face, knew it was true. She watched that race against time, Katherine's life against the King's, in an agony of suspense and prayed with fierce desperation that God would see fit to take her father before he got the chance to change his mind.

And He did. Even Henry could appreciate the fine irony of it as he lay on his death-bed and told his wife that 'It is God's will that we should part'. She knelt and wept, not very convincingly, and if he had had the strength left he would have laughed and told her not to play the hypocrite—it didn't become her. And so they parted on amicable terms. Tom Seymour was waiting outside the chamber when she came out. He had an odd, preoccupied look which she thought she understood; she was careful not to smile as she passed on her way.

And so the old lion died. Having restored *both* his daughters to the succession with a despot's calm disregard for logic, Henry Tudor departed this world, apparently entirely reconciled to all the evil he had perpetrated while resident in it.

'His Majesty died in the faith of Christ,' said Cranmer smoothly and his bland expression challenged anyone to deny it.

So he was dead. A little boy stood devastated by the news that he was King of England and turned to his youngest sister for support. Edward cried so pitifully that Elizabeth found tears stealing down her own cheeks and Lord Hertford, watching them with a jaundiced eye, decided they must be separated immediately; he didn't like the influence she wielded over the boy. Within a week, Elizabeth found herself at Chelsea Palace with her stepmother.

The moment Henry had breathed his last, Hertford had taken command. The King's will had dictated a Council of Regency during the minority of his son; Hertford kept Henry's death a secret for three days while he manipulated the legal details, emerging at the end of it as Lord Protector of the Realm and Sole Governor of the little King's royal person. By February he was Duke of Somerset and the whole of the Council was beneath his heel. Somewhere in the course of usurping power for himself, he remembered his younger brother Tom, and tossed him the post of Lord High Admiral to keep him quiet.

When the news was announced, John Dudley leaned back in his chair at the council table and picked his teeth delicately with an ivory toothpick to conceal a smile of satisfaction. He had seen the murderous look on Tom's face and he was well pleased. He knew resentment when he saw it and what it heralded in an ambitious, headstrong man. The Seymours would drive each other along the inevitable path of self-destruction without any helping hand. And when the power feud between the King's uncles was over there would be rich pickings for anyone with the stomach and intelligence to take them.

The new Earl of Warwick knew he could afford to wait a little longer for the lion's share.

CHAPTER 4

Tom Seymour had spent the last five years waiting for the King to die. Now that moment had come only to see him cheated of his rights by a smug, posturing elder brother who skulked self-righteously beneath the mantle of Lord Protector. When he heard that news Tom could have slit the throat of every creeping lackspittle on the Council, and he moved swiftly to consolidate what was left of his own influence. Casually, as though it were a matter of small importance, he broached the subject of his marriage to the Princess Elizabeth with the Council. It was turned down so flatly and furiously that even Tom saw it would be certain death to proceed with the matter any further.

He asked her all the same though, just for the amusement of watching her reaction; and was rudely disappointed. She was as prim and wooden as a doll beneath his caressing hand and told him she had neither the years nor the inclination for marriage. He could not begin to imagine why the idea threw her into such a rage, when every time he caught her sidelong glance upon him he could feel it heavy with silent worship. Vexed and curiously hurt, he rode back from Chelsea in a grey mood to drown his irritation in malmsey.

She refused me! That little chit had the damned effrontery to refuse me!

He went to bed that night, more drunk than he had ever been in his life; but by morning he had almost forgotten it. Reality had him in a painful grip that left little time to spare for the nursing of injured pride. Every day that he wasted saw Ned a little firmer on his stolen pedestal. Maybe he could not have a princess—but he could have a Dowager Queen and that was no little prize.

So, night after night, he rode in secret assignation to Chelsea Palace, but now it was not Elizabeth he met in the windswept darkness at the postern gate. He took Katherine with pleasure and a clear conscience; a few weeks later they were married in secret, without the Council's consent. And as soon as the ceremony was over, he persuaded his wife to let him break the news to Elizabeth alone.

'But, Tom, don't you think perhaps it would be better—'

'Was I not a highly successful diplomat?'

'Of course you were, but—'

'Then you may safely leave this delicate little matter in my capable hands.'

An hour later, Elizabeth curtsied dutifully to her new stepfather, her eyes downcast, her face wooden, her whole body stiff with furious grief held barely in restraint. She looked suddenly so young that the old tenderness almost checked him—almost, but not quite. He had dwelt unscathed behind the mighty fortress of his charm for more than thirty-five years. Her rejection had undermined the foundations of his confidence, shown him an unfamiliar reflection of himself—the tarnished hero, past the first virile flush of youth, who no longer conquered all. He intended to enjoy this.

'You have been avoiding me,' he observed smugly, looking down on her bent head.

'My lord flatters himself,' she said between clenched teeth. 'Why should I take the trouble to do that?'

'Why indeed?' he mocked. 'Unless, of course, you're jealous of my marriage. Though why you should be, when I offered you first refusal, I really couldn't say.'

She lifted her shoulders with a show of indifference.

'Had I known the Lord Admiral was merchandise for auction I might have been persuaded to bid for him.'

He smiled slowly. He liked a sharp answer when it cost him nothing to hear it.

'What a nasty cruel little tongue it has to be sure—and a temper to match it! Take a lesson from your mother, my little coquette, and learn to say No with less conviction if you want your suitors to knock again at your door. I'm not the only man who won't ask you the same question twice.'

She twisted free of his hand, and ran out of the room, leaving him in a state of rueful amusement.

Five minutes later Katherine swept through the door, saying with gay agitation, 'I knew it, I knew it—I should have told her myself—oh, Tom, what have you done to her?'

'Nothing,' he said hastily. 'Why, what did she say I'd done?'

'She didn't say anything,' cried Katherine. 'She walked past me as though I wasn't there. I knew she'd take offence. It's so soon after her father—think how it must look in a child's eyes. We should have waited longer for decency's sake—a year at least. Oh dear, I did so want her to be happy here with us—such a sad, sad little life, pushed from one to the other, never belonging—Tom, you must win her over. Why, I thought she liked you!'

'I thought so too,' he said, a trifle grimly. 'Perhaps my famous charm is beginning to desert me.'

'What an idea!' Katherine laughed. 'She's just a strange, difficult child who needs a lot of understanding. Be kind to her, Tom, for my sake, and you'll come to love her as I do.'

He coughed. That was fine irony, if she only knew it. He knew a fleeting moment of shame and dismissed it; what she didn't know would do her no harm—and it was true he ought to show an interest. He put his arm around Katherine good-humouredly and half listened to her voice as it went on, soaring in little leaps and bounds of happy concern saying, 'So reckless and impulsive', saying, 'With so many enemies', saying, 'You must take care'—

But he never took care, he despised caution and everything associated with its pursuit, a miserly attitude to life. Caution was his brother Ned personified, afraid to enjoy today for fear he might not enjoy tomorrow so well. Part of him acknowledged that Katherine was right, their hasty marriage had offended those in high places and they would do well to watch their step for a while. He kissed her with hearty affection; he promised to mend his careless ways and went straight out into the garden in pursuit of his stepdaughter.

The young King approved of his stepmother's new marriage; he was arguably the only person at court to do so and his approval was an effective shield against the Admiral's critics, the most vociferous being the Protector's wife.

A heated exchange of words took place in the Duke's private quarters—not in itself a remarkable event; marital harmony had always eluded Edward Seymour. His first union had ended in divorce and his present wife was a notoriously rapacious woman, insatiably ambitious and insufferably haughty. Whatever enemies the Duke failed to make for himself, his Duchess made for him; and her hostility to Tom had long amounted to an obsession. Once again, against his better judgement, the Protector found himself driven to intercede on his brother's behalf.

'Anne, it's hardly a crime to marry a rich widow.'

'The King's widow!' she insisted stonily. 'What if there should be a child?'

'No one could seriously believe it to be the King's after this length of time.'

'People believe what it pays them to believe,' sniffed his wife. 'I've told you before—Tom's a trouble-maker.'

The Duke laid a hand on her arm in what was intended to be a conciliatory gesture.

'And when he makes real trouble, my love, I swear I'll deal with him, but in the meantime you must be patient. I can't over-rule the King in this and brand myself a petty tyrant—you must see that!'

The Duchess subsided, like a crocodile sinking beneath the surface of a muddy lake. It was true that she could safely wait. She was confident the Admiral would hang himself one day without her aid—she had merely to play him sufficient rope for the purpose.

Disapproval of the Admiral's match came from many quarters. From Beaulieu, where the Princess Mary was in residence, it came in the form of a stilted letter offering to take charge of Elizabeth.

'If you want to go, my dear,' said Katherine sadly, 'I shall understand your position. I'm afraid we've made things very difficult for you.'

She went softly out of the room and left Elizabeth sitting at her writing desk with pen and ink. Her first impulse was to go—anything, oh, anything to get away from here. The effort of concealing her misery beneath a brittle cloak of gaiety was becoming insufferable. She must be pleasant to her stepmother, nonchalant with Tom and charming to her cousin Jane Grey, who had recently joined the household, following some shady deal between the Admiral and her parents. She had Jane to be jealous of now, in addition to Katherine, and she was so taut with pent-up, socially unacceptable emotion that she felt ready to burst. Oh yes, she would go, and the sooner the better.

Halfway through the letter of acceptance she paused and imagined the deadly, nun-like regime at Beaulieu. She had stayed with Mary too often during her childhood not to realize that she would be utterly bored within a week, supervised and corrected from morning till night. And if she left the easy-going hilarity of Chelsea where everyone now practised the fashionable Reformed faith, she would be under intolerable pressure to go to Mass. She could twist Katherine around her little finger, but she would never get her own way with Mary no matter how much she sulked or wheedled. At least at Chelsea she was with people she loved, however hopeless and painful that love might be. Katherine, who had been so good to her—and Tom. What torture could compare with that of not seeing him every day?

She screwed up the letter and began again, this time on a formal note of refusal. Outside her window she could hear the Admiral's voice and her pen began to fly across the page. She wrote politely but rather carelessly, declining Mary's kind offer, and at the time never gave a thought to the offence her sister must automatically take from such a refusal. But years later she looked back on that letter, written in such ill-considered haste, and saw it as the pivot on which her whole existence had turned; for if she had gone to Mary then, the rest of her life would have been entirely different.

But she did not go. She remained at riotous, sociable Chelsea, and was more riotous and sociable than anyone else among the gay company that enjoyed the Lord Admiral's ample hospitality. She was a little older now, a little more mature and worldly wise, learning to hide her undesirable feelings and display an amusing front to the world. People turned automatically when she entered the room and gathered around her from choice, rather than courtesy. She began to enjoy the attention she excited among young men, and the Admiral, watching her enjoy it, struggled with his own angry emotions. So the little chit thought she was a woman of the world, did she, just because she had a wicked wit that sent her companions into convulsions of laughter. He'd seen her mother do just that, hold a little court at any gathering and the memory, for no accountable reason, angered him beyond endurance. He'd pull her down a step or two, by God he would—he'd treat her exactly as he used to do when she was four years old—and that would teach her to flaunt her charms at vacant boys and indulgent old men!

Part of this policy was to appear unannounced in her bedroom and start the sort of boisterous horseplay that a man might acceptably show to any four-year-old girl, bounding on the bed in his nightshirt, pulling off the sheets, slapping and tickling and kissing her until she was hysterical with laughter.

Only she was not four now, but nearly fourteen and at the bottom of his heart he knew he had not come to tease a child.

'My lady! My lord, for shame!' The governess, now a respectably married lady herself—Mrs Katherine Ashley—made a futile attempt to maintain order.

'My lord, I must insist you leave Her Grace's room at once. People are beginning to talk.'

'I can't go without Her Grace's express permission—she's a very touchy young lady or haven't you noticed?'

Elizabeth, seeing his back turned, dealt him a resounding thwack with her bolster which sent him sprawling, bare-legged in his night robe at Mrs Ashley's feet. She dived off the bed and began to beat him about the head until the pillow burst its seams and sent a snowstorm of swansdown into the air.

'Mrs Ashley, have you no shame for rearing this wretched Amazon?' he inquired sarcastically from the floor. 'You might at least have taught her not to hit a man when he's down.'

'Is there a better time to hit him?' inquired Elizabeth, aiming a kick. He caught her bare foot and pulled her down on top of him. When at last he had managed to sit on her and kiss her hand with exaggerated humility, he made a mocking bow to Mrs Ashley and clowned out of the room.

Katherine was still in bed when he returned, listening with easy good humour to the sound of turmoil in the room above. He flung himself on his back beside her and she leaned over to pick the clinging swansdown out of his golden beard and hair.

'What a fearful racket!' she said indulgently as she kissed him. 'You must have roused the whole household.'

'Do 'em good!' he retorted. 'Early to bed, early to rise.' He returned her kiss playfully. 'And speaking of *rising*—'

'Oh, Tom!' She pushed him gently away. 'You know we can't—not now—it wouldn't be safe.'

He sighed, but lay back good-naturedly enough; she was right of course. To have conceived a first child after so many barren marriages was a miracle he would not put lightly at risk. He wanted a son—and yet August was such a long way off, a long time to be patient.

Katherine sat up and pulled off her cap, allowing her hair to tumble freely round her shoulders.

'I think you're turning that girl into a positive hoyden,' she said lightly.

He shrugged. 'I'm only releasing her true self from its layers of gentle nurture. Oh, don't deceive yourself, Kate—the girl's a natural guttersnipe at heart, just like Boleyn. She may play the modest maid in your company, but behind your back those pretty prim lips spout words that even I would blush to use in mixed company. You might make a queen out of Bess, my love, but you'll never make a lady.' He paused reflectively. 'What she needs, of course, is a damned good beating!'

'You'd never take a whip to her!'

'Oh, wouldn't I—who's to stop me?' he teased. 'I'm her stepfather, after all, her guardian—oh, Christ's soul, Kate—if you could see your face! You silly goose—would I ever lay a hand upon her, save in fun? She's only a child!'

She's only a child. It was his sole line of defence, to himself and to others, but it grew a little thinner every day; and one chill windy morning, in the formal gardens at Hanworth, he finally acknowledged that he was playing with fire. It began as just another romp and ended with ugly emotions showing through the frayed edges of his control—and all because she was wearing a black dress which reminded him unpleasantly of her mother.

'Strange,' he said softly, 'I don't recall putting the household into mourning, do you, Kate? And no one wears black under my roof without my leave, certainly not a jumped-up chit of twelve.'

'I'm fourteen,' snapped Elizabeth furiously. 'You know I'm fourteen.'

'Is that so, grandmother?'

Katherine laughed. 'Tom, stop teasing her. You make her life a misery these days.'

'And what does she make mine I'd like to know? Listen—' He gave Elizabeth a push. 'We've done with play-acting now, madam. Go in and put on something that doesn't make you look like a whore from the stews.'

'*Tom!* That wasn't called for, dear.'

'I've had enough of her defiance,' he said brusquely. 'I'll have obedience in my own house or know the reason why. Go into the house, Elizabeth, and get changed at once.'

'I *won't!* I won't be ordered about. I'm the King's daughter.'

'You certainly are, madam. And it's time you began to behave like one.'

She backed against a tree, looking desperately at Katherine, who shrugged her shoulders in an amused and helpless gesture.

'You can't make me do anything,' she muttered sullenly.

'Oh, can't I? We'll see about that!' He grabbed her roughly and pushed her into Katherine's arms. 'Hold her for me while I teach her a lesson she won't forget.'

He whipped out his little jewelled dagger and knifed the full skirts to ribbons. Finally he took hold of the bodice and ripped it down the front, exposing her bare breasts. When he had finished he was panting. There was a glazed look in his eyes and his hand was shaking.

Elizabeth and Katherine stared at him in silence and in the cold wind Elizabeth began to shiver. He sheathed his dagger and tried to laugh nonchalantly.

'You wouldn't change it, so I changed it for you,' he said inadequately. Still they stared at him and suddenly, filled with shame, he lost his temper completely. 'God's death, girl, don't stand there like a bloody Bedlamite. Get inside the house and cover yourself decently.'

'Yes, go along, dear,' said Katherine shakily. 'I'll be up later.'

As he watched Elizabeth run up the gravel path to the house, he put a guilty arm around his wife and thought: It's got to stop!

Mrs Ashley was leaning over a clothes press when Elizabeth came into the room. She straightened up, turned round and stiffened with horror.

'What in God's name—'

'Before you ask,' said Elizabeth haughtily, 'it was the Admiral who did it.'

'The Admiral!'

'Yes—and don't take that tone with me, Ashley! It wasn't my fault. The Queen held me while he cut it up. I tell you the Queen *held* me.'

But she would not look at Kat as she said it.

Kat Ashley had never aspired to discipline. She had lost the whip hand with Elizabeth more than ten years ago and she had been endeavouring to lead her wilful charge ever since, with about as much success as a bumbling general attempting to command his army from the rear. Now she was forced to admit to herself that the Princess was galloping away from her ineffectual rein like a wild, unbroken mare. She had been unable to stop the girl slipping out on a barge after midnight on some wild jaunt of the Admiral's, and an uncomfortable premonition of impending disaster had begun to weigh heavily on the governess's mind.

That premonition eventually saw her standing alone in the Admiral's private study, patting nervously at her coif while her small anxious eyes roved over the maps strewn across his desk, over anything in fact which would postpone the necessity of looking into his handsome face.

'My lord—' There was an absurd wobble to her voice, but suddenly the panelled room seemed remarkably small and the Lord Admiral uncomfortably near. Kat was a little afraid of provoking that magnificent rage of his at such close quarters. 'My lord—forgive me if I speak out of turn—'

He looked up and gave her a wry smile.

'Get on with it, woman—I haven't got all day, you know.'

'My lord—I don't mean to question your intentions and, of course, it's not my place to give you advice—'

'Perfectly true,' he remarked sardonically, 'but I sense you intend to give it anyway. Speak out, woman, for God's sake—I'm not going to slit your throat.'

'I have to warn you that there's a great deal of talk—damaging and slanderous talk—concerning the Lady Elizabeth and—and you, my lord.' She took a gulping breath. 'My lord—to come alone, bare-legged, to a maid's chamber—tickling, slapping—and *kissing*—I beseech you to have a thought for her good name and leave off these morning visits.'

He exploded out of his chair with his favourite oath and Kat took a hasty step backwards.

'By God's precious soul, madam, I'll not be told how to conduct myself in my own house by a gossiping busybody of a servant. I'll lay the whole matter before the Protector first. God knows, we've had our differences over matters of state but he wouldn't stand by and see me slandered like this.'

'But, my lord—' wailed Kat.

'Out!' he roared. 'Get out before I forget you're a lady!'

Kat went to the Queen and voiced her fears, but Katherine laughed uneasily and merely promised to chaperone her husband's early-morning visits to Elizabeth's bedroom. Had she not been pregnant, she might have reacted more strongly, but the growing child had made her lethargic and complacent. She would handle this in her own way; she would not be stampeded into acting harshly by malicious gossip. And it would be all right in the end. Many a middle-aged man had a passing fancy for a teenage girl—*But it's me he loves, I know it's me. I mustn't let this get out of proportion.*

And there were other worries to distract her; increasingly strained relations with the Protector for one. Goaded by his wife, Somerset was refusing to hand over the jewels that the old King had left to her—why, he had even confiscated her wedding ring. Tom had been furious; there had been another bitter quarrel. And now Tom was talking of redressing his wrongs, with the little King's help, in Parliament, making the present session 'the blackest that ever was in England'.

He had remarked, in public, on the ease with which a man might steal the King from beneath his brother's nose.

'You must not *say* these things,' begged Katherine, wild with anxiety. 'Don't you see how it could be misunderstood?'

'Don't fret, my sweet. Ned can't see beyond the end of his nose—he never could!'

No, thought Katherine fearfully. But his wife can!

'A chance remark,' said the Duke of Somerset uneasily, 'is hardly evidence, my dear.'

The Duchess glared at him. 'It's a chance remark, is it, when someone speaks of abducting a king? In my day we called it treason! How much longer are you going to sit on your reforming backside waiting for that rogue to bring you down?'

'I have absolutely no evidence—'

'Then find some, you pompous fool. God knows there's rumour enough to hang him ten times over.'

The Protector chewed his pen and stared darkly out of the little latticed window. Oh yes—there was certainly rumour—crooked negotiations with Jane Grey's father—that very unhealthy interest Tom showed in the Lady Elizabeth. There was talk of condoning piracy, of debasement of the coinage, of the Admiral's desire to employ 10,000 men a month.

And what might he want with 10,000 men at his back?

The Protector turned to look at his wife with narrowed eyes. She was a hard bitch, but shrewd; he trusted her judgement.

'I shall have my brother put under surveillance,' he said quietly. 'Will that satisfy you?'

The Duchess smiled coldly.

'For the moment,' she said, and left him to brood.

*   *   *

There was no stepping back from the precipice this time; Tom had known it the moment he entered the room and found her alone with her hair loose.

Afterwards he blamed that hair, rippling in long red waves around her pale face, inflaming his desire, and wondered if she had heard his step in the corridor beyond and deliberately removed her coif to make herself look so abandoned and irresistible. He never knew the answer, never had the opportunity to ask it. He only knew that he wanted her, suddenly, urgently, beyond caution and common sense and decency; and that as suddenly, urgently, she wanted him.

He opened his arms to her as he had done so many times across the years, but this time it was no child they closed around. And he knew that whatever price he had to pay for this stolen pleasure it would be worth it.

It was not difficult to get her to the floor; she sank slowly, willingly, beneath him while he opened her mouth with his own. She wore a loose morning gown, no farthingale or petticoats, nothing to impede his urgent exploring hand. His touch sent a violent spasm through her body and deep in his mouth he felt her gasp. His finger worked with practised skill. Warm, moist, ready—oh, very ready.

He bunched the skirts high about her breasts, burying his face in her taut, bare skin; and it was there that Katherine found them, just in time to stop that moment of wild surrender.

He sprang up, as though her gasping exclamation had stabbed him in the back like a knife blow, and his bronzed face was crimson beneath its golden beard.

'Katherine!'

'Yes,' she said, in a strange, flat little voice, 'Katherine,' and went out of the room.

The Admiral ran after her and Elizabeth was left alone on the floor, burying her face in the dirty rushes, hiding from a shame that was too great to be borne.

Katherine said, 'She's fourteen—scarcely more than a child and just old enough to bear you one. Were you out of your mind?'

He was silent, shamefaced as a little boy caught stealing from his mother's purse.

At last he said awkwardly, 'It meant nothing.'

She stared at him.

'You think it nothing to despoil a girl second in line to the throne? You think your *brother* will call it nothing?'

'She's still a virgin,' he muttered. 'I give you my word on that, Kate. It's the first time I've ever let it go so far.'

'Then give me your word that it will also be the last and I too will be more than grateful to call it nothing.'

As she watched, a slow flush mounted to his forehead. He stared out of the window at the brick-walled garden and was stubbornly mute.

'Then you leave me no choice,' said Katherine dully. 'I must send her away.'

'You asked me to give my word,' he pointed out grimly. 'It would have been easier for me to lie and spare you the truth.'

She conceded the point wearily. She was great with child now and it was several months since he had shared her bed. At such a time, any woman in the household would have been happy to accommodate him. There was no need for him to have chosen Elizabeth unless—

'You love her, don't you?' she whispered.

Abruptly, he turned on his heel and went to the door.

'Just send her away, Kate,' he said harshly. 'And send her quickly. I don't want her in this house a moment longer than necessary.'

When he had gone, Katherine sank into a chair and let the tears roll slowly down her grey face.

It was all the answer she needed.

Torches were already blazing in their wall brackets, despite the evening sunshine, when Elizabeth closed the door of the Queen's room and trailed wearily over the rushes in the Long Gallery. It had been a quiet interview, without harsh words, bitterness or recrimination, but it had been hurtful to them both, leaving them like spent swimmers, gasping on some alien shore. The dignity of Katherine's generous spirit had humbled her, searing her with a remorse which made her squirm and want to hide away in shame. Nothing she could say or do would ever make amends for the wicked mess she had made of all their lives. And the memory of Katherine's anguished face would follow her into her lonely exile, feeding her gnawing sense of guilt, that most self-destructive of all emotions.

She stood still for a moment, grinding her slippered feet into the rushes and watching the cockroaches scatter. The thought of returning to her own apartment, to Kat Ashley's anxious questions and reproachful platitudes, was unbearable. She did not need the ruffled governess to tell her that she had only herself to blame . . .

At the end of the gallery there was an arched bay with a cushioned window-seat. She sank into it with relief and leaned her hot head against the thick glass of latticed panes, glad of its cool touch against the sick throbbing in her right temple. The pain was unfamiliar and intense; it seemed to be growing in severity, obscuring her vision, and it frightened her a little.

She had been too proud to tell Katherine or Kat, lest they assumed it to be a play for sympathy; now she nursed the acute discomfort with a touch of self-pity and fiercely hoped she had the plague. How much easier it would be to face death than to go away, alone, and in disgrace, with everyone knowing why she went . . .

A heavy hand fell on her shoulder, causing her to jump and start round. Beyond the window the sun was setting in a great red ball behind the trees, and a thin shaft of brilliant light cut at a low angle through the greenish glass, making a glory of the Admiral in his russet doublet.

'Has the Queen spoken to you?' he asked brusquely.

'Yes,' Elizabeth swallowed hard. Hot colour was flooding into her pale cheeks; she could not look at him.

He frowned. 'Did she—speak harshly?'

Elizabeth shook her head slowly. 'She was very kind. I almost wish she had been angry. She made me feel like—like an ungrateful hedge-drab.'

'It was no one's fault,' he began uncomfortably. 'When something like this happens we all have to be—sensible about it.'

'As sensible as my father perhaps?' She fixed him with a look of contempt which struck him to the heart. 'What would the Lord Admiral do, I wonder, if he found his wife on the floor with another man?'

Goaded to the limit of endurance, he dragged her out of the window and shook her violently.

'Do you think I'm proud of this day's work, you taunting jade? I swear by God's precious soul I never meant to hurt her. Is it a crime to love two women?'

'No, it's not a crime.' Her lips were curled in a bitter smile. 'Merely a damnable inconvenience to you. And what did poor Uncle Tom ever do to deserve that?'

'You bitch!' He slapped her smartly across the mouth. 'Don't you ever call me that again!'

Both hands flew to her head; she moaned and crumpled up in the window seat in a dazed stupor. The colour drained out of her face before his eyes and for a moment he was afraid he had knocked her senseless. He had hit her hard enough to hurt, it was true, but not that hard—surely not that hard.

'Bess!' Frightened by her colour, he lifted her up and touched the flaming patch at the corner of her mouth with remorse. It was the first time he had ever struck a woman—the first time he had ever felt either the need or the desire to. In all his light love affairs, he had always been the master, carelessly in command, conferring his virility with casual superiority on an enchanting but decidedly inferior breed. In Elizabeth he had met his match—perhaps more than his match—and her taunt was like a burn on his manhood.

But his savage blow now seemed unforgivable to one who looked suddenly so small and forlorn and wretched.

'You have to go away,' he said slowly. 'There is no alternative. If you stay, I couldn't answer for what might befall you. It's too dangerous.'

She said on a little strangled sob, 'I don't care about danger.'

'No,' he muttered, looking at her strangely. 'Your mother never cared either. And you're like her—too much like her. You fey a man worse than a quart of aqua vitae—you too could brew murder—as she did.'

Elizabeth leaned against the wall and drew a shaky breath.

'Then it's you, and not Katherine, who is sending me away.'

'Katherine would keep you here if she could,' he said hoarsely. 'If you were her own daughter, she couldn't love you better.'

Elizabeth bit her quivering lip.

'She said we were not to blame, you and I—that you had a man's appetites and that I was too young to resist them. She begged me to guard my reputation with the people. She said one day—I might be Queen of England.'

'So you will be,' he said quickly. 'A great queen.'

'And a great catch!' Her voice was suddenly soft with venom. 'That's why you asked me first—what a fool I was not to see it before now.'

She tried to push past him, blind with rage, but he caught her roughly.

'Listen to me—*listen*—'

'I don't want to hear your lies,' she sobbed, fighting free of him. 'I won't be used—not by you or anyone else. I've lost my home for nothing. Oh, why did you have to come here and spoil everything? I hate you! I hate *all* men.'

He let her go then, appalled by the pulsing violence in her voice. If she had had a dagger in her hand he would not have given a farthing-piece for his own life in a further struggle. Suddenly he felt he didn't know her, that he had never known her—the real Elizabeth—and he was shocked by the discovery. This morning a woman had sprung to life in his arms, but now that woman had gone, perhaps for ever. It was a child who ran away from him down the narrow gallery of Chelsea Palace; and as he stood and watched that reckless headlong flight he had the morbid fancy that she would go on running for the rest of her life.

CHAPTER 5

Elizabeth's immediate future was settled quickly and without dispute, both guilty parties being anxious to humour the injured. Sir Anthony Denny, a close friend of the Dowager Queen, agreed to take the Princess and her entourage under his own roof at the manor of Cheshunt, and if he was startled by the unprecedented nature of the arrangement, he was sufficiently a courtier to give no outward sign.

They were difficult days for everyone, those few before Elizabeth's departure, hours of feigned gaiety on both sides, alternating with tense, moody silences; tedious meals accompanied by equally tedious conversation. The old, jolly informality of the household was sealed for ever beneath a layer of ice which could not be broken no matter with what goodwill it was attacked; little Jane Grey sat crushed by the atmosphere, fervently wishing her tempestuous cousin were gone.

And at last, a week after Whitsun, she was gone indeed. Jane stood in the arched doorway beside the Queen and waved to the trim figure in the green riding habit, as she cantered down the drive at the head of the great, rumbling retinue of carts and pack horses, riding off into the still green countryside and out of their lives. Long after the drive was empty once more, Katherine stood there, watching the white dust swim and settle behind the tramping hooves and Jane knew, without daring to look, that tears were running down her haggard face. Jane's Greek and Latin were equal to many a Cambridge scholar's but the harsh emotional repressions of her childhood had left her tongue-tied in the presence of other people's distress.

'If it please Your Grace,' she said uneasily, 'my tutor will be waiting in the library.'

'Of course.' Katherine turned and smiled down at her absently. 'Run along to your studies, my dear.'

Jane hesitated.

'Will Your Grace not come inside out of the heat?' she ventured timidly.

Katherine's preoccupied gaze still roamed down the empty drive.

'I think I should like to walk a little in the gardens,' she said slowly. 'Run along now, child. I need no attendant.'

Jane ran up the wide staircase and knelt in the window-seat, watching that sad, shapeless little figure trail away across the lawns until she too was out of sight. Then the grounds were still and silent once more, like an empty stage at the end of some dramatic performance. It would certainly be peaceful with Elizabeth gone, but strange, as though some of the colour had gone out of the world in her absence. And people would miss her—even those like Jane, who did not particularly like her.

Jane leaned her head on her arms and thought sadly: If I were to leave here, it would be a week before anyone noticed I was gone . . .

When Elizabeth arrived at Cheshunt, the Dennys were waiting on the steps to greet her, hiding their curiosity beneath a civil mask of welcome. Some very ugly rumours had preceded her coming—it was even said in some quarters that the Princess was pregnant.

Certainly she was pale enough, thought Joan Denny as she rose from a curtsey and surveyed that slim, rather arrogant figure, but if she was, it was too early to tell by her external appearance. Faintly disappointed, Lady Denny went down the steps to greet Mrs Ashley, who was her sister.

'Well, Kat,' she said with muted disapproval. 'Here's a pretty state of affairs, I must say, when the King's daughter has to be sent away in disgrace. What were you about to let such a thing take place under your very nose?'

Kat stiffened and returned a perfunctory embrace.

'I hope you're not going to take *that* attitude, Joan, or our stay here will be most disagreeable.'

'Well, I'm not blaming you, of course,' added Lady Denny hastily. 'God knows I never envied you the post—always said you'd have more than one body's work. She's a haughty little piece, isn't she? Gives you trouble aplenty, I'd say.'

'She's very young,' said Kat loyally, flushing as though her sister criticized her own child, 'and whatever you've heard I don't doubt has been grossly exaggerated. The Lord Admiral would turn any girl's head. You take my word for it, Joan—she's more sinned against than sinning.'

'Well, my dear, I'm sure you know her best.' Joan sniffed and glanced doubtfully at the girl on the steps. 'She's very pale, don't you think?' she added meaningfully. 'I hope she's not ill.'

'She's been having headaches lately—very bad headaches.'

'Any vomiting?'

'Well, once or twice she—' Kat saw her sister's smile and broke off sharply. 'What are you trying to suggest, Joan?'

'I'm not trying to suggest anything,' said Joan smoothly. 'Merely that if she's ill perhaps we ought to send for the Protector's physician.'

'When I think that's necessary, I'll send for him myself,' snapped Kat, and followed her mistress into the house without another word.

The violent headaches continued throughout the summer and were accompanied by irritability, and a drastic weight loss. Kat was on the very point of sending to London for Dr Bill when, at the end of August, Katherine's child was born, and Elizabeth's fierce tension relaxed. And when she began to eat a little and talk hopefully of going home, Kat was reasonably certain the worst was over.

Late one evening in early September a courier arrived from Sudley Castle where the Seymours were now in residence, and Kat left her seat at Elizabeth's bedside to receive him in the solar. Much later, returning with a slow, wretched step to Elizabeth's room, she found her charge sitting bolt upright in bed.

'Where have you been?' Elizabeth accused wildly. 'I thought you were never coming back.'

'Downstairs,' said Kat vaguely, keeping her face carefully averted from the bed. 'Just downstairs—'

'I heard a horse in the courtyard. Has someone arrived?'

'There's been a message,' Kat swallowed hard. 'From the Admiral's household.'

Elizabeth was silent, staring at her. After a moment she said softly, 'Did the baby die?'

'It wasn't the baby.'

There was no need to say any more; Katherine's name hung unspoken on the air.

'But she was well,' gasped Elizabeth. 'I had a letter—they told me she was *well!*'

'Child-bed fever,' Kat muttered. 'Very sudden. That's the way it always strikes, just when you think they're out of the woods. The courier told me the Admiral is out of his mind with grief—of course, it's a terrible shock for him—'

'He'll get over it!' Elizabeth turned her head away on the pillow; her face was suddenly stony. 'God knows, my father always did. Wives are far easier to replace than a good horse!'

Mrs Ashley recoiled at this unexpected savagery, so uncalled for, so unkind!

'What a wicked thing to say, Your Grace. You must write at once and comfort him in his great sorrow.'

'I won't—I don't believe he needs it.'

'But, Your Grace!' Kat was appalled. 'There must be a letter of condolence for decency's sake!'

'Then write it yourself, for I'm damned if I will.'

Mrs Ashley stiffened, curtsied formally and went to the door.

'Is that Your Grace's final word on the subject?'

'It is!'

'Then I shall deal with the matter as I see fit.'

There was no reply from the bed and Kat went out of the room. Elizabeth waited until her indignant footsteps had died away and then unleashed the tears that threatened to choke her.

In the autumn Dr Bill came down to Cheshunt, and was sufficiently concerned to recommend a complete change of scenery; but his visit and his vague diagnosis did little to disperse the rampant speculation about Elizabeth's condition down in the Great Hall.

'It's not a doctor she needs but a midwife—I never knew a pregnant woman yet that wasn't cured by time—nine months to be exact!'

Oh yes, it was good to get away to Hatfield where her childhood attendants remained loyal and discreet. Change of scenery worked a remarkable change in Kat too. Once removed from the sharp eyes of her sister, the governess, an incurable romantic, found herself viewing recent events in a very different light. So the Queen was dead—very sad, very tragic, of course, but women died in childbed every day and, really, it was an ill wind that blew no one any good. The fact remained that the Admiral was now free once more, to make the marriage he ought to have made in the first place. Certainly he was making tentative overtures in that direction.

'What a man,' said Kat indulgently. 'Never a thought for convention. Imagine sending to know whether Your Grace's buttocks have grown any less —you know what he means by that of course.'

'It hardly sounds like a proposal.' Elizabeth stabbed her needle into the embroidery frame and pushed it aside angrily.

'Don't be coy,' said Kat archly, 'your old husband is free again and you know very well you may have him if you will.'

Elizabeth spat into the hearth.

'I wouldn't marry him if he were the last man on earth. I've told you before, I don't intend to marry anyone.'

'Oh, we're not back to that old nonsense, are we?' Kat sighed. 'I can't understand you at all. He's the noblest man unmarried in the land and you were always his first choice. You'd not deny it if the Protector and the Council gave their consent would you?—and you know you can trust me of all people with—' She glanced up, saw Elizabeth's eyes fixed on her like the cold steel points of twin daggers and subsided into uncomfortable silence.

It was not a restful silence and it grew oppressively; Kat crept out of the room to arrange a hot cordial, reflecting that it was impossible to know what to say for the best these days.

Elizabeth went to open the casement and lean out of the window, letting the sharp autumn air cool her flaming cheeks. Hatfield park spread beneath her, a rambling rustic solitude dotted with great oak trees. The night was black as pitch beyond the flickering lights of the old palace and somewhere in the graveyard stillness she heard an owl hoot.

So it was true then, this crazy whisper of marriage with him! How dared he even think of it? He must be mad to dream of uniting himself with a claimant to the throne beneath the Protector's very nose, and she must be mad herself to listen. And yet she was listening—listening and blushing when she should be writing a furious letter denouncing him to the Council for his presumption.

Closing her eyes she tried to shut out of her mind the ugly rumours which were now filtering down into the countryside, rumours which said Katherine Parr had died of poison as well as a broken heart, poison administered by a husband who wished to be free once more; free to marry the Princess Elizabeth.

Was it true? She knew him to be ruthless and self-seeking, but was he really capable of such a deed? Or were his enemies, led by his own brother the Protector, spreading these rumours preparatory to destroying him? She felt as though she stood on the edge of a whirlpool, waiting for his hand to reach out and pull her forward into complete disaster. Love, passion and death—her mother had trod the steps of that fatal dance; did the same music now await her daughter, the relentless, inevitable dance of death?

Shivering, she closed the casement and crouched down by the fire. His support in the country was growing steadily. It was just possible that he might gain the consent of the Council to the marriage, and if he did what was she going to say when he asked for her hand again? Once he would ask—only once—if she didn't marry him now then he would marry someone else to further his ambition—perhaps Anne of Cleves or even Mary. Her blood throbbed hot with rage at that thought and her body cried out that she could not lose him again of her own free will.

'I hate him,' she said to the flickering fire. 'I hate him.' But even in her own ears the words had the false unsteady ring of a lie.

On a dark drizzling day in November, as the King's retinue wound its weary way through the muddy London streets to Parliament, Lord Russell, the elderly Lord Privy Seal, edged his horse alongside Tom Seymour's to spit in a quarter deck whisper, 'My Lord Admiral, there are certain rumours of you which I am sorry to hear.'

Tom cast a wary glance at the Protector, riding, so he judged, just out of earshot.

'Perhaps,' he said, deceptively pleasant, 'you would care to tell me what they are, my lord.'

Russell sensed the mockery and stiffened. 'It is said in many quarters that you hope to marry either the Lady Mary or the Lady Elizabeth . . .'

'Indeed!'

'. . . in which case,' continued the old man pompously, 'I would say you seek the means to destroy yourself, sir.'

The Admiral slapped his horse's side heartily and laughed—it seemed wise to laugh it off.

'Father Russell, you are very suspicious of me. Who's been telling you these tales of marriage?'

Russell coughed delicately.

'That I am naturally not at liberty to say, my lord.'

'Naturally!' It was a sneer and the old man bridled accordingly.

'I advise you for your own sake, sir, to make no suit to either of these ladies.'

Tom could contain his irritation no longer.

'Good God, man,' he snapped, 'isn't it high time they were married— married within this realm rather than any foreign place—and why not to me, or to another raised by their father?'

Russell shot him a look of pitying contempt. 'I tell you, to attempt such a match would destroy you utterly. Think of the King's suspicions. Married to one of his heirs, he'll think you wish for his death whenever you see him. And anyway,' he veered off at an angry tangent, 'what the devil do you hope to have from either of them?'

'Three thousand a year,' said the Admiral, a little too promptly; he had looked into the matter with Elizabeth's steward, Thomas Parry, some time ago.

The Lord Privy Seal snorted in disgusted amusement and steadied his restless horse.

'I can tell you now that whoever marries the princesses will have no more than ten thousand all told in money, plate and goods. No land at all. And what's that to a man of your charges and estates if you match yourself there?'

The Admiral grew angry, suspecting a trick of his brother's.

'They must also have three thousand a year,' he insisted furiously.

'By God, they may *not!*'

The Admiral resisted a very real impulse to knock the stubborn old fool off his horse.

'By God, none of you will dare say no to it!' he roared, and somewhere in front, the Protector glanced over his shoulder uneasily.

'By God, I *will* say no to it.' A nerve had begun to jump in the old man's cheek, his eyes bulged and for a moment Tom thought he would fall to the ground in a seizure. 'It's clean against the King's will. And I warn you, sir, to have a care how you go about your business!'

Tom caught his brother's agonized glance and repressed the desire to laugh. This had been Ned's idea of a subtle warning, no doubt, the futile roar of an elderly, toothless lion. If this was the best he could do in the way of threats, then the whole affair could easily be settled without bloodshed. Such pathetic opposition—Tom was almost ashamed to encounter it from his own kin.

And there was too much at stake to back down now, with Elizabeth almost his for the taking. Already he had the governess and her steward eating out of his hand. No word from Elizabeth herself, of course, but it would come, it would come. A fresh surge of buoyant confidence had suddenly swept away his earlier doubts of winning her. And if she wanted to play the coy maiden a short while longer he was willing to humour her, waiting until that little flame he had lit within her consumed the last of her inherent caution. A pity Katherine had caught them before and not after the act. He was a rogue but not quite a villain, and even while he thought that, he remembered his dead wife with sadness and a stab of regret for the cruel blow he had dealt her that day at Chelsea. Women! They were all so damnably possessive, wanting to own a man body and soul or else believing his love was false. Every man should have at least four wives—he hadn't much time for the new or the old religion but it might be worth turning Moslem for that!

Well, there it was, the one lost to him now, the other still to be had—and he *would* have her, by God, he'd have her if he had to take the Council apart man by man to do it. He loved Elizabeth and had done so for an uncomfortably long time, but there was a double edge to his determination now. For if the little King should die—and he was a sickly child—that would leave him married to the heir to the throne. If he had his way, with all those men at his back, she would be Queen of England and then—he would be King, and there would be nothing left for Ned to protect.

So whatever happened now, he couldn't lose. First secure the King's person and make his demands from a position of real strength. He was almost ready now to strike—almost ready—just a few more weeks would see him in a position to force the Council's hand—rabbits, the lot of them. They would give their consent to his marriage and abandon Ned—and if they didn't, he would take the King and hold him to ransom. The lad wouldn't mind—it would be a fine adventure for the poor brat. A nice lad—it could be a very satisfying partnership for them both. King or Protector—he'd settle for what came easiest—no point in provoking war. But if the boy died, he'd make damn sure Elizabeth was ready to step into his place.

So the wild plans rioted in his mind and he ignored those tentative warnings to put them aside. Again he approached Parry on the subject of Elizabeth's lands. They were inconveniently placed and he would prefer them in the West Country, adjoining his own.

'Get her to make suit to the Duchess and have them changed,' he told Parry, but when that blustering gentleman returned to London, he dodged the issue until Tom lost his temper.

'Did you tell her what I want her to do?'

Parry looked uncomfortable and twisted his cap in his hands. 'That I did, my lord—and begging your pardon, sir—but she flatly refused to do it.'

'I see.' The Admiral turned away curtly and poured himself some wine. Why was she making difficulties? Was it true—was it really possible—that she didn't want him after all?

From that moment he became anxious and ill at ease; he had lost a measure of self-confidence and, as a result, began to intrigue more clumsily than before, taking less care to cover his tracks. Things were getting tense in London. Mrs Ashley was brought up from Hatfield and rebuked by the Duchess for lax conduct in her post; Parry was increasingly vague about his mistress's intentions.

'You God-damned hedger—are you keeping something back from me? Don't you know your own mistress?'

'No, sir, that I don't.' Parry fingered his thick neck, which was tender from the Admiral's angry grip. 'No one does. She's so close, I'd swear she doesn't even know herself.'

'I don't believe you've even tried to pin her down—she's only a girl—what are you afraid of, man?'

'You don't know her, sir, that's obvious, if you can ask me that. And you're wrong, my lord—I asked her outright what she would do if the Council gave consent to your marriage with her.'

'Well—what was her answer?' He saw Parry's face and was suddenly filled with fear.

'Did she refuse—did she?'

Parry looked at the floor.

'She said she would do what God puts into her mind.' He stole a glance at the Admiral, fearing to see anger. 'I don't know what to make of it, sir. What do you think it means?'

Tom strode to the window and thumped his hand on the thick glass pane. After a while he said darkly, 'I'm damned if I know.'

At Hatfield, the Christmas celebrations had ended with a wine-sodden night in the Great Hall and Mrs Ashley, having seen her young lady to bed, returned on unsteady feet to find Mr Parry sitting alone by the hearth in a reasonably amicable stupor.

'Time for a night-cap,' he said and poured her a large tankard of mulled wine.

Mrs Ashley sank into the chair opposite and accepted the tankard with an amenable grunt.

'Here's to the New Year, Mr Parry—let's pray it brings about what we all desire between my little lady and my lord.'

'Amen to that,' said Mr Parry with feeling. This continual jogging to and from London to meet the Admiral was no joke in winter weather.

Mrs Ashley kicked off her tight shoes with a resentful movement.

'Always supposing I'm still here to see it, of course,' she said darkly.

He watched her carefully over the edge of his tankard. She had returned from London extremely ruffled and he often wondered exactly what the Duchess of Somerset had said to put her in such a temper.

'The Duchess, eh?' he prompted.

'Yes—Somerset's cow!' Mrs Ashley emptied her tankard and set it down. 'The things she said to me that afternoon—you wouldn't believe it, Mr Parry. Only told me I wasn't fit to have the governance of a king's daughter.'

'She never did!'

'Oh, yes—and gave me to understand there'd be another in my place before long. You should have seen Her Grace's face when I told her—well, you know how loyal she is to me—it took me a while to calm her down, I can tell you.'

Parry nodded. 'Stands to reason, she's fond of you. You've been a mother to her all these years.'

'That I have and I'm proud of it. Not that it's been easy, mind. Such a time she's given me this last year, one way and another. I can tell you, Mr Parry, devotion like mine takes its toll on a woman. I've not had a quiet night's sleep since this whole sorry business with the Lord Admiral began.'

Parry nodded with understanding and the candlelight shone on the chain of office as it hung suspended over his ample chest.

'Ah yes,' he murmured knowingly, 'the Lord Admiral, eh? I must say I've often noticed the goodwill between the two of them.'

Mrs Ashley kicked him gently. 'I'd put it a bit stronger than goodwill! Oh, yes—I know the situation well enough and I'd wish her his wife of all men living. And I dare say he'll bring it to pass with the Council soon enough, he's the sort of man who always gets what he wants in the end. Not that it's best spoken of too freely, you understand—not with the Duchess watching like a hawk. Indeed, she gave me such a charge on the subject that even now I hardly dare speak of it. But of course I know *you* can be trusted, Mr Parry— just fill that tankard again, if you wouldn't mind.'

Parry leaned forward obligingly. This promised to be interesting.

'I must say,' he murmured with a discreet cough, 'there's a good deal of bad rumour going about concerning the Admiral.'

'Pooh—there'll always be rumour about a man like him and rumour's never anything but bad.'

'Well—it's said he used the late Queen Katherine very badly. There's even talk of poison.'

Kat choked on her wine and the steward thumped her heartily on the back.

'Talk!' she managed to exclaim at last. 'That's pure malicious gossip spread by his enemies. And we know who *they* are. Mind you, he made too much of Her Grace, there's no denying that. Ah, Mr Parry—' she leaned back comfortably in her chair, wriggled her toes in the firelight and gave him a knowledgeable wink—'the things I could tell you.'

The logs shifted in the hearth and the candles burnt low as that soft reminiscing voice rambled on without a pause until what Mr Parry did not know about the banishment from Chelsea was not worth knowing.

'Well!' he breathed at last, fixing her with a sanctimonious stare. 'Who'd have thought there could be such familiarity between them!'

Something in his shocked voice filled Kat with the first glimmer of unease. She glanced round at the empty hall and leaned towards him urgently.

'Of course, I'm sure I don't need to remind you that all I've said is in the strictest confidence. If it were known, Her Grace would be dishonoured for ever.'

Mr Parry looked positively hurt.

'You can be sure of me, Mrs Ashley.' He leaned forward and patted her arm, gently confidential. 'I'd rather be pulled with wild horses than so much as breathe a word. You have the word of a gentleman on that.'

And at the time he really meant it.

The Lord Protector told his brother, the Lord Admiral, that if he so much as went near the Princess Elizabeth again he would have him clapped in the Tower. When the rumours of the Admiral's 'disloyal practices' and the nagging of his own sharp-tongued wife became more than he could bear, the Lord Protector summoned the Lord Admiral to give an account of his activities in private. The Lord Admiral regretted the time was not convenient; and the Lord Protector clenched his fist, and laid the matter at last before the Council who after 'divers conferences had at sundry times' decided to 'commit the said Admiral to prison in the Tower of London'.

By now Tom realized the plan had miscarried, and staking everything on one last desperate gamble, he went at dead of night to take the King. Using a master key, which he had had cut for just such an emergency as this, he opened the bedroom door to be greeted by the maddened yapping of Edward's little spaniel. In panic he fired at the dog and the single gunshot roused the whole palace, leaving him with perhaps two full minutes to make his escape. But he did not even attempt to make it. He was still standing there, watching the little King weep over the bleeding bundle of fur at his feet, when the guards burst into the room. He threatened to dagger the first man who dared to lay hands on him, but agreed to go peaceably to his own apartments.

It was daybreak when they came to arrest him. He was pale and strained, but he went quietly enough, even humorously, observing over his shoulder that 'No poor knave was ever truer to his prince.'

CHAPTER 6

Across the wide sweep of Hatfield park an arrow sang through the cold January air and struck the target, narrowly missing the bull's eye.

'Well aimed, madam,' said a softly approving voice at her side, 'but if I might suggest the slightest alteration of Your Grace's stance—may I make so bold?'

He moved behind her, drawing back her long fingers to the heavy bow so that his arms for a brief moment almost embraced her. She glanced up at him quickly over her shoulder and the pale sunlight glinted on the brilliant hair caught inside a silver snood.

'Try that now, madam.'

The arrow flew wide, missing the target completely this time and she turned to him with a helpless smile which made him feel distinctly heated.

'I think,' she said innocently, 'you will have to show me again.'

There was very little that Roger Ascham, that young and highly able Cambridge scholar, had ever found it necessary to show his pupil more than once. He had held his new position as tutor for several months now, chosen, at her very particular insistence, in spite of the objections of her former guardians, the Dowager Queen and the Lord Admiral. That fact alone had flattered him even before he took up the post and since then he had found every hour in her presence a fresh stimulus and challenge to his elastic brain. He felt as though in all his life he had never truly lived before this moment, that he would never want, never hope, for anything more but to school the remarkable, retentive mind which was now in his sole charge, a mind which he knew would one day far outstrip his own and conceivably every other mind around it. It was a curious, vital, throbbing entity, the brain of a brilliant boy (he could never quite accept it as a girl's) trapped inside an entirely feminine shell. Body and brain were an astonishing combination which alternately delighted and disconcerted him. He was on fire with the desire to make her the most accomplished royal lady in Europe, but sometimes he suspected the heat originated from an entirely different source. Increasingly, beneath the pleasure he found in her company, he was aware of an undercurrent of shamed confusion. He was glad when the lesson was over and they began to argue over the merits of mathematics. The subject vexed rather than titillated his senses and he welcomed it, for really, he was beginning to doubt the ethics of his position here. She encouraged him quite shamelessly to make a fool of himself. It would be easy to take advantage of her youth and inexperience, but he was in a unique position of trust and the last thing she could afford now was another scandal. Once or twice he had considered resignation and put the thought from him hastily. Things were not quite as bad as that—yet.

'Madam, any change in the itinerary of your studies is quite out of the question at the moment. The programme you propose would be too taxing for—'

'For a girl,' she smiled. 'Roger Ascham, you got this post under false pretences. I understood you were a man with advanced ideas.'

He blushed furiously and thought: A little too advanced, if only you knew, madam!

Aloud he said stiffly, 'Even at Cambridge mathematics is not considered a serious subject.'

'Then it ought to be. Any man of the future—yes, even Robin Dudley—will tell you that mathematics and science are the keys to it.'

The colour left his face, leaving him stiff and formal.

'Lord Robert Dudley? You know him well?'

'Well enough, we were children together.' A thought struck her. 'Were you not his tutor before you were mine?'

'That dubious honour was mine,' Ascham observed drily.

She smiled again. 'So—how's his Latin syntax? Still as abysmal as ever, I'll be bound.'

'It would be a good deal better if he didn't waste valuable time chasing every new fad and fancy in learning,' said Ascham severely. 'Science, astrology, *mathematics*—he's off up each track like a rabbit running wild in an empty warren.'

Her laugh rang out, clear as a bell on the still air.

'Poor Robin! That's too cruel and apt. *And* highly unprofessional etiquette. I hope you speak more highly of me behind my back, sir.'

'I cannot speak highly enough of you, madam.' The colour rose in his cheeks again and he shrugged his shoulders uncomfortably. 'Oh, mathematics are well enough in their place, but I've already told Lord Robert he'll never make a politician if he abandons Cicero for Euclid's pricks and lines. He's a bright enough lad, but lacks Your Grace's perseverance and perception. He'll be a jack of all trades and master of none—no match for you, madam, I fear.'

She threw her gloves up into the air and caught them deftly.

'Shall I ever find my match?' she asked with a mixture of coquettishness and sincere interest.

He stopped and looked at her with a curious thoughtful stare.

'No, madam,' he said slowly, reflectively. 'I don't believe you ever will.' And that, he added silently to himself, may be your real tragedy, so you need not look so pleased about it. A pedestal is a lonely place.

It was bitterly cold and their breath made little feathery clouds in the nipping air as they approached the low brick palace. The sound of stamping hooves was carried to them from the courtyard, and suddenly Elizabeth stood stock still, staring up at the house as though she could not believe what she heard.

Parry had said that the Lord Admiral would visit her soon. Had he dared to come at last? And what would she say to him after all these months? What would she say now when he asked her to be his wife?

Her heart gave a wild lurch beneath the stiff bodice of her shooting gown and suddenly all the doubts and fears and caution flew out of her like little bats from a dark cave. There was nothing left but her love for him, the desire to run into his arms as she had done so many times as a child, to look up into his bold teasing eyes and answer his question now without fear or guilt—yes. *Yes!*

She spun round, and tossed her gloves to the bewildered man beside her. Ascham caught the flash of anticipation in her eyes and knew for certain that not only had she forgotten him—he might as well be an educated mouse!— she had also for once forgotten herself. Picking up her heavy green skirts she began to run towards the house. A mad gust of icy wind blew the silver snood free from its pins and her hair fell unbound to her waist. Ascham saw her stoop swiftly and reclaim it with a careless gesture, saw her run on past the stables and disappear beyond the open double doors into the house. He stood holding her bow and her gloves, like a lackey, and thinking of the Lord Admiral with a twinge of envy, knowing that never in a thousand years would she ever look or run like that for himself.

Beyond the oaken doors, the Great Hall was full of strangers and frightened servants. Elizabeth pulled up short and stared at the tall, rather sharp-faced gentleman who immediately approached her.

'Sir Robert Tyrwhitt?'

'Your Grace.' He inclined his head curtly.

'I demand to know what this unpardonable intrusion signifies.' For a moment he did not reply and she stamped her foot to cover her rising terror.

'What has happened? What are you doing here?'

'I come on the King's business, madam, by order of the Council. I have my written authority here if you should wish to see it. I think you will find it quite in order.'

The silver snood dropped from her cold fingers and she turned away into the adjoining solar. He followed, shutting the door on the chaos outside.

In the centre of the floor she swung round upon him with a great deal more bravado than she felt.

'What is your business here? Answer me!'

Still he said nothing, merely looked her up and down with a steady contemptuous glance, then ensconced himself behind a table, setting down a sheaf of papers. She was aghast and frightened that he should dare to behave with such pointed disrespect. It could only mean one thing, that her position was suddenly deadly serious. But why—why?

He indicated the chair in front of her.

'Perhaps Your Grace will be seated.'

'I will stand in my own house if I choose, Sir Robert.'

'As you please,' he said mildly. He adjusted the papers fussily and ignored her for a moment as though she were a mere serving maid; then abruptly looked up and fired a statement at her.

'The Lord High Admiral is at this present moment in the Tower of London.'

The room rocked around her and she took hold of the back of the chair, but all she said at last in a thin whisper was, 'What has that to do with me?'

He was annoyed at the failure of what he had expected to be a telling shot, one which would bring her defence down in ruins.

'Your servants Parry and Ashley,' he snapped, 'are on their way to the Tower, there to confess the practices between Your Grace and the Admiral.'

'What practices?' she gasped. 'I know nothing of—'

He sprang to his feet and banged his fist on the table; the papers scattered to the floor.

'You planned to marry the Admiral without the Council's consent . . .'

'That is a lie.'

'. . . *and* seize the crown. Such a charge is high treason.'

'No!'

'Oh, come, Your Grace, these dealings are very widely known.' He paused and added spitefully, 'Indeed it is generally said that you are with child by the Admiral.'

'How dare you repeat such a vile and filthy lie!' Her voice trembled and she steadied it with a furious effort of will to say calmly, 'I am quite willing to disprove that, to show myself as I am before the court physicians. I have done nothing and have nothing to fear.'

He decided to change his tactics. Pushing back his chair he came to stand beside her, laying a gentle hand on her arm, his voice soft, insinuating, almost fatherly.

'Come, be sensible, there's no call for you to distress yourself.' His voice became larded with tenderness. 'You are extremely young and the Council will take that into account if you confess your dealings fully. All the blame will be taken by Parry and Mrs Ashley who—'

'Who are the King's good subjects and my true and loyal servants,' she said fiercely. She flung off his arm and rubbed away the tears which had rolled down her white face.

He lost his temper at this ungrateful rebuff and controlled a very strong desire to give her a good shaking.

'When we came to arrest Parry he took his chain of office from his neck and threw it down. He said, "I would to God I had never been born. I am ruined." Madam, those were not the words of a true and loyal subject. The man's a traitor and so are all who seek to shelter him.'

She turned away from Tyrwhitt in stubborn silence and he was put to the undignified measure of placing himself between her and the door.

'By God, madam, your guilt shows in your face—I will have your confession in the end.'

'If my guilt is so manifest you'll have no need of a confession. Kindly stand out of my way.'

'Madam, I would ask you to remember that you are in no position to give commands. You are under house arrest and your servants are to be kept from you until further notice. I advise you for your own safety to consider your honour and your great peril, for you are but a subject—as indeed was your mother before you.'

He wished he had thought of that earlier; the effect upon her was quite remarkable. For a moment he thought she was going to faint. It was as though the full significance of her hopeless plight had struck her like a blow across the face, as though she understood at last that she was utterly alone and friendless and in real danger of her life. She clenched her teeth, but could not bite back the choked sob of terror which escaped them, and suddenly her bold front crumpled and she began to cry wildly, like the child he suddenly remembered that she was.

'What have they said?' she sobbed. 'What have my servants said?'

He was not by nature a harsh man and he was confident now that he had the upper hand at last. Putting one arm around her shaking shoulders he

guided her to a chair, offered his own handkerchief and smiled down be-
nignly on the bent red head.

'Come,' he said gently, 'you had better tell me everything.'

Sir Robert's moment of triumph proved remarkably short-lived and hollow.
Having come down to Hatfield confident that a day or two would see his
business at a satisfactory end he felt he had made an excellent beginning and
wrote to tell the Protector, 'I begin to grow in credit with her.' But in the
weeks that followed he discovered that breaking her will was not after all to
be the easy task he had initially hoped it would prove to be and soon his
reports were less hopeful and frankly baffled: 'She has a very good wit and
nothing is gotten of her but by great policy.'

He began to resort to underhand tricks, a false letter, a false friend, daily
brow-beating interrogations, which in return produced nothing but a host of
trifling incidents told in great detail, not one word of which could be used
against her.

Within weeks he was in a state of baffled irritation, writing to inform the
Protector: 'I believe there has been a secret promise between my lady, Mrs
Ashley and the steward never to confess to death and if that is so, it will
never be gotten out of her . . .'

The Protector took the hint and the savage barrage of questions was repeated on the wretched prisoners in the Tower. Under the intolerable pressure brought to bear on them, first Parry, then Mrs Ashley, broke down and
wrote their confessions, twin documents which in the right hands might be
used to take their mistress to the block.

Now 'I have good hope to make her cough out the whole', wrote Tyrwhitt
gleefully on receiving them.

Elizabeth stood quite still as he marched into her apartment, waving the
papers in a threatening gesture. 'All is lost, madam,' he announced. 'Your
servants have confessed everything. You can have nothing to gain now by
your continued stubbornness.'

Panic closed in on her, making her breath come in a panting gasp, but she
managed to take the documents and pretend to study the signatures carefully, hinting at forgery.

He was infuriated by the gesture. 'Your Grace knows your servants' hand
with half a sight!' he snapped.

Desperately she played for time, while her eyes roved from one hateful line
to another, trying to decide through her sick confusion how bad this could
truly be for her. Parry's confession was a terrified rabbiting of slapped buttocks, of tickling, scuffling in bedchambers, of Queen Katherine's jealousy

and the banishment from Chelsea, of Kat Ashley's muddled, indiscreet and obviously inebriated conversation: '. . . she seemed to repent that she had gone so far with me and prayed me that I would not disclose these matters . . . and I said I would not . . . I had rather be pulled with wild horses.'

How could Kat have betrayed her to Parry? And what had been done to this pair of poor gossiping fools to make them break down like this? Her terror was knifed by sudden fury. Had they tortured her helpless servants? She would see the Protector hanged from the highest tree in the realm if she were Queen—if only she were Queen of England now.

But she was not Queen; and it began to look as though she never would be. The mere thought was treason; but were these confessions treason, after all? They were extremely damaging, they would certainly mean her reputation, possibly even her place in the succession, but as long as she stuck to her ground and denied everything it was just possible that they might not mean her life. Only a lawyer could pick his way through the legal niceties of her perilous plight and she had no one to advise or counsel her, nothing to rely on except her own instinct for survival, and that instinct told her to hold her tongue.

The tension in the room grew by the minute as they waited for her to speak, but she said nothing.

'Mrs Ashley was at first staunch in her refusal to speak,' Sir Robert burst out at last, aware that he was losing once again in this war of nerves. 'She and Parry were brought face to face. When he stood by what he had written she called him "False Wretch" and reminded him he had promised never to confess it to death.'

Her eyes dropped to the final paragraph of Kat's testament, a pathetic plea for removal from a cell where the window had no glass—Kat who could not bear the cold, who spent the winter months scurrying from one fireplace to the next. In her mind she saw that forlorn, harassed little woman stuffing the window with straw in a vain attempt to shut out the knifing February wind. And she saw Parry too, plump, complacent, garrulous Parry, framed in a muddle of account books with the chain of office swinging portentously. Parry, self-important at his furtive little dealings with the Admiral, wooing harmless tales from the governess on a cold Christmas evening assisted by a certain something to loosen tongues and keep out the cold. A domestic life where promises came easily and did not stand the threat of torture—'she prayed that I would not disclose these matters . . . and I said I would not . . . I had rather be pulled with wild horses.'

A fierce protective affection welled up in Elizabeth and swept away her own terror like driftwood before a mighty wave. She swore to herself that if it was the last thing she ever did she would get those two pitiful creatures out of their wretched plight.

Folding Parry's confession, she handed it back with measured civility.

'It was a great matter for him to promise such a promise and then break it,' she said calmly.

A purplish hue rose in Sir Robert's leathery cheeks as he listened to that cryptic little line and knew that the most powerful weapon in his arsenal had failed him miserably. Weeks he had been here, hounding, spying, threatening, an influential member of the Privy Council and as many agents and devices as he saw fit to employ, all the skill and cunning amassed during a lifetime of power politics to be used against an opponent who was still in the schoolroom, and it had gained him absolutely nothing. Without her own confession the signed testimonies of Ashley and Parry alone would be insufficient evidence to convict an heir to the throne. And now at last he saw she understood that, and he knew that for all the good his presence here would do he might as well pack his bags and ride back to court in humble defeat.

He still believed she was guilty, that the reason they all sang the same song was because they had set the note before, but somewhere beneath his fury and his indignation there moved the absurd impulse to salute her. Well, he had done his best and he could do no more. It was up to the Council now to find the means to break her will.

Personally, he was beginning to believe it couldn't be done.

The Duchess of Somerset rounded on her husband like a cat about to strike.

'What the devil do you mean, "nothing more can be done against her"? You're surely not about to let a chit of fifteen get the better of you.'

The Protector threw up his hands in a gesture of frustration.

'I've done everything in my power to get the truth out of her.'

'Not everything. You've not appointed a new governess yet.'

The Protector frowned, 'I can't think that will make any difference. She defends the Ashley woman at every turn. Why, I doubt if she would even accept—'

'Accept?' screamed the Duchess. 'God's death, we're talking about an accused traitor, a girl without a friend or an ounce of influence to her name and you concern yourself about what she will accept! Have you gone soft in the head with all your reforms?'

'My dear, you are too shrill—' the Duke protested nervously. 'Do you want the servants to hear?'

The Duchess lowered her voice an octave in scale and came to stand over him.

'When you fight a cat you use a cat's claws. She defends the Ashley woman, you say? Very well, then, make it plain to her by appointing a new governess that she'll never see Ashley again. I have the very woman in mind.'

'You have?' He was startled.

The Duchess smiled unpleasantly. 'Tyrwhitt's wife would be admirably suited to the post.'

The Duke blinked and cleared his throat.

'But Lady Tyrwhitt was the late Queen Katherine's devoted friend. It would hardly be fitting to appoint a woman who hates the sight of the girl.'

'Did I say it would be fitting?'

'Admirably suited—your very words, my dear.'

'Oh, good God, man, do I really need to elaborate further?'

The Duke flushed, like a schoolboy who has been rapped across the knuckles for daydreaming.

'No,' he said grimly, and went over to his desk to write out the order. 'You don't need to do that. I take your meaning.'

Across the darkening room the eyes of Elizabeth Tyrwhitt met those of Elizabeth Tudor like a clash of swords.

'I don't recognize you as my governess, madam, and I will not obey you. I will have no other governess but Mrs Ashley.'

Lady Tyrwhitt bridled like an angry tabby cat.

'This is a fine welcome, madam!'

'Were you expecting one?'

'I can tell you here and now that this post was no choice of mine. But I am commanded here by the Lords of the Council and I expect you to accept my services thankfully.' *You will be sorry if you don't!* added the stony-grey eyes.

Elizabeth clenched her fists, digging her nails into her palms to prevent herself from bursting into angry, frightened tears.

'I have not so demeaned myself that the Council needs to put any more governesses over me.'

'I regret to say that is open to question. And having been governed by such a person as Mrs Ashley I'm sure you need not be ashamed to have any *honest* woman in that place.'

The room was darkening towards evening and a thin blinding rain obscured the tall windows. Elizabeth swung round upon Sir Robert who was skulking by the hearth, trying to pretend he had no part in this dispute.

'Sir, the world will take it as proof of my guilt if I am appointed a new governess so quickly. I shall be condemned as a great criminal. Is that what the Council wish?'

'Your age and danger considered it is best for you to have one without an hour's delay,' the gentleman orated pompously. He looked at her sharply and added in a feeling tone, 'By God, madam, if I had my way you would have *two!*'

'I shall remember that,' she said coldly and walked out of the room without their leave.

Lady Tyrwhitt stared at the closed door and exploded with rage.

'Oh, she'll remember that, will she? When she's Queen no doubt! Good God, she needs a governess to teach her manners! The brazen little bitch—I remember her at Chelsea, tossing her head at the Admiral and breaking that poor woman's heart. I never could understand why the Queen allowed it to go on for so long.'

Sir Robert tossed another log on the fire and eased himself stiffly into a chair. It was hard work grinding down the Princess's spirit and he had had a long weary day of it.

'I've had a great deal to put up with,' he complained. 'Even the Council have no real idea what it's been like. I can tell you, Bess, I'm worn out by this whole business.'

'Oh, you!' sniffed his wife officiously. 'You've been too soft with her, I've said so all along. It's time we took off the velvet gloves and tightened the vice —let her know how badly things are going for the Admiral. There's more than one way to kill a cat—but then men are no good at this. At least the Council had the sense to see it in time. I'm here to succeed where you've failed, Robert. One week, that's all I'll need with the little madam and she'll be only too ready to talk. You see if I'm not right.'

Lady Tyrwhitt settled to her appointed task with a will. She haunted her charge day and night like a malicious shadow, taunting and insinuating, belittling her servants whom she vigorously defended, and the Admiral of whom she dared not even speak. Lady Tyrwhitt saw that that was the note to hammer home and her low spiteful voice ranted out, spitting filth and venom against him until the last thread of Elizabeth's steely control gave way and she flew out suddenly in his defence, declaring that she would never believe he was a traitor.

'Your Grace's opinion carries no weight,' sneered the older woman. 'All the houses of the Lord Admiral have been sold and his servants are dispersed. His guilt is obvious to all.'

'But not yet proven,' said Elizabeth on a gasp. 'They haven't dared to bring him to trial yet, have they?'

Lady Tyrwhitt smiled contemptuously.

'Your Grace's innocence astounds me. Surely you know that an Act of Attainder can be passed against him without the necessity of open trial.'

Elizabeth stared at her, appalled.

'The King would never allow—'

'The King will see justice done, against his own kin if need be! Uncles, *sisters*—none are above a charge of treason and they will answer as any other subject. Know this for sure, my lady—it will be the axe for him in the end. He has no hope left in this world.'

From the doorway the new governess watched as Elizabeth sat down at table where the morning meal had been served. She sat for a long time, white-faced, staring at nothing, then at last pushed her plate away untouched. When the same thing happened at dinner and supper, Lady Tyrwhitt reported that she was making progress and Sir Robert wrote triumphantly to inform the Council: 'She begins now to droop a little.'

But neither spiritual harassment nor physical weakening loosened her tongue. She remained silent until the day she finally sat down and wrote the letter which defeated the Protector as surely as if she had dealt him a knife blow. She demanded that a royal proclamation should be issued throughout the land, clearing her good name. If she did not receive it she would be ashamed to ask it again, 'because I see you are not well-minded toward it'.

It was a bold personal accusation and the Protector wilted beneath it, knowing he had no option now but to capitulate to her demand. She was appealing to her greatest strength, the goodwill of the English people, and he dared not enter a contest against her on those terms in the absence of any firm evidence with which to convict her of treason. He could not fight her any longer, incredible though it seemed that a girl of fifteen should take on the entire strength of the government and win. He issued that proclamation as meekly as if he had received a royal command and silenced his wife, for the first time in their married life, with no more than a look.

Elizabeth received news of her victory in silence. She had saved her life. All that remained now was to wait for the act which would rob it of all meaning.

The Bill of Attainder had been passed against the Admiral and he had faced thirty-three separate charges, many of them so petty that it was a wonder they dared even to write them. But she knew his end could not be long delayed. The Tyrwhitts had said there was no hope of a reprieve.

In the still silence of her room her affection for Kat was now the only thing which goaded her into activity. She sat and wrote to the Council a long desperate letter pleading for the governess's life and freedom *'because she has been with me a long time and has taken great pains to bring me up in honesty and learning . . .'*

She stared at that line and bit her lip, remembering with anguish just how great those pains had been, how lucky she had been to be cared for by a woman whose heart was twice the size of her brain.

On and on scratched her pen across the sheet of paper that blurred before her eyes. Her head hammered from lack of sleep and her mind reached out desperately to the one for whom she must not plead, clinging to the last blind hope, which he also must cling to, that the little King, his nephew and friend, would save him.

But if the eleven-year-old boy felt anything he gave no sign. He attended to his common round of business and pleasure and authorized the Admiral's execution with the absolute indifference he might have been expected to show at the extermination of a rat. He was disciplined, self-contained and unemotional, a credit to his teachers, a model of virtue; and a travesty of a child. The malleable boy had been transformed into a pretentious little prig, overburdened with the weight of his own royal dignity and unhealthily preoccupied with the spiritual welfare of his people. Under the guardianship of the Lord Protector, Edward had gained stature and lost humanity; and no one was more shocked than Elizabeth to witness the result. She knew, in her own heart, that her brother would have authorized her execution, had it come to it, as easily as he had authorized the Lord Admiral's—to whom he had also owed love and loyalty. It was chilling knowledge from which grew the principles that were to rule the rest of her life: love no one, trust no one, for all affection is false.

The terse, cold comment which would guarantee life to herself and her servants lay unfurled in her mind like an open scroll. For thirteen endless days she waited for the moment to use it, but beyond that moment her mind was a dull blank.

She sat alone at her writing desk staring into the fire until at last her eyes were too heavy to stay open. Her head slipped down on to her satin sleeve and she fell asleep, plunging down, down into an endless dark corridor where there was no hope of light. She was alone, more alone than she would be even in her coffin, surrounded by the darkness, sobbing for Kat. But no one came, no one would ever come.

It was wet on the floor where she huddled. She put out her fingers and felt the wetness. It was warm to her touch, viscid, somehow familiar.

Blood!

She recoiled and began to scrabble in the darkness, seeking escape. And then her fingers, clawing outwards, touched the object that lay across her path and she saw where all the blood had come from. There was no light, but she saw his dismembered head—bleeding a river to drown her!

A log fell into the hearth and she started awake with a strangled gasp, listening to her own heartbeat drumming wildly in her ears. The door behind her opened and as she looked round unwillingly Lady Tyrwhitt's personal maid bobbed an insolent curtsey.

'Sir Robert requests your presence in the Great Hall, madam.'

Elizabeth rose from her chair in a numb daze and somehow the dark little room swam away, exchanged itself for the broad stairway and the great panelled chamber which was full of Tyrwhitt's people. There was some muted whispering and nudging as she crossed slowly to the hearth where Sir Robert and his wife stood in gloating triumph. They described the Lord Admiral's execution in meticulous detail, hoping to shock a response that would justify their wasted weeks of persecution. But she had already lived through every step of this, every look and gesture and word. Her eyes met theirs in a steady unwavering stare and her hard little voice rang clearly through the cold air.

'Today died a man of much wit, but very little judgement.'

She felt the ripple of astonishment from the intently listening audience behind her, saw the Tyrwhitts glance at each other in shock, indignation and disbelief at her callousness. But it did not matter; nothing mattered now. She had fought for her life and the lives of her servants and she had won. Now it seemed there was nothing left worth fighting for and the angry spirit which had sustained her through her ordeal went out, like a candle in her mind, leaving her cold and empty and totally spent.

They went on talking to her, asking questions, but their words had lost the power to hurt. She found it difficult to concentrate on them, for a numb exhaustion had closed in around her, shutting her off from that world of mouthing dolls which suddenly seemed so absurdly shrunken and insignificant. Like a beleaguered castle her mind was husbanding its resources, boarding every window, locking every door, shutting down unnecessary functions.

She went upstairs slowly and found her old nurse, Blanche Parry, waiting for her. It was the first time since the arrival of Tyrwhitt that she had seen any of her own servants, but now she looked at the woman blankly, almost without recognition. She allowed herself to be undressed and put to bed without argument.

And that was the last she remembered for a long, long time.

CHAPTER 7

In Hatfield park the old palace stood silent in the pale spring sunlight. The courtyards had been empty for weeks now, and in the stables Elizabeth's favourite gelding tossed his head and whinnied his protest at his mistress's continued absence. Grooms exercised him now, once a day, careless young lads who were paid to do it and never stroked his nose or brought him fresh apples. His eyes were dull and sad, and his coat was beginning to lose some of its satin sheen.

'Reckon he's pining,' said one of the older hands, and at that everyone in the stable glanced furtively up at the red brick mansion and away again, before going silently about their duties once more.

Inside the house, Sir Robert Tyrwhitt said, 'I quite agree, Mistress Parry, it's gone on long enough. I shall send to London at once,' and stormed down the turret staircase to his own apartments.

'Well?' said his wife, rising from the window-seat, a shade less composed than usual. 'What do you think, Robert?'

Tyrwhitt shut the door with a bang; on his face was the blustering belligerence of a very frightened man.

'I think,' he said unpleasantly, 'that if we're not very careful now, you and I are likely to be facing a hanging mob.' He took an angry turn up and down the room, then paused to add peevishly, 'Of course, if I'd had my way I'd have sent for Dr Bill long ago—but, oh no, you knew best, you were the expert. Nothing to worry about, you said, she's only sulking, she'll get over it. And now—God's blood, woman—she's like a skeleton.'

'I can't force her to eat,' said his wife defensively. 'I'm not to blame if she wants to starve herself.'

'Yes—well, you tell that to the Protector and see what he has to say if she dies on him, a few bare weeks after the people have been told she's innocent. We're responsible for her—a perfect pair of scapegoats, don't you see it? I can tell you this, if the worst happens you and I won't be able to show ourselves in London for a very long time. It will probably cost me my seat on the Council—'

Lady Tyrwhitt was pale and shaken as she went to the table and set out pen and ink and a sandcaster.

'You'd better write then,' she said and sat down anxiously beside him to watch.

The Protector reacted to the news of Elizabeth's grave condition with alarm and cast about frantically for anything that might hasten her recovery, sending his personal physician, a host of kind wishes, and a letters patent guaranteeing her estates and income.

The death of his brother had seriously damaged his standing with the common people, who had previously fallen into the habit of calling him 'the Good Duke'. There were rumours of unrest all over the country and he was aware of John Dudley's increasing influence at the council table. Certainly, if he was to have any hope of outriding the opposition gathering steadily against him, the girl's death was the last thing he wanted on his hands.

When the trim, dapper little figure of his personal physician was shown into his private study, he was waiting at his desk with ill-concealed anxiety. He waved irritably as the doctor prefaced business with a courtly bow and correct inquiries after his own health.

'Oh, there's nothing wrong with me, man!' He gnawed his lip and gestured the physician into a chair. 'What news from Hatfield?'

Dr Bill leaned back in his chair and examined his master shrewdly. The Duke was pale and strained and obviously nervous; he did not believe that statement that all was well.

'Don't sit there gawking—get on with it. I'm a busy man—a very busy man. You know that.'

The doctor cleared his throat and looked ill at ease.

'My lord will recall that I attended the Princess in the autumn. Since that time circumstances—unhappy circumstances—have exacerbated her condition to a serious degree. It was most unfortunate—' He broke off abruptly under the Protector's icy glance.

'Most unfortunate that I was obliged to execute her lover!' snapped the Duke in furious interruption. 'Well, it wasn't a move which gave *me* any particular pleasure either, contrary to public opinion. And I don't want your moral judgement, merely your professional opinion on the girl's health—so stop your damned hedging and come out with what you think.'

'My lord—' The doctor hesitated. 'My lord, I anticipate neither a swift nor complete recovery.'

The Duke swallowed and found his throat as dry as a bone. His hand fumbled out absently to a flagon of wine but he lacked the concentration to pour it.

'God's blood!' he muttered feverishly. 'Are you trying to say you expect her to *die?*'

'I am trying to say, my lord,' replied the doctor defensively, 'that it is possible.'

The Protector leapt to his feet suddenly and began to stalk wildly about the room as though rapid movement might prevent this unwelcome news from catching up with him.

At last he burst out angrily, 'But she's young—she's strong—three times as healthy as her brother, or her sister for that matter. And nobody dies these hard days of a broken heart, least of all a Tudor, a heartless, self-sufficient brood if ever I saw one.' He stopped and looked accusingly at the man opposite. 'So what possible reason can you give me for such an extreme forecast?'

'My lord, she has lost interest in all that life has to offer. Unless she can be aroused from her melancholy she will simply slip away—I would stake my entire career on it.'

The Duke sat down abruptly and chewed his thumbnail.

'If this gets out among the common people it will finish me—God knows, as it is there could be revolt at any moment.' He clenched his fist and then suddenly banged it on the table with a peevish blow that made all his papers jump and scatter. 'Well—you're the physician, God damn you, suggest a cure! What else do I pay you for?'

'My lord—return her governess and steward without delay. That is all I can suggest.'

The Duke frowned at his inkwells. After a moment he said in a slow, puzzled tone, 'I should have thought they were the last people she would want to see again.'

Dr Bill shrugged slightly, hunching his stooped shoulders together.

'Logic is not necessary to love and loyalty, my lord. I believe their return to be imperative to her survival.'

'Oh, very well—very well—whatever you think will help.' The Duke waved his hand impatiently. He seemed suddenly preoccupied, staring inwards, seeing the memory of his royal nephew calmly and cold-bloodedly handing him the Admiral's death warrant. Whatever crimes Tom had committed, he had always been unfailingly good to the boy and yet the King had never questioned that last act, had never shown so much as a qualm of conscience. It was unnerving and it caused the Duke to know what little loyalty he himself could expect from Edward. All his service—less self-seeking than it often appeared to observers—had been wasted on that small waxen doll, who had shown himself to be without heart or compassion.

'*I am a friend not won with trifles nor lost with the like.*' That single line stood out from all Elizabeth's correspondence to his brother and filled him with a moment of poignant regret for the love and loyalty that he would never know.

All his schemes, his hopes and fears seemed suddenly diminished, almost insignificant; he knew at last, without reservation or even self-interest, he desired above all things that she should live.

He rose and grasped the doctor's hand, wringing it hard, with all the moody petulance suddenly gone from his face and his voice.

'My friend,' he said hoarsely, 'for love of me go back to Hatfield and do all you can.'

Outside the window of Elizabeth's bedroom the branches of a tree, heavy with new leaf, tapped monotonously against the little leaded panes as though nodding in permanent agreement with all the pearls of philosophy which tripped in incessant procession from Mrs Ashley's thin lips. Day after day that falsely cheerful monologue buzzed hopefully, like a persistent bee, from one subject to the next, seeking a response, while through it all Elizabeth lay still on the day-bed, like a marionette with no strings, watching the branches dancing madly in the wind beyond her window.

She said yes and no at appropriate intervals and occasionally smiled lest Kat's feelings should be hurt, but in all she said or did there was a tired indifference, a hopeless, resigned lethargy which filled the governess with an increasing chill of fear and made her talk more and more wildly, until at last, in desperation, she found she was talking treason.

'. . . don't you *want* to be Queen of England?' she cried.

Elizabeth turned her head sharply on the cushions and stared at the older woman. Her hands had clenched abruptly and her dull eyes ignited like balefire.

'What are you talking about? You know I can never be Queen.'

'Why not?' said Kat artfully, fanning this spark. 'Your father restored you to the succession—no one now remembers—'

'That I was once the "Little Bastard"? I'm sure Mary does, and if anything should happen to Edward, she will be Queen first and make sure I never succeed her.'

Hope danced in Kat's heart like a crazy imp. 'She couldn't exclude you—the people would never stand for it.'

Elizabeth sighed wearily. 'The people call me a whore,' she muttered.

'Then show them it's a lie! Oh, my love, don't you see it? All you have to do is wait and the crown will fall on your pretty head as surely as day follows night. Not yet—not for many years perhaps, but it will come, I swear it.' She paused. 'But once it's yours of course they will try to take it from you—all your enemies, France, even Spain—and that's why you must get well—to be ready. Ready to fight for your inheritance.'

Elizabeth sat still in stunned silence with Kat's voice like a thunderclap in her mind. It seemed as though all her life she had been waiting for this moment, this sudden conception of her true purpose on this earth, born to rule and so vindicate the mother whose only real crime had been to bear a girl. To be Queen of England—it was all that could ever matter to her now.

She got slowly off the couch and went to open the casement window, pushing it wide with one painfully thin arm so that the wind slapped her deathly pallor. She stood staring at the empty rose bushes beneath, which would bloom red and white for the Tudor emblem, remembering the one Rose which would never open its eager petals to the sun again. 'A Rose without Thorns' Henry had called the child wife of his doting old age, pretty laughing Katherine Howard for whom he had wept bitterly, even as he had done her to death—and one before her. But he had never been seen to weep for that one, not after he had split England in two in pursuit of her. What fools women were to put themselves willingly into the power of men!

The Admiral was dead and she must forget him. He was dead and he had deserved to die; now at last she could admit it to herself. Whatever the fierce link of passion that had sprung between them that day at Chelsea, she believed now that ambition and not love had driven him to the grave she might so easily have shared with him. Only the instinct to hesitate and to hold back had saved her from complete disaster. And now no memory of his bold face and gay bantering voice, however bitter, could alter the knowledge that he had meant to use her like a pawn in his treasonous designs.

No man, be he friend or foe, would ever have opportunity to use her for his own ends again.

She turned from the window to look at Kat, still thin and wasted from the rigours of the prison cell she had endured for the sake of her young mistress.

She said quietly, 'When I am dressed you may ask Mr Ascham to attend me in the solar.'

It was all she said, but Kat knew instinctively that it marked the end of her mourning. Elizabeth began her lessons again, dressed with dark severity in the plainest gowns her wardrobe had to offer, knowing she must win back her reputation in the only manner now available to her, in the role of the austere, high-born, Protestant maiden. The jewels and gay gowns so dear to her repressed childhood vanity were shut away and her image looked bleakly back from her steel mirror, a pale sombre outline, bright hair hidden beneath a plain cap. Every natural instinct within her she curbed—the levity, the co-quetry, the vanity—all the wanton clamourings of her wild Tudor inheritance were ruthlessly stifled until, outwardly, she was a perfect model of learning and virginal propriety. Even Lady Tyrwhitt was impressed. Slowly the scandalous rumours of her conduct began to die away for want of fuel and the people murmured her name with ever-increasing affection.

There were no more mistakes. She stepped with faultless caution around every issue that might draw her into dangerous controversy. Archbishop Cranmer's *New Book of Common Prayer* she accepted without protest, where her sister Mary refused it outright.

She built an impenetrable wall around her heart, and the only outlet of affection she allowed herself was for her childhood attendants. Though Tyrwhitt had discovered Parry's account books 'were so indiscreetly made it appears he had little understanding to execute his office', she demanded his place should not be filled. Parry retained his chain of office and his fatuous sense of importance, while she audited the household accounts herself, behind his back, and made strict economies.

In the quiet backwater existence at Hatfield she shrugged off frequent bouts of illness like an angry cat shaking water from its coat. The only thing she steadfastly nursed was her implacable hatred of the Protector, and she listened with quiet satisfaction to all the rumours which suggested his world was about to collapse around him at any moment. John Dudley, Earl of Warwick, waited in the wings like an actor waiting for his cue. When discontent at the Protector's rule broke out into open rebellion in two serious revolts among the populace, it was Dudley who rode into Norfolk to subdue the uprisings. He did so with a panache that won over to him most of the Council, ambitious lords who now resented the priggish, ineffectual rule of a man who had spilt his own brother's blood. If the Lord Admiral had been a rogue at least he had never been the hypocrite the Lord Protector was now seen to be, cowering behind the little King like an arrant coward. When Dudley returned to London with his triumphant army, Somerset, sensing his real danger, seized his young nephew and fled to Windsor Castle. There for a few desperate, futile days he held siege against Dudley's forces, while Edward regarded him balefully, with an increasingly jaundiced eye, and thought how much better life might be in a world which no longer contained any ambitious uncles.

Somerset was borne off to the Tower, with the memory of his young nephew's icy stare imprinted on his mind, half expecting that his end was in sight. But Dudley was too clever for that. He had seen the effect that Tom Seymour's death had had on the public imagination and he intended to bide his time a little longer. So 'the Good Duke' was released in disgrace, his rule virtually ended, his death postponed until it should prove either convenient or desperately necessary. He was a broken stalk of a man now. Dudley played with him like a cruel cat, reducing him to the status of a hunted mouse who found every hole stopped against him.

Elizabeth, waiting in the shadows to hear news of Somerset's execution, was thrown into a transport of silent fury by this delay. Why didn't Warwick strike the death blow? Surely he would never allow the sneaking white rat to escape! That possibility tormented her day and night and drove her at last to step outside her self-imposed retirement for the first time since her recent disgrace. In December of 1549 she accepted the King's invitation and returned to court for the Christmas celebrations. Whatever it cost she must discover what Warwick intended for the fallen Protector.

She looked at the tall gangling boy who sat on the throne in the Presence Chamber and failed to identify the child she had always thought of as her little brother. He was a stranger to her. Under Warwick's influence, he was striding towards manhood with desperate haste, throwing off the stranglehold of learning and driving his frail strength to the utmost at sports. He was thin, and flushed and racked with a persistent cough that had an ominous sound. She sank to her knees before him, ashamed and a little shocked that her first thought should have measured him squarely for his coffin. She had once loved him very dearly, but he had not lifted a finger to help her when she had been a friendless prisoner in fear of her life; love was an unwelcome invader in the heart of princes.

It was to be a formal interview; she was not sufficiently restored to favour to be allowed the privilege of seeing him alone. It had required half a dozen deep curtsies to bring her to the foot of the throne and as she rose from the sixth, she caught the pale, grave eyes of Protector Somerset's young secretary, Mr William Cecil, upon her. He inclined his head slowly in her direction and she surprised an odd look in his guarded expression. Was it sympathy? It occurred to her suddenly that Cecil must have dealt with all her correspondence to the Council during her imprisonment at Hatfield, had no doubt seen the confessions of Kat and Parry, had likely handled the details of the draft proclamation which officially sanctioned her innocence. He was looking at her now with almost furtive respect. How curious! Could it be then that Cecil did not believe she was a whore after all? It would be invaluable to have a friend at court, and from the cold, sly glances around her she knew there were few indeed prepared to take that risk, and even fewer that she would ever dare to trust. With a sudden irrational instinct she felt drawn towards the man.

'You are welcome to court, my sweet sister Temperance.'

The King held out his hand and indicated that she might sit beside him; he had used his old childish nickname for her. Temperance had been chosen with teasing irony and shortened in private to its more apt version of Temper ever since young Robert Dudley had annotated it, to Edward's huge satisfaction.

Temper, temper! A shrill childish pipe echoed back from a sunny afternoon in her childhood. Robin Dudley, that horrid little boy!

She looked up, and saw him at last standing among the Dudley faction. And all the time she sat listening patiently to her brother's precocious monologue, it was Robin she watched from beneath demurely lowered lashes.

Whitehall Palace sprawled around three sides of the Privy Garden, bounded to the north by the Privy Gallery, a timber structure which they had brought from a house of Wolsey's at Esher at the time of the cardinal's disgrace. At the end of the gravel path Robin Dudley pulled his purple velvet cloak around his broad shoulders, gathered a handful of snow and flung it at a low-hanging tree. He grinned as the minor avalanche which ensued showered an elderly spaniel circling beneath, searching, with maddening procrastination, for the right spot.

The old dog paused in his dawdling and eyed his master with rheumy-eyed reproach.

'Don't look at me like that, you ancient villain, just get on with it! God's death, it's cold enough out here to freeze my—'

A twig snapped behind him. He broke off abruptly and swung round to look down into the cynical face of the Princess Elizabeth.

'Yes?' she said with a cool smile. 'Do continue your conversation—I should imagine Caesar sympathizes with you, being considerably nearer the ground than you are.'

She watched with amusement as the young man turned red to the tips of his ears, thoroughly embarrassed to be caught talking to his dog by this superior girl and the smug governess who was her permanent shadow now. But as he knelt gracefully in the snow to kiss her formally outstretched hand, he forgot his quick annoyance beneath a flicker of vulgar curiosity. There were so many questions burning within him about the Lord Admiral, questions which he knew he must never dare to ask. And what could he say to her now that would not sound prying, that would take the cold wary expression from her pale face? Shocked to see how strained and frail she looked, he said, unable to think of anything better, 'Will you walk with me, madam?'

'*Madam?*'

He smiled suddenly, took her hand with all his old familiarity and laid it on his arm. She turned and nodded to Kat, who knew what was required of her and reluctantly fell back several paces behind them.

'Show me the gardens,' Elizabeth said. 'It's a long time since I've been at court.'

'Too long,' he parried swiftly. 'Much too long. I would have ridden over to Hatfield to see you but—' He hesitated.

'But your father wouldn't have liked it.'

'Well—' He was uncomfortable. 'You know what Father is—'

'You don't have to apologize, Robin, I'm not offended.'

A look of real relief crossed his face and they began to talk of other things.

Thirty-four columns, each surmounted by a fantastically carved animal, lined their way as they strolled towards the huge fountain in the centre of the garden. A sturdy vein of self-confidence marked Robin's conversation, based on a belief, as yet unchallenged, that the world was a pleasant place and life was his own particular oyster. He was cheerful company and Elizabeth found herself studying him from the corner of her eye with a warmth of interest that amazed her. She was astonished to see just how handsome he had grown and very careful not to let him see that she had noticed. She was accordingly astringent, and as he strutted beside her, boisterous, bumptious and buoyant as a half-grown hound, she put him down several times with verbal cuffs that began to penetrate his healthy depth of thick skin. So he tried a little of the flattery that had paid him handsome dividends in other circumstances.

'They say you never wear your hair loose any more.'

'Well?' She gave him a frigid glance.

'Don't you think it's a waste to hide it like that—no one else at court has hair to match yours?'

Against her will she was faintly mollified.

'Courtier!' she said suspiciously. 'Where have you been polishing your tongue?'

'In Norfolk, on a softer stone,' he admitted with a shrug.

'Norfolk?'

'Syderstone—we were quartered there for a few nights after the rebellion. You mind old Robsart's daughter? We marry in June.'

She stared ahead, unable to look at him, hiding an emotion that seemed as irrational as it was unexpected. For what was it to her, after all, if he married?

At last she turned with a crooked little smile and slapped his arm playfully.

'Wild oats,' she said softly. 'Pleasant enough to sow, but very tedious to reap. Poor Robin!'

'Men pay for whores,' he snapped angrily, needled by the sly insinuation. 'They don't take them to wife.'

He watched her go white as a bleached bone and was suddenly on fire with guilt, ashamed of pricking holes in that hard, careless front of composure which was her sole defence against the knowing leers and sniggering talk. At seventeen, with nothing ahead that he could see for himself but success and happiness, her taut misery hurt him, made him feel small and mean-minded. How tactless and insensitive to have spoken of his marriage, with the Admiral rotting at this moment in a dishonoured grave. He stole an uneasy glance at her. She shivered in the frosty air and he flung his cloak around her shoulders with a curiously heavy heart. So it was true then, all the rumours—she had loved a man old enough to have been her father— And why should she give the time of day now to a callow, shallow youth who had as good as called her a slut . . . ?

'I didn't mean to imply—' he began awkwardly.

She smiled faintly and put her finger to his lips to close them. The clumsy lie had touched her. Certainly he believed the rumours, but unlike the rest, believed them unwillingly. In spite of evil gossip and wealthy heiresses, he was still her friend and would always be; it was as though he simply couldn't help it.

'Tell me about your bride,' she said gently.

Suddenly bashful as a schoolboy, he told her a little, packing the snow to ice beneath his boot and not looking at her as he spoke. When he had finished there was silence between them, a silence it was incumbent upon her to break with the greatest care.

'So,' she said guardedly, 'hardly an *arranged* marriage.'

He laughed, 'If I'd proposed to a peasant it couldn't have caused more trouble. Oh, she's wealthy enough, even Mother couldn't fault her there— but of no standing, you see, nothing to further the family's interests at court. But I'll be hanged before I play a pawn on Father's chessboard. If I ever find power in England, no man shall say I first went hunting it beneath my own wife's petticoats.'

There was a curious expression on her face. She lifted her hand to her lips as though to hide a smile and he instantly took the gesture for mockery.

'I have amused you,' he continued stonily. 'Doubtless you prefer men to be cold-blooded, ruthless graspers like—'

'Like your father,' she finished for him pleasantly.

He smiled uneasily and conceded the point. Did she know just how close he had come to flinging the Admiral's name at her, like a gauntlet? Her eyes regarded him steadily, hard and bright, quietly superior with an unvoiced depth of knowledge that touched him with the first moment of self-doubt. His world had been uncomplicated, coloured simply in black and white, and he had been sure of himself and his desires. Now suddenly, unexpectedly, there was confusion, an area of indistinct greyness and uncertainty which he did not care to examine too closely—

It had been easy to fall in love with Amy—too easy, he thought suddenly, remembering the rough kick Warwick had dealt him beneath the cover of the Robsarts' table.

'Paws off, Robin, I know that look of yours! When we leave here tomorrow I don't want old Robsart running after us yelling "rape".'

It was an indignity and it had stung deep, transforming a moment's normal, healthy lust into a pitched battle for independence. Marriage with the Robsart heiress was the first serious campaign Robin had ever waged against his father's authority and he won it sooner than he had expected. Warwick, preoccupied with pressing matters of state, had neither the time nor the inclination to master a belligerent man-cub whose stubborn wilfulness was vaguely reminiscent of his own. He had always had a soft spot for Robin, of all his sons the nearest mirror image of himself—and the girl had money that might be useful. So he gave way; the contract was drawn up, a date agreed and Robin was complacent at his victory; or had been, until this moment.

'Seventeen,' remarked Elizabeth casually, 'is very young for a man to put his head willingly into a noose.'

He was silent, shaken, infuriated. Young! Now what exactly did she mean by that—naïve, immature, ignorant? He, twelve months her senior in an age when many lads of his station had already fathered the next generation—he, *young?* Too young to recognize a passing fancy in time to retreat from it? Was that what she meant to imply?

'You must come to the wedding,' he said curtly and they walked on in hostile silence for a while, with the old spaniel padding between them.

The fountain was still, supported by frozen cherubs. Close by stood a sundial designed to show the hour in thirty different ways, but today, thickly covered by a layer of snow and ice, it showed none of them. Elizabeth chiselled at the frozen mass with a stick. After a while she asked casually what he knew of the Protector—it was safer ground.

'Somerset's finished,' said Robin flatly.

'He's still alive.'

Robin smiled. 'For the moment.'

She paused, with the stick suspended in one hand and her eyes met his across the sundial.

'*When?*' she whispered.

He was silent, weighing the risks of indiscretion.

'When it pleases the people?' she persisted.

'Oh—the people don't count!' Robin shrugged carelessly. 'When it happens—*if* it happens—it will be at my father's convenience.'

She asked no more. She had learned all she wanted to know; the Duke's days were numbered. Snow began to swirl around them and they went back to the palace, where she returned Robin's cloak in silence.

Further down the corridor there was a sudden movement. A sombre, unimposing figure began to walk steadily towards them and she recognized him at last, in the winter half-light, as Somerset's secretary.

'Here comes that bloodless wonder, Cecil.' Robin's voice in her ear was contemptuously amused. 'He'll have to shift soon if he wants to save his skin. They say you'll always be able to judge which way the wind's blowing by the way Master Cecil trims his sails. Father's cultivating him, thinks he might prove useful. Personally, I wouldn't bother. He's just a spineless weathercock like all the rest of the Council.'

Elizabeth turned to look at the gentleman in question, a small man, dull and insignificant to look at; she wondered why her heart should jump at the sight of him. It was the second time now that she had felt this extraordinary jolt, as though something had touched her soul at its very core.

Cecil stopped in front of them and bowed sketchily, taking the hand she automatically extended to him. He seemed about to speak when an angry voice cut between them, rebounding down the empty passage from an open door beyond.

'Robin! Devil take that boy, he's never about when I need him. Mary—cut along and find the lovesick lout—'

The door closed abruptly, cutting off the strident tones in the middle of an oath. Robin didn't wait for his sister to appear in person.

'Damned dog,' he said, bending to slap the spaniel's rump affectionately. 'If I had more sense and less heart I'd have you put down and save myself a deal of trouble.'

He straightened up briskly to kiss Elizabeth's right hand and found Cecil holding it. There was a moment of pointed silence while he glared at the older man, waiting for him to give way. Then Elizabeth offered her left hand and he was forced to take it, so that for a curious second the three of them stood physically linked in a triangle. The moment lengthened past convention, charged with significance beyond their present ken, until Elizabeth laughed and withdrew her fingers from Robin's fierce grasp.

'Dogs and horses,' she remarked to the secretary, 'I believe they even follow him to bed when they can. You're a married man, Mr Cecil—you had better warn him that his wife will be jealous.'

Robin made her a mocking bow.

'Your Grace may keep an easy mind on the matter. However crowded the bed, there's always room to fit in a wife—wouldn't you agree there, Cecil?'

The secretary stared with vague distaste, and Elizabeth's sudden laughter confirmed his suspicion that he had missed the point of some vulgar jest. The knowledge irritated Cecil, and his precise mind, trained to a lawyer's obsession with detail, began to gnaw at the innuendo. *Always room to—* He stiffened in disgust as the young man departed cockily—fast, foul-tongued, symbolic of a jumped-up race he instinctively despised.

The geriatric spaniel, sensing hostility, gazed at him balefully, before ambling after his master in a leisurely fashion; Elizabeth and Cecil were left alone in the dimly lit corridor, wrapped in a pulsing silence.

'Do you too jump when Warwick roars, Mr Secretary?' she asked at last, wondering why he stood and stared at her in that strange manner. 'I understand that soon you may be in need of a new master.'

'We must all seek out one whom we can serve with love and loyalty, Your Grace. However long the search I shall find my true master—or mistress—in the end.'

The words had an indescribable ring, and for a moment it was as though the outer world had faded, leaving them to face one another on a spiritual plateau, divorced from time and space, a sixteen-year-old princess of doubtful reputation and a colourless, twenty-seven-year-old lawyer, whose morals and intellect were equally impeccable. Her right hand still lay in his, as though some unseen force had suddenly soldered them together.

When she spoke at last it was in a whisper.

'It may be that soon I shall need a surveyor to handle my landed properties —it would be a minor post with a salary of roughly twenty pounds a year.' Her voice was now charged with that same strange ring. 'I need someone to watch over my interests, Cecil. Are you prepared to take on that extra duty?'

At last he raised her hand to his cool lips.

'I believe the position you have in mind would in no way hamper the discharge of my present offices. I shall be happy to serve your interests, madam—in whatever direction they may lie.'

Their eyes met and held and in that moment they both knew they were bound together until death.

* * *

Kat curbed her delighted curiosity until she was alone with her mistress.

'Well,' she said at last, unable to hide the thrill of pleasure in her voice, 'what did you think of him, Your Grace?'

Elizabeth looked up with a start.

'I don't know who you mean.'

'Such a fine figure of a man, but then I always said he would be—did Your Grace say whom?—why young Robert Dudley of course.'

'Oh, him!' Elizabeth affected a bored yawn and removed her coif; Kat's excitement visibly disappeared, like a pricked bubble.

'He has no more to recommend him than when I saw him last—and that as I remember was precious little.'

'Your Grace! How can you say such a thing about so handsome and charming a young man who—'

'Who is to be married in June.'

'*Oh!*' It came on a note of bitter disappointment. Kat picked up a comb and began to draw it slowly through Elizabeth's hair.

What a pity, she thought, and was silent.

CHAPTER 8

Elizabeth attended Robin's wedding later that summer, one of many unwilling guests obliged to show their faces at a series of Dudley unions. Only the day before, Robin's eldest brother, Jack, had married the Duke of Somerset's daughter, a shrewd political move which had thrown many off the scent. Men had begun to remark on the 'outward great love and friendship between the Duke and the Earl'; but the Duke still went about the court looking haggard; and his daughter wept.

Then it was Robin's turn, and the congregation sweated through the vows in the hot sunlight which filled the chapel at Richmond.

'. . . with this ring I thee wed, with my body I thee worship . . .'

The Earl of Warwick, fingering his prayer book with bored indifference, let his idle glance fall on the Princess Elizabeth, and surprised a look on her face that made him smile with fond pride. Robin was a fine young ram, there was no mistake about that—he had left more than one thin-lipped young lady watching enviously. But Elizabeth—still mourning the Admiral? Somehow he did not think so. The extreme pallor spoke of a more immediate cause and Warwick was faintly amused. A low-born Dudley, hey? Her tastes were not what they should be, but they were healthy—by God, he'd say so!

The day was depressing for Elizabeth, the jousting dull, the feasting repugnant, the increasing round of frivolity meaningless and exhausting. Amy was insipidly pretty and Robin was attentive. Elizabeth withdrew to the hearth with her ladies and mentally wandered back down that dark path which ended in a dead man's arms.

She had not retreated far, when a shadow fell over her and a quiet voice jerked her back into the uncomfortable present. Looking up into the thin, strained face of the Duke of Somerset, she froze into wary immobility.

'I must stand,' he said softly, 'unless Your Grace invites me to sit.'

'Stand then,' she retorted with barely controlled venom, 'stand until you rot—my lord.'

A look of distress touched his ravaged face; he looked suddenly ready to weep.

'There is something I must say to you,' he muttered hoarsely, 'something I must beg you to hear whether you will or not.'

Her hostile stare burnt him, like the touch of black ice, and she was grimly silent.

He glanced nervously about the crowded room and then his eyes swivelled back to hers, filled with all the servile appeal of a beaten dog.

'Five minutes of your time, madam, is all I ask to tell you how it was—how it truly was between myself and my brother.'

She opened her mouth to protest, but he gave her no chance. The broken words flowed out of him like a bloody flux.

'I never desired his death—I swear it. I did what I could—begged him to account for his activities in private. He refused my help—after that it was taken out of my hands. Madam, I have suffered torments of guilt since the deed was done—'

'I pray daily for a speedy end to your suffering on this earth, my lord.'

He smiled tiredly, almost with admiration.

'Yes,' he murmured, 'you are your father's daughter and like him spare no man in your anger. You could prove very powerful.'

Her eyes widened, shocked out of their hostility.

'Remember me when you are Queen, madam,' he continued quietly, 'remember how I failed and learn from my mistakes. I was a fool to trust the men who served me. Trust no one, madam, not even your own shadow, and beware of this land you covet so badly. England is a fickle shrew that may break even your stony heart.'

'You would know more about shrews than most, my lord,' she said unsteadily. 'God knows you married one.'

He shook his head slowly, without bitterness.

'Madam, let me make my peace with you.'

'Make it with God,' she said curtly and turned away to speak to an attendant.

He bowed low and shuffled away into the milling crowds, a sad and weary figure, aged beyond his years by guilt, the heaviest of all human burdens. Elizabeth looked down at her hands and found they were trembling violently; the music echoed dimly around her and the guests frolicked before her unseeing eyes. Black thoughts claimed her, fencing her off from the merriment with a stone wall of hatred.

At the far end of the hall, Warwick was holding court beside the King's chair, with Henry Grey toadying to him, bobbing his silver head in obsequious agreement to every word the great man uttered. Guildford Dudley was dancing in sulky silence with the Greys' eldest daughter, Lady Jane. He looked bored, and at the end of the measure seemed disposed to return to the wine table. Warwick said nothing, merely fixed a steely glance on the boy, and Guildford immediately turned back and led Jane out on to the floor for the galliard.

This curious little side play penetrated Elizabeth's vacant gaze just sufficiently to prick her sense of self-preservation; it was a rather more sturdy plant than it had been the previous year. She had a small stake in life now—not much, but enough to make her care whether or not she would celebrate her next birthday, and what she saw now between Warwick and Grey was sufficient to alarm her. The King was plainly sick, no matter how many doctors cheerfully said otherwise, and Jane was third in line to the throne. After today, Guildford Dudley was Warwick's only remaining marriageable son. And Guildford had plainly been told to dance with Jane. So—

Following Guildford's progress across the hall, Elizabeth saw Robin bend his head swiftly and steal a kiss from the pretty little nobody he had married. Tears pricked suddenly and unexpectedly at the back of her eyes; she smoothed the feathers of her fan and stared into the fire, willing them not to fall.

Robin, looking over to the yawning hearth, saw her sitting surrounded by her ladies and thought that she looked more solitary, more isolated, than if she sat alone. He turned to his wife and said suddenly, inexplicably sharp, 'Come, I shall present you to the Lady Elizabeth.'

If he had offered to introduce her to an adder Amy could hardly have shown more alarm.

'Oh no, Robert, don't! Please don't do that.'

He stared at her in honest amazement. She fumbled with the ribbons trailing down from the bodice of her gown and muttered something about already being presented.

'That was mere court formality,' he insisted. 'Two words and a curtsey are hardly sufficient to make anyone's acquaintance.'

Against his impelling arm Amy hung back like a reluctant child.

'Don't make me, Robert. I can't. She's so clever and so—' But there were no words to describe what she felt about Elizabeth, who had chilled her at first glance. She gave him the look of kittenish appeal which had never yet failed to move him, but in his present mood it glanced off him without effect and his hand remained firm beneath her elbow.

'You must learn to be at ease with my friends, my love,' he said pleasantly enough, but in a tone that brooked no opposition.

Short of making a public scene, there was nothing Amy could do but accompany him to the hearth with precious little grace. Resentful and agitated, she sank down in her wedding gown before a remote figure that raised her to her feet with the cool touch of a long white hand.

Elizabeth's hand fascinated and intimidated Amy; she had never seen anything so delicate, so flawless as those beautiful fingers, each capped with a perfectly formed nail. She could not recall any other hand ever riveting her attention in this unnatural fashion and was suddenly uncomfortably conscious of her own. Well kept, even by court standards, they now felt as clumsy as a row of sausages on a pair of wooden platters.

Hands like Elizabeth's, she thought darkly, had no place in this mortal world; hands like that must surely be reserved for the Devil's work! She recalled a few things her father's chaplain had told her of how evil disguised itself under beauty's mantle: and she clung a little harder to Robin's arm.

The opening gambits of conversation passed over her head, quick, clever sallies of court wit which she scarcely heard and would not have understood even had she done so. She said, 'Yes, madam', 'No, madam', where it seemed appropriate and was just beginning to be satisfied that that was all that was required of her—to stand at his side and look decorative—when a boy in livery summoned Robin to the King's side. He went at once, leaving Amy, alone with Elizabeth, staring after him in dismay.

For the space of roughly two minutes Elizabeth exerted an honest effort to be civil to this overdressed country mouse.

It was wasted breath. Amy's dislike was instinctive and she was not sufficiently disciplined to hide it beneath a polite veneer of conversation. Elizabeth sensed the hostility and took the point off her rapier with a clear conscience and disarming smile.

'You are nervous,' she remarked silkily. 'Is it me or the thought of the marriage bed that ties your tongue in my presence?'

The indelicate suggestion sent a wave of beetroot colour creeping up Amy's neck. Elizabeth sat back on the bench and watched her with satisfaction. This promised to be amusing.

'Have they told you all men are brutes? Oh yes, I'm sure they have! But not Robin. I think I have seldom met a man more gentle with animals.'

Amy, not quite as stupid as she had made herself appear, caught that barb and stiffened.

'They say he is the best horseman in England,' continued Elizabeth innocently. 'Do you also love horses, Amy?'

'No, madam.' She was coldly, pointedly formal. 'I am afraid of horses.' *And of you—you are dangerous!*

'But you do ride, I suppose.'

'Never, madam. I travel by litter.'

Elizabeth's delicate eyebrows arched in genuine astonishment.

'Is that not inconvenient for a horseman of your husband's stature?'

'He doesn't mind,' said Amy, defensive now. 'Why should he?'

Elizabeth smiled contemptuously behind her fan.

'When you have been a little longer at court you will understand the necessity of mastering a horse for the hunt.'

'I have no intention of living at court,' said Amy stiffly. 'Father wouldn't like it.'

'Father gave you away—remember?'

Amy flushed.

'My estates in Norfolk will keep my husband fully occupied, Your Grace.'

Suddenly, inexplicably Elizabeth lost her temper. She said very low, very controlled, very spiteful, 'Madam, you're not married to a simple country squire with no thought in his head beyond next lambing! If that's all you have to offer him you won't hold him past the first encounter!'

Amy stared, silent, stunned. She was spoilt and smug and in all her sheltered life no one had ever said such a terrible thing to her. Her pretty face went first very red, then deathly white and she swayed a little where she sat.

Elizabeth knew a moment of shamed panic. She did not want the girl to cry or faint at her feet; the last thing she could afford, in her tenuous position, was to draw the hostile attention of the bride's father-in-law.

'Kat, fetch Lady Dudley some wine. I'm afraid the excitement has been too much for her.'

Kat departed with a hard, accusing look at her mistress and returned with a goblet of malmsey. Amy accepted it with a trembling hand and took a few gulping draughts. Slowly the colour crept back into her face and her lips set themselves into a thin, sulky line.

'Amy.' Elizabeth leaned forward a little to touch a ruffle at the girl's wrist. 'Don't look for kindness at court or anywhere else. The world is a hard place.'

'Certainly,' said Amy pointedly, 'it is full of cruel people.'

Elizabeth smiled faintly.

'I have found treason in trust and learnt to strike before I am stricken. Let us dispense with pretence—there can be no friendship between us. I fear neither of us desires it.'

'Robert shall know how unkind you have been, madam.'

'Only if you are fool enough to speak of it. What I told you was the truth and if you have any sense you will learn from it. Open your mind to his world and study the things that interest him. Be prepared to grow with him, Amy, because if you don't you'll wake up one day and find him gone. And believe me—the woman who takes him from you won't be prepared to give him back without a fight.'

Amy sat still with her hands clenched in her lap. She was no longer shocked or offended; she was simply sick with terror in the face of a declared enemy. She fixed wild eyes on the figures before the throne, until at last Robin turned, intercepted her distress signals and hurried back, vaguely irritated by her obvious inability to hold her own for less than five minutes without him.

Side by side they still sat; Amy agitated, almost dishevelled, as after some physical encounter of which she had plainly got the worst; and Elizabeth, with her finely chiselled poise, looking very—very as he had never seen her look before. Was it beautiful or merely mysterious? He could not have said, but on impulse he bowed over her hand and begged her to dance with him. Amy drew in her breath sharply but he ignored it.

Elizabeth glanced at Amy, laughed and shook her head.

'My lord, you should ask your wife.'

'I have the rest of my life to dance with my wife.' He was annoyed, a little drunk, inclined to be heartless and belligerent. 'And you owe me this measure, madam. Listen.' The musicians were striking up a haunting refrain. 'Remember the day we learnt this at Hampton Court?'

'Greenwich.'

'Well—wherever! *"Andante andante"*, you said and pinched me because I went too fast.'

'You'll always go too fast, Robin Dudley—'

They were out of Amy's hearing by now, but not out of sight. Her jealous eyes followed them, two bodies joined by the perfect harmony of rhythm. They laughed rather more than was in keeping with the sombre stateliness of the measure and when it was over they stood for an endless moment talking. *Saying what?* screamed a voice in Amy's head.

There was no opportunity to ask. Even as Robin raised Elizabeth's hand to his lips, his eyes resting all the time on hers, a crowd of laughing women descended on Amy and bore her away to the bridal chamber. There she was undressed, teased mercilessly and put naked into the big bed to wait for Robin.

'Don't worry,' someone said kindly. 'After the first time it's not so bad.'

'Oh, don't cozen her with nonsense, you know very well that it takes months—you take my advice, my dear, and give him a son quickly. Once you've done your duty they take their pleasures elsewhere and leave you in peace.'

The matrons drew off, arguing good-naturedly and Amy lay very still, trying not to overhear snippets of their dreadful tales.

'. . . it's the last thing a man does before they put him in a box, you know.'

'Aye—they're all the same there—well, *most* of them, hey?'

The conversation became muted, laced with sly laughter. *Oh, Robert, why don't you come and send them all away?* . . .

He came at length, wrapped in a long satin robe, and it seemed to Amy as though he had brought the entire court on his heels, a host of vulgar, drunken wedding guests who milled around the bed, laughing and shrieking like grotesque devils from the mouth of hell.

But there was one who did not prance or shriek or sing rude innuendoes, one who was stone-cold sober and whose slender presence terrified her more than all the rest.

She shut her eyes and did not open them again until the noisy multitude had jostled itself out of the room. What she saw then made her shrink into the shelter of Robin's warm nakedness.

Elizabeth was standing alone beside the bed. One hand rested lightly on the bedpost and the other on the curtain, so that her sweeping Boleyn sleeves unfurled like an angel's wings. Candlelight made a red-gold halo of her hair and softened the sharp contours of her face to a gleam of extraordinary beauty. Beneath her hand, Amy felt Robin's body stir and stiffen.

No one spoke. Elizabeth laughed suddenly and swept the curtain across the bed, shutting them together in the little brocaded prison. They did not hear her leave the room, but they knew instinctively the moment she was gone; it was as though something beyond this world had withdrawn to its own sphere.

The room was very quiet after the noisy crowd. Robin lay rigid beneath the sheet, staring at the dividing curtain, and Amy sensed some fierce emotion had him in its grip. Before she could speak, he had wrenched the curtain aside with a violent jerk and strode naked into the room. By the hearth he paused to pour a goblet of wine and she watched him throw it down his throat as though it were water.

'Robert.'

'Be quiet!' he snapped.

'But I don't understand—what's wrong?'

'I said be silent, God damn you! Didn't you promise to obey?'

He flung the empty goblet across the room. It bounced off the wall and he stood staring at it for a long time. At length he returned to bed and made love to her in the rough, selfish fashion she had been led to expect. Afterwards he was moderately kind and wiped away her tears, reassuring her until she fell asleep beneath his arm.

He lay awake, with her hair streaming across his bare chest and watched the room grow steadily lighter. He thought of Elizabeth, wondering what it would be like to lie beside her in the half light: and suddenly he was filled with a hollow sense of loss.

All through the next day, as he followed the hunt, he was dogged by a curious depression which spoiled his pleasure in a good kill. He lingered over cards in the Great Hall and Amy was asleep when he came up; so he went back downstairs to find Guildford and the pair of them got roisteringly drunk.

It was a curious relief to have been spared that nagging disappointment two nights in a row.

Once installed in Norfolk, it was less easy to avoid his wife; and when nothing in the length and breadth of that whole county gave him any satisfaction, he began to escape to court as often as he could without exciting comment. Discreet inquiries from his mother over the state of Amy's health, coupled with puerile jests from Guildford ('Not got that mare of yours in foal yet, Robin?') suddenly focused a new light on his nebulous dissatisfaction. How could a man be content, burdened with a barren cow who showed no sign of giving him a son and heir? After eighteen months he had at last succeeded in convincing himself that the sole cause of his bitter frustration was this persistent inability to be presented with a miniature replica of himself. And one dull, rainy evening at Syderstone saw them quarrelling peevishly on the subject.

'Perhaps if you came a little more often to my bed—' she said on a sudden sob.

He turned away impatiently.

'For Christ's sake, Amy—I've sown seed enough in you to father a dozen sons by now.'

'That makes it my fault, of course.'

'I suggested you should see a doctor. I never *said* it was your fault.'

'But it's what you meant.' Amy bit her lip. 'And you were right. There'll be no child. How could there be, when a witch overlooked me on my marriage bed?'

His irritable stride up and down the room halted abruptly; he swung round to look at her with the curious, cautious look that people reserve for the mentally deranged.

'Of all the brain-sick gibberish—' He stopped and his tone changed sharply as understanding dawned. 'God's blood—you mean Elizabeth, don't you?'

The casual use of that Christian name stung Amy like a pebble from a sling and made her reckless.

'Everyone knows her mother was a witch—the King himself accused her. And it's passed on in the blood to the next generation, like the French Pox. Father says that every witch—'

He took a step towards her and slapped her silent; his face beneath its tan was quite white.

'If you say just one more word,' he spat, 'I'll take my whip to you.'

'You wouldn't dare,' she whispered, holding her flaming cheek.

He gave her a tight smile, glacial, contemptuous, and turned away in silence.

'I'll tell Father,' she flung after him, suddenly desperate.

'Please do,' he said evenly, from the door, 'and when you do you might also ask him to send you a lawyer.'

She began to tremble then. 'A lawyer?'

'You know on what business,' he announced curtly, and went out of the room.

She knew. It was not the first time he had clubbed her into silence with that hefty cudgel labelled 'divorce'. She couldn't afford to provoke him any further by giving free rein to her jealous tongue.

She would not speak of the Lady Elizabeth again.

Robin stood alone in the half-lit hall, marshalling his resentments like a man inspecting a regiment.

He had been a fool to marry the first pretty heiress to cross his path—just how great a fool was being revealed more clearly to him with every day that passed. Events were moving fast at court. As the King's health failed, Warwick had said it might be necessary to alter the line of succession and Guildford was being schooled for marriage with Lady Jane Grey. Guildford—timorous and effete, always so afraid that life might have something nasty up its sleeve. Guildford Dudley to be King of England, for no better reason than that it *had* to be Guildford; while Robin rotted in Norfolk, married to a snivelling little country bitch who couldn't even give him a son!

And Elizabeth—

He broke off there, as though faced with a grievance too painful even to acknowledge.

Oh, yes. She was the catalyst in his simmering cauldron of discontent.

But he would die before he admitted it to anyone. Least of all to himself.

What remained of Edward Tudor's reign ticked relentlessly away in a welter of petty storms. Elizabeth lived like a nun at Hatfield, impeccably Protestant and beyond the reach of Warwick's hand; she was not, in any case, his primary target. If Edward died, it was Mary who stood next in line to the throne, and it was Mary he persecuted mercilessly for her stubborn adherence to the Catholic faith, hoping to drive the sickly woman into exile, or better still, into the grave.

When the King created him Duke of Northumberland he was at the zenith of his power, great soldier, wily diplomat, the most feared and hated man in all of England. The time had come when he could afford to rid himself of liabilities and secure his position as undisputed ruler. And first and foremost on his list was the Duke of Somerset.

As the net of intrigue tightened inexorably around him, Somerset confided in Mr Secretary Cecil that he suspected some ill.

Cecil's bland face had the look of one who has stepped straight from boyhood into middle age. Loyalty to the Duke was a damp cloak around his bowed shoulders, uncomfortable to wear, easy to shake off.

And Cecil said coldly, 'If Your Grace is innocent you may be of good courage. If you are guilty I have nothing to say but to lament you.'

After this rank desertion, the Duke appeared to slip into apathy, making little effort to escape the fate that was closing in upon him so relentlessly. They came to arrest him at Hampton Court shortly afterwards and he accepted the charge of treason with curious indifference.

Alone in his stone chamber in the Tower, he looked back down the inevitable path of his failure to that night of Edward's christening. Life had seemed so full of promise that night, marred only by the disagreeable need to carry a little girl in his arms. If he could only go back to that night and walk down that corridor again, how differently would he have chosen his allegiances.

Elizabeth walked endlessly across his mind and her eyes were hard and unforgiving. The longing to atone for his crime had become an obsession, and suddenly he knew the only way to do it, the one thing that could give her greater pleasure than his death. He took the last of his pride and offered it to her, in the form of a letter begging her shamelessly to intercede for his life.

When her answer came—a cold, merciless little note calmly regretting that 'being so young a woman I have no power to do anything on your behalf' —he imagined the immense satisfaction it had given her to write it.

And he was suddenly at peace with himself.

CHAPTER 9

Northumberland's triumphant dictatorship lasted a little over a year. By May of 1553 he was face to face with the event which would spell ruin to his family when at last the King's doctors were bullied into privately admitting the truth. There was no more to be done for the sixteen-year-old boy who lay in silent agony on his bed, coughing blood and black mucus. Northumberland swore the physicians to secrecy on pain of death and insisted that reassuring descriptions of the King's health should be widely circulated. Meanwhile, he worked desperately against time to salvage his own future.

The court was sealed like a tomb against any unwelcome interference from either of the King's sisters. Elizabeth's last, desperate attempt to force a meeting in April had been forestalled by armed guards and the message, supposedly from Edward himself, to return to Hatfield until further notice.

All her letters to Edward were skilfully intercepted by Northumberland and she waited in vain in her outer darkness for a reply from her brother.

On Whit Sunday, physically beaten into submission by her ruthless parents, Lady Jane Grey was married to Guildford Dudley in a hasty ceremony. Some time later, Northumberland bowed himself to the King's bedside and there explained the absolute necessity of a new will, bequeathing the crown of England to his daughter-in-law.

'The late King himself named your cousin, the Lady Jane, in direct line of succession,' he pointed out.

'*After* my sisters.'

'Half-sisters,' corrected the Duke smoothly. 'And both bastards by English law.'

The King's eyes stared up at him confused by tortured logic. They could not *both* be illegitimate—not at the same time. That indeed had been Henry's final dilemma, one which, in his usual autocratic fashion, he had simply chosen to ignore in his last testament.

'To go against my father's will—'

'Is your duty, sire, in this instance. Only consider what the Lady Mary would do to wreck our work for the Protestant cause.'

'Then surely Elizabeth—my sweet sister Temperance—'

The Duke coughed uncomfortably. He had his reasons for overruling Elizabeth but this was hardly the time or the place to reveal them.

'The Lady Elizabeth might be persuaded to marry a Catholic, in which case her accession would be equally hazardous to the future of the Protestant faith in England.'

Doubt crossed Edward's white face.

'She would never willingly marry a Catholic,' he protested.

'Her hold on the throne would be tenuous, sire, she might have no alternative means of securing her position.' Northumberland rose and bent ominously over the wasted figure against the pillows. 'Let me remind Your Majesty that when the good of the country and the glory of God are at stake, it is the bounden duty of a prince to set aside all considerations of blood. Neglect of that duty will procure you everlasting damnation at the hands of God's dreadful tribunal.'

The boy in the bed was bald, shrivelled and nail-less. Gangrene had already claimed several of his toes and he was close enough to death to be swayed by fear of what he would find waiting on the other side of that threshold.

By the end of June, Northumberland's new Device for the Succession was signed, sealed and witnessed by the Privy Council, waiting in a locked drawer to be used.

*   *   *

On the sixth day of July the air was hot and heavy all over England. At Hatfield, where park, gardens and orchard shimmered beneath a stifling heat haze, the dove-house had emptied its sleepy inhabitants along the low red roof of the palace and in the solar the bees droned lazily.

Dusk came in a violent thunderstorm. Streaks of blue lightning split the sky and giant hailstones pummelled the manor house. Shortly after midnight a deluge of rain lashed against the windows of Elizabeth's room, and she got up from her desk to close the casements. Tendrils of hair had crept from beneath her cap and coiled damply about her forehead, for the heat was still oppressive. She was tired and tense and a sudden unexpected tap at the door made her start round violently.

'Come,' she said sharply and the door opened to reveal a nervous maid, clutching a candle. A howling wind was springing up beyond the ill-fitting casement, causing the flame to waver drunkenly in a strong draught.

'What is it, Meg? I thought the whole household was in bed by now.'

The girl made a flustered curtsey and hesitated in the doorway, reluctant to intrude into the room without direct invitation.

'Begging Your Grace's pardon, but there's a man in the Great Hall asking to see you urgently. Soaked to the skin he is, and his horse spent from hard riding. Well, I told him of course Your Grace could receive no one at such an hour, what with Mrs Ashley retired—and Mr Parry too—and really, madam, he was downright rude—'

'My business is not with underlings, Your Grace.'

A tall man with urgent, hunted eyes stepped into the room unannounced and stood with his heavy cloak dripping steadily on the bare floor.

'Business?' echoed Elizabeth warily.

'A private message, madam—from one who wishes you well.'

She weighed him for a moment in silence and then waved away the curi-ous-eyed girl. His voice was well modulated and his cloak of good cut; he was obviously no ordinary messenger.

'You come from court?' she demanded.

He ignored the question and took a step towards her, extending a small slip of folded paper.

'Read it, madam. It may save your life.'

She took the paper unwillingly, concealing it in the palm of her hand.

'Who sent you?' she repeated.

'Please, madam,' he said uncomfortably.

'Don't you trust me?'

She let both her hands rest a moment on his wet sleeve and he was dizzily aware of her oval face, those extraordinary eyes which seemed to see inside his head. He had heard it said that she was beautiful and at first glance had been vaguely disappointed. But now—

'Madam,' he whispered, 'I gave my word. My master's life may depend upon my silence.'

Her slow smile sank into his memory like a caress, as she stepped back from him. She had tested his spirit and not found it wanting; she was not displeased.

'You are a loyal servant, sir—I wish you were mine.'

He flushed and opened his mouth to babble inarticulately of his sudden irrational desire to throw himself and his life at her feet, but she took pity on him and held up her hand. Immediately he was silent. She picked up the little handbell on her desk and its imperious tinkle was shrill in the silent house.

'Tell your master of my gratitude,' she said gently. Again he would have spoken, but the return of the serving girl forestalled him. The fleeting moment of intimacy was gone and might never be recalled. He felt curiously depressed as she addressed the girl in a clipped businesslike manner, kind enough, but distant, as though she were discussing the stabling of a horse.

'Take this gentleman to the kitchens. See he is warmed and well fed before he leaves.'

'Yes, Your Grace.' The girl withdrew, waiting for him, and miserably aware of his wet clothes, his dishevelled appearance and inferior status he bowed low and would have backed out of the room. Then he saw that she was holding out her hand to him. He was a messenger, in this instance no more than a lackey and no lady of the manor would waste such a gesture on a man of his standing—

He went down on one knee and pressed her fingers to his lips.

'Remember me,' she said quietly. 'My time will come.'

The door closed behind him; and he went down the stairs with the curious girl at his side like a man in a trance.

When the soft sound of footsteps had died away in the corridor, Elizabeth returned to her desk and opened the paper in the tremulous candlelight.

Seven words in a hand she did not recognize: *Avoid the court. The King is dead.* She sat down suddenly, staring at the paper and a kaleidoscope of memories whirled in her mind. Edward at two, wearing the cambric shirt she had painstakingly made for him; Edward at nine, King of England, a frightened little boy cowering in her arms; and Edward at eleven, with the Lord Admiral's death warrant in his steady hand—

Mentally she shook herself. The King had been dead for perhaps a few hours; the boy she had loved as her brother had been dead to her for almost four years. No time to waste in tears when her own life hung in the balance. She bit her lip savagely and lit more candles with a trembling hand.

Ever since news had come of Jane's marriage to Guildford, Elizabeth had known which way Northumberland would leap when Edward died. She herself had left him with no other choice. It was several months now since she had received the neat outline of his outrageous proposal to divorce his wife and marry her; *'together we will take the throne'*. She had laughed and turned away, without even troubling to reply, but not before she had seen his features harden into an expression of fear and dislike. Several times since then she had wondered whether the pleasure of snubbing him had been worth the price he could make her pay if his new scheme succeeded. He would eliminate Mary with passionless efficient speed—but for her, he would surely reserve some special suffering, a lingering end that could be savoured. For once, she had allowed anger to override her common sense; she ought to have kept him dangling. Even now an armed force might be marching on Hatfield—

She stared into the flickering candles, while her mind galloped forward into the blind night, seeking desperately for intuition to guide her through the pitfalls now gaping at her feet.

Everything depended on Mary, and Mary was a dark, untried horse. Would she give up at the first sign of danger in meek surrender; would she flee to the armed support of her uncle the Emperor Charles V, the mightiest power in the Christian world; or would she stand and fight doggedly to the death?

Elizabeth privately suspected the last course. Mary didn't lack for courage, and when she believed she was in the right she could be as stubborn and mulish as ever her father had been. So—unquestionably Mary would fight. But would she *win?* Who in this largely Protestant land would now support a Catholic claimant? Northumberland controlled the Council, the soldiers and the ports; and on any purely logical assessment of the facts he must win with ease. Mary had no hope at all, save for the goodwill of the English people. Fickle as the toss of a coin, whose side would they come down upon now?

Elizabeth moved to open the casement and looked out at the raging storm. It was a night fit for treason. It seemed as though the heavens themselves had cracked open in fury, as though her dread sire hurled mighty thunderbolts against those who dared to tamper with his will and take the Crown from the Tudor line. She shivered with a delicious thrill of terror. Here she stood between Mary and Northumberland, utterly alone save for the anonymous goodwill shown by the author of that curt little note.

She looked again at the slip of paper in her hand, the words illegible in the gloom at the window. Who had risked his life to warn her of Northumberland's trap? Was it Robin, acting behind his father's back, or Sir William Cecil, about to desert yet another master? She would have liked to believe it was Robin, but the brief line bore the stamp of Cecil's personality—cautious, calculating, saying just enough and no more, trusting her intuition to reward him when she came into her own. Robin would have signed it, in terror that she might prove obtuse.

No, it was Cecil. She knew it as surely as if she had seen him write it. She also knew that if she failed to use this warning to advantage she would hear no more from him. If the Duke won, Cecil would be at his side to serve him. She attached no censure to the knowledge, for he had a family; and a man had to live—

Avoid the court! That suggested she would shortly be summoned to her brother's death-bed. But when the Duke's messenger arrived he would find her in bed, too ill to move from the house, certainly too ill to declare her partisanship for either side. Do nothing, say nothing, for as long as possible, and pray that Northumberland would be unable to spare sufficient men from his desperate venture to take her by force of arms.

A sudden flash of lightning threw the shadowy furniture into sharp relief against the dark walls. She held the slip of paper to a candle, let it shrivel to her fingers and then dropped the smouldering remnant into the empty hearth. Across the empty miles of rain-lashed countryside her gratitude stretched out towards a silent, clerkly man whose true stature was a closed book waiting for her opening hand.

'My Spirit,' she said softly to the wild night beyond her window.

And on the streaming latticed pane she traced an inverted cross.

In the dark hollow of the courtyard an armed body of men mounted on restless horses awaited the appearance of the young man who was to lead them on their mission. They knew precisely why they were gathered here and one or two muttered among themselves that it began to look as though the great Duke of Northumberland might have bitten off more than he could chew this time.

'Bit of a bad job when it's left to a young fellow-me-lad to salvage the game,' someone muttered, and a little furtive, nervous laughter travelled along the ranks.

In the torchlit corridor beyond the courtyard, Robin Dudley paused with his feathered hat in his hand and glanced uneasily at his father. All the Duke's composure did not disguise the anxiety at the back of his dark eyes, for by now they were certain there was a traitor in their camp and that their intended coup had been betrayed to their two enemies. The Princess Mary and the Princess Elizabeth had both received urgent messages summoning them to their brother's death-bed. Mary had set out for London immediately, having apparently swallowed the bait as everyone had anticipated. They had traced her progress as far as Hoddesdon, but there all information of her activity abruptly ceased. And while Mary had failed to arrive, the Lady Elizabeth, conveniently struck with another of her mortal illnesses, had not even set out.

Evidently someone had talked and Robin strongly suspected that ingratiating lawyer, William Cecil. But there was no time to waste now in idle accusations. The entire design depended on Robin's ability to ride out and capture the Princess Mary before she got the chance to do any serious harm to their cause. And when he returned her to London, he knew, without a shadow of doubt, that he would be returning her to her death. That much did not trouble him. It was inevitable and he had neither attachment nor loyalty to that dull old maid. But something else had been weighing heavily on his mind in the tense atmosphere for the past week or more. He had not dared to mention it to his father, whose brooding temper had become increasingly uncertain these last few days; but now he knew he could remain silent no longer. He had to know.

Twisting his hat in his hand, he averted his eyes from his father's fine-drawn face and stared out into the noisy courtyard.

'Father—' He hesitated a moment and took a quick breath. 'What will become of the Lady Elizabeth?'

Northumberland's restless eyes narrowed on the younger man's with an inscrutable lack of expression; knowing his son as he did, he was not unprepared for this awkward question. He was also acutely aware that he could not afford any more wavering loyalties at this critical stage in their venture. It was largely for that very reason that he was packing the young man off on this desperate gamble when he would have much preferred to send one of his older and more experienced sons. It would be a great deal safer to get Robin actively involved as far away from Hatfield as possible; by the time he returned, Elizabeth would no longer be complicating the issue.

He said in his calm, precise courtier's voice, 'I will settle with the Lady Elizabeth.'

'But you wouldn't—' Robin's voice faded out and the Duke shook his head quickly.

'Oh, I don't think it will come to that. I have a certain proposition to make which I'm quite sure the young lady will accept. But let's not take chivalry too far, Robin. I want the other one and I want her damned quick—you understand that, don't you?'

'You'll have her, sir. I swear it.'

Robin saluted his father, marched down the steps two at a time, vaulted effortlessly into the saddle of his favourite mare and galloped out of the courtyard at the head of the troop.

The Duke watched him go with a frown. The moment he had Jane safe on the throne, he would invite the Lady Elizabeth to attend the Coronation festivities, where, at some convenient point in the entertainment, she would be taken violently ill. A fatal recurrence of that earlier malady, which only a few weeks earlier had prevented her travelling to her brother's death-bed. Very sad, but hardly surprising with such precarious health!

As for Robin—well—he was young and he had a wife; he would get over it eventually.

But in the meantime, as a representative of the family's grief, he would make an extraordinarily convincing chief mourner at the funeral.

Mrs Ashley stirred three heaped tablespoons of salt into a small goblet of water, hid the container beneath the curtained bed and looked at her mistress doubtfully.

'Is it really necessary to go this far, madam?'

'Yes,' said Elizabeth curtly. She took the goblet and frowned.

'Are the Duke's emissaries in the anteroom?'

Ashley nodded.

'Give me time to stuff this goblet under my pillow and show them in immediately.'

The salt water was spectacularly effective. The Duke's messengers, openly suspicious in the anteroom, hovered in the doorway, horrified, embarrassed and suddenly uncertain, bumping into each other in their haste to back themselves out again.

They were readmitted a few minutes later and Elizabeth watched them arrange themselves around her bed like a flock of nervous vultures. She coughed and was amused to see two of them start and step back warily. How oddly squeamish in men who would cheerfully stand around a scaffold to see her head fall.

'Your business, gentlemen,' she said at last in an extinct whisper and lay back on her pillows.

Their business, suitably bolstered by a welter of legal jargon, was to inform her that on the tenth day of July, in accordance with the will and testament of the late, lamented King Edward, the Lady Jane Grey had been proclaimed Queen of England.

They waited for her to speak. And waited. The moment lengthened intolerably, forcing their spokesman to abandon ceremony and explain the Duke's proposition in blunt layman's terms.

'. . . and that, madam, is the proposition as it stands. The Duke—' He amended himself hastily, '*The Privy Council*, is prepared to be magnanimous to the—the natural daughter of the great King Henry. Withdraw all claim to the throne, madam, acknowledge the lawful succession of Queen Jane and you will be handsomely provided for.'

With a coffin, thought Elizabeth and closed her eyes against their steely gaze. So that was the bait! Make it easy for us, you will not find us ungrateful.

Dudley was sharp, she gave him that. To buy her acquiescence, keep her at court just long enough to parade her approval of his coup, and then quietly remove her from the scene—it was a master stroke; one could only admire the man's nerve! And he had placed her on a razor's edge of insecurity. One wrong word now to his minions and she would be arrested and hauled off to the Tower anyway. But cornered like this by the Duke's henchmen, how could she neither accept nor reject this offer?

She opened her eyes; she said coolly, 'My sister is the only one concerned with the Duke's proposal. As long as she lives I have no claim whatsoever to assign.'

They stared at her amazed. The quick, clever twist of logic had thrown them momentarily off guard and she gave them no chance to recover their wits.

'Ashley, show the gentlemen out.'

Swept out of the room by the belligerent governess, they rode back to the Duke, who swore. Damn the bitch, damn her to the deepest pit in hell, and damn these spineless fools who had allowed her to slip out of his net. Must he see to everything in person, was there no one on the Council with an ounce of courage or common sense? But rage was useless, self-defeating; he had no more time to waste on her at present, more urgent matters pressed. No news of Robin for days, and Mary still at large, safely installed at Framlingham Castle, rallying large numbers to her cause. Of course he should have sent Jack, older, more experienced; and had it not been for Elizabeth he would have done so. Elizabeth, Elizabeth—that crooked little white-faced whore had put a spoke in all his wheels; nothing for it now but to take the field against Mary Tudor himself.

On the 14th of July, Northumberland rode out from the Tower with a vast escort of horse and artillery to settle with this stupid, middle-aged woman for good. What did she know of men and battle tactics, what did she know about anything for that matter, this semi-cloistered near-nun? He'd smash her forces without mercy and when they trotted her into his camp he'd make her sorry for this undignified scramble to arms. All the way through Shoreditch he sat his horse in grim silence and thought of ways to teach a sheltered old maid the folly of playing fast and loose with soldiers. The crowd along his way stood mute and at last their ominous silence penetrated the armour of his rage.

He turned in his saddle and looked back in surprise towards the city.

'The people press to see us,' he remarked bitterly, 'but I see not one of them cries "God speed".'

Northumberland's desperate coup took exactly nine days to crumble into ignominious defeat, foundering on the treachery of the Council and that most unpredictable of all factors, the mood of the people. Behind his back, unwilling and cowardly associates began to waver and when they heard that the crews of the royal ships at Yarmouth had gone over to Mary's side to a man, it was inevitable that they too would do the same. On the 18th of July Mary Tudor was proclaimed the rightful Queen of England and the city of London erupted into a sea of waving caps and blazing bonfires, as the people came out to dance in the streets, singing and cheering while the bells rang furiously.

There was no accounting for the people, that moody, headstrong, fickle race. It was against all rational supposition that Protestant England should now rise in support of a Catholic Queen, but it happened, and no one was more astonished than Mary Tudor to find herself at the heart of a resounding victory over the most powerful man in the land.

The news of Mary's unlooked-for triumph was swiftly carried to Hatfield, stunning the entire household, but not its mistress.

'Nothing surprises *you*, does it?' said the governess tartly, sweeping an assorted jumble of books and sweets off the bed. 'I suppose you're about to say you expected this all along?'

'Had I expected it,' said Elizabeth with an infuriating smile, 'you and I, my dear Kat, would now be sunning ourselves at Framlingham in the royal favour. But nothing about Mary would ever surprise me—she's a tangled mass of contradictions.'

'It must be in the family,' sniffed Kat and ducked the pillow which immediately flew at her head. After a moment, Elizabeth followed the pillow, running barefoot across the room like some wild creature suddenly let out of a cage.

'If you get up now,' said Kat severely, 'everyone will say your illness was feigned.'

Elizabeth mocked a deep curtsey.

'It was a highly contagious affliction, Your Majesty. I understand there's been a lot of it about.'

Kat stared down at her in alarm. In her present mood she looked quite reckless enough to say it, and impertinence, flippancy, were the very last things to display before Mary Tudor.

'Madam, are you mad? You of all people must guard your tongue in your sister's presence.'

'Oh yes, I know she's never liked me.'

'Then you must admit the need to stay in bed and play out your farce to the end.'

Elizabeth pouted. 'But I'm so bored.'

'Better bored than dead,' snapped Kat, sharp-tongued with nerves. 'For the love of God, madam, get back between the sheets before someone sees you prancing at the window.'

Elizabeth turned and regarded the curtained cave with repugnance.

'I hate beds,' she said slowly. 'They stand there night after night waiting for you to die in them. It's like lying in a tomb.'

She shivered in the hot sunlight and Kat, watching her bleakly, recognized the signs that heralded a new cycle of nightmares and migraines. For all her hard self-sufficiency that childhood legacy could still reduce her to suffocating panic each time she woke in mindless terror, screaming for lights. Kat knew she would be needed tonight, when the brittle air of nonchalance had run its course. But for the moment, high as a kite and careless of the risk, Elizabeth sat in full view in the window-seat and her eyes, scanning the parched gardens below, sparkled with taut anticipation. Kat had once heard it said that people who lived overlong with danger were sometimes unable to live without it; increasingly, she was beginning to fear that Elizabeth was one of them. That look on her face was a euphoria more properly appertaining to the steady consumption of wine.

Certainly, she was still in peril. Everyone knew the new Queen instinctively disliked her sister and had more reason than most to consider her a bastard. She was now in a position to secure her own legitimacy by Act of Parliament and to bar Elizabeth from the line of succession. A treacherous quagmire of ugly emotions surrounded Elizabeth and one false step while crossing it was likely to prove her last. Already, by sitting quietly on the sidelines during Northumberland's coup, she had let the first round with her sister go by default. She had measured the situation with the yardstick of expediency and Mary, who so despised compromise, would distrust her for it. But that could not be helped and however quickly the Hatfield entourage was assembled now to join the new Queen, it would still be too late to allay Mary's suspicions.

So why hurry? It would only look ignoble, place her on the same level as those rats of the Council who had already scuttled towards the rising sun. She might as well take her time and go in style. What could not be done with any hope of success could at least be done with panache. And the people dearly loved a good show—

Kat, waiting with scant patience for her mistress to return to bed, tapped her foot ominously, but Elizabeth uncurled her legs in a leisurely fashion and began to study the curls which tossed loosely round her shoulders in an auburn cascade.

'I think I'll wash my hair,' she announced thoughtfully. 'It ought to dry well in this heat.'

Kat was speechless. An hour later she exploded into the antechamber to inform Blanche Parry that certain people had no sense of priority.

'. . . and they say Nero fiddled while Rome burned—doubtless the Lady Elizabeth would have taken a *bath!*'

Elizabeth met Mary on the road to Wanstead, with an escort of a thousand strong sprawling behind her spirited gelding. The Queen beckoned her forward and she dismounted, kneeling on the roadside to kiss the shrivelled little hand so formally presented.

'Madam, permit your humble servant to lay her loyalty at your feet.'

A trifle too glib, it irked the new Queen, rubbing an old sore. With veiled insolence such as this had Ann Boleyn curtsied to Mary's mother in the days when Henry had first begun to show his preference. The gesture, the voice, even the arrogant set of her head—oh, the likeness was unnerving!

Dear God, is it really only I that see it?

But Mary could not complain of any genuine lack of respect on her sister's part, and she had already sworn, in gratitude for her wonderful delivery from Dudley, to allow no past bitterness to mar the future. So when the two retinues halted at White Chapel, she dismissed her ladies, detained her sister and made a deliberate effort to be pleasant.

'How well you look, my dear.'

Even as she spoke, Mary was aware of saying the wrong thing with that old lack of tact for which she was renowned. Elizabeth's pale cheeks instantly suffused with hot colour.

'The news of Your Majesty's victory did much to restore me, madam.'

'I'll warrant it did.' Mary's smile was not pleasant. 'I imagine you were warned of Northumberland's intent?'

'No, madam.' Cecil had publicly made his peace with the Queen and been duly acclaimed as 'a very honest man': she owed him silence.

Sensing the lie, Mary frowned and began to finger her crucifix. In spite of good intentions, the old, unreasoning hostility was clamouring suddenly for expression. Everything about her sister irritated and alarmed her, even to her choice of dress. Virgin white—after all that scandal!

Mary's shortsighted eyes narrowed on the girl's face.

'You swore to serve me,' she began slowly. 'Your mother served mine—in what manner the whole world knows.'

Elizabeth fell to her knees in the dusty straw, frightened by that far-off look in Mary's eyes.

'Madam, I beg you, let the dead past go, and remember the loyalty of blood ties.'

'As you remembered it, sister, when you chose to sit safe at Hatfield rather than ride with me against the traitor's forces?'

Mary's hand beneath her chin tilted her face sharply upwards, and Elizabeth was silent, trapped for once by her own instinctive need for subterfuge. Safer by far to have confessed to her sham, admitting deceit and making fear her excuse. But lying to Mary had always come naturally to her. She did it on almost every occasion they met, because the temptation to do it, as a sort of mark of her own mental superiority, was irresistible.

But now, it was no longer safe to play games with Mary—

She was not even aware that she had begun to bite nervously at her fingernail, until the moment the Queen reached out and tapped the offending digit away.

'I thought Ashley would have cured you of that silly habit by now,' Mary sighed, and her voice was suddenly quite sane and kind. Her mood had shifted in the manner which made her so unpredictable. She was the officious elder sister now, reaching for the pair of scissors which hung at her waist, a relic of those years of cloistered domesticity.

'Such dreadful nails,' she grumbled, snipping with quick efficiency, 'like an eagle's talons! No wonder they irritate you. There now—doesn't that feel better?'

Elizabeth looked at the Queen's handiwork. Nails grew again; heads were not quite so obliging. She agreed it felt much better, and for a while their conversation was devoid of rancour and suspicion. At length, aware of time pressing, the Queen laid both hands upon her shoulders and kissed her cheek lightly.

'It gives me real pleasure to have you at my side again, Elizabeth. You and I have known so little family life these past troubled years. But now, once we are safe in London, the two of us shall hear Mass together once more as we used to do when you were a small child. Remember how you would say a Paternoster for me before you went to bed? Barely two and every word in perfect Latin. You were such a forward little girl—'

'Yes, madam—I remember.' Elizabeth had stiffened and the faint note of hesitancy was unmistakable.

Mary removed her hands from the girl's shoulders and the light of indulgence went out of her eyes like a snuffed candle.

'You do of course intend to support the restoration of the Roman Church by attending Mass with me? There can surely be no question of you continuing in your heret—' she broke off and continued hastily, 'in your misguided practices.'

Elizabeth looked away uncomfortably.

'Madam, did you not yourself demand freedom of conscience in our late brother's reign?'

'Naturally,' Mary rejoined frigidly. 'Mine was the true faith, for which I would gladly have died. Would *you* die willingly, sister, for the beliefs you now profess to hold?'

Talking to the Queen, thought Elizabeth suddenly, was like walking a tightrope over a yawning chasm. The prospect of weeks, even months, of these swift veering confrontations set all the nerves in her stomach jumping. She was suddenly very glad to see Susan Clarencieux appear in the doorway looking flustered.

'By Your Majesty's leave, the night is drawing on. If we are to enter London while it's still light—'

'Yes—yes, of course. Tell them I am coming.' Mary turned to look at her sister steadily. 'Elizabeth, you had better go down. We will speak further on this issue when I have more time. But think on what I have said—think very carefully.'

Suspicion, like bread, rises rapidly in a warm environment. Though London was red-hot in its welcome for Mary, there was no mistaking the tremendous ovation which greeted Elizabeth's entry to the capital, and the Queen, with the cheers for her sister ringing hollowly in her ears, struggled with a serpentine quiver of jealousy. It was no use, even in this sweet moment of victory, pretending that the years between them did not show. The girl was nineteen and the people worshipped her glowing youth.

Mary rode on stiffly and bit her lip until she tasted blood.

Oh, God, teach me how to trust her . . .

CHAPTER 10

The new reign began briskly with the trial and execution of its principal opponent. Most unsuccessful traitors displayed a certain degree of dignified restraint, even cheerful resignation, to this inevitable act. Northumberland took the opposite course. All that could be done by recanting his Protestant faith, grovelling and begging shamelessly for mercy he did and more.

'Oh that it would please her good Grace to give me life, yea the life of a dog, that I might but live and kiss her feet . . .'

People said it was a disgraceful exhibition and only went to show what Dudleys were, a low lot that wanted breeding as badly as they would shortly want heads. But Northumberland cared nothing for the ridicule. Even at the last moment, when he stood on Tower Hill, he was still gazing steadily down at the city, scanning the narrow streets desperately for a royal messenger bearing his written reprieve.

But that message never came. The Tower guns boomed and Robin Dudley, alone in his damp cell at the bottom of the Beauchamp Tower, awaiting his own imminent trial and execution, sat on his flea-bitten mattress and wept harsh, difficult tears for the fallen idol of his childhood.

Further along the river, Elizabeth, sitting with the Queen a little apart from their attendant women, heard that same dismal booming and thought of Robin. Her throat closed and her fingers trembled as she drew a thread of gold silk through her tapestry frame.

Mary leaned forward a little in her chair and frowned.

'Unpick that rose, Elizabeth, it's wildly uneven.'

Elizabeth looked up, carefully expressionless.

'Madam—do you not hear it?'

'Of course I hear it, do you imagine I'm deaf?'

'Then—the Duke is dead.'

'I think we may safely assume that,' said the Queen drily. 'Never sit there and tell me that his death disturbs you.'

'Not *his*, of course,' retorted Elizabeth hastily, 'but some of his sons are very—young.'

'The youngest will naturally be pardoned,' said Mary primly. 'Henry is barely fifteen, I understand.'

Elizabeth took a tremulous breath.

'Only Henry, madam?'

Mary dug her needle deep into the tapestry and pushed the frame aside with a pettish gesture of irritation.

'Guildford, as Jane's husband, I cannot possibly pardon. Both Ambrose and Jack are of an age to answer for their crime. And as for that impertinent young man who set out with armed men to capture me,' she snapped her fingers impatiently, 'the wretch's name escapes me—'

'Robert.' It came on a whisper.

'Oh yes, Robert! I can well imagine what my fate would have been had he succeeded. There can of course be no question of clemency for *him.*'

The needle slipped through Elizabeth's nerveless fingers and was lost in the dusty straw at their feet.

'But, madam, he was only obeying his father's instructions. Surely, in your great mercy—'

Her voice wavered to a halt; Mary's gaze was hard and shrewd.

'You must not concern yourself so greatly with the fate of traitors, sister,' she said coldly. 'It could be quite grievously misunderstood.'

Elizabeth took her embroidery scissors to the ragged rose and was silent.

In the event, however, Mary proved remarkably merciful to those involved with Northumberland's disastrous *coup d'état.* Jane Grey, though tried and found guilty, was kept in honourable custody and given to understand that her life was in no danger; Jane's father, Suffolk, was released; winter crept closer and still the Dudley boys lived on under sentence of death in their comfortless prison cells. For Mary had better things than revenge to occupy her narrow mind.

After all the bitter, barren years of persecution, she was free at last to consider matrimony, assured, in fact, on every side, that it was her duty to consider it. The list of suitors made her blush like a schoolgirl. There was Edward Courtenay, of course, the last of the Plantagenets, recently released from his lifetime's imprisonment in the Tower, very young, very handsome, but frankly not very ardent—at least not to her. At every evening reception he made it blatantly obvious where his interests lay. He ogled Elizabeth quite shamelessly, admittedly, Mary was forced to acknowledge, with very little active encouragement from that young lady, who retired pointedly behind her pomander whenever he approached.

But Courtenay was merely a red herring in the ambassadors' nets, disguising the Queen's true interest which lay with Prince Philip of Spain. Simon

Renard, the Spanish Ambassador, had done his job well, painting a haloed image of his young master which was irresistible. Mary, in love with the idea of love, wished to be left alone with her dream for a while and forget the unpleasant. And by the unpleasant she meant Elizabeth.

But Renard would not let her forget. He was a smooth, polished, ruthless little Spaniard, working with single-minded purpose for marriage and alliance with Spain, and he had rapidly become the Queen's closest adviser. As such, he was acutely aware of the steady hostility from his rival.

De Noailles, the French Ambassador, was equally smooth, polished and ruthless and his immediate response to Spain's suit was to gravitate ostentatiously to Elizabeth's side at every available opportunity in public. To Renard's suspicious eye, Elizabeth's nebulous role at court had taken on a new and sinister significance. This unspoken Protestant heir presumptive was suddenly the greatest obstacle to Prince Philip's path to England and Renard had already resolved to dispose of her at his earliest convenience.

Accordingly, he invited her to dance and tried his hand at a little subtle flattery. They manoeuvred delicately down the Hall, like two scorpions locked in mortal combat, but no matter how he tried, he could not get close enough to sting. And all the time as she smiled and parried his thrusts like a seasoned fencer, he was aware of men's eyes following her. There was something indefinable about her that aroused intense male excitement—he himself was not entirely proof against the extraordinary promise of her smile. As for Courtenay, the lad was hopelessly lost, ready to jump through a hoop at a snap from her fingers—all the more so, it seemed, because she scarcely gave him a second glance. Oh yes, she was dangerous, there was no doubt of that. She had the power to seduce the loyalty of every man at court—all she needed was the inclination and the incentive to do it. And unless he was very much mistaken, de Noailles was already fostering that—the Queen must be made to see it.

'Madam, she is too prominent in the eyes of the court.'

'How can she be otherwise? I can hardly hide her behind screens at every court function—she *is* my sister!'

'Is she?' echoed the Spaniard softly. 'I very much doubt it. Her mother was executed on grounds of adultery and incest. Madam, have you never wondered whether—'

'I have not,' retorted Mary, very defensive of a sudden. 'What you suggest is unthinkable.'

Was it? He did not think so. In his experience women were always prickly and sanctimonious when you touched them on a raw nerve. Certainly he was on the right track; but it would be necessary to follow this particular path with some care.

'Grant that the relationship stands, madam, and you will still look in vain for sisterly affection on her part. Has she once attended Mass to please you?'

Mary averted her eyes hastily.

'I shouldn't wish her to attend simply to please me. Whatever her creed, I could better brook her stubbornness than her hypocrisy.'

'The only creed she will ever hold is self-interest—madam, don't you see that she mocks your tolerance daily? Is it likely that she would embrace the very faith which denies her legitimacy?'

'She was not responsible for the circumstances surrounding her birth,' said Mary uncomfortably.

'She is responsible for her own actions now, madam—both responsible and answerable! Test her loyalty and I assure you it will be found wanting.'

'*Test?*' Mary stared at him uncertainly and Renard shrugged his elegant shoulders.

'Your Majesty must offer an ultimatum. She must enter the true Church or suffer the consequences.'

Mary got out of her chair and began to pace the panelled room, chewing her lip. At last she said hoarsely, 'In what form do you envisage these—these consequences?'

Renard gave her a smile bespeaking exquisite patience. In all his distinguished career it had never been his task to deal with anyone so naïve and guileless as Mary Tudor.

'In my country,' he remarked pleasantly, 'the penalty for heresy has always been death at the stake.'

'But my brother's laws expressly forbid the persecution of heretics!'

'Your brother is dead,' Renard reminded her pointedly. 'And laws can be changed.'

Laws can be changed . . . Elizabeth leaned against the stone parapet and stared into the dark river swirling below her feet. She threw a stone into the water and watched it disappear so sharply, swiftly, that her eye was unable to record its descent. Death too could be like that, mercifully quick—but not by burning, never by burning. Laws could be changed; and she did not want to burn!

'Madam.'

She spun round wildly and sucked in a breath of relief.

'Cecil!'

'I must speak to you, madam, but not here in full view of the palace. A little further down the river we shall have the shelter of the trees.'

She turned without question and walked away; a few minutes later he joined her in the appointed place and knelt beside her where she sat on the river bank.

'Is it true you are to accompany the Queen to Mass tomorrow?' he demanded bluntly.

'It is!' Elizabeth sighed and stared bleakly across the river. 'What does it matter, after all, now that Parliament is to endorse the validity of my father's first marriage?'

'Whatever is settled in the matter of the Queen's legitimacy no Parliament will bar you from the succession,' said Cecil. 'If the Queen makes a stand on that issue she will be defeated—I give you my word on it.'

He reached out to take her hand and again she felt the affinity between them, a natural bonding of the spirit, utterly devoid of sex.

'If I go to Mass I shall alienate every Protestant in the realm. If I don't go it may be I shall not live long enough to alienate anyone. I'm in a cleft stick, Cecil—advise me!'

He looked at her steadily, without a flicker of emotion on his pale face.

'I believe Your Grace will feel unwell tomorrow—so unwell that you can scarcely attend to the ritual. I believe your enemies will see that you conform, but your friends will be reassured you do not do so *cheerfully.*'

'I can't perform like a shamming schoolboy at every service.'

'Once will be sufficient to make your point. Certainly after that there must be rigorous conformity. Avoid intrigue. De Noailles haunts you because Renard has the Queen's ear, but he is not your friend, nor is his master. The King of France seeks only to advance the interests of the young Queen of Scots, that she may bring a united Britain in her marriage portion to the Dauphin. Fear France, madam, as greatly as you fear Spain, for both countries seek your death.'

She smiled faintly. 'And in what manner am I to pass safely through that formidable gauntlet of hostility?'

'Softly, madam, like a cat in the dark.'

She leaned over and laid her hand on his plain sleeve.

'It *was* you who warned me of Northumberland's trap, wasn't it?'

He inclined his head in silence.

'Why?' she demanded, with sudden passionate interest. 'Why do you put yourself at risk for me?'

'You are the future,' he said gravely. 'And you will survive. That is all I can tell you.'

She held out her hands and allowed him to pull her lightly to her feet.

'We both know how to survive,' she said softly. 'And when the time comes we will know how to rule—you and I.'

When the little bell rang to announce the elevation of the Host, Mary bent her head over hands clasped rigidly together. For most of the service she had been forced to hold them in that same furious grip, tensing herself against the urgent desire to lean over and slap her sister's face.

It was intolerable! The procession to Mass had been marred by Elizabeth's persistent and remarkably loud complaints that her stomach ached, but once inside the chapel, the fuss and performance had been truly unbelievable. Even now, at this most sacred moment, one of her ladies was ostentatiously rubbing her back. And Mary was not a fool; she knew a public gesture when she saw one.

When the farce was over, they walked back through the gardens together in frosty silence. Elizabeth stole a glance at her sister's stony face and knew she had gone too far.

'If it please Your Majesty,' she muttered uncomfortably, 'I should like to retire to my own apartments.'

'You will stay,' hissed the Queen in a desperately controlled undertone, 'until I am satisfied as to your true belief in the Holy Sacrament.'

Elizabeth lowered her eyes hastily.

'Madam, I have attended Mass of my own free will, without fear, hypocrisy or dissimulation.'

Suddenly Mary took her arm in a vicious nipping grasp and hastened her further along the path, well out of the hearing of the curious court.

'Don't play the hypocrite with me!' snapped the Queen furiously. 'What was the meaning of that disgraceful exhibition back there? Speak! Tell me what you truly think for once.'

Elizabeth's eyes were suddenly fixed on Mary's like gimlets. She said in a steely whisper, 'I think I'm going to be sick.'

Shocked by the brazen threat of those shamelessly amoral black eyes, Mary released her hand. Threatened by the ultimate, unthinkable sacrilege to the Host, the very Body of Christ, there was nothing she could do for the moment but capitulate with some tangible token of appeasement, symbolic of her trust and approval. In icy silence, she unfastened a diamond and ruby brooch from her gown and pinned it to Elizabeth's plain bodice, then handed over her personal rosary of white coral beads. Elizabeth curtsied demurely and made a show of fastening the beads to the stomacher of her gown. And under the eyes of the court, they returned to the palace with what passed for goodwill between them.

When Elizabeth entered her own room, whirling the coral beads carelessly, she found Kat waiting for her anxiously.

'What are you doing with that popish trinket?' inquired the governess with mild distaste.

'What a heretic you are, Kat!' mocked Elizabeth, slinging the beads carelessly across a table. 'It was a present from Her Majesty—like this!' She flaunted the brooch at her breast and Kat's eyes widened in astonishment at the size of the diamond.

'The Queen gave you that?' she echoed suspiciously.

'A small bribe, to help me to stomach the Mass in a rather literal sense.' Elizabeth sank down in the chair and fingered the beads slowly. Her cynical smile was suddenly strangely sad. 'I hope Cecil was right about this, Kat. Because after today, she's never going to trust me again.'

'My dear child,' said Kat drily, 'it's my belief she never has.'

'I could have killed her, Renard—I swear I could have killed her with my bare hands. But of course I should not have been surprised—her mother was a spleeny Lutheran.'

Renard discreetly placed his hands behind his back, controlling a sudden urge to rub them with glee. This response was rather better than he had hoped for.

'I did warn you, madam. The Lady Elizabeth is sly and clever, she will be plotting against you at the first opportunity.'

'No doubt,' said Mary shortly. 'What do you suggest I do to prevent it?'

'What I have most respectfully suggested for some time now, madam—stabilize your position with a wise marriage.'

'By which you mean Prince Philip?' She frowned. 'Gardiner will oppose it in Council, you know. He still favours Courtenay.'

'With respect,' remarked Renard smoothly, 'the good bishop was many years imprisoned in the Tower during your late brother's reign—he has lost touch with affairs in Europe and even here at home. Courtenay is a young fool who will bring you nothing but Plantagenet blood and trouble from court factions. Madam, you, a daughter of the royal house of Spain, cannot mate with a mere subject—and such a subject! A libertine, a profligate.'

The hot colour flared into Mary's cheeks and he noted it with quiet amusement. 'And as I'm sure Your Majesty must have noticed, he smiles very warmly on the Lady Elizabeth, herself, I fear, no stranger to scandal.

Madam,' he sat down beside her uninvited, and presumed to pat her hand gently, 'look to your true friends in this matter.'

'Ah yes,' said Mary, suddenly soft-eyed and reminiscent. 'Your master has always given me his support. I was contracted in marriage to the Emperor as a child, did you know that? but I fear it came to nothing. You see, my dear father felt—'

Renard hastily intervened before the floodgates of past memories were opened to swamp him. He had made the mistake of listening once before and knew that such talk would wash away his political arguments like a burst dam. She dwelt too much on the past, brooding over the wrongs done to her mother at the hands of Anne Boleyn.

'Madam,' he said briskly, seeking to rally scattering forces, 'the Emperor now offers you his beloved son and you would find the Prince of Spain a true gentleman in every sense of the word.'

'But he is so young!'

Renard coughed.

'Young in years only, his great sense, his judgement, his moderation and experience bespeak a man old in wisdom.'

Mary shuddered from complex causes.

'You understand that as a maid I am quite ignorant of—of what men mean when they speak of love in the flesh. Is he indeed so—accomplished?'

Renard spread his hands in an expansive gesture and rolled his eyes to heaven dramatically.

'Madam, he is perfection itself.'

It was hot in the Abbey and the coronation seemed endless. The pews were densely packed. Elizabeth, dressed in pure white, sat wedged in uncomfortable proximity to de Noailles, who had plumped down beside her before she had a chance to avoid him. The coronet on her head was heavy and far too large; she was forced to sit like a ramrod to prevent it slipping down over her eyes.

'I wish this wretched thing fitted me better,' she complained to him at last in a low voice. 'It's giving me a headache.'

He glanced up at her with amusement and replied in a tone which carried clearly into the aisle and beyond.

'Have patience, madam. It is only the preliminary to one which will fit you better.'

'It was only a chance remark,' said Kat doubtfully, as she removed the infamous coronet from her mistress's head.

'Chance remarks like that,' muttered Elizabeth, 'repeated in the right quarters could cost me my place at court—which is no doubt what de Noailles intended.' She leaned back against her chair and closed her eyes while Kat began to brush her hair. 'Granted, I'd be glad to go, the way things are, with Renard's dagger at my throat and de Noailles' at my back—and Courtenay's clumsy advances make me want to heave. He has about as much finesse as a bull trying to serve a cow!'

'Poor lad,' said Kat tolerantly, 'with all his youth wasted in the Tower, what does your Grace expect?'

'I expect him to take a bath occasionally and drown a few of those Tower fleas.'

'But he's so handsome, you must admit that he's very attractive!'

'So is a pig I suppose—to another pig! Oh God, Kat, he *stinks*, haven't you noticed?'

Kat sighed. Elizabeth's fanatical fastidiousness was a great trial to her.

'No one's good enough for you,' she grumbled. 'You'd find fault with Adonis himself. There are times when I really despair of you.'

'Never mind,' Elizabeth patted her arm, 'I'm not likely to plague you much longer. If Renard and de Noailles have their way my head will probably roll before the end of the year.'

Standing in front of the mirror, she laughed and circled her neck with her fingers.

'And I have such a little neck, don't you think, Kat? Just like my mother's.'

Kat met the steady black gaze of the reflection in the steel mirror, and crossed herself in the old, instinctive fashion of her childhood.

Small strands of greying red hair were escaping from the Queen's head-dress as she paced feverishly up and down her room.

'Opposition,' she muttered, looking harassed. 'Gardiner tells me I can expect opposition on all sides to Prince Philip's suit.'

'Opposition to the desires of a reigning sovereign should surely be overcome, madam.' Renard's voice held just a touch of impatience. 'Is it possible that the policy of the state can be satisfactorily left to the rabble?'

'Of course not!' said Mary testily, and swung away from him down the room once more. 'But I'm not sure—not sure, do you understand?' She flung out her hand in a weary gesture of frustration. 'Oh, if only I could see him before I commit myself.'

Renard restrained a strong impulse to tell her that the Prince of Spain was not to be inspected like a stud horse in the market place.

'Madam, you could not possibly find him wanting in any respect.'

'Then he is truly all you say?' She caught at his hand and he saw with acute discomfort that her faded eyes were full of tears. 'Or do you speak purely as a subject,' she continued fretfully, 'whose duty is to praise his master?'

Renard disentangled himself from her feverish grasp to say solemnly, 'Your Majesty may take my life if you find him other than I have told you.'

'Pray with me,' she said suddenly, and he duly knelt. During the long silence he glanced up at a full-length portrait of Philip and thought peevishly: If I bring this thing to pass it's small thanks I'll get from you . . .

Mary rose stiffly from her knees and he came forward to take her outstretched hand.

'God has inspired me with this decision,' she said huskily. 'I shall marry Prince Philip. I swear to you now that my mind is made up and will never change. I will love him perfectly and never give him cause for jealousy.'

Renard hid a smile as he bowed over her hand. That much he did not doubt, for one moment.

'So it is to be marriage with Spain,' purred de Noailles in a silky voice, drawing Elizabeth's hand on to his arm as they strolled by the river. 'I cannot think the country will approve. What is Your Grace's opinion on that?'

'Oh, my opinion is of no importance, sir.'

'Come,' he said gallantly, 'I cannot believe that.'

She smiled at him coyly. 'I would never dream of touching a man's beliefs.'

'Nor anything else, madam?'

She slapped his cheek lightly with her fan and drew away. If de Noailles were not her enemy she would find him an amusing companion. All the same it was becoming as hard to avoid him as it was to avoid Courtenay; it was hardly safe to step outside the palace without one of them pouncing on her. She retreated strategically out of reach and he attended to the ruffs at his wrist while he murmured pleasantly, 'You may speak freely with me, madam. I understand the Queen does not display the kindness towards you that might be expected.'

She looked at him with the blank innocence of a child.

'The Queen is my good sister, sir.'

De Noailles smiled faintly, showing a row of discoloured teeth.

'I understand your *good sister* has transferred Your Grace's right of precedence to the Countess of Lennox and the Duchess of Suffolk? Madam, it is unseemly that you should be forced to walk out of rooms after these ladies. It is shameful that you should be so coldly treated that only the youngest and most daring members of the court visit your apartments.'

She looked away angrily and he was aware that he was rubbing a very sore point. The two sisters had just had their first public quarrel on the subject and Elizabeth was now almost entirely isolated from all except the younger, male faction. She had already demanded leave to retire from court and been coldly refused. Her position was becoming an intolerably humiliating strain and de Noailles privately admired the self-control with which she masked her temper.

'Only the young and the daring,' de Noailles repeated softly, 'are willing to be your friends. But the King of France is constant in his affection for you, madam.'

She smiled contemptuously.

'Your King has a spacious heart. It has already embraced the Queen of Scots, who will soon be his daughter-in-law.'

'The Queen of Scots is a mere child, and our beloved Dauphin is not strong. There might after all be no marriage between them.'

'Your king has other sons.'

'My king,' said de Noailles smoothly, 'is concerned at this time only with Your Grace's marriage.'

'*Mine?*' He saw her turn pale.

'With Edward Courtenay. He has powerful friends in Devon, madam, friends who are reluctant to see the Spaniards set foot in England, who would see a younger queen grace the throne of England.'

'I will hear no talk which tends to treason! You may tell your master—and Courtenay!—that with my blessing.'

With no further pretence at civility she swung round and returned in the direction of the palace, followed by a flustered lady-in-waiting. De Noailles lounged against a tree and watched her go, admiring the swift grace of her carriage. He was a connoisseur of women, but he had never seen anyone carry herself with such unconscious majesty, like a well-bred cat. There was something about her which made her stand out in any crowd, a unique ability to make every other woman look colourless that owed almost nothing to beauty, something she would possess even in unlovely old age. No one remained indifferent to Elizabeth; she engendered violent feelings of love or hate among her associates. And he was beginning to see the effect of her allure in the uneasy, half-concealed glances of the young men at court, drawn towards her in spite of their common sense, as though to a siren or a mermaid. Yes, a mermaid, he decided, with a cool enchantment drawn from borders just beyond humanity. What else could be expected of the daughter of a witch and the old Devil himself?

Naturally, she was too clever to commit herself irretrievably to his plans, but he was confident that he would be able to count on her furtive support.

She wanted the crown of England more desperately than anything else in this world; he'd swear to that!

And he did not see why she should be too squeamish as to how it came her way.

'Madam, I beseech you! Send her to the Tower.'

'I cannot! I have no evidence.'

'Then send her from the court, madam, and I swear you will soon have it!'

Candlelight glinted on the blue lights in Renard's neat moustache and reflected in his brilliant black eyes. Behind him the portrait of Philip stared down with wide-eyed gravity as Mary paced beneath it.

She stopped suddenly, fingering her crucifix nervously.

'What do you mean by that?'

'Let her return to the country believing she has your trust and we will watch her every move.'

'You think she will betray me?'

'Madam, it is inevitable. Her Protestant friends are waiting for this very opportunity. But she must not suspect your motives. Send her kindly, promise anything she asks. It is your turn to dissemble with her now.'

The Queen wandered sadly to the portrait and stared at the smooth, bland face. He was so young! Without looking round she muttered almost inaudibly, 'My sister is not alone in her apartments, is she? She is a disgraced outcast but she is not alone.' Mary turned and there was that in her face which pleaded for him to deny it.

'No, madam.' He paused, then added spitefully, 'The young are with her.'

It was his final thrust and he saw that it had been successful. The small lined face shut into a hard little mask.

'I will do as you say,' she muttered grimly and returned to her restless pacing.

It was late in the afternoon of a cold December day when Elizabeth returned from her formal interview with the Queen. She was dressed for travel with a heavy fur cloak over her riding habit and she was wearing a new sable hood and a rope of pearls which Kat had not seen before.

'New Year's presents this time,' said Elizabeth in answer to her speculative gaze, 'to appease her conscience while Renard stabs me in the back, I suppose.' She sighed suddenly. 'No—that's unjust even for me. She was always generous to me, I'll never know why.'

'But what did she *say?*'

Elizabeth shrugged and walked to the mirror to admire the softly furred hood.

'It doesn't matter what she said—or rather what Renard said through her —he works her like a puppet! As long as I go quietly to Ashridge, say nothing, do nothing, they can't touch me. Oh Kat, I shall be free of her after all these miserable months. Free! Free!' She pulled off the sable hood and pirouetted round the room. 'Free of their hot little hands clutching at my soul—free of God too,' and on a sudden spurt of laughter she added, *'anybody's* God.'

'Shh! Your Grace, for pity's sake, you will be heard.'

'Oh, I'll be heard, always—in my own defence. It was her last promise to me, her word as Queen.'

'And you trust that?' asked Kat doubtfully.

Elizabeth turned to look at the governess and her face was suddenly serious.

'My sister is the only honest human being I have ever known,' she said slowly. 'If I can't trust her word I shall trust nothing in this world again.'

You may not need to, thought Kat sadly and went in grim silence to fetch her riding crop.

CHAPTER 11

In January, the signing of the marriage treaty between England and Spain sparked off open unrest in the streets of London. There was a spate of physical assaults on priests and a shower of anti-Catholic propaganda found its way even into the palace. On the day after the public announcement, a dead dog was thrown through the window of the Queen's chamber; its head had been shaved and a label round its neck read: 'All priests should be hanged.' Mary stared at the wretched corpse in silence. This then was what Gardiner had meant by opposition from the fickle-hearted mob. It was less than six months since she had ridden in triumph to take possession of this same capital city, which now seethed with hostility against her faith. She could not believe it was really happening.

De Noailles, too, was alarmed at the prospect of an imminent alliance which would encircle France with enemies. All that would prevent this marriage now was open rebellion, so rebellion they must have. His network of intrigue spread out all over the country, but was centred in Kent, where Sir Thomas Wyatt was presently rallying and directing his supporters. Jane Grey's father, the Duke of Suffolk, had sworn to raise the Midland counties. There remained only one serious drawback, the need for a convincing figurehead, and with Jane in the Tower, and Elizabeth secluded at Ashridge, they were left with Courtenay in that role. Not a very happy choice, this last sprig of the White Rose, reflected de Noailles sourly, as he wrote home complaining bitterly of the young man's 'weakness, faint heartedness and timidity'. But, needs must when the Devil drives, and it was the Ambassador's lot to rein in this high-born lout and hold him to their course, in itself no mean feat. Years of imprisonment had scattered Courtenay's powers of concentration to the point where they were virtually non-existent. After that long period of physical and intellectual deprivation, women and clothes were now the sum total of his interest. And though he was quite willing to be king, he was very unwilling to exert himself in the process of attaining his crown.

He was posing now in front of a mirror, in his private chamber, impatient as a child for the Ambassador's approval on his choice of suit.

'The red is striking—but I suppose the gold would be more becoming to my state. Don't you agree?'

'What? Oh yes—um—very becoming.'

'Of course, there is the green,' Courtenay continued doubtfully.

De Noailles set his goblet down on the table with an irritable bang.

'Perhaps we might continue with our more urgent business, my lord.'

'Oh, urgent is it, now? You ambassadors are all the same, always stirring and meddling, rushing around without a minute to live. There's nothing like a few years in the Tower for slowing the pulse, you know.'

If yours slows any more, thought de Noailles irritably, it will stop altogether.

'Provision for revolt,' he rapped out sharply. 'Item: castles all over the country are being stocked with gunpowder—'

Courtenay gave him a sly glance. 'Not at Ashridge I trust, with that bright spark in residence. What a girl, hey? Armoured like a porcupine! I swear her tongue's stabbed me in more places than a pincushion—splendid bitch, isn't she?'

De Noailles forced a smile and began again.

'As I was saying—castles are being stocked with gunpowder, ammunition and food. We have relays of horses and men waiting for the signal. We have provisions in hand for the capture of the Mint, the Tower and the Queen's person.'

Courtenay swung round upon him.

'But have you got Elizabeth? That's what I want to know. What's the good of all this grand plotting when she can still slide through our hands like a slippery fish?'

'If the Lady Elizabeth refuses to join us she will be taken by force of arms,' said de Noailles shortly.

Courtenay laughed on a shrill note and clapped the Ambassador on the back with a force that made him spill his wine.

'God's death, man, show me the fellow who can take her without it and I'll take off my cap to him—aye, and my crown with it!'

At Ashridge, Elizabeth sat on a bench in the monks' garden and stared up at the old stone manor, silhouetted against a dirty blue sky. The house was encircled by a bleak wood of oak, beech and sycamore and the barren branches were like twisted fingers, reaching down to her with silent menace. She ran her hand across the back of the bench and held the gathered snow against her temple for a second, until contact with the burning skin turned it instantly to water and soaked her satin gloves. She had been taken ill on the journey to Ashridge and she had been ill more or less ever since, with headaches and pains in her back and recurrent bouts of vomiting. When her face and body began to swell, her private physician, fearing a kidney infection, had advised complete bed-rest, but she had perversely resisted his advice. Rumours of spreading unrest were filtering daily into Ashridge and had caused her to briefly consider whether she was being slowly poisoned on Renard's orders. But whatever it was, she could not afford to give in to it at the very moment when she needed all her faculties about her. Shut away in her bedchamber, she would be unable to question the pedlars and travelling entertainers who gathered in the Great Hall and provided so large a part of her information.

She knew by now, from several sources, that her own case was growing increasingly desperate. Fear that the rebels would swoop on Ashridge to take her by force had prompted her to place the house in a state of defence. But how bad that would look in London, and how easy for Renard to misrepresent that action to the Queen. And now with Suffolk's force encamped nearby, she was surrounded by armed men, like an animal in a snare waiting for the hunters to close in for the kill.

From the rebel leader, Thomas Wyatt, had come an urgent note advising her to move to Donnington without delay and fortify it against siege. Even now, several days since she had returned that letter without reply, she could not rid herself of the paralysing horror born at the sight of his bold signature. Of all the men in England who could have led this revolt, why did it have to be Wyatt, whose father had loved her mother with all-consuming passion and chosen to immortalize it in verses that were still quoted all over Europe?

> Forget not yet, forget not this,
> How long ago hath been, and is,
> The mind that never meant amiss
> Forget not yet!

The wind which tossed the skeleton trees seemed to whisper the words to her with cruel mockery. For she was not likely to forget, any more than her sister Mary, how the first Thomas Wyatt had gone to the Tower, along with five other men, accused of adultery with his cousin Anne Boleyn. And how Wyatt, conceivably more guilty than the rest of them put together, had been the only one to come out again alive and cheat the axe. Was it mere coincidence or perverted fate that now drove his son to challenge his lawful monarch for the sake of Anne Boleyn's daughter? Perhaps after all, the axe could not be cheated of its clients . . .

As she sat there shivering, staring at the eerie ring of trees, it seemed to Elizabeth that all her life was twisted by these haunting shadows of a previous existence, shadows reaching out now to join hands with her living enemies and wind the coils of treachery tighter round her own neck.

'. . . and I have such a little neck.'

She could sit still no longer, with Wyatt's verses for her mother running riot in her head. Chilled to the bone with cold and fear she fled down the icy paths of the monks' garden, back to the house which brooded against the sheltering woods.

The armed guards before the door saluted her and stared curiously as she mounted the steps, spent and breathless. One, forgetting himself, took an anxious step towards her, then froze at her furious look and hastily resumed his position, scarlet with shame at his presumption. At the top of the steps she paused to look at him and he stiffened, expecting the curt reprimand which he deserved. But she only smiled a little with pale lips and let her hand touch his sleeve for a fleeting moment. Then she was gone, swallowed up by the cool darkness beyond the great door, leaving him, redder than ever, to face his companions' jealous twitting.

In the hallway three greyhounds bounded to greet her and almost knocked her over in her weakened state. She cuffed them down affectionately and they followed her back into her private chamber, settling around her as she sank down on the cushions in front of the log fire and peeled off her gloves. She put her head down on one smooth, short-haired flank and let the warm fire bathe her closed eyelids; a clock ticked steadily on the chimney-piece, lulling her towards sleep.

Suddenly, all three dogs sat up with one will, pricking their ears and staring at the door. A moment later, it opened to disclose Mrs Ashley, white with terror, dithering on the threshold.

'Your Grace,' she whispered stupidly. 'Oh, Your Grace,' and became totally incoherent.

It was sufficient to make Elizabeth leap up from the hearth and snatch the document from Kat's trembling hand, breaking the seal with her long nails. There was a deathly hush in the room while she read rapidly and supported herself with one hand against the chimney-piece.

The letter was in the Queen's own hand and ordered her to London at once, lest danger befall her 'either where you are now or about Donnington, whither we understand you are shortly to remove.'

The paper fluttered to the floor, and Kat pounced on it, reading it quickly with bulging eyes.

'*Donnington,*' was all she whispered at last, but it was enough; and they were silent, staring at each other. For there was no way Mary could know of the rebels' suggestion to move to Donnington unless Wyatt's letter had been intercepted by spies.

'What shall we do?' moaned Kat helplessly. 'Child, what *can* we do?'

Elizabeth said nothing. The room was growing dim around her and a curious sound, like the rushing wind, seemed to drown her panic-ridden thoughts. Kat caught her as she swayed dangerously near the fire, a Kat suddenly restored to the full stature of calm common sense.

'No more argument, my lady. You are going to bed immediately.'

Against her shoulder, Elizabeth laughed weakly.

'Yes,' she said slowly, 'that's it. Put me to bed, Kat, and say I am too ill to travel.' Lifting her head she looked at the shifting shadows on the stone wall and shivered convulsively. 'It will gain me a little time—and time is all I have left to hope for.'

They went out of the room together and slowly up the stairs with the three dogs tumbling gaily around their heels.

'Too ill to travel!' Renard tossed Elizabeth's letter aside with a gesture of contempt. 'Madam, that is a card she has played too often!'

'This time it would appear she plays it with some justification,' muttered the Queen, refusing to meet his gaze. 'They are saying here in London that she has been poisoned, that she is so sick and swollen that her life is despaired of.'

The corners of Renard's mouth began to curl up in a rather cruel little smile.

'Sick and swollen, heh?' he echoed softly. 'Then depend upon it, madam, Wyatt's contact with her has gone considerably further than a letter.'

Mary stiffened and a slow purplish flush mounted in her cheeks.

'I know you to be my friend,' she said uncomfortably, 'but was that really necessary?'

'Very necessary.' Renard twisted the end of his moustache with quiet enjoyment. 'I would ask Your Majesty to remember that Wyatt's father was the Concubine's lover.'

'That was never proved.' The memory twisted deep in Mary like a sword thrust in an old wound. 'Wyatt was a gentleman and my father was satisfied with his personal integrity.'

'*Whoso list to hunt, I know where is an hind,*' quoted Renard slyly in his impeccable English and was rewarded by seeing the Queen flinch as though from a physical blow. 'Are *you* satisfied now with the integrity of Wyatt's son and Boleyn's daughter?'

'You know I am not.'

'Then I humbly and most desperately beg Your Majesty to act. Bring the Lady Elizabeth to London by force and commit her to the Tower for examination.' He waved the letter in his hand, in what was almost a threatening gesture betokening his angry despair. 'You have every justification. A copy of this letter of hers was found in de Noailles' mail to the French King. I tell you plainly, madam, as I have told you before, she is working with France.'

'That might be difficult to prove. And of her involvement with Wyatt we still have no evidence that will stand up in court.'

'Under your brother's laws we would have circumstantial evidence sufficient to hang the lady three times over.'

Mary turned away.

'But as you are so fond of saying, my friend—these are *not* my brother's days. And I have never regretted the repealing of those tyrannical acts.'

I have! thought Renard bitterly. Aloud he said smoothly, 'May you never have cause to regret it, madam!' and tried a new line. 'She has set an armed guard around Ashridge—do the implications of that act not strike you as sinister?'

The Queen shrugged thin shoulders. 'With Suffolk encamped so near, it is quite conceivable that Elizabeth fears attack.'

Renard choked back a curse and took the Queen's hands in his urgent grasp.

'The only thing Madam Elizabeth fears,' he said evenly, 'is the failure of this attack on *you*. For the love of God and His mother, bring her to London now, before it is too late!'

At the first breath of danger, Courtenay bleated all he knew to the Queen's chief minister, Bishop Gardiner, who had been both friend and father-figure to him during the long years of their mutual imprisonment. The news of his betrayal reached Kent four days later, forcing Wyatt to act alone, seven weeks before their original schedule. The church bells rang the alarm, rousing all who feared the heel of Spain and the wrath of the Inquisition. Wyatt raised his standard in Rochester, seizing vital arms and ammunition from the Queen's own ships, and began the march to Greenwich.

In London, those who had dismissed the Queen scornfully as a tear-sodden old maid, Renard included, watched the metamorphosis with amazement as once again the natural warrior kicked aside the vacillating middle-aged woman and Mary Tudor rose in defence of her crown. She ignored the pleas of her councillors to take refuge in the Tower or better still flee to Windsor Castle, ordered the arming of her capital city and rode out to the Guildhall to appeal to the goodwill of the people, to assure them of her love and devotion and to ask theirs in return.

They listened, and they gave it. At the end of the most stirring speech she would ever make, the loyalty of London spoke back in a sudden deafening roar.

'God save Queen Mary! God save the Queen!' And suddenly, inexplicably, unbelievably, the cry of support for he who was now her dearest hope, 'God save the Prince of Spain!'

She rode through the cheering, waving crowds to take her barge to Westminster, and then, in the sudden flush of triumph, ordered her oarsmen to row her as near as possible to London Bridge.

Across the Thames, an army of two thousand rebels sprawled along the Southwark banks, their banners fluttering defiantly in the wind.

Mary stood beneath the canopy and smiled the challenge of a Tudor prince.

Silence hung over the Thames, silence deep and penetrating, and Wyatt stood in his camp, scorning the £100 price on his head by wearing a velvet cap boldly stamped in large letters with his name. Having sworn he came 'only to resist the coming in of the Spanish King' he was proud of the orderliness of his men who had obeyed his stern commands. There would be no rape and pillage on this campaign! But for three days now he had puzzled over the silence of that barricaded city which he had been led to believe would welcome him with open arms. Five hundred of the Queen's guard had deserted to him at Strood, but since then, nothing. Not a single shot had yet been fired as each side waited for the other to make the first move.

Integrity, which had once saved the father, now betrayed the son. By the time Wyatt accepted the need for an assault upon the city, the fatal delay had already lost him the offensive. His nightmare march led him through rain and ice and confusion to a muddled furore at Charing Cross. And there, as his followers were mown down by cannon fire, he came face to face with the traitor, Edward Courtenay, fighting now on the Queen's side. Courtenay panicked at the sight of him and fled to the Queen at Whitehall crying that all was lost. And for a moment his panic threatened to sweep the whole palace. Men and women ran like frightened rabbits until Mary's voice rang out above the pandemonium like the lash of a whip; she swore to take up arms herself before she would 'yield one iota to such a traitor as Wyatt . . . God will not deceive me.' The panic died; the palace held firm; God had not deceived her—not yet!

Wyatt struggled to Ludgate only to find the city gates locked against him, and it was there in the rain, staring at the impenetrable thickness of wood, that he suddenly realized he was beaten. He sat on a bench at the Belle Sauvage inn and watched his men slip away down the side streets. The day had gone against him and further resistance would be a senseless bloodbath. He surrendered his bedraggled person to Sir Maurice Berkley and rode through a bristling, insulting mob to the Tower, where the Lord Lieutenant greeted him contemptuously.

'If it were not for the law which will pass just sentence on you, I would dagger you myself, sir.'

Wyatt drew his hand across his face, wiping away blood, mud and tears. 'It is no matter now,' he said sadly, and stepped inside.

Renard said grimly, 'Madam, the time has come for you to cut out the cankers in this realm. They must all die—*all* of them.'

Mary hunched a little further down in her chair; her face in the candle-light was an old woman's.

'Not Jane,' she muttered dimly, 'not Jane.'

'Show mercy again and the heretics will call it weakness. Madam—do you want bloodshed for the rest of your reign? What are three lives when the safety of your realm and the preservation of your faith are at stake?'

Three lives. Jane, Guildford—and Elizabeth. She had heard the same argument from countless sources: *What were three lives . . . ?*

The candles burnt low and had to be renewed; she agreed at last to sign the warrants for Jane and Guildford.

'And Elizabeth?' Renard prompted coldly.

She shielded her face with her hands.

'I will leave my husband to deal with her.'

'Husband?' he echoed blankly.

She looked up at him wildly and felt suddenly cold with apprehension. Renard spread his beautiful hands in a helpless gesture of frustration.

'Madam, is it possible that the precious person of Prince Philip could set foot on English soil while Elizabeth still lives?'

'But he would have every conceivable protection!'

Renard shrugged and made a slight bow.

'No protection would be adequate in the Emperor's eyes, madam. I fear our business is concluded and by your leave I shall retire.'

He was not more than halfway across the room when she called him back and promised to despatch doctors, her personal litter and an armed guard to Ashridge.

He came back, concealing a wry smile, and reflected with unkind amusement that Philip was in for a most unpleasant surprise.

The state bedroom at Ashridge was dominated by an enormous carved bed, and Elizabeth lay in its cavernous depths, playing chess in the yellow candlelight. She made two shrewd moves in succession, then lunged suddenly across the mattress and was violently sick into the big silver bowl at her side.

'Play on,' she commanded cheerfully in the panting pause before the retching convulsed her again, but Isabella Markham had risen in alarm.

'For God's sake, madam, let me fetch Mrs Ashley.'

'Don't be silly, Markham, there's nothing she can do for me.' Elizabeth leaned back on her pillows, white with exhaustion, and pressed a handkerchief to her lips. 'There are some sweets in that cabinet over there—fetch me one of those instead.'

'You'll be sick again.'

'So?' Elizabeth shrugged carelessly. 'We're not short of bowls, are we?'

Markham sighed and went across the room to pull out a box of sugared violets and marchpane. Over her shoulder she said severely, 'All your teeth will go black one day.'

'Only if I live to be old,' remarked the invalid smugly, 'and under the present circumstances, that prospect hardly seems likely to concern me.'

Isabella bit her lip and was aware of a sudden tightness in her throat. It was a moment before she had schooled her face sufficiently to return to the bed in a brisk and uncompromising manner.

'Medicine first,' she said and put a tiny goblet firmly into Elizabeth's hand.

'Be kind to me, Belle,' wheedled the younger girl. 'You know how I hate physic. I'll take it later before I go to sleep.'

'No, you won't,' said Isabella bluntly, 'you'll throw it in the chamber pot—the doctor warned me not to trust you.'

'Oh, did he?—the impertinent old fool! You could balance the sum total of his medical knowledge on the head of a pin.'

'He may not know much about medicine, madam, but he certainly knows a good deal about *you!*'

Elizabeth shrugged her thin shoulders against the pillows.

'Well, what if I am a poor patient? My father was too. It's part of my royal inheritance.'

'Madam, your *royal* brother bore all manner of unpleasant treatments in his last illness with saintly patience.'

'Much good it did him!' muttered Elizabeth, pushing the goblet to the back of the bedside table. 'And for your information, Markham, when that little painted saint was four years old he once kicked old Doctor Butts and yelled: "Go away, fool!" '

Markham looked up in astonishment, with a knight suspended in her hand.

'Why, madam, the late King never put a foot amiss in all his life! You're making it up.'

'I'm not! And I'll tell you something more—Butts fell on his knees with joy and swore that if he tarried till the child called him knave he would say *Nunc Dimittis*. It's the first rule they teach at the College of Physicians—as long as the patient can still kick you there's every chance you'll be paid for your services.'

'You're a dreadful cynic, madam.'

'So I am and so was Butts in the end. So would you be if someone took the most spectacular achievement of your career and threw it on the dung heap.'

Isabella looked at her curiously.

'What was that? Oh come, madam—you have to tell me now!'

Elizabeth was silent for a moment, staring at the tester of the bed, as though she half regretted embarking on this tale. Her eyes were pits of ebony and Isabella for no accountable reason felt suddenly chilled and uneasy. The door was shut, they two were unquestionably alone in the room, and yet . . . and yet . . . .

Markham's trembling fingers crept up to her throat.

'Why,' said Elizabeth at last, in a voice which seemed to come from a distance, 'did you never hear how Butts was sent to cure my mother of the sweating sickness—and how my father wrote to her: 'I would willingly bear half of what you suffer to cure you?' Elizabeth laughed, and the dreadful splintered sound made Isabella shiver. 'People openly prayed that she would die—but she didn't die, not then. Butts had rather more skill than most doctors—too much perhaps. God knows, half the world called it the worst day's work he ever did.'

She smacked her greyhound playfully on the rump to make him jump down off the bed and lay back with candlelight making an amber glory of her eyes. Isabella released her breath in a slow sigh of relief, freed from the crazy, fleeting sensation of something lurking in her mistress's steady gaze.

'Checkmate,' announced Elizabeth calmly and began to collect her winnings from Isabella's hanging pocket. 'Three games in a row, that's fifteen crowns. You play a miserable game of chess, Markham, do you know that?'

'I was the victim of devastating strategy, madam.'

'Quite so,' agreed her mistress drily. 'I seem to recall that every time I threw up it was your move. Pure coincidence, of course.'

Markham smiled and said, 'Shall I set the pieces out again, madam?'

'No, put them away. You're too tired to play again.'

The girl's head jerked up indignantly.

'I'm not tired, madam, far from it.'

'Look in your mirror, Markham,' said Elizabeth gently and saw the tears seep suddenly into her friend's eyes. 'Don't cry for me, Belle,' she continued uncomfortably, 'I'm not dead yet.'

'No, of course you're not.' Markham pulled herself up sharply. 'Forgive me. It's just that all this waiting and uncertainty are driving me out of my mind. None of us can bear not knowing from one day to the next if the Queen's men will come. Oh, madam, we do nothing in the Great Hall now but listen for hoof beats in the snow.'

For the last two weeks Elizabeth had been aware of the increasing tension that was slowly crippling the household. With nerves reduced to flapping strings, her close attendants snapped and quarrelled with each other when they believed themselves to be out of her hearing; even Kat, who seldom had a cross word for anyone, scolded the kitchenmaids without mercy.

Why do they care so much what becomes of me, wondered Elizabeth idly, it's not as though I were an easy mistress . . .

Aloud she said kindly, 'Everything seems worse at night, Belle. Put out the lights now and go to bed.'

She lay in the increasing gloom as her friend moved quietly around the room, dousing the candles with a brass-capped pole. The familiar little ritual was strangely comforting with its unspoken promise of continuity and one by one the candles were snuffed out until at last the room was lit only by the red glow of the fire. Outside snow was falling softly, swirling against the uncovered windows which seemed to be made of black glass. She burrowed under the sheets, glad of their warmth and security against the cold hostility of the outer world, ready to fall asleep like a tired child.

Markham turned to the bed and swept a deep curtsey.

'Goodnight, Your Grace.'

The outer door to the ante-room was abruptly flung open and the sudden tramp of boots, the jostling of spurs that announced the arrival of armed men, froze Markham to the floor in her graceful gesture of obeisance. Elizabeth sat up with a jerk and stared into the rosy half-light as Mrs Ashley's voice soared into an indignant wail of protest in the next room.

'My lords! Her Grace is far too ill to be disturbed at this hour of the night.'

'Madam,' said a gruff voice in reply, 'the Queen's business will not wait. Her Grace is to be examined immediately by Her Majesty's own physicians—and I'm sure you will agree she cannot possibly be too ill to see a doctor.'

Markham found her feet and fled to her mistress's side.

'Oh God, madam—they've come to take you! What shall I do?'

'Be calm—you must be, Belle, for my sake. Any panic among my servants will be taken as a sign of my guilt. Be surprised, be indignant, but don't be afraid.' She squeezed the older girl's hand. 'There—that's better! Now you can go and let them in.'

Markham turned away mutely, not trusting herself to speak again and went to light a taper. Elizabeth lay imperiously against the high pillows, ready to show affronted regality, but her heart was hammering beneath her ribs, making her breath come in painful jerks, threatening to spoil all her practised poise. Light-headed with fever and lack of food, she had a curious sensation of falling slowly into some nameless void—a little white pawn, with no hope left of being queened, tumbling quietly off the chessboard of life.

CHAPTER 12

The snow-bound countryside was filled with a white brooding silence as Elizabeth's great-uncle, Lord William Howard, lifted the Queen's prisoner into the waiting litter. They had been told to bring her back 'either quick or dead' and everyone knew the examination by the Queen's physicians which had pronounced her fit to travel had been a mere formality. Just as they were about to leave, there was a sudden anxious skirmishing of servants between the house and the litter; when Howard returned to poke his great head between the curtains, he discovered that she had been sick all over the velvet cushions.

'The Queen's personal litter,' he muttered, with a horror that quite robbed him of formality. 'Oh, *Elizabeth!*'

She looked up at him with a white-lipped smile of urchin innocence.

'Yes,' she agreed quietly, 'such a shame, isn't it?—and velvet never washes. I expect she'll have to have the whole thing refurbished.'

He suddenly saw there was absolutely no point in inquiring why she had not managed to lean over the side in time.

'Get her a bowl,' he said curtly, and turned away before anyone could surprise a rather disloyal smile on his heavy face.

They set out along the frozen lanes at a snail's pace, with Howard stubbornly insisting they could travel no more than seven miles a day. It was an unheard-of pace, even in this weather, but he was more fond of his great-niece than he dared to admit, and was deaf to all protest from the Queen's officers of deliberate delay.

The news of Lady Jane's execution eventually reached them at Redburn, and Elizabeth was crushed into silence when she heard it. Behind the swaying curtains, her mind flew back to Chelsea, to those jealous days when Jane had first intruded on her gay life with Queen Katherine and the Admiral.

'If it please Your Grace, the Lord Admiral says you are to play with me.'

'Tell the Lord Admiral I don't play with little girls.'

She wept for the cousin to whom she could have shown more kindness, and now, for the first time, she began to weep a little for herself. Of what use to struggle for delay and plan the best line of defence to the Council? If Mary could kill Jane, then there was nothing left to hope for.

An icy gale sprang up, swirling snow and sleet under the curtains of the swaying litter, and she huddled beneath her furs, her long fingers blue with cold. By the time they reached Highgate, the storm had become a blizzard and Elizabeth was too ill to care any more what waited at her journey's end. She was only dimly aware of Howard carrying her upstairs to her bed and standing over her while Kat forced aqua vitae between her rigid lips.

'It's barbarous,' Kat was sobbing wildly, 'truly barbarous, my lord. She's the King's daughter and she'll be dead before we reach the palace—is that what they want?'

Howard chafed Elizabeth's cold hands and swore softly, for he too had begun to think it more than likely. Cardinal Wolsey had died on his way to the Tower and therefore spared Henry the unpleasant necessity of disposing of him. But Howard was damned if he'd hand his great-niece over to the Queen in her coffin, however convenient it might prove to the government. He stormed out of the room without a word and five minutes later the Queen's doctors scuttled in, took one look at their patient and hastily advised complete rest.

And so there was a whole week's respite at Highgate while Renard spread the rumour across London that the swelling in her body had an excellent and obvious cause since she was no doubt with child again—whose child he neglected to say. Most assumed it was Courtenay's; one or two pockets of opinion inclined towards Wyatt.

Elizabeth seethed with rage when she heard the rumours and on the morning of her departure insisted that her corset should be laced so tightly she could scarcely breathe. She dressed in white to proclaim her innocence, flung off the fur covers and insisted the curtains of the litter should be drawn back so that the people who pressed to see the truth of that rumour would know it for the lie it was.

The London crowds who lined her way were silent and frightened and the gibbets which swung on every street corner were explanation enough for the mute eyes which followed her. The whole city was like a charnel-house.

'The most beautiful sights that can be seen in this town and indeed all over the country,' de Noailles had written home triumphantly, 'are the gibbets on which hang some of the bravest and most gallant men that she had in her Kingdom. The prisons are full of the nobility and some of the most prominent people . . .' He was confident that prison would shortly contain the most prominent person of all—but not for long, not for long, eh? De Noailles was like a dog with two tails on the day Elizabeth was carried through the city gates, all displaying their fine array of heads and dismembered bodies like so much bunting. London stank with decaying flesh and Elizabeth stared ahead with unblinking eyes, swallowing hard, grimly determined not to disgrace herself before the watching crowds.

At Whitehall, the Lord Chamberlain hurried her to an obscure suite of rooms and separated her from most of her household, who were told to find lodgings in the city. She demanded to see the Queen and was told that was impossible; she would be denied all visitors and an armed guard would stand outside her chambers day and night. The rooms, which were cold and damp, had clearly not been in use for a long time and her few remaining servants fell to unpacking her belongings and lighting a fire. They put her to bed and she fell immediately into sleep, to be woken a little over an hour later by a resounding crash overhead. The noise was repeated at roughly ten-second intervals and sounded for all the world like heavy metal pots being flung around in the room above.

'God's soul, Kat, what the hell is that?'

Kat went to inquire from the guards and came back looking grim.

'Apparently Your Grace is lodged beneath the Countess of Lennox's apartments. The room above is a kitchen.'

Elizabeth stared at her, seemed about to flare up into one of her sudden rages, then suddenly sighed with tired resignation, and lay back on her pillows.

'Oh well,' she muttered, 'I don't suppose it can go on for long.'

But it did. Lady Lennox's household were evidently insatiable eaters and her servants appeared to work in shifts. In desperation, Elizabeth sent a request that the activity should cease, and the racket was promptly doubled. By midnight she lay rigid with tension, bracing herself against the next crash, and her eyes were misty with unshed tears. She wanted to scream, but knew that once she had begun she would not be able to stop; and she would not give her tormentor that much satisfaction.

'How can she be so cruel?' whispered Markham dully from the side of the bed.

Elizabeth laughed shortly. 'You don't know the Countess of Lennox if you can ask that.'

'But she's your *cousin!*'

'Just so,' Elizabeth's voice was grim, 'and if the Council should make a swift end of me, she and her pretty son, Darnley, will be a good step closer to the throne. It's in her interests, you see, making sure I get no rest. Exhausted prisoners make mistakes—and one mistake is all they need now to take my head.' Suddenly she clenched her fists and bit savagely at her pillow. 'If I get out of this alive, I'll settle with that bitch one day, and her precious son! When I am Queen you bitch-whelped Darnleys . . . oh God, when I am Queen . . . take care!'

Elizabeth clung to her sanity through a month of sleepless torture, while the Council collected its evidence against her. Lennox's tactics, coupled with her illness and the endless weeks of waiting, shook her nerves beyond repair, but whenever her mind grew numb with exhaustion, she whipped it mercilessly into a frenzy of activity. Latin, Greek, mathematical formulae—she used her formidable education like a stone, sharpening her wits against it, honing it to a razor's edge. When they came at last to interrogate her, the day after Wyatt had been sentenced to death, she was ready for them. She sat on a low stool with her hands demurely folded on her lap and stared squarely at the ten hostile men who faced her across the plain table.

Gardiner had primed them well and questions fired at her from all sides in quick succession, but she would not be panicked or stampeded into hasty answers. They could not budge her from her story, whatever angle they attacked it from. She had done nothing; she knew nothing.

Gardiner got to his feet in excitement. He thought he had found the first chink in her armour.

'Madam, you overplay your innocence—Wyatt himself admits he wrote to you—can you deny it?'

Slowly she raised her eyes to his in cool challenge. 'Where is my reply, my lord?'

A low mutter ran through the assembled councillors, like a rustle of wind through a field of corn, but Gardiner stilled it with a furious look.

'Wyatt will testify that he received a verbal reply,' he said quickly, aware, even as he said it, that that would not do, and seeing the faint curl of her lips which showed she knew it too. As he glared down at the ashen face beneath him, he took spiteful comfort from the black shadows under her eyes, like the smudge of two thumbprints on alabaster. In poor health himself, the long interrogation was taking its toll upon him and he could not believe that this sick, friendless girl was still defying them all.

'Madam,' he said grimly, 'your only hope is to confess your fault and seek the Queen's pardon.' But she had heard that tune before and knew it for the cruel trick that it was.

'Pardon is for the guilty, my lord,' she replied calmly, 'I cannot be forgiven for a crime I have not committed.'

The arrogant assertion blotted his vision with red spots of rage. His face was livid as he pointed a finger at her and suddenly roared, '*You!* You are of equal guilt with the traitor Wyatt!'

'Prove it,' she countered softly. 'Bring me to trial in open court and prove your case. Only then will it be time for you to give me advice.'

'She must go to the Tower, my lords!' Gardiner's voice splintered the tense silence of the room and immediately the orderly air of the council chamber erupted into violent uproar. Above the shouting and pounding of fists upon the table came one indignant cry which voiced the feeling of many present.

'Good God, my lord, what evidence justifies so violent a measure?'

For a long time the quarrel raged to and fro in a bitter debate, until at last Gardiner got to his feet and banged on the table for silence. When it had descended, he glared balefully down their ranks.

'May I ask instead if any of you *noble* gentlemen would care to take charge of the lady in question?'

Even her staunchest supporters gawked at him in horrified disbelief. No one dared to be responsible for so notorious a lady and no one took up Gardiner's sarcastic offer. He glanced down the table with a little smile of satisfaction and re-seated himself in quiet triumph.

'Then I perceive, gentlemen,' he said sardonically, 'that we are in unanimous agreement at last.'

The Tower!

All the waiting, all the suffering, all those smooth clever answers for nothing. One hundred soldiers, their torches flickering in the darkness, paced the gardens beneath her window; and tomorrow they would take her away and shut her in 'that place', unless the Queen personally intervened.

All that night she sat and waited in vain for a summons from her sister. Early the next morning, the door opened at last and she started up from her stool; the Earl of Sussex and the Marquis of Winchester stood there, with their hats in their hands.

'My lords?'

'Madam,' announced Sussex gravely, 'the barge is ready and the tide is right. You must come at once for the tide waits for no man.'

She stared wildly at Winchester's blank face, and found it a carved mask of hostility, immovable as stone. To plead with him would be wasted breath. Instinctively she scanned Sussex's stolid features, a huge weathered face framed by a shock of grey hair and grizzled beard. His nose and lips had an uncompromising line, but his eyes were a soft grey glimmer that might just mean pity. She reached out and laid her hand on his sleeve.

'My lord, let me see the Queen. Let me speak with her.'

But it was Winchester who answered, brisk, half angry.

'Out of the question, madam. Her Majesty refuses to see you under any circumstances.'

'Then let me write to her.'

'There is no time.' It was Winchester still, tugging his beard. 'Totally inconvenient, and in my opinion,' he sniffed officiously, 'it would do you more harm than good.'

Sussex remained silent, staring at her, and she saw his grey eyes were in agony now. Those eyes were her only hope and lifting her own she assaulted him with the full force of her charm.

'A few words only,' her voice was a soft throb of appeal, a siren's whisper which smote him to the heart. 'I beg you, sir.'

The eyes capitulated, body and soul; his voice roared out suddenly. 'Get her pen and ink. By God, I say she shall write.'

Winchester gasped. 'My lord, are you aware—'

'Fully aware. I'll answer to the Queen for it.' He went down on his knees and kissed her hand. 'I'll take your letter with my own hand, madam.' He had his reward; she smiled at him and said she would never forget. As he left her to write her letter in peace, he felt that smile would burn against his eyelids for the rest of his life.

She took her pen and began to write frantically, not a letter—there was no opening salutation—but a plain statement of her innocence and her loyalty, the first lines of which were a hammer blow to Mary's conscience, the only part of her sister's heart she now had any hope of touching.

If ever any did try this old saying 'that a King's word was more than another man's oath' I most humbly beseech Your Majesty to verify it in me and to remember your last promise and my last demand, that I be not condemned without answer . . . which it seems I now am . . .

Beneath her window the soldiers tramped steadily, beating a tattoo in her mind. The Tower! The Tower! The Tower!

. . . To this present hour I protest before God whatsoever malice may devise, that I never practised, concealed nor consented to anything that might be prejudicial to your person or dangerous to the state . . . Let conscience move Your Highness to take some better way with me.

The pen scratched on, ran dry and as she leaned forward to ink it, she heard the screech of fiddles and the gay babble of voices, she was once more sitting beside a great fireplace staring up into the haggard face of the man who had killed her lover. Against her conscious will, the painful memory poured out across the page.

I have heard in my time of many cast away for want of coming to the Presence of their Prince and in late days I heard my Lord Somerset say that if his brother had been suffered to speak with him he would never have died. But the persuasions made to him were so great that he was brought to believe he could not live safely if the Admiral lived . . .

She stared down hopelessly at the words. Why had she written that when after all it could serve no purpose other than to remind her sister that she might well have been a whore, like her mother before her. If she crossed it out, Mary would only wonder what she had tried to hide and there was no time to start again. She turned the page. Panic sent her words wavering drunkenly across the sheet; crossings out, omissions and frantic insertions began to litter her final paragraph.

. . . and for the copy of my letter sent to the French King, I pray God confound me eternally if ever I sent word, token or letter by any means and to this, my truth, I will stand to my death.

My death. The finality of that last phrase wiped her mind utterly blank. Almost two-thirds of the page was still empty, open to the forger's pen. There must be something else she could say, but her mind, exhausted by the effort, crawled away into a dark corner and refused to play any more, like a sulky child. She scrawled slanting lines down the page, signed her name frantically and looked up to find the Earl of Sussex looking down at her. He was staring at those lines and his face, slowly flushing with dark colour, wore an expression of real pain.

'Forgive me,' she whispered as he reached over for the paper. 'No, wait— I've thought of something more.'

There was a momentary tussle as she snatched the paper back and a huge blot half obliterated her signature at the foot. Over the top of it she scribbled quickly:

I most humbly crave but one word of answer from yourself.

She did not receive it.

Mary's response to Elizabeth's letter knocked all the breath out of Sussex's stolid body.

'You, sir, are travelling on the wrong path!' she screamed, and her rage held an undercurrent of half-demented jealousy. Sussex, one of her own staunchest supporters, was another helpless victim to the deadly lure of that witch's daughter; no man was safe in Elizabeth's presence, no man!

'You would never have dared do such a thing in my father's time,' she roared. 'Would to God he were alive again for a month to deal with you.'

Privately, Sussex saw precious little need for that. The great Henry himself could hardly have demoralized him more than this ferocious little woman in the grip of her father's murderous rage. Both he and Winchester were very relieved to get out of her presence suffering nothing worse than disgrace.

'I hope you're satisfied, you damned fool,' muttered Winchester. 'I thought a man of your age would have had more sense than to let himself be taken in by a pair of pretty eyes.'

Sussex was strangely preoccupied.

'Yes,' he said vaguely, 'it was the eyes that snared me—have you ever seen any quite like them?'

'No, I haven't,' Winchester replied shortly, 'and you can think yourself lucky it was only a letter and not your precious prisoner that you took to the Queen. In her present mood I swear she'd have killed her. For God's sake, get a hold on yourself, man, and remember where your loyalties are supposed to lie. You can't afford another show of partisanship.'

Sussex sighed. 'We can't leave now, we've missed the tide.'

'Which is no doubt what the young lady intended in the first place. Another night in the palace—another chance of a rescue. By God, we'll need to keep our men vigilant tonight. I don't suppose I need to tell you that if she escapes you and I will pay for it with our heads—we'd better double her guard.'

Next day it was Palm Sunday and rain was sluicing down steadily, misting the palace gardens with a grey cobweb curtain. While all good Londoners were in church, receiving their palms, Elizabeth was hurried down the lawn at Whitehall to the waiting barge. She noticed the Earl of Sussex staring straight ahead as though he was afraid to look at her. She cried out that she marvelled the nobility of the realm would suffer her to be led into captivity, but still he would not look at her.

'The tide,' whispered Sussex anxiously as they reached the barge at last, 'the tide is still unsuitable—'

'We dare not delay any longer,' snapped Winchester. 'We leave at once.'

Elizabeth gathered from the indignant protests of the boatmen that something was very wrong. The grey, rain-splattered river rushed by the barge as they swerved towards London Bridge and there was a sudden cry as they struck a whirlpool which rocked all the occupants to the floor. Soaked with dirty water, Elizabeth was flung into Sussex's arms for a moment as the barge struck against the bridge supports, while the rotting heads impaled on spikes above glared down upon them sightlessly. And when at last the bargemen had regained control, they were washed up at the grim portal of Traitor's Gate, bumping against the landing steps that were submerged with black water.

Soaked to the skin, with her hair hanging loose down her back in damp snarling curls, she stood at Traitor's Gate filled with such rage that she felt she could fell old Winchester with one blow. How dared they half drown her in their haste!

'I will not be landed here,' she cried furiously, 'I'll be over my shoes in water.'

'Madam, you have no choice,' grunted Winchester. He had hurried back in annoyance to discover she was making more trouble, but suddenly found himself so horrified by her appearance—so like a proud but bedraggled tawny cat—that he pulled off his own cloak and flung it round her shoulders.

But she was in a blazing temper and blind to all chivalry. She dashed off his cloak and stepped into the icy water, her voice ringing through the rain with a shout of defiance.

'Here lands as true a subject, being prisoner, as ever landed at these stairs. Before you, oh God, I speak it, having no other friend but you alone.'

'If that is so, then so much the better for you,' sneered the Marquis who had already regretted that unaccountable act. He bent down, fished his cloak out of the filthy water and shook it out angrily.

She turned from him and looked beyond him to the rows and rows of guards and officials. There was an angry laugh in her voice now.

'What—all these harnessed men for one weak woman?'

Her scornful gaze swept their ranks and to the fury of the Lord Lieutenant, Bridges, the men began to fall to their knees murmuring, 'God save Your Grace', and there was absolutely nothing he could do to prevent it.

The rage died in her eyes then and suddenly she looked up, seeming to see the Tower for the first time. Somewhere within that beautiful stone fortress what was left of her mother's headless body lay buried in an arrow chest, picked clean by countless maggots. The sound of the river had lapped in her dreams for seventeen years, waiting to sweep her home to this moment of reunion with her mother's blood.

She sank down upon the streaming stones and bowed her head. No force in this world would make her enter that place, no, not if they chose to kill her on this very spot.

There was a moment of horrified silence, during which all the men exchanged uneasy glances, for none of them had been prepared for this. After a minute, the Lord Lieutenant came forward uncomfortably and knelt beside her.

'Madam, you had best come in,' he said anxiously, uncertain what the effect upon his men would be if they were obliged to resort to physical force, 'for here you sit unwholesomely.'

'Better sit here than in a worse place,' she muttered darkly, tracing one long finger across the wet stone.

Little rivulets of water were running past her, soaking into her gown, and her mind like a boat gently slipping its mooring rope drifted with them, aimless, thoughtless, towards oblivion. If, in that critical moment, they had dared to lay hands upon her and drag her inside the fortress, they would have found it necessary to restrain her in chains.

But no one dared. The rain hammered down and as she floated swiftly and painlessly to the very brink of insanity, one of her young men servants began to weep noisily.

Slowly, incredulously, she raised her head and looked round: Cornwallis, her gentleman usher, a shy, sensitive young man, who blushed and was overcome with stupid confusion every time she had cause to address him.

'Stop it!' she ordered, getting to her feet and giving him a gentle poke in the ribs. 'Stop it, do you hear? I'm not in such a plight that I need to be wept over yet.'

'No, madam,' he mumbled and little knew what service he had just rendered to her. She was in command of herself once more, able to give her hand to Sussex and sweep haughtily into the fortress, even to smile graciously when the Earl whispered brokenly, 'Madam, I am sorry I ever lived to see this day.'

At length she stood in a bare, semi-circular, stone chamber, listening to the turning of the key in the outer door.

'See her doors are locked straightly at all times,' said Winchester's nervous voice, addressing the guards.

There was a sudden angry jangling of heavy keys in the lock and Winchester's voice became a whine of protest.

'My lord of Sussex. They *must* be locked—for safety's sake.'

'There's nothing in our orders that says anything about locked doors,' retorted Sussex heatedly. 'You talk of safety? Then let us take heed that we do not go beyond our commission. She was our king's daughter and is the prince next in blood. By God, let us deal with her now that we do not have to answer for our dealings hereafter.'

Winchester was silent.

And Elizabeth's door remained unlocked.

The outer world had ceased to exist for her; there was nothing to do except embroider quietly with her women before a petulant fire and wait for the daily interrogations from the Council. Once they brought her face to face with the prisoner, James Croft, hoping the sight of her would loosen his stubborn tongue.

He stood for a moment staring at her white face, then fell on his knees at her feet and declared her innocent.

'I have been marvellously tossed and examined touching Your Highness, but I take God to record I know nothing of the crime which is laid to your charge. If they bring me to trial, madam, I will take my death upon that oath.'

Her hand went out in helpless rage to the broken wretch at her feet and she wondered how many they would have to torture before they found one willing to testify against her. She wanted to say she would pray for him, but that could be twisted, misunderstood, and so she said nothing; but her eyes were soft with compassion.

Gardiner, enraged by this dismal failure, returned to the subject of Donnington. Could she deny there had been talk among her household of moving there?

'What if there was!' she snapped, turning on him suddenly. 'May I not go to my own house whenever I choose?'

Evidently the logic of that was too much for the elderly Earl of Arundel who, likewise, went down on his knees before her and declared, 'Your Grace speaks the truth and we are very sorry to have troubled you.'

We! It was unbelievable. From the corner of her eye Elizabeth saw Gardiner's face suffuse with purple fury and his lips contort into a twisted line. She lowered her eyes demurely, held out her hand to Arundel and said on a maddening note of ineffable sweetness, 'May God forgive you all.'

James Croft's dirty shivering form was instantly bundled out of the room and Gardiner, barely able to speak, all but threw the rest of the Council after him. When the door had slammed, Elizabeth found she had begun to shake with wild laughter.

Gardiner stormed away to inform Renard that as long as Elizabeth lived he had no hope of seeing the kingdom in peace.

'A reasonable conclusion,' said the Ambassador testily. 'I'm surprised it took so long for you to reach it.'

He was truly astonished at the laxity with which the English government conducted its affairs. Mary assured him that fresh proof against the Princess was arriving every day, but he saw little evidence of it. And now that Lord William Howard had taken up his great-niece's cause in good earnest, it began to look as though they might actually be forced to let the young bitch go. 'Unless—' said Gardiner; and let the sentence hang significantly. *Unless . . .*

* * *

April had touched the Tower garden with little riots of spring flowers and a blustery wind. Tucked in the shelter of the high wall, three small children knelt on the gravel path beside Elizabeth and watched as she traced her name with a stick.

'Do you always write it like that, Madam Elizabeth?' Henry Martin was a sturdy, opinionated five-year-old. 'With all those twirls and loops?'

'Every time.'

'But it takes you so long.'

'I know—that's why I hate writing letters and have a secretary.'

Henry sighed. 'I wish *I* had a secretary.'

She tapped him playfully on the tip of his nose with the stick.

'Even if you had one it would still be necessary to add your signature. A signature is a unique part of yourself, it tells people things about you.'

'Like whether you are full of loops and twirls?'

She laughed and would not answer.

'Do dragons have singy-tunes too?' demanded Susanna suddenly.

'Oh yes,' said Elizabeth cheerfully. 'They all write in a fine Italian script. Some of them even write books. I knew one once, his name was Remnarc— Remnarc the Coward.'

They settled around her avidly in the pale April sunlight while she drew Archbishop Cranmer for them, making him a timorous weedy little dragon cowering in a dark cave for fear of burning himself with his own flames. And burn he might in good earnest, she thought dispassionately, if Gardiner had his way and Cranmer's *Book of Common Prayer* became an outlawed heresy.

She liked her dragons; they were fuel for her starved imagination, by-products of a frivolity which had surprised her. And if the children missed the finer points of her malicious characterizations, it hardly seemed to matter. They loved the simple adventures and the subtle innuendo was her own private delight.

A week is a long time in the Tower; this one had transformed her life. It was her first experience of children, her first real opportunity to discover how infinitely preferable their company was to that of adults. And her first discovery of her own unique affinity with the infant mind. It had cost her very little conscious effort to make these children worship her. They were only Tower brats, offspring of the officials who lived and worked here, but they were suddenly the centre of her world, bringing her gaiety and hope; and—inadvertently—contact with a fellow prisoner.

It was little Henry Martin who began it all, a lively chatty child welcomed in more than one dull cell by the more respectable inmates. When he began to arrive daily in the garden with a posy of flowers, Elizabeth was touched and amused, but hardly suspicious. Then one day she unloosened the bundle of stems and found a tiny pellet of paper concealed there.

It was not a letter, just a short list of names which she instantly recognized as her dragons' *alter egos*, accredited with an impertinent postscript.

'Not very subtle! Robin Dudley.'

The blood rushed into her cheeks with a sharp mingling of anger, alarm and pleasure. She tackled Henry next morning with some care, but it was soon evident he knew nothing about the note. Certainly he had been often to visit Lord Robert and repeated her stories.

'. . . he said Trebor the Brave was the best.'

'Oh!' she exclaimed and put her hands up to her burning cheeks. 'Did you have to tell him that one?'

Henry looked bewildered.

'But it was a good story, Madam Elizabeth—I liked it best too.'

Oh, what was the use? She looked at her latest posy, lying in splendid isolation where she had left it under a bush. It contained another stupid note, she knew it did, and suddenly she didn't care about the risk. Not since her disastrous love affair with the Admiral had she felt such wildly happy anticipation. She was young, she was still alive, and this long, breathless moment, stolen from Time's bleak march, had made her curiously reckless.

Her guard was coughing discreetly, delicately attempting to indicate that her hour of exercise had ended some time ago. The children danced around him, protesting vigorously.

'Aw, Will—five more minutes.'

'Five and twenty you've had already,' he grumbled. 'Your Grace—if you please now.'

She clapped her hands and the children ran to her; one by one she hugged them and swung them round in the air until they squealed with glee. She watched them sidle out through the gate, then ran up the stairs in the Governor's house to her room in the Bell Tower.

When she was alone, she slit the binding round the posy with her fingernail and spread the stems across the table. There between the leaves lay another tightly folded pellet of paper, containing one line in the old familiar writing she remembered from her childhood.

'Dismiss your dragons tonight.'

Between the Bell Tower where she was lodged and the Beauchamp Tower where Robin Dudley was held captive under sentence of death was a narrow walk known as the Leads. It stretched roughly seventy feet from one door to the next, between the battlements of the outer walls and the gables of the

King's and the Yeoman Gaoler's houses. From that high vantage point she had seen the far sweep of the Essex marshes and freedom, for it was there that they had first allowed her to walk for exercise, before she gained the greater freedom of the Tower garden. She remembered glancing at the door to the Beauchamp Turret and thinking how strange it was to be so near and yet so far from her childhood's best friend.

So—he would come to her tonight! It could be done, she knew that, knew that stranger, darker and more mysterious things had taken place before now in this stone kingdom where money talked with a louder and more persuasive voice than anywhere else in England. Meetings could be arranged easily enough for those who were not out of reach in the dungeons and she was not there yet, though she could think of some who would like to see it arranged. But Robin Dudley, even committing rank treason at his father's command, was not among them.

Now, in the darkest moment of their lives, when they were both too near to death to fear the consequences, they could afford to be reckless. They were neither of them likely to see another spring, so what the devil did it matter anyway if they met once more to say goodbye?

'What the devil!' she said softly to herself and dropped the small pellet of paper into the fire with a little smile.

And so it had come to this. Her life had turned the full circle of love and death and she was waiting for life to end or begin that strange circle again, waiting in the Tower, listening to the wind and staring at the unlocked door.

Death was all around her in this place of dark memories. Anne Boleyn; Katherine Howard; the Lord Admiral. All had met their violent ends within the confines of the fortress which now held her captive.

She sat very still in the cold, stone window-seat and rain drummed heavily into the moat outside.

Who would come to her through that door which was scarcely visible in the half gloom—a living breathing young man, or a gay, teasing, reckless ghost?

As she watched, the door creaked open and shut again, and a tall figure stood at last with his face in the shadows. She rose from the window-seat and they stared at each other for a long moment in the twilight, before he came across the room and knelt to kiss the hem of her gown. He lifted his head to look at her and the light of the single candle fell not on the golden beard and hair of the Lord Admiral, but on a face as darkly handsome as a gypsy's.

In that moment, when she held out both her hands to Robin Dudley, it seemed to her that she held them out to life itself.

PART TWO

The Woman

*'I hate the very idea of marriage for reasons I would
not divulge to a twin soul.'*

ELIZABETH

CHAPTER 1

The Lady Elizabeth was one admirer short on her morning walk in the little Tower garden and found herself disproportionately distressed by the lack.

It was not as though Katherine was her favourite. She was not high-spirited like Henry, or half so amusing as Susanna; in fact she was a dull little thing, with hardly a word to say for herself, a child one might easily overlook in a crowd. But her solemn, tongue-tied adoration had been a trophy, a tribute to Elizabeth's power, and she was shaken by this unexpected desertion.

Where's Katherine?

The nagging little question gnawed at the back of her jealous mind, and neither hide and seek nor a vigorous game of tag shifted her growing depression.

'Madam Elizabeth!'

She turned eagerly towards the gate and held out her arms in welcome to the little figure who came running towards her.

'Look what I found for you, Madam Elizabeth. Look!'

Flushed and animated, the child held up a bunch of keys with a triumphant flourish. Never in all her life would Elizabeth have believed it possible that the plain, rather plump little face could look so beautiful.

'Where did you find them, sweetheart?'

'Where indeed, madam?' The guard was at her side. 'Forgive me, Your Grace, but I must see.'

He held out his hand for the keys and Katherine, that quiet, colourless, well-behaved little girl, suddenly let out a scream of fury that almost made him drop them.

'No! The keys are for the lady so she may unlock the doors and go abroad. Give them back to her—give them *back!'*

Elizabeth swung the child up into her arms and straddled her on her hip.

'Are you always so full of tact?' she demanded of the guard, who flushed uncomfortably.

'I'm sorry, madam. I shall have to report the matter.'

'Surely that's not necessary. You can see well enough what has happened. Have you no children of your own?'

He lowered his eyes. 'I have five, madam—and another on the way. That's why—' he faltered.

'Why you can't afford to risk your place.' She smiled suddenly. 'Yes—I understand. Do whatever you feel is necessary.'

Immeasurably relieved, he bowed and hurried away with the keys. The other two children crowded round Elizabeth, jealous of the sudden prominence of one they only permitted to tag along on sufferance.

'Cry-baby,' mocked Henry, as Elizabeth took out her own handkerchief to wipe Katherine's face. 'They were the wrong keys anyway. *Yow!*' his voice shot up an octave in pained surprise as Elizabeth's hard hand came down sharply on the back of his head.

'You nasty little turd!' she said furiously. 'If you don't say you're sorry for that I'll turn you inside out!'

He took a halting step backwards, with one hand to his ear, and looked at his fairytale princess with wary respect.

'How do you turn someone inside out?' piped Susanna.

Elizabeth glanced ominously at the silent boy.

'Watch very closely and I'll show you how it's done.'

The children scattered before her challenge and Henry ran for his life. Elizabeth cut off his retreat to the gate, chased him round the flowerbeds and finally cornered him against the high stone wall, where his belligerence crumpled into screams of delighted terror.

'Don't—oh, please don't! I'm sorry, Katherine, I'm sorry, I'm sorry—'

He flung his arms around Elizabeth's waist and buried his face in the stomacher of her gown. She held him close until the quivering sobs died away, then sat on the grass in a puff of dull green skirts and pulled him down beside her. She kissed the top of his tumbled hair and looked down on him with quiet amusement.

'I didn't frighten you, did I?'

'Oh no!' he lied on a hasty gulp. 'Not one bit.'

'That's what I thought. So that's all right then, isn't it?'

'Yes.' He was watching her long hair flying out like copper snakes in the breeze and Elizabeth studied him calmly; there was nothing in her manner to suggest the sudden panic which had seized her. The guard would take those keys to the Lord Lieutenant of the Tower, who in his turn would lay the matter before the Council. And if everything that had taken place in this garden was suddenly subjected to close scrutiny, it might be that her life and Robin Dudley's lay unbelievably in the hands of a five-year-old boy.

A boy, moreover, whose ear was still brilliant red from her ill-considered blow.

'Harry,' she said softly, 'will you do something for me—something secret, like a knight of the Round Table?'

'A *real* secret?' he breathed. 'Something the others don't know about?'

She nodded. 'Just you and me. Our own very special secret about the flowers you bring me.'

'But Lord Robert sends the flowers.'

Mentally she cringed, and had to force herself to smile nonchalantly.

'If anyone should ask you questions, you must say nothing about Lord Robert. Nothing at all. It's very important, Harry—will you promise me?'

'Can we swear a pact?'

She laughed with relief. 'If you like.'

And so they sat in the cool April sunlight, spitting on palms and pressing thumbs, while the Lord Lieutenant watched from a window above and absently fingered the keys in his hand.

Henry Martin stood in a narrow, ill-lit room surrounded by the bearded faces of men who ruled his father's life. They did not threaten to turn him inside out, but they were looking at him as though they would dearly like to do it.

'Come here,' said the Lord Lieutenant and Henry came, not very willingly.

'Do you know what a lie is, young man?' inquired the mighty master of this domain.

'Oh yes, sir. A lie is a very wicked thing.'

'Just so,' agreed the gentleman severely. 'So you will not tell lies to us, will you, Henry?'

'No, sir.'

The Lord Lieutenant glanced along the row of faces and back to the boy before him.

'You visited the Lady Elizabeth and took her flowers. We would like to know what was in those posies, my boy.'

'Well—' Henry considered a moment. 'They were mostly bluebells and just a few of those tall—'

The Lord Lieutenant coughed. 'Did anyone give you a letter to put in with the flowers?'

'No, sir!' The small face was quite genuinely baffled now; the ring of elderly gentlemen congealed into a tightly knit whispering group and then re-formed around him once more.

'Have you ever visited a prisoner called Edward Courtenay?'

'No, sir.'

'Sir Thomas Wyatt?'

'No, sir.'

More muttering and mumbling followed, only splinters of which were audible to the boy.

'*Gardiner's furious—who allowed it to take place?*'

'*The prison's crammed to bursting point—can't have eyes everywhere you know—and besides it's obviously been innocent enough—*'

'*Aye, innocent this time, thank God—there'll not be a next.*'

The Lord Lieutenant swung round at last to the boy's father.

'You, sir! You're responsible for all this trouble. You will keep your crafty knave at home in future—and you, my boy, you are not to see the Princess again, do you understand?'

'Yes, sir.' The voice was obedient, but the face was fiercely mutinous as he walked out of the room with his father's hand on his shoulder.

Henry's parents took the Lord Lieutenant's rebuke very seriously and it was three days before the little boy was allowed to set foot outside their apartments on the sound promise of a good whipping if he dared to disobey.

He hung around outside the garden, kicking a stone in apparent indifference, and then, seeing no one was watching, he sidled over to the garden gate and pushed it hard. It was locked now, but through the chinks in the wood he could see her walking, alone except for her guards. He hammered on the gate and yelled her name and a minute later he heard her low, breathless voice on the other side.

'What happened, Harry—tell me quickly.'

'I can't come any more. I can bring you no more flowers.' He stopped shouting and his voice became a whisper she could only just hear, 'I didn't tell, Madam Elizabeth—I didn't tell.'

Through the gaps in the wooden gate she watched him flee down the path and felt an absurd pricking at the back of her eyes. She never saw any of them again. The children were gone and with them the dragons and the dreams; life was real once more and threatening to prove terrifyingly short.

News came that Mary had collapsed with what might well prove to be a fatal illness, and Gardiner, knowing how little he would have to hope for if Elizabeth came to the throne now, at last took the desperate gamble which had been at the back of his mind for a few weeks.

Hard on the news of the Queen's illness, came the death warrant for Elizabeth's immediate execution.

* * *

The Lord Lieutenant of the Tower sat close to the fire in the stone hearth and stared at the death warrant which had been delivered with strict instructions to act at once and in secret.

The warrant had been signed by Gardiner for the Queen in her indisposition; Gardiner, the head of the Council, the most powerful man in England; Gardiner who must be very sure of the Queen's secret desires to dare this.

The Lord Lieutenant buried his face in his hands and told himself that no one could blame him for acting on the authority of this document. Indeed, refusal to act upon this direct command would very likely cost him his post—and Gardiner would see to it that he got no other. So he must go to her now and tell her that she must die tomorrow, die secretly and shamefully without trial or legal warrant.

He rose slowly with the document in his hand and stared out of the window to the place where so short a time ago the Lady Jane's scaffold had stood. It would take several hours to build a new one and he would have to give the order immediately if it was to be done in time. He wondered, with idle curiosity, how she would go to that death and with the memory of that scene at Traitor's Gate still fresh in his mind, he imagined she was likely to kick up quite a fuss. It was always unpleasant when they had to be dragged and held down, much better when they behaved with calm dignity, in a decent manner—and oddly enough most of them did when it came to it. Guildford Dudley had been a blubbering wreck, but he had found courage at the last moment, while his young wife had conducted the whole business like a lesson in deportment. Only once, when they had tied the blindfold around her eyes, had Jane groped for the block in a wild panic, crying, 'Where is it? *Where is it?*'

Bridges had watched it all without a flicker of emotion for it was a familiar part of his job and he was not a sentimental man; proprietors of the slaughterhouse seldom are. He turned calmly to the door, and there he paused and remembered the Queen, so notoriously sentimental, so very unpredictable. And suddenly his vision was clear and true. He saw Gardiner smoothly disclaiming all knowledge of the warrant in question, once the deed had been safely executed.

'*Bridges exceeded his authority and anticipated your order . . . oh, yes, madam, I quite agree . . . a gross dereliction of duty . . . an outrage. And I'm afraid I must suggest, for the sake of Your Majesty's good name . . .*'

Bridges cut off his vision, like a man snapping shut the pages of a book; he knew damn well what Gardiner would suggest to the Queen!

His desk was only a step away; he took up his pen and inked it firmly. Let Gardiner find himself another scapegoat.

Disgrace was unpleasant, but it was infinitely preferable to the hangman's noose at Tyburn. He wrote at once to the Bishop, regretting his inability to act on so great a matter without the direct authority of the Queen.

'. . . It is not only difficult, but well nigh impossible to foresee what the English may do, whose natural character is inconsistent, faithless and treasonable; a character they have always exhibited and which the whole course of their actions and of their history has proved to be just.'

Simon Renard had written his general curse against the perfidy of the English several months earlier and by April he had very little cause to change his opinion. Wyatt had gone to his death at last, exonerating Elizabeth from all part in his rebellion, and the people had danced in the streets in spite of all the efforts to suppress the information. The entire city was racked once more with religious agitators, opposition to the Spanish match and fierce popular support of the imprisoned princess. Renard wrote home glumly that the whole Council was split from top to bottom, with quarrels and ill-will becoming so public that several councillors, out of spite, no longer attended the meetings. The Queen was powerless to control the divisions.

'She spends her days shouting at the Council but with no results.'

No results, stalemate, impotent futility—they were crumbling bricks upon which Mary seemed to have built her entire life. She had martyred herself for her mother's sake during her father's reign and martyred herself for her faith during her brother's, with nothing to show for it. 'Nothing' was the keynote of her whole existence; even her marriage hung in meaningless limbo. Legally she was now Philip's wife, but Renard still insisted that the Prince of Spain could not set foot in England while London remained in such turmoil. And his advice was constant: remove Elizabeth!

But it was no longer so simple. Elizabeth's image had taken root in the popular imagination with wart-like tenacity; to execute her now would be to kill all hope of reconciling England to Philip. Gardiner's attempt Mary had allowed to pass unpunished, and the half-heartedness of her rebuke had only emphasized her bitter disappointment at the failure.

Remove Elizabeth, said Renard—if not from the world then certainly from the capital. And so a new prison and a new jailer were chosen—the place Woodstock Palace, a broken-down hunting lodge barely fit for human habitation, the guardian Sir Henry Bedingfield. The very name alone would be sufficient to strike fear into her sister's heart, for Bedingfield's father had had custody of Katherine of Aragon at Kimbolton Castle, presiding over her dispirited and neglected death within those walls. A fitting choice, thought Mary. Elizabeth's notorious charm would make no inroads on Sir Henry's loyalty. He was a stickler for rules and regulations; wooden, humourless, incorruptible—and *old*, too old to care for natural curls and a pretty smile. Bedingfield was safe from her wiles.

Mary sat alone in her bedchamber, staring darkly into the flickering red fire. She knew what Renard expected of her now, once Elizabeth was quietly out of the public gaze. She knew too that it would be easy to arrange. There were poisons that killed slowly, evincing the symptoms of recognized illnesses. If Elizabeth were to die quietly, privately, at Woodstock, after a decent interval of time, who could point a finger at the Queen who had already saved her from execution, against the advice of her own chief ministers?

Bedingfield was loyal—a devoted Catholic. She had only to give the word and it would be done. It would be done; and how many problems it would solve. The Protestant opposition, bereft of its figurehead, would fall into disarray. The next claimant to the throne was Mary Stuart and the malcontents of England were unlikely to champion a French Catholic against their reigning monarch. Remove Elizabeth and the seething unrest would wither away into sullen resignation to the status quo. And there were times—dark soul-searching nights like this—when Mary knew she was capable of giving that order.

Kill her! whispered a cold serpent of fear in Mary's head. Kill her before Philip sets eyes upon her! She is possessed—I know it is so. How else could she seduce good men from their allegiance—men like Sussex and Arundel who were her sworn enemies? She will take Philip from me, as her mother stole my father. So kill her, kill her soon, before she has the chance. It will be no sin to do it, it will not be murder but—exorcism. I shall set her soul free and when we meet again in eternal life, she will thank me for it—my little sister—the child I once loved . . .

She got up stiffly and went to kneel at her prie-dieu, praying for guidance until the velvet cushion was wet with her tears. Was it God's will that she should kill her father's child—or was it her own, born of a jealousy that placed her on the same level as the woman she hated?

'*Murder is always murder,*' said Katherine of Aragon's voice, pure and true above the whispering darkness in her mind. And it was so, she knew it was. Murder could not be dressed up in a cloak of respectability, and motives could not be hidden from God who would one day judge her, as she was already judging herself. She could not imperil her immortal soul by sinking to murder.

A gleam of light stole through the casement and played upon the benevo-
lent stone smile of the Virgin. It was morning and Mary had not slept again,
but the shadow on her soul had lifted a little. There *was* an alternative.
Marriage would remove Elizabeth from England almost as effectively as
death. The Duke of Savoy had sued for her hand more than once and as a
Spanish vassal would control her more surely than any jailer.

It was the best solution, the only solution.

Mary left the prie-dieu for her desk and there wrote out the order that
would release her sister from the Tower.

When Sir Henry Bedingfield with a hundred men at arms, all dressed in blue,
approached the Tower and surrounded the Princess's apartments, Elizabeth,
who had been informed of nothing, jumped to the very reasonable assumption that they had arrived to escort her to execution.

'But they'll have to wait,' she muttered savagely. 'Oh yes, I'll make them
wait until they send me the sword of a French executioner! Where is the
Lord Lieutenant of the Tower? Say I demand to see him at once.'

He found her waiting for him in the window-seat, clasping her hands
firmly in her lap so that he should not have the pleasure of watching them
tremble.

'Has the Lady Jane's scaffold been removed?' she asked bluntly.

'Yes, madam. Why do you ask?'

She laughed shortly and pointed to the window.

'Do you tell me all those armed men are not for me after all?'

'For you certainly, madam, but there's no cause for alarm I assure you. You
are to leave the Tower.'

'Leave!' She stared at him with open disbelief. 'Never tell me I am to be
set at liberty!'

'No, madam.' He shifted his weight to the other foot, a little uncomfortable to see the colour flood into her pinched face. 'My orders are to consign
you to the charge of Sir Henry Bedingfield.'

'And what are *his* orders, do you know?' her voice was sharp with sudden
anxiety; she was beginning to sense the possibility of even greater danger.

'You are to be conveyed to Woodstock, madam.'

She nodded absently, as though his words had just confirmed her private
suspicion.

'So—' she whispered, 'it is to be murder after all.'

The Lord Lieutenant stiffened indignantly.

'Madam, Sir Henry is an honest and courageous gentleman who will do
you no harm. He is a true knight.'

'Yes. My sister's!' She stood up suddenly and fixed him with a piercing glance. 'Can you deny that if murder were secretly committed to his charge his conscience would be too dainty to execute it?'

Beneath her steely gaze Bridges lowered his own eyes to the floor.

'Madam—as to that—'

'You cannot say, of course, how could you?'

He looked up and found she was smiling.

'May my next jailer be as courteous as you, sir. I thank you for your gentle care of me.'

She knew about the death warrant, he was suddenly certain of that as he bent clumsily over her hand. And as he went out of her room he found himself hoping with curious intensity that she was mistaken over Bedingfield's instructions.

Sir Henry Bedingfield, that grey-bearded incorruptible, escorted his prisoner to the waiting barge in unencouraging silence. He had an unbending air which sent her heart plummeting; a cold, correct formality which offered her little hope of winning him for a friend.

As the barge pulled away from the landing steps, she looked back at the Tower with a sudden pang of real regret. She was leaving Robin Dudley alone in his prison cell and the odds were high that she would never see him again. In the short time that remained before her departure, there had been no way of sending a message; the sense of loss was unexpectedly strong and she felt strangely depressed. There would be very little to look forward to at Woodstock, she saw the promise of that in Bedingfield's stony face.

As the barge glided steadily towards Richmond Palace, all the city bells began to peal madly and the merchants of the Hanseatic League fired a royal salute for her from the riverside factories of the Steelyard. From the corner of her eye she saw Bedingfield half rise from his seat in anger. His grim fury would be but a pale reflection of the Queen's when news of this outrage was carried to her.

What need have I for enemies, she thought bitterly, my friends will hang me yet . . .

When they landed at Richmond, where they were to spend the first night, she had no thought of being received by her sister, whom she understood to be at Whitehall, and did not even trouble to ask it. So she was taken by surprise later that evening when Bedingfield arrived to conduct her to the Queen's private chamber.

Mary was alone, hunched in a high-backed chair beside a blazing fire, and Bedingfield withdrew at her gesture. Elizabeth glanced after him with regret.

She did not feel safe with Mary and she would have preferred the security of a witness, however hostile.

'Come here.'

She came, like an errant child, and as she sank into a deep curtsey before the chair she had time to be shocked at her sister's face, so shrivelled and sallow in the yellow candlelight. She reached out to take the hand which lay on the tapestried arm, but Mary snatched it away, as though her touch might be leprous.

Elizabeth moistened her dry lips.

'No—don't speak,' said the Queen curtly. 'I have not brought you here to listen to your lying protestations of innocence. No words of yours will move me again.' She made an irritable gesture. 'Stand up, I will not be mocked by your feigned humility.'

Elizabeth rose slowly to her feet. Her throat was parched and she was trembling like a bird in the clutch of a cat. She could not believe this bitter woman, half demented with hatred, was truly her sister. All through her turbulent childhood she had received nothing but unstinting kindness from this selfless, dutiful lady. A dozen memories of Mary's generosity distracted her mind when it should be struggling to think of words safe to utter to her most deadly enemy. Yards of yellow satin to make a gown—the curious pomander ball set with its own clock—she wore it now on a chain about her narrow waist in the hope that the sight of it might please her sister. She had always taken Mary's generosity for granted, the kindness of a dull, unbending old maid, reliable as a rock. How could Mary, who had always been so unfailingly good to her . . . ? Her question stopped abruptly. Mary had been good to Jane too, had certainly liked her better; and Jane was dead.

Mary was staring hard at the pomander ball, knowing full well why her sister had worn it and not liking her any better for the calculating instinct it revealed. She had come to the point where she could no longer bear Elizabeth in the same room without being stricken with a sickening desire to inflict some physical assault upon that smooth elegance, so terribly reminiscent of Anne's.

'I hear you were royally entertained on your journey from the Tower,' she remarked.

'I beseech Your Majesty to remember that I was in no way responsible for the merchants' gesture.'

'Ah, no—you are never responsible for anything, are you, sister? A helpless victim of malign fate!'

Elizabeth ignored the direct invitation to a quarrel.

'Your Majesty sent for me,' she prompted nervously.

'I did,' snapped Mary. 'Merely to remind you that you have exchanged one prison for another. And to promise you that you will find the guardianship of Sir Henry Bedingfield more irksome than the closest Tower surveillance. You will discover he has little time for women—do you understand me, madam? There is no way that even *you* will find to undermine his guard.'

Elizabeth was silent.

'You are to be shut away from all you hold dear,' continued the Queen coldly, 'shut away indefinitely from laughter and music—and men. Ah, yes—that last touches you, does it not, sister? You need men as a flower needs the sun. Without their attentions you wilt and wither. Your mother was just the same—the *Concubine* they called her.'

Elizabeth stirred uneasily. 'Madam—'

'You never speak of your mother do you?' mused Mary with narrowed eyes. 'Even as a child, you never asked awkward questions. I always thought it odd —unnatural even—it was as though you already knew all the answers.'

'Madam, *please*—'

'Do I make you uncomfortable? It is in my power to make you more than that, Elizabeth. It is also in my power to set you free if I choose. Shall I so choose, sister? Shall I give you the one key that will unlock your prison door?'

Elizabeth's head jerked upwards and Mary smiled faintly and sat back in her chair.

'Hope springs eternal, is that not so, sister? There are terms, of course, to that freedom.'

'Name them, madam.' Elizabeth was cautious.

'The Duke of Savoy has renewed his suit for your hand in marriage. Take him, Elizabeth. Swear to leave my kingdom in exile and you shall have your full liberty.'

Elizabeth stared down into her sister's eyes and said with soft vehemence, 'Madam, I would rather die first.'

'That too can be arranged,' the Queen shouted suddenly. 'Never be in doubt of it.'

'I have never doubted it,' said Elizabeth wearily. 'I only wonder why Your Grace does not give the word and free me from this cruel suspense.'

That touched on a very sore point and Mary's face contorted with rage. She started out of her chair and Elizabeth instinctively shrank back.

'You think I'm *afraid* to do it, don't you?— Afraid of the people who chant your name in the streets. You think to rule here one day—but I swear before God that you will never succeed me. How could you—heretic, hypocrite, traitor and bastard that you are? *Bastard*—but not my father's. Oh, no! Your mother was an infamous whore and you are the living image of her lute player, Mark Smeaton, who died for his adultery with her.' Hysteria was welling up in Mary. She clutched her crucifix as though it alone stood between her and the Devil. 'So, who are you—Smeaton's brat—to question my command? You'll marry Savoy and count yourself fortunate that the man is still willing to take you. God knows why he should be, after all he must have heard—perhaps his taste runs to whores.'

'Or corpses,' suggested Elizabeth, and stood aghast at her insane remark.

Without warning, the Queen stepped forward and struck Elizabeth full in the face with a violence that rocked her to the floor. There was ecstasy in Mary's panting frenzy as she stood over her sister—the sudden achievement of a long-delayed satisfaction.

'Do you *dare* to mock me to my face, you—you low-born strumpet? Oh, yes—bring tears to your pretty eyes, you were always very good at that as a child. Do you think I don't remember all the times you deceived me? But it's too late now to try that trick on me again, too late, do you hear? I shall bear a son to the Prince of Spain and the moment my child is born I will see that you are shut away for the rest of your miserable life! You tell me you would rather die than marry—go now and lie in your chosen grave.'

Somehow she got out of the Queen's room and back to her own where her terrified servants flocked round her, aghast at her colour.

'Madam, are you ill?'

Her gentleman usher, Cornwallis, was clinging to her hand and trying to help her to a chair. She started to answer him, then stopped as the door flew open and Bedingfield marched into the room.

'Out! Out all of you. It is Her Majesty's command that Her Grace should be left quite alone this night.'

Alone!

They stared at him, their eyes wide with fear, for this could mean only one thing and Elizabeth, too, now appeared to think it.

'Pray for me,' she sobbed suddenly, as Cornwallis bent over her, 'for tonight I think I am to die.'

Cornwallis blazed round upon Bedingfield.

'If the Princess Elizabeth is in danger of death, sir, I and my companions wish to die with her.'

'God forbid,' said Bedingfield with cool irony, 'that any such wickedness should be intended.'

He indicated the door once more and one by one, weeping and kissing her hand, they bowed and curtsied and trailed from the room until she was alone, facing her jailer.

'Goodnight, madam.' He bowed curtly and went out, locking the door behind him.

Silence weighed in upon her and she lay on the bed too exhausted to undress. She was to be shut up for the rest of her life because she refused to be shipped away from all hope of the Succession, because she refused to give up her dream. But that dream was all that gave meaning to her life and without it she might as well be dead. Suddenly she no longer cared whether a dagger came to her in the still darkness behind the curtains; for why should she fear the end of this wretched existence?

Neither hope nor terror remained to disturb her mind. She curled her arms around the lumpy pillow and fell dead asleep.

Next morning, strange women were sent to attend her, Catholic ladies from the Queen's household who performed their duties in taciturn silence. Breakfast was set before her, but she pushed it away without a second glance and then looked up in surprise to find the girl who had served her still hovering at her side uncertainly.

'It will be a long journey—will Your Grace not take just a little of the meat?'

Elizabeth shook her head slowly and glanced around the room; the matrons had withdrawn and for the moment they were alone.

'What is your name?' she asked guardedly.

'Sands, madam.' The girl dropped a pert curtsey and returned her smile cheerfully. 'Elizabeth Sands.'

'Elizabeth?' The Princess laughed. 'Not a very fortunate name. I'm afraid it will bring you little favour at this court.'

'I have been appointed to serve Your Grace,' said the girl steadily. 'The only favour I shall seek now is from your hands alone. If there is anything—anything at all—that I can do to ease Your Grace's lot, you have only to ask—'

Behind them the door opened to admit Sir Henry; Elizabeth Sands curtsied formally and withdrew, leaving her new mistress curiously elated. Bedingfield watched suspiciously as she left the room. He did not care for Mistress Sands—she had a stubborn look and a frivolous manner which irritated him. When he looked at her side by side with his prisoner, he had the shrewd suspicion that it was more than a name they shared. Well—he would watch the girl. And at the first sign of active partisanship he would send her packing.

Aloud he said gruffly, 'The litter is waiting in the courtyard, madam. We leave at once.'

Elizabeth was vaguely amused by the litter that awaited her. It was a shabby, broken-down vehicle which had plainly seen better days, eminently suitable for the worst of travel-sick children; she wondered idly whether the Queen's litter had been refurbished yet. As the entourage rolled out of the courtyard, she realized she was in for a very uncomfortable ride. There was a broken mechanism on the litter which caused a constant jolting. Pure coincidence? Somehow she did not think so as the miles stretched behind her and her head began to reel.

But the journey had compensations. Word of her coming had spread in spite of all Bedingfield's efforts at secrecy, and the people along their way flocked out of their houses treasonably to cheer their imprisoned princess and shower her with flowers and cakes, until the floor of the old litter overflowed with them and she cried out, laughing, for them to stop.

But they did not stop. An almost magical transformation was turning a journey of disgrace into a royal progress of triumph and there was nothing Sir Henry could do to stop it. In vain he ordered them back in the Queen's name and heard their fearless hoots of derision. The boys of Eton College flocked around her, cheering and waving their caps in the air. At Aston they rang the church bells for her and Bedingfield had the two culprits jailed for it; but he could not imprison the inhabitants of every village and hamlet through which they passed and his futility mocked him.

'God save the Princess Elizabeth!' The cry reverberated through Oxfordshire.

Inconstant, faithless and treasonable . . . given so much to change and infidelity, the people left their hovels and their poverty to join the girl who already reigned in their hearts, to tell her that in this dark moment of her life she was not alone and friendless. She looked out on the cheering, loving crowd and saw her life before her, the life that their love alone had preserved. England was like a storm-tossed ship, rolling helplessly on the tides of fear and unrest, a ship in desperate need of an anchor. She would be that anchor, strong enough to hold this perilously bobbing vessel from the rocks.

She owed her life to England's love and she saw that in return she must give that life. It was the only way to repay the debt she owed, perhaps had always owed from the moment of her birth. She would justify her birth and her existence that had cost so many lives, her own mother's among them. Bloodshed and waste, bitter controversy and religious war had attended her entry to this world. But she could atone for it by becoming the greatest monarch in the history of her country. She could atone for it all when she was Queen—and she *would* be Queen. Suddenly, for the first time, she was sure of it. She had been right to hold her ground, to refuse Savoy, to spurn hope of sanctuary and safety.

The people pressed about her litter in hope and she swore in that moment never to betray their trust. Now when she was only twenty, when her coronation might be ten, even twenty, years ahead, when the world had narrowed to the short distance between one prison and another, she could swear to do it. Now, surrounded by guards, without benefit of an abbey and choirs and candles, without the holy oil of the annointing and the high solemn voices— now in the midst of a hot, loving crowd she took the final vow of service.

All semblance of a royal progress ended at their destination.

The old stone palace of Woodstock stood on a small slope, surrounded on all sides by enormous trees. Even from a distance Elizabeth could see the broken windows and the crumbling stonework. The privy gardens were choked and overgrown with weeds and the countryside littered with uprooted trees. Winter was evidently unkind in this area.

Bruised and weary from the constant jolting of the broken litter, Elizabeth stood on the uncut grass and stared with horrified disbelief at the dilapidated building. It had not been in use as a royal residence for many years and it was not difficult to see why.

Bedingfield escorted her to the primitive little gatehouse, where he told her four rooms had been prepared for her use.

'Prepared?' Elizabeth blew on the chimney-piece and a thick cloud of dust flew up into his heavy face.

'I can't stay here—the damp is running down the walls.'

He glanced in a cursory fashion at the mildewed tapestries and the paltry furniture. A fierce draught blew in through a broken window and the ancient rushes were alive with cockroaches.

'I shall see what can be done about the window, madam, but I have no orders to lodge Your Grace elsewhere in the meantime.'

She bit her lip and turned away. Mary had been right—she had been a great deal better off in the Tower! She sat down wearily on the rickety window-seat and stared out at the bleak countryside through the hole in the dirty green glass. Dimly she became aware of Bedingfield's angry voice in the next chamber.

'How can I be expected to keep her close confined if only three doors out of the four can be locked? You—fetch me a locksmith from the village—and you, arrange the rota for her guard. I want sixty soldiers around the house by day and forty at night. I want—' He broke off abruptly as he suddenly saw her standing in the doorway. 'Your Grace desires something? I shall send your ladies to attend you.'

He treated her as though she were a high-born leper, avoiding her company and the touch of her hand on his. Her eyes narrowed as he bowed curtly and withdrew from the room; she had heard the tales about him—taciturn, intractable, immune to all female charm.

So he thought he could safely keep his distance, did he?

We'll see about that, jailer! she thought. A month from now will see you eating out of my hand like a tame wolfhound. You'll go the way of all the rest, my friend. I swear it!

CHAPTER 2

Philip of Spain sat with stiff dignity beneath the canopy of estate and his bride sat beside him. She was smiling and holding his cold hand and chattering nervously like a young girl, though she was by no means a girl, and he could see, with a flicker of mild distaste, that it was some considerable time since she had been one—rather longer than he had been led to believe by Renard and his father.

Grey spectacles of distaste had coloured Philip's view of England since the moment he landed in a summer downpour. Had he been a man to show his feelings, he would be kicking his personal attendants in his private apartments, strangling Renard, or maybe losing his frustration in the soft curves of a whore's body, on this, his last night of freedom. Instead he sat here dutifully performing in this public peep-show, following the Emperor's orders to the letter, as always. No one could say he hadn't done his best—he always did his best. He had been impeccably charming to these crude barbarians; he had drunk their foul beer, kissed the Queen on her dry lips and tried not to notice that none of her simpering women were on the right side of thirty. But all the time he was bored and wretched and a little voice at the back of his mind whined persistently: What have I done to deserve this?

The same thought found an echo in Mary's mind, but on a note of ecstasy rather than despair. She could not tear her eyes away from him, this handsome symbol of her unity with Spain and the Catholic Church, her husband

—her *lover!* She kept him endlessly at her side, while they conversed in broken foreign tongues, but at last, with her rigid sense of etiquette, she knew she could delay the moment of parting no longer. One more night alone in the big state bed and then tomorrow—oh, tomorrow!—she would be a woman at last.

'What shall I say?' His hand was on her arm, his bland face vaguely anxious; he had a horror of losing his dignity in public, of being made to look foolish and inadequate. 'What shall I say to your court, madam, as I take my leave—the correct form of address?'

His French was surprisingly poor, it took her a moment to follow his meaning. And then she smiled gently.

'Goodnight, my lords and ladies,' she said slowly, in English.

He practised the phrase with grave persistence and Mary listened indulgently. They had told her he was serious and moody, that he never smiled, but he had smiled upon her tonight—smiled upon everyone. She never noticed how cool and expressionless the china-blue eyes remained. She thought only how truly Renard had spoken; they had indeed sent her perfection itself!

Philip bowed courteously to the nobles of England and mumbled the objectionable line; and at long last his duties for that day were behind him.

A lifetime of unremitting duty lay behind Philip, who had spent his twenty-seven years mastering the rigid servitude of a Spanish prince. In all of Europe there was no court which equalled the cold formality of Spain and Philip had learned to subordinate his own personal desires beneath the needs of the state. This would be his second marriage. The fruit of the first remained behind in Spain—Don Carlos, a deformed, half-witted creature of whom Philip was secretly bitterly ashamed. No one spoke openly of Carlos's disabilities because nobody dared to; but Philip knew the Emperor looked now for a sane heir, rather than a gibbering lunatic. He was stuck in this miserable, rain-sodden land until he produced the goods and this time the raw materials were less than promising. A withered old maid in place of the lusty little cousin he had first married—he was frankly less than hopeful. He lay alone in his bed the night before his wedding, stiff as a sacrificial offering on an altar, and wondered why God, whom he had always served so faithfully, should have chosen to lay this extra burden upon his shoulders.

For if he *had* to marry one of Henry Tudor's misbegotten daughters, surely it was only human to wish that it might have been the younger one.

Winter crept on Woodstock, making the tumbledown palace bleaker and more uncomfortable than ever. Sir Henry Bedingfield felt old and cold.

Seven months of his prisoner's company had changed him almost beyond recognition, into a weary elderly man pressingly aware of his years.

He had come to this post in full command of his faculties, a wooden, uncompromising, vigorous knight who knew his orders and his own mind. Accordingly, he had been quick to dismiss Elizabeth Sands, an outspoken girl overready to complain on her mistress's behalf. He had believed that by exerting his authority so early and in so cavalier a fashion, he would totally demoralize his prisoner. With the loss of her friend, she was quite alone in a house full of unfriendly women and he ought, from that time on, to have had little further trouble with her.

But the incident merely served to mark the beginning of his problems. Nothing cowed her. Nothing discouraged her endless, outrageous demands for one indulgence after another. She had even asked for an English Bible, in spite of the Heresy Bill which was presently in Parliament. He couldn't understand her. She was like an irritating moth flitting round him in a dark room and there was no way he could avoid the touch of her wings against his face. Slowly he was being ground down, reduced to a state of dithering mental anarchy which found him 'marvellously perplexed whether to grant her desires or say her nay.'

There were times when she flatly refused to speak to him. She would withdraw to her room in a huff and against his will he would find himself coaxing her out again, wooing her to walk in the gardens. Day after day he scurried between her rooms and his own like a hunted lackey. Her pitiful tears wrung his hard heart; her continual indispositions caused him countless hours of anxiety; her outbursts of temper unnerved him. And her smile—he had learnt to fear her smile above all else; it manipulated him mercilessly. He was like a puppet dancing jerkily on the strings of her emotions. She even persuaded him to act as her secretary and write her long list of complaints to the Council in his own hand. Afterwards, he was in such a flat panic at what he had done that he was forced to send a desperate covering note with the document excusing, 'this my evil writing, trusting Her Highness will forgive my rudeness, and you, my lords, also.'

What had happened to him? He did not know. He only knew that he was behaving like a fool and that all his letters to the Council marked him as a very silly old man, so interminable and confused were they.

He resorted frequently to his written commission from the Queen, by now much thumbed and rather crumpled, seeking desperately for some indication of where he had gone wrong.

'Item: he shall, at convenient times, suffer our said sister for her recreation, to walk abroad and take the air in the garden . . . as he himself shall be present in her company.'

Behind this apparently innocuous instruction lay long hours of panting up and down the winding gardens locking and unlocking endless gates behind the teasingly restless figure of 'our said sister'.

'Item: he shall generally have good regard not only to the Princess, but shall also do his best to cause the country thereabouts to continue in good and quiet order.'

But down in the village the Bull inn was swarming with her undesirable friends, of which the most suspicious was her Steward, Thomas Parry, who complained loudly of the fare provided for his mistress and exhibited 'great doubts' over the strain on her funds.

Bedingfield was so terrified of what might be hatching down at the Bull, that he summoned three of his brothers from their comfortable estates and begged them to keep watch for treason.

But inside the house, he was mesmerized by the endless circles Elizabeth ran around him. At every opportunity he besieged the Council, with many apologies, to grant 'the importunate desires of this great lady', and he wrote 'this great lady' without realizing how much it betrayed his capitulation to hostile outsiders. He was harassed from morning to evening by an endless series of small crises, while his charge mimicked his orders to his face and called him 'jailer', and uttered all manner of reproaches 'too long to write'.

But the day she called him jailer, he went down on his knees and begged her not to give him that harsh name.

'I am only an officer appointed to serve you and guard you from danger on the Queen's instructions.'

'God bless the Queen,' observed her sister sharply, 'and from such good officers, dear Lord deliver me!'

She looked down on his bowed head and knew a moment of intense satisfaction. This old stallion had had more kick in him than most—but she had broken him in the end and could now trot him off to that menagerie which still housed Sussex and Arundel, elderly pets of whom she was mildly fond.

And they say you can't teach an old dog new tricks!

She turned away hastily lest he see the smile which hovered at her lips.

Woodstock held more than one prisoner . . .

Philip was utterly bemused by the muddled accounts which came in a steady stream from Woodstock.

'My dear,' he ventured one evening, looking up at his wife in irritation, 'was this old dotard the best custodian you could find?'

'He wasn't a dotard when I appointed him.' Mary flung her embroidery across the room. 'Oh, don't you see, have I not said it often enough?—it's *her!* She corrupts all men with her evil wiles. If you had met her you would understand what I mean.'

'But I have not met her,' said Philip pointedly.

'No!—nor will you!' Mary leapt from her chair. 'Oh I will hear no more of her, no more, do you understand? As for those disguised and colourable letters of hers—I swear I shall not receive another one. She shall be forbidden to write—absolutely forbidden.'

He shrank from the scene he had provoked and turned away to his letters; he hated these hysterical outbursts, so undignified, so ugly, so frequent. In Spain, no one ever raised their voice—even orders for torture and execution were given with placid courtesy. It seemed to him that the English, as a race, had no self-control and that everyone from the Queen down to the rabble mob delighted in making an exhibition of their emotions.

He was ill at ease in this marriage; and in this adopted country of his, where he seemed like a fish out of water. Every night as he climbed reluctantly into the state bed and regarded the Queen's withered little body, eager enough—oh God, almost indecently eager!—but scarcely inviting, he reflected that some duties were decidedly more distasteful to perform than others. It was then that his thoughts turned unwillingly to the sister-in-law of whom he had heard so many odd tales. He was assured on every side that she was a bad lot, and the more firmly he was assured, the more perversely his unhealthy interest grew.

Loneliness was growing on him steadily, and loneliness was an emotion to which Philip was a complete stranger. Since childhood, he had possessed those recluse-like qualities which would have placed him happily in a silent Order, so this restless, unaccountably strong desire to meet Elizabeth was quite beyond his understanding. Why should he feel such vulgar curiosity about an ill-bred courtesan, whose very existence placed him at risk in this realm? Barring the little Queen of Scots, whip-hand of his French enemies, Philip honestly considered Elizabeth to be the most dangerous person in Europe. Oh yes, he wished to get the measure of that tricky young lady—but was that the *only* reason he was quietly manoeuvring to get her back at court?

He put his pen down and leaned his chin moodily on his hands. He had precious little to look forward to in this land, beyond that meeting. Eighty of his disillusioned grandees and retainers had already left for home, and those who remained complained pitifully that, 'We are miserable here, much worse than in Castile . . . the English cannot bear the sight of a Spaniard, they would rather see the Devil.' There were open brawls on the streets between the two races and in every shop and market-place the Spaniards were mercilessly fleeced. Even the religious settlement, effected by Mary's cousin, Cardinal Pole, showed little sign of bringing peace and reconciliation. The Papal Legate had been escorted to England by no less a person than that 'very honest man', Sir William Cecil, and the country was now officially Catholic. Yet no one would part with church lands plundered during Henry's break with Rome, and Protestant opposition remained vociferous in the streets.

Compromise had failed and the rigours of persecution were slowly taking its place. Gardiner's Heresy Bill had legalized the examination and punishment of all heretics who publicly persisted in practising their creed and in February the first martyrs had gone to the stake. The former Archbishop of Canterbury, Cranmer, had been forced to watch while Bishops Latimer and Ridley burned, and knew his turn would come.

The burnings had not increased Philip's popularity. Indeed, if Mary should die while he was still in England he would be fortunate to escape with his life. The rabble howled against him and circulated crude lampoons which mocked his dignity and his manhood. Even Mary no longer spoke hopefully about his coronation. The heir to half the world had been reduced to the status of a stud horse, but at least there his selfless devotion to duty had achieved its purpose.

The Queen—God be thanked!—was with child at last.

They told this to Elizabeth at Woodstock and in the next breath asked her the fatal question.

Did she believe that the bread and wine at Communion was transformed into the actual body and blood of Christ?

Her fingers tightened on the rosary beads which hung from her waist. Her life depended on her answer. If she denied belief in the Sacrament she would burn as a heretic; if she publicly avowed belief she would lose her Protestant support and be cut adrift in the future like a rudderless ship.

It was a moment of terror and supreme loneliness, that showed her the gulf between herself and the rest of the world. For to her this issue was a dispute over trifles which threatened to tear the Christian world apart. She saw no purpose in dying for any creed—did that make her wicked? Certainly it made her different; she knew, as she gazed into the bigoted faces around her, that her mind stretched out beyond the narrow confines of this century towards a more enlightened age of tolerance.

When I am Queen I swear I will make no windows into any man's soul . . .

But now she had to speak and mock the infallibility of this test of faith. And suddenly, the words revolving in her head resolved themselves into a neat little riddle.

> 'Christ was the Word that spoke it,
> He took the bread and broke it.
> And what His Word did make it,
> That I believe . . . and take it.'

Slowly she raised her eyes in a coolly defiant gaze that dared them to probe any further. And one by one they lowered their eyes to the ground. Not a man of them took up her pointed challenge, for the slight emphasis on 'take it' had been unmistakable and they were all well acquainted with her dutiful attendances at Mass. Too clever by half was the general opinion, but they had no knife long enough to reach her; and at length they had to let her go.

Bedingfield was waiting to escort her back up the narrow staircase to her room, and once there she went across to the window where the light of a bleak day was rapidly failing. Somewhere in the distance she could hear a milkmaid singing as she crossed the meadow to the barn with two pails swinging from a yoke across her shoulders.

'Your Grace is weary,' ventured Bedingfield with cautious sympathy.

'Weary of this miserable existence,' Elizabeth muttered, 'I wish I were that milkmaid out there.'

'Madam.' He laid his heavy hand on her arm. 'You must not despair. The Queen is with child and will surely soften towards you in her great joy. We must all rejoice in the news and pray for a son.'

Elizabeth looked out into the dusk through blurred eyes and wondered if she would ever set foot again outside her prison door.

'Yes,' she said dully. 'We must all rejoice and pray for a son.'

Pray—oh, God forgive me—that it is still-born!

Philip had been sitting for over an hour at his meticulously tidy desk, staring at the letter he had received from Renard, recently recalled to Spain. It was full of advice on what to do with Elizabeth and, frankly, what to do with Elizabeth was rapidly becoming a very urgent question.

Renard had been blunt, as was his wont.

'Should the Queen's pregnancy prove a mistake the heretics will place their hopes in Elizabeth, and here you are in difficulty whatever is done, for if Elizabeth is set aside the crown will go to the Queen of Scots.'

Philip frowned. That was Elizabeth's trump card, should he choose to set her free and let her play it. In due course, the Queen of Scots would be Queen of France. Add the crown of England to Scotland and France and you altered the entire balance of power in Europe. And Mary Tudor, nearing forty and in poor health, was at a dangerous age for bearing children. If he should lose wife and son at the birth, Elizabeth was all that stood between France and England.

'Before you leave the country you should see the Princess yourself and on your part promise that you will be her friend and assist her where you can find opportunity.'

Philip folded the letter and locked it in his desk. A sound fellow, Renard—he'd always thought so. Well then, there was no choice, was there? He must see the Princess and become her friend—he owed it to himself and to his father. Self-defence, common sense, nothing more, he told himself firmly. And yet that subdued, lecherous dog, kennelled in the cellar of his mind, was sitting up with wagging tail and drooling tongue. He felt extraordinarily pleased with himself as he made his way to his wife's apartments.

'Bring her to court?' echoed Mary, wild-eyed against her pillows.

'She should surely be there to witness the birth.'

'She should be *dead!*'

'My dear, you had the opportunity to take her head and let it slip away.'

'Next time I may not be so foolish.'

He came out of the shadows and looked down on her in alarm.

'Next time?'

Mary stared at him with tired jealousy.

'How careful you are of her safety. Is her power so great it can enslave a man she had not even met?'

'You are distressed,' said Philip coldly. 'You must not excite yourself in this manner—it is bad for the child.'

Mary turned away to hide her tears in the pillow.

'Once you set eyes upon her you will go the way of all the rest. I know it.'

He was vaguely offended by the suggestion.

'You think I cannot handle the young lady? You are mistaken, madam. I am no callow boy to be taken advantage of by a pretty woman. I merely make a political suggestion in the spirit of duty.'

'The same duty that tied you to me?'

Her thin shoulders were shaking with sobs. There was nothing for it but to get on the bed beside her and speak a few soft words of comfort.

'It distresses me that you should doubt my motives,' he said at length in a pained tone. 'Don't you trust me, Mary?'

'Oh, yes.' She buried her ravaged face in his doublet. 'Of course I trust you, my love.'

'Then you will show that trust by obliging me in this matter.'

She clung to him in terror; she had heard the threatening note in his voice. He was bored and homesick, it would take very little to drive him away.

'You will write to Bedingfield soon?' he prompted.

'Yes,' she said hopelessly against his shoulder, 'I will write at once.'

So he had turned the key in the lock and opened the prison door. In spite of his satisfaction he felt a moment of real apprehension.

He was not entirely sure what he was releasing upon the world.

> Much suspected of me
> Nothing proved can be
> Quoth Elizabeth, prisoner

That crude little phrase, etched on her window with a diamond ring, was Elizabeth's defiant farewell to her imprisonment at Woodstock.

On a blustery April day, when early flowers were struggling in the hedgerows, she rode away from the gatehouse with a retinue of servants. It was more than fifteen months since she had been on horseback.

A teasing wind billowed out the ladies' skirts and flung petulant bursts of rain in their faces. Bedingfield would not budge above a clumsy canter, and Elizabeth, feyed by the squallish weather, resisted a crazy impulse to take off across the fields and frighten the life out of him. She had grown curiously fond of him, but oh, what a bore he was with his endless authority.

Christ, if I am ever Queen no man in this world will ever say 'must' to me again . . .

To the left of the muddy road lay a large house and along the track a well-dressed young man was running to meet them.

Elizabeth thought rapidly. The wind had already blown the sable hood down her back. When Bedingfield's attention was diverted, she lifted her hand to her head and removed the central pin which held her heavy hair in place.

The next gust of wind brought a mass of loose curls tumbling wildly about her face. She cursed loudly and reined to a halt; when Bedingfield glanced round in alarm she gave him a helpless shrug and in that moment the young man drew abreast of her horse.

'Your Grace! We had word you would pass this way today. May I offer you the shelter of my own poor house in this abominable weather?'

She gave him that smile and held her hands out to be lifted from the saddle.

'Sir,' she said gaily, 'if you were to offer me the shelter of a pig-sty I would be grateful.'

'Madam! I can't possibly allow this!' Bedingfield had leaned over to take her arm aggressively. Anxious, blustering, he was quite unable to deal with the slightest change in plans and also most uncomfortably aware that she was not to be trusted with any young man of unknown loyalty.

She rounded on him furiously.

'Why, in God's name?'

'Madam—my instructions—'

'I *know* your instructions. I have them by heart if you remember, but I don't recall any item that says I shall sit under a hedge to do up my hair simply because you refuse to countenance a simple act of chivalry.'

'I repeat, madam—I cannot permit you to enter this gentleman's house.'

She stared at him stonily. 'You should be ashamed to call yourself a knight!'

She jumped down from her horse without assistance and swept across the road to sit down under the hedge in question. Two of her women hurried over to her and began to do battle with her hair. Bedingfield was left holding her horse's bridle and staring at the young man in embarrassed silence.

Presently she came back, with the sable hood jammed on her head and her green riding habit covered with mud.

'Well,' she demanded coldly, 'are you satisfied now?'

Clumsily he lifted her into the saddle and groped for her gloved hand.

'Your Grace knows I bear you no ill will. To receive discharge from this service without offence to the Queen would be the joyfullest tidings that ever came to me, as our Lord Almighty knows.'

She laughed outright as she looked down on him.

'Oh yes, I know how dearly you would love to be rid of me, Sir Henry. And, who knows, it may be sooner than you think, if I've misread the reason for this summons, after all.'

As she slipped her reins out of his quivering hand, she was amused by his horrified glance. Clearly he had not considered the possibility that he might be taking her to her death.

She rather hoped that Mary had not considered it either.

When they arrived at Hampton Court she was hustled in the back way so that none should see her and was packed off at once to the Gatehouse, once more the disgraced prisoner, almost the poor relation. The doors were locked upon her and for more than a fortnight she paced her rooms like a caged lioness. Oh, what a fool she had been to raise her hopes; nothing was changed. She had two heated confrontations with Gardiner and then the dreadful silence closed in again, leaving her to imagine the worst.

She lost track of time and the days began to merge into each other in endless tedium; even Woodstock had been better than this isolated limbo. Outside her window she could hear the laughter of the courtiers who came and went into the palace, but she had no part in their world. It was as though she had ceased to exist.

And then, at ten o'clock on a cold spring evening when she had just begun to go to bed, the door opened to admit Susan Clarencieux, Mary's Mistress of the Robes. Behind her came Bedingfield, grey-faced with fright.

'Madam, you are commanded to wait upon Her Majesty at once.'

Elizabeth stood up. Her women had removed her coif and brushed out her hair which now hung to her waist.

'Now?' she whispered stupidly. 'Now?'

Across the room her eyes met Bedingfield's and saw them mirror her thought.

Queens don't give audiences at ten o'clock at night. I am going to my death and he knows it.

Bedingfield shuffled across the room to take her cloak from the arms of a trembling maid. Wordlessly he wrapped it around her shoulders, fastened the clasp and pulled the hood over her head exactly as though she was a small child.

'Come, Your Grace.' His gruff voice was hoarse as he took her hand and began to guide her forward. In the doorway she glanced back at her terrified attendants and asked them to pray for her, since she could not tell whether she would see any of them again. Bedingfield, she noticed, made no protest to that, but his hand on hers tightened its pressure. She was suddenly very glad of him.

It was pitch black and cold as she followed torch bearers over the gardens to the foot of the staircase which led to the Queen's lodgings. A guard stepped forward and gestured to Sir Henry.

'You are to remain here, sir, with the rest of Her Grace's attendants.'

So it was to be a dagger in the dark, after all! But why bring her all the way to court to do it and how would they explain it to the people?

She glanced at Bedingfield's face and saw there were tears glistening in the eyes of that stern, upright figure. He feared the worst and so did she, and hardship made odd allies. She reached out and squeezed his thick arm, then turned and went alone into the darkness.

Breathlessly she mounted the stairway, spinning round at the sound of footsteps behind her. Susan Clarencieux was mounting the steps in her wake and motioning her through the door ahead, so perhaps after all she was not to be murdered. But it was still a full minute before she found the courage to step over the threshold into Mary's bedchamber.

The Queen was hunched against her pillows and her distended figure was obvious beneath the coverlet. At the far end of the room stood a tapestry screen and Elizabeth, who did not recall it, wondered whether this interview would be heard by Mary's ears alone. Where was Philip after all this time? Why had he not chosen to show himself? She glanced again at the silent screen and wondered.

At the foot of the bed she fell on her knees and let the hood fall back to reveal her loose hair.

'Madam, I am your true and loyal servant whatever reports have said of me.'

Silence. Mary's short-sighted eyes peered down at her, sliding over her white face and away again. She did not offer her hand for the formal kiss and her voice was grim.

'You will not confess your fault, I see. Pray God your tale is true.'

'If not I will look for neither favour nor pardon from Your Majesty's hands.'

That answer though mildly made seemed to anger Mary. As her face creased into a frown and she twisted the bedclothes over the swollen mound of her stomach, Elizabeth found her eyes drawn irresistibly to that visible evidence of her own danger, the unborn child which was the living symbol of her own destruction. Once that child was born her position would be hopeless; she would be lucky even to be offered exile . . .

'So,' said the Queen darkly, 'you have been wrongfully punished then.'

Elizabeth bowed her head hastily.

'I must not say so to Your Majesty.'

'But you will to others!' snapped the deadly little voice from the bed. 'Is that not so, sister?'

It was useless. This interview, like the last, was sliding away from her, and every word she spoke increased the Queen's hostility. She said at last in a voice only just above a whisper, 'I most humbly beseech Your Majesty to have a good opinion of me.'

Oddly enough that childish request seemed to touch Mary in spite of herself. She gestured irritably for the girl to get off her knees and waved her hand as though dismissing the whole sordid business. She seemed suddenly too weary to continue the conversation.

'You may be speaking the truth—God knows!' she muttered and then repeated in Spanish, '*Dios sabe!*'

Elizabeth whirled round instinctively to look at the screen and a moment later a small, sombrely dressed young man stepped out and stopped to look at her. He bowed and walked towards her, his pale eyes fixed on hers. She knew who he was; she also knew that she should curtsey, but she remained defiantly standing. For a moment he stood gazing at her, as though he expected the sheer force of his presence to force her to her knees; their bright, fair heads were exactly level. There was a long, long moment of silence before he realized she would not submit, and then he spoke for the first time.

'You are welcome to court, my sister.' He held out his hand and drew her close to kiss her formally on the lips as befitted the greeting of a sister-in-law.

And when he released her, having prolonged the moment just a second or two longer than was strictly necessary, Mary saw that his eyes were smiling at last.

Across the brilliant green English countryside they galloped ahead of their attendants, hunting, hawking, spending the long spring days in idle companionship. In the light evenings they danced and raised their wine goblets to each other beneath smiling eyes and slowly, inexorably, relentlessly Philip found himself falling in love against his will and against all the promptings both of conscience and common sense.

Years later, he reflected bitterly that it had been inevitable. He had been as vulnerable as a puppy to her charm, miserable, disillusioned, frustrated. And she had set out to catch him like an angler with a fish, until at last there he was, hooked and helpless on the end of her line, labouring under the incredible delusion that their feelings were mutual.

He had never meant it to happen. He had intended to observe her closely for treasonous intent, sound her religious beliefs and finally see her married safely to his vassal, the Duke of Savoy. He had tried to prepare himself and be armed against her wiles. for Renard had warned him darkly that 'she has a spirit full of incantation'.

But no armour of Spanish dignity was proof against her; she cut through his defences like a knife through butter, effortlessly, casually, as though she was not even trying. He might have been any other handsome young man in her company, rather than the omnipotent heir to half the world. When she spoke to him it was as an equal, occasionally, he suspected through her teasing, as a superior. Her speech was littered with lies and insincerities; he tried to cling to his doubts and suspicions of her, but she laughed them away. And no one—man or woman—had ever laughed at Philip before. In all the dark formal years in Spain, years of duty and discipline governed by a rigid code of etiquette, he had never met a woman like Elizabeth. In all the hard cruel decades which followed he never met her like again. A few brief weeks he was held fascinated, like a wild animal dazzled by a bright light, weeks which later seemed to exist in a vacuum and hung in his bitter memory like a locket, which from time to time he would take out and examine with slow disbelief and wonder—did it really happen? Sometimes it seemed to him that he spent the rest of his life in penance for it.

They had told him she was clever; on close acquaintance, he found her brilliant and was intimidated by the formidable list of her accomplishments. He considered it a personal affront that any woman should be fluent in six languages.

'Is there anything you cannot do?' he asked her at length, stung to a jealous awareness of inferiority.

She smiled demurely.

'I can't swim, Your Highness.'

'If you ever learn,' he said softly, 'I shall *kill* you for it.'

His command of English was still uncertain. It was quite possible he had misused the word. But as she stared into his steady eyes she knew he meant exactly what he said and was amused by the knowledge. After that, she went out of her way to flaunt her talents and her charm. And all through that spring, while he deliberately engineered occasions on which he might be alone with her, he was swept off his course like a helpless twig on the restless tide of her energy.

'No, we shall not hunt today,' he said as he followed her to the window one dark morning. 'Can't you see it's raining?'

She looked out of the glass and laughed and said in her faultless Spanish, 'That's not rain—it's only a fine drizzle that will soon lift. In England Your Highness must learn to call such weather fine and be glad of it.'

Must!

He stared at her. It was more than twenty years since anyone of lesser rank had used that word to him. Her audacity amazed him.

'You are so restless,' he complained suddenly. 'You dance and ride and shoot as though you may never be free to do these things again. If you continue to live each day as though it was your last—'

She swung round from the window and smiled at him. 'I shall burn out like a firework before I am thirty, no? But that is no new thought—I hear it from my governess quite regularly.'

Again he was shaken by her daring. To speak so lightly of burning with Gardiner's Heresy Bill now the law of the land—was she mad?

'Your governess is optimistic,' he said severely. 'In my opinion you may be exceedingly fortunate to reach twenty-two.'

'That doesn't give me long, does it, my brother?'

Her eyes slanted a direct challenge that made him take her roughly by the hand and lead her to the virginals. This way she had of playing with her own danger excited his physical desire. And it alarmed him.

'Sit,' he commanded, 'and play for me.'

She made a deep mocking curtsey and seated herself at the instrument. He felt vaguely relieved to see her still at last, for somehow he knew that if she went on talking and laughing and weaving her slender body around the room, he would not be answerable for what he might do to her. When she lost herself in the music she would forget to tease and tantalize.

There was nothing to disturb his ears now except the tinkling notes, nothing to disturb his eyes except those extraordinary fingers, mesmeric as snakes, moving lightly across the keyboard and lulling him gently into a trance-like state of contentment. He sat and watched them until the failing light forced her to stop; then he leaned over and took her hands in his, lifting them alternately to his sensual lips.

'You have beautiful hands,' he mused, turning them over in his grasp and staring at them with an odd intensity, 'such long fingers—almost too perfect to be human.'

She waited patiently. After a moment she frowned.

'Is that all? I rather hoped you would go on to say they matched my face.'

His pale skin turned furiously red.

'Madam,' he muttered, suddenly gauche as a boy, 'your face is beyond compare.'

'So is a vulture's!' She gave him a wicked smile. 'Oh—you are not accustomed to paying compliments, are you, my brother?'

'I am not accustomed to being *asked* for them,' he retorted drily. 'In my country no lady would dream of such brazen talk.'

She laughed and sat back on her stool, watching him.

'But this is not your country,' she said softly, 'and I am not a lady—surely the Queen has told you that.'

He looked away for a moment.

'Certainly she has told me that you are not to be trusted—as indeed has one other.'

'What other? Come, Your Highness, you may safely tell me—was it Renard? What did he say of me?'

'That—' Philip hesitated, 'that you have a spirit full of incantation and are greatly to be feared.'

A cold shiver touched Elizabeth's spine. As an accusation of witchcraft it could hardly be more plain, and superstition ran deep in Philip. Suddenly his preoccupation with her hands took on an ominous meaning.

Too perfect to be human—

Not since the day they took her to the Tower had she been so terrified, and yet she knew instinctively that to show fear before this man would be the worst thing she could possibly do. He would relish it and believe at the same time that it betrayed her guilty conscience.

She leaned forward boldly and took his hand in her warm grasp.

'Is that what you believe of me, Philip?'

'I do not know,' he said slowly, staring at her very hard. 'I know nothing about you even after all these weeks in your company and I think that is how you mean it to be. You hide your true self behind a mask. You are charming, witty, accomplished—'

She pouted.

'You might try beautiful.'

'I might.' Against his will he was moved to smile. 'Oh I concede you are fair of face—but beneath that pretty shell, I fear—'

'Oh dear—a natural savage at heart?'

'Madam, I would not venture to suggest what you were—at heart.' They were very close, close enough to kiss. 'But perhaps one day—I shall find out.'

His pale eyes were locked on hers, urgently trying to suggest what his pride and rigid breeding still forbade him to put into words. She saw with amazement that he was desperate for her to make the first move, so that he could call her whore in his heart and enjoy her without a qualm of conscience. What a prig! What a hypocrite! She wanted to slap his suave face, but if she did that it would be an end of her, for he was not a man who would ever forgive an insult. So it was better to play the modest virgin, to blush and withdraw to a safe distance, while indicating with a subtle glance that he might still pursue his elusive quarry. She dared not risk slighting him with an open rebuff. Too much depended on his friendship and her perilous attempt to hold it without running foul of the Queen's possessive heart. Already there had been whispers of peevish quarrels between Mary and her husband, and Elizabeth suspected that she was the cause. She must step warily, for once the child was born Philip would return to Spain and she would be at Mary's mercy once more, shut away perhaps year after year until she was old and withered. At the end of that month she was abruptly given leave to retire from court—leave which she had not requested—and she knew her suspicions of Mary were well grounded.

A fierce tension hung over the country that spring as England waited for the birth of a new heir. And waited. Mary was many weeks over her time; the doctors said there was a miscalculation in their dates; the doctors said it was quite normal. But the days slipped into weeks and the weeks into months, while Mary lay heavy and moribund on her cushions waiting for labour to begin. The country was explosive with unrest. Philip lived in terror that the pregnancy might indeed prove to be a mistake, that his wife was merely ill with a tumour and had never been with child at all. And if that was so then the most disagreeable of his duties would have to begin all over again, to say nothing of the humiliation which would attend the announcement. He knew the epithet which the English would hurl behind his back.

Another impotent foreigner!

It was August before the Queen finally accepted that there would be no child and Philip, making his father's abdication his excuse to go, prepared to escape from England at the first opportunity. Elizabeth was summoned to Greenwich and in a small panelled room the Prince of Spain stood alone to bid farewell to his sister-in-law.

She sat on a little footstool at his feet, spreading her skirts around her like the petals of a flower; and when he reached for her hand, she raised her eyes slowly to his face with an expression which could only flatter his taunted manhood, a look which promised an exquisite surrender.

'I have things to say to you,' he said quietly, 'things that must not be heard outside this room.'

'You can trust me, Philip, surely you know that by now.'

He shook his head slightly. All he knew was that he had to trust her, because he was too deeply lost in her coils to do otherwise.

'Savoy is very close to Spain,' he began haltingly, 'and the Duke is my vassal. If you marry him he would not be a possessive husband and I would look to see you often at my court.'

She smiled.

'You disappoint me, Philip. I had hoped for something better than a place in your harem.'

His breath caught in his throat. Was she telling him that in the event of Mary's death she would be prepared to give herself to him in marriage?

'Dare I hope—' he began and faltered.

She held out her hands to him and he lifted her to her feet; they stood staring into each other's watchful eyes.

'When I am Queen of England, Philip,' she said softly, 'you will not find me ungrateful for your protection.'

The bargain was now quite plain to him. *Keep me and my inheritance safe from Mary and you shall have your reward!*

His hands moved to her bare shoulders; his mouth was dry with sudden excitement.

'Will you not show me a little of that gratitude before I leave?'

As though on impulse she put her arms around his neck and kissed him deeply. Drowning in her embrace, he pressed her close against his codpiece. Suddenly she pulled away, shaken with what he could only interpret as the violence of her desire.

'Not now,' she whispered. 'Not here. Anyone could walk in.'

She saw the real horror in his eyes; to be caught in a compromising situation would be worse than death to him. She laid a fragile hand regretfully on his sleeve. 'Wait for me, Philip—as I shall wait for you.'

He bowed and went to the door, a stiff, courtly figure in his black suit. There he turned to look back with longing, and in his eyes was the question he could not bring himself to ask.

'Trust me, Philip,' she said steadily, 'trust my love for you—as I know I can trust yours.'

He smiled his rare smile and was gone.

When the door had closed behind him, she went to her own apartments and scrubbed his kiss from her lips with a rough cloth.

Mary knew she must not weep. She must sit quiet and calm and listen with borrowed dignity, while Philip held her limp hand and spoke to her with the forced kindness she had grown to dread.

He was angry beneath that dignified exterior, and she bowed her head before his cool eyes, shutting out the mask of pity which cloaked his contempt. Her failure had exposed his sensitive pride to the worst of insults. She had brought him to England and humiliated him, and now that he was leaving and promising absently to return in a few weeks only, he was speaking not of her, but of Elizabeth.

Always Elizabeth!

'If you wish to please me, madam, you will treat her with kindness when I am gone. And in my absence the Act of Succession must remain unaltered.'

When I am dead she will be Queen. And then he will take her . . .

But after she was dead, what did it matter? There was that in his face which suggested he would not set foot again in England if she refused him. And so anxious was she to bring him back that she agreed without murmur to his terms.

When Philip had sailed away, pity chained Elizabeth to her sister's side. The empty cradle still lay forlornly in the empty nursery, mocking its cruel inscription:

The child which through Mary, oh Lord of Might has
   send
To England's joy, in health preserve, keep and defend.

Elizabeth stood in the doorway and watched her sister rock the gilded thing with her foot, and thought that in all her life she had never seen so sad a sight. Impulsive words of sympathy rose to her lips, but she turned away quickly before she could be seen, knowing she would do more harm than good by voicing them.

With Philip gone there was nothing to keep Elizabeth at court.

She went back to Hatfield and lived as quietly as she could, while the Protestants burned.

CHAPTER 3

A few weeks only' lengthened into nineteen long months before Philip set foot in England once more. He stayed just long enough to muster English forces for his war with France and within a month of achieving this was gone again, leaving his wife behind, once more indulging in a phantom pregnancy which deceived no one but herself.

The war began well enough for the Anglo-Spanish troops, with a great victory at St. Quentin; but Philip failed to make the vital march on Paris at the critical moment and the French rallied their forces. On the 10th of January came news of the greatest English disaster in more than a hundred years: Calais, the last outpost of England's influence in France, had fallen, 'the heaviest tidings to London and to England that ever was heard of'. After that the French war dragged on and became a sieve, draining the life force of the English crown to the point of bankruptcy.

Among the many young Englishmen who had accompanied Philip to France was Robert Dudley. Released at last from the Tower, but not permitted to show their faces at court, he and the rest of his brothers had been kicking their heels in poverty around London and their country houses until the god-sent chance of employment came. Robin had seen Philip retire inexplicably from the furore of St. Quentin at the very moment when Paris lay open to their troops. He was filled with contempt for that military blunder. But later, when called to Philip's tent to be commended on his bravery, he was careful not to let that contempt show. One does not tell the master of half of the world that he is a spineless fool—particularly when one is a penniless young lord seeking one's fortune wherever it may be made.

Philip's personal request sent Robin back to England with dispatches for the Queen and within a few weeks, in recognition of his services at St. Quentin, the Queen restored to the Dudley family lands which had been escheated to the crown. But of the five Dudley boys who had set out on their father's desperate venture in 1553, only Robin and Ambrose were now left to claim the rank of a duke's son. Guildford had died on the block; John of his rigorous imprisonment; Henry in the French war. Whenever Robin surveyed the wreck of their once notorious family, he knew it was left to him to restore its fortune.

Accordingly, he spent a short time making himself agreeable at court, and gleaning information as to the nature of the Queen's illness. When at last he was satisfied that there was no longer any hope of a recovery, he returned to his country estate and began to make plans for the future.

Amy Dudley stood in the low arch of the doorway and watched her husband sadly. He was sitting at an old writing desk, with his back towards her, poring over deeds and documents with taut interest. A candle burned on either side of him and his favourite hound lay at his feet in the sweet straw.

Misfortune had hardened him. He was no longer the easygoing boy she had fallen in love with at Syderstone; they lived together in this big house like strangers and made love occasionally in cursory silence. Ever since his return from the Tower he had been like this, tense, preoccupied, distant, driven by a burning restlessness which kept him hunting till dusk and prowling through the quiet house at night. Often he went down to the village alone, galloping out of the courtyard on that wild black stallion which frightened her so much. She believed he met women there, but dared not ask. He seemed to be waiting for something, consumed by impatience, and the longer he waited the more moody and irritable he became.

'Robert,' she said diffidently from the doorway, 'what are you doing?'

He was silent. She sensed his displeasure at being disturbed.

'I'm selling some land,' he said curtly as she came over to his side. 'I need the money.'

'For what? You lack for nothing here, Robert.'

'I intend to make a small investment for the future. That's all you need to know. Go to bed now, Amy—I'll be up soon.'

Her eyes were steady on his face, but the hand resting on his shoulder had begun to tremble.

'It's for *her*—isn't it?'

His lips tightened; he flung down his quill.

'It's for Elizabeth, if that's what you mean. She will be Queen before the end of the year with any luck and then—'

'And then you will go to her,' said Amy dully.

'Naturally I shall go to her,' he snapped. 'She is the only one who can bring me to power and fortune again. For Christ's sake, Amy, don't you understand —she will be Queen of England.'

'She's always been your Queen. Do you think I haven't known it all these years?'

He began to gather up his papers in angry silence. Amy caught desperately at the fur robe which hung loosely round his broad shoulders.

'Robert, listen to me, I beg you. Listen to me this once even if you never do again. I'm not a fool. I know how attractive she is to you, and to all men. She's handsome and clever, and amusing—but her eyes are like ice. And you won't melt them, Robert—no man could. There's something cruel and twisted deep inside her. Oh, Robert, keep away from her. I know she's dangerous.'

He unpicked Amy's hot fingers and put her from him; his face was hard and contemptuous.

'I shall be leaving at the end of the week for Hatfield,' he announced with measured calm. 'When you have finished embellishing your absurd fancies, you will find me waiting upstairs.'

'Wait as long as you like,' she sobbed, 'I will not lie between the two of you again.'

He shrugged indifferently and blew out the candles on the table.

'As you please, my dear. I shall not lack for comfort if you come no more to my bed.'

He whistled to his dog and went quietly out of the room, leaving her alone in the dark.

Robin crossed the small ante-room and stared through the narrow window out on to Hatfield's great park. From the corner of his eye he could just see the bags of gold which he had placed on the table over an hour ago, and the sight made him frown. A whole hour he had been hanging around here like a lackey waiting to be admitted; evidently she was in no hurry to see him again. Discouraged and vaguely ill at ease, he sat down on a stool, remembering the Tower and that secret visit with a rueful smile. It did not rank in his memory as the greatest love scene of all time. Until that moment he would have confidently said that no other man in England had more skill when it came to parting a woman from her clothes. Yet strangely, alone with Elizabeth, he had not even tried; and the memory troubled him. Why had he not tried? God knew, he had been desperate enough for a woman after all those months of monk-like existence. Was it the fear of rebuff, the sneaking, uneasy feeling that she would laugh at him, the suave, the utterly irresistible Robert Dudley? That brief hour, how quickly it had passed in feverish conversation, and in all that hour he had done nothing more significant than hold her hand. Oh God, the shame of it made him squirm. From then until now, he had been haunted by the memory of that candlelit scene in the semi-circular stone room, that golden opportunity lost. He had tried to forget it in the eager arms of a dozen other women, but her image would not be pushed away. It mocked him daily, lay steadily between him and fulfilment, until he knew that for the rest of his life he would know no peace until he had had her.

The door opened and he looked up expectantly.

'Her Grace will see you now, Lord Robert.'

The wide-eyed girl who stood in the doorway smiled coyly and tried to catch his eye. He did not appear to notice and she turned off the smile in disappointment as he walked past her into the room beyond, without a glance, taking the gold with him.

A great fire was burning brightly in the stone hearth and Elizabeth was sitting beside it in a high-backed chair, with a long, ringless hand resting on either tapestried arm. She was regally composed, dressed all in white with her few jewels scattered in the myriad of bright curls which framed her face. She was rather more beautiful than he had remembered.

He bowed very low, much lower than he had first intended; he had not been prepared for such formality.

'Your Grace.' He had been on the point of saying 'Elizabeth' and suddenly thought better of it beneath her steady watchful gaze. In the window-seat he noted the ubiquitous Kat Ashley with a prick of annoyance.

'Welcome to Hatfield, my lord. What is it you want?'

He blinked. He had not expected that. Struggling to regain the offensive, he swept a courtly bow and said smoothly, 'I want nothing but the pleasure of speaking with Your Grace and of placing myself and my possessions at your service.'

Her eyebrow rose very slightly with just a hint of irony. She had made that sort of pretty speech herself before now and she thought she knew exactly what it was worth. She said nothing and he grew uncomfortable.

'May we speak alone, madam?' There was a note of desperation in his voice and she looked him up and down with a glance that might mean amusement.

'Leave us, Kat, and wait in the next room.'

Mrs Ashley went with a sniff and a reproachful look and he breathed a sigh of relief, for surely it would be easier now they were alone.

She leaned forward quickly to pick up one of the bags which lay at her feet and he was reminded of the swift, swooping movement of a falcon.

'So these are your possessions? They seem remarkably portable, my ragged Robin. But you are not so ragged now, are you, and hope to be even less so in the future—my future.'

How shrewd she was, and how cynical, when he had hoped to find her so amenable. He stood in awkward silence as she opened the bag and then he saw the quick glint of pleasure in her dark eyes as she looked at the gold within. She glanced up and smiled at him.

'Does this come with Amy's blessing?'

'Does that matter?' he countered swiftly.

She shook her head and the jewels in her hair flashed fire.

'Would you take it back if it did?' she asked wickedly.

He looked at her extraordinarily long fingers, delicate hands far stronger than they seemed, hands which he knew to his cost could deliver a blow at astonishing speed and which would never let go of anything that had once fallen into their grasp.

'I wouldn't give much for my chances on that score,' he said drily.

Their silence lasted a moment more and then exploded into laughter. She had raised the invisible barrier between them. He sat down on the stool at her feet and they began to talk unguardedly, like old friends. For nearly two hours, Mrs Ashley paced the ante-room in annoyance and occasionally applied an eye to the keyhole. Then at last Elizabeth glanced regretfully at the clock on the chimney-piece and held out her hand.

'Robin, you must go. I'm sorry I can't ask you to dine, but even now it wouldn't be safe. You should not have come and I should not have received you. The Queen still has spies in my household.'

'The Queen is in no condition to listen to spies' tales now.' His voice was serious suddenly, his glance urgent and compelling as he leaned forward to take her hand. 'She's very near to death, but if she fails to name you as her successor you may have to fight for your crown. Cardinal Pole could oppose you in his own right and rally the Catholics against you. Use that gold to arm yourself.'

'And you?' she asked quietly. 'You will fight for me?'

'To the death if need be.'

She clasped both his hands between her own in the ancient symbol of allegiance.

'Till death us do part then.'

He bent his head swiftly and kissed the hands which covered his own, knowing that the dice were thrown, that she had sworn him for life into her service and that death alone would release him from her jealous possession. Where she led he must follow, but must he only follow? He dared to ask it and received an ambiguous little smile in return.

'Good friends should travel side by side, like parallel lines.'

'Parallel lines never meet,' he reminded her meaningfully. 'Even in eternity.'

She looked up at him and there was no laughter in her eyes now. They were cool and clear as they rested on his face for a moment.

'You are the mathematician, Robin. If you tell me that is so I shall believe it. But surely you remember Roger Ascham saying you would never make a politician if you gave up Cicero to study Euclid's "pricks and lines".'

He was shrewd enough to know when he was being mocked and warned off. He would need to be a strategist to win her love; he would have to stalk her like prey. She was daring him to go to war, to enter a battle where all the odds were against his ultimate victory. She had flung down the gauntlet of challenge and he was too great an adventurer to resist taking it up, knowing the value of the prize at stake. And just to show her he was not daunted by the prospect, he told her that if she chose to play chess with him, he knew all the right moves.

'The right moves, yes,' she conceded mockingly, 'but *not* necessarily the right order in which to make them.'

There was a glint of amusement in her eyes as she held out her hand and rather carelessly dismissed him. He was very glad then that he had not pushed his luck by attempting to kiss her; he saw with uncomfortable clarity what a crass blunder that would have been.

All through the long journey back to Norfolk, the memory of her pale, enigmatic face tormented him. It was always her delight to speak in riddles and that curious ability to obscure her real meaning had saved her from death on more than one occasion. He spurred his horse angrily and wondered why she should feel the need to exercise that talent on *him!* It gave him the uneasy feeling that she did not entirely trust him, and he knew instinctively that until he had that trust he would never gain his heart's desire.

The new Spanish Ambassador, Feria, arrived in England in November and went at once through the rapidly emptying palace to the Queen's bedside.

The great room was dark and the state bed resembled an elaborate mauso-leum. He had brought a letter from Philip, but the little shrivelled figure in the bed was beyond reading it.

'Will he come?' she whispered, groping for the Spaniard's hand.

Feria launched into what he had evidently prepared. His master was deeply grieved at the impossibility of returning to England, but pressing business detained him in Spain. The welfare of the state must come first. He sent his good wishes—The smooth voice continued to flow over her, glibly repeating the empty excuses, but Mary was no longer listening.

She lay on her death-bed, with her courtiers already flocking to Hatfield, and Philip sent—*his good wishes*.

She held up her withered hand and stayed the Spaniard's eloquence.

'Peace, my friend. I am content.'

Feria's eyes swivelled round to the few women who still hovered in the room. He seemed relieved as he bent closer over to the bed to convey his real message.

'His Majesty begs that as your last duty you will declare the Lady Elizabeth your sole successor.'

Yes, she had known he would ask that. And even now in this last moment of bitter disillusion she could deny him nothing.

'If Elizabeth will discharge my debts and maintain the True Faith, I will acknowledge her as my only heir.'

So, she had said it at last! Yet, strangely, this second betrayal of her con-science was not so clear in her mind as the first all those years ago when her father had forced her to sign that paper recognizing his authority as Supreme Head of the Church in England. Oh, the strokes of her pen upon that evil document had gleamed newly wet in her memory ever since. And this was her final punishment—to hand her country over to a bastard heretic!

She lay very still with her eyes closed, lest the wretched tears of failure should steal down her cheeks.

Feria bowed himself out with very little further pretence at solicitude and the November afternoon darkened towards evening beyond the tall windows. She watched as her women built up the fire and her mind began to wander, flickering and bobbing as wildly as the dancing flames.

Fire.

The futile burnings at Smithfield. For every heretic that burned, three sprang to take his place—the plague of heresy would never be contained in England now.

War.

Military defeat, financial disaster—and *Calais!* Calais was engraved upon her heart.

Marriage.

Two cruel and delusive mock pregnancies which had given false hope to the last stages of a fatal illness—no child, no love.

Fire; war; marriage; her mind, feverish and confused, revolved increasingly around those three words. They had brought her nothing and, worse, brought nothing to England but disaster, religious schisms, bankruptcy and national shame. It was a poor, threadbare inheritance, but even now she need not will it to Elizabeth: she could bequeath her crown to the Queen of Scots. And if she did, there would be civil war.

I should have killed her when I had the chance, but I couldn't do it. Why couldn't I do it?

Now she could not do this thing either, could not disinherit her sister and leave a legacy of anarchy to crown her failures. What John Knox had denounced as the 'monstrous regiment of women' must continue in England—but not in the safe, Catholic hands of a Scottish queen.

It was the last choice between the fate of her beloved religion and the fate of the realm. It was the only choice for a Tudor monarch.

Elizabeth would rule.

The Great North Road was swarming with excited figures, some on horseback, some on foot, all leaving the capital in a steady stream for Hatfield. Day after day the exodus went on and Elizabeth sat in the Great Hall, receiving those anxious to swear fealty to the Queen who was to be. Even Feria came and was suitably ingratiating, while reminding her of all she owed to Philip's friendship. The days ticked away slowly in unbearable suspense, and the news came to her that the Archbishop of Canterbury, Cardinal Pole, was now gravely ill and unlikely to outlive his mistress and cousin by many days. *The crown will fall on your pretty head as surely as day follows night.* If Pole died, there would be no one to lead the Catholics against her and for the present, at least, there would be no fight.

The 17th of November was as hot as any summer's day, a freak of nature which caused some comment. She stood in the early morning sunshine watching the new arrivals flock through the gatehouse below. They couldn't get here quick enough, or bow low enough when they arrived, and her cynical amusement was touched with faint disgust.

'Rats, deserting the ship of state,' she murmured with an unpleasant smile. 'Poor Mary.'

'*Poor* Mary!' Mrs Ashley rustled to the window and looked at her in indignant amazement. 'Your Grace can say *that* after all we've gone through!'

'Why not? The same thing could happen to me one day. If this is what naming your successor does I'll keep my mouth shut till they lay me in my coffin.'

She shivered in the hot sunlight and swung round to collect an armful of books.

'What are you doing?' Kat was alarmed.

'I'm going out—as far away from them as I can get. I'll be in the park somewhere if the news should come.'

'You'd better wear your sun hat then.' Kat tossed her a red and white bonnet. 'I don't want you ascending the throne covered in freckles!'

Elizabeth put on the sun hat and ducked out of the crowded manor, avoiding the obsequious bows and curtsies which greeted her appearance, waving back the women who hurried forward to attend her. She wanted to be alone now in these last hours before her destiny closed in upon her, alone to think and remember the past.

She went out of the quadrangle through the central arch in the loggia at a stately pace, crossed the green before the palace, and took the archway that would gain her the park. Once through that gateway she began to run like a child, away from the very thing she had coveted for more than ten years.

When she could run no longer, she turned and faced the hateful sense of duty like an enemy.

'I will be Queen,' she screamed to the old house glowing rusty red in the distance, 'I will do as I please.'

You will be Queen. And you will do what pleases England. She sank down beneath an oak tree and buried her face in her hands. She did not want her throne on terms, but she could not fight her own conscience. She knew what she owed; and she knew how to pay. She would rule England, rule it alone. And England alone should rule her.

The utter loneliness of splendid isolation closed in around her as she sat beneath the bare oak tree, a proud young tigress ready to stalk wild and free in the forests of Europe, unshackled by human bondage. There was a shout in the distance and she raised her head slowly in its direction. Across the broad sweep of grass a great crowd had begun to move.

So it had come. The long apprenticeship was over.

It had come and she was ready. She stood before them and heard Cecil's voice above the rest crying that the Queen was dead.

'*Long live the Queen!*'

The roar of their acknowledgment died away and they were silent, waiting for her to speak.

There, in the strangest moment they ever experienced, they saw her kneel to them, like a Druid sacrifice beneath the ancient oak.

She said, very low, in Latin, 'It is our Lord's doing and it is marvellous in our eyes.'

The hot November sunshine blazed down on her bent head. No one else spoke.

And one by one the men who had sworn to serve her sank down on their knees around her and likewise bowed their heads.

CHAPTER 4

It was far into the night before Hatfield's hive-like activity ceased, and the jostling bodies who had packed into the old manor house each found themselves an uncomfortable niche in which to spend the remaining hours of darkness.

Finally, the heavy doors of the new Queen's private chamber were opened by the discreetly yawning figure of Mrs Ashley, and the young man who had waited so patiently without for so many hours was admitted. The clock in the Great Hall struck two as he stepped into the room and went humbly down on one knee with his hat in his hand.

The Queen was dressed in a loose robe edged with sable and her hair fell freely down her back. She looked very young as she rose from her chair and gave him her hand to kiss.

'Robin!'

'My Queen.' He bent his head over her hand and the reverence of his voice and gesture amused her. She allowed him to hold her fingers a shade longer than the moment demanded before she took a step back from him.

'I saw you arrive this morning,' she said.

He was immediately disheartened. All these hours she had been aware of his presence, yet had not summoned him till now.

'I have been busy.'

Her eyes reproved him. It was as though she had answered his unspoken question.

'Of course, madam. It was gracious of you to receive me at this hour.'

She smiled and half turned her back on him.

'That white mare of yours is beautiful,' she continued thoughtfully. 'May I have her?'

He inclined his head hastily. 'Gladly, madam.'

'It will not break your heart to part with her then?'

'She was intended as a gift for Your Majesty. Indeed I would have presented her—' He hesitated.

'Had I not asked for her first.' She laughed and held out both hands to him. 'Did you *really* think I had forgotten you?'

'It is Your Majesty's privilege to keep me waiting.'

'Half the night?'

'All my life—if you choose.'

'You *are* offended.'

He smiled drily. 'Madam, I am always offended when I go hungry.'

'Why, have they not fed you?' she asked in surprise.

'Not so that my stomach noticed. Do all your retainers subsist on these sparrow rations?'

'I was not prepared for such company,' she said demurely. 'Kat, set that tray before the fire. And bring wine—two goblets. Half water in mine.'

She withdrew to the couch before the log fire and he followed in accordance with her gesture.

'Water?' he echoed questioningly.

'I don't like wine.'

A word began to tumble round his mind, nudging him unwillingly along an uneasy train of thought.

Temperance.

A stupid, inappropriate nickname, he had never understood it, but now, face to face with this extraordinary frugality he could pause and wonder for one anxious moment how far these nun-like habits extended. Once, as a very small boy, he had been soundly cuffed for trying to touch a lighted altar candle. Now his family was Protestant and they no longer held with sacred candles. Yet, kneeling at the feet of his Queen, he experienced that same guilty, hopeless feeling of something beautiful just beyond his grimy reach.

'Eat,' she commanded lightly, and he obeyed. She watched him in the dancing firelight, turning the goblet stem slowly between her long fingers.

She said softly, 'Cardinal Pole is dead.'

He looked up startled. 'Madam, are you sure?'

'I have reliable sources.'

He shook his head slightly and bit into a chicken leg.

'I find it quite remarkable that two of your mortal enemies should drop dead on the same day. And this extraordinary weather—it's almost like an omen.'

He drained his goblet and set it down with a slight frown.

'I suppose this means there'll be no fight after all.'

'You would have preferred civil war?' she inquired ironically.

'A little healthy conflict—nothing serious, of course—'

'Just enough to distinguish yourself as my true knight!'

Unnerved by the ease with which she saw through him, he flushed and was silent for a moment.

'A man must prove his worth to his monarch,' he said slowly, 'if not in battle, then perhaps—in other ways.'

The urgency of his glance was charged with meaning. She chose to ignore it and sat back on the couch, winding a tendril of hair around her finger.

'Tell me what is happening downstairs.'

He was silent a moment, regarding her steadily in the soft candlelight, completely at a loss as to how to reconcile the snub with that decidedly seductive gesture. He would have said he could read any woman like a book, but with Elizabeth there were too many pages missing. She was an elaborate code that he must crack.

'The palace,' he mused, 'the palace is bursting at the seams, but it's quiet now. The news of Pole's death is not generally known yet—there will be great excitement tomorrow. For the present most of them are asleep on the floor like dead flies.'

'Flies,' she repeated, looking inwards. 'Flies around a honey pot. Yes—I suppose that's how it will be from now on.'

Now he was truly ill at ease. Hell—was that how she saw him—a parasite like the rest, hanging around in the hope of what he might get from her?

'Madam—' he began haltingly.

She leaned forward swiftly and poked him roughly in the ribs.

'Fool!' she said gently. 'I didn't mean you. We have been friends for many years. But I do have a position for you—something that will suit you very well. Guess!'

'Secretary of State?'

She frowned. He tried again.

'Lord Chancellor?'

She kicked him, furtively, so that her women should not see.

'Master of the Horse?'

'You knew all the time!'

'Madam, you don't have a royal monopoly to tease. What other post could suit me half so well?'

'Then you don't want to be Secretary,' she remarked thoughtfully. 'That's good.'

'Why?' He looked at her, suddenly suspicious. 'Why is it good that I don't want to be Secretary?'

'Because I intend to appoint Sir William Cecil.' There was a shade of coolness in her voice as she saw his face harden. 'Yes—I can see you are delighted to hear of his elevation—indeed, as delighted as he will be to hear of yours.'

Cecil, that sneaking, wily snake! Who had advised her in this?

'Throckmorton,' she continued softly, and again it was as though she had heard his unspoken thought, 'Throckmorton tells me he is the only man for the job.'

'May his advice prove sound,' Robin said stiffly.

She held out her hand in dismissal and he rose to his feet, kissed her fingers and bowed himself to the door; where she called him back.

'One thing more, my lord. Do you wish me to find a place at court for your wife?'

There was a gasp, a suppressed snigger of amusement from the few women who attended her, and he knew instinctively that he looked every inch the fool he felt. And yet, humiliated as he was, a small part of him laughed in grudging admiration and said she was a clever bitch.

He had still to get out of this with panache. He bowed to her with exaggerated formality.

'My wife has been in poor health for some time, madam. Unless Your Majesty expressly commands otherwise I know she would prefer to remain quietly in the country.'

The Queen seemed to eye him with satisfaction.

'And your sister Mary—will *her* health permit attendance on me at court?'

'Mary will come with the greatest of pleasure, madam.'

Oh, it would suit him finely to have his favourite sister among her women. He wondered briefly if that was why she had suggested it and then the door closed behind him and he was alone in the ante-room, still none the wiser as to where he really stood with her. Charming, familiar, generous—she had been all three, but what did it amount to? He really could not say. Beneath that casual intimacy she remained unshakably in control, invulnerable as a fortress.

And no matter which way he looked at it, he knew he still had a long way to go.

On a brisk November morning Elizabeth rode through the cheering crowds which lined her way, to take possession of the Tower, dressed in the royal mourning gown of purple velvet, with Robin Dudley following immediately behind on a black horse.

The crowds pushed forward and challenged the cannon fire which echoed down the narrow streets with their great full-throated roar of affection. It was a sound that had not been heard in England for many years. They called out to her and saw her turn in the saddle to laugh and wave in reply. They had waited through many gloomy years, through poor harvests and rebellions and religious controversy for this moment, and she had waited with them. The moment was theirs as much as her own; she wanted them to know it.

On Tower Hill she drew rein and the cannon fire ceased as she looked down on the fortress. It lay silent and submissive, girdled by a grey curtain wall, with the pinnacles of the White Tower spiking upwards in the winter sky. She had cheated death and conquered the dark force of 'that place' and as she stared down at it in the deep silence which had descended all around, it seemed to her as though the Tower itself was shrinking, dwindling in significance before her eyes until it was no more than a toy fortress. She might reach out one hand and toss it into the River Thames beyond.

Shaking herself out of her reverie, she became aware of the wondering faces about her. They clearly expected her to say something and she caught Robin's grave eyes upon her as she began to speak.

'Some have fallen from princes to be prisoners in that place; I am raised from a prisoner to be prince of this land.' Her eyes swept the rows of eager faces. 'Let me show myself thankful to God and merciful to all men.'

Entering the Tower as a prince, she asked to be conducted to the apartment she had occupied as a prisoner and as many as possible crowded into the semi-circular room on the upper floor of the Bell Tower. Those unfortunate enough to be last were squashed against the three latrines between the inner and the outer door.

She wanted never to forget this room—the uneven floor, cold and rough beneath her feet, the tall windows capped with hoods, the deep, stone window-seats and the sound of the east wind outside.

Oblivious to the staring crowd behind her, she walked to the window and looked out, resting her fingers against the rough wall. Cold stone. The words of an old psalm came suddenly into her mind. 'The stone that the builders refused has become the headstone of the corner.'

And she was that stone—smooth, hard, impregnable. She too would stand for ages in the memory of men, for she wished to make her fame spread abroad in her lifetime 'and after occasion memorial for ever'.

Robin was beside her, silent, a little overcome by the significance of this moment, and as she turned slowly she saw her own memories reflected in his eyes, memories which isolated them together from the rest of the crowd. He was the only one who understood—truly understood—what this moment meant to her, for it meant almost the same to himself.

Smiling and laying her hand familiarly on his arm, she walked out to the state apartments in the White Tower.

Sir Henry Bedingfield knelt before the throne and kept his eyes on her jewelled slippers, because he did not dare to look into her face. He was mortally afraid of what he would find there. Face it—should she choose, she had ample cause for taking revenge on many, and Gardiner, chief among them, was no longer alive to receive his share, having conveniently died of natural causes three years before her accession.

Her summons had filled Bedingfield with stark terror. He wished he had not removed all her servants that night at Richmond; that he had not insisted on locking gates behind her; that he had not dismissed the Sands girl. He wished with incredible fervour that he had not made Elizabeth of England sit under a hedge to do up her hair.

'Look at me,' she said.

He lifted his eyes unwillingly. She sat above him like a statue, glittering, unsmiling.

'Well, gaoler—what shall I do with you?'

'Your Majesty—' His voice was an absurd croak in his throat; his legs were trembling.

'Get up, my friend.' Her finger brushed his grizzled cheek. 'Get up, go home, and live in peace. And when I need to keep someone close confined I shall send for you.'

'Madam,' he stammered. 'Gracious Madam—'

She smiled and covered his clumsy incoherence by offering her hand. Behind his back the polished courtiers were rude at his expense, but they could not take this moment from him. Slowly he made his way out of the thrumming palace where the candles now burnt till dawn took over. He did not belong here, he knew it and he was glad to go, back to rustic obscurity where there would be no more teasing assaults on his wooden dignity. And yet his relief was tinged with regret. So young, so full of life and he not there to see it. Too old—too old! Ah—he knew it. The pace would kill him. So walk out of her palace, walk out of her life and forget her.

But he never forgot. He took with him the shining memory of a laughing girl—brilliant curls dressed with diamonds, white gown crusted with gems spilling over the arms of her chair. And whenever at dinner someone raised his tankard and said reverently: 'Gentlemen—the Queen,' he saw that image in his mind, untarnished by time.

When Bedingfield had gone, Elizabeth came down the steps of the dais and walked slowly through the crowded room, pausing frequently to talk with anyone who caught her fancy, until at last she reached the two she had marked for attention.

'Margaret!'

The Countess of Lennox sank into an uneasy curtsey at her feet and kissed her hand.

'And this must be Henry. I should hardly have recognized him, he is so well grown—but of course you feed him well—day and night, I seem to remember. I trust you have found a quieter set of menials to service your kitchen by now, cousin.'

Elizabeth gave Lennox a smile which sent the Countess's stomach plunging with fear. She took a step past her and then glanced back over her shoulder.

'I think your mother looks a little pale, Henry. Perhaps you should take her to the window for some fresh air. The room is vastly overcrowded.'

She inclined her head pleasantly and moved on, with Robin Dudley at her side, leaving the Countess to fan herself vigorously.

Sweat a little, Lennox. Your time will come.

Robin said questioningly, 'Kitchens, madam?'

'Just a little private jest among relatives, Robin. Nothing to excite concern.'

Robin glanced over his shoulder thoughtfully.

'It certainly appears to have excited the Countess. I thought she was going to faint when you spoke to her just then.'

'She's a very excitable lady. It takes very little to go to her head.'

Robin looked hard at his Queen; her expression was inscrutable, but he sensed her hostility to the Countess and was surprised by it. She possessed more pressingly dangerous relatives than Lennox—the Duke of Norfolk, mouthpiece of the old nobility, the Queen of Scots, now Dauphine of France. France might yet declare war in support of Mary's claim to the English throne; Norfolk could prove disloyal. And the claims of Margaret Lennox were certainly subsidiary to those of the two remaining Grey sisters,

Katherine and Mary. Suspicion was a vital force, so why waste it? Frankly, he would have said the Greys were the greatest threat of all—Katherine was truculent and opinionated, and considered herself heiress presumptive. Some said she should be Queen—His hand on Elizabeth's arm tightened its grip. She looked up at him in surprise and followed his glance across the room.

Lady Katherine Grey was in conversation with the Spanish Ambassador and her voice rose and fell on a complaining note.

'Watch her,' said Robin softly. 'Watch her well. And Norfolk. You can't afford to turn your back on any of them for a moment. You're not safe yet.'

Elizabeth smiled at him.

'I'll never be safe,' she said and went on down the room to give her hand graciously to Katherine.

CHAPTER 5

The gayest court in Europe was like a golden hive under the rule of a Queen bee, no place for the old or the fainthearted. The new Queen was never tired or idle and the courtiers who shared her life found they were not expected to be tired or idle either. They rose at dawn and few could hope to see their beds again before the small hours of the morning.

There was something quite insatiable in Elizabeth's mad pursuit of activity. In the eyes of half of Europe she was a bastard and usurper; it was as though she stretched out both hands to snatch all that life now had to offer her, and snatch it greedily for fear it might be gone tomorrow. Her restless energy, her total inability to relax, affected everybody's life; but to no one was her wild mood of more importance than her principal Secretary, William Cecil.

He could not complain that it affected her work—she was killing him with work! No one had ever stretched his mind like this before and her ability to manage her affairs and her court never ceased to amaze him. Oh no, he had no qualms about her conduct in Council.

It was her private hours of pleasure that gave him real concern. He allowed for her youth, allowed for the years of miserable restraint—but he simply could not make allowance for her relationship with Robin Dudley. And that relationship was becoming quite impossible to ignore.

Cecil stood unobtrusively in the doorway of the Great Hall, glowering at the court masque, waiting for some appropriate moment at which to catch her eye and draw her aside. There was news from France—not pressing, admittedly—but news he would prefer to discuss before she went to bed—if she ever went to bed! Sometimes he doubted it. They were dancing—well, he had nothing against dancing, he was no Puritan—but was it necessary to dance all night with the same partner? By the same token, was it necessary to wear a green wig?

The music rose to a climax and every partner exchanged a formal kiss.

Only there was nothing *formal* in the way Robin Dudley kissed his Queen; and Cecil found his own hands were clenched with anger.

They must be watched. Later, I shall arrange it—

The masque ended and the court applauded as Robin led the Queen back to the dais. She sat down in the chair of state and handed him her heavy mask on its silver handle. Robin, in turn, handed it to his sister, pretty, dark-eyed Mary Sidney, who curtsied and withdrew tactfully out of hearing.

'You make a better mermaid without the mask,' said Robin thoughtfully. 'That pale mysterious face of yours beneath a green wig has quite an eerie fascination. You look like—'

'Like death, Kat said.' Elizabeth's eyes were smoky with kohl, her smile was provocative.

'Ashley is a silly old fool,' said Robin seriously. 'There can't be another woman in England who could wear that wig and get away with it. Why shouldn't you wear something that suits you so extraordinarily well? You are the Queen.'

'True.' Elizabeth nibbled the plumes of her fan aggressively. 'I am the Queen and answerable to none save God. If I should wish to be outrageous, eccentric, even *dishonourable*—' She caught a sight of the grim figure by the door and broke off with a sharp sigh. 'Damn! There's Cecil hanging around like the ghoul at the feast. I swear if he had his way I'd be locked up in a glass cabinet and only trotted out for Council meetings and state occasions. Judging by his face I'd say *he* doesn't approve of my green hair either.'

Robin followed her glance with sudden hostility.

'It's not his place to approve or disapprove of you, madam. I wonder you don't box his ears and tell him to go to the Devil.'

Elizabeth laughed and shook her head.

'Ah no, to lay a finger on all that dignity would be sacrilege.' She leaned back in her chair, fanning herself lazily. 'Now you, on the other hand, have the sort of face that simply asks to be slapped.'

'Is that all my face moves you to, madam?' His eyes were steady on her face. 'It did not seem so to me just now when we danced.'

He moved close, leaning over the arm of her chair with the boldly painted hunter's mask hanging from a ribbon on his strong wrist. She was acutely aware that the talk and laughter in the hall had become muted, that all eyes were fixed upon them in vulgar curiosity.

'You must not kiss me again like that.'

'How would Your Majesty prefer me to kiss you?' he inquired pleasantly. 'Like that wooden idiot Pickering?'

'Not at all for the present,' she said coolly. 'I would prefer you to leave the court for a while.'

His hand on hers tightened angrily. 'For what purpose?'

'To perform a small service for me. But, of course, if you are unwilling I can easily find someone else—Tom Heneage perhaps—or that wooden idiot, Pickering—'

Robin kissed her hand hastily.

'You don't need those fools. I can provide anything Your Majesty may desire.'

'Anything?' she mocked. 'Anything at all?'

'Tell me what you wish me to do.' He was suddenly eager and humble. 'Please tell me, madam.'

It was always 'madam' now, whenever he was uncertain of her, whenever he was afraid he had taken familiarity too far. It was something to hold power over such an arrogant young man.

'I want you to consult your astrologer, Dr Dee,' she said slowly.

'On your behalf?'

She nodded. 'To discuss the most propitious day for my coronation—if there ever *is* a coronation. Cecil's yet to find a bishop willing to crown me.'

Robin frowned. 'Catholic bishops! Why wait on them? The Protestant clergy will soon be flocking back from Geneva, ready to slit each other's throat for the honour!'

'It's too early to risk trouble, Robin. I dare not be crowned by Protestant rites.'

'Have *all* the Catholic bishops refused?'

'All save one, and who can blame them? Once I'm safely crowned I shall be quite at liberty to start a reign of persecution worse than the last.'

'But you won't,' he pointed out reasonably. 'You've given your royal word—'

She looked up at him quickly, with a slight smile.

'And knowing what my royal word is worth, you as a Catholic bishop would be prepared to trust your life to it?'

He coughed and supposed not; they shared a smile. After a moment he said cheerfully, 'So there's not much point in my going down to Mortlake to see Dee, is there?'

Elizabeth shrugged.

'Well—there's always Bishop Oglethorpe. He's too scared of the Pope to say yes, and too scared of me to say no, but since I'm nearer than the Pope I may well win in the end. And the minute he agrees I want to be ready, with the stars on my side. If you go I shall be endlessly grateful.'

'May I know what form that gratitude will take?' he inquired significantly.

'Leave of absence,' she said mischievously, 'to visit your wife.'

'My *wife!*'

'Yes—with this ring I thee wed—remember?'

He wrenched the hunter's mask from his wrist with a savage twist that snapped the ribbon, and his sister glanced round in alarm.

'I won't be mocked,' he said darkly. 'Even by the Queen.'

'I'm not mocking—merely reminding my Master of Horse that he has not ridden his own mare for many weeks. You are a married man, Robin.'

'And if I were not?'

The rash words were out and could not be recalled. He knew a moment of acute unease, until he saw that she was still smiling, her gaze bright, amused and tolerant.

'If you were not you would be in need of a wife, my Robin. And I rather think I should have to find you one with some alacrity.' She stood up abruptly. 'Now let loose my hand—I must go to Cecil.'

Robin left the court for Mortlake in a mood of baffled exasperation and Elizabeth was conscious of some relief. There was a great deal requiring her attention and it was easier to concentrate without those predatory eyes constantly following her about. Cecil relaxed, too, in Robin's absence and lowered his guard against fear of disillusion. She was not going to disappoint him, as others had. It was almost ten years now since he had singled her out as his personal protégée, and so far she had not put a foot wrong along the slippery ledge she walked. She was young and totally inexperienced, yet she behaved like a seasoned statesman. At her first public reception Philip's Ambassador had challenged her to be 'very careful' in religious matters.

'It would indeed be bad of me to forget God, who has been good to me,' she had replied innocently, and Cecil had been astonished at the ease with which she slid round the direct threat from Spain. Everyone knew she must keep friends with Philip, yet to lose faith with none of her Protestant allies while doing it—now that was truly remarkable! Her own personal leanings were still an ambiguous question mark in Europe, and she had taken the heat out of religious controversy by forbidding all public sermons for the present.

No English sovereign had ever sat on a more uncertain throne. The Catholics considered her a bastard; the influential Protestants, now flocking back into the country from exile, expected to see an immediate return to the religious regime of King Edward. Religion could make or break her, and quite honestly Cecil saw no way of effecting a settlement that would make her safe. With her claim to the throne so tenuous, she could not afford to alienate any large section of the population; but clever as she was, she had to alienate someone soon. She could not sit on the religious fence for ever.

They talked long on the issue and he looked forward to each personal interview, because he could talk to her like a man. It was his pleasure to guide her; she learnt so quickly. On Christmas Day she walked out of the chapel before the elevation of the Host—if there was uproar they could always say she had felt ill. There was no uproar. On New Year's Day she proclaimed all future services would be held in English. Still no outcry. It was working, this gentle easing away from Rome, each step so small it was hardly noticeable, yet inexorably showing the way they would go. Soon they would be ready for Parliament.

What surprised Cecil most was her complete lack of illusion. She deceived everybody, but she never deceived herself. She knew all the odds were against her success. She was surrounded on all sides by rival claimants to the throne whose legitimacy was beyond question. And England was weak, riven by internal divisions, virtually bankrupt since Mary's disastrous campaign in France. What a task! He had seen strong men, able men, go under with less than half the opposition that waited for Elizabeth. Her enemies said smugly that it was only a question of time and waited gleefully for her brief hour of triumph to collapse like a speculator's bubble.

But if she was nervous and insecure, no one knew about it. She had a calm, unquestioned air of authority which had caused even Feria to admit grudgingly that 'she never gives her orders and has her way as absolutely as her Father did'.

Fluent in six languages, she was uniquely independent in her dealings with foreign ambassadors; and her Council she had tamed by the end of her first week. Not a man among them seriously entertained the hope of becoming the power behind the throne. Even Cecil knew his place.

Only a husband could hope to challenge her power. She had said many times in private, and in public, that she did not intend to take one.

But, naturally, no one believed her.

The Count de Feria was not enjoying his ambassadorial duties in England. Communication with King Philip had led him to believe he would step effortlessly into the same unique position of influence that Renard had held in the previous reign.

But it simply had not happened. Far from becoming her chief adviser, he was finding it extraordinarily difficult to get close enough to give any advice at all. He was hedged in by an unseemly press of envoys and special emissaries of foreign suitors and no one seemed the least impressed by his credentials as Spanish Ambassador. And he was not accustomed to being treated as though he were of no account.

He wrote home in alarm to inform his master that, 'I am afraid one day we shall find this woman married and I shall be the last person in the palace to know anything about it.'

Personally he considered the Queen's attitude to be suicidal. Without Philip's support her petty, insignificant little crown would be knocked off her swollen head inside six months. And yet this jumped-up, low-born baggage still behaved as though she were the centre of the universe—and more to the point, succeeded in getting everyone around her to treat her accordingly. Feria had never seen so many men compete for the honour of making utter fools of themselves—Lord, they fell over themselves backwards to keep her in a pleasant humour. It was a ridiculous sight. Give her a year at this rate and there would not be a single *man* among the lot of them. Already they showed disturbing signs of losing their initiative, and more incredibly, their self-interest.

Feria had found he could not even bribe with success. One very promising candidate, accepting his delicate overtures with interest, had come back to tell him the next day that 'the Queen says it is quite acceptable for me to take the money and I should be glad if you would let me have the first payment.'

Feria was deeply concerned. What sort of diplomacy could be conducted in a court where one could not bribe? And what manner of woman could reduce ambitious, self-seeking predators to tamed birds in less than two months?

He looked at her with new respect—and suspicion. Every day that passed saw this cocksure, confident madam sitting a little more securely on her uncertain throne, and consequently a little less dependent on the goodwill of her brother-in-law. And still he had no inkling of her true intentions.

It occurred to Feria that once she was safely crowned there would be no holding her. And the coronation was rapidly closing in upon them . . .

When Robin left Dr Dee's mysterious riverside house with rolls of astronomical calculations coiled in his saddle-bag, he deliberately dawdled over his return. And when he finally sauntered into court, it was to find the Queen waiting for him with ill-concealed annoyance.

'The 15th of January,' she said coldly, and pushed the documents aside after a cursory glance. 'Dee took his time to come to that conclusion. Is he in his dotage?'

Robin lifted his broad shoulders and gave her a look of practised surprise. 'Madam, you gave me to understand there was no urgent need of my return.'

'So? Where have you been till now?'

'Visiting my wife,' he replied calmly, 'at Your Majesty's kind insistence.'

'I see.' He saw her fingers tense as she began to roll up the documents with unnecessary vigour. 'And was the visit of benefit to her in her sad state of health?'

'I believe I managed to raise her spirits, madam—among other things.'

Her hand quivered towards the heavy sand caster and for a moment he was quite convinced she would throw it at him. But then she appeared to think better of it, clasped her fingers resolutely together on the desk and looked at him with something curiously like grudging respect. It was not often that she got as good as she gave and she was half furious, half amused by his nerve. She wanted a man at her side, a *real* man—one who would not be afraid to stand up to her when the occasion demanded. And Robin was suddenly aware that if he wanted to get any closer to her, he was going to have to be prepared to take a few risks.

Certainly for the moment his strategy appeared to have succeeded. He had never known her so charming. There were no more uncalled-for remarks about Amy, and he was the Queen's constant companion. By the time the fifteenth day of January dawned, cold and brilliant with snow clinging to the narrow streets, even the lowest court scullions were whispering about their intimacy.

Plans for the most spectacular coronation in English history had been held in abeyance by the need to find a bishop willing to officiate, but Oglethorpe, Bishop of Carlisle, had finally capitulated under pressure. Reluctantly, with all the grace of an unwilling bull being herded into the ring, he had agreed to crown her at last, and after that, Cecil had seen to it that no more time was wasted. With half the world ready to question her legitimacy, the sooner she was safely crowned the happier he would be.

Strenuous ceremonies led up to the great event and by the day of the coronation, Cecil, in company with the majority of the court, was completely exhausted. But Robin was young enough to cope with the extra work, and insensitive enough to remain impervious to the tension. And as he strode through the crowded corridors he was amused by those glances of deference which were already becoming his due. His new suit of carnation-gold silk perfectly complemented his dark features; he looked like a king and had begun to feel like one. He could hardly wait for the Queen to see him in all his magnificence and when he managed, amid the press of people, to get close enough to kiss her hand, he was sure she would remark upon it.

'Are you actually *related* to Jonah,' she inquired in a fierce undertone, 'or just a close friend?'

He straightened up abruptly and released her fingers with alarm. She moved on immediately to give her hand to the Duchess of Norfolk, leaving him feeling deflated and very uneasy, wondering what he had done. Or not done. Or said—

The questions gnawed at his mind until he saw her enter the Abbey, and there in that solemn moment, he briefly forgot the fortunes of Robert Dudley. His quick intake of breath was echoed by the whole congregation, clearly audible above the fanfare.

The cold air was heavy with incense. She walked slowly towards him, dressed entirely in crimson velvet, an ermine cape around her shoulders, her red hair falling loose to her waist beneath a tiny crimson cap. In the glow of a thousand candles she looked suddenly like a living flame, remote, splendid, immortal.

Untouchable, he thought, and lowered his eyes as from a brilliant light that caused him pain. It was in that moment that he first knew he loved her, and the knowledge filled him with despairing humility. There was no shame in aiming for a crown and failing—some of the strongest men in England had done that. But to truly want the one woman in this world who might just refuse him—that was madness. He could wander the surface of the earth and never find his pride of manhood again, if the worst happened. If she said no—

For five hours he craned his neck to get a glimpse of her between the flowing arms of Oglethorpe's robe and when it was over he was as weary as the rest. Elizabeth's crimson gown was changed for cloth of gold after the Anointing and by the time she sat down at the state banquet in Westminster

Hall, it was three o'clock in the afternoon and she was wearing violet velvet. Eight hundred guests were attended by an army of servants, all dressed in red, while Norfolk and Arundel supervised the proceedings on horseback. Robin sat like a man in a trance, absently eating whatever came within reach of his hand. His eyes were fixed continually on the Queen, who had not once glanced his way.

She sat on a raised dais beneath a lofty window, with the Earl of Sussex and her great uncle Howard standing behind, ready to serve all she ate and drank. The violet gown did not suit her so well, thought Robin suddenly—in the harsh winter daylight it made her look quite ill. She was extremely pale and she had eaten nothing—

Jonah!—ill-omened messenger of the Lord, his name for centuries synonymous with bad luck.

Understanding dawned upon Robin in an unpleasant moment which made him sweat with horror. It was one o'clock in the morning before she left her place and he was able to calculate dully that she had endured over fourteen gruelling hours of ceremony on a day she should have spent in bed. A day he personally had guaranteed as propitious.

She was not going to forgive him for this, he knew it. Dee was to blame, but Dee was safely buried at Mortlake beyond her immediate reach. The damned charlatan would doubtless get away with it, while Robin paid the penalty, like the Greek messengers of old. And the penalty would be withdrawal of her favour—

Hopelessly, he dared one more glance at her and found her eyes suddenly fixed upon him. Her face was waxen with fatigue, but her smile was warm, reaching out to him like a friendly hand. To the end of his life he never knew how she found the strength to walk out of the Hall and back to the palace unaided.

When she had gone he found his eyes were wet with unshed tears. And it was no surprise to him next morning when he was told his tournament must be cancelled because the Queen was too ill to attend it.

The opening of Parliament was also delayed by the Queen's illness, the first real indication to the court that they might all be living in a fool's paradise. Cecil conducted state business at her bedside and was aware of a nagging anxiety. Evidently she was not as strong as her blazing energy had seemed to suggest. The official explanation that she had a bad cold hardly seemed sufficient to account for her pinched pallor and her listless lack of appetite. She seemed to have dissipated all her reserve of strength and he was suddenly aware of the pressing need to get her married and safely with child. If she should die without leaving an heir of her own body, the country would be thrown back into the dynastic feuds of the previous century, the Catholics plumping for Mary Stuart while the Protestants championed Lady Katherine Grey. There would be utter chaos. Surely she could see that.

While he was there, they brought her a bowl of steaming beef broth which she pushed to one side without interest. He was driven then to interfere and beg her to take some nourishment.

'. . . for the sake of this country which depends on Your Majesty's well being.'

She glared at him but picked up the spoon, like a sulky child, and began to toy half-heartedly with the contents of the bowl. As he took his leave, he told himself feverishly that there was no time to waste, no time to waste at all.

I must find her a husband quickly—

The shadows over her crown were rapidly growing longer. In France Mary Stuart had officially quartered the English royal arms with those of France and Scotland and now appeared at all public functions under the title of Queen of England. It was the first serious challenge to Elizabeth's legitimacy, and it could only mean that sooner or later the French King would enforce his daughter-in-law's claim with an army. And England was in no position to wage war at the moment. So much depended on the uncertain life-span of one delicate, wilful young woman—it hardly bore thinking about.

And yet he thought of it continually, while snow fell soundlessly outside his narrow window. Waking and sleeping Elizabeth was never far from Cecil's thoughts. Her pale, oval face seemed to be permanently engraved on his mind and in any other man there would be only one word for such obsession in a woman. But he was not in love with her. How could he be when he was so utterly devoted to his bluestocking wife? He was a simple, respectable married man who had neither the time nor the inclination for other women.

And yet she was everything to him, he could not deny it. His career, his future, almost his twin soul. He had never felt this way for any other human being. He had served and abandoned several men in cold blood, but deep in his heart he knew he would never be able to abandon Elizabeth, no matter what she did against him. It would be like abandoning himself.

On the day she officially swore him into her service, her eyes had looked straight and unafraid right into his soul.

'It is my command that at all times, without respect to my private will, you will be faithful to the state and give me always the counsel you think best. I know you will not be corrupted by any manner of gift . . .'

Her words had moved him immeasurably, her riveting glance had made him tremble with the magnitude of the burden she laid upon him. She had said in public that he was a man who could not be bought. How did she know it? Many would say his record for loyalty was not an impressive one. Indeed he could think of only one other who would have given that judgement of him—his straight-laced, unexciting, but entirely reliable wife, Mildred. Was it possible that the Queen, on such a relatively brief acquaintance, could know him as well as his own wife? Because if she did, then her judgement was not only sound—it was quite uncanny.

For Mildred was the key that unlocked the inner man in Cecil. He was a loyal husband and a loving father in an age where those qualities were rare. He and his wife had a happy, stable union and they had dwelt for many years behind its dull fortress in secure harmony, no hint of restless dissatisfaction on either side.

Now suddenly there was the Queen, volatile, unpredictable, demanding— the very antithesis of Mildred in every way. And Cecil knew the quiet, happy existence of his home life must lose something in consequence of his extraordinary relationship with Elizabeth.

He accepted the loss gladly and felt guilty because of it. Once he would have said nothing in this world could come between him and Mildred, but now holding his place at Elizabeth's side was his sole concern. He had a dream—a strong, united England guided by his hand—and Elizabeth was the answer to that dream. He had sensed her kindred spirit years ago, and known that there might yet be one worthy of his selfless devotion, one he would not need to desert.

She owed him loyalty, a debt of gratitude and already she had begun to repay it. He was jealous of his influence, terrified of losing it, prepared to hate anyone who might place it in jeopardy. And fierce resentment had begun to gather in his mind around the name of Mary Stuart. She was sheltered behind the might of France and there was no way they could strike at her directly. But in her native land of Scotland her crown was not so strong, defended virtually alone by her Catholic mother, the Regent Mary of Guise, struggling to uphold the lost cause of the Catholic faith in a land ruled by the Puritanical kirk. Oh yes, it was in Scotland that they must strike at Mary Stuart, strike hard and soon, aiding the rebellious Protestant lords. They could rely on help from the Scottish preacher John Knox, who held the populace under his thumb—Knox who had denounced the 'monstrous regiment of women', but would surely bend his scruples to the wind of necessity in alliance with a Protestant Queen.

Cecil frowned and tapped his quill on the crowded desk in front of him. There was much to be done and little time left in which to do it. Elizabeth had given him leave to speak his mind freely on all occasions and he hoped she had meant it; for he was about to tell her two things that he knew instinctively she would not like. First that they must make war on Scotland. And second she must stop flirting with a married man in order to attend to the serious business of choosing her husband.

CHAPTER 6

Everything depends on the husband she chooses . . . If she decides to marry out of the country, she will at once fix her eyes on Your Majesty.'

Feria could not believe he had ever written those confident words, as he sat now surveying the failure of his diplomatic mission. He had thought her 'a young untried lass, sharp, but entirely without prudence', and she had succeeded in making him and his master look utter fools. There had been a point when he was quite sure of her, so sure that Philip had finally abandoned his tortuous and contradictory instructions and come out in the open with a marriage proposal and the command—extraordinary from Philip!—to 'spare no expense in the matter'.

So Feria had spared no expense. Gifts she had had aplenty—boxes of jewels, God only knew what—but in return she raised continual objections to the match. She feared Philip would spend very little time with her, he would come and go even if she were pregnant . . . Indeed her objections began to sound so remarkably like echoes of Philip's complacent letters to him, that Feria was quite certain his correspondence was being tapped.

True, he could no longer complain of her neglect. She told him gossip, invited him to plays and listened to his advice with flattering attention.

'I often wish,' she had told him innocently, 'that religion had played a larger part in my upbringing.'

Feria had fallen for the bait and that was the beginning of their happy theological discussions, when he brought her doctrinal books, assuring himself—and his master—of her good intentions to remain true to the Roman faith. And while he was lulled on the soft tide of her charm, she was duly crowned and held her first Parliament . . . which made her Supreme Governor of the Church of England.

Then suddenly there was no further need for deceit.

She took off the charming smile and told him curtly that she could not possibly marry the King of Spain because she was a heretic.

A heretic! The word was thrown at him like a lighted torch and mentally he stepped back from it, aghast. All those books, all those soul-searching little talks where he had marked her for a true Catholic at heart! How could she use such an inflammatory, undiplomatic expression?

'Madam, I cannot believe you are a heretic.' He spoke soothingly, half suspecting she was feverish. 'You know that you would not separate yourself from the true Church for all the thrones in the world.'

'So much the less,' she snapped, 'would Philip do it for a woman!'

He found he had begun to sweat copiously. 'Men,' he ventured uneasily, 'sometimes do for a woman what they would do for nothing else.'

'Oh, *men!*' she spat, and walked away from him. The rest of the interview was like awakening from a pleasant dream to a nightmare reality. He heard her swear and say she meant to do absolutely as her father had done.

Ashen-faced, he bowed to her and told her she was no longer the Elizabeth he had known. She was not quite quick enough then to conceal her smile of satisfaction and he actually shouted—from the safety of the doorway—that if she continued in this fashion she was a lost woman.

In Spain, Philip was jolted out of his comfortable complacency by the unbelievable news that he had been turned down.

Wait for me, Philip . . .

And he had waited patiently—for this insult!

He went to his private altar and tried to pray for guidance, but he could not hear God's voice for his own, screaming silently in his head.

She'll pay for this. One day I swear she'll pay . . .

But not just now. Now he had to save face in the only way open to him, by finding a wife as soon as possible to negate his assumed interest in the Queen of England.

There was only one royal bride instantly available, the little French Princess Elisabeth already betrothed to his son, Carlos. Philip broke the betrothal and married her himself—and saw to it that the Queen of England should be one of the first to hear the news.

'My name is a fortunate one,' said Elizabeth, and pouted so convincingly that Feria was instantly uneasy. Oh Lord, had he been too hasty, misunderstood a passing mood of petulance for declared intent—botched the whole thing after all?

'Madam,' he cried, exasperated beyond endurance, 'The fault lies with you —you *know* how unwilling I have been to accept your refusal.'

'Surely he could have waited three or four months—I might have changed my mind, you know.'

Was she laughing at them—was she? He went away to record his angry opinion for the edification of his master and posterity.

'The country is lost to us now, body and soul, for it has fallen into the hands of the Daughter of the Devil and the greatest scoundrels and heretics in the land.'

But Elizabeth had many other suitors and had already discovered that no other creatures in the world were quite so easy to exploit. She had had more than her money's worth out of Philip.

Now she was ready to take on the rest.

Cecil found himself living on a razor-edge of anxiety. They had gambled high with Philip, gambled to the very limit, and that July, when the French King died in a jousting accident and Mary Stuart became Queen of France, it began to look as though they had exhausted their run of luck. With Mary's uncles now in command of the French government it seemed unlikely that the Scottish rebellion would be allowed to continue unchecked. Once a French army had marched into Scotland to deal with the rebel Protestant lords, it was uncomfortably obvious where it would advance next. Philip was allied in marriage to France and Elizabeth could no longer count on his active support. They were saying in Europe that the reign of the bastard Tudor would be fortunate to reach the end of its first year.

And in the back streets of London they had begun to take bets on the outcome . . .

The new King of France had claimed the English throne in the name of his wife, and everyone at court was devastated by the news.

'Let him have a care,' snapped Elizabeth savagely, 'or I will take a husband to make his head ache!'

An uneasy silence fell over the courtiers assembled round the archery butts, suddenly irritating her beyond bearing. She flung down her bow and walked away from them before the caged fury inside her betrayed her insecurity any further. After a moment's hesitation, Robin handed his own bow to a page and hurried after her.

'Madam!'

She stopped and swung round upon him angrily.

'Damn you! How dare you run after me like a wretched little dog?'

He could have bowed and backed off as most men would have done faced with that curt reception. Instead he calmly took her arm.

'What good will brooding alone do? Whatever you feel like saying you may say to me and know it will go no further.'

She sighed and a little of the fiercely coiled tension went out of her as she allowed him to fall into step beside her.

'You're a thick-skinned devil,' she muttered, 'I'll say that for you.'

'Family trait,' he asserted cheerfully.

'Yes—you are your father's son.'

'And you,' he ventured carefully, 'you are to be married?'

'So it would seem.' Her face was suddenly stormy again. 'France leaves me precious little choice now.'

'You would let an insult force your hand?'

'This is more than an insult. It's a direct challenge.'

'Perhaps.'

'How can you doubt it? That grasping Scottish bitch collects crowns. She can't have a man in her bed because her husband is an impotent, half-witted Valois—so she'll have England instead to console her. But I know this—she'll rue the day she laid her greedy hands on my sceptre—by God she will!'

'She's very young and ruled by her uncles. She may not be directly responsible—'

He broke off abruptly beneath Elizabeth's unwavering gaze.

'I was not aware,' she said icily, 'that I was in conversation with the French Ambassador.'

Jealousy! There it was again, peeping out beneath her studied indifference, a shadow in her eyes, a tightening of her lips which filled Robin equally with excitement and fear. Sweet as it was, one did not court this woman's jealousy without risk.

He said hastily, 'I'm no friend of Mary Stuart's.'

'No?'

'*No*, madam. Indeed I know very little about her save that she must be a fool to think she can play against you to win.'

Elizabeth smiled faintly, as though for once he had paid her a compliment she really valued.

'How formidable you make me sound.'

'You *are* formidable in this mood. I tell you this much—I wouldn't care to be your enemy.'

She laid her hand gently on his sleeve and said softly, 'I don't think you will ever be that.'

They were silent for a while, comfortably, harmoniously silent, with their hands intertwined.

'Will there be open hostilities with France?' he asked at length.

She shook her head.

'Not if I can avoid it. Oh, I know Cecil wants war in Scotland—he'll bleat even louder now.'

'You don't have to take his advice on all issues. He presumes on his position.'

She frowned. 'It is my cousin who presumes.'

'You have too many cousins.'

'I know. And all of them legitimate.'

He squeezed her fingers between his own.

'They say the Queen of Scots has poor health. Perhaps she'll die.'

'That would solve nothing. Her death is the last thing on this earth I would wish for. I need her alive.'

She saw genuine surprise on his face.

'You *need* her?'

'She is my shield against Philip. If he would unseat me he must then put her in my place—he cannot deny her right to succeed. Consider the implications of France and Britain united under one ruler and you will see why Philip will never make war on me during her lifetime. I must live with her shadow, I have no choice.' She sighed. 'There's no place for personal hatred in the heart of a prince.'

'Or love?' he demanded suddenly.

She looked away from him uneasily.

'I value your friendship, Robin. I acknowledge you are good for me.'

'I could be better,' he said bluntly, 'much better. As good as you would be for me. I love you, Elizabeth, can't you see that? Is there no place in your heart and your bed for me?'

She twisted her hand away from his grasp.

'Don't ask me that—I don't know.'

'Is it because you do not know that you give no answer to your suitors?' he persisted urgently.

'You ask too many questions.'

'And you never give a straight answer.'

She laughed unsteadily and took a step back from him.

'Christ set us all a good example. Never answer your enemies' questions.'

He stiffened angrily. 'I want to be your lover, not your bloody enemy!'

'For me it is the same thing.'

He stared at her in astonishment and she bit her tongue. Too near the truth, that—and he must not know the truth. It could destroy all their precarious happiness.

She said flippantly, 'Ask me again when I'm in a better frame of mind,' and turned to look back across the lawns to where the little crowd still hovered around the archery butts, uncertain whether they could consider themselves dismissed or not. 'Come—you had better take me back. They are beginning to talk.'

'Talk about what?' he demanded irritably.

'They say you come too often to my rooms—and I to yours.'

'Oh, for God's sake—you never come alone!'

She shrugged and began to retrace her steps across the lawn, with the train of her russet shooting costume trailing over the parched grass.

'The Council doesn't like your familiarity with me.'

'You mean *Cecil* doesn't like it.'

She was silent and Robin knew his guess had been correct.

'I can't begin to understand why you put your trust in that man. He's a treacherous, self-seeking bastard.'

'I hear much the same song of you from him—admittedly in a lower key,' Elizabeth gave him a quick sidelong glance. 'Why do you dislike him so much?'

'He betrayed my father. If it hadn't been for him—'

'If it hadn't been for him,' Elizabeth cut in sharply, 'I would be dead now at your father's hands.'

Robin shook his head.

'Your life was never in any danger—only Mary's. Father swore you would not be harmed.'

She looked at him incredulously.

'And you believed him?'

'He gave me his word. And no matter what he may have done as a public man, once Father gave his word to any of us—'

Elizabeth's glance was suddenly curiously full of pity.

'Your father gave his word before God to your mother. He also gave her thirteen children.' Her voice was quiet and controlled. 'Shortly before Edward died he offered to divorce her and marry me. I refused. If I had not done so I would now be your step-mother and what you ask of me would be near incest.'

He was silent, utterly stunned, demoralized by this final disillusionment with a dead man. He could not question the truth of her assertion. Even Elizabeth would not lie on such a matter.

'Robin,' she said gently, 'I would not have told you that for all the world—but when you speak so lightly of treachery in a loyal man—'

'I understand,' he muttered stiffly. 'It ill becomes me. And I see now that you were right. Once Father had you in his hand your life would not have been worth a farthing piece. So when Cecil castigates me for a traitor's son you naturally listen to him. Under the circumstances you would be a fool to do otherwise.'

'I don't always listen to Cecil's tales,' she remarked lightly, 'or to his advice.'

He turned to her eagerly, grasping her hand so hard that she winced.

'Is he out of favour?'

She smiled evasively. 'Let's just say that some of his pearls of wisdom have fallen on deaf ears lately. Now forget him and fetch my bow. I still intend to win this match against you.'

He smiled suddenly.

'And I still intend to beat you hollow—*madam.*'

She laid her fingers lightly on his arm.

'That's why I love to shoot against you. You're the only man in this court who would dare.'

'Here is a great resort of wooers and controversy among lovers,' Cecil wrote irritably in October. 'Would to God the Queen had one and the rest were honourably satisfied.'

Certainly he had some cause for complaint. The court was a veritable bear garden of foreign envoys and lesser suitors, all clamouring for attention and all quite shamelessly encouraged by the most sought after young lady in Europe. She discouraged no one. They sent expensive gifts and while they were all planning to marry her, they were far too busy to consider any less friendly line of action. Let them all come, bearing jewels, furs and tapestries —she was quite happy to play them off, one against the other.

She was quite blatantly enjoying the farce, but Cecil was not amused.

'It can't go on much longer, madam—it really can't. You must,' he quailed as she looked up pointedly from her papers, 'it is—essential—that you marry soon.'

Elizabeth rose from her chair and arched her back like a lazy cat; he had never noticed before how decidedly feline all her movements were.

'Who can I marry?' she inquired with studied innocence. 'The people will resent a foreigner, the nobility will resent an Englishman—you must admit that doesn't leave a lot of choice.'

'Surely the Earl of Arran, as a Scot, would offend no one.'

'Except me!'

'Madam!' He flung out his hand hopelessly towards her. Of late all his gestures had become a little more exaggerated when he spoke to the Queen. 'I thought you liked him!'

'I liked him so well I hope never to see him again,' she said drily.

'But, madam, you said—'

'I said nothing of any consequence.'

'Yet Arran was convinced of your intentions.'

'My dear Cecil, they are *all* convinced of my intentions. I spend a great deal of time and effort to that very purpose. When I marry—*if* I marry—I trust it will be a man with more to sustain his role than six stiff inches of manhood. A mind for one thing wouldn't come amiss. Arran was more than half out of his—surely you noticed.'

Cecil coughed to cover his discomfort.

'A few unfortunate mannerisms, madam, nothing to cause real concern.'

'I fear they would concern me greatly,' she said coolly, 'in the bedchamber.'

He looked at the floor and she eyed him with amusement.

'Arran is overbred and unstable—like half the crowned heads in Europe. I will go virgin to my grave sooner than raise a brood of vacant lunatics to menace England after my death.'

'They're not *all* madmen' he began uneasily.

'No? You'd call the King of Sweden sane? Perhaps you should read some of his love letters. And the Spanish heir tortures live rabbits in his private apartments—roasts them alive on a spit so that he can hear them scream.'

'Rabbits?' he echoed vaguely.

'Distant relatives of yours, perhaps—they too are obsessed with perpetuating the species.'

'With respect, madam,' he said pointedly, 'this matter deserves serious discussion.'

She gave him a hard little smile that made her lips look like a closed trap and said silkily, 'I stand corrected, Mr Secretary.'

It would have silenced any other man, even Robin. But Cecil had courage. In spite of the sudden prickle of sweat above his upper lip, he had his teeth into the subject now and he did not mean to let go without a struggle.

'Your Majesty, I repeat, the present situation is insupportable. Your suitors—'

'My suitors,' she interrupted with a hostility that was now unmistakable, 'are a box of rotten apples. Show me one without a maggot big enough to consume me and England too and I'll marry him tomorrow!'

Retreating hastily from his blunder he said uncomfortably, 'Madam, I don't deny there are grave difficulties—'

'I've had enough of the subject,' she snapped. 'If you have nothing else to say then get out of here and leave me in peace.'

'Your Majesty.' He inclined his head automatically and began to talk of other business, giving in to her once more as he was finding it necessary to do with increasing frequency these days. She was easily ruffled of late, flippant and cantankerous by turns and it was extremely difficult to judge which way her mood would turn. Their relationship was suffering in consequence and he believed he knew the reason why. There was only one man in this court who could make her behave like an adolescent girl in love, stubborn and intractable, blind to all reason. Robert Dudley, that undesirable young upstart, a married man it was true, but with a meek little wife who kept herself discreetly in the country, childless and divorceable. If the Queen should choose Robert Dudley to be her consort, Cecil had a shrewd idea what his own fate would be.

They began to discuss arrangements for armed men to march on Scotland; and the atmosphere between them as they did so was decidedly frigid.

Soft yellow candlelight filled the Queen's bedchamber, winking on the jewels of a select little group of courtiers, the favoured, privileged few who had spent the evening in her company. Talk and laughter faded slowly in their wake as they kissed her hand and began to file out into the Privy Chamber.

Robin lingered long over kissing her hand. He was always the first to arrive and the last to leave and now he stood with her hands in his as though force alone would make him tear himself away.

She was beautiful tonight, an elegant column of black velvet stamped with golden oak leaves, her chin framed by a ruff of finely worked lace. Slowly, deliberately, he drew her forward into his arms and there was a breathless silence as their lips met. For a long moment she was locked in his urgent embrace, and then at last she drew away and pressed her hands against his shoulder, gently pushing him back. He whispered something in her ear; those by the door heard her laugh softly and saw her shake her head, then he bowed deeply, reverently, and backed out of the room, his eyes never leaving her face. The door closed behind him and she stood staring at it, smiling, oblivious to the tense, uneasy glances her women exchanged as they materialized from the corners of the room and came forward to begin the arduous ceremony of the Disrobing. Nobody spoke; nobody dared. Elizabeth sat down at her dressing-table and stared into her mirror with distant eyes.

Lettice Knollys removed the little pearl-studded cap and began to brush the Queen's long hair until her arm ached. Lettice was one of her many Boleyn cousins, a light-natured, impudent chit of a girl with a sharp malicious tongue that often amused her cynical mistress. But the woman who watched her now in the mirror was not preparing to be amused. She had caught

Lettice smiling very warmly at Robin this evening, and consequently felt less than cousinly towards her.

When the brush tugged at a tangled curl and flew from Lettice's grasp, she was more than ready for her.

'I'm sorry, Your Majesty—'

Elizabeth turned very slowly from the mirror, holding the moment for her embarrassment.

'Take care how you treat your Queen's possessions,' she remarked pointedly.

The cold formality of Elizabeth's challenge covered Lettice with confusion as she groped uncertainly for the brush.

'Shall I—shall I continue, madam?'

'Thank you.' Elizabeth took the brush out of the girl's quivering hand. 'I think I would prefer to keep what little hair is left after your clumsy ministrations.'

'I'm truly sorry, madam—I swear I never saw the snarl.'

'Yes—I have observed your eyes to be elsewhere more than once this evening.'

Lettice turned a dull brick-red and tiny beads of perspiration broke out above her upper lip.

'Madam, I beg—'

'I have no further need of you tonight, Lettice. You may withdraw.'

Lettice curtsied and hurried out of the room and the Queen leaned her chin on her hands, still staring dreamily into the mirror. It was seldom necessary for her to put anyone in their place more than once; she put Lettice out of her mind as easily as she might have closed a book.

'Your Majesty—I must speak to you.'

Elizabeth dragged her eyes unwillingly from her reflection and looked up to find Mrs Ashley at her side, nervously twisting her wedding ring.

'What the devil's wrong with you, Kat? You look as though all the hounds of hell are on your tail.'

Kat slipped painfully to her knees and groped for the Queen's hands. The hounds of hell would be the least of her worries once she had said what she knew she must.

'Madam, forgive me—forgive me, but I must say this. Lord Robert Dudley —' she hesitated, groping for the right words, and Elizabeth sighed faintly.

'Madam, to allow him such freedom—such liberties with your person—'

Elizabeth smiled and touched the faded face at her knee with affection.

'Kat! Lord Robert is like a brother to me. Why shouldn't he kiss me goodnight?'

Kat glared up at her through red-rimmed eyes. When a brother and sister kissed like that there was a very ugly word for it.

'Such behaviour will ruin your reputation,' she insisted.

Elizabeth picked up the brush and began to brush her hair lazily.

'If you continue to cluck like an old hen I shall simply ignore you, Kat.'

In all her years of tending Elizabeth, Kat had never once lost her temper. But she lost it now.

'You can't behave like this—do you think the people will stand for it?'

'Kat—'

'By Christ's soul, madam, I would I had strangled you in your cradle before I let you live to see this day.'

The room was suddenly utterly silent. All the women waited with taut anticipation for Katherine Ashley to have her ears boxed, but they waited in vain. Elizabeth turned from the mirror and laughed.

'I was four years old when I first came into your care, Kat. Never tell me I was still in a cradle!'

Mrs Ashley dissolved into hopeless, incoherent tears.

'Oh, yes—that's Your Grace all over—mocking, poking fun—but it won't do, I tell you, it won't do. For God's sake, madam, marry him and put an end to all these terrible rumours.'

'What rumours?' inquired the Queen steadily. Kat's angry gaze fell to the floor.

'The whole of Europe is saying that—that you and he—'

'Then the whole of Europe is wrong, as you quite well know. I have done nothing that would bring me into dishonour.'

Elizabeth rose slowly from her chair and her loose ermine robe hung open over a white nightdress embroidered with diamond-eyed butterflies. Her narrow face was suddenly weary and strangely sad.

'Kat,' her voice was gentle, as though she spoke to a dull-witted child, 'I have lived in this world for twenty-six years now with very little joy. Robin is my loyal subject, my best friend and I don't want to hear another word against him—do you understand?'

'But Your Majesty—'

'I said, enough!' suddenly the patience exploded like a treacherously dormant firecracker. She picked up the hairbrush and hurled it at the door.

'God's death, woman, are you stupid? Outside that door are guards and ministers and courtiers. Have I a chance in hell of leading a dishonourable life?'

In the deathly silence she stalked to the curtained bed, threw off her robe and plunged between the sheets. First Lettice, now this. It was intolerable!

She glared across the room.

'But I tell you this, Kat Ashley, if I ever had the wish to live in dishonour, I'm damned if I know of anyone who could forbid me.'

The silence deepened and she punched her pillows furiously before burying her face in them. The women who had frozen, horrified, about their various duties, now came forward warily to curtsey and bid her goodnight. She did not look up or reply to any of them.

Mrs Ashley signed to them to leave and blew out the remaining candles; Elizabeth was left alone to stare hot-eyed and miserable through a sleepless night.

CHAPTER 7

Cecil paused in the doorway of the Privy Chamber and was aware of instant irritation at the sight which greeted his eyes.

The Queen was sitting on cushions in the window-seat, virtually surrounded by Dudleys. Robert sat beside her, as though it were his right, Mary and Katherine sat on the floor, and Mary's husband leaned against the panelled wall. The whole room was ringing with their rude laughter—evidently, from its shrill, spiteful sound, they were having fun at someone's expense. And Cecil immediately felt threatened and uneasy.

No one had noticed his arrival and for a moment he hesitated in the shadows, wondering how best to break the news which had brought him here. Always laughing these days, he thought sourly, never serious, never listening to him as she had sworn to do. 'Put not your trust in princes' said the old adage—he was beginning to think it might be sound advice!

He was very close, close enough now to hear their conversation and see Robin, with familiar ease, snap shut the Queen's comfit box and hand it to his sister Mary.

'Take them away or Her Majesty will eat no supper.'

It was a bad sign, thought Cecil bleakly, that the Queen, instead of responding to this rank insolence with anger, merely smiled at Mary.

'Temperance is a virtue, as your brother so rightly reminds us,' she said calmly. 'Perhaps he would be happy to set us all a good example by following the diet I shall draw up for him.'

There was a moment's silence, followed by immediate laughter at Robin's expense.

'Dear madam, Mother told him years ago he would eat his way into an early grave. If you put him on a diet, I beg you, hold him to it.'

'Aye,' said Henry Sidney slyly, 'the wing of wren for breakfast and the leg for supper.'

'The twentieth part of a pint of wine and as much of St Anne's sacred water as he cares to drink—'

'Poor Robin—he'll fade away.'

'My dear Kitty, where *could* all that flesh fade to?'

Robin got up with dignity and pulled the Queen lightly to her feet.

'Madam, let me remove you from the presence of these gaggling geese. Come riding with me and I will show you that exercise is more beneficial than any diet.'

'Oh, but I believe the kind of exercise you have in mind cannot be conducted on horseback!'

He drew her firmly away from the others with no difficulty.

'You'd be surprised what I can do on horseback when I put my mind to it.' He smiled meaningfully. 'I'm a man of many parts.'

'Yes,' she said with a sly glance at his jewelled codpiece, 'some of them more prominent than others.'

Suddenly they both caught sight of the Secretary and halted; the raucous laughter behind them also stopped abruptly in that same moment.

Robin's hand rested possessively at the back of Elizabeth's waist in a gesture that was just short of an embrace. Cecil was aware of hostile glances from the Dudley faction and a certain coolness in the Queen's eyes.

'I don't recall sending for you, Cecil.' Her voice was neutral, faintly bored.

'Madam, I bring news from Scotland.'

'Oh? From the length of your face I take it to be less than good.'

'Cecil never smiles,' remarked Robin spitefully, 'but with your leave, madam, I could instruct him.'

Cecil directed a look of contemptuous loathing at the young man and turned to appeal quietly to the Queen.

'Madam, I should be grateful for a private audience.'

'If you bring bad news we can all hear it.' She stepped away from Robin's encircling arm; her face was suddenly like finely chiselled stone. 'Spit it out and be quick about it.'

Cecil was appalled by her change of tone. Impossible to remind her in public of the promise she had made to give him private audience whenever he desired it.

'Madam,' he took a faltering breath, 'our troops have been defeated at Leith.'

'What!' Her eyes narrowed on his face like splinters of ice. 'Did I not tell you to let the Scots slit their own throats? How many dead?'

He looked away in the tense silence that had fallen.

'Five hundred, madam.'

A gasp echoed round the room and was stilled on the next breath. Robin was not alone in hoping to see the distinguished Secretary get what was clearly coming to him.

Then suddenly, inexplicably, she decided not to make a public scene of this after all and snapped her fingers to the little group behind her.

'Leave me—yes, Robin, you too—Sir William has a little explaining to do!'

Cecil watched them go with grateful relief, and thanked God that she was going to be reasonable after all. But when the door had closed behind them and he dared to look once more into her face, his heart sank into his boots.

He emerged from her room more than an hour later, pale and exhausted after the most blistering interview he had ever endured in his life. He had known she had a temper, but never, never had he dreamed she would ever speak to him like *that*—so coldly, contemptuously, as though she would never trust his opinion again. The fact that he had eventually persuaded her to send more troops counted for nothing against that memory. He was suddenly so bitter with disillusion that he felt quite murderous with rage. How could she have changed so soon, promised so much and then gone back on her word, when he had been so sure—so certain—that she was different from all the rest. Put not your trust in princes!

He was not a violent man; he could not even remember the last occasion on which he had lost his temper. He was dimly aware of his servants' glances of surprise, as he sat at length in his small, panelled study, drumming his fingers on the desk and gazing stonily at the wall. It took a long time for the unaccustomed rage to leave him, but when it had gone it left him stone cold, like iron forged in heat and left to cool. And in such a mood, this quiet, unassuming man was infinitely dangerous.

With complete dispassion, he began to examine the policy that appeared to have so deeply displeased her. At first she had liked it well enough. Lending underhand assistance to the Protestant rebels in Scotland had suited her nature admirably. It committed her to nothing and it had worked quite handsomely, until the Earl of Bothwell intercepted three thousand pounds of English gold in transit to the rebels. The scandal provoked by that would

have precipitated open hostilities, had not Elizabeth's convincing lying mollified the French and Scots ambassadors. In all his life Cecil had never met a
more plausible, smooth-tongued woman. She could tell you black was white
—and you'd believe it! For weeks she had lied like a Trojan and after she had
made such a good job of smoothing the situation it had been very, very hard
to get her to agree to open war. During the course of a heated disagreement,
he had threatened to resign over the issue. It had been a calculated risk and it
had paid off. Quite suddenly she seemed to change her mind and in March
an English army had advanced into Scotland. Philip of Spain promptly responded with such threatening gestures that Elizabeth was obliged to humour him with a promise to marry Spain's latest candidate for her hand, the
Archduke Charles.

A delicate situation admittedly, but not one without hope of success even
now. The defeat at Leith should prove no more than a temporary setback;
indeed Cecil had it on good authority that the Scottish Regent, Mary of
Guise, was near to death and in despair of receiving help from her French
allies.

Why then was Elizabeth suddenly so hostile? Because he had almost certainly committed her to marriage with the Archduke—was that it? And if
that was so, then it needed little imagination to see who was stoking the fires
of her indignation—Dudley, panicking at a move which would be the death
knell of his own ambitions. For weeks now Cecil had suspected that Dudley
was behind his own unlooked-for disfavour with the Queen. History was full
of incidents which proved how easily a malicious tongue could pour poison
into the royal ear. Anne Boleyn had destroyed Cardinal Wolsey by that very
means—slow, insidious, but devastatingly effective!

The scandal of Dudley's undesirable association with the Queen had already run the length and breadth of Europe. The English Ambassador to
Brussels had written back in December to tell Cecil that the rumours were so
bad he dared not repeat them. Everyone who loved the Queen and England
longed to see 'the Gypsy' dead or disgraced. The young Duke of Norfolk had
said publicly it was a disgrace that the realm could not produce one man of
sufficient spirit to dagger the knave. But no one would dare to do that and
risk facing the Queen's vindictive wrath. She would rend to pieces the men
she held responsible for that deed, and Cecil knew that he, along with Norfolk and Sussex, would certainly be suspected if the event took place. It could
be arranged of course, easily enough, but it was far too dangerous even to be
seriously entertained as a last resort. No, the elimination of Dudley, however
desirable, was not the answer to the Secretary's dilemma.

Evening drew on and a body-servant lit candles on his table with respectful curiosity.

'Will there be anything else, Sir William?'

'What? No—no—get yourself to bed.'

'You've had nothing to eat, sir.' The man paused in the doorway uncertainly. His master was a man of regular habits, reliable as a clock; he was not wont to sit brooding with that odd fierce look on his face. But the fellow received no answer and at length closed the door and hurried away.

Cecil sat with his hands clenched on the desk in front of him and surveyed the ominous facts before him. The Queen was cold with him, cold in a manner she had never shown him before and in her moody preoccupation with Dudley he read a woman on the brink of a disastrous love affair. If Dudley obtained a divorce she might well be tempted to marry him. And then—and then it was simple. Once Robert Dudley was King Consort, there would be no place in the government of England for the man who had betrayed his father. Cecil knew that a few weeks might be all that were left before he was fighting to keep his place, and perhaps—since it seemed he could no longer depend on the Queen's loyalty—even his life!

Change of fortune was not unfamiliar to Cecil. Twice now he had attached himself to men who had fallen, yet had failed to take him with them to the block. He had a shrewd politician's instinct which told him when to risk a desperate gamble. He was ready to risk one now if it should prove necessary, but it would be a risk, probably the greatest he had ever taken in his life. And certainly the most unscrupulous.

It was a risk because it involved the Queen's whole future; and in many ways the Queen remained an enigma to him. He did not really know her and he doubted if anyone ever had or ever would. But he knew this: the crown of England meant more to her than anything else on this earth. She guarded her power with animal-like intensity. If Dudley could be discredited in the eyes of the world, if there could be a straight choice between her lover and her crown—Cecil swore he knew which way the cat would jump.

The spies he had planted in Amy's household at Cumnor Place informed him that her servants had begun to keep a careful watch over her food. Rumour was rife all over England and Europe that Dudley would soon dispense with his unwanted wife. Divorce was the obvious means to gain his freedom and, after King Henry's matrimonial escapades, was no longer the scandalous procedure it had once been. The Protestant Church permitted it —even the late Duke of Somerset had once availed himself of the legal loophole. But the scandal-mongers of Europe were not trafficking talk of divorce; they were waiting with gleeful anticipation for murder. Speculation was at such a pitch in foreign courts, that if Amy were to die now, even of natural causes, there would not be one voice raised in Dudley's defence.

Not even the Queen's. Cecil was ready to stake his whole career on that. She might in a rash moment risk marrying a divorced man, the son of a traitor, and hope that her popularity would weather the storm. But she could not possibly hope to marry a murderer and survive the scandal.

Cecil buried his face in his hands. It was a gamble—too great a gamble. And he was not without conscience. He remembered Amy well—a pretty, innocent creature already wronged by two utterly selfish young people. Oh no, he did not want to do this; there was too much that could go wrong.

But if it came to it, if there should be no other way of restraining the Queen before she ruined them both . . .

Oh God, let her come to her senses before it is too late . . .

The candles wilted on his desk and he sat on in the darkness, a quiet, eminently civilized, middle-aged man—with murder in his heart.

'I have this theory,' said Robin complacently, 'that the complete man at some point in his life must make war to fulfil a basic need. It goes without saying, of course, that the complete woman must make love.'

Elizabeth pirouetted beneath his hand.

'And the complete monarch?'

'Makes both, naturally, madam.' He smiled and continued to glide down the crowded ballroom at her side. 'So—since you are already at war with Scotland—may I not come to you tonight and complete your royal fulfilment?'

'No,' she smiled and made him an exaggerated curtsey. 'Not tonight, not tomorrow, not next week, next month, next year—'

'Why is it always *No?*' he interrupted with a sigh.

She lifted her face to his and her eyes slanted a gleam of open mockery.

'I should have thought the complete man would know the answer to that. Perhaps he'd better ask Cecil, since an heir for England, and who best to get it from, is the sum total of his conversation these days.'

'Is he pressing you to marry?' Robin was alarmed.

'It would be closer to the truth to say he's squeezing me in a damned vice!'

Robin's hand tightened angrily on hers, causing the coronation ring to bite into her flesh.

'I knew he'd make trouble for you. The man's a snake in the grass—get rid of him while you still can.'

'While I still can?' she raised her fine eyebrows slightly. 'Perhaps you would care to explain what you mean by that?'

'I mean that he's beginning to be resented.'

She laughed. 'By you!'

'And others,' he countered swiftly. 'A great many others.'

'Oh?' she turned, glided to the right and looked at him over her bare shoulder. 'And with what snake should I replace him, my cunning mathematician—an *adder* perhaps?'

He acknowledged her sly wit with a sulky frown.

'I tell you this, madam, no man at court will be able to fart soon without asking Cecil first.' He saw her smile complacently and lowered his voice. 'But there's something else that won't amuse you quite so much—something they've begun to call him behind your back.'

'And that?'

'*King* Cecil.'

Her glance impaled him like a spear and made him catch his breath; she was suddenly no longer safe to tease. Daring to hint at Cecil's dominance had placed him on very treacherous ground. She moved away again, this time to her left, swung back and touched hands with him. Her eyes were a hard, brilliant gleam of challenge.

'There is no king here,' she said coolly, 'and as long as I live there never will be. You had better remember that Sweet Robin—and choose your words with more care.'

'While he chooses your husband! Marries you off to some impotent, imbecile princeling who'll make your life a misery!' Robin's voice dropped to a note of desperate daring. 'He'd never let you marry me now—would he?'

Elizabeth halted abruptly in the middle of the measure and stared at him. The music in the gallery above trailed into uncertain silence, and the rest of the dancers also stood still, watching them with speculative eyes.

'Play on!' she said curtly and walked away to the table at the window to pour ale. Robin followed with his heart in his mouth, knowing that if he had misjudged this moment his whole future lay in the balance. It was the first time he had ever dared to mention marriage; had he presumed too much at last?

'Madam—'

She handed him a tankard of ale and spoke without turning to look at him.

'So that's what's behind all your pretty love talk—I should have known, of course—'

His hand groped out towards her and fell back to his side.

'Elizabeth—' he whispered.

She turned to look at him then and there was a crooked little smile on her lips. He had laid his cards on the table and he was entirely at the mercy of her whim. She rather enjoyed watching him sweat.

'Why should I want to marry you?' she inquired at last with quiet amusement. 'Women marry for security, for wealth or power—I need no man to give me these things.'

'Some women marry for love,' he ventured softly and she laughed out loud.

'Some *men* like to think so.'

Well—at least she was not angry! He drew a breath and dared a little further.

'If I were free of Amy would you marry me?'

'You?' she shrugged carelessly. 'You are unsuitable on every count—a low-blooded upstart descended from a tribe of traitors.'

'In that case why keep me with you?'

'I suppose because I've got no taste.' She set down her tankard and he felt his confidence mounting. She had the hesitant, uncertain look of a coy female hedging for delay and he felt suddenly masterful and decisive enough to force a decision.

'I shall seek an immediate divorce,' he said quickly. 'Amy won't stand in our way. I know that.'

Something moved behind the Queen's eyes and was gone almost before he saw it. For a moment he could have sworn it was fear.

She shook her head.

'No divorce. Not yet. There is scandal enough.'

'When I am a free man the scandal will die. I don't see any point in prolonging this meaningless relationship with my wife.'

'I forbid it, Robin!'

There was a sharp note in her voice now that warned him to push no further for the moment.

'Very well,' he said ungraciously. 'If that's what you wish—but will you give me no reason?'

The bitter disappointment on his face softened her and she reached up to pat his cheek.

'*Andante andante,*' she said softly and led him back into the centre of the floor where all the dancers swept back to make room for them. 'Step softly round my crown.'

She swung into the bedchamber an hour later with the heavy satin gown swirling out from her tiny waist like the upturned petals of a tulip. The new fashion she had set had led to an outburst of billowing gowns, with skirts so full and wide that sheer lack of space enforced many of her ladies to dine on cushions on the floor. Fashions were becoming preposterous, muttered the elderly—they matched the new Queen's morals!

She swept past her women with an impatient wave of her hand.

'Leave me,' she said.

The women left with the speed which was beginning to characterize obedience to Elizabeth and only Mrs Ashley dared to linger, observed the slight flush in her mistress's normally pale cheeks and thought: Something has happened between them.

'Kat,' said her mistress, but not unkindly, 'I told you to leave me.'

For a moment Kat's eyes appealed to her.

Trust me, take me back into your confidence. I will never betray you again. You need to talk to someone, to share your hopes and fears. Let it be me. Please!

Elizabeth looked at the woman who was all she had ever really known of a mother and for a moment the need to pour out her confused emotions almost overwhelmed her common sense. But she dared not trust Kat, or anyone, with her confidence. She had lost the power to surrender herself. Kissing the old woman lightly on the cheek, she turned away to the window; after a moment she heard the soft click of the door closing and knew that Kat had gone.

She began to pace up and down the room and felt the prickle of cold sweat breaking out over her body in spite of the heat. Suddenly her whole life was in turmoil once more, and she felt an unwilling rage surging up in her towards the author of her distress. In a few short moments he had altered the entire course of their lives, for he was no longer a pleasant friend, a casual, harmless flatterer. He was a threat to her power and nothing could ever be the same between them again. He had spoilt everything!

She had expected him to make some clumsy bid to become her lover, but she had never dreamed he would have the sheer effrontery to suggest marriage. He had shot that arrow when she was totally off guard and sure enough it had pierced to the core of the barricaded citadel which she called her heart. And she had been so sure that no man would ever have the power to do that again.

The summer of her reign these first two years had been; her power, her glorious power, untouched by her harmless flirtation. And now it was spoilt, spoilt, spoilt! She threw an inkpot from her desk into the empty hearth in a tearful temper. Could she really have been so *stupid* as to fall in love with him? Had she learnt nothing from the past, after all? She sank into a chair and covered her face with her hands in an attitude of despair. What a fool she was, what a fool! Was it about to happen all over again, the whole ugly sordid business? She did not doubt his friendship, but she doubted his love, and her suspicion, now suddenly thrown into clear focus, was like a physical pain.

She sat very still in her chair, utterly miserable. He wanted her crown—all very natural, she could even understand it—but she could never take the risk of believing in his love.

I will not trust my body or my soul to anyone in this world.

How in God's name had she ever let it go so far, permitting a court flirtation to become a determined pursuit of her crown? And all because she had thought she was clever enough to play with fire and not be burnt! There was only one thing to do and that was to put an end to it by sending him away, lightheartedly, casually, as though the whole thing were no more than a joke to her. Let him ride back to Norfolk and cool his ardour with that silly little country bitch! Yes—that was it—she would send him away tonight, tomorrow, next week. *Soon!*

And the future? Bleak years of using herself like so much political merchandise, buying time for England, time and peace and the chance of prosperity. There was no one else who shared the memories of her traumatic childhood and miserable adolescence, no one else who made her laugh and forget her worries as he did, covering his ambition with a cloak of sincere affection so that she was almost—almost—tempted to believe in it. No, there was no one else she would ever love as she loved him. Without him, her world would be cold and empty, a gorgeous, glittering, lonely shell and she who had prided herself on her ability to face life in splendid isolation was suddenly terrified at the prospect of that existence. To be alone—utterly alone for ever—would be a living death!

God damn it, she would not send him away—and the devil take any man —yes, *any* man—who tried to spoil what little happiness she might find in Robin's company. His company was all she wanted. Was it too much to ask to remember that she was human?

She turned as the door opened and Mary Sidney bobbed an apologetic curtsey on the threshold.

'Your pardon, madam—but Sir William Cecil is waiting in the ante-room and begs to remind you that you promised him an hour this evening.'

King Cecil!

All her furiously bottled-up rage rushed out at the thought of that whey-faced lawyer. What did he want now? More nagging about the damned succession? All he cared about was pushing her into bed with some crowned nonentity; he didn't give a damn whether or not she would be happy, just as long as she did her duty and gave England a son. And if she died in childbirth, he would stand beside her coffin with reproachful eyes and say she had failed them all! She wanted to storm out into the ante-room and stuff his state papers down his throat, to scream and kick and shout: *I hate you—it's all your fault!*—to behave as she had done as a spoilt, wilful two-year-old when she could not have her own way. Years of deadly danger had forced her to learn a rigid self-discipline but, beneath the iron core of control, that petulant little girl still existed. She was always there, threatening to break out, and sometimes it was very hard to keep her out of sight.

Swallowing her temper, Elizabeth crossed the room slowly and deliberately, took a book from a table and settled herself to read.

'I'm busy, Mary. Tell him—' She paused and met her friend's even, puzzled stare, 'tell him to wait.'

Cecil waited almost thirty minutes in the antechamber, chafing at the delay which kept him from the stack of papers waiting in his room. Mary Sidney sat in the window-seat and uncomfortably avoided his questioning gaze each time he pointedly glanced at his timepiece.

When he was finally admitted, the sight of Elizabeth sitting idly in her chair turning the leaves of a book was the final straw. How dared she treat him as though he were the lowest counting clerk!

Stiff-necked with indignation, he informed her of the progress their troops had made in Scotland. There seemed every opportunity of a favourable peace treaty in which England would dictate the terms.

She patted a yawn and he had to put a hard grip on himself to hold his tongue.

'I hoped the news would please you, madam.'

'I think you are quite pleased enough for both of us,' she said unkindly. 'And since this is so plainly a personal triumph for you I feel you should see it through to the end.'

'Madam?' He was alert and uneasy.

'You will travel to Edinburgh and handle the terms of the treaty yourself.'

So she was sending him away from court! Why? What was she about to get up to behind his back?

She saw his face stiffen with alarm and laughed at him.

'Poor Cecil. You've no spirit for such a journey, have you? But I'm sure my cousin's Protestant subjects will make you very welcome. Take Mildred with you if you can't bear the separation. The Scottish air may bring a little colour to your sour face—God knows, it wouldn't come amiss!'

'I find it rather difficult to believe in Your Majesty's concern for my comfort.' He was coldly incredulous. The jibe at his wife was intolerable.

She shrugged indifferently.

'I desire it as I would my own.'

'But it is Your Grace who destroys it!' he burst out at last. 'Forgive me, madam, it is my duty to warn you of danger. Your conduct with Lord Robert Dudley will be your ruin.'

She looked at him calmly and he was unaware that he had just set fire to a very short fuse.

'Guard your tongue, my friend,' was all she said. Her voice was deceptively mild and again he was misled.

'I believe it was Your Majesty who asked me to speak my mind plainly, without respect to your personal will.'

Her book snapped shut and her eyes blazed suddenly hard and hostile.

'You may say what you like over matters of state, but leave my private life to me. I'll brook no interference there from anyone.'

'Madam, you have no private life. Your smallest action is a matter of state, you are the Queen—'

'Yes, Cecil, as you so rightly say but seem to be in danger of forgetting, I *am* the Queen. And I warn you now that the man who tries to use the spur with me will take a fall from which he'll never recover!'

She stood up suddenly and he stepped back from the smouldering fury in her eyes.

'You may leave me now, Cecil. Come back and speak to me again—' She turned her back on him and spoke spitefully over her shoulder—'when you have remembered your place!'

As he stared at her jewelled back something Sir Thomas More had once said of her father echoed ominously in his mind.

'If the lion knew his true strength it were hard for any man to rule him.'

And now he was finding it hard—perhaps impossible—to rule the lion's cub. He had thought himself in partnership with this splendid young lioness, but now he saw how easily she might break the chains of discipline and dignity, and turn upon him with rending claws, as the great Henry had turned on his loyal servants Wolsey and Cromwell. Never trust a cat, the least domesticated of all animals!

Bowing coldly, he left the room with heightened colour and in the doorway of the Privy Chamber met Robin Dudley, who inclined his head curtly and said with a smirk, 'Good evening, Mr Secretary. I trust you had a pleasant interview with Her Majesty?'

'I believe, my lord, that you would know that better than most,' said Cecil icily. 'And now, if you will excuse me, *someone* in Her Grace's court must see to the business of the realm!'

Robin watched triumphantly as Cecil stalked away into the Presence Chamber.

CHAPTER 8

Mary of Guise stared out over the stone battlements of Edinburgh Castle into the grey mist of another freezing Scottish dawn.

Never before had the narrow little streets of her capital city seemed quite so bleak. Sixteen years she had looked out upon them alone, sixteen years since her husband had died and left her to fight for the rights of a six-day-old daughter. She would not look out upon them much longer—her fight was over. She had lost; and just for once she had not expected to. The English troops had been so heavily defeated at Leith, at the very least she had expected a breathing space, time in which to receive help from France. But the slaughtered troops had been replaced with unbelievable speed to continue the besiegement without mercy. And in France, the uncovering of a Protestant conspiracy had drained the forces of her Guise relatives. Whatever aid came now from Mary's homeland would be too late to save French influence and the Catholic faith in Scotland.

Crossing the battlements with a slow, dragging step the Queen Mother returned to her rooms. They were bleak rooms, as cold and comfortless, even in summer, as the life she had led in this barren land since the day she had sent her little daughter to safety in France. She would never forget that French galley drawing slowly out of Dumbarton harbour, its precious cargo a five-year-old child, queen of the most barbarous country in Europe. It had been a mighty slap in the face for the English, who had hoped to take her captive to London; but now those wretched years of separation seemed so pointless.

Long, hard years they had been since that day she rode away from Dumbarton harbour, years filled with treachery and violence that had found her many enemies and a handful of loyal friends. And when she thought of friends, she thought of the Earl of Bothwell, surely the most unlikely man in this world to embrace a lost cause. Bothwell was a lone wolf and a loyal villain, the one member of the Protestant kirk who refused to run with Knox's pack. And it was Bothwell who had waylaid that three thousand pounds of Elizabeth's and embarrassed the English government—not that Elizabeth had been embarrassed for long. Her glib lies had disgusted Bothwell, who lied himself when it suited him as well as the next man, but had never thought to see a woman sink so low. She did not share his surprise or even his outrage, for it was the underhand which ruled the world now, the stab in the back rather than the honourable duel. It was the age of the serpent, and the tongue of the English snake was long and forked in the darkness. No one could yet be sure how far it reached.

But whatever followed this humiliating peace with England would not be Mary's concern. Her battle was over and with it her life—the doctors had been plain and already she felt distant and indifferent. An hour later, when they brought the news to her bedside that a delegation of English commissioners, headed by Sir William Cecil, was on its way to Berwick, she did not even turn her head on the pillow.

Cecil was glad of his lawyer's training, his ability to function with passionless efficiency while his mind was totally preoccupied with another matter. Reports from his spies came in a steady and unencouraging succession from England. The Queen and Lord Robert were everywhere together—they were shut up for hours at a time in the palace—they were alone— There seemed little doubt that their affair was rapidly moving towards some kind of emotional climax and Cecil was in a mad fidget to get back to the scene.

He cursed and railed against them in private, but it never affected his work for a moment as he juggled the complicated legal details which would result in an invaluable diplomatic triumph for England. The Scottish Regent had died shortly before his arrival; a military disaster in Tripoli had prevented Philip's active interference by obliging him to look to his own territories; France was still desperately occupied overthrowing the Protestant conspiracy of Amboise. Never had there been a more perfect opportunity for the English to throw the French out of Scotland and place power in the hands of the Protestant nobility, led by Mary Stuart's bastard brother, James.

By the 6th of July his work was completed. The Treaty of Edinburgh formally recognized Elizabeth's right to the English throne. The French, but for a mere handful of troops, were finished as a power in Scotland and the government of the realm could be safely left in the hands of Protestant allies. All that remained was the acquisition of Mary Stuart's signature to ratify the document, and the back door to England would be firmly locked. Cecil knew he had reason to be well pleased with his achievement and the knowledge raised his spirits, causing him to view his recent fears and discontent in a new light.

Whatever was happening in England, Elizabeth had to be grateful for this, for it altered her whole standing in Europe. He had made her as safe as she could ever hope to be and what had Dudley to offer to compare with that? It would surely win back her trust, that unique and deeply satisfying trust which had been his before Dudley stepped between them with his malicious innuendoes.

Suddenly, he could not wait to get back with his wonderful trophy; he was as eager as a hunting dog to lay a rabbit at his master's feet. She would not pat him on his head and say: 'Good boy', but she might lay those beautiful fingers on his arm for a moment and tell him he was her right hand. It was the same thing really, he supposed wryly, but what did it matter if only he could win her back again?

And perhaps he had been wrong to suspect her motive in sending him away, for who else could have handled this tricky business half so well? She had been right—he had needed this break from court, this chance to think things over and see how small and petty his fears really were. She would never let him down, not after all he had done for her, Elizabeth—*his* Elizabeth!

He went out into the courtyard and affably patted the placid mule which waited for him; and as he began the tedious jog south to Windsor, he found he was full of hope.

Passing through the cool corridors of Windsor Castle on his way to the royal apartments, Robin noted with satisfaction that no guard or gentleman usher presumed to bar his way or question his right of access to the royal presence. Nobody questioned him now. Of late it had pleased him to flaunt his unique privileges quite flagrantly in the face of the old nobility, and chief among those it amused him to irritate were the Earl of Sussex and the young Duke of Norfolk. Sussex castigated him openly as an upstart gypsy; Norfolk, during the course of a dangerously heated exchange, had advised him to abandon his 'preposterous pretensions' to Her Majesty's hand. The envious eyes of every man at court were upon him and few doubted that he would shortly be their new master. But while the fawning deference of the court was deeply gratifying, it did not serve to mask Robin's growing unease; he was still far from sure of winning that prize which everyone supposed to be so nearly in his grasp. He had rooms adjoining the Queen's so that he might be on hand day and night should she need him; but the arrangement was not made, as the ill-informed fondly believed, that he might play the lover with greater convenience. As yet, he had not played the lover at all and the lack of that role had begun to disturb him greatly.

Cecil's absence from court had seemed the answer to his anxious prayer at first—he had been certain it was Cecil who held her back from him. As soon as the dust settled behind the Secretary's entourage, Robin had begun to lay siege to the Queen's affections, like a man beleaguering a castle. He had been sure of his ability to breach her defences. No woman he desired had ever denied the final intimacy, and the removal of Cecil from the scene had seemed to herald his approaching triumph.

Through the lazy summer days he had bound her closer; mornings riding in the Great Park, afternoons on the sun-dappled river, evenings strolling hand in hand across the wooden terrace. She no longer seemed to care who saw their transparent happiness. Her attendants discreetly kept their distance —soon they were alone in her rooms and there, as he began to urge the natural conclusion of their love, he became slowly aware of something wrong, something missing in her response. She had become as tense and wary as a hunted fox and the previous evening a serious quarrel had blown up, causing him to depart in a towering rage to his own apartment.

He had woken in a sullen mood and gone down to the stables, where he relieved his feelings by finding fault and bawling at the grooms. He took a vigorous ride in Windsor Great Park and returned in a better frame of mind to discover the arrival of the Irish geldings he had ordered. In spite of their journey they were in prime condition, with proud heads and gleaming flanks and the promise of good speed. His first thought was of Elizabeth—she would be pleased. He wondered whether to go to her now with the news or wait until she joined him for the hunt and have the pleasure of her surprise.

And then his sister Mary had come down the path with a basket of roses on her arm, to tell him that the Queen had a headache and would not be riding today.

His face darkened. He took his sister's arm and steered her away from the prying ears of stable boys.

'She doesn't want to see me—is that it?'

Mary withdrew her arm from his urgent grip. Her voice was curiously cold.

'The Queen is ill, Robin. If you weren't so wrapped up in your own interests you might have noticed that she's not been well for several days.'

He stared at her uncertainly.

'But we've hunted and hawked and danced all week. She never said anything.'

Mary shrugged.

'She never says anything. Mrs Ashley has taught me to recognize the signs.'

He stood grinding the heel of his riding boot into the soft mud, tense and preoccupied.

'I wish I'd known,' he muttered. 'Perhaps it explains—'

Mary watched him for a moment and then laid her hand on his sleeve.

'Robin—what happened last night?'

'Nothing happened,' he said absently, kicking the caked mud off his boot. 'That's the trouble.'

'But you must have done something to make her so angry. Did you quarrel with her?'

His head jerked up angrily, as though she had jarred a painful nerve.

'That's none of your damned business,' he snapped, and turned away abruptly across the paddock, striding so fast on his long legs that she had to run to catch up with him.

He had no desire to talk of last night; how for the first time he had lost his temper, asked what the devil it was she expected of him, told her he was not cut out to live like a monk; how he had stormed to the door remarking angrily that he would settle with Amy whether she liked it or not, that he was damned if he needed the Queen's permission, or anyone else's, to divorce a wife who was a useless burden; how she had looked at him with icy contempt and told him that if he left the court now he need not trouble to return. An ugly quarrel that had placed everything at risk and all because he had lacked the sensitivity to look beneath her unreasonable attitude.

But, Christ—what *did* she want of a man? What had the Lord Admiral offered to sweep away her resistance? Was it necessary to throw her on a bed and cut her dress to pieces to arouse her interest? Perhaps he had been too much the gentleman—

Mary was at his side, her pretty face creased with anxiety.

'Robin, it's not safe to quarrel with her. You can't back her into a corner and take her by force.'

He stared across the paddock to where the grooms were trotting the Irish geldings for his approval.

'I must have her, Mary. I *must.*'

'But—if she does not want you—'

He swung round and grabbed her arm roughly.

'What has she said to you?'

'Nothing.'

'For Christ's sake, she's fond of you—and there's precious few women she does like—she must have told you *something.*'

Mary moved away angrily.

'I won't spy on her for you, Robin. She's been good to me since I came to court and I owe her loyalty.'

'You owe me a sister's loyalty.' He shook her roughly by the shoulders. 'Doesn't that count for anything any more?'

'You're so like Father,' she said suddenly. 'Always wanting the moon, never happy with anything less—if you're not careful you'll end the same way. You're pushing too hard and no one's indispensible to her.'

'Except Cecil!' he said bitterly and let his hands fall in a half-shamed gesture. 'He seems to be the only one she really trusts. I wish to God I knew what it is between the two of them.'

Mary was silent and her glance was touched with pity. She was very close to Robin, but she knew his faults and her primary attachment was now to Elizabeth. If she had to take sides, she would support her mistress.

'Robin,' she said softly, 'give it up. The Queen is not for you.'

'We'll see,' he said grimly and tugged the basket from her arm. 'Give me those roses. I'm going to her now, alone and unannounced—and I mean to find out, one way or another, where I stand.'

And so it was that he wound his way through the Presence Chamber and the Privy Chamber, to the door of the Bedchamber, where the Captain of the Guard, meeting his arrogant glance, let him pass without a murmur. He stood at length in the inner sanctum, a large, sunny, stone-walled room which housed the state bed, where the heavy curtains were partly drawn to shield the occupant from the bright light.

Mrs Ashley sprang up from her tapestry screen and her chair creaked with the violence with which she had vacated it.

'How *dare* you come in here unannounced!' she hissed. He put both hands around the waist of this elderly viper and swung her gently out of his path to the bed.

Once there, he drew the curtain quietly and hesitated. Elizabeth lay quite still on her pillows, her unpainted face very pale, her eyes closed. Only the faint tremor of her lids betrayed the fact that she was fully aware of his presence and only pretending to be asleep. If his intuition had played him false, the piece of lèse-majeste he had in mind would probably catapult him into an outer darkness from which he might never emerge. On the other hand—

He turned the rose basket upside down and emptied the contents over her; Mrs Ashley blanched with horror as the Queen sat up.

'You *bastard!*'

He caught Elizabeth's hand, kissed it and said with an impertinence that was almost suicidal, 'So *that's* what makes us such a perfect pair!—I've often wondered.'

Behind his back, Kat sucked in her breath with a sharp, gurgling gasp of incredulity. The Queen stared at him in silence and there was an endless moment in which he heard his own heartbeat hammering louder and louder inside his head, before she lay back on her pillows and, still watching him, said with inscrutable calm, 'Kat—you can go now.'

'Go, madam—go?'

'Oh, I don't think he's about to rape a sick woman—we all know what a perfect gentleman he is!'

Mrs Ashley withdrew in frigid disapproval and Robin watched her departure with satisfaction.

'Get these damned things off me,' said Elizabeth when the door had closed, 'and if just one of them pricks me, you insufferable pig, you'll be extremely sorry.'

He smiled. 'Madam, if I ever prick you it won't be with a rose.'

He leaned over the bed with an exploring hand and she bit him.

'Vampire!' He jerked back and sucked his finger. 'Look at that! You've drawn blood.'

The Queen reached out and took a golden paperknife from the bedside table, then lay back on her pillows and touched its gleaming edge with the tip of her tongue.

'Come closer,' she smiled, 'and I may draw a good deal more.'

The point of the knife flashed in the sunlight, teasing, provocative, edged with just sufficient genuine danger to make him pause for a second before he lunged forward and pinned both her hands behind her head on the pillow. The knife slipped from her grasp and fell to the floor; they rolled together across her bed, laughing like small children romping in a meadow.

At length he lay beside her on the coverlet, smoothing the hair back from her temples.

'About last night,' he began uneasily, 'if I had known, then naturally—'

'You would not have behaved like a boring boy in search of his first whore?'

'I could have been more—reasonable.'

'Oh,' she said innocently, 'were you being unreasonable?'

'You certainly appeared to think so.' He smiled cautiously, not quite sure of her mood even now. 'You were in such a rage I half expected to find myself under guard this morning. It's the first time we've quarrelled since we were children.'

She began to unfasten the silver buttons on his doublet.

'We're not children now,' she said softly.

He smiled at her, suddenly sure of her invitation.

'Sometimes I think you never were,' he said and bent his head to kiss her deeply. Her arms closed around him. He loosened the ribbon at the neck of her nightdress and slipped his hand inside to cup the warm softness of her breast. Her body arched with desire beneath him, a sudden urgent arousal which told him that at last it would all happen. Everything.

Deft from years of practice was the hand which freed him from the cumbersome cod-piece and then explored with knowledgeable skill, finding no need to delay the moment of their satisfaction. He lowered himself for the final act. In that same moment her eyes opened full on his face and every soft, seductive curve of her body went rigid in his embrace. He was strong enough and mad enough to have forced her on to the end, but she struggled free of his lips just long enough to cry out. One word, one anguished syllable made him release her as though she were suddenly white hot to his touch.

For the name she cried was not his!

He stared down at her, and she clawed away from him into the pillow. He was left kneeling beside her with his codpiece dangling absurdly, feeling, for all his sudden limpness, as though he had been turned to stone. He could not believe it had happened to him and he was too amazed, too demoralized even to feel anger. Not knowing what to do or say, he hung there, staring at her in a bemused stupor.

It was a full moment before he even realized that she was crying and then, in spite of everything, he was moved by a curious tenderness. He had thought her so hard, so clever, so invulnerable and now her tears hurt him beyond belief.

He leaned over and laid a hand on her shoulder, touching her gently, without demand.

'Tell me about the Lord Admiral,' he said simply.

There was no sound except her tortured sobbing, a dreadful sound which knifed his senses. It affected him like the wild anguish of an animal in a trap. He tried to gather her up in his arms and hold her close.

'Tell me and have done with it,' he begged. 'Tell me—how can I help you unless you do?'

It was a mistake—oh, he knew it the moment the words were out. He could not hold her now, she was like a wild animal in his arms, savage with fury. She sat upright, with the tears still running down her face, and he recoiled from her.

'You insolent bloody knave—I don't want your help. Get out of here. Get out, God damn you!'

She reached out for the little silver bell and his hand went out to her in a hopeless gesture of bewilderment.

'Elizabeth—wait!'

The angry, imperious jangle cut across his protest and brought Mrs Ashley sweeping back into the room with alacrity.

She paused on the threshold and took in the scene with one glance, the Queen's face still wet with tears and Dudley, struggling with frantic, humiliated haste to fasten his cod-piece. Her lined face settled itself into a mask of strict neutrality as she approached the bed, where Elizabeth, unable to meet her gaze, lay down and stared up at the tester.

'Your Majesty?'

'Show Lord Robert out,' said Elizabeth shakily, 'and see to it that I am not disturbed again.'

Ashley curtsied and turned away in silence. From the opposite side of the bed, Robin caught Kat's gaze with an urgent, questioning look that she ignored.

For the first time he was angry. As soon as they were alone in the Privy Chamber, he turned masterfully on the old lady and manoeuvred her to a window-seat.

'Well, my Lord?' She was looking at him with ill-concealed hostility. 'What do you want?'

'Information,' he said bluntly. 'You've been with the Queen since she was a child, she can have no secrets from you.'

Kat's lips set into a thin line of pain.

'If she had, my lord, you can rest assured they would be safe with me.'

She got up abruptly and made to step past him, but he blocked her path.

'What holds her back from me—is it only the Admiral? Or is there something more—something I've not even begun to guess?'

Kat's stubborn silence was infuriating, following so hard on the heels of his humiliating failure. He caught her wrists in a bruising grasp and his handsome face was suddenly savage with rage in the harsh sunlight.

'You damned old fool! If you know what ails her, then for Christ's sake tell me!'

Kat's eyes were stony. After a moment he released her and stepped back, ashamed and vaguely alarmed by his behaviour. She was the second woman he had bullied in the last hour, and all for desire of one on whom he dared not lay a hand in anger.

'There's only one thing you need to know,' said Kat with icy dignity, 'and I will tell it with pleasure. You will never be King of England while my lady lives. So—if that's all she means to you, get out of her life. Take your wretched little wife and go abroad and don't come back. Heed my advice, my lord—there's nothing ahead for you but misery if you don't.'

He let her pass and did not watch her leave the room. Beneath the narrow window where he sat, the brightly clad courtiers and ladies walked to and fro, like mechanical dolls, across the wooden terrace. But he neither saw nor heard them as he stared out through the little leaded panes. Only Kat's voice walked slowly up and down his mind, like the doleful tolling of a death bell.

There's nothing ahead for you but misery . . .

Somewhere, in the depths of unwilling consciousness he knew that he had heard an awful truth.

It was stiflingly hot in the curtained bed, but Elizabeth found she was shivering. She got up slowly, instinctively avoiding a sharp movement which would jar her throbbing temple and groped her way blindly to her writing table. For a long time she sat in the faint stream of cooler air that blew in from the open window, with her head in her hands. Hot tears burned tracks down her fingers and soaked the tiny ruffles at her wrists.

The coils of her brain writhed with the conflict of opposing desires. For twenty-five years she had lived in peace with her shadow, her mirror image, her other self, unaware of its consuming malevolence, its need to destroy one man in the name of love. But she was aware of it now, terribly aware. And afraid of its power to hate.

One man. Only one. It was all that shade demanded as it looked from time to time out of her amber eyes, turning them to mirrors of black glass, waiting quietly, unobtrusively for its ultimate revenge on manhood. The shadow slept, but how little it would take to wake it.

Death waited in a lost corridor of her mind, waited for Robin in the glittering guise of her love. She knew now what she feared, what held her back from taking the very thing she desired. She could not trust herself with his life.

For marriage would not content him. Men like Robin were never content, and men like Robin were all she would ever love, grasping, ambitious reflections of herself. Once he knew that the crown matrimonial would never be his, that she would not make him king in his own right, he would begin to plot and scheme behind her back, building up a court faction to force her hand. Robin was too like his father, neither men to be ruled by their wives. To emerge from that final conflict as the victor, it would be necessary to kill him. And she knew she was capable of doing it—it was as simple as that. His company, his friendship, his passionate attachment were all that she dared to take from him; she loved him too much to let him pay the price of owning her, body and soul.

What woman could keep a man by her side for a lifetime on such terms? She had no choice but to let him go on hoping, hoping, till he saw that she had let him waste his life in a vain pursuit, and hated her for it; as she would hate herself.

She was alone with her secret, her dark legacy of the past; there was no one she could trust enough to tell, who would not think her mad. And yet she must tell it somehow and release a little of this caged anguish which seemed to rock her sanity.

She took up her silver pen and stared down at the blank sheet of paper before her. The words poured out of her agonized soul and spread themselves across the page like gleaming drops of black blood.

> I grieve and dare not show my discontent
> I love and yet am forced to seem to hate.
> I do, yet dare not say I ever meant,
> I seem stark mute, yet inwardly do prate.
> I am and not: I freeze and yet am burned,
> Since from myself, my other self I turned.
> My care is like my shadow in the sun,
> Follows me flying, flies when I pursue it,
> Stands and lies by me, does what I have done.

When she came to her senses, the pen was still in her hand and the words were long dry. She had no conscious memory of writing them. For a moment she felt inclined to destroy the whole page, then found she could not bring herself to do it. She put the sheet of parchment in a drawer, locked it safely away and then turned her guilty attention to the state papers which waited in a neatly reproachful stack.

Behind her back, the door clicked open and shut. Soft footsteps went across the room to Kat's chair and became a quick rustle of silk that betokened a curtsey. Then there was pointed silence from the tapestry frame. The afternoon darkened with a threat of thunder and they sat and worked in the failing light without looking at each other or speaking a word.

There seemed to be nothing left to say.

CHAPTER 9

Cecil stood in the Queen's room in icy, disbelieving silence, aghast and immobilized by the storm of invective that was raging in his ears. His tentative reference to the Archduke Charles, Spain's current choice of suitor, had brought a hornet's nest of ungrateful abuse upon his head.

Through narrowed eyes he watched her pace up and down the room, twisting a lace handkerchief between her trembling fingers. She looked pale and strained and there were dark circles beneath her eyes, as though she had not slept for many nights.

Her voice flayed him with spiteful and unreasonable hostility; nothing in his conduct of the Scottish treaty appeared to please her. She had been obliged to spend freely on the campaign, so why was there no financial recompense written into the terms of surrender? Why had he failed to get Calais back from the French? What had he been doing all these weeks idling in Scotland? She did not want to hear about the cost of his journey—if he had incurred expenses, he would have to foot the bill himself. She was not made of money!

The incredible injustice of her accusations stung him deeply; and if she carried out her threat and refused to pay him, he had no idea where he would find the money. But for a moment longer he valiantly put aside his personal considerations and tried to reason with her, to bring her back to the question of the Archduke.

The handkerchief ripped in two; she flung the two pieces in his face and stamped her foot savagely. Marriage, marriage—she was ill of the miserable word. Had he nothing else to say for himself?

'Only this, madam—that I see you are neglecting your business and half way to ruining the realm.'

She drew in a sharp breath; for a moment he was quite certain she was going to hit him.

Then abruptly, she turned her back on him so that he could not see her face.

'Get out! Quickly! And pray for my forgiveness, Cecil—pray very hard.'

He went with his mind made up at last. She was on the very edge of disaster. He knew he had no choice but to save her from herself and the evil influence of Lord Robert Dudley.

The plump, episcopal shadow of the Spanish Ambassador, Bishop de Quadra, hung on the panelled wall of Cecil's study, quivering, like its owner, with intense interest. It was the most curious interview, held between a spy of His Most Catholic Majesty and the arch-heretic detested by Spain, and Quadra was sharp enough to see it was not being held by accident.

He knew the Secretary was in some kind of disgrace, having heard from various sources that Lord Robert Dudley was endeavouring to deprive him of his place. Cecil was evidently a man with a serious grievance, but even so his behaviour now seemed strangely out of character. Since Quadra had been in England he had never seen the Secretary display a flicker of emotion, or heard him speak a single word that had not been carefully weighed before hand. Was this really Cecil speaking now, speaking with the wildest indiscretion in an open disloyalty that bordered close to treason?

'What I am about to say must never be repeated, Bishop. Will you swear to absolute secrecy?'

Quadra smiled faintly in ironical disbelief.

'Men of my calling are not without discretion, Sir William. No one will hear of it, I assure you.'

No one except the whole of Spain and ultimately the rest of the world, thought Cecil calmly as he poured wine from a glass decanter. He deliberately slopped the wine into the tray and mopped at it in a gesture of distraction.

'I tell you this, sir, the Queen conducts herself so strangely that I am about to leave her service.'

'Indeed?' It was almost a purr. Quadra stroked his crucifix thoughtfully. 'That, if I might say so, would be a grave loss to your country, Sir William.'

Cecil shrugged irritably and handed him a goblet.

'That's as may be, but it's a bad sailor who fails to make for a port when he sees a storm coming—though God knows I shall probably end in the Tower for it.'

'A storm?' Quadra blinked like an owl.

'The Queen is heading for utter ruin with Lord Robert Dudley.'

'Certainly there have been rumours—disquieting rumours.'

'I don't traffic in rumours, Bishop, I deal with pure facts. And the facts are that the Queen is shutting herself up in the palace to the peril of her health. Dudley plans to marry her, of course, but the realm will never tolerate it. He'd better be dead, Quadra—better in Paradise.' Cecil paused and laid his hand on the bishop's with an air of desperation. 'Sir, I implore you, for the love of God, to use your influence with Her Majesty and persuade her not to throw herself away in this manner. Remind her what she owes to the people.'

'I am grieved by what you tell me.' Quadra shifted uneasily in his chair. He had no influence whatsoever with the Queen and he believed Cecil was perfectly aware of that fact. So where was this leading? 'Deeply grieved,' he repeated solemnly. 'I have, of course, always done my best to persuade your Queen to live quietly. If it is of any comfort to you, sir, I will naturally do what I can with her now.'

'I fear—it may be too late for that.' Cecil leaned forward to fill Quadra's goblet again, meeting the steady gaze of those globular brown eyes. 'I have heard it said that Lord Robert Dudley is thinking of destroying his wife.'

Quadra's gaze flickered and held.

'Reliable sources, sir?'

'Oh yes,' said Cecil grimly, 'most reliable. He has given out that she is ill, hoping, of course, that her death will cause no comment. But I happen to know that she is perfectly well and taking good care not to be poisoned. I trust God will never permit such a foul crime to be accomplished.'

Quadra crossed himself and looked suitably shocked. Cecil sat with his head in his hands, a man in the dregs of despair who had unburdened himself of a dark confidence. After a moment he felt Quadra's soft hand patting his arm.

'A bad business for you, Sir William. You have my sympathy.'

'Your most *discreet* sympathy, I trust.'

'Without question,' Quadra placed a fat finger to his lips and Cecil gave him a bleak smile. A moment later the bishop was reaching for his timepiece and sucking in his breath with feigned surprise. Was that really the time? Ah, these light nights—so deceptive. And he had work to attend to.

'Of course, Bishop—I must not keep you from state business.'

Thus, murmuring affable trivia, the two men parted, both knowing precisely what business would take Quadra to his ambassador's pen.

And two days later, on Sunday the 8th of September, Amy Dudley's household returned at dusk from Abingdon fair to find their mistress's dead body at the foot of a shallow stone staircase.

'Dead, madam. Dead of a broken neck. And in what I'm afraid can only be called suspicious circumstances.'

Elizabeth sank into a chair and stared at Cecil's innmobile face.

'Suspicious?'

'She was alone in the house, madam. All her servants at the fair. No witness to say how she came to fall—if indeed she *did* fall.'

Elizabeth stood up abruptly.

'You think he killed her, don't you?'

Cecil raised his shoulders in a noncommittal shrug.

'My opinion is immaterial, madam, it's the opinion of the world that counts. Guilty or innocent, he will always be tainted by suspicion. Marry him now, or at any time in the future, and he'll bring your throne down within a month.'

She turned away. Her fists were clenching slowly and unclenching, her face was pale and hard as marble, her eyes black pits of fury.

'The fool,' he heard her mutter, 'the blundering dolt!'

She swung round upon Cecil suddenly.

'So! Where is he now, the bereaved husband, the merry widower?'

'I believe he is waiting for audience with Your Majesty.'

'Send him in to me.'

She dug her nails savagely into the carved wood of the chimney-piece until more than half a dozen of her scarlet talons were smashed and ragged. The sound set his teeth on edge. He stood by discreetly while she examined the wanton damage with an angry glance.

'Cecil.'

'Your Majesty?'

'There will be an inquest.'

'Naturally, madam, under the circumstances.'

'The matter will be tried in open court. Nothing is to be hidden, do you understand? If he's responsible I want to know.'

Cecil bowed to hide the smile which hovered at the corner of his lips.

'It shall be exactly as Your Majesty instructs. I commend your wisdom, madam.'

She nodded absently and wandered away to the window, taut as the string of a bow, chewing at a broken finger-nail. After a moment she turned to look at him hesitantly over her shoulder.

'Is your wife expecting you home tonight?'

He bowed. 'If Your Majesty has need of me I can easily send a message.'

She smiled distractedly and held out her hand to him.

'You're very kind, Cecil—more kind than I deserve, perhaps. Remain at court then and I will send for you later. I would be grateful for your advice.'

He kissed her hand, dizzy with elation. The lilt in her voice, the charming grace of her diffident gesture, they were things he would have sold his soul to win back. She needed him. *I will send for you later.* Had it been a lover's invitation, it could not have pleased him more.

He walked slowly into the ante-room and inclined his head in ironical greeting to the impatient young man who paced the small floor like a frantic tiger.

'The Queen will see you now, Lord Robert,' he said in his even voice and passed on with a slow, limping step.

When Robin came through the heavy double doors and closed them angrily behind him he looked so genuinely pale and shaken that momentarily she was taken aback. For a long, horrible minute they stared at each other in bleak silence and then at last he made a faltering move to kiss her hand.

She struck his arm away and her voice was harsh and ugly with suspicion.

'Don't touch me with your bloody hands—you!—you are no better than my father was. Did you honestly think you could murder your way into my bed?'

The last vestige of colour drained out of his face; his voice was a thin, reedy gasp.

'You can't seriously believe that I had anything to do with this?'

'What else am I to think? I forbade you to seek a divorce—now, conveniently, you no longer need one! But are you such a clod, such an imbecile, as to think I could ever marry you now? You bury your wife, and your hope of the crown, in the same coffin!'

He shook his head and looked at her with bitter disillusion.

'Cecil digs the grave and the world fills it in,' he said slowly. 'How pleased he will be to know that yours is the first hand to lift a spade.'

She came a step towards him and her eyes glittered dangerously. He was suddenly acutely aware, like Feria before him, that this was no longer the Elizabeth he had known.

'Cecil?' Her voice was ominously quiet. 'What the devil has Cecil to do with this?—he's been in Scotland for weeks!'

'He has agents,' said Robin shortly. 'And he's been back at court long enough to see how the land lies. He's a frightened man, madam—and a frightened man will stoop to anything.'

'Repeat that accusation outside this room,' she said steadily, 'and you will join your wife. Indeed, you may join her anyway, for if this crime is proved against you, I shall execute you.'

He laughed unsteadily. 'For murder?'

'No,' she said icily, 'for rank stupidity! For insufferable vanity!'

He caught her arm violently, goaded by her heartless injustice.

'And what will you say when they bring you the news of my execution—

today died *another* man of much wit and very little judgement? You had best take care, madam. They will say you have a most unhealthy preference for fools in your bed!'

Without warning, her right hand swung up and struck him full in the face. He staggered back a step from the violence of her blow and lifted his own hand to his cheek, feeling the trickle of blood where a diamond ring had split the soft skin at the corner of his mouth. The rage left him as suddenly as it had come, purged by a stark terror greater than he had felt even in his worst moments in the Tower under Mary. She had threatened to kill him and with cold, incredulous horror he realized now that she had meant it. In the last resort nothing mattered to Elizabeth Tudor but her crown; if it was necessary, she would abandon him to his fate in order to save it.

'I have many enemies,' he said dully, suddenly quiet and despairing. 'They stand outside that door ready to rejoice at my downfall, waiting to tear me to pieces like a pack of wolves! Will you desert me now when I need your help most—is that all our love is worth, Elizabeth?'

She stared at him in an agony of doubting silence, then slowly, deliberately, turned her back on him in a cruelly symbolic gesture. He fell to his knees at her feet in a blind panic and his voice was edged with tears.

'Don't turn away from me—oh God, why won't you see it?—You with the sharpest mind in Europe! For months now they've been talking of murder. My worst enemy could not have found a better time for Amy to die mysteriously and Cecil *is* my worst enemy—not Sussex or Norfolk who so plainly hate me and don't trouble to disguise it—but Cecil! He's made you choose between me and the crown.' Robin smiled bleakly. 'Only I could have spared him the trouble. There never was any choice, was there—I see that now. And seeing that, all I ask of you now is the opportunity to clear my name. Let me go down to Cumnor and find out what really happened.'

She turned to look at him and the hand he had stretched out to her in desperate appeal dropped to his side hopelessly as he saw her face. It was pale and cold, entirely without a flicker of emotion. In her glittering gown, she stood in judgement upon him like a stone effigy; she looked unreal and terrifying and her voice seemed to come from a great distance.

'You may send your own men, but not yourself. You will go to Kew under house arrest and stay there until the inquest is over. You will make no attempt to communicate with me.'

He looked at her with disbelief. 'Not even a letter?'

'Nothing. You may leave me now.'

He lowered his eyes wearily. After a moment he got off his knees and turned to go.

'Robin.'

He looked back with wild hope, but her expression was unchanged.

'Guard your tongue in captivity, for I meant what I said. If you breathe a word against Cecil, I'll hang you like a felon at Tyburn.'

Across the sunlit room, he thought he heard the echo of an anguished cry.

Her eyes are like ice and you won't melt them . . . no man could. There's something cruel and twisted deep inside her. Keep away from her, Robert . . . I know she's dangerous . . .

Now, at last, he knew it too, and wondered why he had never seen it before. Gone was the teasing playmate who had shared his childhood, and the tortured, vulnerable woman he had glimpsed in the preceding weeks. In their place he saw the Queen and saw her for the first time with the mask of friendship removed, a figure suddenly as ruthless and terrible as ever her father had been. He knew now that in any personal crisis it would be the Queen who ruled and not the woman. All their dazzling intimacy was an illusion, a mere straw in the wind, for in the last resort he was but a subject, as her mother had been. What a fool he had been to forget it, even for a moment!

He bowed formally to that icy and unbending figure.

'I understand you, Your Majesty,' he said at last. 'And I thank you for your plainness.'

The scandal ran through the length and breadth of Europe, reverberating like a single gunshot in an empty canyon. English ambassadors were too humiliated to show their faces once the Queen of Scots, with schoolgirl wit, had put the world's opinion in a neat nutshell: 'The Queen of England is going to marry her horsemaster who had killed his wife to make room for her.'

Everyone expected it and everyone knew it would be the end of her. It was patently obvious that the Protestant bastard would 'lie down Queen Elizabeth and wake in the Tower plain Madam Dudley'. Even the Spaniards said so, and they had more cause to fear it than most.

Philip was in agony, for the scandal touched him on an old wound. She had refused his hand to play the harlot with that handsome, penniless nobody, and had the matter been on a purely personal level, he would gladly have stood by and applauded while her people burnt her for a whore and a murderess.

Trust my love, Philip . . .

He was on fire with rage at the memory of her cool caress, for cool it had been, he knew it now. Cool and calculating and filled with mockery. Did she laugh at him with Dudley behind the curtains of the state bed? Did she? Oh, how he longed to see her dead—but he must stand by her yet again, because he had no alternative. To see England fall to France was just too high a price to pay for the removal of his eternal embarrassment—the woman who had publicly rejected him.

During the inquiry, Robin sweated at Kew in a fever of anxiety. He had sent his servant, Thomas Blount, to Cumnor Place with strict instructions to get to the bottom of the matter without 'respect to any living person'. It was the nearest he dared get to any open accusation.

Reports from Cumnor were complicated by descriptions of Amy's curious behaviour on the day of her death. She had sent her whole household to the fair—to their considerable annoyance for it was a Sunday and only the lowest of the low attended the fair on the Sabbath—and had grown quite hysterical when one of her companions had refused to comply with her request. There had been something close to a quarrel and the offended woman had stalked off to her own apartments. Robin puzzled over that for many hours. Amy was terrified of solitude—why should she suddenly wish to be left entirely alone? Had she been led to expect a secret visit from a very influential man, a man offering to do all in his power to keep her husband and the Queen apart? Was it a condition of that visit that it must not be witnessed by gossiping servants, that the Queen must never hear of it? What had happened during those last, lost hours of Amy's life?

He would never know for sure. Amy's maid, Pinto, described her as being in 'strange mind' and praying daily for deliverance from despair. The implication of suicide was a straw that Robin clutched hopefully, for Blount could find no evidence of foul play, though he sifted the household from top to bottom. Cecil's arrangements had been made with his usual masterly care, a clockwork precision which left no trail.

Housed in luxury, surrounded by servants, Robin lived out his lonely nightmare as the Queen's prisoner, cut off from the world and all he held dear. Every day he rose with new hope expecting some message from Elizabeth; and every night he went to bed, disappointed and despairing. After all there had been between them, how could she abandon him like this? Was it possible she did not care—had never cared? Did he mean nothing to her? Hour after hour he combed his memory, seeking crumbs of her affection, balancing the gifts with which he had been showered since her accession—this Dairy House at Kew was one—against the memory of her face that day at Windsor. She had looked and spoken as though she hated him and whatever the verdict of the inquest, he feared he had lost her. He tried to visualize a life without her; and ended most nights by drinking himself into a stupor of forgetfulness.

The great and the influential stayed clear of Kew as though it were infested by plague, for disgrace is a highly infectious disease. He expected no one and the day his nervous valet bobbed into his room to announce, 'Sir William Cecil, my lord,' he stood and stared at the door as though he had been pole-axed.

It was Cecil at his most benign—mild mannered, courteous and under-standing, very apologetic for any inconvenience his unexpected visit might have caused. And it was Cecil also at his most ostentatious, for this was not a visit he intended to go unnoticed. The scandal was sufficient now to finish Dudley's hopes for good and Cecil felt he could safely afford to give the lie to his own conversation with the Spanish Ambassador. He could afford to show the world his belief in the young man's innocence and intimate at the same time that the way back to court could only be opened up by his own unassailable influence with the Queen.

Cecil's visit spelled out Robin's position in no uncertain terms and the unmistakable air of patronage was difficult for the angry young man to bear. He wanted to take Cecil by the throat and shake him like the rat he believed him to be, but Robin was no fool. He knew when he was beaten, and when it paid to be humble.

He went to meet the grey-clad figure with guarded civility and extended his hand coldly.

'I shall never forget your kindness in coming to see me, Sir William—it's all been like a bad dream.'

Cecil's thin fingers, discoloured with years of paperwork, administered a sympathetic squeeze to his companion's arm.

'At such a time, Lord Robert, a man is fortunate when his friends will stand up and be counted. The whole court is with you in your tragic bereavement and we are in mourning at Her Majesty's personal request.'

At the mention of the Queen, a desperate light shone in Robin's eyes.

'I had hoped to have some message from her by now, but there's been nothing. Not a word, not a gesture, just a silence that—that I find very hard to bear. She's not ill, I hope.'

Cecil looked at him gravely.

'The Queen is not as well as I could wish to see her, my lord. This sorry business has exposed her to considerable stress.'

Robin stiffened. 'If she's ill, then for Christ's sake let me go to her.'

'I regret, my lord, that under the circumstances, that would be most inad-visable. I myself have often chosen to bear my personal anxieties with patient silence sooner than overtax Her Majesty's uncertain health. I know you will be happy to do the same.'

Robin stared at him aghast.

'You have advised her not to receive me?'

'For the time being.' Cecil smiled slowly. 'A little forbearance, if I might counsel it, would be in order now, my lord. I shall of course be very happy to speak on your behalf to Her Majesty—if I judge her to be well enough to hear what I have to say.'

Robin met the Secretary's steady gaze and knew very well what he intended to convey: *You are in no position now to make demands!*

He took a deep breath and managed to say with impeccable restraint, 'I repeat, Sir William, I shall never be able to thank you enough for the service you have done me.'

An hour later the distinguished visitor took his leave and Robin watched the neat little figure ride slowly out of the courtyard on an elderly nag with loathing in his heart. The audacity and cunning of the man took his breath away, for he knew no shadow of suspicion would ever touch that ruthless little worm, so quiet, so eminently *respectable!*

Robin turned from the window at last and took stock of his position. It was patently obvious he could no longer afford the luxury of Cecil's enmity. If there was still any remote possibility of uniting himself with the Queen it could now only be done through Cecil's good offices—and he would have to grovel for that friendship. Cecil's cool gaze had made that very clear.

A certain grim philosophy came to Robin as he reached for pen and ink; if he had to grovel he might as well begin now.

'Sir, I thank you for your being here and the great friendship you have shown towards me I shall not forget . . . I pray you let me hear from you what you think it best for me to do . . .'

Cecil, receiving that humble letter, folded it quietly and indulged in a satisfied smile.

'The jury returned an open verdict, madam.'

Cecil watched, without appearing to do so, as the Queen's hands tensed on the arms of her chair.

'An open verdict condemns no one,' she said cautiously.

'Nor does it clear any man's good name, madam. It merely records the fact that no one knows what happened and leaves the world to speculate as it will.'

Cecil was well pleased with the verdict—in many ways it could not have suited him better. Delighted as he had been with her behaviour in these last difficult weeks, he was uncertain that he could have pushed to the extent of persuading her to sign Dudley's death warrant. It was better the way it was, a sensible compromise of the kind he had built his life upon.

He admired the steely grip she had kept over her own emotions. Whatever she felt, she gave no sign as she went about her daily business. She was once more the heartless, dispassionate entity that he delighted to serve and already in his heart he was offering himself excuses for her unbecoming conduct. What was more natural than that, after years of dancing on the whims of others, she should suddenly run wild with the freedom to indulge whims of her own? All her youth had been stolen from her, corroded by fear and suspicion. It was a great pity her heart didn't seem to match her brain, but he was certain that after this fiasco he would have no more need to concern himself with her wayward affections.

Beneath heavy lids he stole a glance at her and was suddenly touched with pity. She looked thin and pale, as though all the bright life had gone out of her. Even her brilliant hair seemed muted to a dull copper. He felt like a guilty father who has locked a dangerous toy away in a cupboard.

When you are sensible enough to use it properly you shall have it back, but not until . . .

His conscience gave him precious little trouble, for he was well satisfied that the end had justified the means. She would outride this stormy scandal and allow him to lead her down that path which would end in a foreign alliance and a wise marriage, to an heir with no traitor's blood flowing in his veins. Their spiritual reunion was complete, their dreams once more in perfect harmony; together they would serve this land and make it great. He was quite certain that no golden apple, however sweet its promise, would ever turn her from her chosen path again.

Elizabeth sat in moody silence, twisting a ruby aglet on the bodice of her gown; when it came away in her hand, she cursed and got up. A mantle of silver-spangled lawn fell from her shoulders and trailed in the rushes as she walked away to the empty hearth.

'Now that the inquest is over,' she remarked casually, without looking at him, 'I shall recall him to court.'

'If you think it wise,' he said guardedly. His glance had flickered. She turned to smile at him a trifle unpleasantly.

'Wise or not you have nothing to fear from him now, my friend—have you?'

'Your Majesty?' He kept his gaze steady, but of a sudden all the colour had drained out of his face and he was acutely aware of his own heartbeat.

She ran her fingers caressingly across the chimney-piece and still he saw that twisted little smile about her lips.

'It occurs to me, William Cecil, that you cannot be unduly displeased by Lady Dudley's timely demise.'

He had known some bad moments in his varied life, but never one to equal this.

She knows!

But that was impossible—inconceivable! There was nothing to link his name with this, no careless mistake, no apparent motive. She could not know —but if she did, would he walk from this room to a cell in the Tower?

Panic touched him, throwing his ordered brain into chaos, but by some remarkable effort of will he stood his ground and faced her calmly. Whatever she suspected, she had no evidence—she could prove nothing in any court of law.

And yet there were other ways for a monarch to dispense with the services of a minister who exceeded his authority—he, like Amy Dudley, could meet with a well-timed accident.

The evening light was failing rapidly and the pupils of her eyes had grown enormous, obliterating all colour from the iris. Black eyes in the pale face of a stranger—and yet not unfamiliar. Where had he seen them before?

Suddenly she held out her hand to him. As he took it and pressed it fervently to his lips, he heard her soft voice and knew, without looking, that she was still smiling.

'I don't know who murdered Amy—I don't think I want to know now. But whoever it was I am grateful to him.'

'Madam,' he whispered.

'I won't be held, Cecil, not by you or any other man. I won't be harnessed by snaffle and bit. If you would ride an unbroken mare, you must learn to do without a saddle.'

He smiled faintly. 'I'm a poor horseman, Your Majesty.'

'I never promised you an easy journey—nor a safe one. Only a unique destination. I am the only person in this world who can give you what you crave. So come with me, Cecil—I need you.'

He released her hand and stood back from her; his face was pale.

'And Dudley? Do you need him too?'

'You must not be jealous,' she said slowly. 'I give you my word, now and for all time, that I shall not marry the man, nor take him to my bed. I give you the word of a queen—and a virgin. Is it enough to make you trust me—or would you prefer that I submit to the indignity of medical examination?'

She saw the sudden rush of purple colour in his sallow face, and wondered idly how long it was since anyone had made William Cecil blush like a bashful schoolboy. When he knelt solemnly at her feet and told her that the Queen's word was as sacred in his mind as the word of God, she was vastly amused by her power to move him, and rapped him lightly on the head with her fan.

'Then pray that I don't come to confuse the two—as my father did, several times.'

He rose to his feet, inflated by a bubble of triumph that remained invulnerable to the needle of her mockery. She was safe for ever from Dudley's vulgar grasp; she had given her word, her royal word. And he believed it, because he needed to believe it.

As he left, it occurred to him that it was rather a pity his hand in this remained unseen. It was the triumph of a lifetime that surely ought to be accorded the honour of verse.

Some years after his death, the playwright, John Webster, unwittingly obliged him: *'The surest way to chain a woman's tongue is break her neck; a politician did it.'*

Short and to the point, it would have pleased his fastidious taste in epitaphs.

When Cecil had gone, Elizabeth sat alone in the empty room and played the virginals by candlelight. For a short while her fingers moved with their customary skill across the keyboard, then suddenly struck wildly, savagely, making a jarring discord of the tinkling notes. She slammed the keyboard shut and gave way to the uncontrollable laughter which had seized her, an uncanny echo of her mother's wild levity, which had laughed even at death. For, like her mother, she too was laughing at a travesty of love, laughing to find herself caught in a fierce emotional tangle with two men who had nothing in common but ambition and the English language. Two men prepared to fight like dogs for the right to possess her, one desiring her body, the other her soul. Only now did she realize how closely she was bound to them both.

They pulled in opposite directions, and if they pulled long and hard enough no doubt she would split in two, like a rag doll, so that each could run off to his lair, gloating over his dead and useless trophy. Only now she knew how to turn this deadly game to her own advantage. She could be the apex of that triangle, controlling every force within it; Cecil, unwittingly, had just handed her the very means with which to do it.

She was free of Robin now, free of his predatory affection and her own dark uncertainty. She could indulge her love for him within the limits she chose to set. All the world knew she could not marry him, and because she could not marry him he could not expect her to risk the threat of pregnancy. Iron-cast bars of logic would keep him out of her bed and keep him safe—as safe as that terrible secret which need never be told.

But the cream of the jest for her was Cecil—her dear, wily Cecil who imagined he had been so very clever. As indeed he had been—perhaps a little too clever for his own good. He imagined, as they all did, that her reluctance to accept a foreign prince lay in her secret longing for Robert Dudley. Even Cecil believed her public statement that she was wedded to England and would live and die a virgin was just the empty protestation of a coy female. No one took her seriously, and perhaps in the game she had elected to play it was just as well.

Above and beyond her own emotional conflict, the choice of spinsterhood burned free, fuelled by the purest of political considerations. She had seen only too plainly the disaster her sister's foreign match had brought in its wake. Marriage to France or Spain would reduce England to a vassal state once more, while marriage to an Englishman raised the spectre of faction warfare among her jealous nobility. There was only one way for a Queen Regnant to survive and that was alone. As she was now she had perhaps another twenty years to play her enemies off against each other, to drive a wedge between France and Spain by keeping both in perpetual fear that she would marry a candidate of either side. It was a game that only a woman could hope to get away with and, if it worked, it would gain her the time she needed to rebuild a nation which was spiritually and financially bankrupt. She would cultivate this country till it bloomed like a fine rose; she would cosset trade, stimulate education, encourage piracy and fling her ships wide to the wealth of the new world. She would not be too nice about her methods; whatever paid was worthwhile and when trouble threatened she would wriggle out of it with a cunning facade of lies. She was probably the most accomplished liar in the world, and proud of it! She had no illusions about what lay ahead—there would be years of endless struggle, perhaps even heartbreak, years in which she would have to fight herself and her own desires as hard, if not harder, than the myriads of enemies around her. In many ways it would be a nun's existence.

She stood at the crossroads of her life and stared at the deep forking of the ways. Down one lay the ultimate fulfilment of a woman; down the other the fulfilment of a queen. And for a moment, as she saw the steep and barbed path before her, she quailed. She wanted to ride to Kew and throw herself into Robin's arms and beg him to lay the ghosts that haunted her; she wanted to love and be loved and bear him a dozen merry, black-haired children. But it wouldn't work. In her heart she knew that, knew that she was not fit to be any man's wife.

Yet those very things which flawed her womanhood could be made to serve England and make her a great queen. She could play them all off against each other, France and Spain and the Papacy, people and Parliament, Cecil and Robin—

Poor Robin!

She was aware of tears in her eyes and rubbed them away with a fierce gesture. Great queens did not wail like little girls for what could not be! She went to her mirror and took up the tiny pots of paint which would remove the marks of grief from the mask of majesty. When she had finished, her reflection looked back at her calmly, a bold, clever face that was both composed and utterly resolute.

Two men and one woman, she thought suddenly and smiled, for she knew she could make it work. She could have the pair of them on her own terms and take from them everything they had to give. And she could do it for no better reason than that one of them—normally the most clear-sighted of men —had allowed fear to make him act like a fool.

One small mistake, with devastating consequences, had given her the whip-hand over them both.

PART THREE

The Queen

'She fished for men's souls and had so sweet a bait none could escape her network . . . She caught many a poor fish who little knew what snare was laid for them.'
SIR CHRISTOPHER HATTON

CHAPTER 1

The chamber of mourning was silent and lit by the glow of black candles, the heavy curtains drawn to shut out the bright light of day. The death of a French king was traditionally followed by forty days of isolation for his widow and not even the irreverent rays of the sun were permitted to intrude on this formalized period of grief. Apart from her four handmaidens, Mary Stuart had seen no one for over a month and, in spite of her genuine sorrow for the loss of one who had been a playmate rather than a husband, she was beginning to find the compulsory inactivity tedious.

Outside, beyond the courtyard of Orleans, the bells were ringing, as indeed they were still ringing out all over France: *The King is dead, long live the King!*

But the King for whom they rang was a frightened nine-year-old boy cowering in the apartments of his dominating mother. Catherine de Medici was a mysterious, vindictive woman, waiting only for a decent interval to elapse before she might have the extremely personal pleasure of ejecting her detested daughter-in-law from French soil.

Mary knew in her heart that a few months' respite was the most she could expect from the woman she had once carelessly castigated as a tradesman's daughter. And then it would be goodbye to France for the girl who was Queen of Scotland by birth, Dowager Queen of France by marriage, and Queen of England by right in the eyes of every good Catholic in Europe.

There would be no opportunity to arrange another marriage on French soil, with her mother-in-law, as Regent, blocking every diplomatic avenue. No matter which way she looked at it, Mary could see no alternative for the time being but a return to her native land.

She remembered very little of Scotland. The country was just a faded nightmare, an echo of wild hoofbeats in the night, bearing her away from her English enemies, a smell of damp and decay and sweat. All that was proud and fastidious in her recoiled at the memory, so that her mind writhed like an animal in the snares of a net, seeking the loophole that would mean escape.

And when she thought of escape she thought of England—rightfully hers, snatched from her grasp by a greedy Protestant usurper. It was hard to believe that the English could first take a bastard for their Queen and then support her through the most disgusting scandal since the days when old King Henry's matrimonial farces had entertained the courts of Europe. Elizabeth was not only a bastard, she was a whore; so what dark arts did she practise to keep a people as proud as the English in submission beneath her amoral rule?

Mary had stared long into her Venetian mirror asking herself this very question, and now believed she had the answer. Lack of choice had cramped the English into mutinous acceptance of this 'live dog'—Mary smiled to think how close the Bishop of Winchester had come by that remark to calling his Queen a bitch. But once the Queen of Scotland sat on her throne beyond the border, it would be a different case. With the right marriage and foreign troops to enforce her claim, she could be Queen of England within six months. There remained one distasteful obstacle in her chosen path. To reach Scotland it would be necessary to pass through English waters; to do that without jeopardy required a written safe-conduct from the so-called Queen of England; and to ask for that was to imply that the usurper had authority to grant it.

All that was young and impulsive in Mary cried out that she would rather enter a French convent than submit to the indignity of asking Elizabeth Tudor for anything. But ambition, warring against her finer sensibilities, told her that for once she must lower her high-stomached Stuart pride. First get home in safety to Scotland and then—England would be her footstool.

So ask—where was the harm? Elizabeth would never dare to refuse. Indeed, the only obstacle Mary foresaw lay in getting the English jade out of the Horsemaster's bed just long enough for her to sign the necessary document.

Mary laughed and turned from the mirror; she often laughed when she thought of Elizabeth. A horsemaster, a low-born knave, a traitor's son—was it possible such a harlot could stand in her way for long?

She rang the bell for her ladies and smiled gaily when they entered. Tomorrow the black candles would be doused to mark the end of her official period of mourning and she would begin to build herself a new life beyond the safe haven of French shores.

Fierce July sunlight streamed in gold shafts through the latticed windows of the Long Gallery and struck green fire from the emeralds in Elizabeth's hair. She smoothed the plumes of her feathered fan between her fingers and stood looking out over the busy river which was dotted with barges and small boats. Beneath her gaze, London heaved with activity like a huge ant-hill; it was a sight she never tired of watching from this splendid vantage point, the throbbing heart of their kingdom.

Cecil, who waited at her side, shifted his weight on to his good leg and glanced at her face, which as usual told him nothing. She had flown into a public rage when news of Mary Stuart's request had reached her, but since she was perfectly capable of producing rage, grief or pleasure in appropriate proportions whenever it suited her, he was uncertain of her real reaction.

For himself, he was horrified by the news, and knew his alarm was shared by most of the Council. The Queen's most significant rival installed in close proximity across the border was a grim prospect for the future. It was bound to excite unrest in the Catholic North. Mary's refusal to ratify the Treaty of Edinburgh had nullified its most important clause. Her claim to the English throne still stood and in all essentials they were right back where they had started.

He was tired and vaguely depressed; his foot was throbbing with gout. If only the Queen were not so fond of standing! He eyed a footstool with regret and coughed discreetly, to remind her of his presence.

'Shall I draft a reply to the Scottish Queen, madam?'

'If you will.' She turned from the window. 'I think I have made my feelings quite plain. Unless she signs the Treaty and renounces her claim I shall not guarantee her safety in English waters.'

Cecil fingered his plain buttons uneasily.

'And if she refuses, madam—what then?'

Elizabeth raised the plumed fan so that only her dark eyes and brilliant hair were visible above the white feathers.

'Then, my friend, it will be my life or hers in the end. Instruct Throckmorton of my terms.'

Cecil bowed bleakly, and took himself and his gout away.

'—and so, madam, under the circumstances,' Throckmorton's voice quivered with embarrassment, 'I fear Her Majesty is obliged to refuse your safe conduct.'

A gasp of disbelief came from the little group of attendants surrounding the Scottish Queen and Mary rose with icy dignity from her chair.

'Draw back,' she said to the women closest to her. 'I have no desire to make a vulgar display of *my* temper in public.'

She swept away to a pink-cushioned window-seat and the English Ambassador, miserably humiliated, followed her.

'I'm sorry, madam,' Throckmorton said quietly. 'There was nothing I could do to spare you this—nothing anyone can do with Her Majesty in such a mood. And yet,' he groped hopefully for her hand, 'if you would only sign this treaty, you would find her more than amenable. My mistress can be a loyal friend,' his voice dropped very low, 'or a deadly enemy. I beseech you from the bottom of my heart not to win her as the latter.'

Mary smiled gently and touched his arm. She was not afraid of his mistress, as Throckmorton so plainly was, and it was time she made that fact quite clear.

'The enmity of the English is nothing new to me, sir,' she said pleasantly. 'Your late King attempted to prevent my journey to France when I was but a child. I will not relinquish what I know to be my rights simply to spare myself your Queen's displeasure. I shall sail without her permission, and regret only that I so far forgot myself as to ask a favour of her in the first place.'

Throckmorton gnawed his lip uneasily.

'And if a storm should chance to throw you upon English shores, madam?'

Mary raised her slim shoulders with indifference.

'Then your Queen may make a sacrifice of me.' She gave him a slight smile. 'And who knows, my friend, perhaps that would be for the best after all.'

He did not know how to answer that. It seemed the strangest thing for her to say and he wondered what she saw as she stared past him for a moment. Whatever it was, it made her shiver.

He bent to kiss her hand tenderly, with real regret. She was so vulnerable —beautiful, charming, full of those feminine frailties which appealed to a strong man; but, frankly, he would not hazard a week's pay on her chance of surviving any serious confrontation with Elizabeth. His mistress had long claws and would have no compunction about using them on any cocksure kitten who strayed across her path.

There was nothing more he could do to help Mary; an ambassador must take care. He had given his advice and further argument would only compromise his position with Elizabeth.

He walked out of the room sadly, and left the Queen of Scots to make her own mistakes.

'Bitch!'

Elizabeth's clenched fist crashed down on her desk and sent Throckmorton's despatch spinning to the floor.

'Stupid, stupid little bitch! Who the devil has advised her in this madness?'

Cecil bent automatically and retrieved the scattered papers in silence. Privately he doubted that anyone was advising the Scottish Queen at the moment. Dictated to equally by pride and courage, she was plainly acting on a heated emotion which boded ill for future negotiations. Intrigue, unrest and foreign interference were the natural corollaries to her arrival in Scotland. Even if she held fire for a year or so to consolidate her influence, she would be a constant menace to Elizabeth's life. And for the moment their position seemed stalemated.

Elizabeth stared down at her papers, fingering her temple in an unconsciously fretful gesture that alerted him.

'This summer progress into Suffolk,' he began cautiously.

'Yes,' she said lightly. 'What of the progress?'

'There's still time to cancel it, madam.'

She looked up startled.

'Cancel it? On what grounds? There's no unrest in that county.'

'Madam, you are not fit to undertake such an arduous journey.'

Elizabeth's eyes narrowed and she pushed her papers to one side angrily. 'Have you been talking to my women?' she demanded.

'I was concerned,' he admitted nervously, 'and certainly several of your ladies agreed—' He broke off, uncomfortably aware that he was about to be indiscreet.

'Well,' she prompted ominously, 'what have my women said? By God, you had better tell me!'

'Forgive me, madam—but they say you are the colour of a corpse and that all your bones may be counted.'

Elizabeth stood up and he instinctively took a step backwards.

'Damn them!' she snapped. 'Damn their meddling tongues! Do I employ them to count my bones and put the fear of God into my chief minister?'

He was crimson with a mixture of alarm and pleasure. *My chief minister*— had he really heard her say it?

She watched him shift his weight awkwardly from one foot to the other and suddenly gave him a devastating smile, which caught him right off balance. He was not in love with her; but he could see, with startling clarity, why so many men were.

'Who was it?' she laughed. 'Cobham—Northampton?'

He looked at the floor and she nodded slowly.

'Oh, yes, I might have known. Those two are the greatest panic-mongers in this realm. Extraordinarily fond of seeing death written on someone's face —usually mine. Wishful thinking, I fear.' She waved her hand as he began to protest. 'For God's sake, Cecil, confine your spying to its proper sphere. Bedchamber gossip could be the end of you.'

'With respect, madam—my anxiety remains.'

'Without foundation, my friend—I shall outlive you all, I swear it.' She sat down again and leaned her chin on her hands as she watched him sigh and look unconvinced. 'Listen. If ever I have the slightest intention of departing this world I shall see that you receive a month's notice in advance. Even allowing for your gout, that should give you plenty of time to flee to safety in Geneva—wouldn't you agree?'

'Madam!'

She lifted her hand to silence him.

'Sit down. I have something to show you.'

He eased himself into the chair opposite, deeply aggrieved by her assumption that self-interest alone motivated his concern. He had a fierce paternal feeling for her which defied logical analysis. All his life he seemed to have been marking time and waiting for her service. And now little else mattered beyond those hours when he was challenged, stimulated, and alerted in every mental faculty by the most difficult and exacting human being he had ever met.

Mildred was not amused by his obsession. She had once told him tartly that if he could not leave the Queen outside their bedroom door, he had better sleep alone. The incident had jolted him. In all their cosy, domesticated existence it was the only time he ever remembered Mildred raising her voice; and in the interests of marital harmony he no longer discussed his royal mistress with his wife.

The Queen signed a document and pushed it across the table for his attention. As he looked down at it, he blinked in astonishment.

It was the authorization of Mary Stuart's safe conduct through English waters.

'That leaves England the moment she sets sail.'

'Too late to be of use to her?' Cecil raised a puzzled eyebrow. 'Why sign it at all then?'

'To cover myself. Should she reach Scotland in safety I shall simply tell her Throckmorton misunderstood me—but make no mistake, Cecil. If she slips through our fingers when we have the chance to take her, someone will hang for it.'

Cecil rolled up the document hastily and got to his feet with difficulty.

'I shall see that the fleet patrols the Channel in search of unauthorized vessels, madam.'

'Good.' Elizabeth laid her pen aside. 'Give me five minutes alone with her at Hampton Court or Greenwich and the Treaty of Edinburgh will be ratified beyond all question of doubt. By God, she'll sign it, if I have to guide her hand with my own.'

'And then, madam?'

'And then I have no further quarrel with her. She can count on my friendship, for what it's worth—God knows she'll find precious little when she gets to Scotland.'

Cecil frowned. 'All this diplomacy hinges upon her capture, madam. But the Channel is vast and the elements are in God's hands. A storm—a sudden fog—and it will be like searching for a needle in a haystack.'

'Well—you're on the best of terms with God, aren't you, my friend? See what you can arrange.'

He found her cynical irreverence disturbing and coughed to cover the break in his composure.

'I shall certainly do everything in my power, madam. If the Scottish Queen lands in her native land with this issue unresolved I fear Your Majesty's fair head may not sit in safety for long.'

'Well,' Elizabeth gave him a sly smile, 'that ought to cure my headaches permanently.'

'Quite, madam,' he said drily, 'yet I and every other loyal Englishman should prefer a less drastic remedy. And to that end—touching this matter of the progress—Your Majesty will consider my advice?'

Her smile was disarmingly reproachful.

'I always consider your advice, William Cecil. You ought to know that by now.'

He went out of the room feeling flattered and topsides with the world.

When the door had closed behind him she added softly to herself, 'But of course, I don't always take it.'

Ipswich, in the height of summer, was surely the last place on earth God made, thought Robin.

He stood at a window, pulling uncomfortably at the high ruff that had a stranglehold about his throat, while below him a vast, swaying crowd chanted the Queen's name with maudlin affection. The combined stench of so many unwashed bodies drifted up to him and forced him to withdraw, holding a pomander to his nose. Oh, to be at Richmond in the cool breeze which blew in from the river, to be at Hampton in the graceful shade of the herb garden —to be anywhere in the world but on progress with the English court, surely the most exquisite form of torture ever inflicted upon man.

He glanced at the Queen, sitting white-faced and grim at her dressing table, and wondered again why she did not spare herself this annual ordeal of travelling among her people. Personally, he found all close contact with the rabble crowd highly distasteful, and how she could bring herself to mingle so freely with a stinking mob of disease-ridden peasants was beyond his understanding. He was beginning to realize that there was a great deal he did not understand about her . . .

Almost a year had passed since Amy's death and he was still unable to make sense of his position with the Queen. She had greeted him with quiet affection on his return to court—he might have been returning from a holiday in the country rather than exile. She now made show of her belief in his innocence in public, but in private she never spoke of it and he did not dare reopen the subject. She had not apologized for her outrageous accusations that day at Windsor, but superficially all was as it had been between them before the tragedy. Only the smug superiority of Cecil reminded him that his ambition was still unfulfilled.

'Whatever reports and opinions say,' Cecil had written confidently to Throckmorton in Paris, 'I know surely that Lord Robert himself has more fear than hope . . .'

Now Robin stood in limbo, frustrated and insecure, weathering Elizabeth's wildly varying moods. She had more sides to her than a cut diamond and loving her had all the complications of conducting a love affair simultaneously with half a dozen different women. And yet there had been moments of hope. On Midsummer's Day he had given a water party, a riot of fireworks, music and pageantry that had cost him a small fortune. Elizabeth sat on cushions beneath the canopy of the royal barge, clutching his arm every time a million coloured sparks exploded over their heads. Her mood was so responsive, so gay and utterly abandoned, that he had turned to Bishop de Quadra and demanded that he marry them on the spot. There had been a crazy moment when she had laid her head on his shoulder and he had honestly thought she was going to go through with it. Silence had fallen all around them and Quadra, looking vastly excited, had begged her, in rapid Spanish, to rid herself of Cecil and his gang of heretics first. '. . . and then, madam, I shall be glad to do it.'

Everything hung on the cobweb thread of her mood, and her mood was wild. Robin had begun to draw a gold ring off his finger and Quadra was moving forward portentously. Then suddenly she sat up and laughed and said she doubted the Bishop had enough English to perform the service. She slipped away from Robin's encircling arm and turned the whole thing into a joke.

The incident had only served to increase Robin's sense of insecurity, his bitter knowledge that sooner or later he was going to lose her, either to a foreign husband, or to another handsome young upstart, with the same ambitions as his own and no legal impediment to stand in his way. He was jealous and mortally afraid of every man who approached her, however briefly.

But he would be making no proposals to her tonight, lighthearted or otherwise; no man in his right senses would risk attracting her moody attention. He was familiar with all the signs that heralded a tantrum and he was not surprised when she suddenly tore off a pair of emerald earrings and threw them back into the velvet-lined jewel box.

'Robin! Those earrings of yours pinch me!'

He hurried across the room to where she sat glowering at her reflection in the mirror.

'I'm sorry to hear that, madam,' he replied cautiously, 'I understood them to be a perfect fit.'

'Well, your understanding is at fault, my lord, like your miserably inferior jewellery! What am I going to wear tonight?'

She pushed the box towards him peevishly. 'Find me something suitable, I'm tired of looking.'

He examined the contents of the huge box with unease. He had good taste and was not unused to this task, but tonight whatever he selected would be wrong, he knew it. Over Elizabeth's jewelled hair he met Lettice's despairing glance and for a moment his eyes rested with interest on her full lips. It was the first time he had ever really noticed what an extremely attractive girl Lettice was.

Glancing into the mirror, he saw the Queen watching him with hostility, and hastily selected a neutral pair of pearls.

Elizabeth struck them out of his hand.

'Fool! If I wear those I shall have to change the gown again.' She glanced around her, as though seeking something else on which to vent her irritation. 'Lettice, are all those windows open? It's like an oven in here.'

'There was one I couldn't unfasten, madam, the latch was too stiff.' Lettice lowered her eyes demurely. 'Perhaps Lord Robert could loosen it if I show him?'

Elizabeth glanced at her sharply, then sat down again with an indifferent shrug.

'Very well. See what you can do with the thing.'

Robin and Lettice retired together to a window at the end of the room and exchanged a smile behind the Queen's back. Lettice extended the tip of her tongue in a rude and risky gesture and Robin laid a warning hand on her wrist. Their glance met again and held, but the rest of the women in the room were too hot and too intent on their mistress's dark mood to take any notice.

The court was on progress through the counties of Norfolk and Suffolk, and Robin, as Master of Horse, was responsible for all the transport arrangements. As much as any other courtier he disliked the wretched inconveniences of these annual excursions. It was essential for the sovereign to see and be seen by as much of the population as possible and Elizabeth had begun to travel more adventurously than any of her predecessors had done. Her vast entourage moved around the countryside all through the long summer months, staying in large country houses and crowded little towns, equal prey to bad roads, foul weather and the risk of plague or smallpox. Nothing deterred Elizabeth from this arduous practice and no one who played host to her was ever quite the same again after the devastating experience. The court, and the rabble which followed in its wake, descended like a swarm of locusts, a horde of quarrelling courtiers all intent on getting a decent bed for the night. The cost to the noblemen who entertained her was virtually ruinous, but none of them could resist the honour or the need to outdo one another with entertainment on a lavish scale. The Queen, delighting in any opportunity to ease the burden on her inadequate purse, traded heavily on their vanity, oblivious to the trail of chaos left in her wake, and the common people loved her for it. In public she was unfailingly gracious, informal and witty, accessible to the lowest of her subjects, captivating whole towns with a simple, charming gesture and stopping to speak to any child who offered her a ragged bunch of flowers. But as the summer temperatures soared, and the list of engagements became steadily more impossible, those who waited on her in private found her almost impossible to please.

Primitive sanitary arrangements were not calculated to improve her temper either. She was fastidious over matters of hygiene and an iron travelling bath bumped along beside the state bed wherever she went. Robin lived in constant terror of losing it between one destination and the next and his minions mounted a virtual armed guard over it. At Windsor Castle she had had two stone rooms set aside for bathing with the ceilings tiled with mirrors, and everyone in close attendance on her was obliged to adopt her habits or suffer the consequences. Only Robin had dared to tease her privately, insisting that a whole new generation of fleas had found itself obliged to take swimming lessons.

She kept her court clean and surprisingly sweet, but on progress she was entirely at the mercy of provincial manners and a general belief that there was no harm in a stink. Certainly they flushed the streets clean of refuse and removed the dunghills for her coming—but nobody could fumigate the masses. She would never permit the people to be held back as they pressed around her and this year she was suffering more than usual from the heat and the stench and the unceasing round of ceremony. The knowledge that Cecil had been right had put her in such a dark mood tonight that Robin was vividly reminded of a keg of gunpowder waiting for a stray spark. The tension in the room filled with nervous women was mounting; it was the kind of atmosphere in which anyone who made a wrong move might find themselves with the leisure to regret it in the Tower.

Directly behind the Queen's jewelled back, Lady Katherine Grey was unpacking a vial of French perfume, moving mechanically like a creature in a trance. For several months she had been tense and preoccupied, seldom talking to the girls who crowded around the Queen. The peevish complaints about her lack of status, voiced freely to anyone who would listen in the early days of Elizabeth's reign, had trailed to a halt of late and she was no longer to be seen making friendly overtures to the Spanish Ambassador. In fact she was seldom to be seen anywhere outside her hours of compulsory attendance on her cousin, and the air of timid silence, so alien to her earlier aggression, had begun to arouse Elizabeth's interest.

She watched the girl now in the mirror, studying the slightly ponderous step which had first alerted her. When Katherine swayed a little and put out an unthinking hand to steady herself against the Queen's chair, Elizabeth turned to place her own fingers over her cousin's.

'You look pale, Katherine. Are you not well?'

Beneath her own, she felt Katherine's fingers tense on the back of the chair.

'It's nothing, madam, truly. I fear the heat affects us all.'

Elizabeth smiled up at her slowly.

'Are you sure that's all it is? Your health is very dear to me, cousin, I think perhaps you ought to see my doctor.'

The vial of perfume dropped from the girl's hand and smashed on the floor, filling the room with the scent of musk. Everyone looked round in the sudden, electric silence to see Lady Katherine staring down into her mistress's steady eyes like a hunted fox.

'Madam, forgive me—forgive me!'

Katherine dropped on her knees, catching the Queen's hand and pressing it to her dry lips.

'Forgive you for what?' laughed Elizabeth lightly. 'For breaking a silly bottle of perfume? Get up, you foolish girl, and go and change your gown—you're covered with the stuff. You smell like a French brothel!'

The tension in the room broke up into hysterical amusement as all the women relaxed with the swing of Elizabeth's mood. Katherine flushed hotly and fled from the room in a wake of muted sneers and titters. The prim haughtiness of the Grey sisters had not endeared them to the court, and most of Elizabeth's ladies were glad to see Katherine flustered and embarrassed.

'Wretched girl!' muttered Mrs Ashley, kneeling down to mop up the mess with flimsy handkerchiefs. 'I can't think why Your Highness makes so much of the proud trollop—I swear she did it purposefully! Your Majesty's favourite perfume too, and *so* expensive!'

'Oh—Robin will give me another bottle—won't you, beloved?'

Elizabeth held up her hand to him and he came to take it passionately, laying his lips daringly on the top of her brightly jewelled hair and watching her face in the mirror.

'I would give you the moon and the stars, madam—if you asked for them.'

She smiled and drew both his hands over her shoulders, clasping them just above her breast.

'I'll settle for the perfume just now—as I rather think you will when Kat tells you the price. Here—put these on me, will you?'

She handed him the emerald earrings which she had rejected five minutes earlier.

'I thought they pinched,' he reminded her playfully as he bent to fasten them.

'These?' She glanced up at him in mock astonishment. 'But these are my favourite pair—they were given to me by someone very special.'

She allowed him to lift her from the chair and kiss her with his accustomed familiarity. Everyone laughed and applauded softly as the kiss deepened, except Lettice who stood, abandoned and forgotten where he had left her at the window, glaring down at the drunken crowd outside. She took no part in the malicious female conversation which followed.

'Katherine Grey's such an insufferable prig, madam—how can you bear to keep her with you?'

'Oh—I have my reasons, believe me. Now—where's that dratted fan?'

'Here, madam—and so rude to Your Majesty at times, after all your kindness.'

'I swear she'd do anything to spite you, madam.'

'Mrs Ashley's right—she dropped that bottle deliberately.'

'Oh, I don't think so.' From the window-seat near Lettice, Mary Sidney's lazy, good-humoured voice cut in. 'Your Highness knows how easily these things are done. Lord knows, when I was carrying Philip I broke almost everything I laid my hands on—'

'Pregnant women are noted for dropping things,' observed Elizabeth thoughtfully. She looked at Robin, who looked back at her, blank and uncomprehending.

It was not until the early hours of the morning that he gauged the significance of that casual remark. For it was only then that he awoke with a start to find Lady Katherine Grey on her knees at the side of his bed, beseeching her 'good brother' to come to her aid with the Queen.

'I'm not your brother!' he snapped. 'I'll thank you to remember that any family connection between the Dudleys and the Greys has long since been severed.'

He got out of the bed with ungallant speed and stared anxiously at the door. Any beady-eyed spy of Cecil's could have seen her enter his room—and if Cecil got to hear of this he would make sure the story reached the Queen in its most ugly form.

He pulled her roughly to her feet and looked at her with distaste.

'Stop bawling, woman,' he said shortly, 'or I'll give you something to bawl about! What the devil are you about coming here in the middle of the night anyway?'

She took a shuddering breath and stepped back from him. She had heard it said that he had a violent temper when roused and for the first time she believed it.

'Well,' he demanded, 'are you going to tell me what this is all about or not?'

'Oh, Robert,' she whispered, 'I'm pregnant!'

He stared at her—the proud, the loudly virtuous young lady who had once made it so plain where her ambitions lay. And he could not help it—he began to rock with laughter.

'You stupid little harlot—the Queen will throw you out of the court for a common whore!'

'You don't understand.' Katherine was stung by his contempt, 'It wasn't like that. We were married—'

'In that case,' he remarked heartlessly, 'she'll have your head—and since it doesn't appear to have been much use to you I don't suppose you'll miss it greatly!'

Her mouth opened and shut again and she swayed where she stood; he cursed and caught her, holding her against him for a moment and feeling the sobs welling up in her. He was horribly reminded of Amy's soft, clinging hands as he pushed her helplessly into a chair.

'Treason,' he muttered. 'You do realize that what you have done is treason —or as near as makes no difference? In your position so close to the throne how could you be fool enough to marry without the Queen's consent?'

'I loved him—I couldn't go to him differently. And now he's in France—and I'm here—and I can't keep it secret much longer. This evening when she looked at me, I was almost sure she had guessed. And she hates me, Robert—for all her sweet words I know she hates me—she's been waiting for some excuse to destroy me.'

'Very likely,' he said drily. 'So why come to me with this fiasco? What do you expect me to do, for God's sake?'

Katherine caught his hot hands and covered them with kisses.

'Speak to her for me—put my case and beg for mercy. She'll listen to you, she likes to please you—everyone says that she—'

'You would have done better to have gone to Cecil if that's what you believe,' he said bitterly, 'but, God knows, you could expect no quarter from him. I hope you realize what a difficult position you've placed me in—'

'But you *will* speak to her?'

'I haven't got much choice, have I? If she hears of this visit from anyone else but me I'll be finished. Come—you had better tell me the whole story—I'll go to her first thing in the morning.'

It was a sorry tale of a secret wedding to the young Earl of Hertford and some of the details were so ludicrous that he would have laughed again if the matter had not been so deadly serious. Hertford's sister, who had been the only witness to this hole-in-a-corner marriage, had died in March and Katherine had mislaid the relevant legal documents. By the time she had finished her tale, he was reasonably convinced her true destination should be a madhouse; but at the same time he knew very well where she would be going once he had broached the subject to the Queen. She had signed her own death warrant, and he did not have the heart to tell her that the only cause he would be pleading with the Queen was his own! He had troubles enough without being sucked into this stupid quagmire.

When at last he managed to be rid of her, he went back to bed in the steamy, mosquito-ridden heat and lay awake for the rest of the night rehearsing his lines for the morning.

He had expected anger and Elizabeth did not disappoint him. His nervous revelation of Katherine's crime was greeted by a string of enlightening oaths and the immediate despatch of that unfortunate girl on the first stage of her journey to the Tower.

When the dust had settled and her women had been driven out of her presence for a pack of clacking hens, Elizabeth sat down in her chair and began to laugh.

'It's safe now,' she said mockingly. 'You can come out of the shadows, Sir Galahad, and stop bleating about your integrity.'

Robin took a few uncertain steps towards her, unnerved by this volte-face. 'I never knew you were so afraid of me,' she remarked calmly.

'Afraid?'

'Yes—flattening yourself against that wall and hoping I wouldn't notice you were still here. Come now—it wasn't a very chivalrous performance, was it? Pushing her out of your room and working yourself into a muck sweat for fear of getting involved.'

'Mud sticks,' he pointed out coolly, 'and I am smeared enough.'

She nodded.

'A sensible attitude—if not very noble. Sometimes I think it must be the baseborn dog in you that attracts the bitch in me.'

'So I do attract you?' He took her hand and smiled.

'Perhaps. You and I deserve each other. We are so passionately devoted to ourselves.'

'And Katherine?'

'I was certain yesterday. I have been suspicious for some time.'

'Then—you are not truly angry?'

'Not in the least. It is remarkably obliging of her to remove herself permanently from the scene.'

Permanently. He knew what that meant—or thought he did. Well—it had been inevitable.

He said quietly, 'You can't execute a pregnant woman. You'll have to wait until the child is born.'

All the colour left the Queen's face and she shivered in the hot sunlight. 'I shall not execute her at all,' she said faintly.

He was startled.

'You are actually going to leave her alive and let her raise a brood of children to menace your throne?'

'Bastards are no threat to me.'

'But the child won't be a bastard,' he said patiently, 'she's married.'

'She'll have difficulty proving it with the relevant documents lost and her only witness dead.'

He began to smile slowly with admiration. She was so quick, so clever. Banished to the Tower as a slut, Katherine would lose all the puritanical support of those who, until now, had been parading her virtue and her legitimacy and comparing it so favourably with the Queen's questionable birth and even more questionable honour.

'So—'

'So I graciously commute her sentence—to life imprisonment.'

He laughed and bent over her chair to kiss her lips in a sort of salutation.

'You cunning cat—is there anything you can't twist to your own advantage?'

'Ask me that again,' she said softly, 'when I have all my rivals safely under lock and key. Both the Greys—and Lennox—'

'And the Queen of Scots?'

They laughed at the absurdity of his suggestion and at length Elizabeth leaned back in her chair, studying him with amusement.

'Oh, Robin,' she said wistfully, 'if I ever got the chance to turn the key in *that* lock I should throw it into the Thames.'

CHAPTER 2

In August, the French galley bearing Mary Stuart eluded the English warships in the Channel in a thick fog and arrived at Leith. There was no official welcome, her bastard brother James having been under the impression that she would be making an unplanned detour through England first. The dour Protestant preacher John Knox screamed at his cowering congregation that the haar which shrouded her entry was the devil's work, an ill omen; but the Queen's party were inclined to thank God for its shelter, having lost to the English ships, which had plainly been lying in wait for them, only the vessel carrying the royal stable.

James arrived at last with his Scottish courtiers, sombrely dressed and most apologetic, trying hard not to betray his surprise that she had arrived at all. Mary entered her capital city on a clumsy, battered, old nag and her heart sank as she rode through the winding streets to the bleak and uninviting edifice that was Holyrood Palace. A clumsy celebration followed, reminding her of the forced gaiety of a funeral feast and she recoiled from the hulking, grubby figures of the Scottish lords, pounding their tankards on the bare tables, scratching, belching, and spitting in the dirty rushes. They were little better than savage chieftains, thought Mary. She was privately appalled to find herself Queen of such barbarians and was bitterly aware of the cynical glances among her lofty French attendants.

A huge fire roared in the stone hearth but it made no more impression on the Great Hall than the flame of a candle. Mary shivered. The long, elegant feet inside her satin slippers were like ice and the damp hung so heavily on the air that she fancied it to be solid. She could not believe this was really happening to her; it was a distorted nightmare from which she would surely awake.

The night dragged to an end with members of the Scottish kirk droning tuneless Protestant dirges beneath her window. She was glad to retire to the tiny stone-walled bedroom, where her women stood on the hems of one another's sweeping trains as they attended her.

'It won't be for long,' she said cheerfully, and they tried to smile; they had already seen their own sleeping-quarters.

It wouldn't be for long, for Mary had no intention of staying; Scotland was an uncomfortable resting place, not a destination. Lying back on the hard bolster pillow she became aware of the spider busily spinning a large web between the far post and the tester—she too could spin as fast and furious on a web of intrigue.

Spain was her best hope. The Spanish heir was misshapen and mad, but such things scarcely mattered when set against the advantages of a Spanish match. A Catholic army at her back would certainly force Elizabeth to ac-knowledge her as her successor. Invasion might not be necessary after all. There were encouraging rumours that suggested Elizabeth's health was fail-ing and doubt had been cast on her ability to bear children. Mary glanced about her with a resigned sigh. With the candles lit and the tapestries hung, the bleak little room was now moderately comfortable. It would suffice for a time if she chose to wait a little longer for her prize. Waiting would mean winning Scotland to her and courting the English Queen's favour; waiting would mean lies and pretence and pretty artifice.

But I am young and I have time on my side—

The fire died and the shadows on the stone wall grew longer. In the twilight zone between waking and sleeping, Mary imagined Elizabeth's scream of rage at being presented with horses in place of a royal captive. No doubt a few ears would be soundly boxed—they said the woman had a spitfire temper and no qualms about making a disgusting exhibition of it. No control, of course, lack of breeding; it always showed. Poor Elizabeth—one could almost pity her unquestionable inferiority. So let her enjoy the jewels and the fine dresses, the little group of fawning lovers and everything else that deco-rated her outrageous reign. Let her have a few fond memories to take to an early grave, for one way or another her dance would soon be ended.

And then, thought Mary, as she turned her face into the lumpy goose-feather pillow, it will be my turn.

October 1562 was a cold, squally month which seemed to echo the distress of English soldiers fighting a lost battle in the French civil wars. Plague had broken out among them, decimating their ranks to the point where retirement from the venture now seemed inevitable; and since Ambrose Dudley, Lord Warwick, was leading those forces in France, the Dudleys had more cause than most to fear what was happening across the Channel. Certainly the Queen had had her fill of war. Twice now she had humoured Cecil's military ambitions, once with success, once, it now seemed, with failure. In future she would avoid war at any cost.

A fierce wind was buffeting the palace casements and driving showers of dried leaves across the lawns at Hampton Court. Elizabeth stood at the river's edge, feeding a cluster of hungry swans, and occasionally leaning against the balustrade, shaken by a dry, rasping cough.

'This wind is like a knife,' said Mary Sidney in an anxious whisper. 'She ought not to be out in it. Can't you persuade her to go in, Robin?'

Robin did his best. Twice he remarked that it looked like rain; twice he complained peevishly that he was cold. Finally he took to stamping up and down beside the parapet, swinging his arms across his chest and remarking rudely that no one in their right senses would have ventured out of the palace on a day like this.

Elizabeth emptied the last crumbs from her hanging pocket and turned to look at him with amusement.

'You're growing soft with good living, Rob. Perhaps I should push you in the river with the swans—then you'd know what it means to be cold.'

He smiled. 'Any time you care to try your hand at that, madam, I shall be happy to put money on the outcome.'

'Done!' Elizabeth reached across Mary and drew Robin's sword from its scabbard. She pressed the sharp blade against the olive skin which showed between his chin and his ruff and forced him steadily backwards to the water's edge.

He raised his hands in submission and began to laugh uneasily.

'Now, madam—you know you don't really mean this.'

'I took a bath this morning—did you, my love?'

'What—in this weather?'

'In that case, you won't mind taking it now, will you?'

With his heels on the edge, he was forced to hold on to the blade to keep his balance; beneath his feet the dirty river, swollen with rain, rushed on downstream.

'If I fall in there I shall stink for days.'

'True. But then I don't have to receive you, do I?'

For one moment he considered how easy it would be to overpower her and shake the sword out of her hand. Had they been alone he would have done it, but with his sister present he did not dare to risk such an assault upon her dignity. It was nothing for him to help himself to her handkerchief in public or stand in her rooms while she dressed, handing her her shift or choosing her jewels. It was nothing for him to kiss her uninvited—though certainly the Duke of Norfolk had objected—but there was a fine distinction between familiarity and insolence, a line over which he must not step in front of witnesses—even when that witness was his own sister and the Queen's best friend. So, now, he played it safe.

'All right,' he said, as the pressure at his throat tightened inexorably. 'Name your price, madam, and let me go.'

'Fifty gold pieces.'

'Fifty!' he was outraged. 'Judas sold the Lord for less.'

'The River Jordan,' said Elizabeth calmly, 'was considerably cleaner than the Thames. Fifty gold pieces spares you a soaking—and a forfeit, of course.'

'Madam?' he looked at her suspiciously; he knew that smile.

'Fill your boots with water—and put them on again.'

Mary held her breath as her brother stared at the Queen, terrified that this might prove the final straw. In spite of its outrageous absurdity, it remained a direct command, a test of her ultimate authority. If he defied her—and what man of Robin's temper would not?—it could be the end of his career at court.

She watched, with her hand pressed to her mouth, until she saw him shrug and bend down to pull off a boot. Wild relief coursed through Mary; she began to laugh and found she could not stop. The Queen turned towards her and for a moment the two women clung to each other for support, squealing like over-excited schoolgirls, until Elizabeth's cough intervened.

'I shouldn't laugh,' gasped Mary, 'he'll never forgive me for it. Oh, madam, if only you had told him to jump in!'

'I know, I know—he would have done it too, wouldn't he? Oh look! The great fool is actually going to put them back on.'

Elizabeth ran the few steps to the water's edge and laid her hand on his arm.

'Don't,' she said, and became incoherent as the cough seized her again.

Robin took her hand and stood up in alarm, his ruined boots suddenly forgotten.

'Your hand is burning—you've got a fever, madam.'

She shook her head.

'It's nothing. Just a chill, the doctor says.'

'Perhaps.' He put one arm firmly around her waist and began to walk her in the direction of the palace, with Mary hurrying behind. 'I'd be happier with a second opinion on that. There's that German doctor Hunsdon speaks so highly of. Will you let me send for him?'

'All this fuss,' grumbled Elizabeth. 'You know how I hate doctors.'

'At least consult the fellow—just to please me. And if he too says it's just a chill I shall be very happy to believe him.'

It was smallpox.

She had the good Dr Burcot thrown out of her room for making the dreadful diagnosis, screaming he was a knave and could get out of her sight; but a week later she lay in a coma, without a mark on her body, and the court physicians told Cecil that her death was imminent.

In desperation they sent again for the pear-shaped, opinionated alien, but Dr Burcot had been insulted. He said with a curse that she could die for all he cared, and was only returned to her bedside with a knife at his back.

Once there he took in her condition at a single glance. Still no eruption on the skin, the worst possible thing that could have happened.

'Almost too late,' he announced grimly. 'Build up the fire and set a mattress in front of it. The infection must be sweated out—'

While Burcot worked, the Council met in confused and terrified debate to determine her successor. It had begun to look as though Lady Katherine Grey would have to be trotted out of the Tower after all, but in their hearts they all knew nothing would prevent the Scottish Queen sweeping down from the North to claim her inheritance.

They were poised on the very brink of civil war when Burcot emerged exhausted from the Queen's room.

'The fever has broken,' he announced pompously, 'with care, she will live.'

The councillors surged about him, yelling like schoolboys, thumping him on the back and wringing his hand, laughing and weeping so that he felt like God. When they had all dispersed in a mad scramble to celebrate, the Secretary, who had taken no part in the hysterical frolics, came quietly to shake his hand.

'You will be well rewarded for what you have done, sir. The Queen's gratitude—'

'Do not speak to me of your Queen's gratitude,' snapped the doctor with an angry laugh, 'she does not know the meaning of the word—her first conscious words were a complaint. Her hands—her beautiful, incomparable hands, if you please—are marred by a few spots and may be marked. She will never forgive me, never.'

'Delirious, perhaps,' suggested Cecil cautiously.

'No, sir, quite in her wits. I asked her by God's pestilence if she would rather be dead!'

Cecil discreetly neglected to inquire what her reply had been and the doctor did not trouble to enlighten him. Instead he kicked his bag across the room in an excess of irritation.

'The woman *deserves* to be disfigured—yet on her face, virtually nothing. I might add that she almost paid for her face with her life.' Burcot swung round and glared at Cecil. 'I never saw a woman in greater need of a master, sir. I advise you to find her a husband with a strong whip hand without a moment's delay, or you will have trouble there. Oh, yes—a great deal of trouble.'

Cecil opened his mouth to comment and shut it again as the door opened behind him.

Robin stood there, dishevelled and pale from his long vigil.

'Burcot,' he said brusquely, 'the Queen requests your attendance.'

The German turned to look at him with faintly raised eyebrows.

'Your Queen *requests?*'

'My sister is ill. The Queen fears—'

'Of course.' Burcot bent automatically to retrieve his bag and walked to the door. 'I will come at once. You will be very fortunate, my lord, to avoid contagion yourself—'

Cecil was left alone to ponder that delightful possibility and all that the natural elimination of Dudley would mean to him.

Only an informed observer would have described Elizabeth's gaiety as false, as she sat on the edge of Mary Sidney's bed with a shawl around her wasted frame.

'It's a rough sort of justice that allows *him* to walk back to the palace in his stockinged feet and not catch so much as a cold,' she remarked cheerfully.

Mary smiled up at Robin, standing beside the Queen, and held out her hand to him.

'I am glad he was spared, madam.'

'Well, he's never ill, is he? There ought to be a law against being so horribly healthy—and so damned smug about it. He thinks he's no end of a man for being exposed twice and not catching it. The devil looks after his own, of course.'

'And who would know that better than you, madam?' Robin's smile held that same faintly forced brightness and the pressure of his hand upon the Queen's shoulder tightened a little, as they both looked at the masked woman in the bed.

There was silence for a moment. Elizabeth played with the fringe of her shawl, sucking it and twisting it round her fingers. Suddenly she leaned forward and gently touched the gauze mask which covered her friend's face.

'Take it off, Mary. I don't want you to hide your face from me.'

Mary shrank back uncomfortably against the pillows.

'Please, madam,' she protested faintly. 'It's truly better that you don't see.'

Elizabeth looked at her gravely.

'You nursed me night and day. Let me see what it cost you.'

With mute reluctance, Mary pulled the ribbon. The gauze mask fluttered to the coverlet and, in spite of her determination to show nothing, Elizabeth gasped. Robin had warned her, but no words could prepare her for the dreadful sight of her friend's ruined face. The skin, which had been so smooth, now had the spongy consistency of long-congealed porridge, an ugly lunar landscape of blistered scabs and deep pitted craters.

She wanted to cry, but knew she must not do that for Mary's sake, so to stifle her tears she began to talk feverishly of sending abroad to find a doctor who could help—there were many treatments—

'But no cure,' said Mary quietly, 'only resignation to God's will.'

'*God!*' The Queen seemed to choke on the word. 'God didn't do this to you. I did.'

'Madam—' Mary faltered and looked at Robin for support. He nodded and she reached out for the Queen's frail hands. 'Madam, I beg you, let me leave your service. Let me go home and make a life in retirement—I can't stay at court like—like this.'

Elizabeth stared at the coverlet and Robin saw the struggle in her eyes, the struggle of a selfish woman in the act of making a real sacrifice. There were very few women that she cared for and he knew how much she had come to depend on Mary's affection. Her instinct was to talk her friend out of this, to beg her to stay, but she strangled it, knowing that, if she asked it, Mary would not deny her.

'Of course.' She looked up and forced herself to smile. 'You must go home to your family. I have kept you from your children over long and no doubt Henry—pest take him!—will want more sons. But you will come back and see me from time to time, won't you? Your room shall be set aside in all my palaces.'

Mary lifted the Queen's hand and treasured it against her ravaged cheek. Elizabeth felt hot tears spilling through her fingers.

'Thank you, madam—you have been so understanding, so kind—'

The Queen flushed hotly, and looked hastily away.

'I'm not kind, Mary, I'm as hard as a nail and twice as selfish. Ask your brother if you doubt it.'

Mary looked at her and a slow smile touched her face with a fleeting gleam of its former beauty.

'Dearest madam,' she said softly. 'You do not know yourself.'

In the corridor beyond Mary's room, Elizabeth released her caged emotion in a flood of savage curses.

'With all the mean, sly, ugly bitches in this palace to choose from—why did it have to be *her?*'

'You must not blame yourself,' Robin said uneasily.

'She bears my disfigurement in addition to her own—how then can I be blameless?'

He started to say that was untrue, absurd, that she was overtired by the visit and morbidly fanciful, but she cut him short.

'Look at me,' she commanded, and he lifted his eyes hesitantly. 'Is there a mark upon my face?'

He shook his head slowly.

'And do you call that natural?'

'It's not for me to—'

'*Is it natural?*'

The words pummelled his unwilling ears with the icy force of hail; his eyes rolled over her face and then quickly away.

'No,' he said at last in a strained whisper, 'I've never seen anyone survive unscathed.'

'Nor anyone so disfigured as your sister—is that not so?'

'Don't question God's will,' he said quickly, 'it's never wise.'

Her eyes seemed enormous in her pale face. She laid her hand on his arm and he felt it trembling.

'Someone grants me a charmed life,' she said softly, 'I wish I could believe it was God.'

He was silent as he escorted her back to her rooms, remembering things he had heard whispered about her. Renard had said she had 'a spirit full of incantation', Feria had called her the daughter of the Devil; even Quadra had written home to tell Philip, 'I think this woman must have 10,000 devils in her body.'

Certainly she appeared to have more lives than the proverbial cat—

Robin found that he too had begun to wonder.

Elizabeth's illness galvanized Parliament to life with all the maddened ferocity of a half-broken stallion that has felt the cruel sting of a spur. They had been patient long enough and now in the certain knowledge that miracles, like lightning, are notoriously disinclined to strike twice in the same place, the Lords and Commons joined their voices in an irritating parrot cry for marriage and a settlement of the succession.

She could do neither of these things—both, for many reasons, were equally impossible politically and personally—but she could not tell them so, and it took all her charm and cunning to wriggle through their grip and emerge at the end of the session with her financial grant and their affection still intact. Parliament was dissolved before the members truly appreciated that the royal fish had slipped their line again, but she was angered by the intolerable pressure to which she had been subjected. And when she was angry with those it would never do to punish, it was Robin who suffered for it.

Their relationship had become a permanent source of curiosity to the court. At the height of her fever, she had begged the Council to make Robin Lord Protector of England in the event of her death, swearing, with God as her witness, that though she loved him well, nothing improper had ever passed between them. Robin had been first amazed, then deeply moved by the news; but later, when she had recovered consciousness and he dared to question her about it, she had merely blushed furiously, then laughed and said she must have been delirious at the time. It was the first time he had ever seen her at a loss for words, and, however light she tried to make of the incident, it marked a change in his anomalous position. She raised him almost immediately to the Privy Council, giving him for the first time an active say in the government of the realm. Cecil maintained an ominous silence on the subject, but he was past panicking now. And when she raised the Duke of Norfolk to the Council, he was duly reassured that a balance would be maintained. There was bitter rancour between Dudley and the premier peer of the realm; whatever ambition Robin still entertained would be amply restrained by Norfolk's influence at the council table.

Robin's seat on the Privy Council turned out to be no more than one further step in an unheard of series of ups and downs in the royal favour which left him in a permanent state of uncertainty.

'He is like my little dog,' Elizabeth was heard to remark in public, 'whenever people see him they know I am near by.'

And a dog's life was precisely what she gave him. She showered him with favours; she slapped his face. She drew up the letters patent to create him Earl of Leicester; she publicly slashed it to pieces with a penknife in front of his eyes, saying that Dudleys had been traitors for three generations and she did not choose to raise another above his station to threaten her. In March 1563 she stunned the court by offering him to the Scottish envoy as a suitable husband for Mary Stuart.

When Robin appeared in the doorway of the Privy Chamber unannounced, Elizabeth could see he was in the grips of a murderous rage. She had anticipated a scene and dismissed her women hastily.

When the door had closed behind them, Robin snatched the silks out of her hand and threw the tapestry frame across the room. His expression suggested that for two pins she would follow it and she was suddenly breathless with excitement.

'Am I a toy, to be given away when I no longer please?' he shouted. 'Or is this some low trick of Cecil's to be rid of me for good?'

'I see you've heard,' she said calmly.

'It seems everyone's damn well heard from here to Scotland—everyone, that is, except me! Don't you even owe me the courtesy of an explanation?'

She laid her silks back in their basket and smiled faintly.

'I don't owe you anything, Robin—you'd better remember that before you start shouting at me. Now—sit down and hear me out or you'll cool your temper in the Tower tonight.'

As he sank down beside her in the window-seat, she was conscious of an irrational sense of disappointment.

'Then you *are* tired of me,' he said wretchedly.

'Oh, don't be a fool!' She touched his cheek gently. 'If I really wanted to be rid of you I could take a considerably cheaper course than this.'

'Cheaper?'

'It will cost me your earldom at least.'

His face was suddenly stony and he released her hand abruptly.

'Like the last time? Are you about to make a public fool of me again for your perverted amusement?'

'No,' she countered evenly. 'I told you then that the Bear and Ragged Staff was not so easily overthrown. And this time I shall sign it. A place in the nobility to complement your place on the Council—it's what you wanted, isn't it? Well, now you can have it, under such circumstances that not even

Cecil can complain. I shall offer the Earl of Leicester to the Scottish Queen with my personal recommendation of his prowess.'

'In bed?'

'It will be convenient to let her think so. I have already suggested that the three of us should form one household—at my expense.'

Robin laughed shortly.

'What do you expect in return—an open declaration of war?'

'The only war she will declare is on her own judgement—this will blow her self-restraint to pieces. You need not worry, Robin—you're not going to Scotland. You're merely the bait in my trap, a stalking horse—a red herring if you like.'

'Worms make the best bait, don't they?' he remarked bitterly. 'Yet even worms can turn. Perhaps you'd care to explain a little further. I'm afraid it's all too deep for my humble powers of perception.'

'It has to be deep,' said Elizabeth slowly, 'she's cunning and she's been well trained in France. Given time she could control all the division I've fostered in Scotland—already she's too strong and confident for safety. She's waited patiently for two years for me to drop dead of my own accord, but, being mighty unneighbourly, I haven't obliged her. I think she's beginning to suspect that I may not be so frail as she hoped and all the signs are that she's not going to wait much longer. One strong foreign marriage will put an end to all this pretty pretence of friendship between us and the first thing she'll do is to march against me. I can't allow her to make a good match—I dare not! The man she marries must bring her trouble. And by the time she's finished chewing over her resentment at your suit, she might just be ready to choose the one I really have in mind for her.'

'Oh, you have a man in mind, do you? And who might that be?'

'Lennox's eldest son—Henry Darnley.'

They were silent for a moment and he gaped at her. The light from the window danced on the crown of diamond spikes that held her blazing hair in place, and suspended a transparent cobweb veil beyond her bare shoulders. There was a little glow of malicious pleasure in her face, almost a touch of the sinister, and as he looked at her he felt, not for the first time, a small prickle of fear.

'But surely you don't intend to let her marry a man who has a claim to your throne! Won't marriage with your cousin's son simply strengthen her position? What's to stop them invading anyway?'

Elizabeth toyed thoughtfully with her fan.

'If she marries Darnley, she'll find she's got her hands too full to even think of my crown. She'll be too busy hauling her husband out of every beer barrel and whore's bed in Edinburgh. There's a little more to dear cousin Henry than that angelic face suggests. Haven't you ever wondered where he gets to whenever he's excused attendance? Well, I happen to have made it my business to find out, and believe me, Robin—if Mama knew what her precious blue-eyed boy does behind the doors of a whore-house she'd beat him black and blue for it.'

Robin frowned. 'I've never noticed anything amiss in his conduct.'

'Oh, he wouldn't dare to bring his nasty little habits to court, not with Mama watching. He lives in terror of the bitch, like his father and the rest of her household. But once he's off the leash in Scotland he'll run mad as a rabid dog. We'll hear no more of Mary's pretensions once she puts a crown on Darnley's head!'

'But what makes you so certain she will want him?'

'His pretty, pouting face—his Tudor blood—his claim to my throne—oh, he's certainly got his assets! Superficially he's a great match and I shall appear to move heaven and earth to prevent it. I shall scream and stamp and probably threaten war—that should really convince her that he's worth the having! When she takes him—as she will—it will be with a crow of triumph at having out-manoeuvred me at last. And the minute that marriage takes place, the Countess of Lennox will go to the Tower for plotting it against my spoken wishes.'

Robin gave her a speculative glance and touched her clenched fist on her lap.

'God knows I'm no lover of the Countess, but I've often wondered why you hate her so much.'

Elizabeth stared into space with narrowed eyes.

'Oh—it's an old grudge and I suppose I should have let it go by now, only every time the old harridan flounces into my presence, I remember how she made me suffer and I want to wring her scrawny neck all over again.'

She told him about the kitchen and saw his eyes widen in surprise and anger.

'Traitors suffer less on the rack,' he muttered. 'You might have gone out of your mind.'

Elizabeth laughed shortly.

'I wouldn't have given her the satisfaction, I knew it was what she wanted. But even so I still bear the scars of her malice.' She held out her hands at arms' length, palms down and for the first time he noticed their continual tremor. 'Ever since then I've slept badly, disturbed by the smallest sound, I snap and slap for no apparent reason, so that behind my back my women curse me for a bad-tempered bitch—oh yes, they do, and it's true!' She frowned. 'A lot of other people had a hand in wrecking my nerves, Robin, but Lennox was the only one who did it out of spite. And Lennox alone will pay for it—as I swore at the time.'

'By seeing her son made a king? Won't that be worth at least ten years in the Tower to her?'

Elizabeth smiled slowly at him, and something about that smile made him shiver involuntarily.

'The Scots have sharp daggers and a long-standing tradition of killing their kings. I imagine they'd make short work of any mincing he-bawd who tried to lord it over them—and Darnley's just fool enough to try it. One sniff of power and he'll think he's God Almighty.'

For a moment Robin was silent, staring at the floor.

'You intend to send him out to his death, don't you?' he said at last. 'That's your true motive—your ultimate revenge on Lennox!'

She looked at him coolly.

'My only true motive is to restrain Mary's ambitions and protect my crown. That's all that really matters. Anything else that accrues from this is purely incidental, but I think it will work very nicely—don't you?'

'No, I don't,' he said. 'I don't see how you can possibly expect to play chess with the emotions of half of Europe.'

She smiled and ran her fingers through his hair playfully.

'In that case you'll be prepared to put a thousand gold crowns on the outcome.'

And that truly staggered him, for where money was concerned she had all the instincts of a miser. She would never bet such an amount on anything she did not consider to be an absolute certainty, but the possibility of winning such a wager from her was irresistible. It would upset her for days if she lost!

So at last he agreed to play the part she had assigned him, took on her wager and watched incredulously as events unfolded steadily, almost entirely as the Queen had predicted.

In order to make him a suitable candidate for Mary Stuart's hand, Elizabeth raised Robin to be Earl of Leicester and Baron of Denbigh. It was a royal title which had never before been bestowed on one without a drop of royal blood, but as she had surmised, under the circumstances even Cecil could not breathe a word against it. Sussex and Norfolk held their tongues with remarkable restraint, so that the only person at the English court who looked as though he might choke on the issue was the Scots envoy, Melville, who was forced to watch the ceremony of investiture and witness the Virgin Queen of England tickling the neck of the new-made Earl who knelt before her. Robin looked up at her with a familiar grin and she parted her lips in a burlesque of a kiss, while Andrew Melville held himself rigid to suppress his burning desire to stride up and slap her presumptuous face. He had already suffered a great deal from the English Queen in the preceding weeks. On more than one occasion, she had backed him into an impossible diplomatic corner, demanding to know whether he considered her to be more beautiful than his own mistress. Who was the better musician, the better dancer? He had grown scarlet with embarrassment beneath her wicked gaze as the outrageous questions became increasingly personal and he was uncomfortably aware that her attendants were doubled up with amusement at his acute discomfort.

'And which of us is the taller, Sir Andrew?'

'My mistress stands several inches above Your Majesty.'

'Ah, then she is too tall, for I myself am exactly the right height for a woman—do you not agree, sir?'

What could he say? How could he ever face his own mistress again? He had never in his life been made to look such a wooden idiot, but this investiture was the final straw. How dared she insult his Queen by offering this shabby adventurer, the man who was commonly reputed to have murdered his wife in order to find a place in the royal bed? And how dared she publicly demonstrate the relationship which was obviously still between them as though her original suggestion had not been insolence enough! Tickling his neck on a solemn state occasion—what did they do in the privacy of her apartments if this was how she behaved in public? And as for that disgusting suggestion that the three of them should form one household—he glanced up and quailed, for the ceremony was over and she was bearing down upon him once more. And if she made one more tasteless remark—just one!—he was going to throw diplomacy to the winds.

'Well, Melville—what do you think of my new creation?'

'No doubt he will adorn his place,' said Melville drily. 'He is fortunate indeed to have a princess willing to reward him for his services.'

She knew what he meant by that and was amused.

'I detect a certain lack of enthusiasm, Melville.' She glanced pointedly at Darnley, who bore the Sword of State and a bored expression. 'I hope you don't prefer that long lad over there for your mistress.'

Melville was startled. How in God's name had she got wind of their interest in Darnley? Did she want Darnley for herself? Certainly her tone implied that she would not consider Mary's interest in him in a friendly light.

'Why, madam,' he replied hastily, 'no woman could prefer that beardless lady-faced boy to so fine a man as Lord Leicester.'

She smiled coyly, inclined her head in approval of his answer and beckoned the new Earl to her side. Melville drew aside in some relief. As far as he could tell, he had assuaged her suspicions, but her attitude had confirmed his private opinion: Darnley was a good catch that must be netted with the minimum of delay. For if she knew, she would stop it—her tone had made that quite clear.

The reaction in Scotland to the Earl of Leicester's suit was exactly what Elizabeth had hoped for. Mary was blind with rage and deaf to the most elementary promptings of common sense. Neither her advisers, nor her half-brother, were able to reason with her and persuade her to call Elizabeth's bluff. The insult was intolerable. The Horsemaster, the murderer, the son of a traitor and—worse than any of these—the cast-off lover! How dared Elizabeth try to pass him on as though he were a well-worn slipper whose comfortable fit she could heartily recommend. It was disgusting—*disgusting!*—and she would not give the proposal a moment's serious thought, no, not even with the subtle promise of the English succession as a wedding present.

Rage stripped away the mask of patience and restraint which Mary had cultivated for nearly three years, exposing her raw emotions to the air. And Elizabeth allowed Darnley to escape to Scotland at the precise moment when she judged her cousin to be ready to fall in love with the first handsome candidate who crossed her path. Darnley was an English subject—he would bring Mary nothing but his Tudor blood and his remote claim to the English throne, as Mary's outraged bastard brother, James, did his best to point out to her before it was too late. As he watched his half-sister's helpless infatuation take its natural course, James pleaded, begged and finally threatened; while Elizabeth, apparently furious at the turn events were taking, demanded Darnley's immediate return to England. The open hostility from James and Elizabeth was sufficient to convince Mary that Darnley must be a good match. He was also a Catholic and the most handsome and charming young man she had ever had the good fortune to meet. The choice seemed patently obvious to her—she was heartily tired of humouring her enemies. Her marriage to Darnley was conducted in almost indecent haste, simultaneously satisfying a physical lust and a personal spite against her half-brother and her English cousin, the two people she had begun to hate more than anyone else on earth.

Within a month, the marriage was celebrated by civil war. James led her outraged Protestant nobility in open rebellion against her and she rode into the field against him, nursing a devastating personal knowledge of the perverted drunkard who was now her King-Consort. The peace which Mary had so skilfully preserved in Scotland since her arrival was shattered beyond repair, while in England Elizabeth smirked as the new Earl of Leicester paid out his thousand gold pieces and seriously began to wonder if she had second-sight.

After six months of degradation and misery with a debauched brute for a husband, pregnancy was Mary Stuart's sole triumph, all she had to show for the marriage that had split her kingdom, and turned her half-brother into a traitor. Only the devotion of her closest adviser, the stunted little Italian musician, David Riccio, saved her from abject despair, as slowly and carefully he began to rebuild the bridges which her hasty marriage had destroyed. It was soon obvious to Darnley, to the Scottish lords and to the anxiously watching English councillors that Mary was receiving too much good advice and that something drastic would have to be done about it. So on a bitter March night, with a savage brutality unparalleled even in Scottish history, Riccio was stabbed to death in the presence of a mistress six months gone with child. Darnley held Mary while the Lords Ruthven, Morton, Lindsay, Kerr and Douglas plunged their daggers into the little Secretary in a frenzy of blood lust; he stood by, with quiet satisfaction, while Kerr pressed a cocked pistol against Mary's side and threatened the life of his unborn child. He was a king at last, taking a kingly revenge on an inferior rival and his conscience never stirred; but later, alone with his wife, his sense of self-preservation did and the signs of nervous agitation were unmistakable to Mary. She had neither time nor strength to waste voicing her loathing of this spineless traitor—that could come later when she was safe. Now she needed the pitiful craven to engineer her escape, and she began to play mercilessly on his fears with such success that a mere night later saw her riding with Darnley to the safety of Lord Bothwell's castle at Dunbar. And when the news was brought to England, Elizabeth astonished her own advisers by applauding the courage and cunning by which Mary had won free of her enemies.

'I'm only sorry she didn't stab Darnley with his own dagger at Dunbar!' she cried. 'The mean-minded knave should be boiled alive for the way he's treated her.'

It was too much for Leicester's logic. He had to point out to her that it was she who had sent the mean-minded knave to her cousin in the first place, but she did not appear to hear as she stalked up and down the room with an angry swish of brocade.

'They say he held her and forced her to watch it all—a helpless girl carrying his own child.'

'Madam, that helpless girl is your deadly enemy, you've said so yourself before now. And you knew Riccio was to be murdered. I showed you Randolph's letter weeks ago—you approved of it.'

She shot him a look of hostility.

'I approved the principle, not the means. Neither you nor Cecil told me that it was to be done in her presence with the poor devil clinging to her skirts and screaming like a stuck pig. They say her gown was soaked with blood—.'

Elizabeth stood in the centre of the room, clenching and unclenching her hands. They were alone, so he could not accuse her of play-acting for the benefit of watching ambassadors.

'If I'd known it was to be done like this I'd have warned her—I swear I would.'

He was silent, trying to reconcile this angry sympathy with the cold cunning of her diplomacy. Increasingly, he was beginning to see the woman and the Queen as quite separate entities. A pity one never knew which one would be called to face!

At last he said cautiously, 'Well, it's done now. Does it really matter how?'

'It could have caused her to miscarry.'

Robin shrugged. 'I'd say it's not too late, even now, to hope for that.'

'*Hope?*' she picked up an inkwell from her desk and flung it at him wildly. 'You think I hope for the death of unborn children? God, what an insensitive pig you are. Get out of my sight and don't come back until you've wiped that gloating smile off your face.'

He picked his way carefully over the trail of ink and bowed himself out of the room, reflecting that it was rarely possible to know just what she would welcome. Evidently the only kind of treachery she seemed to approve of was her own.

In the corridor beyond he met Cecil, who glanced at his ink-splashed doublet with a quizzical expression.

'Still angry, I see,' the Secretary remarked. 'This is perhaps not the time to seek audience.'

'Not unless you aspire to decapitation by inkwell,' said Leicester drily.

The two men exchanged a guarded smile. For a fleeting moment there was an alliance of puzzled male sympathy, as strong and irrational as that which had suddenly united Elizabeth with her sworn enemy.

They withdrew together beyond the Privy Chamber, civil with each other now, as political necessity had increasingly forced them to be.

'What do you make of this business with the Scottish Queen, Sir William?'

Cecil frowned and glanced round cautiously to ensure they would not be overheard.

'I think it a great pity they allowed her to escape. Given time and the right support, she will regain her full power and influence in Scotland.'

Leicester gave him a heartless little smile.

'Time is the one thing no one can give her—from what I hear she has no hope of surviving the birth. Three more months, Sir William, and God may resolve our problem for us.'

Cecil sucked in his lower lip and gnawed the edge of his greying beard.

'The fortunes of every Englishman may now depend upon the fate of Mary Stuart in childbed. I hope you're right, my lord—indeed I hope you're right.'

CHAPTER 3

All the windows of the Great Hall had been pushed open and a gay riot of music and laughter spilt out into the sweet dusk beyond. It was a sultry June evening and not a breath of air stirred the silent trees in the rambling riverside gardens of Greenwich, as Sir Andrew Melville rode hell for leather into the empty courtyard and tumbled from his spent horse. Grooms hurried forward to take the reins from his hands and he paused a moment to draw his sleeve across his sweating face, before stumbling through the clouds of midges into the palace.

In the hot, airless corridor beyond the Great Hall he encountered the Secretary of State who stiffened visibly at the sight of him.

'Melville! What news?'

'It's a son, Sir William—a fine, bonny prince.'

'And your Queen?' Cecil's voice was sharp with anxiety.

'A hard and difficult labour—but, God be thanked, the doctors say she will recover.'

Cecil gave him his cold hand.

'You bring us wonderful tidings,' he said stonily, his sombre face as fixed and unsmiling as a death's-head. 'I know Her Majesty will be overjoyed when I inform her.'

Melville made a quick step towards the door of the Great Hall.

'But surely I should deliver news of such moment in person.'

Cecil's cool eyes looked him up and down, from dust encrusted beard to muddy riding boots.

'You could not possibly appear before Her Majesty in such a state, Melville. You are familiar with Her Majesty's fastidious taste and if I may say so without giving offence, sir—you do stink of horse and sweat. Go to your chamber and rest and I will see food is brought to you. Her Majesty will receive you tomorrow.'

'*Tomorrow!*' Melville opened his mouth to protest further, but the resolute little figure had already turned away and begun to thread his way through the swirling mass of silks and satins. Melville crept close to the door to watch.

The Queen was dancing with Leicester, but at the Secretary's approach they swung out of the measure and stood waiting for him to reach them. Leicester murmured something in her ear. She laughed, tapped his cheek playfully and stepped forward alone to hear what Cecil had to say.

Even from that distance Melville saw the colour leave her complexion. She staggered back a step and fell into the chair behind her, turning her face away from the company and covering it with one long white hand. The music died in mid-beat, the dancers froze and stared as a cry of savage anguish tore through the summer air and splintered the gay, informal atmosphere into a deathly hush.

'*The Queen of Scots is lighter of a fair son and I am but a barren stock!*'

For a dreadful moment no one moved, then Cecil made a quick commanding gesture. A clutch of women rushed around her, closed her from sight, and a moment later hurried her from the crowded room. Melville drew into the shadows as they swept past, but Cecil, limping slowly in their wake, caught a glimpse of his triumphant face, and his own lips set in an angry line.

He went at once to her private apartments expecting to be refused admittance, but, to his surprise, he was shown into her bedchamber almost immediately. He found her alone, standing with her back to him and with one hand resting against a carved bedpost. She did not look round, but with her free hand she made a quick, furtive gesture and he guessed that she was hastily wiping away tears.

'You've come to scold I take it. "An appalling loss of self-control in public, madam!" So what do you propose as punishment? Shall I go to bed with no supper?'

Standing there, listening to her petulant defiance, he suddenly saw her as she must have been as a child and he forgot to be angry.

'It's not my place to criticise you, madam,' he said gently. 'I came merely to tell you that Melville saw and heard it all.'

'And will tell his mistress, who will gloat!' She clenched her fist. 'Well, I'll give him the lie tomorrow. I'll dance with joy for him—I'll even be godmother to the infernal brat! Will that suffice?'

'For Melville, no doubt,' he said grimly, 'but not for the rest of your countrymen, I fear. Madam, you described yourself as barren—have you any idea what uproar that will cause among those who fear for the Protestant succession?'

'Oh, the succession—good God, I'm not dead yet!'

'Not yet—pray God not for many years—but the birth of a Scottish prince will cause a public outcry for your own marriage from Parliament and people alike.'

She swore softly and swung away from him.

'Cecil, I rule this country and I rule it well—is that not so?'

'You know it is, madam.'

'Then why can't they be content? Why must they try to force me into something that I cannot—'

She broke off and he stared at her in silence. After a moment he went over and put his hand on her arm.

'Is it still Leicester?' he asked quietly. 'Is it?' She did not answer and he shook his head.

'If I had known it was going to mean this—' He stopped as he saw her look and continued hastily, to cover his slip, 'I sometimes think Your Majesty does not mean to marry at all.'

She turned away from him impatiently.

'Is it a crime then, not to marry?'

'Madam,' he was suddenly aghast at the implication behind her truculence, 'in your case it would be a crime against the state—aye, and an unnatural crime at that. No woman can be happy in your position, alone and childless.'

She looked over her shoulder with a sudden, mocking smile.

'You speak very knowledgeably on the pleasure of womanhood Cecil—when did you last climb out of childbed?'

He refused to be baited or side-tracked. He had come here tonight to know the answer to one question and he did not intend to be gainsaid by any of those 'answers answerless' with which she placated the Commons. And because the empathy between them was now so sound, she knew the question in his mind, and held up her hand to stay him.

'Don't ask it, my friend—believe me, you don't want to know the answer. I have reasons against marriage that I would not divulge to a twin soul. All I will tell you now is that I do not mean to marry—ever!'

He went out of her presence like a man in a trance.

*   *   *

Among the first to make capital out of the birth of Mary's son was the new Earl of Leicester. Still flushed with the triumph of his title, he brooded long and hard over Elizabeth's curious outburst and managed to convince himself that their marriage was its only natural corollary. Nothing would induce him to abandon his dream and he was ready to bully or grovel to anyone who might help him attain his object. Less than a year since, he had even approached Cecil openly, begging him to give up his plans for a foreign marriage and to support his own suit, promising that he would see Cecil handsomely advanced in return.

It had been rather worse than just a waste of effort. Cecil had smiled, thanked him warmly for his confidence, and then repeated the whole conversation to the French Ambassador, carefully accentuating Leicester's presumption in a manner which was calculated to infuriate the Queen when she heard of it. Leicester had not dared to approach the Secretary again on the subject.

His tentative overtures of marriage to Elizabeth resulted in some of the bitterest quarrels they had ever had. There was a succession of ugly, public scenes between them and once they were both seen to be in tears. He simply could not understand her attitude. Since the sudden death of Kat Ashley the previous June she had been very difficult to live with. After the first day when she had been utterly silent and bewildered by the shock, she had thrown herself into the pursuits which filled her life, working, hunting and dancing like one driven by the devil, until everyone around her was on their knees with exhaustion. Leicester had waited patiently for the passionate breakdown which he sensed lurking beneath the surface of her indecent gaiety and insatiable restlessness, waited to take her in his arms and comfort her. But it never came. If she wept, he didn't know about it; and whatever comfort she craved she appeared to find in the attentions of another man.

When she transferred her favours to Thomas Heneage, Leicester was devastated. She announced publicly that she was sorry for the time she had wasted on him—'and so is every good subject . . .' wrote Cecil with acid triumph in his diary.

The court turned cool to Leicester and Cecil gloated quietly, watching him panic and resort to desperate means. An ostentatious flirtation with Lettice Knollys brought him nothing but a long exile from court and the knowledge that there was little to be gained by provoking the Queen's jealousy.

Exile was costly and showed him great glaring gaps in his own defences. His enemies closed in gleefully, reviving the scandal of Amy's death by persuading her half-brother, John Appleyard, to intimate that he knew more than he had said at the time. There was loud talk of payments to Appleyard by his brother-in-law and a strong implication that they had bought his silence. Leicester's recall to court came only just in time to warn his enemies off. John Appleyard faded back into the limbo from which he had been bribed to emerge, and for the time Leicester was spared the indignity and the danger of answering these libellous accusations.

The incident had unnerved him and shown him the depth of his dependence on the Queen's protection; he was less the man for the experience. He dropped Lettice hastily and rushed back to court in a hopeful mood, expecting to find the Queen waiting tearfully for him with open arms, as all his women waited for him after a quarrel. Instead he found her so surrounded by younger men—Heneage, Christopher Hatton, the Earl of Ormond—that he could hardly get near her, and he was aghast at the apparent ease with which she seemed to have replaced him. It was hard, very hard, to admit that he might not be indispensable to her happiness. And she played her part so well that only a man as perceptive as Cecil could have gauged the depth of her suffering.

Jealous, frightened, tormented beyond endurance, Leicester cursed the cruel fate that had made him want the one woman who did not want him. Savage desire had begun to eat into his nature, making him ruthless and haughty and aggressively virile. He snapped his fingers about the court and a woman was his—any woman, except the one who mattered. He took them all wherever he found the opportunity, without love or gratitude or inner satisfaction, and indulged in violent fantasies. He wanted to drag Elizabeth from her exalted pedestal and rape her in full view of the court; he wanted to beat her into abject submission and cover that alabaster body with bruises. He suspected that she had a taste for rough handling, but he lacked the basic courage to follow that conviction to its logical conclusion. For he just might be mistaken; and, if he was, he knew that raping Elizabeth would be the last mistake he ever made.

So he was forced to stand by and watch while she behaved like a goddess promising favours to a fawning group of humiliated men. None of them could resist the oblique suggestion that at any moment she might indeed be prepared to take a lover—or a husband—from their midst and so they hovered like moths around a candle. She had a cruel genius for stalking men's hearts.

When she could bear the game no longer, she softened at last, agreed to see him alone, and laughed at his jealousy, telling him that all her friends were men and he need read no more than that into it. He was unconvinced, but so grateful to be taken back into her affections that he returned meekly to the place she had allotted him, like the lap-dog she had once called him. Her attendants tiptoed discreetly from the room and he sat at her feet in the bright firelight. There was a relaxed and comfortable silence between them and neither of them spoke, as if they feared to disturb some magic spell.

It was as though they both felt it was the only way to avoid another quarrel.

It was a bad year for lovers. While Robin was struggling to cement his return to favour, the Queen of Scots began to eclipse all lesser events with the scandal of her own private life. With a sudden, shocking pace her life was circling in a downward spiral to disaster beyond her control, and Elizabeth watched with genuine horror as her rival fell helplessly into the trap of personal relations, which she herself had eluded so successfully eight years before. No one shed any tears when the villainous Darnley met his deserved end in an explosion at Kirk-o'-fields, but everyone knew—or at least believed they knew—that Mary's lover, the Earl of Bothwell, was responsible for it.

Mary now stood on the edge of the very same disaster which had once threatened her royal cousin. Her only hope of escaping the consequences of Darnley's murder was to abandon her lover to his fate and a public execution. It was a plain choice between her lover and her crown, and Elizabeth, who had already made that painful choice, was filled with a terrible foreboding, a sharp, anxious sense of watching her own younger reflection in a mirror, rushing relentlessly towards self-destruction.

For the first time, acting a little out of self-interest, but a great deal more from a wealth of sympathetic understanding, she stretched out her hand to Mary in a gesture of real friendship with a frantic, scolding letter that begged her to come to her senses before it was too late.

'Oh, madam, I should not fulfil the office of a faithful cousin or an affectionate friend if I studied rather to please your ears than to endeavour to preserve your honour; therefore I will not conceal from you what most persons say about the matter, namely that you will look through your fingers at taking vengeance for this deed and have no intention to touch those who have done you this kindness, as if the act would not have been perpetuated unless the murderers had received assurance of their impunity.

'. . . I exhort you, I advise and beseech you to take this thing to heart and let no persuasion hinder you from manifesting to the world that you are a noble princess and also a loyal wife.'

She sanded the letter and stared down at it, gnawing the paint on her lower lip. After a moment she pushed it across the ivory inlaid table to

Leicester, who read it in silence, arched his fine dark eyebrows, and handed it back.

'Well?'

'A remarkable achievement, madam—anyone who didn't know you better would say that was written from the heart.'

His tone made her look up a trifle sharply. 'When I ask your opinion on a matter of state I expect to hear a Privy Councillor reply—not a petulant lover.'

'I'm not your lover,' he reminded her.

'Be glad of it. One of us must maintain a little common sense. Or would you prefer to stand in Bothwell's shoes?'

'Poised to marry his queen—is that so far from my desire?'

'When lovers play for kingdoms desire is not enough. A marriage between Mary and Bothwell will cost her the crown, and that, as I believe I have told you before, is the last thing I want. So,' she tapped the letter with a brisk forefinger, 'is that strong enough to make any difference?'

Leicester raised his broad shoulders in a noncommittal shrug.

'That rather depends on how much he means to her. Not all women abandon their lovers when the going gets rough.'

Elizabeth tucked her bottom lip under her teeth and let her mocking gaze travel slowly over his extravagant suit, from rich doublet slashed with gold-thread embroidery to soft leather boots studded with pearl buttons.

'You look singularly unabandoned to me, Robin.'

He followed her gaze and smiled faintly.

'The well-kept lap-dog! I sit on a jewelled cushion chewing whatever bones you choose to throw to me, and come to heel when I'm called. I know damned well what I can expect if I don't.'

She laughed outright.

'You know where the door is, Robin—I shall not lack for company if you go.'

'And you know I couldn't stay away from you if I tried.'

'I know you couldn't afford to stay away,' she said softly. 'I'm afraid it's not quite the same thing.'

He was silent a moment, staring at her.

'Take any man at court,' he said at last, 'use him as you have used me all these years and see if pillage alone will hold him.'

She left her desk and went over to him, stroking one long finger over his taut cheekbone.

'Why do you treat me as you do?' he asked seriously. 'If you love me, why does it give you pleasure to give me pain?'

'I don't drink and I don't whore,' she countered lightly. 'Surely I'm entitled to one unfortunate habit.'

'It's not a habit,' he said quietly. 'It's an obsession.'

Her soul quivered like a plucked lute string and she stepped back from him, unnerved.

'I know,' she said uneasily, 'that I am not always—kind. I try to make it up to you.'

'Oh yes,' he conceded wearily, 'with lands and money and fine titles. I can't complain you're not generous. You give me everything I want—except yourself.'

'And my crown.'

'Keep your precious crown,' he snapped suddenly. 'God only knows how much I've grown to hate it.'

'And me,' she whispered, looking away from him. 'You hate me too, don't you?'

He put up his hands to cup her chin between his fingers.

'Sometimes,' he said slowly, as though each word gave him pain, 'there are hours, even whole days, when I think I'm quit of you for good. I can tell myself that I despise you, that I'll never care for you again and for those few hours I'm a free and happy man, gloating over my possessions and ogling your women. But you are a fever in my blood. Each time I think my manhood restored you strike me down again. You fall ill and I am sick with terror; you smile and melt away all my resentments. If I could find a doctor to cure me of my love for you, believe me, madam—I would make him a wealthy man!'

She laid her head on his shoulder and his arms stole around her, holding her very close.

Don't stop loving me Robin—don't ever stop. Because the day you do my dearest, my beloved—God help me—I know I shall kill you for it.

Mary paced her ill-lit chamber with Elizabeth's letter in her hand. It was more than an hour since it had been delivered and still she could not dismiss its urgent wording from her mind.

I exhort you, I advise and beseech you—

It was not the sort of letter she had ever expected to receive from the woman she regarded as her worst enemy, and the naked warmth of its friendship had shocked and shamed her. Was this woman really a contemptible whore, a bastard bitch devoid of all Christian feeling? How easy it would have been for Elizabeth to stand by and laugh, to make the sort of cruel and tasteless comment that she herself had made in similar circumstances: *The*

*Queen of England is going to marry her horsemaster, who has killed his wife
to make room for her.*

Suddenly she was deeply ashamed of that quip.

In all the weeks of her tempestuous relationship with Bothwell, no word of
warning from friends or ministers had penetrated the crazy fortress of her
infatuation. But this letter had moved her, unnerved her, made her suddenly
begin to question her own actions with torpid bewilderment, like someone
stirring at last from a drugged sleep. Elizabeth was the only woman in Europe who truly understood what it meant to choose between a lover and a
crown.

*If only she was here. If only I could talk to her. Throckmorton was right. I
could have trusted her—*

In an agony of doubt she turned at the sound of footsteps on the private
stairway and a moment later Bothwell was before her, towering above her
with his magnificent weatherbeaten face laughing down into hers, a face hard
and brutally handsome, like rough-hewn granite. Here was a man indeed, a
man who, given the opportunity, might even have tamed her cousin, and for
a moment she wondered just how hard Elizabeth would have fought for her
honour, that dark night on the floor of the Exchequer House.

He seized her exultantly and swung her round as though she was as light as
a doll, but carefully, gently, remembering that already she carried his child.

'What's amiss, my little white Queen? You look as though you've just seen
a ghost—not Darnley's, I trust.'

It was the tasteless joke of a tasteless man and she shuddered as she
handed him Elizabeth's letter.

'You had better read this—it concerns you.'

He read it in silence, then cursed and flung it on the floor with an angry
laugh. 'So the Virgin Queen offers you the advice she took so well herself!
But that bitch's game won't work for you, madam. You'll never keep me for a
tame bird as she keeps Robert Dudley—I'm no horsemaster or kept man. I'll
leave you to your enemies first, so take your choice.'

For a long moment Mary hesitated, weighing her future in the balance,
until he bent her backwards in his arms and took her chin between his strong
fingers in a vicious grip that made her cry out with pain.

'I am your destiny. You'll marry me and we'll fight for your crown if we
have to. Tell Elizabeth to go to hell—it's where she belongs anyway.'

Gladly she surrendered to his will and stood perfectly still while he tore off
her cumbersome gown and carried her through into the tiny bedchamber.
And while they made wild, passionate love on the very brink of disaster, the

Queen of England's letter lay face down and forgotten on the stone floor of the ante-room.

Disaster followed Mary like a patient spaniel from that day on as, relentlessly, the very scandal men had expected to see in England years before was enacted inexorably, like a morality play. Mary married Bothwell and swore that she would follow him to the end of the world in a white petticoat before she would abandon him. And it was the end of the world, as she had known it. Scotland rose against Bothwell in the righteous fury of a civil war and the lovers gathered their forces at Carberry Hill, only to watch their followers melt away in a bloodless battle which betrayed the utter hopelessness of their course. Torn from her husband's side, Mary was stripped of her power, imprisoned on the lonely island of Lochleven and forced to the final act of abdication. But for the fear of Elizabeth's retribution she would have been executed, and increasingly Mary looked on her cousin as the only friend left to her in a world turned suddenly treacherous and hostile. For a few short months, in spite of the miles between them, each felt a curious closeness to the other, two women against an army of men. Elizabeth was working furiously for her release and reinstatement, confident that it could only now be accomplished on terms favourable to herself, when Mary plunged everything into chaos by escaping. Her few days of wild liberty ended in a resounding armed defeat at the battle of Langside, and Mary fled across the bleak Scottish countryside as a fugitive in fear of her life.

In May 1568, against the advice of her staunchest supporters who begged her to flee to France, Mary turned to the last relative she trusted. She crossed the Solway into England in a tiny fishing boat, wearing the only gown she possessed, to throw herself upon the mercy of her cousin and dearest friend—Elizabeth.

'Well, madam, you have the wolf by the ears now, and no mistake.'

The comment fell from the Secretary's lips, as flat and heavy as a lump of lead, and she did not trouble to stop writing or look up.

'That's not an original remark, Cecil, I had expected better of you.'

He promptly began to give it in a tone deliberately casual, but spiced with malice.

'I hear she is holding a pretty court in Carlisle, madam, for all her ragged state—a dispossessed princess makes a most appealing damsel in distress. I hear it said on all sides that, even in rags, she is very beautiful.'

Elizabeth looked up at that and eyed him with respect; he was perhaps the one man at court who would have dared to mention it.

'You have no scruples, have you, Cecil? You would have made a good woman. Are you actually daring to suggest that I have good cause to be jealous?'

'Jealous of your people's loyalty, madam. Remember that most of your northern lords are Papists. Within months the whole of the North could be aflame beneath her banner. The Catholics—'

'You,' she interrupted waspishly, 'have Catholics on the brain.'

'Certainly I maintain that the statutory measures against them are hopelessly inadequate under the present circumstances.'

She pursed her lips angrily; she was beginning to grow annoyed.

'Did you learn nothing at all from my sister's reign, Cecil?'

'Madam, I fail to see—'

'Then open your bigoted eyes and look around you, my friend. Perhaps you will see that the majority of my Catholic subjects are quiet, law-abiding folk whose only real desire is to live out their lives in peace. It's my belief that half of them couldn't give a damn who is on the throne. But start a reign of terror and they'll begin to care heartily enough—they'll take up her cause like a crusade and you and the rest of my godly Council will have so much to answer for you'll still be excusing yourselves on the Day of Judgement. I've told you more times than I care to remember that persecution is the last resort.'

'The last resort will come, madam, no matter how you try to avoid it. If the Pope should excommunicate you now in favour of Mary, the very word Catholic will become synonymous with traitor. Parliament will cry out for action against them.'

'And you can't wait for that day to dawn, can you, Cecil—you and the rest of your Puritan mob? Well, I can tell you this much—I'll stand against it as long as I am able. I will make no windows into men's souls!'

She leapt out of her chair and swirled away from him in her billowing russet skirts, and he sighed inwardly. She was a sad disappointment to him in religion and indeed he had the sneaking suspicion that she would rather be a Catholic, if only it was politically expedient. The circumstances of her birth had allied her in a marriage of convenience to the Protestant Church, but her personal taste inclined distressingly towards Catholic ritual and her private chapel was a hotch-potch of the new and old religions. She liked music and candles, even a crucifix, and was downright rude to her married clergy. But, much as it grieved him, there was nothing he could do about it; he knew better than to pass comment.

And just now, there were more pressing concerns than her orthodoxy.

'May I ask what Your Majesty intends to do with the Scottish Queen?' he ventured at length. Waiting in vain for her answer, he continued uneasily, 'I trust you don't intend to bring her to court.'

She glanced over her shoulder and gave him a wicked smile.

'Would the monstrous regiment of two women be more than your sanity could bear?'

'I merely suggest it may be as well if the two of you do not meet. It might cause—complications.'

'You think she may win me for a friend? Oh Cecil, how little you know me.'

He smiled thinly. 'Of late Your Majesty has shown some sympathy for her plight. I beg you to remember that she is still your enemy.'

'But this alters everything. The bird has flown to me for protection from the hawk, and by God I'll see she gets that protection—from you if need be. I shall clip her wings and put her in a golden cage where she will sing safely for the rest of her life.'

'Mere imprisonment,' he said discontentedly, 'will scarcely restrain her violent appetite for your crown. Madam, such mercy on your part is suicidal.'

She shook her head slowly.

'You call it *mercy* to wake day after day in a living grave?'

He avoided her eyes and knew his instinct had been true; certainly a meeting between the two of them must be prevented at all cost.

He said bleakly, 'She will demand to see you, madam, and I beg you to refuse. It is hardly fitting for you to receive a harlot accused of such outrageous crimes.'

Elizabeth laughed. 'Move her to Bolton Castle then, under guard. But, Cecil—no little accidents on the journey. I want her alive.'

'To sow a canker of treason throughout the land?'

'To stand between me and Philip. She is the most valuable hostage in the history of Europe.'

'And the most dangerous,' he said bluntly. 'This puts a premium on your murder, madam—your life hangs by a thread from this moment on.'

'Then you must be vigilant, my Spirit.' Elizabeth held out her hand to him. 'I trust you beyond all men and you have never failed me yet.'

'Then don't set me an impossible task,' he burst out suddenly as he closed her fingers between his own. 'The best spy system in the world could not protect you under such circumstances.'

'Assassination is the occupational hazard of any monarch,' she said calmly.

'But to court assassination in this manner is madness. As long as you have no heir and the Scottish Queen lives in England, you will never know a minute's peace. I can't answer for your safety, not now. No man could. All I can promise you is that sooner or later a dagger or a bullet or a poisoned cup will do its work. For God's sake, madam, reconsider your decision and dispose of her.'

'Stop panicking,' she said gently. 'I shall dance on your grave even yet. Always supposing that you don't desert me first, of course.'

'*Desert* you!' he stiffened in horror. 'What do you mean, madam?'

She turned back to her desk and began to tidy her papers casually; she was not looking at him now.

'Ten years of loyalty is something of a record for you, isn't it, Cecil? Some would say it was high time you were looking for your next mistress.'

He was not a demonstrative man, but he went down on his knees then in a clumsy gesture of obeisance and pressed her fingers to his dry lips.

He said, 'I would rather die than desert you, madam. You are the last person on this earth that I shall ever serve.'

She had not expected that and found she had to bite her lip to govern herself. She raised him to his feet and looked into his worn face, wondering a little at her power to trap the heart and loyalty of such a hardened man. He had been a chameleon before she swore him into her service, but he would not change colour again, she knew it.

The moment was charged with emotion. She had only to take one step towards him and their unique relationship would be altered for ever.

Instead she stepped back from him and allowed him to recover his composure; she did not want him to become like all the rest, reduced to the squalid level of panting for her body. She let the dangerous moment pass them by and knew it would not come again.

And yet she was still curious. Precious little material gain had come his way through serving her—he was not even a member of the peerage. So what held him? What had she done to deserve such unswerving loyalty from the most accomplished politician in all Europe?

When she asked him, he smiled and sighed and replied with flattering exasperation, 'Madam, I would to God I knew the answer myself.'

CHAPTER 4

Trouble came to England in the wake of the Scottish queen, just as Cecil had feared, and rather sooner than he had first anticipated. Fear of Mary and the action that Spain might take on her behalf, jealousy of Cecil's undisputed position with Elizabeth and sheer terror of the Queen's uncertain health, was soon concentrated in a cabal of her foremost Privy Councillors. The intensely vigorous life which the Queen led no longer lulled the men who surrounded her into a false sense of security; they were morbidly obsessed with the possibility of her death. It was obviously necessary to make some provision for that event now that the next heir was resident in the country, to find some way of circumventing the possible accession of a Catholic queen who would take revenge on her rival's supporters.

To protect their own interests, Elizabeth's closest advisers, with the notable exception of Cecil, sought to ensure against the future by arranging a marriage between Mary Stuart and the foremost Protestant peer of the realm, the Duke of Norfolk. Norfolk had buried three wives already; he was confident of controlling Mary and his confidence won over the anxious men who formed the English Council and who were now convinced that disaster was about to overtake them at any moment.

Superficially, it seemed they had good cause for concern, for relations with Spain had been strained to breaking point. In December 1568 Spanish ships carrying bullion intended for the payment of Philip's armed forces in the Netherlands were harassed by pirates and forced to seek refuge in an English port. When Elizabeth discovered that the money was a loan from Genoese merchant bankers, she promptly entered negotiations to transfer that loan to herself, leaving Philip and his commander, Alva, in desperate straits. For a time the incident looked certain to precipitate war; but Elizabeth and Cecil were quietly confident that Philip's hostile gestures would prove as empty as his coffers. Both politically and economically they had him in a stranglehold; for the time being they held all the trump cards and could afford to gamble high.

Lesser minds found this hard to accept and soon a combination of fear and outright panic had concentrated into a conspiracy to sweep Cecil from office to the block. Cecil's execution was the bait they dangled before Leicester and he charged after it with a will. Remembering bitterly how readily the Queen would have abandoned him after Amy's death, Leicester was suddenly convinced that in the face of united opposition she would desert Cecil too.

So Leicester allowed his fellow conspirators to talk him into the role of spokesman and on a cold Ash Wednesday he got to his feet in Council and told the Queen bluntly that England would be ruined unless Cecil answered for his policies with his head.

It was the first and last time he ever dared to challenge her face to face in public, and within minutes he was wondering what had possessed him to open his mouth in the first place. White-lipped with fury, she whipped him with scathing contempt, until he bent like a stalk of corn before the blast of a hurricane. Soon he was cowering on his knees and then to his relief she turned her searing rage on the rest of his confederates.

When she had chastised them all to her complete satisfaction, she swept out of the room with Cecil at her side, for all the world like a tigress with her cub, leaving Leicester collapsed in his seat at the council table with his head in his fine hands.

Terror and jealousy warred within him. She could not have defended Cecil more vehemently if he had been her lover. What was the secret of her relationship with that colourless statesman which transcended all other ties? She had begun lately to bestow deeply symbolic nicknames on the men who were closest to her, an echo of the playful dragon allegory she had created in the Tower for her own amusement. Robin was her Eyes, Hatton her Lids, Cecil her Spirit—her familiar spirit some said, and to Leicester the implication was obvious. Without her Eyes she would be blind, but without her Spirit she would be dead. If it came to a fight to the death between the two of them he believed he knew which she would support. They were a formidable combination and now that they had closed their ranks against him, Leicester could see that his blunder had merely served to bind them even closer together. Theirs was an unholy union that no mere lover could ever hope to put asunder.

One by one, crushed and nervous, the councillors stole away from the chamber, until at last Norfolk and Leicester were left alone in the chill atmosphere.

Norfolk rolled his quill back and forth across the polished oak table and said peevishly, 'She never wraps it up, does she? Spares no one's feelings!'

'Neither woman in her anger nor man in her lust,' muttered Leicester, misquoting deliberately and darkly. 'I feel drained, don't you—as though she's sapped every ounce of blood out of my body.'

A great pity she hasn't, thought Norfolk maliciously, it would be an im-
provement that's long overdue. When I mount the English throne with
Mary Stuart, I'll make sure *you* are not around to bask in the sun!

Aloud he said, 'As I see it, there's only one course left to us, and that's to
take a lesson from the Scots—they have a quick way with overmighty ministers. I suggest that we arrest Cecil and finish him ourselves, since we can't
persuade her to do it for us.'

Leicester emerged from his hands in alarm.

'Are you out of your mind?' he breathed. 'She'll hang the lot of us! If you
persist in this mad plan, I shall have no alternative now but to warn her of it.'

Norfolk bowed ironically and flicked his small, pie-dish ruff in an insolent
gesture.

'The loyalty of the Earl of Leicester to Her Majesty has of course always
been beyond question.'

Robin took the premier peer of the realm by the throat and lifted him
forcibly out of his chair.

'I'm afraid I didn't quite catch that, Norfolk. Perhaps you would care to
repeat it.'

Duels at court were expressly forbidden by the Queen, and Norfolk felt it
was safe to speak freely. There had always been hostility between the two of
them—once they had almost come to blows on the tennis court. Despite
being an earl and one of the most powerful men in the kingdom, Leicester
still never had such a thing as a handkerchief about him. When he had
casually helped himself to the Queen's to wipe his sweating face, Norfolk
went purple with rage and threatened to break his racquet over the Earl's
head for his presumption. Now they made uneasy allies in a bid to rid themselves of Cecil, whose influence threatened them both.

Norfolk's smile was calmly superior and he made no attempt to free himself from Leicester's grip.

'I have said it before and I say it again, Leicester—you will not die in your
bed unless you give over your preposterous pretensions to Her Majesty's
hand.'

Robin laughed shortly and flung the Duke back into his chair with a force
that winded him.

'Well—I'm not alone now, in my pretensions to the hand of a queen, am I,
Norfolk? And since Elizabeth has said that the Queen of Scots may soon find
some of her friends the shorter by a head, I beg leave to suggest that it may
be *you*, my lord, who will not die in bed.'

'A neat prophecy!' sneered Norfolk. 'I suppose we can expect to see you backing out of this and creeping back under Her Majesty's skirts. She named you well—by God, she did—you're the next best thing to a lap-dog.'

'Even lap-dogs bite when goaded,' said Leicester shortly. 'If you don't want my teeth in your precious windpipe, Norfolk, I'd advise you to remember that.'

He turned on his heel and flung out of the room, leaving Norfolk alone, tenderly fingering his neck.

Alone with the Queen in her withdrawing room, Cecil watched his mistress pace the room in an ecstasy of rage. Her magnificent fury would have cowed the strongest man and he could not imagine anyone daring to make a stand against her in this mood, certainly not Leicester whom he had always suspected of being an arrant coward at heart.

What could have got into the man? Surely he understood by now that she was the last person in the world to be constrained by violence. Cecil had never seen her so angry. She was swearing and pacing and working herself up to such a pitch that he was truly alarmed.

'Madam, be calm,' he protested at length. 'You will bring on a migraine.'

She pulled up in front of him and smiled grimly.

'I'm not concerned with my head at the moment, Cecil, but with yours. Your *life!* Those ignorant clods and cowards who can see no further than the ends of their noses—how dare they threaten you! By the living God, I swear I'll play no Mary to your Riccio! If anyone lays a hand on you, my friend, I'll see the whole pack of them hung, drawn and quartered for it—and Leicester will be the first to die!'

Cecil smiled faintly and laid a fatherly hand on her arm in an effort to restrain her.

'I hardly think we need be over concerned with Leicester, madam. I have rarely seen a man so shaken—indeed, I'd go further and say we can probably rely on him to betray any further conspiracy as soon as it hatches. His cowardice could make him a useful ally now.'

She smiled suddenly and to his immense relief sat down in an armchair by the fireside.

'Yes,' she said thoughtfully, tapping a finger on the arm of her chair. 'As you say, he could be useful to us. When he's had time to consider his folly, I shall show him how he can make amends for this outrage. I'm afraid it won't make him very popular with his fellow councillors, but that's no more than he deserves. He won't intrigue against you again, Cecil—I give you the word of a prince on that.' She sighed and sat back in her chair, suddenly weary. 'So —Norfolk wants the Queen of Scots, does he?'

'Nothing has been said directly, madam, but there would appear to be some support for the match among the Council.'

'And you approve?'

Cecil spread his hands in a noncommittal gesture.

'One could make out a reasonable case for it, certainly, since Norfolk is your cousin and a loyal Protestant. If Mary forswears the Catholic faith and marries him it would be possible for you to settle the succession on her without the risk of civil war. And yet—I have reservations.'

She leaned forward in her chair, holding out a hand to the blazing logs in the hearth.

'I'm relieved to hear it. Christ's soul, Cecil, you know Norfolk by now—the pride of Lucifer and the brains of a sheep. Marry him to Mary Stuart and you and I will find ourselves in the Tower within a few months.'

Cecil frowned.

'Then you believe he would forswear his faith?'

'He'd forswear his own mother if it would gain him two crowns. I will not give my consent to this marriage, Cecil, and, if he ever finds the courage to ask, that's exactly what I shall tell him.'

They were silent, staring at each other in the pale March sunshine, a chequerboard of light dancing on the polished floor between them.

'Guard your back, Cecil,' she said quietly, 'for I fear they may yet move behind mine. And however many I hang for it, it will not bring you back to me.'

He kissed her hand affectionately.

'Don't worry about me, madam—I have had long experience of shifting for myself. If they should force this issue to a head, abandon me and look to your own safety. I am not indispensable.'

She lifted her hand to touch the tip of his beard—a great deal more grey, she noticed, than it had been on the day he first entered her service ten years ago.

'When we have ridden out this storm,' she said gently, 'I shall raise you to the peerage for that.'

The grey spring light was fading into an early dusk as Robin knelt humbly before his Queen and begged forgiveness.

'. . . you were right, madam—I was an arrogant fool and I should have known better than to meddle in this affair.'

'That is true,' she said calmly, 'but now I am going to ask you to meddle a little longer. I don't trust Norfolk and I want a spy in his camp. Will you do that for me, Robin, just to prove how sorry you really are? And for God's sake get off your knees—I really can't bear to squint down at you any longer.'

He got up abruptly and sat beside her in the window-seat, trying to read behind her unexpected friendliness.

'You're asking me to play double agent,' he said slowly. 'You realize, of course, they will probably slit my throat if they find out.'

'They won't find out,' she said coolly, 'not until it's too late. I want you to watch Norfolk for me and the moment you sense the possibility of real danger, you will retire to one of your country mansions apparently struck with a mortal illness. There you will be seized by an overwhelming desire to confess all to your Queen and love, in order that you may die in my arms with a clear conscience. We will enact a very touching death-bed scene and I will weep copiously and beg you to consider yourself forgiven. By the time you have recovered Norfolk will be cooling his bridegroom's ardour in the Tower. I doubt that anyone will suspect. No amount of cowardly grovelling on your part could excite the least surprise among your peers.'

He laughed suddenly and tried to take her in his arms, but to his surprise she pushed him away quite roughly.

'I wouldn't presume too much on my forgiveness if I were you, Robin.'

Before he could recover from that unexpected rebuff, she rose swiftly and walked away from him, pouring a glass of Alicante wine from a silver decanter and mixing it with water. She did not offer him any and it was so rare for her to drink wine that he suddenly understood she must be far more anxious than her cynical, rather careless manner indicated. So far there had been no active treason in this, but he trusted her shrewd political instinct rather more than his own. If she was anxious, he knew it would be with good cause. He watched for a moment in silence as she stood before the log fire. The blazing orange flames leapt upwards into the dark abyss of the chimney and winked on the dozens of tiny diamonds suspended in the hollow lace folds of her ruff, flashing on the crescent moon of emeralds which spiked her red curls in place. The finely drawn face, rose-hued in the firelight, held an endless fascination for him.

'What is it you really fear, madam,' he asked her at last, watching her steadily. 'It's not Norfolk alone, is it?'

'No.' She turned to look at him over the rim of the silver goblet. 'I'm not afraid of that overweening idiot, but of the effect this business may have on the North. There's no backbone of loyalty there, Robin—I'm just a name without a face. If the Catholics should rise in Mary's cause they'll play straight into Cecil's hands, and there'll be no way I can stand out against the outcry for stronger measures against them. My people are as dear to me as children, but it's a foolish parent who spares the rod and spoils the child. I don't want to punish or persecute—but I'll do it, if it becomes necessary, if there's no other way. I pray to God it won't come to that and that's why I want you to help me.'

She set her goblet down on the chimney-piece and stared into the fire, preoccupied and tense, like a wary cat surveying hostile surroundings. He crossed the room to her side and looked into the flames with her.

'I am your Eyes,' he said quietly. 'I will keep watch for you. And you know that you can trust me, madam—say that you trust me, that you depend on my affection.'

He laid his hand on her jewelled sleeve but she looked away.

'I trust no one,' she said softly. 'It is the sole reason I have lived this long.'

'But after all these years you *must* trust me.' He was aghast. 'I may have worked against Cecil—you more than any know what cause I have to hate him—but I could never betray you.'

'Any dagger you aim at Cecil's heart passes first through my own—his enemies are mine. Between us we have kept peace in this realm now for ten years and I will not allow you and the rest of your gaggle of short-sighted self-seekers to make him the butt for your own cowardice and lack of confidence.'

He had been a fool to aim at Cecil, he could see that now. But suddenly it no longer seemed important. He reached out and tilted her chin upwards so that she was looking deep into his dark eyes.

'I can't bear to see you look at me like that, full of doubt and suspicion. At least say you trust me a little further than the rest of the pack—for God's sake, Elizabeth, *say it!*'

She said nothing. There were weary lines etched at the corners of her eyes and lips and she looked as though she wanted to cry, but she did not do that either. And suddenly he could no longer bear her steely self-control. He caught her roughly, clamping his mouth over hers in a savage, bruising kiss; and when at last he released her, he said bitterly, 'Does *that* lie to you, madam?'

'No,' she said quietly and the tears spilt down her pale cheeks at last. 'If I can't believe that then I may as well be dead.'

Throughout the tense summer months, Leicester carefully courted the confidence of his old enemy Norfolk, watching and waiting as the latter trembled towards treason and a rebellion with the Northern earls of Northumberland and Westmorland. At last, scenting the real possibility of a rising, Robin felt he had played the farce as far as he dared and retired to his bed at Titchfield

Manor, sending an urgent message to the Queen which begged her to visit him in his last hours.

She came immediately with a very convincing show of panic, and he confessed his faults loud and long for the benefit of her women, who could be relied upon to spread the tale.

When she had dismissed her attendants, Leicester sat up against his pillows.

'So,' she said seriously, 'what have you discovered?'

'Not as much as I would like to,' he replied grimly, 'but sufficient to disturb me. I think Norfolk's working with Spain.'

'Can you prove it?'

Leicester shook his head. 'He doesn't trust me—I think he's becoming suspicious. I wouldn't leave him at liberty much longer, if I were you. Put him in the Tower before the whole thing gets out of hand.'

Elizabeth smiled and patted his hand on the coverlet.

'Don't worry. I won't let him cut your throat for this, nor Throckmorton and the rest of the pack. You will be perfectly safe as long as you take your medicine and stay quiet.'

'Medicine?' He eyed her suspiciously. 'That wasn't part of the bargain, madam.'

'I thought we ought to be convincing.' She reached for the vial she had brought from her personal physician and poured a large measure. 'Drink it,' she commanded cheerfully.

He took the goblet warily and hesitated.

'Drink it!'

He swallowed a large mouthful and gagged.

'Christ! What is it? Poison?'

'It's only a purge—roughly sufficient to keep you on the close-stool for the rest of the day.' She got off the bed briskly and handed him his velvet chamber robe. 'I'd move if I were you, my love. I believe it works quite quickly.'

He got out of bed and glared at her as she wrapped the gown solicitously round his shoulders.

'We can't have you catching a chill while you sit there,' she said gaily.

'Is this your idea of a joke?' he demanded.

'As a matter of fact I thought it might save your neck. Anyone who doubts your condition has only to come in and see you there.'

He tied the belt around his waist and went to draw the curtains around the close-stool.

'I hope you've got something equally fitting in store for Norfolk,' he grumbled meaningfully over his shoulder.

'Leave Norfolk to me,' she said and went out of his room.

The news of Leicester's betrayal acted on Norfolk like a bullet from a gun on a startled rabbit. He rushed away from the court in a blind panic, first to his London house, then to his estates in Norfolk. Elizabeth immediately closed all her ports, and his attempt to get a message to Alva, the Spanish commander in the Netherlands, met with failure. Without Spanish support he knew he was lost, and when a peremptory royal command summoned him to the Queen's presence at Windsor, he gave in to the inevitable. In a frantic attempt to avert the planned rebellion, he sent a message begging the Earl of Westmorland not to stir now or it would cost him his head, and set out himself to surrender to the Queen's mercy at Windsor. As soon as he came within sight of the great stone-walled castle, he was surrounded by an armed guard and diverted to the Tower, there to pace and sweat and pray that his allies would obey his desperate command.

But it was too late now to retract, even though the northern earls themselves had begun to lose their nerve. Westmorland was goaded into action by his sharp-tongued wife, and Northumberland by the urgings of a loyal servant. On the 14th of November, with an army at their back, they stormed Durham Cathedral to tear up the English translation of the Bible and trample it underfoot, proclaiming their rebellion to be an act of religious warfare, the first blow in the battle to maintain the Catholic faith in England. Then they marched south to free their figurehead, the Queen of Scots, only to find that Elizabeth had already spirited her 'guest' away by force of arms to Coventry. The Catholic population, which they had expected to fall upon them with open arms, looked on in polite bewilderment, reluctant to trade peace and growing prosperity for the claims of a foreign sovereign who had already wreaked havoc in her own country. The rebels were defeated before they had begun by the ten years of security and plenty which Elizabeth's rule had bestowed on England; and when the Queen's army moved into the field against them under the leadership of the Earl of Sussex, the leaders fled in ignominious defeat across the Scottish border, leaving the humble peasants, who had followed their landlords blindly, to face the consequences.

And the consequences were severe. The most hardened members of the Council were shocked to learn how Elizabeth intended to handle her rebellious subjects, for it was the first time she publicly revealed the iron hand which now governed England beneath that velvet glove of loving care. Some six hundred peasants were hanged at her personal insistence, while the landowners who had raised the rebellion were spared, so that the crown might take their estates forfeit to cover the cost entailed in crushing it. Justice was sacrificed on the altar of hard economic fact. It was savagely cruel and unfair; but it worked. The North of England learnt the reward of treason and learnt it so well that it was to be the last blood shed there for the rest of the Queen's reign. Elizabeth knew when it paid to be cruel.

In the Tower of London, Norfolk drew his first breath of relief when he heard that the Privy Council did not consider that he had actually committed treason. He smiled to himself and admitted that, thanks to Elizabeth's prompt action, they were technically quite correct. His plans might have been nipped in the bud with a vengeance, but they were not quite extinguished. He was smuggling letters out in bottles hidden in the dark, dank privy, making good use of the Tower's shortcomings as his royal cousin had once done before him. Already there was public agitation for his release and he was not unduly concerned to hear that Elizabeth had screamed at the Council that she would have his head on her own authority if the law could not provide for it. They also told him that she had fainted outright in the council chamber immediately after saying that and he thought he knew his royal cousin by now. She might kill six hundred faceless peasants without a qualm, but her own flesh and blood was an entirely different matter.

In the triumph of his reprieve, the amorous overtures from Mary and the veiled hints of assistance from Spain remained an irresistible temptation. Whenever common sense and timidity assailed him, he comforted himself with the plain fact that no one—no one at all—had been beheaded in England since the Queen came to the throne.

Could it be that she was a little squeamish when it came to the axe that had already claimed her mother, her step-mother and her first lover? Mulling over the possibility, Norfolk began to feel remarkably safe. She was only a woman after all, a weak and feeble vessel destined to be taken advantage of by men. And it was becoming increasingly obvious that she could not continue to hold the premier peer of the realm captive without hard evidence. He had no difficulty at all in signing the paper which reaffirmed his oath of loyalty to her and he swore publicly to have no further dealings with the Queen of Scots.

Leicester looked at the paper with undisguised disgust. He had been sure that he had heard the last of the man who would now be his most deadly enemy, but there he was riding off to liberty, cock-a-hoop at having escaped virtually scot free.

'I had to release him,' said Elizabeth quietly. 'For his own good I would have preferred to keep him under guard, but they were growing restless down in Norfolk. I dared not provoke another rising.'

'And what now, madam?'

'Now I am afraid I shall have to give him enough rope to hang himself. Cecil's spies will watch his every move—it can only be a question of time . . .'

Norfolk wrote hastily to Mary's agent, the Bishop of Ross, explaining that his signature on Elizabeth's deed meant nothing. He had signed it under duress and he hoped the Queen of Scots would understand that he was as ready to become her husband as he had ever been.

Within months, the perfect opportunity presented itself. The Pope, justifying Cecil's worst nightmares, chose that moment to excommunicate Elizabeth officially, thus freeing all Catholic subjects from their allegiance to her and issuing an open invitation for someone to stick a dagger in her heart in God's holy cause. From that moment on, everyone accepted that her ultimate assassination was a foregone conclusion and that sooner or later she would meet a violent and untimely end.

Elizabeth cursed the act which now made Cecil's persecution inevitable, knowing its trumpet call to martyrs would shatter the compromise by which she had kept religious peace for over twelve years. But she shrugged her shoulders at her enemies at home and abroad and raised the arch-heretic Cecil to the peerage at last, as she had promised. In February 1571 he became Baron Burghley and his unassailable position was recognized by everyone of influence; Leicester was particularly ingratiating in his congratulations.

The inevitable intrigue between Norfolk and Mary was soon flourishing with the assistance of the Spanish Ambassador, de Spes, and the services of a Florentine banker, Ridolfi. The murder of Elizabeth was the spearhead of the plot and Norfolk requested 10,000 Spanish troops to effect the *coup d'état* that was to follow. He did not receive them, for though Philip was bent on making as much trouble as possible for his sister-in-law, he was the last one to intervene actively merely to place Mary Stuart on the English throne. To the end of her life Mary was to believe blindly in Philip's friendship for her and never see the naïvety of her request to the Spanish Ambassador: 'Tell your Master that if he will help me, I shall be Queen of England in three months and Mass shall be said all over the kingdom.' Philip had no doubt that once Mary had come into her own, her Guise relatives would rediscover their old affection for her; and he had no wish to see Mass said in England by French priests!

So there were no troops from Philip; instead, Cecil's army of spies ferreted out every piece of information which illustrated the Duke's guilt, the Scottish Queen's acquiescence and the half-hearted collusion of Spain. The Spanish Ambassador was sent packing to his homeland, while Norfolk found himself back in the Tower, this time under sentence of death.

Elizabeth calmly signed the warrant for his execution by the axe, the scaffold on Tower Hill which had rotted away from disuse was rebuilt, and everyone expected that would be the end of the matter. No one who had seen her at the time of the Northern Rebellion entertained the slightest hope of a reprieve and no one was more astonished than the new Lord Burghley to be summoned to the Queen's bedchamber in the middle of the night and be told that Norfolk's execution must not take place the following morning.

Looking absurd in his chamber robe and furred slippers, Cecil stared at her as she sat up in the state bed, sheet white, biting her lower lip.

'But why, madam?' he gasped. 'Why?'

'I don't know why!' she sobbed furiously. 'Don't ask me why—just do as I say, God damn you, and cancel it!'

For the next two months there was a raging battle between the Queen and her advisers to obtain her signature once more on Norfolk's death warrant and to persuade her to have Mary's drawn up. For more than eight weeks the lives of Mary and Norfolk hung on the balance of Elizabeth's whim, while the clamour of the English Council for their deaths rose to a furious pitch. And then, on a cold March night, the disaster they had all feared for so long struck at last.

Leicester could not recall the last occasion on which he had taken a game of chess from the Queen, but he was going to win tonight, he knew it suddenly as she moved her knight. It was a rash move, careless, indifferent, curiously unlike her and it gave him his chance for a quick kill. He was so elated at the prospect of victory, so ruthlessly absorbed in his own strategy, that when she suddenly rose from the table and told him curtly to put the pieces away, his first impulse was to vent his bitter disappointment in a string of obscene oaths. One win, one little win, it was all he had wanted from her and she must even deny him that much satisfaction! In moody silence he began to throw the gold chessmen back into their box. When he had finished he sat in sullen silence, staring into the fire, waiting for dismissal. He never knew precisely what made him look up at that moment, sixth sense, intuition, but whatever it was it came just a second too late. She fell across the little table so heavily that it overturned and sent the chessmen scattering into the four corners of the room.

Elizabeth!

Sweat broke out all over his body, as he fell on his knees beside her and turned her over.

Spasms of pain convulsed her and she clutched at his sleeve, grey-lipped in her panic for breath. When he lifted her, hampered by the weight of the court gown, she went suddenly limp in his arms. He carried her into the bedchamber, through a wake of panic-stricken women, with her vast sweep of black satin skirts spilling over his arms and trailing to his feet like the magnificent plumage of a dead bird.

As he laid her on the bed he spat curt commands at the hovering women.

'Get her doctors—get Burghley—and help me to get her out of this damned gown before she suffocates.'

Glancing round, he saw them staring at him wildly, paralysed with fear, like rabbits caught in a bright glare.

'Move!' he roared, and they dispersed immediately, leaves in the fierce gale of his authority.

When Burghley came through the door of the bedchamber, Leicester went to meet him and their eyes locked in an agonized glance, the certain, grim knowledge that if the worst happened now, then their heads would be the first to roll under the revenge of Norfolk and Mary.

'How is she?' Cecil's voice trembled as he scanned the Earl's white face.

Leicester shook his head, chewing his lip, and Cecil stiffened in fearful anticipation.

'So bad?' he whispered hoarsely.

'I've never seen her like this before—never! She's in such pain she can scarcely breathe. To me it looks like poison.'

Cecil felt his brain reel at the suggestion.

'Impossible,' he said woodenly. 'We've been so careful, every precaution—'

'Don't be a fool!' snapped Leicester. 'Are you telling me you can answer for the loyalty of every woman in her service, every page and scullion with access to her comfit box?'

'No.' Cecil shook his head grimly. 'It was always a hopeless task and I warned her—God knows, I warned her. But she's so careless and reckless—sometimes I swear she believes she's immortal.'

'She'll need to be immortal to come through this.' Leicester gave him a hard, searching look. 'Are you squeamish?'

Cecil swallowed and spat out a lie.

'No more so than the next man, my lord.'

'Good.' Leicester glanced darkly towards the bed. 'There's only one path open to her now, and it takes its course straight through the centre of Hell.

I've spoken to the doctors. And, believe me, what they intend to do I wouldn't see done to my worst enemy let alone to my—' He broke off short. 'She asked for you,' he continued brusquely. 'So take that look off your face before we go to her. She doesn't need our personal fears at the moment.'

Cecil nodded mutely and side by side, suddenly drawn close together in a brotherhood of mutual terror which suspended all their many differences, they approached the state bed. It was hung with cloth of silver and its four posts were topped with bunches of ostrich feathers, all spangled with gold, a magnificence in stark contrast to the crude treatment which took place within its hangings. Emetics and purges were administered in steady succession, accompanied by a savage letting of blood; but as the hours dragged slowly into days and still she tossed and turned, shivering with a raging fever and violent pains which nothing alleviated, they began to fear that their frantic efforts to rid her body of its toxin had failed. By the third evening she was so weak that Leicester sat on the edge of the bed, waiting for her to die in his arms, while the doctors squabbled and contradicted each other in a fierce huddle by the fireside. A little ring of black-robed professionals, pecking at each other's opinions like a flock of frightened crows—he watched them with savage contempt.

'Useless bastards!' he muttered. 'Not one of them fit to doctor cattle— what keeps them clacking all this time?'

'Arrangements—for the post-mortem—perhaps,' suggested the Queen wearily. 'I would—I had the arranging—of *theirs.*'

'I know. All that suffering, my poor love—I should never have allowed it.' He stroked the wet tendrils of hair back off her forehead, and held her close, remembering with hot anguish all the pointless misery she had endured without a single tantrum or complaint.

'I'll put my dagger through the next quack who lays a hand on you—I swear it!'

Elizabeth turned her head with difficulty to look up at him and slowly traced the wet tracks on his cheeks with one trembling finger. After a moment she gave him a tired little smile which tore at his heart.

'Robin?'

'It's nothing.' Hastily he brushed his cheek against her hair. 'Something in my eye, that's all.'

'Both of them?'

He bent his head and kissed her for that, not caring who should see it. The doctors came back to stare down at her hopelessly, but beneath Leicester's steely gaze they dared suggest nothing more, and retired once again to the hearth. She was beyond their aid now; it was in God's hands.

Leicester never knew how he managed to live through the rest of that night. His hand was numb from the convulsive grip of her fingers, his arm aching as though it was broken, but he kept his lips closed on his agony. It seemed to him that her grip on his hand was her last link with this world and he had intense, almost superstitious, terror of her letting go. Life and vitality seemed to be draining slowly out of him through the touch of their fingertips, a physical fusion more intimate, more complete than copulation could ever be. The hours meant nothing to him. He was impervious to thirst, hunger, exhaustion, even to the calls of nature, impervious to everything and everyone except the intensely personal battle he felt himself to be fighting with the Queen's restive soul.

Around the great room, her attendants drowsed from exhaustion, but Burghley still hovered on the other side of the bed, grey with fatigue, and at last the Queen turned her head from the pillow of Leicester's arm, searching for him with sudden urgency.

'Cecil—'

He came forward hesitantly, as though aware that he intruded on something personal, vital—sacred. She held out her right hand to him and as he took it the three of them were once more linked in their unholy triangle. Cecil, too, experienced a curious sensation, as though the last vestige of strength had been sucked out of him. He swayed a little when she released his hand and had to steady himself against the bedpost.

Her pain-crazed eyes were smiling at him.

'You look ready to drop,' she said gently. 'Go and sit down somewhere. You must not steal a march on me—by dying of exhaustion first.' He had to bend over the bed to catch her fading voice. 'Robin will call you—if I should require—the last rites.'

Walking away from the bed in slow disbelief, it came to him suddenly that this might be the last time his narrow religious sensibilities were outraged by her irrepressible irreverence. He was shocked, but not surprised; even at her coronation in the most solemn sanctified moment of the Anointing, she had scandalized her women by complaining that 'the holy oil was nasty grease and stank', as though the moment which had been the supreme culmination of a lifetime's desire meant nothing to her. She was teasing God, as she had once teased her dread father, careless of the consequences, and Cecil found he had begun to pray with feverish intensity, not for her life—he no longer hoped for that—but for her salvation. He could not be comfortable with the thought of her burning for all eternity; and he honestly did not see how it could be avoided.

Shortly after dawn he jerked awake in a panic to find Leicester bending over him, and he suffered himself to be led out of the room, half crippled with stiffness, leaning heavily on the Earl's arm. The Queen was sleeping, colourless as a corpse against the high pillows and the doctors were exchanging muted congratulations with each other. He received the news in silence and went with Leicester without argument or rancour; he knew it was a miracle.

The ante-room was as cold and cheerless when they entered it as only a room in a chill March dawn can be, and from the Privy Chamber beyond came the muted murmur of anxious councillors and courtiers, waiting for news.

Leicester flung himself wearily upon a wooden couch and reached for a flagon of wine. Burghley paused to lean on his staff and look at him curiously.

'Were we not commanded to retire, my lord?'

Leicester drained the goblet and filled it again without looking up.

'Commanded or not I stay until I know for certain she's out of danger.' He filled another goblet and held it out to Burghley. 'Here—since it looks as though you and I may be keeping our heads after all, you ought to join me. We'll drink a toast to the Queen, the most remarkable woman who ever lived. My God, I thought we'd lost her this time.'

The goblets fell to the floor, spilling wine everywhere, as he suddenly buried his face in his hands and his great shoulders shook with the racking sobs that were welling up inside him.

Burghley watched him weep and was aware of pity and shame. Oh, he had seen so much these past three nights, things which had made him learn a new respect for the man he had always so contemptuously dismissed as a self-seeking adventurer. For Leicester loved the Queen; Burghley having witnessed the man's tireless tenderness, now had no doubt of that.

And that knowledge altered everything. Over the years a steady conviction had grown that his early fears had been groundless. There would have been room for them both—had she not shown it over and over again? But he could still look back on the disposal of Amy with a clear conscience and reassure himself that his act had saved the Queen from the clutch of a greedy, selfish predator.

Now it was no longer possible to deceive himself and he suddenly saw how his perfectly executed device had backfired upon him. They were all of them balanced precariously on the tightrope of Elizabeth's life and he, the brilliant, the dedicated chief minister, was to blame for it!

He went stiffly to retrieve the goblets and refill them with wine; then he eased himself on to the couch and offered one of them to Leicester.

'To the Queen's health,' he said softly, 'and to our own increasing understanding. I pray it may serve Her Majesty better than our enmity.'

Leicester lifted his head and through a blurred haze saw Burghley's gnarled hand extended towards him. After a moment's puzzled hesitation he met it with his own.

'All the Queen's men in the last resort, eh?' he said shakily.

Burghley shrugged his rounded shoulders.

'Our service is our vocation and vocation has its own reward, my lord. The time draws near when men of loyalty and the true religion can no longer afford private quarrels.'

Leicester inclined his head in brooding silence. He too sensed the gathering of clouds above England and feared that even Elizabeth could not trade on the devil's luck for ever. And if she was in danger, he was ready to stand by anyone, even Burghley, in her defence. It marked the end of the tense, armed truce between the two of them, for they were both bound body and soul to the Queen and now each recognized the true value of the other in her eyes. Within the security of their eternal triangle they must muster their forces against attack from without, defending the apex, the mutual pivot of their existence.

Cecil laid down his goblet at last and stared at the door of the silent bedchamber.

'She's cheated death twice—a third time would be too much to ask. There's a limit to God's favour.'

'And the Devil's!' muttered Leicester darkly.

Cecil ignored him. 'You realize, of course, that it is now more urgent than ever that Norfolk should meet his fate. I simply cannot understand it. She was swift and terrible enough after the northern rising, why in God's name does she hesitate over Norfolk?'

'Perhaps, my friend, because he must die by the axe.'

Cecil looked round at him in surprise.

'Now what difference could that make? She's not squeamish.'

Leicester smiled faintly beneath three days' growth of thick black beard and leaned forward to fill his own goblet again.

'You really don't know her very well, do you, even after all this time? Is it mere coincidence that no head has fallen in England in fourteen years? I lost my father, my brother and my grandfather to the axe, but perhaps you who have lost no one in such a manner cannot be expected to understand. I have sat with her at night more than once, calming her nightmares when no one else can soothe her, because I know her, you see, better than anyone else alive. And I can tell you now that if you want Norfolk's head, it will take Parliament to force her hand.'

'And the Queen of Scots?'

'Forget the Queen of Scots,' advised Leicester seriously. 'She has friends in high places—the highest of all barring one, did the stupid bitch only know it. You'll never get Elizabeth's signature on *her* warrant.'

Burghley shook his head. 'It has to come to that sooner or later, Leicester. Nothing in this world will induce Mary Stuart to live quietly in an English prison. I tell you this much, the poor fool will never cease until she loses her head.'

He got unsteadily to his feet, looking old and harassed in the cruel daylight.

'Get to bed, man,' said Leicester, not unkindly, 'the Queen won't be best pleased if she has to bury you after all this.'

A wan smile touched Burghley's lips.

'There was a time when I thought my nerve was quite unshakeable, Leicester, but God knows I've never seen anyone sail so close to the wind as Her Majesty, without sinking.'

'Witches never drown,' remarked Leicester thoughtfully. 'Surely you know that.'

A glimmer of the old hostility suddenly narrowed Burghley's steely blue eyes. 'I don't know what you mean by that, my lord, I'm sure.'

'Don't you?' Leicester's smile was cynical; the wine had hit his tired brain and loosened his tongue. 'King Henry said her mother was a witch. Surely you must have wondered about her before now. I know I have—'

Burghley opened his mouth to protest heatedly, then closed it again, seeing the utter futility of arguing with a man who had been drinking heavily on exhaustion and an empty stomach.

'That's a highly dangerous allegation, Leicester,' he said at last very drily. 'I trust you won't repeat it to anyone else. Some people might think it constituted an act of treason.'

He went out of the room, determined to forget the incident, for it brought back an uncomfortable picture. Try as he might he could not dismiss the memory of her light, laughing voice, promising to give him a month's advance notice of her death. In spite of all the laws of nature, she had not yet broken that promise.

Was it possible? Was he really serving a witch?

He was unnerved by the intense disloyalty of the thought.

* * *

It was almost ten o'clock before Elizabeth stirred. She opened her eyes briefly to find Leicester sitting by her side, and her fever-cracked lips parted in a dazed smile.

'I told you to go to bed.'

'Did you, madam?' He kissed her hand playfully. 'Then I'm afraid I must have misunderstood your meaning.'

She drowsed again and woke shortly before midday; he was still there. She made no comment this time but allowed him to place extra pillows behind her head and swallowed a mouthful of milk to humour him. Then she asked for her mirror.

He handed it over with some reluctance and when she looked at her reflection she saw why.

'Hell's teeth—I look like a corpse!'

'How would you expect to look,' he inquired gently, 'after an attempt on your life so damn near successful as this was?'

She laid the mirror face down on the coverlet and sighed a little.

'Must we play Hunt-the-Traitor every time I have a stomach ache?'

He stared at her in disbelieving silence for a full minute, incredulous, outraged.

'God's death,' he swore softly at last, 'surely even you can't believe this illness had a natural cause. All the doctors agree it was something taken by mouth at supper.'

She gave him a maddening smile.

'Almost the Last Supper, then—but I've yet to see them hang a fish for treason. Norfolk's arm may be long, but it certainly doesn't stretch from the Tower to my plate.'

'Don't jest,' he said testily. 'The Tower has its shortcomings—you and I had good cause once to know just how short they can be!'

'That was a long time ago, Robin.'

'Long or not, it makes no difference. The Tower never changes. You know that money buys virtually anything there and to a man of Norfolk's means and desperation poison would be cheap at any price. He had everything to gain from your death and precious little to lose—you must see that.'

'You really hate him, don't you?'

'I hate anyone and anything that threatens you. But it's not just my opinion—the rumour is all over the court.'

'Is it?' She bit her lip angrily. 'And what else does Madam Rumour have to say?'

'That Norfolk must die swiftly, before he gets the chance to try again. There is no way you can hope to save him after this.'

Elizabeth lay back on her pillows in silence, her face closed suddenly against him into a mask of secrecy.

'What are you thinking?' he asked anxiously, sensing that devious brain fiercely at work.

'As a matter of fact I was thinking that I am far too ill to hear of business,' she said demurely, stealing a glance at him from beneath her heavy lids. 'I shall probably be too ill to hear of it for a long, long time—'

'You invite assassination,' he said darkly, 'and next time you may not be so fortunate.'

'But I am always fortunate—isn't that so?'

He shook his head gravely. 'You really don't care, do you? You play with kingdoms and men's lives like pieces on a chessboard—you won't be satisfied until you've put both me and Burghley in the same grave.'

'Poor prisoners,' she said quietly, 'the two of you should have let me go when you had the chance.'

Her eyes, like bottomless wells of black water, held him frozen in the bright stillness of their gaze. So—he had not imagined that physical link; and in the deepest recess of his mind he acknowledged that his bondage to her was now complete.

Later, in his apartments which still adjoined the Queen's, he paused to look into his own mirror, encrusted with ivory figurines, and there saw his face, handsome still, yet blurred and indistinct, his jet black hair touched at the temples with silver grey. Once, in fun, he had called her a vampire, and that jest had assumed a strange form of truth—she took her strength, not from blood, but from the love of men.

He looked at his reflection sadly—the signs of age were unmistakable. Slowly the flame of her life was consuming him, eating away his manhood, almost his identity; he had sunk his life in hers, lost himself so deeply in her shadow that it seemed without her he would no longer exist.

He wondered briefly if Burghley felt the same.

CHAPTER 5

Elizabeth signed five warrants for Norfolk's execution and rescinded four of them. For five months she ran a gauntlet of opposition from her Council and her Parliament, maddened wolves howling for the two lives she held just beyond reach of their snapping teeth. She whetted their appetite with frustration and then, at the very point when they were blind with blood lust, she tossed Norfolk to them like a choice bone. Immediately the pursuit was thrown into confusion. They fell upon her chosen sacrifice in a frenzy of delight, never noticing that they had given her the time to escape with the real prize; and for a little longer Mary Stuart clung to a perilously thin ledge of security, just beyond their reach. So, in the panting pause between the plots and counterplots which now formed the basis of her life, Elizabeth found she had achieved her object. But she had not enjoyed playing shuttlecock with a man's head, and Norfolk's humble letter, begging forgiveness and mercy for his poor children so soon to be orphans, distressed her deeply. She told Burghley to see to it that the brats were cared for; she had been an orphan herself . . .

At dusk on the first day of June 1572, the eve of Norfolk's execution, she found herself pacing up and down the Privy Chamber, unable to eat or settle to any of the pursuits with which she normally passed the evenings. Her first execution by the axe—the first of many, no doubt! So what ailed her? Why this unlooked-for guilt and squeamishness so alien to her nature?

On a sudden whim she ordered her barge and had herself conveyed to the Tower, throwing the unfortunate constable into a fidget of agitated unease by her unheralded arrival. He asked her with great delicacy if she desired to visit the condemned Duke and watched her walk up and down his narrow room, twisting a pair of silk gloves between her long fingers.

It was, after all, what she had come for, to see him, to explain and excuse the tortured suspense she had kept him in for the last five months. But now she shied away from it, reluctant to raise his hopes falsely yet again, afraid that her resolution would crumble at the sight of his broken penitence.

Instead she wandered aimlessly out to the site of the Green where her mother and Katherine Howard had lost their heads, where little Jane Grey had died and they had told her, *'the torrent of blood was quite extraordinary'* as she waited in the Bell Tower to follow in Jane's footsteps. Through the falling light she saw the Chapel of St Peter-ad-Vincula that held the remains of her mother and that tomorrow would receive yet another mutilated body. And she shivered in the hot twilight, drawing the heavy cloak more closely round herself as she swept past the hovering constable with a curt salutation and returned to the barge. They sailed away over the black river and she watched the mighty fortress dwindling in the distance to the toy she had once imagined.

She could not sleep that night. She sat in a window-seat and watched the darkness recede into a bright orange dawn, while her lady-in-waiting snored in careless oblivion on a pallet at the foot of the state bed.

This, then, was what it meant to be Queen, the murder of relatives who had sought first to murder you. Strike or be stricken was the simple rule of every ruler. Her father had followed it with sublime indifference to the end of his days—why then could she not do the same?

But she would never be able to do it. And when at last the roar of the Tower cannon announced the death of a traitor, she stood alone in her room, pressing her hands over her ears in a vain attempt to shut it out.

The years of Philip's reluctant and deluded friendship with England were now at an undisputed end. England and Spain had slowly and inevitably drawn apart over a long series of mutual grievances and Philip comforted himself now with the certain knowledge that one day he would settle with England's Jezebel. But for the moment his hands were firmly tied, by the defensive Treaty of Blois which Elizabeth had just wrung from his old enemy, France, by the ever present risk of her marriage with a French prince, and by the unrest of his own Protestant subjects in the Netherlands. As long as Elizabeth held the Queen of Scots hostage, she was safe from any overt aggression on his part. His ostensible championship of Mary masked a very hearty desire to see the woman dead and he believed that sooner or later, as the plots in her favour grew in magnitude, Elizabeth's advisers would force their Queen to dispose of her. He could afford to wait until that stumbling-block in his path to England had been removed and, while he waited, he steadily noted each English outrage, from the seizure by Elizabeth's ships of Spanish treasure galleons, to her disgraceful treatment of his ambassadors. He sheltered her Catholic exiles, while her ports were always open to his Protestant refugees. It seemed inevitable that they would end as deadly enemies, that in his attempt to dominate Europe, he would be forced to subjugate England and destroy the Queen whose very existence was a threat to his kingship and an insult to his manhood. He watched anxiously from afar as she began to toy with fresh marriage negotiations, first with the French heir, Anjou, then with his brother, the Duke of Alençon. France was fawning round Elizabeth like a spaniel and Philip did not care for the way things looked—he did not care for it at all.

Leicester, too, was ill at ease with this new marriage project. Initially, he had regarded the negotiations as yet another of Elizabeth's brilliant diplomatic farces. Anjou was an overt homosexual; Alençon was a rake and an ugly pock-marked dwarf to boot. She could not be serious—the match was impossible! And yet, as she approached her thirty-seventh birthday, he sensed a subtle change in her attitude. She had always been happy to stand as sponsor —had indeed collected a veritable army of godchildren—yet now weddings and christenings seemed to depress her equally. She watched the children of her friends with increasing wistfulness, and Leicester, watching her with anxiety, recognized a quality his mother had once described as 'broodiness'.

One evening, goaded beyond the boundaries of common sense by fear, he remarked that if she had really set her heart on taking a stunted, pock-marked imbecile to her bed, there were plenty in England to oblige her without looking to France.

The backgammon board swept to the floor between them as she stood up. 'Get out!' she said; and he went with some alacrity.

In the Privy Chamber, where the more favoured courtiers hovered, the Queen's women were engaged in various quiet pursuits. Leicester paused for a casual word here and there, with forced civility, as he edged his way towards the windowseat where Lettice Knollys, Countess of Essex, sat reading.

The Queen's cousin raised her almond eyes and smiled impudently at him. 'Good evening, my lord.'

As he bent to kiss her hand with cool formality, he whispered curtly, 'The usual place. Don't keep me waiting,' and was gone before she had time to reply.

Ten minutes later, having pleaded a headache to the Queen, Lettice slipped away from the gossiping maids and matrons and followed the torch-lit corridors that led to a small room on the other side of the palace.

As soon as she stepped inside, he locked the door and tore the cloak from her shoulders.

'Get your clothes off,' he said roughly. 'I want you now.'

The incipient violence of his mood excited her. He was always like this after a quarrel with the Queen and she was a woman who appreciated crude emotions in a man. Not for Lettice the well-mannered lover. She had married one, for the sake of a title, and wished him dead within a month. When

Leicester flung her across the narrow Indian couch and took her with a bruising violence that was little short of rape, she writhed with ecstasy beneath the savage beating of his body in hers.

The arrangement had been in existence for some time now. There had been other women, of course, over the years, even a bastard son to Douglass Sheffield, but somehow it had been inevitable for him to drift back into this old liaison with Lettice. He needed Lettice; she preserved his sanity, slaking the fire which the Queen delighted to raise.

When at length he lay beside her, with one arm across her breast, relieved of his fierce tension and desire, staring at nothing, Lettice wanted to laugh out loud. Oh, how he loved to be the master, to remind himself that he was truly a man; and how well their mutual need of each other suited them both; he chained to a frigid mistress, and she to a mild, meek bore of a husband. If she knew whenever he took her in this angry manner that his thoughts were not really of her, it made no difference to the intensity of her pleasure. She lived for his moods of naked savagery and revelled in the animal-like quality of their fierce lovemaking. Leicester satisfied her as no man had ever done before and when at last he rose in moody silence, dressed and left her, she lay alone on the old couch, treasuring her bruises and thinking smugly of Elizabeth.

Danger enhanced the quality of this stolen pleasure. Lettice knew she risked her position at court, possibly even her life, every time she accommodated Leicester's frustrated manhood. There was only one step more perilous and already her perverse, possessive nature had begun to set itself on the idea of secret marriage. It was impossible, of course, while her husband lived, but he was a weakling and his service in Ireland was taking a heavy toll of his health. Ireland had hounded better men than Walter Devereux to their dispirited deaths. And if she should ever be fortunate enough to find herself a lusty young widow, there was only one man who would do now for her next husband.

Her throat was dry with excitement at the thought. To goad Leicester into a permanent, legal relationship, to make him relinquish his vain pursuit of that royal butterfly—it was madness, sheer insanity, almost a death wish for the pair of them. He would never do anything so grossly suicidal—or would he? She remembered a night not long ago when he had drunk deep and given free rein to his resentment in a burst of inebriated self-pity.

'I was full of hope after her last illness, Lettice. We were so close that I truly began to think—' He had turned away angrily. 'But I was wrong, of course—I'm always wrong about her. And now it's all just as it was before—Hatton, Ormond, Oxford—Tom, Dick and Harry for all I know—I must take my place in line again and wait until she remembers to throw me a smile. I can't bear it, Lettice, it's destroying me. I never know for sure just how far she goes with them, but one day she'll goad me too far. There'll be one laugh and one slap too many—and I'll kill her, I swear it. I'll put my hands round that beautiful white neck and squeeze every last mocking breath out of her body. And when she's dead in my arms, she'll be mine at last—mine only!'

'Treason,' said Lettice softly. 'You know that's treason.'

He went to stand at the window, staring bleakly at the swaying trees and for once she was moved by pity for the depth of his despair.

'Come here,' she said. He came back to the bed and lay down beside her dully.

'There is a better way to kill Elizabeth,' she whispered, 'a way that may just leave your head on your shoulders for you to enjoy it.'

When she had told him, he laughed and slapped her bare buttocks and told her she was an impertinent little minx. She could see he had not taken her suggestion seriously and at the time it had angered her, made her aware of the inferiority of her position as his mistress. But she had had the good sense not to show it and they had parted amicably.

'My dear,' he had said, in a sudden excess of maudlin gratitude, 'if only it were possible.'

The seed was safely sown, and each unkind rebuff from Elizabeth would nurture it tenderly—Lettice was quietly confident of it.

Now she slipped off the couch and began to dress slowly, fastening the lawn ruff over the red love bites on her neck, and smiling with soft malice into a tiny pocket mirror.

'You had better be careful, Elizabeth, my bastard bitch cousin,' she whispered to her reflection, 'very, very careful with your precious possessions from now on, or I may deal you a blow which will make you wish you were dead.'

While the court was on progress at Leicester's castle of Kenilworth later that year, news came of an event which seemed calculated to destroy the new alliance between England and France.

Elizabeth was out riding with a small party of courtiers when a despatch from Francis Walsingham, her ambassador in Paris, was brought to her side.

Leicester brought his horse alongside hers as she opened the seal and began to read. He saw the look of incredulous fury which stole over her face and heard her curse vehemently under her breath.

'Bad news, madam?'

'I must return at once!' she said curtly and swung her horse's head around.

They rode back in total silence and he hurried after her to her private apartments, where she flung herself into a chair.

'Find Burghley—have him brought to me at once, and the rest of you women, out of my sight. Leicester—you stay!'

She was in no mood to be questioned, that was obvious, so he took up his position beside her chair and waited until Burghley hobbled into the room.

'Sit down,' she said before he got the chance to bow, 'and read this.'

Burghley took the despatch. As he read, his white eyebrows knit together and his normally bland features hardened.

While he absorbed details of the most unprecedented religious massacre in history which had taken place on St Bartholomew's eve in France, Elizabeth paraphrased the more horrific passages for Leicester's benefit.

'. . . the Protestants lie dead in their thousands, the nobility in Paris, the rest in villages throughout France. Women, children and babies—yes, *babies!* —were dragged from their homes and butchered in the streets—the River Seine is choked and rotten with festering bodies. And all done at the hands of the French king—or, to be more precise, his damnable mother—simply because she botched the assassination of a political rival.'

'Not *Coligny?*' murmured Leicester, aghast. Coligny was the leader of the French Protestants.

'Yes, he's dead! The rest were murdered for fear of revenge when blood lust took control. Catherine has wiped out the entire Protestant faction in France—the Puritans here will make an endless meal out of this!'

Burghley looked up from the despatch and announced with awesome pomp, 'Madam, this is the greatest crime since the Crucifixion.'

She had expected this and her glance was suddenly hostile.

'Oh, for God's sake, Burghley, spare me the noble sentiments—I happen to know that were this only a massacre of Catholics you personally would be lauding it to the heavens. Why is it that all bigots are such hypocrites?'

Burghley flushed as red as a beetroot at her rebuke and Leicester was unable to resist a smile. There was an uncomfortable silence as the Queen swept angrily up and down the narrow stone room across an oriental carpet, then stopped and glared at Leicester, who turned off his smile hastily.

'Well? And what have *you* to say about this—as if I couldn't guess!'

Catching sight of Burghley's pleading glance, he coughed and took up his cue at once.

'Madam, when the news of this gets out the fury against the Scottish Queen will become uncontainable.'

She put her hands on her hips in what he read as an uncomfortably threatening gesture.

'You dare to tell me to my face that Mary is responsible for this outrage?—the woman is a friendless prisoner, not a second Eve.'

'The Daughter of Debate can scarcely be called friendless,' Burghley interposed quietly. 'She *is* the Queen of the Castle and her friends will be held responsible for this, justly or not.'

'Then God preserve her from her friends, my lords, as I once prayed he would preserve me from mine!'

It came on an angry note and the two men exchanged looks of alarm. These odd moments of personal and political sympathy with her rival were quite beyond their comprehension. Leicester cleared his throat hesitantly.

'Surely Your Majesty will not continue to protect her after this? France is in no position to object to her execution now—it's the perfect opportunity to be rid of her.'

'I fear I must agree with Leicester, Your Majesty,' said Burghley drily and the Queen laughed outright.

'I suppose that is indeed a miracle—the two of you in agreement after all these years! But you waste your breath, both of you. I will not take responsibility for the judicial execution of a sister queen.'

'Assassination then, madam,' suggested Leicester, a trifle too smoothly.

Elizabeth frowned.

'If she dies mysteriously in an English prison every finger will point to me.'

'She could be returned to Scotland,' said Burghley calmly. 'The Scottish Regent would no doubt be glad to execute her for us—at a price, of course.'

Elizabeth walked away from them, as though suddenly deep in thought. Whatever the price, it would be too high, she would see to that. Once it was accepted that a sovereign was answerable for common crimes, like any ordinary man, the whole concept of monarchy would be in the melting pot. She wondered why they could not see what a dangerous precedent it would set. They were too obsessed with Mary to see the issue objectively, worrying at her life like dogs with a bone, blind to all reason. Even a man as astute as Burghley was unable to divorce himself from the present and see that Mary dead might ultimately be a great deal more dangerous than Mary alive.

She glanced at the two men, so dear to her in different ways, both desperately trying to read her mind. The advice they gave was but an echo of what she could expect to hear from her Council and the country at large, 'Cut off her head and make no more ado with her,' Parliament had said months ago, 'The axe must give the next warning.' One day there was going to be real trouble with Parliament; Elizabeth sensed it in the growing outspokenness of the Commons. Each session seemed just a little more difficult to rule than the last, testing her powers of autocracy, making her stoop to flattery and dissemblance. She was not afraid of the Lords—they were easily brought to book—but she had a deep, instinctive wariness of conflict with the Lower House. Their readiness to consider judicial disposal of a monarch filled her with foreboding, for what was done once might be done again.

So—play for time now—dissipate their energies on a wild goose chase by pretending interest in Burghley's plan. Negotiate terms for Mary's execution in Scotland, knowing she could thwart them whenever she chose—indeed, she could probably rely on the greedy treachery of the Regent to do that for her. And in the end there would be another negation, one of those perfect impasses for which she had gained a formidable reputation.

She turned to Burghley and sighed.

'You may approach the Regent, my lord, but be discreet. I shall want exact details of his terms before we proceed any further.'

Burghley exchanged a quick look of triumph with Leicester, and Elizabeth bit her lip to curb a smile. How easy it was to manoeuvre them all when she wished, little men—little chessboard men—who never felt the hand that moved them.

'As for the French,' she continued calmly, 'my ports will naturally be open to refugees—but there are to be no attacks on French shipping. A little restraint now will salvage the alliance.'

'But not the marriage, of course,' said Leicester aggressively.

'No, not the marriage, I fear.' She answered Leicester without looking at him and glanced obliquely at Burghley. 'I will leave it to you, Robin, to keep the French Ambassador out of my sight until I can bring myself to receive him civilly.'

'It will be my pleasure, madam.' Leicester bowed and retired in accordance with her gesture. When he had gone, she sat down again and looked up at Burghley shrewdly.

'How long before we can resume the marriage negotiations?'

'When the outcry has died down, madam—six months, perhaps a year— who can say?'

She nodded and picked up the despatch once more, glancing at it with a frown.

'What kind of maniac can murder children and believe that God will say "Well done!" '

Burghley shrugged.

'Madam, when a country tolerates two religions forever at war with each other, I fear such atrocities are inevitable.'

'One castle must fall, eh?' She glanced at him sardonically. 'I hope that's not the preamble to a cry for more persecution here.'

'Madam, I feel most strongly on the subject. Do you wish to see St Bartholomew's Eve repeated here in England?'

'Don't take that sanctimonious tone with me, Burghley. You had your way after the Excommunication Bull, against my better judgement I may add. I advise you not to make capital out of this, if you value your place.'

He bowed, his dignity ruffled as only the Queen was capable of ruffling it.

'I am, of course, Your Majesty's to command in all things,' he said stiffly.

She gave him a strange, compelling look, a piercing gaze that suddenly made him feel very uneasy and caused him to drop his eyes to the floor.

'Just see that you remember that, my friend—at all times.'

The words went on ringing in his ears as he left the room and he was suddenly rather relieved to get away from her. It was as though he had received a warning not to overreach himself again.

Fenelon, the French Ambassador, spent three days of ostracism at Woodstock, kicking his heels among hostile glances and waiting uneasily for a summons from the Queen. When at last he entered the Privy Chamber, he augured the worst from the stony silence which greeted him and he walked awkwardly past rows of courtiers, all dressed in mourning black, who pointedly turned their faces away from him as he approached. His own footsteps clicking nervously across the floor seemed to be the only sound in that tense room.

At the end of the Chamber the Queen awaited him, likewise dressed in black and surrounded by a semicircle of long-faced councillors; her own face was pale and sad and very stern. She advanced a few steps to meet Fenelon, drawing him coldly aside to a window embrasure.

'Well?' she said quietly, looking at him with just a small glimmer of sympathy. 'You had better make your excuses, if you have any.'

Whatever diplomatic suavity had been left to him deserted him abruptly beneath the glare of so many hostile eyes.

'Madam,' he began hesitantly, 'it would seem a conspiracy was discovered against the King's life. Justice demanded the most severe reprisals—'

'Did it demand the murder of women and children—the slaughter of babes in arms?' she inquired coolly.

He flushed with humiliation and muttered something hopelessly inadequate about the confusion of the moment.

'The King and Queen Mother,' he continued hastily, 'are most anxious that you of all people, madam, should understand that no enmity was entertained against the Protestant powers in Europe.'

Her eyes were cynical, hard as polished stones.

'I fear those who led your King to abandon his natural subjects will easily persuade him to abandon his alliance with a foreign queen.'

'Madam, my King has sworn to take revenge for this outrage. I swear he had no hand in the matter, no say at all in this as in other—'

'Enough.' She laid her hand on his sleeve, but her command was gentle and he realized that his efforts to exonerate his master would only reveal the unfortunate man for the hagridden mother's boy he was. 'Tell your master that I grieve for him,' she continued gently.

There was something quite genuine in her voice as she said that and the warm pressure of her fingers on his hand was remarkably reassuring. He watched her leave the room with regret and as he turned and saw the hatchet-faced council descending upon him, like a pack of black wolves closing in for attack, he was even more sorry to see her go. By the time they had finished with him, he wrote home that no one would speak to him 'but the Queen, who treats me with her accustomed urbanity'.

Elizabeth, satisfied that she had handled a sore situation with kid gloves, made a mental note to recall that Puritan hothead, Walsingham, from France before his rudely expressed outrage earned him a dagger in the back. The recent promotion of Burghley to Lord Treasurer had left a gap in the Secretariat which would need more than one man to fill it. She had no liking at all for Francis Walsingham, but he knew his job and did not object to footing his own bills for his expenses. There was not a great deal of that sort of loyalty about and she was inclined to agree with Burghley that Walsingham would be a fitting choice as Secretary—always supposing she could stomach that long Puritan face about her apartments at all hours. Certainly she could make far better use of the man's fanaticism at home—a less able brain and a more tactful tongue would serve her better in Paris for the moment.

Burghley sent his own brother-in-law up to Scotland with the offer of Mary's life and found the Regent interested, but greedy; in return for staging the execution he would expect 3,000 English troops as a safeguard and an annual payment equal to that being spent on Mary's upkeep at the moment. In short, the English would have to sanction the deed to such an extent that they might as well have it done in England.

Having made his outrageous demands, the Regent promptly dropped dead after dining out; Scotland dissolved into chaos once more and the negotiations faded into limbo, to the intense chagrin of Elizabeth's ministers.

Elizabeth, tongue in cheek at the failure, moved Mary to closer confinement at Sheffield Castle, doubled the guard and talked no more of murder,

judicial or otherwise, continuing to protect the woman Walsingham castigated as the 'bosom serpent'.

The months following the St Bartholomew massacre were curiously quiet
and uneventful. Days were long and memories were short, the outcry against
Mary slowly died. But when Elizabeth talked of reopening marriage negotiations with France, Leicester was truly alarmed. Throughout her reign, suitors
had risen and fallen with the ceaseless regularity of the tide, to be used
shamelessly and then cast aside, but this little Frenchman seemed inclined to
linger on the scene with remarkable persistence. The Queen's interest grew
steadily and that broody look was more prominent than ever. It occurred to
Leicester that if she was really sickening for a severe attack of maternal
instinct, he would do well to incubate it on his home ground.

So in the summer of 1575, with the desperation of a gambler who has
placed everything on a long shot, he threw a fortune into preparing a fairytale
scene for her at Kenilworth, an entertainment which was to become a legend.
His great castle was a show-piece of scintillating grandeur, a brilliant setting
awaiting the finishing jewel; and no one was left in any doubt of the identity
of that jewel.

When Elizabeth entered the castle to a cannon salute, the great blue-
dialled clock with gold figures that stood high and solitary on Caesar's Tower
was stopped; and at the same moment every clock in the castle was stopped
also. 'Time stands still for you,' he whispered and saw her smile.

It was the hottest summer in living memory and the glittering pageants
shimmered beneath a July heat haze. The air was filled with the savage roars
of bears in the baiting pit; music, dancing, plays and masques passed the days
away in endless frivolity and at night the black summer sky was hidden
behind a multicoloured blaze of fireworks which lit the countryside for miles
around. Night after night the castle windows shimmered in the light of
thousands of perfumed candles, all supported in glass candelabra, while
within the company dined from a choice of three hundred dishes served on
plates of crystal.

One sultry evening, Elizabeth stood on the long drawbridge which
spanned the castle moat and watched the Lady of the Lake float towards her
on an artificial island lit with tiny lights. A mermaid drew a tail eighteen feet
long through the dark water and on the back of a giant mechanical dolphin
Arion prepared to address his Queen. A hush fell over the watching court for
the climax of this spectacular water extravaganza, but Leicester's hospitality
had been generous, even to minions, and Arion was gloriously drunk. At some
critical point in his speech he forgot his lines and pulled off his mask, waved
it at the Queen and informed her that he was none of Arion.

'Not I, ma'am—honest Harry Goldingham, that's me!'

The Queen glanced at Leicester's murderous face and went into paroxysms of laughter, from which she eventually emerged sufficiently to inform honest Harry that he was the best part of the show.

Leicester was aggrieved as they strolled back into the gardens in the summer dusk.

'That fool—that village idiot!—I'll hang him for this!' he grumbled.

Elizabeth glanced sideways at him with amusement.

'Would you hang a man for making me laugh?'

'The man was drunk in *my* employ! Madam, do you have any idea what it *cost* to build that dolphin?'

'What dolphin?'

He had pulled up short, on the verge of an angry retort, when he saw her smiling.

'Well,' he muttered, laying her hand on his arm, 'you can't expect me to be best pleased. Not when I can see Hatton and the rest sniggering like schoolboys—'

Elizabeth laughed. 'If Hatton had paid for that dolphin wouldn't *you* have sniggered too?'

Leicester smiled faintly and conceded the point—it had suddenly dawned on him that this trivial incident had put her in a remarkably good mood; it might be that honest Harry had not failed him after all.

The Queen's attendants had dispersed discreetly to the pleasure ground beneath the terrace, leaving Elizabeth alone with her host. The parapet was dotted with stone effigies of Leicester's crest—the white bear—and she stood looking down over the gardens, idly patting the cold head of one of them. She felt suddenly relaxed and happy, as though all the tension of these last troubled years was flowing out of her on this balmy evening. Beyond this haven of peace, the outer world of documents and treason seemed strangely unimportant. Sometimes it was good to forget reality . . .

'It's so beautiful here,' she remarked after a moment. 'You should not make me too comfortable, Rob—I may outstay my welcome.'

'Impossible, madam.' He came to stand beside her. 'If I entertained you for eternity it would seem too short a time.'

'*To serve you is Heaven, to lack you is more than Hell's torment,*' she mocked.

Leicester glanced at her jealously.

'I suppose Hatton said that to you!'

Elizabeth shook her head. 'He wrote it. I imagine some would say it reads rather better in reverse.'

He said, with a sudden catch in his voice, 'Don't count me among them! I despise the man, but I envy his gift with words. I would I could have put it half so well.'

There had been a time when she regularly showed him her love letters from Hatton and they had laughed at the man's extravagant sentiments—until the moment it occurred to Leicester that she might be doing exactly the same with his own correspondence. He had promptly declared the practice obscene and since then he had seen no more of Hatton's letters—or anyone else's.

But tonight he was warmed by that little touch of self-deprecation in her voice and sufficiently encouraged by the expansiveness of her mood to take one final throw at the dice.

Moving closer, he covered her hand with his own where it lay on the white stone bear.

He said softly, 'For sixteen years I have begged you to marry me, Elizabeth. Now I lay my heart and my possessions at your feet and ask you for the last time to be my wife.'

She stood very still and he scarcely dared to breathe, feeling her spirit leap suddenly towards him. Below them jets of water rose and fell in an octagonal fountain of white marble. A faint breeze carried the scent of strawberries and roses to her, as she listened to the sleepy flutterings of the aviary and the soft, steady spray of the fountain. For one moment the temptation to unite herself with the author of all this homage was irresistible and she admired the skill and cunning with which he had baited this trap. Leaning a little on his arm, she looked up into his face and answered him gently, without mockery.

'Then for the last time my answer must be No. You can stop the clocks, my love, but you can't turn them back. It's too late for us, Robin—sometimes I think it always was. Outside your fairytale the real world still exists and calls you a murderer. If I married you even now it would destroy us both.'

He slammed his clenched fist against the stone bear in an agony of bitter disappointment.

'For Christ's sake—must I spend the rest of my life answering for a crime I didn't commit? I was *not* responsible for Amy's death.'

'I know.' It was the first time she had ever admitted that to him and he was staggered.

'How long have you known that?' he asked sharply.

'It doesn't matter.'

'It does to me! How long?'

'Since the verdict of the inquest.'

'And all this time you've let me believe—' He broke off, seeing suddenly how he had been used. What a dance she had led him, what a cruel dance! 'Sometimes I think you have no heart at all, madam!' he muttered.

'You're wrong, Robin—my heart knows its place, that's all. Look—you have cut your hand.'

'Perhaps it would suit you better if I cut my throat!' he said bitterly.

She sighed, took the little lace handkerchief from the golden girdle at her waist and dabbed his grazed knuckles with it. He submitted to her ministration like a sulky little boy and she was gently amused by him.

'Oh, Robin, did you really expect me to fall into your arms because of a few fairy lanterns?'

'I don't know,' he said wearily, 'I just hoped, as I always hope, so perhaps I am the fool you appear to count me, after all. I suppose that is your last word on the subject—you don't want me to ask again, do you?'

She lowered her eyes demurely.

'You can ask as often as you like, if only you agree not to fall about in a rage whenever I refuse.'

In spite of his angry disappointment, he had to smile faintly at that. Vain as a peacock and so inherently sure of her damned power over them all that it was impossible to protest against that vanity. It was part of the unique audacity that set her apart from the rest of her sex.

He put his hand on the back of her waist and drew her closer into the warm shelter of his own body. She did not draw away.

'At least promise me one thing, that you will think no more of Alençon,' he begged.

'I can't give you that promise, Robin—not with Europe so unsettled—but if ever I should be forced to marry anyone but you, then it will only be for policy and nothing will change between us.'

'You expect your husband to accept me?' he said incredulously.

'He'll do as I tell him if he wants a quiet life. Does that satisfy you?'

'No,' he said ungraciously. 'But then that's of no consequence, is it? I've no choice in the matter. You will do exactly as you please and it is your right for you are the Queen and I am merely your humble servant. Parallel lines, madam—how right you were all those years ago. We shall never meet now.'

They went back inside the castle and spoke no more on the matter. The extravaganza at Kenilworth served no active purpose other than to put him deeply into debt; the marriage negotiations continued and with each month that passed Alençon loomed larger and more menacing on the horizon.

Despair attended the ultimate death of Leicester's last hope and made him an easy victim of Lettice's machinations. When the Earl of Essex died in

Ireland during an outbreak of dysentery, she brought a mental battering-ram against her lover's defences.

And in September of 1578 Robin married her at Wanstead with the deepest secrecy—and resignation.

CHAPTER 6

So you have finally given her up! I always wondered just how long it would take before you conceded defeat.'

Burghley placed a heavily bandaged foot on a low stool and slowly sipped the tankard of mulled ale which Leicester, suddenly remarkably solicitous of his comfort, had offered him. 'And I suppose the meaning of all your pathetic letters grovelling for my friendship is that you hope I won't seek opportunities to tell the Queen what you have done—is that not so, my lord?'

Leicester tugged uncomfortably at his beard and avoided the Lord Treasurer's frosty blue eyes.

'I knew you would find out, so it seemed best to confess it to you. You are the only man who would dare to tell her.'

Burghley smiled coldly and shifted his painful foot on its cushion. 'My dear Leicester, you grossly overestimate my courage. The Greeks used to execute messengers who brought bad news—I've no mind to provoke Her Majesty into reviving the custom.'

'Now *you* exaggerate.' Leicester turned away, gnawing anxiously on a fine golden toothpick. 'She has so many men I doubt if she'd have time to notice my domestic arrangements. It's hardly likely to break her heart, is it?'

Burghley stared at him steadily and balanced the tankard on the arm of his chair.

'Forgive me—is that not exactly what you desire? I understand the lady in question has been your mistress for some considerable time. What possessed you to marry her now, knowing what it will mean if the Queen finds out?'

'Why the devil shouldn't I marry?' Leicester burst out in peevish self-defence. 'Why shouldn't I get myself a legitimate son to carry on my father's name? You've seen the way she treats me, it must have given you enough delight in the past. She has no feeling for me—no feeling at all—'

'If you believe that, Leicester, then you really are the fool I always took you for.'

Leicester sank on to a hearth stool and flung the toothpick away with an angry gesture.

'She has a damn peculiar way of showing her love then!'

'So for that matter have you.' Burghley looked at him shrewdly. 'Oh, you don't deceive me, Leicester—I know how deeply you love the Queen. God knows, over the years I have come to consider it your only saving grace. You at least can boast of her cruelty—yet better men than you have loved her and left no mark at all on her heart. You may spare a little pity for Hatton, who finds himself physically unable to take a mistress while she lives—yes, he told me that once. And how he will end I do not care to think, for a man must take his comfort somewhere. So you see, my friend—you are not alone in your affliction.'

'That is a great comfort,' said Leicester bitterly. 'I believe she collects men's souls and locks them in that casket by her bed—mine, Hatton's, countless others—all neatly labelled and preserved in vinegar like specimens in a laboratory, meaningless trophies, souvenirs of a past conquest. The moment you're conquered she loses interest, leaves you caught in her web like a fly, struggling to remember where you left your manhood. What she's searching for God only knows, but she's never found it yet.'

Cecil looked away into the fire.

'It may be safer if she never does,' he said darkly.

Leicester's eyes were suddenly alight with curiosity. He leaned forward to fill Burghley's tankard again.

'Well,' he said slowly, 'I've been in her power for a long time, ever since I was a child. She hooked me young and I need her, like some men need opium. I know how she snares the rest, but *you*—now, you're the riddle. Perhaps you're the key to her whole mystery. A devoted husband, viceless some would say.' Leicester's lips curled maliciously. 'Only you and I—we know better, don't we, Sweet William? You're the coldest, shrewdest, most ruthless devil I've ever met. So tell me, man to man, all differences aside— what's the secret of her hold over *you?*'

Cecil gave him a thin-lipped smile. His eyes were suddenly veiled.

'It was you who once spoke of witchcraft,' he said coolly, and got abruptly to his feet. He had no desire to continue this conversation any further. It smacked of the confessional and a great deal more that he assured himself he did not hold with.

Leicester rose with him, snubbed and uneasy once more, sensing he had offended Burghley.

'I didn't mean to pry. Every man to the Devil his own way—as the Queen would say.'

Burghley laughed suddenly and Leicester's head jerked up at the dry, rasping sound, so utterly alien to this humourless man.

'My lord?' he said cautiously.

Burghley shook his head slowly.

'I am not entirely the humourless bore you think me, Leicester—I can smile at irony like the next man.'

'Irony?'

'You and I and the Queen. I never thought I should live to say this, my lord, but you have your uses. She's a great deal easier to work with when she's happy—and you have made her happy, I grant you that. But that won't save you if she ever finds out about your marriage. Should that day dawn, I for one pray I shall not be in the same palace. And as for you, my lord—well, I rather think you will wish you were not in the same world.'

Europe was in ferment. In the Netherlands the Dutch Protestants waged eternal war against their Spanish overlord, while vague talk of 'the Enterprise of England' loomed now big, now small, according to Philip's doubts and fears and hesitancy—and the state of his exchequer. There were anxious moments for him when the French crown passed to Henri of Anjou and the power of Mary Stuart's Guise relatives threatened to become supreme once more. The new King's brother, Alençon, became heir to the French throne and his position as a confirmed troublemaker in France took on consequence. It was soon evident that the King of France would be thankful to see the back of him, preferably by packing him off to England . . .

Having fanned Philip's unease by her overtures to France, Elizabeth swung the see-saw of negotiations back to Spain. Her treasury was swollen by the spoils taken from Spanish ships by English pirates, and Philip would dearly have loved to snub her. But the terms of the treaty she offered, with its promise of trade, was irresistible to him in his straitened means and after a brief struggle with his finer feelings, he agreed to sign it. Elizabeth was complacent. Nominally at peace with Spain, she continued to lend secret aid to the Dutch rebels, in her customary underhand manner, anxious to keep Philip's attention on his own territories. She flatly refused to come out in the open as the acknowledged leader of the Protestant world, knowing that such an action would plunge her into war within six months. She could accomplish a great deal more, at a fraction of the expense, by skulking in the shadows, her dealings shamelessly unfettered by scruples; she had become a past master at the diplomatic knee in the groin.

When Philip's bastard brother, that romantic young knight-errant, Don John of Austria, descended on the Netherlands to crush opposition, she rapidly disgorged £20,000 in aid for the Dutch. She had no patience with religious warfare and had scandalized Philip's envoy by pointedly inquiring why the King of Spain could not allow his subjects 'to go to the Devil their own way'. But she knew Don John's intention was to use the Netherlands as a springboard to launch the 'Enterprise of England'. She dared not allow him to install himself safely there—equally, she dared not risk open war. Secret aid was as much as she was prepared to hazard.

When Don John's troops began to flatten resistance, Elizabeth's Council panicked and demanded immediate intervention and open war. Against the war fever she hung back, ignoring their bleating that only a miracle would save her if she did not act decisively now, gambling on her personal knowledge of Philip's character. He was on the brink of bankruptcy, jealous and suspicious of his heroic half-brother's loyalty, starving his troops of money and reinforcements. Philip did not seek war with England at the moment and she was not going to hand it to him on a golden platter of armed intervention.

The policy of inaction horrified the Council, and even Burghley, who did not lack for cool nerves, began to wonder if she had pushed her luck too far at last. It seemed that nothing in this world would prevent the Spaniards overrunning the Netherlands and invading England.

And then she got her miracle. Unsupported, Don John's venture floundered, crumbled and ended with his dispirited death, some said of a broken heart at his half-brother's treatment of him.

'God deals most lovingly with Her Majesty in taking away her enemies,' remarked Walsingham with awe.

This uneasy belief that it was not healthy to be an enemy of the English Queen was finding followers all over Europe. Men said such luck was beyond the boundaries of pure coincidence; many remembered that her mother had been accused of witchcraft, and strange rumours were afloat.

Now the Spanish embassy in London, closed for the past eight years since the expulsion of its ambassador after the Ridolfi Plot, was reopened by that very thin olive branch of peace, Don Bernadino de Mendoza. And Elizabeth believed she had discovered the perfect solution to her dilemma in the Netherlands.

She extended a thin hand, almost transparent in the sunlight, and bent her long fingers to examine their scarlet talons, flexing them gently like claws.

'A cat's-paw,' she murmured, more to her hand than to Burghley who stood watching her—'that's what we need now to stir the troubled marshes of the Netherlands and hold Philip at bay. I think Alençon will do very nicely, don't you?'

'We have yet to persuade him to undertake the mission.'

'Don't fret, my friend, I know how to handle little pock-marked donkeys.' She held out her hand—that very marriageable hand—and smiled at it tenderly. 'This is the thing that will hold him until he has served our purpose—this,' her smile deepened, 'or to be more precise—the promise of this. This hand has served me as faithfully as you, my Spirit, for over twenty years. It is about to enjoy one long and very satisfying last performance before I ring the curtain down for good on its charade.'

Burghley stooped to kiss that hand with a faint quiver of emotion. It was true that no one had played the marriage game with greater skill or more profit than Elizabeth. Over and over again he had seen her do it, balance Europe on the slender promise of her hand, and it honestly amazed him that after twenty years the fish were still gullible enough to swallow the bait. He could not deny the remarkable success of her methods, but he was too upright and correct to admire them wholeheartedly for they smacked of brothel principles and offended his image of her as an incomparable deity. If only she were not so brazenly amoral about the business, so full of cheap political tricks, hawking her body and her crown to the highest bidder as shamelessly as any whore who walked the London streets. For though she might be a goddess, she was not a lady and somewhere, between his respect and his love, there hovered a small niggle of regret for her lack.

He had never met Alençon, but he could find it in his heart to pity the man. He stood no chance against Elizabeth's inborn gift for manipulating men, her remarkable ability to take advantage of her sex. Her physical frailty had saved her from the serious limitations of a total virago and he suspected, at times, that she was not above making use of that too, when it suited her. The same woman who rode roughshod over the dignity of the men who served her was also likely to restore their feelings of male superiority by fainting outright at their feet, a move which never failed to send them into a fiercely protective fuss for vinegar and restoratives, however murderous with exasperation they might have felt with her five minutes before. Play-acting or genuine, it was always impossible to tell which and it always had the desired effect. She had made her sex into the most formidable weapon in her armoury. And Alençon was to be her next victim.

The soft, tinkling notes fell on the air like pure, clear drops of rainwater; as the last one died on a throb of exquisite melancholy, there was a genuinely reverent silence before the burst of furious applause.

Jean de Simier, special envoy of the Duke of Alençon, bent to offer his arm to the player who sat at the keyboard of the virginals, attempting, not particularly with much success, to look modestly embarrassed by the spontaneous ovation.

'My master will be entranced—Your Majesty plays like an angel.'

She smiled a little smugly, familiar enough with fulsome flattery to know the man spoke sincerely. She was very proud of her accomplishments—there was no woman in her court who could rival her, for she played and danced, as she did everything, to perfection.

She glanced up at the virile Frenchman and smiled mischievously.

'Don't you think your master would find marriage with an angel a great trial? Surely wings and a halo would be a great inconvenience to any man in bed.'

He returned her smile and leaned over the virginals to take her hand, caressing it with his lips.

'The Duke would overcome any obstacle for the joy of meeting with Your Highness in that same place—'

'Yes—we have heard it said that he always *rises* to the occasion.'

A ripple of amusement ran round the little group of listening courtiers and Simier bowed, acknowledging her sly wit.

'You are too quick for me, madam. I fear I cannot deny my master's reputation with the ladies. It is true that his virility exceeds that of many men.'

'Alas—then I can scarcely expect a faithful husband.'

'Not so, my Queen. I swear you will drive all other women from his mind.'

'It's not his mind that troubles me, Simier, it's his *bed.*'

Leicester laughed out loud and the Frenchman shot him a look of dislike and distrust before spreading his hands in an expansive gesture.

'Madam—surely experience is an asset in every field.'

Elizabeth rose from the virginals and leaned familiarly on the Frenchman's arm.

'When I've tried him in a field,' she said wickedly, 'I'll let you know.'

Simier had been at court since Christmas, wooing the English Queen by proxy with a dextrous mixture of charm and outrageous gallantry. He was never absent from her side now and he had caused more scandal in the last few weeks than Leicester and the rest had done in twenty years. His overt physical advances were cloaked in the thinnest guise of respect and were never repulsed. He was an aggressive, dangerous man who had murdered his wife and his brother for infidelity and he was attracted by Elizabeth's feline charm—she was perhaps the only woman he had respected all his turbulent life. At the age of forty-five she was playing her favourite game for all it was worth, more successfully than she had ever played it before. Her mirror showed her hard, handsome face positively radiant beneath the flamboyant diamond-threaded curls of her fashionable red wig. She felt as though she had shed ten years in as many weeks and tonight the intense gaze of Simier's eyes, and of all those furiously jealous ones behind him, filled her with an ecstatic sense of power.

She glanced beyond Simier to the men who shared her government. Sussex, his weathered features ageing and benign, looked on with approval—he longed to see her with an heir. Burghley's face was noticeable only for its lack of emotion in that very emotional room; he knew more of her game than most and was not deceived by her performance. Walsingham, who had spent four years in the Secretariat, serving her with passionless efficiency and infuriating her with his Puritan bigotry, was irritated at the apparent success of the Catholic Frenchman. And Leicester was intensely and bitterly jealous, making no secret of his fierce hostility to the match. Poor Robin! But she would make it up to him, when at last it was all over. She saw no reason why she should not enjoy her last fling.

Beneath the light of a hundred candles, she danced with Simier until dawn and knew that beyond the palace gates the people had begun to grumble faintly and say that she had lost her senses. Robin said quite openly that she was bewitched by the Frenchman.

She wondered in half-idle amusement if she was.

Simier sat in the royal barge watching the sweating oarsmen, tightly bunched up in their Tudor livery, dipping their long white oars in and out of the water in perfect rhythm.

He stared out over the Thames, gnawing the inside of his lip, for he was a man who found it hard to relax at the best of times, and relaxation was a commodity in short supply at the English court, where everyone from the sovereign down appeared to live on their nerves. He had been over six months in England and the Queen gave him every reason to think she found him and the cause of his mission as fascinating as ever; but still he had not persuaded her to sign the vital passport which would allow the Duke to come to England. She painted a pretty picture of herself as a weak and defenceless woman in the hands of statesmen who could not agree, but it was a picture which did not quite accord with the totally unquestioned obedience she appeared to command from all, even Burghley. Simier knew she was playing for time and he believed he knew why—Leicester's enmity had been steady and pointedly obvious since his arrival in London. Well, he had discovered a secret which would cook Leicester's goose, and if necessary he would disclose it at some suitable opportunity, if the man did not back off soon.

Certainly the French marriage was not being hailed by the English people, and public opinion was beginning to speak out against it. The Duke should be here now, pleading his own cause; they would be less ready to offend a prince personally than they were to offend his shadow.

Simier sighed and arranged the lace ruff at his cuff. A slight breeze was skirting the river now, rippling the water into small waves, and boats passed them on either side. Idly he noticed a small sculler's boat which seemed suddenly to be out of control, its occupant struggling with an unwieldy gun. Simier stiffened. What in God's name would a man want with a gun on this peaceful river?

He was about to cry out, when suddenly the gun discharged. A grey lead bullet grazed the royal canopy, missing the Queen by inches, and struck a bargeman who collapsed to the floor with a scream of pain. The peace of the river dissolved into pandemonium.

Calmly the Queen snapped her book closed and smiled at the French Ambassador who was watching her closely, hoping she would panic at this attempt on her life and provide him with a nice tid-bit for his next despatch. She waved back the anxious onslaught of courtiers who flocked around her and insisted on going at once to the injured man. A respectful silence fell as her bargemen parted to let her pass and followed her with worshipping eyes.

The bullet had passed clean through the man's arm and blood was streaming down his wrist. Elizabeth unwound the silk scarf that flew at her neck and bound the wound tightly. When he swayed unsteadily, her hand beneath his arm guided him back to his seat.

'Don't be afraid,' she said gently. 'You took that bullet for me and I shall see that you never want.'

Leicester had pushed his way to her side anxiously and now handed her a handkerchief to wipe her fingers.

'The culprit has been arrested, Your Majesty,' he said quietly.

She glanced out across the river to the muddle of small craft and sighed.

'Won't you come back and sit down, madam? You've had a shock.'

She smiled faintly. 'I'm all right, Robin, stop fussing. Tell them we will return to the palace—this man needs attention at once.'

Leicester gave her his arm and they walked back towards the royal canopy. As she passed Simier she noticed how pale and shaken was his dark face and the thought crossed her mind that he firmly believed the bullet had been meant for him.

The trial of the would-be assassin took place at Windsor where one

Thomas Appletree was found guilty, not of treason but of creating a danger-ous disturbance in the presence of the Sovereign. The point was merely academic—the penalty for both charges was still death—and he was brought to the scaffold through a violently hostile crowd which screamed abuse and tried to attack him. He wept bitterly, declared that he deserved death and had hoped for nothing else, but he did not get his wish. Elizabeth sent a personal reprieve to the foot of the gallows and the crowd, as though to prove their notorious fickleness, cheered him down the scaffold as heartily as they had just booed and hissed him up it.

She was quite prepared to believe his story that it had been an accident and not only saved his life but got his employer to take him back. Burghley, who lived in constant terror of her assassination, was dumbfounded by the incredible implications of her unwarranted mercy; but she told him that she did not slay mice.

In July, after a furious quarrel with Leicester on the subject, Elizabeth signed the passport which would permit Alençon to travel to England, and the Earl retired to Wanstead to sulk and announce loudly to anyone who would listen that he was ill with grief and chagrin. Elizabeth strongly sus-pected him of shamming, but she had to make sure and so she hurried down to Wanstead with a small train and spent two days reassuring her offended lover that he had nothing to fear.

'I couldn't put him off any longer without arousing the suspicion that I'm not serious about the marriage.'

'And are you serious?'

'Of course not, haven't I told you so often enough?' She looked at him shrewdly. 'Have you dragged me here on a wild goose chase? There's nothing wrong with you, is there, you sly devil?'

'Indeed there is, madam.' His jealous fear had relaxed at her quick con-cern. 'My feelings have been deeply wounded—you will have to kiss them better.'

She laughed and leaned over the bed to tweak the grey-streaked beard.

'You're absurd, do you know that, Robin Dudley, and I'm too busy to waste any more time on your nonsense.' She kissed him briskly and got off the edge of his bed. 'Stop acting the fool and come back to court. We're getting a little too old to play these silly games with each other.'

She was tired when she got back to Greenwich and not at all pleased to hear that during her absence another pot shot had been taken at Simier in the palace gardens. She changed her gown hurriedly to receive him, prepared to humour the man's injured dignity and smooth the situation before it got out of hand and caused real trouble with France.

'Jean!' She came across the room with her hands outstretched to him, at her most charmingly informal. 'Jean, I was so sorry to hear. I cannot imagine who can be behind such a foul act.'

'I can,' he said grimly, bowing over her hand and allowing her to lead him to a window-seat. 'I know who opposes your marriage with my master more strongly than anyone else.'

'Robin?' She burst out laughing. 'Oh, Jean, how little you know him to suggest that. If you had seen him as I have today, sulking in bed like a little boy, you would not walk in fear of him. I promise you, he would not dare to do it.'

'Why not, madam? A man who found the courage to marry your cousin, the Countess of Essex, twelve months ago would certainly dare to silence me.'

'What!' It came on a whispered gasp. 'What did you say?'

'I said he was married, madam.' Simier opened his eyes wide in feigned astonishment. 'But surely you knew—why, everybody knows—it's common gossip around the court.'

As he watched, the blood drained out of her face so that the small patches of rouge stood out in stark relief on her ashen cheeks. She stood up suddenly and took hold of the heavy curtain to support herself. Her mouth was a thin, twisted line clamped tightly shut as though to prevent any cry of anguish escaping and her eyes, suddenly unable to meet his knowing glance, looked away through the window in mute misery. It was as though the ramparts of her world were crashing in upon her and though he was not a sensitive man, he knew he was looking at a woman reeling from a mortal blow. She began to breathe in quick, laboured gasps and one hand crept to her heart, as though she felt a physical pain.

A cold sweat broke out over Simier's body, for if she dropped dead at his feet of a seizure, as she seemed in a fair way to do, then all his clever diplomacy would count for nothing. He touched her arm in a panic. Suddenly she swung round to look at him and he fell back a step from the dreadful expression in her blazing black eyes. He felt he was looking into the eyes of a creature from the darkest regions of Hell, as though he stood on the crust of a seething volcano.

'Leave me!' she said, and he fled from the room like a man who has dabbled in forces beyond his control and understanding. He was halfway across the Privy Chamber when a scream of unearthly rage splintered the air behind him; something hit the closed door with a crash, and again he heard that terrible cry. Whatever had broken loose in that room, he knew for certain it was no longer sane or even human. He hurried away to his own apartments, feeling the startled glances of courtiers as he passed. When at last he dared to emerge, a few hours later, he heard the news that the Earl of Leicester was already under arrest in a small fortress in the palace gardens, waiting to be shipped to the Tower on the next tide.

Bets were being placed on the date of his execution.

That evening saw the members of the Council's inner ring ranged about the council chamber in various poses of nervousness, as restless and uneasy as a cluster of frightened rabbits cowering from the presence of a mad dog. It was absurd, thought Burghley, truly absurd that half a dozen of the most influential men in England should be skulking in here, too terrified to face one woman in the mindless grip of a hysterical tantrum. But there it was. Not one man or woman had the courage to go in and slap her to her senses, putting a timely end to that appalling frenzy before she caused permanent damage to herself and to the state. He had never counted himself a coward until this moment when he knew that he could not face her. Oddly enough it was the sort of situation which Leicester alone might have been expected to handle and in any other set of circumstances they would all have been looking to him to calm her back into sanity. Now it looked as though the magic cure of his personality was about to be lost to them for good.

If anyone had told Burghley twenty years ago that one day he would be desperately debating how to save Leicester's skin, he would have laughed aloud at the impossibility. Now he reflected grimly on life's little ironies. Thanks to the Queen, Leicester was a man of very considerable standing— 'The Great Lord' they called him at home and abroad—his voice counted for something among their Protestant supporters in Europe and throughout England. If Elizabeth struck him down now, in a moment of jealous rage, the scandal of her injustice would never die. Such a blot on her name would send her prestige plummeting like a falling star. So she could not be allowed to execute the man; she could not even be allowed to send him to the Tower. And someone was going to have to risk his own fortunes and freedom— possibly even his own life—to tell her so. Burghley tapped his gouty fingers on the table in front of him and looked around the room, seeing the others hastily avoid his cool gaze.

'Well, my lords, we are all agreed that someone must do it. Walsingham— you have been the man's friend.'

Walsingham started and stared, his long thin face quivering like that of a cornered rat.

'Her Majesty threw a slipper in my face the last time I contradicted her opinion—I hardly think I am your man. Surely someone who is known to be the Earl's sworn enemy would infuriate her less—a man known for his courage and physical presence—a man she holds in high esteem . . .'

He licked his dry lips and looked over to where the old Earl of Sussex sat gnawing his thumb and frowning. Suddenly everyone in the room had followed Walsingham's hopeful gaze and the elderly soldier could feel their eyes boring into his head. A moment longer he glowered at nothing, then he got painfully to his feet and shrugged his great shoulders ruefully.

'Well—I'm nearer to the grave than the rest of you. I suppose it had better be me. I stuck my neck out for her with her sister when she was just a slip of a girl and she said she would never forget it. I suppose I'll never have a better chance to test the word of a prince.' Across the table he met Burghley's anxious glance. 'I can't promise anything, of course, my lord—but I'll do my best.'

As he went out of the room he heard someone mutter darkly that that would make a good epitaph.

Sussex went at once to her ante-room, sent in his name and begged an audience. A maid of honour, her pretty face convulsed with terror, returned to sob the refusal. 'I am to admit no one, on pain of death, my lord.'

The Earl frowned and turned to wave his gnarled hand at the pitiful group of females huddled in a corner. 'Go into the Presence Chamber and shut the doors. Stay there until I send word.'

Mute with fear, they obeyed and he watched them go. With one thumb in his belt in a gesture which gave him courage, he stared for a long moment at the door which led to the Queen's bedroom; then he stepped through it, without a knock or a second thought.

He stopped and stared; and the frantic, headlong pacing which he had interrupted stopped in that same second. He was a hardened soldier and he had heard strong language from her on many occasions, but when she rounded on him the torrent of obscenities which greeted him momentarily took his breath away. Her eyes seemed enormous in her livid face, glittering, vicious, quite insane. A vase shattered in thousands of pieces at his feet and his heart sank. How could he hope to reason with this wild, wounded creature?

'How dare you!' she screamed at last, when he did not turn and flee in terror. 'How dare you come in here?'

And suddenly, unexpectedly even to himself, he heard his own voice bellow back, 'By God, madam, how dare *you* try to keep me out.'

The mad light went out of her eyes, as though a candle had been suddenly snuffed, leaving them black, opaque and quite hopeless. In that same moment he went down on his knees to her and his rough voice became quiet and gentle.

'Madam—many years ago when you stood in danger of your life, it happened that I was able to do you a service which you swore never to forget. At my command the door of your prison in the Tower remained unlocked. Will you now lock your door against me when I come once more to plead in your interest?'

Drained with exhaustion, she closed her eyes for a moment and felt time roll away beneath their heavy lids to the moment on that cold, rainy day when she had laid her hand on his sleeve and begged for his help. *'By God I say she shall write!'* Had she ever really been so young? Now she only felt as though she had been born old—old and unloved and wretched beyond endurance. And yet here was this ancient champion of her cause still risking the royal wrath for her sake, a little remembered affection and warmth. Stripped naked of all her scant emotional security, his loyalty was like a tiny glow in a dying fire. She held out her hands to him in real gratitude.

'Get up, my friend.'

'You will listen?'

'I owe you that courtesy at least,' she said wearily. 'What is it you want of me? What is so urgent that it cannot wait till I have rid myself of an unworthy traitor?'

For a second he hesitated; and then dared to say it.

'Leicester is no traitor, Your Majesty. I must beg you to reconsider the order for his arrest.'

She gasped and her eyes widened in furious disbelief; she dropped his hand and stepped back from him.

'Are you mad, Sussex—are you quite senile? Can it be that you do not *know* what he has done?'

'Yes,' he said quickly. 'Yes, madam—I fear I do know.'

She had swung away from him and resumed her maddened pacing.

'I want him dead—*dead*, do you hear? I want to see the crows pick his head clean on London Bridge—he never had such joy in his marriage as he shall have agony in his death. I shall never rest until I have spilt his blood on Tower Hill. By God, he'll die for this, I swear it.'

Sussex swallowed hard. 'Your Highness knows that is not possible.'

She stamped her foot and screamed, 'I am the Queen.'

'Even the Queen cannot act without recourse to the law—and he has committed no offence, in law.'

'Then I'll bend the law!' she spat, 'find another pretext, as my father did when it suited him—fabricate evidence for some new plot against my life. Are you daring to tell me that can't be done?'

'It can be done,' he said quietly, 'but you will not give the order, madam, because you are ten times the monarch that your father was, feared and respected by friends and enemies alike. Even the Pope reveres your name! You cannot throw all this away to be revenged upon an inferior scoundrel who has betrayed your affection.'

She turned away from him, trembling with the intensity of her rage, struggling to control it before it leapt out and destroyed him, too, for his audacity.

'You have said enough and I have listened. Now you will leave me. My order stands unchanged. He goes to the Tower and he will leave it only for the block.'

'Madam, I beseech you, be reasonable.'

'Reasonable? *Reasonable?* He commits bigamy with that whore and you ask me to be reasonable—'

He caught and held both her hands; he was truly desperate now.

'For the love of God, madam, will you tell me how a man can commit bigamy against a woman he has never married?'

She hit him for that and turned away, sobbing bitterly.

'I won't be mocked—I won't, do you hear?'

'No one is mocking you, madam, except yourself. And you know I speak the truth, not as Leicester's friend but as yours. Whatever you feel for him, he is *not* your husband. He was as free to marry in honour as any other man in England and if you act now, in a moment of blind passion, it will destroy everything you have worked for. The damage it will do to your standing in Europe and with your own people will be beyond repair.'

She pulled away from him and sank into a chair before the empty hearth in despair.

'Then I am helpless—tied hand and foot by my good name. There is nothing I can do to punish him.'

'You can banish him, madam. In many ways that will be a worse punishment for him than death. You have made him so much your creature that if you cast him out now you destroy him utterly. He has no place in this world but at your side, no protection but yours against the enemies you have made for him.'

'Of which you are one,' she reminded him, now suddenly very quiet, staring at the floor.

'Yes, madam,' he admitted bluntly. 'My pleading for his freedom does not alter my enmity for him. I would gladly see him driven from this realm in ignominy and poverty. Leave him to his enemies and they will grant you a better revenge than execution—should you really wish it.'

She looked up, sharply incredulous.

'You cannot mean that I might forgive him.'

'You have forgiven him many things before,' Sussex said quietly.

'But not this.' She buried her face in her hands. 'Not this!'

He stood and watched her in pitying silence for a moment.

At last he said gently, 'Is it still to be the Tower, madam?'

'No.' Defeated, humiliatingly close to tears, Elizabeth shook her head slowly. 'Let him go in peace to Wanstead. Let him go to Hell for all I care. What does it matter that a traitor's son has shown his true colours after all? It's finished—truly finished between us at last.'

'I'm glad, madam,' said Sussex simply. 'He was never worthy of you. You are well rid of him.'

'Yes,' she repeated mechanically, like a child learning a difficult lesson by heart, 'I am well rid of him.'

The hysteria had passed, leaving her to face the unpleasant physical symptoms of reaction, and she found herself shaking uncontrollably. She had to force herself to stand erect, to hold out her hand to him, and smile. And when he saw that, and reckoned the immense effort it had cost her to face him with grace and dignity, he suddenly knew why he had risked his neck to come in here today.

'Thank you, my lord. I shall not forget your courage.'

Almost, to the word, precisely what she had said that day he took her letter to Queen Mary. Her image blurred suddenly before his old eyes and he blinked to clear it as he bowed low and went out, sending in her most trusted woman, the Countess of Warwick. And if in that moment he could have obtained access to the imprisoned man, he would have killed Leicester with his bare hands and saved the executioner the trouble.

In tactful silence, Lady Warwick undressed her and put her to bed.

As she sank into the welcoming softness of the mattress Elizabeth felt herself succumbing to the same numb stupor which had overwhelmed her thirty years ago, after the Lord Admiral's execution. Behind these heavy curtains lay sanctuary from the sniggering world outside her door, refuge from a shame and misery too great to be borne with sanity. She had only to let go of reality and nothing would exist for her beyond this bed, no grief, no pain. Already the sounds of the palace were fading, the Countess of Warwick was dwindling before her eyes, and she was slipping down, down into that melancholy state where nothing and no one could matter to her and her only desire would be to sleep and never wake again.

With the last vestige of consciousness she struck out and grasped the anchor of sanity. This pain alone was sharp enough to pierce the great dam of emotion which she had kept welled up for over forty years. Now she turned her face to the pillow and wept for every tragedy that she had suppressed since her childhood; for Katherine Howard and Katherine Parr, for Thomas Seymour and her dead governess, Ashley. And last of all for Robin, the ultimate traitor, who had betrayed her into finally admitting she was a woman, with a woman's heart—and a woman's needs.

CHAPTER 7

In his extravagantly furnished bedchamber at Wanstead, Leicester sat as he had done every day, week in week out, since his banishment, in a low chair before the fire with his great white hound, Boy, at his feet. He had not stirred from the room, nor visited his precious horses, and he had seen no one but his servants. Fever and depression had wasted a body which had already begun to grow stout and no amount of soaking in a hot bath seemed to ease the rheumatic aches in his legs. He was forty-six and he looked and felt every year of it, suddenly feeling as though he had grown old overnight. His face was covered with an unkempt beard and his thinning hair was ruffled by the despairing hands which constantly thrust among it. Rising from his bath, he had not troubled to dress, but sat for hours on end, hunched in his fur-collared chamber robe, drinking a great deal and eating very little, contemplating his stupidity and his ruin with abject misery.

It was over between them. She had cut him out of her life as surely and effectively as if she had followed her original impulse and taken his head—and he knew with grim certainty just how narrowly he had escaped that penalty. There was nothing left to him now without her. The creditors would be lining up, his many enemies closing in with gloating triumph on the best hated man in England. He had few illusions about what lay ahead—persecution, obscurity, poverty—and all to be faced alone, for he doubted that Lettice would follow him into exile. Loyalty had never been one of her virtues.

She followed where her physical senses led, and in time they would lead her to a younger man, with a future to offer. He accepted that with quiet indifference, for he had discovered that he did not greatly care what Lettice did. He cared for nothing and no one but himself and the Queen and the life he had thrown away to satisfy a petty spite.

The enormity of his crime had overwhelmed him at last and the depth of Elizabeth's resentment no longer shocked him; he had been mad to think he could ever get away with it. And now that it was finished, he found himself remembering only the good times, for in spite of their many quarrels there *had* been good times, moments when he was truly proud to be acknowledged as the man she cared for.

In the flickering firelight, memories leapt out at him, like sparks from the burning logs, each one searing the sense of loss a little more deeply into his soul. In every way, except the true one, he had been her husband, and in his heart he knew her bitterness was justified, that she was right to cast him away.

Across the years he chased the elusive images of their love, until at last he came to Ricote—Ricote, in summer, at the height of a hectic progress, home of Henry and Margery Norris, their mutual friends. Only a skeleton train had followed them to Ricote and informality reigned, shooting parties and candle-lit dinners, a time to laugh and love and be themselves in good company, away from the inhibitions of the court. If he could take her just once more to any place in England, it would be to Ricote; and yet, even there, in the midst of their roistering quartet, the shadow had intruded.

The night stood out in his memory as though it were yesterday—a warm summer evening with the scent of roses and newly scythed grass drifting in through the open windows. Dinner finished, the servants dismissed, and Henry Norris serving increasingly large measures of his very best claret. Leicester and the Norrises had been pleasantly intoxicated for an hour or so, and the Queen, who had for once not watered her wine, was as near to drunk as anyone had ever seen her. Norris's father had been one of those five executed with Anne Boleyn, and Henry had a special claim to Elizabeth's affection; she would not hurt his feelings by committing sacrilege against his prize vintage.

They were boisterous and rowdy as school children, absurd as only inebriated adults can be and they had reached the point where any remark was liable to send the listeners hysterical with amusement. A game of question and answer, so popular in court circles, hung in abeyance because Henry was too sodden to think of a question to put to the Queen.

'Don't belch like a pig in the Queen's presence,' said his wife tartly. 'If you don't think of something soon you must pay a forfeit.'

'A dip in the fountain might sober him up,' suggested Leicester cheerfully. Norris got to his feet with haste and asked the Queen to marry him. Everyone laughed, except Margery, who kicked her husband under the table.

'What's amiss?' he grumbled amiably. 'Is it not the most popular question in Europe? Hasn't everyone asked her except the Pope—and he only needs a little more time.'

More irreverent laughter wafted out into the falling dusk, but the prospect of Norris sitting in the fountain now appealed hugely to everyone and even Elizabeth would not let him off the hook. He would have to think of something good if he was to escape a soaking.

'All right—I have it—even Margery can't fault this.' Norris bowed solemnly to the Queen, who leaned her chin on her hands to listen. 'I ask Her Majesty, as the fount of all justice in this land—what is the greatest crime a woman can commit?'

'To kill the man she loves,' said Elizabeth automatically, and looked straight at Leicester as she said it.

There was a moment of quivering silence that sobered that cosy candle-lit quartet like a douse of cold water. Norris arranged nutshells in drunken formation along his plate, and his wife chewed her handkerchief, aghast at what the game had suddenly precipitated.

Leicester stared at the Queen, but was the first to regain composure. He laughed and slapped his host heartily on the back with a force which sent him sprawling among the nutshells.

'Well—that rather rules me out—but if I were you, Norris, I'd watch my step. Everyone knows how fond she is of *you*.'

There was more laughter, of a rather forced quality, until it was discovered that one of the nutshells had nicked Norris's lip. And at that point some semblance of normality returned to the conversation, as everyone got to their feet at once.

Derisive scorn from Margery.

'Oh, God's blood, Henry, you'll live!'

Profuse apologies from Leicester and excessive concern from the Queen.

'Take my handkerchief, Hal—Robin, what a brute you are—you don't know your own strength!'

Leicester caught her hand and swung her over to the empty hearth, away from the other two.

'Do you know yours?' he demanded quietly.

Elizabeth did not answer. She smiled and released herself from his hand

and went back to the table. The evening ended, as convivially as it had begun, but the Queen did not come down next morning; and Leicester had never seen her even remotely intoxicated again.

It was late. The clock on the chimney-piece ticked on, the big dog yawned by the hearth and the door behind him opened with a soft click. Staring moodily into the flickering flames he spoke without looking up.

'Take the food away—leave the wine.'

'I think you have drunk quite enough, don't you, my lord?'

Incredulously, he turned his head and stared. She stood calmly just inside the closed door, pushing the sable hood back from her bright hair and unfastening the gold clasp at her throat. As she walked across the room to the hearth, she let the heavy velvet cloak fall from her shoulders to reveal a simple riding habit. There were no jewels in her hair or at her breast and her fingers were unadorned, save for the coronation ring which, like a wedding ring, never left her hand. It was as though she had deliberately stripped herself of all the accoutrements of majesty, but to his shocked and bewildered glance she had never looked more beautiful or truly regal as she stood looking down on him.

To sit in the Queen's presence, without her express permission, was an outrageous breach of etiquette and yet he went on sitting and staring in dazed and frozen silence, unable to move or speak or do anything to make use of this unimagined opportunity. It seemed an eternity before he managed to stumble out of his chair and fall on his knees at her feet, lifting the dark velvet hem of her skirts to his lips.

'Isn't it a little late to play the devoted subject, Robin?'

He buried his face in his hands and sobbed in a broken voice, 'Oh, God—I never expected this—I don't know what to do—I don't know what to say to you—'

'I suppose,' she said very softly, 'you could say you were sorry.'

There was something in her voice which gave him the courage to lift his eyes to hers and, as he did so, she held out her hands and helped him to get clumsily, unsteadily, to his feet. They stood very close, with their hands linked and their eyes locked together. He did not say he was sorry, there was suddenly no need.

'I can't believe it,' he mumbled inadequately, 'I can't believe you are here —you haven't ridden alone from Greenwich have you?'

She shook her head.

'Lady Warwick came with me, and a young groom I can trust to hold his tongue. No one else knows.'

'But why?' he whispered, not daring even now to hope. 'Why have you come to me?'

She bit her lower lip and laid her head against his shoulder.

'Don't you know?' she said.

For a long time they clung together wordlessly, while Leicester's dog regarded them curiously, with his big head on one side.

Slowly, silently, Leicester undressed her in the warm firelight, until at last she stood naked, with the velvet gown at her feet. He had seen her in various states of undress, but never entirely naked before and he stared in amazement, for her body was still a girl's, straight and slender and firm, white as alabaster. Shame touched him then, a poignant moment of regret that he could no longer offer the fine athlete's physique that had once been his. He had nothing to give her now but experience and skill learned in countless beds.

Oh God, let it be enough . . .

He carried her to the bed and laid her against the pile of pillows stamped with his crest. She lay very still, watching as he let his robe slip to the Turkey carpet. Her eyes travelled slowly down from his face to widen in an amusement that did not quite conceal her alarm.

'The complete man,' she mocked gently, 'is well equipped to meet every demand made upon him.'

He smiled as he lay beside her on the bed, for he was not deceived by her flippancy; he knew she was terrified. Beneath his caressing hand her heart was thumping like a hunted doe's and with some good reason, he admitted. For he had her now to use her entirely as he wished. There were no guards here—she had stripped herself naked of protection and placed herself at the mercy of his goodwill; and for years he had dreamed of raping her.

Yet suddenly, inexplicably, he no longer wished to do that; the desire to humble and degrade her flawless body might never have existed. He only wished to give and take such pleasure as no man and woman had ever found before in each other's bodies.

He loved her with knowledge and infinite tenderness, until her eyes were a soft gleam of urgent desire and the slow-built, shuddering fire could be contained no longer. The volcanic eruption of their love flooded them out of the universe, to a place where time and space had no meaning, where the outline of known things was dim and the world dwarfed within the four posters of this sacred bed. There was nothing but their quivering joy, enshrined for ever in the unimaginable significance of her surrender. She was his at last and his only, at the very moment when he had believed her lost to him for good; and he wondered why he had never seen before that the only way to win this woman was to break her pride and her heart.

When it was over, he cradled her in his arms and felt her tears on his cheeks.

'Don't cry,' he whispered. 'Next time there will be no pain.'

She laughed shakily against his shoulder.

'Was that pain? God preserve me then from joy!'

'I will show you such joy as you have never dreamed of.'

She turned to him and it was suddenly his turn to laugh. 'But not just yet,' he added hastily.

'Why not?' she pouted.

Hugely amused, he kissed her hair.

'You know remarkably little about men, except how to rule them with an iron hand,' he said gently. 'The male must rest a little before the next encounter.'

'So,' she sighed, 'one is not a flagpole, to be run up and down at a moment's notice.'

Oh, he could not believe this. She was like a kitten in his arms, soft and playful with all her claws sheathed, the Virgin Queen—a virgin no more. He could not imagine in that moment how he had ever gone in fear of her.

'Will it take long?' she inquired seriously.

'At least five minutes—if you can spare the time.' He pinned her firmly back in his arms. 'Lie still,' he commanded. 'You and I have many questions to answer first.'

Involuntarily, she shivered and hid her face against his powerful chest, listening to the steady beating of his heart. It had come so much sooner than she had feared, and she was suddenly touched with dread.

'Let's not ask questions, Robin,' she begged. 'Not just now.'

But he did not heed her, did not even notice how thin and anxious her voice had become. He was the master now and she was no longer the Queen, just the woman he had always wanted in his bed. He would never be afraid of her again and he would ask his question, because it had only one answer. He would hear her say it tonight, as he had longed to hear it for over twenty years.

'*Why did you come to me?*'

'*Because I love you.*'

She had to say it now—there was no escape from his arms. He pulled her close, and asked her; and for a long moment she was silent.

Even without answering directly, there was much she could tell him that would set his heart at rest. She could tell him how she had spent the long, lonely weeks of his banishment, whipping her resentment in the hope that her pain and rage would resolve itself into undying hatred. How every day that passed had been more empty than the last, so that with each hour the enormity of his crime receded before the bitter realization that there was no happiness without him. She could tell him how she had steeled herself to kill him and found she could not do it—how she had begun to believe and to hope that she would never do it now—for what more could he ever do against her than to turn away?

So many reasons, all of them true and none of them the right one. Something else had brought her submissive to his bed, an unshakeable decision made at the end of those weeks of misery. And this she must tell him now, because she could not hope to keep it from him; it concerned him intimately and he had to know.

But she was afraid to tell him, terrified of spoiling the only moment when their love had met. Given the choice, she would have been entombed in this bed, safe for eternity, crystallized in time within his arms. But time would not stand still for her, no matter how many clocks were stopped. It marched on relentlessly even now, stealing the magic moment away from her, while the unsaid words lay burning on her tongue. She lay stiff on the pillows, staring at the tester of the bed as though it were a sword suspended above her head. In all her life no single sentence had required such courage of her.

He repeated his question with a shade of aggression and she turned on her side to look at him.

'Because I am going to marry Alençon,' she said.

The tiny crystal of their love shattered in a million fragments as he slapped her face.

'You bitch!' he spat. 'You damned, unholy bitch! Was execution too good for me?'

She shrank away from him on the pillows, holding her cheek in dazed disbelief; even her darkest fear had not prepared her for the savagery of his reaction.

'Robin,' she sobbed. 'Oh, Robin, let me explain—'

'You don't need to explain—I understand!'

He caught her by the throat and began to shake her like a rag doll, his thumbs pressing on her windpipe in a murderous grip. In that moment, driven by an ecstasy of rage, he would have killed her without another thought, but the violence in his voice disturbed the big dog slumbering peacefully by the fire and the animal leapt up, baying like a hound at the hunt.

That sound, so sudden, so unexpected, so *loud*, was sufficient to penetrate

388

his dementia, distracting him in the final moment, as a man making love may be distracted by just such an interruption to his concentration. He threw her back on to the pillows and flung himself off the bed, cursing the dog into silence, kicking it brutally in the frenzy of his frustration. The dog yelped in hurt astonishment, slunk back to the hearth and flopped down with his head on his paws; and Leicester turned to look at Elizabeth, lying still where he had left her, with red marks like burns on the whiteness of her neck. He picked up the pile of clothes and flung them at her.

'Get out of here,' he shouted, his lips curled back like a snarling wolf. 'Get out of my bed and my house! Take your damned French prince and treat him as you've always treated me! He can accommodate your death wish without hanging for it!'

Pulling on his velvet robe, he turned his back on her as he would never dare to do before witnesses and went over to the hearth, draining the cup of wine which he had left there with one gulp. Boy sat up with a quick thump of his tail, cautiously pushing his nose into his master's hand and Leicester knelt and gathered the huge animal in his arms, burying his face in the thick bristling fur to shut out the sight of all that hurt him in that room.

For a long time there was silence broken only by a soft rustle of satin and the occasional whimper of the dog. Slowly Leicester lifted his head and looked round. Elizabeth was standing by the side of his bed, pulling at the fastenings of her gown with hopeless ineptitude. She, whose hand shaped the fate of Europe, had no more idea of how to dress herself than a small child, and for some unknown reason that sight cooled the last of his fury against her. For a moment more he savoured her clumsy struggle, then he went over and fastened the gown with his own hands. She did not flinch at his approach, nor at his touch and when he had finished, he turned her slowly about until she faced him.

'I almost killed you,' he said with a sort of dull wonder. 'Don't you realize that, you stupid woman?'

She smiled faintly and touched one of the bruises on her neck with a gesture that was almost satisfaction.

'I shall have to hide these marks from my women,' she said slowly. 'It won't be easy.'

He shook his head in amazement, recalling numerous occasions when she had turned on him like a vixen for a real or imagined fault, a wrong word, an ill-timed gesture. Even after all these years she could still surprise him, and he wondered if that was not the secret of her power over him, the real reason why in spite of everything he had never tired of her, as he would tire of every other woman in his life.

He put his hands on her shoulders and said with a touch of irony, 'Doesn't that concern you—just a little?'

She touched his pale cheek.

'I'm not going to punish you for it, if that's what you mean. I think you and I have punished each other quite enough.'

'If you marry Alençon—' he began belligerently.

She put her fingers on his lips to silence him.

'Not to spite you,' she said softly. 'To make it safe for us to be lovers at last. I want you to come back to court and support my marriage to the Duke—'

'What?'

'Oh, Robin, don't you see, there's no other way. When I bear your son no man shall dare to call him bastard.'

His hands slipped off her shoulders and hung lifelessly at his sides. He had met immorality many times—even indulged in it—but this was his first contact with amorality, and he was too amazed to be shocked.

'You are mad,' he said quietly, 'quite mad, if you think I will be party to such an arrangement.'

She sighed wearily. 'Is your pride to be greater than mine? If I can live with your wife, surely you can live with my husband. Bend a little, Robin— think of the child.'

'Oh, God, if that's all!' he burst out suddenly. 'How can you delude yourself like this? Christ, you're forty-five—the chances of your conceiving a first child at your age must be virtually non-existent.'

Her eyes narrowed into blazing slits of hostility. She could forgive him his marriage, even his physical assault on her, but that blow to her insane vanity was beyond the pale.

She was Queen again now, as taut and dangerous as a baited cat.

'You'll be sorry for that,' she said, and flinging her cloak around her shoulders she turned to go.

'Why?' He barred her path to the door and caught her arm. 'Because I'm the only man in England who dares to cross your will and tell you what you don't wish to hear?'

'Get out of my way—I was mad to come here! If you don't want your son to sit on the throne of England that's your loss, but mine will. I shall marry the Duke of Alençon and fill my womb with or without your aid.'

'Not while I live,' he said furiously. 'Not after tonight.'

She laughed in his face.

'You honestly think you can stand against me in this? Do so, if you dare!'

'Oh, I'll dare.' There was a note of deadly, acid calm in his voice now. 'I'll break your world in two like an apple before I stand by and see you marry another man. Leave me alive now and I'll split the Council, the court and the whole country on the issue. By God, I'll make things so hot you'll think you already burn in hell!'

'So be it!' She inclined her head curtly and there was silence, as after the formal challenge that precedes a duel.

She walked out of his room as an enemy; and from that moment on they were truly at war.

'Burghley!'

Halfway across the room, the Lord Treasurer turned back slowly to her desk and looked at her curiously.

'I have something to tell you and you had better sit down, it's going to come as a shock.'

He sat down and looked at her in sudden alarm.

'Your Majesty?' he prompted cautiously, as she rose and wandered away from him uneasily.

'This French marriage—I intend to make it.'

His mouth fell open, surrounded by a snow-white beard.

'But Your Majesty said—'

'Never mind what I said. I've changed my mind,' she retorted sharply. 'It's a woman's privilege, isn't it?'

He gave her a quick, suspicious glance, as though wondering whether this was another of her jokes, and read the steely determination in her eyes with a mixture of elation and concern. He got up stiffly and groped for her hand.

'Do you really mean this, madam?'

'Am I in the habit of saying things I don't mean?' she snapped and then, as suddenly, burst out laughing. 'No—don't answer that. Just bear in mind what I have told you and see the negotiations are conducted accordingly. We can expect opposition in Council from—from a certain quarter. I shall expect you to overrule it and guide the final verdict. Do you understand?'

He nodded grimly. It was not going to be easy.

'I shall do my best, Your Majesty.'

'I don't want your best, Burghley—I want my own way. And I expect *you* to see that I get it.'

'Yes, madam,' he muttered.

'That's all. You may go now,' she said curtly and turned away.

Alençon arrived at Greenwich shortly after dawn on an August morning which promised to be sultry. He was bundled unceremoniously into Simier's bed, still wearing doublet and hose, where he promptly fell asleep after his trying journey. Simier settled in the early morning light to scribble a note to the Queen, telling her how narrowly he had restrained the Duke from bursting into her bedchamber.

'. . . with great difficulty I got him to bed at last—' Simier eyed the sleeping lad with an ironical eye—'and I would to God you were with him there as he could then with greater ease convey his thoughts to you.'

Elizabeth received the note with unsmiling silence. She was in deadly earnest now and weary of exchanging indelicate innuendoes with Simier—when this business was concluded it would give her great pleasure to send the French ape packing.

It took the Ladies of the Bedchamber two hours to array their mistress for the first meeting and they were in a fine twitter of nerves as they fastened the long rope of pearls around the white neck, placed a small cartwheel ruff beneath the pointed chin, dressed her hair high and decked it with shimmering diamonds. They watched her stealthily for some sign of emotion, but she was calm and perfectly composed, her mood unfathomable.

When Alençon was led before her at length, her eyes smiled and coolly appraised him at the same time; she looked him up and down with the same calculating glance she might have given to a stud horse. She had expected nothing; she was not disappointed; he would serve her purpose. And at least he was not ugly and hunchbacked, as his enemies said. Plain and a little short in the leg, but the brown eyes were intelligent and sophisticated and they rested on her with a flattering look of relief.

Alençon could hardly believe his good luck. He had come with an air of martyrdom, prepared to marry a vain, middle-aged spinster for the sake of a crown, in much the same sort of mood as Philip of Spain had prepared to sacrifice himself in Mary Tudor's bed. He was pleasantly surprised by the woman who met his eyes. She was astonishingly well preserved for her age, tall and elegant with an indefinable air of majesty. So Simier had not been lulling him with the description he had sent home in despatches. He edged closer, his critical glance sweeping over her. The hair was a wig, but wigs were fashionable and worn by much younger women than the Queen. There was a network of fine lines around her striking eyes and a slight furrow on the high forehead, the result of years of terrible decisions and constant anxiety, but she was still a handsome woman by any count, and he was immediately conscious of her magnetism. He stayed for twelve days, playing the attentive suitor and at the end of those twelve days he was a lost man, raving to Simier of his good fortune.

'No delays, Jean. Whatever her terms—agree to them.'

Simier inclined his head dubiously.

'As you wish, my lord.'

'Forty-five,' murmured Alençon, shaking his head in slow disbelief. 'What's her secret, Jean—does she drink the blood of new-born babies? They say that works, you know—never fancied it myself, mind.'

Simier turned away abruptly.

'She devours *men*, my lord—and devours them whole.'

'Then I shall be gladly consumed. Get me back as soon as this damned country will allow, Jean—and when I'm gone, don't let her forget me.'

All the Duke's close attendants were aware of the change in their master. Alençon the rake, the cynic, the irrepressible little egotist, was behaving like a schoolboy in love for the first time. He wept when he took his leave of Elizabeth and a shower of passionate letters swamped her in his wake, enough, remarked the French Ambassador, Mauvissière, to set fire to water. A superb diamond betrothal ring glittered on her finger and Elizabeth quietly congratulated herself on uniting pure political gain with personal ends in a masterly fashion. She had ignored her physical needs for more than twenty years, allowing the interests of the state to supersede them, while she squeezed every last ounce of benefit from the marriage game. She had surmounted the huge emotional obstacle in her path at last and she felt entitled to a taste of happiness. Now and then in the quietness of her room she had an odd, uneasy memory of an empty cradle rocking forlornly in the corner of an empty nursery, but she pushed it aside and refused to dwell on it. It was absurd to even think of comparing herself with her sister Mary. There *would* be a child and she would survive its birth, as she had survived everything else —threat of execution, smallpox, even poison. Did she not possess the luck of the Devil?

But England refused to share her optimism and the Duke had scarcely left when the inevitable discontent, vigorously fanned by Leicester and his associates, broke out in a dangerous outcry. A widely circulated and intensely loyal pamphlet told her none too politely that though she was the 'crowned nymph of England' she was too old and too delicate to be thinking of children and that her suitor was no less than the 'old serpent himself' and his advances 'unman-like, unprince-like'.

The pamphlet was an open insult to France, and Elizabeth was savage with anger. There was nothing for it but to reassure the Duke of her good intentions and she ordered every copy to be seized, condemning the author and the publisher to suffer the public loss of their right hands. More cruel and vindictive than anyone had yet seen her, she declared it a pity the author could not be hanged, and she remained unmoved when they told her that when the deed had been done he had promptly pulled off his cap with his left hand and shouted 'God save the Queen'.

She affected to be unconcerned by the incident, but inwardly it had deeply unnerved her. She woke in alarm for several nights and fancied that a bloody hand was pulling the fringed coverlet on her bed. Always profoundly aware of public opinion, she now sensed the need for firm support from her advisers and in October she formally asked for the advice of her Council. For twenty years they had begged her to marry, and she expected them to beg her now, confident that Burghley could control the divisions in spite of Leicester's virulent opposition.

The Council sat, and went on sitting in sterile argument on a cold October day from seven in the morning until eight at night, without stirring from the room to take food or drink or to answer the calls of nature, until at last five were for the marriage. And seven against it.

For once all Burghley's elderly, assured leadership seemed to fail him in the bitter debate and it was as much as he could do to keep an open verdict. His hostile glance reached across the table and was mirrored in Leicester's dark eyes and for a moment it was as though the old wounds of personal enmity had never healed. The meeting concluded in the general agreement that the Queen must make her own decision on the issue and there was a dignified stampede for the privy.

The following morning they waited on the Queen—Burghley, Sussex, Hatton, and Leicester—a sombre, uneasy little group who knew their message would not please.

'Well, gentlemen?'

Burghley cleared his throat and stared at the floor. Suddenly he could not look her in the eye.

'The Council feels that as a whole, madam, it cannot advise you on this matter.'

'*Cannot* advise me!' She stood up and her steady hawk's eyes blazed black and hard. Each councillor felt a terrible sinking feeling in the pit of his stomach and Leicester's dark face turned pale and tense.

'God's death, you call yourself my Council and dare to come in here and say you cannot advise me!'

'Madam.' It was Sussex, anxious, trying to avert the storm he saw gathering. 'If the Council only knew your own feelings on the matter—'

She laughed shortly, bitterly, and turned away from him.

'My feelings! Which one among you has ever thought to consider them? I looked for a unanimous request for me to proceed with the marriage. You surely will not dare to say you doubt the wisdom of continuing my father's line with a child of my own body!'

Their silent, doubting faces looked back at her blankly and she clenched her hands into fists. How dared they haggle and barter over her as though she were a barren cow for whom no good price could be found. Christ's soul, the insolence—the mealy-mouthed self-righteous insolence of these little men who surrounded her, whom she had made and could as easily ruin by lifting one finger. Little men, little men! What would they be without her?

'I was a fool to ever consult you all in the first place.' There was a curious, choked sound to her voice as she flung out her hands to them in despair. 'Why am I alone to be denied children? I want a child—is there no man among you who can understand that?'

Suddenly she began to cry, wild, hopeless sobs that shook her frame and made her hide her face from them. Instinctively Leicester would have stepped towards her, but Hatton laid a restraining hand on his arm and shook his head quickly. They all stood in helpless silence, not knowing what to say or do—it was so unlike her!

Aware of their acute embarrassment, she walked to the window, wiping the back of her hand angrily across her cheek, infuriated with them, but more infuriated with herself.

'Get out,' she said. 'All of you—come back this afternoon.'

She watched them go in stony silence.

Leicester was the last and for a moment he hesitated in the doorway as though wondering if he dared to make some gesture of sympathy after what he had done.

Abruptly, contemptuously she turned her back on him and he left in silence; and when at last she knew she was alone, she sank into a chair at the table and buried her face in the jewelled brocade of her monstrously puffed sleeves.

No sooner had the great double doors swung shut than a row broke out among the fiercely opposed councillors, all shaken by what was obviously a very genuine reaction on the part of their mistress.

'Satisfied are you now, Leicester?' Sussex taunted him bitterly. 'Haven't you done enough against her lately?'

'I never expected that—never! I thought—'

'We all know what you thought, Leicester—I thank God now Her Majesty knows too.'

'I opposed this marriage from the soundest of political motives only. If you are trying to imply what took place in there gave me any personal pleasure—'

'Gentlemen! I hardly think this is the time or the place for a brawl.'

Burghley banged his walking stick on the floor and the two rivals subsided into angry silence. He fixed Leicester with an icy, authoritative stare and the Earl flushed darkly, removed himself haughtily from their group and stalked away.

But he had won. Long before they returned that afternoon, Elizabeth had admitted that to herself as she stared moodily into the harsh reflection in her mirror, and saw the pale, sad face of defeat. To marry now without the full support of her Council, in the teeth of her people's opposition, would be to make the same mistake her sister and her cousin had made and place her own interests before those of the state. Selfish and self-willed as she was in lesser matters, her vow of service to England transcended everything and she knew she could not do it. As she sat and accepted the final sacrifice of her womanhood, she reined in the corroding resentment that threatened the whole purpose of her life. She must not hate England, that nameless, faceless mass of people who were the strength of her throne; and in reality it was far more easy, if unfair, to pin the blame on Leicester, who had given her that womanhood at last and then denied her its fulfilment for his own petty personal reasons. *Men!* They were all the same at heart, as she had always known—self-righteous and possessive, like her father, incapable themselves of the fidelity they demanded of their women.

Oh, what a fool she had been to go to him that night at Wanstead. How much easier it would have been to bear this defeat without the bitter-sweet memory of his body beating in hers, reminding her so poignantly of what she had lost, of all that she would never know. He would pay for what he had made her suffer today—oh, God, he would pay! She knew exactly how to punish him, not with disgrace or exile, but by her refusal to re-live that encounter at Wanstead. He thought he had conquered—he was mistaken! She had lived the past twenty years without his love—she could live the next twenty; not happily, perhaps, but at least with her pride intact.

That night when her women drew the curtains around the state bed, she felt the act to be deeply symbolic—the Maiden Queen shut up in a prison of her own making, trapped for ever in the mirror image of a virgin goddess. The silence of the room oppressed her and, when her women had withdrawn, she sat up and reached for her hand-mirror, seeing not her own reflection, but the life she had chosen for herself, stretching out bleakly into infinity.

She was not going to marry Alençon, yet she must go on convincing him and the rest of the world that she would, until she had used him in the Netherlands to contain Philip's aggression. The pretence must continue, perhaps for more than a year, and she must not seem indifferent to it, even for a moment, but must go on acting a lie, as all her life she seemed to have been acting, first one role, then another, until now she scarcely knew the real woman underneath. All through the summer of her reign, she had wrapped the layers of deceit more tightly round herself and enjoyed the game, like a child playing in the hot sun at noon. But now the sun was lower in the sky, lower and cooler, casting shadows on a path where once there had been only light. And in the shadows, with the chill breath of autumn already in the air, she chose to walk away from the only fire that could give her warmth.

It was a hard decision, and a hard, embittered woman made it, punishing herself to punish another and warping the fibres of her soul. The seeds of resentment were sown in her that night, a resentment which would grow rapidly out of all proportion, until the mere mention of love and marriage among her intimates would be sufficient to lash her into a vindictive fury.

She sat very still, staring into the mirror, and slowly became aware of her own face, so terribly altered that she could only gaze at it with shocked resignation. Thin lips set in a cruel line, eyes harsh with suspicion, shadowed with paranoia—her father's face, the face of a tyrant.

She laid the mirror on the table beside her bed with a trembling hand and stared a moment at the small square of Venetian glass, immeasurably expensive, a gift from abroad. Then she took up the silver candle-holder and brought it down in a single savage blow that splintered her reflection into a million lethal shards.

PART FOUR

The Goddess

'What a pity it is that Elizabeth and I cannot marry . . .
our children would have ruled the world.'
POPE SIXTUS V

CHAPTER 1

Plymouth harbour had changed little in the three years since Francis Drake last set eyes upon it—it was just as dirty and disorganized as he fondly remembered. Well—he was none too clean himself if it came to that, and who would have guessed that his little ship with its shabby paintwork could now lay claim to being the most celebrated vessel in Europe?

Fame sat awkwardly on Drake's shoulders, interfering with his personal freedom to scratch and belch and fart whenever the mood took him. Such things were unacceptable at court, and the court was the final destination of his incredible journey. He had circumnavigated the globe, but there was, regrettably, no way he could possibly hope to reach the Queen's presence by circumnavigating a bath.

Still, it was a small price to pay, he supposed ruefully, in return for a knighthood. The Queen had been the principal investor in his enterprise; and now with the hold of the *Golden Hind* packed with loot plundered from Spanish and Portuguese ships in the Pacific, a cargo of silver and jewels worth over one and a half million ducats, the principal investor stood to gain over a hundred per cent on her outlay.

A sound businesswoman—Drake had never been in any doubt of it—her only condition that he should keep her name out of it. He had always understood that if he fell into Spanish hands she would be obliged to publicly disassociate herself from his activities; but if he came back in triumph, he would have his just reward. And so, he was for the court, to kiss the fair hand of the glittering chameleon who had sent him out upon this venture, a woman half goddess, half guttersnipe, whom he was privileged to call his friend. He thought of the blatant acts of piracy with which he had filled his hold and of the Spaniards' outraged demands for restitution and reprisals; finally he thought of the Queen's pale avaricious face—and found himself cheerfully secure in his arrogance.

*   *   *

Don Bernadino de Mendoza was perhaps the most volatile and vinegar-faced ambassador ever to come out of Spain, eminently unsuitable for the briefest of diplomatic encounters with Elizabeth. It was a matter of common knowledge that these two could not bear the sight and sound of each other and no one was surprised when Mendoza took up the cudgels on behalf of the Spaniards' treasure with his usual crass obstinacy.

He marched forcefully into the Queen's presence, determined to have his say, and found himself unable to get a word in edgeways. Elizabeth sat on her throne like a graven image, and looked down on him with distaste, as though he were something particularly nasty that had just crawled out of the rushes. She began to complain haughtily of Philip's interference in Irish affairs. When Mendoza produced a written apology from his master for that gross breach of international etiquette, she would be prepared to discuss the matter further. Until then, she regretted she would be unable to receive the ambassador again. A wave of her hand—and Mendoza was standing outside her closed door, opening and shutting his mouth, with a speechless rage that made him look as vacant as a fish.

Barred from the Queen's presence, Mendoza skulked about the court, gleaning information from his spies. He heard that the Lords Burghley and Sussex had discreetly declined to partake of the treasure, too principled to be seen as the receivers of stolen goods. The Queen, who never allowed scruples to interfere with business, welcomed Drake to court at Christmas and showered him with attention. Drake, in his turn, commissioned London jewellers to fashion a fantastic crown set with a vast quantity of pilfered diamonds and five enormous emeralds, which she shamelessly paraded about the court on New Year's Day—Mendoza swore to himself that she was the greatest pirate of them all!

In April she went down to Deptford to dine with Drake on board the *Golden Hind* itself, for the greatest banquet which had been seen since the days of that famous gourmand, her father, making her support of the rogue more flagrantly public than ever and taking with her, for diplomatic protection, the Duke of Alençon's confidential agent, Marchaumont, a subtle reminder to Spain that England was far from friendless.

As she stepped on board, one of her purple and gold garters slipped off and Marchaumont promptly pounced on it and held it up before her horrified gaze, saying impudently, 'Madam, I claim this as a forfeit. You must permit me to send this to the Duke as a love token.'

She glanced sideways to where her maids of honour stood blushing on her behalf, and decided there was nothing to do but laugh and carry the situation off with an immodest high hand.

'You shall have it as a token,' she said, snatching it back, 'but not just yet. I've nothing else to keep my stocking up with.'

There in full view of polished courtiers and hardened seamen, she promptly extended a slender silk-stocking leg and tied the garter back on herself, deliberately prolonging the moment for their amused appreciation. The applause, warm and manly, started among Drake's crew and spread instantly, like bush fire, along the deck. Marchaumont applauded too and laid her hand upon his arm with amused respect. Oh, one had to get up very early to catch this woman at a loss—he would be the first to admit it.

The festivities would end with the knighting of Drake—everyone knew it. Yet when her favourite pirate knelt on one knee before her with his curly head bent, Elizabeth fingered the sword thoughtfully and frowned.

'Francis Drake, you are a rogue and for the sake of my honour I wash my hands of you.'

All around the crowd an indrawn breath of shock; Drake lifted his head uncertainly to look at her and in that moment she turned swiftly and handed the sword to the Frenchman at her side.

'But I am sure,' she continued innocently, 'that Monsieur Marchaumont will be happy to perform the accolade for me.'

It was a clever move, implying French approval of Drake's activities, and Marchaumont, neatly cornered in a public place, had no choice but to go along with her outrageous demand.

Mendoza was duly infuriated. The diplomatic impasse continued till October, when he received curt word that the Queen would see him at two o'clock that afternoon. The message was served with such short notice, that Mendoza was obliged to rush a meal and take a barge for Richmond at once. Arriving with time to spare, he went up the water steps and into the palace where some jumped-up official in the Presence Chamber informed him that he was late for his audience. Mendoza took out his time-piece pointedly and examined it with compressed lips, but the usher only shrugged insolently and opened the door to announce him.

In the room beyond, Mendoza found the Queen lying on a cushioned couch and he checked in astonishment. There was a pinched look to her face which suddenly caused him to feel positively genial as he bowed over her hand.

'Good afternoon, madam. I trust I find you well.'

'You do not,' she announced peevishly. 'I have been troubled by a pain in my hip for several days.'

The look which accompanied this implied: *And you are to blame for it, as you are for everything.* She had actually screamed that at him during a previous meeting.

He schooled his expression into appropriate lines of sympathy.

'I'm sorry to see you suffering, madam.'

'Yes,' she said ironically, 'I have no doubt you would arrange a very speedy end to all my sufferings were it in your power to do so, Mendoza.'

He did not answer that, knowing how near the truth it was, and their interview minced along the usual irritable lines, winding its way inevitably to the question of the Spanish treasure. Mendoza, at first patient, became patronizing and belligerent in quick succession. He begged leave to point out that the patience of His Most Catholic Majesty, though great, was not without its limits. He begged leave to remind her—

Elizabeth sat upright on the couch, with two bright spots of colour flaming into her thin face.

'Hold your damned rattling tongue, you insolent minion—I will hear no more!'

Something snapped in Mendoza. After all these months of holding his temper in bare restraint, he began to shout like a hysterical woman.

'Then if you will not listen to words, madam, you may shortly hear cannon in their place!'

Her eyes narrowed suddenly and riveted his as she leaned forward a little from her cushions.

'Speak to me like that once more, my friend,' she said softly, 'and I will put you in a place from which you will not speak again.'

She meant it—he could see that. Diplomatic immunity would count for nothing with this woman if she were pushed too far. The steely hold of her eyes battered down the last of his defences and in a moment of stark terror, he began to flatter her, fingering his ruff with a nervous gesture, smiling uneasily, and curbing an urgent desire to urinate.

'Your Majesty has misunderstood my meaning—I spoke in jest, merely to take your mind off your pain. No threat was intended—indeed no. Who would wish to gainsay such a beautiful lady as Your Highness?'

The eyes released their hold and permitted him to step back from the precipice. There was an acrid tang of sweat emanating suddenly from his clothing and she held her pomander pointedly to her nose when she dismissed him.

As he bowed stiffly and backed out, he reflected on the depth of his hatred for her. It seemed to have taken control of his whole personality, colouring and dominating every aspect of his existence. There were times—today was one of them—when he could cheerfully have daggered her without pausing to consider the cost. His only comfort was the certain knowledge that her days were numbered—Spain, the Papacy, the Guise party in France, she could not hold them off her trembling throne much longer. It was a miracle she had lived so long.

It was true that many of her Catholic subjects remained loyal to her—the English had no *zeal*, it was his continual complaint! Yet Mendoza knew that the Council lived in daily dread of a Catholic assassination, and deplored the moderation to which the Queen had clung throughout her reign. The act of conversion to the Catholic faith had been made illegal since Elizabeth's excommunication and in that measure lay the core of Mendoza's hopes. In Douai, the famous Jesuit College was presently training a whole new batch of young priests for their calling in England; and once this formidable, dedicated band had infiltrated the country, their avowed mission would be to sweep a wave of conversion across the land. Faced with a steady growth in the numbers of English Catholics, Mendoza knew that Parliament would panic, raising a clamour for harsher measures which even the Queen could no longer ignore. There would be active persecution at last, and under persecution even the most loyal and docile Catholic might be prepared to put an end to England's cunning Jezebel.

Mendoza went out of Elizabeth's presence convinced that her charmed life was in sight of its end, and determined to further that end himself by any means available to him. In the doorway he almost collided with the Earl of Leicester, who smiled and bowed with mock civility, receiving in return a salutation so curt it was almost a snarl.

Leicester went across the room and eyed the Queen cautiously before sitting uninvited on the arm of her couch. Although she had been expecting him and showed pleasure at his arrival, he was never entirely sure of his welcome these days. The final departure of Alençon for his armed mission in the Netherlands had made her more unpredictable than ever and Leicester, above anyone else at court, found it necessary to tread very gingerly around her moods.

'Something appears to have bitten Mendoza,' he looked at her shrewdly, 'or would it be nearer to the truth to say *someone?*'

Elizabeth sank her teeth into a fruit sucket and smiled.

'He is a trifle ruffled, I grant you. Probably consequent on the fact that he just declared war.'

'War?' Leicester stared down at her in alarm. 'You mean *real* war?'

Elizabeth laughed shortly. 'I don't imagine even Mendoza would dare to threaten me with toy soldiers!'

She sat upright on the couch and Leicester sank down into the space she had made for him, looking extremely shaken.

'Good God!' he muttered, studying her face with anxiety. 'This could be serious.'

'Oh, I don't think so. I'm afraid Philip simply won't oblige him in the matter, not while I continue to hold Mary under lock and key. Poor Mendoza will have to ease his spleen by sticking pins into my wax effigy a little longer.'

Recalling the ambassador's expression of demonic rage, Leicester was uneasy. Like most men of his age, he had a very healthy respect for all manifestations of witchcraft and he did not take such an accusation lightheartedly.

'If you really think that then the Spanish dog ought to be arrested and sent packing.'

Elizabeth sighed.

'I can't expel Mendoza without indisputable evidence that he intends me harm—and I don't have any evidence.'

Except, this stupid pain in my hip . . . which in anyone else I might call rheumatism, only of course I know it's not . . . it couldn't be . . . by God, I'll hang the first doctor who dares to even suggest it . . .

She stood up with slight difficulty and the great drum farthingale flung out a wide sweep of pearl-encrusted skirts about her hips.

'Don't lose any sleep over Mendoza, Robin. If that spineless little turd was really capable of doing me any mischief he'd have done it by now, I promise you.'

'And the treasure?'

'The treasure stays.' She smiled suddenly. 'Only consider how it would distress dear Francis if I returned it.'

'Quite,' conceded Leicester drily. 'And we mustn't upset dear Francis must we?—I thought you were going to hang the knave!'

'I will, when I find a piece of rope long enough to do it.' Elizabeth glanced out of the window where the sun was peeping sulkily through patches of cloud. 'Saddle that new gelding for me, Robin, and we'll ride out in the park when I've changed my gown.'

As she walked away from him towards the Privy Chamber, he suddenly noted the slight, but unmistakable, limp which marred her old graceful carriage and the sight made him frown.

'Madam,' he called after her quickly, 'let us play cards or backgammon instead—it will be more restful.'

She stopped abruptly with her back still towards him and every muscle in her body tensed with sudden fury. She had been confident it didn't show, would have sworn she could defy the most observant eye to pick out that one tiny, disabling detail so symbolic in her mind of encroaching age. But he had noticed—the one person in all the world from whom she would have died to conceal it!

'*Restful?*' She repeated the word slowly as though it was an obscenity and wheeled round to fix him with a look of absolute loathing. 'It's not rest I need, Robert Dudley, but exercise. And be assured I'll find it with a man who's nimbler on his feet these days than you are!'

The door of the Privy Chamber slammed in his face and he sat down on the couch with rueful resignation. She had not forgiven him for Alençon and there were times when he felt she never would. He never knew for sure now just when she would turn on him without warning or provocation; since the birth of his son to Lettice she had been downright hostile on occasions. Once she had appointed his old enemy, Sussex, to inquire into his previous liaison with Douglass Sheffield, seeking proof of a pre-contract which would automatically invalidate his union with her cousin. There had been no proof, thank God, and the matter had served no purpose other than to make him look an absolute fool in the eyes of the court and drive Lettice into a transport of vindictive rage. For some considerable time his home life had been conducted in frigid silence, and he knew in his heart that that result had been the Queen's only motive in the whole distasteful affair. Yet, curiously, he could not hate her for it. In a warped way, it had made him love her all the more, for he was satisfied that her attempts to humiliate him made her suffer at a far deeper level than he did himself. He had a family and she had nothing—nothing but the crown which had cost her so dear in terms of private happiness. In spite of his bondage, he had snatched a small part of his life back from her, setting up one petty boundary beyond which she could never pass. He felt able to cope with whatever she might choose to do against him, for he understood that she was a deeply unhappy woman. And because of that understanding, he found he was able to forgive her a great deal.

The Parliament of 1581 was, as Mendoza had anticipated, panic-stricken at the rising level of recusants. Elizabeth was faced by a bill which prescribed the death penalty for anyone found guilty of converting a subject to the Church of Rome. She moderated it as far as she dared without alienating Parliament, insisting that conversion itself was treasonable only if accompanied by withdrawal of allegiance to her; but she was forced to accept that recusants should be taxed out of existence by staggering fines, far beyond the reach of the majority of her Catholic subjects. She didn't like it and she made no secret of the fact, but Burghley had made it plain that there was now no choice.

In May of that year the most famous Jesuit priest of all entered England. Edmund Campion had once been Leicester's cultured protégé and had stepped in court circles, basking in the warmth of the Queen's friendship and favour; but now he travelled through England like a hunted fugitive. For over a year he eluded all Walsingham's efforts to capture him and his stature and reputation soared in the eyes of the Catholic population as he slipped from village to village, ministering secretly to the spiritual needs of the persecuted. He was doing more than the entire Jesuit force to put heart into the Church of Rome in England and his supporters were beginning to think him invulnerable, when Walsingham's spies finally took him on a hot July day from a priest's hole in Berkshire and imprisoned him in the Tower.

Elizabeth stood very still in the window embrasure, twisting the coronation ring that of late had begun to grow uncomfortably tight on her finger. Leicester, who had brought the bad news to her, stood beside her, glad even of this tragedy which had suddenly brought them so close together.

'It had to happen,' he said softly, 'sooner or later. With Walsingham's spies all over the country it was inevitable. I didn't find out until today or I would have told you sooner—they put him in Little Ease to make him talk.'

'What!' The Queen swung round and stared at him. Little Ease was a grim hole at the far end of the Torture Chamber in the bowels of the Tower, so built that a man could neither stand nor lie full length. Sunk in utter darkness, crouched in the foul reek of their own filth, men had gone blind and raving mad in Little Ease, reduced to poor gibbering wrecks, covered from head to foot with lice and sores. And Edward Campion had once been their trusted friend—

'How long has he been there?' she asked furiously.

Leicester swallowed and looked out of the window.

'Four days—so Walsingham said.'

'Four days! By God, I'll break that damned Puritan's neck!'

Leicester caught her hand as she moved to walk past him.

'You can't blame Walsingham, madam—he's only doing his job—and doing it well, you have to admit.'

She compressed her lips with rage. 'Yes! Thanks to him my prisons have never been so busy, nor my streets so full of gibbets—and that shrivelled spider gloats over every new victim, I swear he does. Well, he won't add Campion to his list—I shall write out an order for his immediate release.'

'Madam, you know that can't be done unless he recants and forswears the Pope's authority—do you want riots in the streets?'

Elizabeth sank on to the window seat and bit her lip. He was right of course—Parliament would expect her to make an example of such a famous man. After a moment she looked up uncertainly.

'Suppose we were to see him—you and I as old friends. Suppose we persuade him to affirm his loyalty by one attendance at a Protestant service—'

'Yes—yes, by God, you're right, madam! Even Walsingham would admit it's worth a try for a man of such public standing.'

She stood up and the sunlight turned her curls to burnished copper.

'I don't give a damn for Walsingham's opinion—or even Burghley's in this instance! If Campion yields just one iota to show his good faith, he can say Mass in St Paul's Cathedral for all I care! How soon can you arrange the meeting, Robin?'

Leicester frowned and examined the watch which hung on a golden chain around his neck.

'Well—he can't be brought to court. It would have to be my house in the Strand—say this evening?—and there would have to be witnesses of course—Burghley and one or two other members of the Council.'

She nodded and touched his arm with gratitude.

'See to it then. And when he recants, I'll bring him back to court in my own barge.'

For a moment Leicester regarded her steadily in the harsh July sunlight, disquieted by her sudden optimism. Campion had been a member of his own household. He had known the man very well before his defection to Rome, rather more closely than the Queen had, and what he remembered most vividly about him was his absolute integrity and stubborn sense of right. Suddenly, in Leicester's own eyes, the outcome seemed frankly less than hopeful.

'Madam,' he began slowly, 'if we fail to move him in his resolution, pardon will be out of the question. The Catholics will take it as a sign of weakness and that is the last thing we dare to show at the moment. You do understand that, don't you?'

She turned her head away from him and looked out of the window.

'When I want Walsingham's advice I will hear it from his lips,' she said curtly. 'Go now and make the necessary arrangements.'

He bowed and left her.

The hours that Campion had spent cramped in a space rather less generous than a coffin would afford had bent and stiffened his joints. He stumbled when they dragged him out and poured cold water over his naked body, scraping the caked filth from his skin. Dried and dressed in rags, he was bundled into the waiting barge, bent double between his guards like an old man, and he blinked in the cool dusk of the summer evening as the plain prison barge floated down the dirty river.

They landed at the water stairs among a flurry of swans and he looked up at the great house silhouetted against the clear sky, the roof rising in four gables, terminating at the eastern end in a battlemented tower which made the building resemble a church. Campion felt a wave of shock flood through him. Leicester's town house! Surely he was not to be granted the privilege of seeing his old friend and patron after all this!

As he mounted the stairway, his reeling senses recorded the fleeting, familiar glimpses of portraits and furniture and the smooth, polished wood of the banisters beneath his gaunt fingers. At the top of the staircase, the heavy double doors swung open before him and momentarily he was dazzled by the blaze of candles from the room within. At last his eyes focused on a small group of soberly clad gentlemen standing around an oak table, equipped with pen and ink. Beyond them he saw Leicester and beside him, in absolute disbelief, he recognized the Queen, dressed in black satin blazing with diamonds, a fantastic stiffened ruff framing her thin face. He noted that the blazing hair was a wig, the face a mask of skilfully applied paint and he was reminded of a wax effigy. She no longer looked quite real and he failed to identify the gay, laughing woman who had dazzled him with her attention more than fifteen years before. Leicester, too, he scarcely recognized with his silver-grey hair, ruddy face and considerable girth, the penalty of too many years of good living and unrestrained indulgence at the table. He felt a little shock of pity for them both, two glittering but jaded personalities who had lost their immortal souls for a ride on fortune's wheel.

The Queen came a step towards him and held out a long pale hand which shimmered with huge gems in the candlelight; as he knelt to kiss it, he closed his eyes and felt time roll back in his feverish memory fifteen years . . .

Hot sunlight playing on the stately stone buildings of Christchurch, church bells pealing in mad welcome, the high-pitched Latin paean of young boys' voices:

Vivat Regina! Vivat Regina!

Edmund Campion had shouted as loud as anyone in that crowd for the red-haired Queen whose reputation as a scholar was a byword in Oxford. Leicester lifted her down from the litter and the President of Magdalen College, that notorious Puritan, hurried forward to kiss her hand. She smiled her charming smile and admired his outfit.

'Loose gowns become you, Doctor—how sad that your opinions should be so narrow.'

A ripple of laughter ran through the students as her words were picked up, repeated and passed on, and Campion had been close enough to see the hated President blush hotly. The Queen's eyes, dancing with sly and subtle humour, had made the young man burn with desire to capture her amused attention.

Later, in the long round of intellectual debates, his chance came. He had prepared a brilliant paper on the influence of the moon upon the tides and all the time he spoke he was aware of those eyes upon him, keen with interest. When he had finished she smiled and beckoned him to her side, where the Earl of Leicester still stood, tall, magnificently dressed, flat-stomached as an athlete.

'You speak too well, sir, to be lost among this crowd again.'

'Robin, surely you can find a place for him?'

'It would be a pleasure, madam.'

'And your name, sir?'

'Edmund Campion, madam—Your Majesty's most loyal and devoted servant.'

'Edmund Campion, do you acknowledge me as your Queen?' The panelled room rushed back into his sight. The Queen's voice was harder and harsher than he remembered it, as though the long years had worn away some of its musical intonation. Looking up into her face he saw she no longer had laughing eyes.

'I acknowledge you as my Queen.' He paused, and added firmly, 'As my lawful Queen.'

'Then it is not your belief that the Pope may lawfully excommunicate and depose me?' she continued eagerly.

His eyes flickered but did not leave her face.

'Madam, it is not for me to judge between Your Majesty and His Holiness.'

She sighed and made a quick movement to still Lord Burghley who had leaned forward to ask the vital question upon which the man's life hung.

'Campion, long ago I believe we were friends. My lord of Leicester showed you great favour, did he not?'

'He did indeed, madam, and I was deeply grateful for it.'

'Your gratitude has taken a strange form—defection to Rome—treason,' she said softly.

'Madam, there has never been any treason in my heart. I am a priest. My mission is to save souls, not to engage in seditious activities.'

His eyes as they rested on her face were gentle and humorous, and even now she could not quite see them as those of a fanatic or a martyr. So much wit and humour in that rather gallant frame would have brought him the Presidency of St. John's, if not a bishopric in the English Church, had not his sudden and unlooked for defection to Rome ruined a promising career, making him an outcast and a fugitive in his native land. If he recanted now he would be a trophy for the Protestant Church. His example would weaken the roots of the entire Jesuit mission and prove that more could be gained by reason and bribery, than by harsh, repressive laws which shed the blood of the guilty and the innocent without distinction.

'Lord Burghley will ask you one question,' she said gently. 'Think well before you answer.'

The question, a device of Burghley's, was to earn the title of 'the bloody question' because there was no reasonable answer that could satisfy both the demands of the state and the demands of the Roman faith.

Burghley cleared his throat and Campion turned to look at him with quiet respect, then bowed his head.

'If the Pope should send an army to depose Her Majesty, Edmund Campion—what would you do?'

There was a pause, a moment of breathless stillness in the evening air.

'My lord, I would do as God should give me grace.'

Burghley grunted and pressed his lips together in vexation at time wasted on a fool. The man had signed his own death warrant and as far as Burghley was concerned there was no more to be said. Instinctively he began to tidy the papers on the desk before him and had opened his mouth to summon the guards, when the Queen shook her head and held up her hand in a quick, commanding gesture.

'One moment, my lord. Rise, Campion, and look at me.'

He did as he was bidden and she held out both her hands to him once more. Automatically he knelt at her feet, pressing her fingers fervently to his lips as though in mute apology.

'You mean me no harm, I know that, but you must recognize the threat you present to the English Church and through that, the state. I have a proposition to make to you and I hope you will listen.' Over Campion's head she saw Burghley stir indignantly and ignored him, concentrating all her will and all her charm on the man who knelt at her feet. 'All I ask is that you show your goodwill publicly by attending one Protestant service. I give you my word it need only be one and that you will be free to worship as you please after that, in total freedom. Campion, I believe you to be a good and gentle man. I am asking you to prevent bloodshed in this land we both love.'

She was clever, he admitted that, very very clever and the quiet, sane, pleading voice brought him to the very brink of spiritual chaos. It would be so easy to do what she wanted in the spirit of self-justification, to bend a little to the wind of necessity, and say—*What does it really matter?* Just once! Just once, she said, and looked at him almost tenderly, as though she really cared, with just enough weariness in her eyes to make him ashamed of laying yet another burden on her shoulders. She knew exactly how to play on a man's feelings; she was not ashamed of emotional blackmail and he could feel himself sliding effortlessly into her trap, lured to the rocks by a siren's voice.

He opened his mouth to agree and closed it again, seeing the rocks on which his soul would be torn asunder just in time. He would not barter his place in Heaven to buy a little extra time on earth and spend it in comfort.

'Madam, forgive me,' he said gently, 'I cannot do as you ask.'

She withdrew her hands from his and let them fall into her lap in despair as the summer evening darkened steadily beyond the tall casements. The reasons of state and the reasons of faith had met and clashed and fallen apart, irreconcilable. Campion, like Sir Thomas More in her father's day, remained the Queen's good servant—but God's first. There was nothing more to be said. She could not help him now.

She snapped her fingers curtly. At Leicester's command the guards returned to remove the prisoner and in his wake the council members filed silently from the room, leaving the Queen alone with her host.

Elizabeth walked to the empty hearth, laid a hand on the chimney-piece, and leaned her forehead against it. Leicester watched her for a moment in silence, staring at the high lace collar which stood out around her shoulders, hiding her jewelled hair from view. Presently he came up behind her and put his hands on her shoulders.

'Don't reproach yourself—you did everything you could to save him.'

She shook her head.

'I could offer him nothing he held important.'

'You offered him his life,' said Leicester firmly, 'and if that's not important to a man, I'm damned if I know what is! He's brought this on his own head and, fond as I was of the fellow, I can't say it surprises me. Since I first knew him he was a stubborn devil.'

'But not a traitor.'

Leicester frowned. This was exactly the reaction he had feared.

'Madam, according to law—'

'I know the law!' she said irritably, moving away from him. 'God knows I ought to—I made it! And may God forgive me for it.'

'Elizabeth—'

'No—don't humour me! Don't cozen me with your logic. There is no way

I can escape the consequences of what I have done. When I came to the throne, this land was sick with religious persecution. I hated it then and I hate it now. How many more loyal men am I to lose through this bigoted madness?'

'For every one who is loyal there may be five waiting to strike,' said Leicester patiently. 'Nothing disturbs me more than your belief that the increase of Catholics in this country can be no danger to you. They are saying in Europe that the Pope has given England to anyone who will undertake to go and get it. The danger to your life—'

'Oh, my life!' She swung round upon him contemptuously. 'Is my life really worth all this?'

He put his hand gently beneath her chin and raised her face to his.

'Your life,' he said slowly, 'the continuance of your reign, is the only thing that matters now in England. And if it costs the death of Campion and a thousand like him, it will be worth it. You are the rightful Queen of England.'

'In English law,' she said steadily, 'I am illegitimate.'

He was silent. It was something no loyal Protestant spoke of—but certainly there was no denying what lay on the Statute Book. Uneasily he watched her toy with the contents of his fruit bowl; there was something in her expression, oddly intense and preoccupied, that disturbed him greatly.

'All the evil in the world God took and locked in an apple, forbidden fruit of a blighted tree.' She held an apple in one hand and scored its smooth skin with a sharp fingernail, squeezing till it bled a little juice on to her gown. *'Such an incredible fierce desire to eat apples . . . the King says it means I am with child . . .'* Suddenly she looked over her shoulder at him. 'Do you know who said that, Robin?'

A cold finger touched his spine, setting the hairs at the nape of his neck on end. He knew the tale of old, how Anne Boleyn, in those very same words, had announced her pregnancy to a gallery of startled courtiers, had laughed and run from them in her ecstasy of triumph, leaving them all abashed and uneasy, knowing the break with Rome was now certain because 'The Lady' had conquered. If Anne had not conceived Elizabeth so quickly after her surrender; if the King had had time to weary of that long pursued pleasure so suddenly, unexpectedly attained; if there had never been that added spur, the promise of a son and heir . . .

If I had never been born . . .

That was her thought; he saw it in her face and heard it in her voice, so full of anguished doubt and uncertainty, almost revulsion. It was a very short and easy step to the next thought: *If I were dead . . .*

Or had she already reached that conclusion? Was that subconscious desire at the root of her indifference to safety, the secret of her reckless, at times almost deliberate, courting of assassination?

He took her hands in an urgent grip.

'There is peace and prosperity in this land now where once there was discord and bankruptcy. Our status in Europe is unparalleled—how can you doubt that your power is for good?'

She shook her head sadly.

'You have eaten of the apple and lost the ability to judge. I am embarking on a reign of terror—is that not evil?'

'It is not of your choosing,' he said grimly, 'your enemies have forced it upon you.'

'Who will remember that—innocent victims like Campion?'

'God will remember,' he said quietly. 'God is your only judge.'

She turned her back on him to stare out of the window and remember how she had come to the Tower as a prince, thanking God for His mercy and in His name pledging mercy 'to all men'. As she looked out of the window into a growing gloom lit by the flaming torches of Campion's escort, she saw bitterly how she must show that mercy from now on. The prisoner, limping slowly down the sloping lawns to the waiting barge, stumbled on his crippled legs and fell down on the gravel path. For a moment he lay still, exhausted and bemused, until an impatient guard cursed and kicked him to his feet, dragging him on to the hideous death of a traitor which was all that awaited him now. She bit her lip, angry with Campion for his stiff-necked stubbornness, angry with Walsingham and his kind who had brought it to this, angrier still with herself that, for expediency, she would stand by and let it happen. She felt degraded, unclean and faintly sick. The ruling of men was a dirty business—

Out along the dark river went the burning, orange lights, flickering and bobbing as gaily as festival torches. Leaning against the casement she watched them disappear, swallowed up in the enveloping mouth of nightfall.

Leicester put one hand around her narrow waist, twining his fingers round the gold chain, girdled with pearls. He sensed her despair.

'Let me get you some brandy.'

'Get my cloak instead,' she said, closing the shutter firmly, as though she had closed a door in her mind. 'It's late. Burghley will be waiting for us in the barge.'

For a moment he hesitated, wondering if he dared; but when at last he found the courage to take her into his arms, she laid her head on his shoulder and seemed glad of the physical comfort. He held her close, with rising hope and remembered that once before despair had brought her to his bed . . .

'There's no need for us to return to court tonight,' he said softly, 'I can send word to Burghley that you're too weary to make the journey—it will cause no surprise and little comment. Stay with me here and I will make you forget them all—Campion, Philip, the Queen of Scots. In my arms all your enemies are defeated.'

She stiffened and drew away from him. She had just sent an innocent man out to death and Leicester, who had been his friend, had the disgusting effrontery to suggest they went to bed and forgot all about it! Pretty much she supposed as her father must have done the day after her mother's execution.

He watched her eyes harden, her hands clench into fists and, misreading the cause of her anger, became angry himself.

'So that's the way it's to be, is it? Just because I sent your little French prince packing, you'll waste the rest of your life and mine, for spite—for pure spite! You never loved him—you'd have hated him within a month! So what did I do that cannot be forgiven?'

'You killed my child,' she said softly and his anger went out like a doused candle, taking his hope with it. He understood at last that the price he had paid for his victory was to lose her for ever and he looked at her sadly.

'You accepted the challenge and you lost. Can't you be gracious in defeat?'

'I'm a bad loser, Robin, like my father. I should have thought you had learnt that by now.'

He picked up her cloak and came to wrap it round her shoulders in a gesture of resignation.

'Come,' he said wearily, 'I will take you back to Whitehall if that is really what you wish.'

Her wish was his command—always had been and always would be. And she would never change; perversity was second nature to her now. But it was a waste, a sad and wicked waste of love; and one day she might be sorry for it—

His steward lit them down the wide staircase into the Great Hall and out on to the terrace, down a flight of steps to the knot gardens, down another flight to the lawns, cut in whimsical shape, two stately figures in gleaming court costume trailing noiselessly away over the twisting paths to the waterfront. They might have been ghosts, sad and silent in the darkness.

Burghley stood as he saw them approach, but they did not speak to him or to anyone else. In silence Leicester handed the Queen into the waiting barge, joined her on the cushions beneath the royal canopy, and snapped his fingers curtly to the oarsmen.

Slowly the great barge, fluttering gay pennants, slipped away into the pitch black night.

Campion and five others stood trial in Westminster Hall, charged with plotting the Queen's dethronement. He said with the little glint of humour which never deserted him, even at the end, 'If our religion makes us traitors we are worthy to be condemned, but otherwise we are as true subjects as ever the Queen had.'

On the scaffold he prayed out loud for Elizabeth 'to whom I wish a long quiet reign and all prosperity'. And in return for that prayer he was allowed to hang until completely dead, before his internal organs were slit from his body.

'. . . There is no doubt whatsoever who sends her out of the world with the pious intention of doing God's service not only does not sin, but gains merit . . .'

Secretary Walsingham repeated this official edict from the Vatican with fierce indignation, but the Queen merely yawned and shrugged and went out hunting, while Walsingham went away to brood darkly on the forces of evil.

He was one of the few men in her service who had failed to get on to a warm, personal footing with the Queen. He was cold and sly and fanatical, but he was also brilliant and efficient; she tolerated him for that. She was generally unkind and often downright rude to him, but he bore the kicks and served her with endless diligence, because there was nothing he abhorred more than the prospect of Mary Stuart on the English throne. Walsingham's few emotional needs were satisfied by the fierce demands of his work, his lifelong devotion to the task of crushing the Catholic faith in England and extinguishing its most illustrious flame and figurehead—the Queen of Scots; his hatred of the woman he had never seen was an obsession.

He maintained, at his own expense, a flourishing and ruthlessly efficient spy system which was already a byword in Europe. 'Knowledge is never too dear,' he had once said sanctimoniously, and he had found Elizabeth quite happy to let him prove that. He lavished his personal fortune and ceaseless vigilance on this unique system and the Queen already owed her life to it several times over. His unstinting service was given without love and received without gratitude; and they were both content that it should be so.

Early in 1583, searching desperately for news of 'the Enterprise of England', Walsingham stumbled upon a new plot against the Queen's life. His money had left a trail of corruption in every foreign embassy throughout the length and breadth of Europe. It was thus that he had come to tap the regular, secret correspondence between Mary Stuart and the French Ambassador and through it discovered the activities of Francis Throckmorton.

Throckmorton was seen creeping away from Mendoza's house late one night and was placed under close surveillance. Walsingham's men seized him at his lodgings at Paul's Wharf in the very act of writing a ciphered letter to the Scottish Queen and he was removed to the Tower, where he withstood the rack three times before breaking down and revealing the internationally based plot which had embraced the Guise party in France, the King of Spain, the Spanish Ambassador, the Queen of Scots and several Catholic nobles at the English court. The massive conspiracy was revealed in a welter of impressive circumstantial evidence based on Throckmorton's verbal confessions under torture and Walsingham was gratified by the hysterical response his publication of the issue provoked among the Council and the English people. Burghley promptly drew up a long list of elaborate precautions for the Queen to take in an attempt to avoid assassination, which she glanced at with a wry smile, and largely ignored.

Throckmorton perished in anguish at Tyburn, but, to Walsingham's intense chagrin, no one was able to persuade the Queen to press the vague evidence discovered against her Scottish cousin. Mary's imprisonment became as stern and uncomfortable as her jailer could make it, but that was all. Walsingham was tempted to believe, along with the founder of the Jesuit College, William Allen, that the Queen of England had no religion at all. And Elizabeth, if she dared to admit it publicly, would now have agreed.

In December she rode from Hampton Court to London, with the French Ambassador at her side. Men and women knelt in the thick mud, their sharp, hungry faces blue with cold as they hailed her as a goddess and clamoured for the punishment of her enemies.

She smiled and waved and called out to them gaily, slowing her horse to snail's pace in the icy wind, so that they might all feast their eyes upon her.

It was pagan idolatry of a kind Mauvissière had never witnessed before and he found it rather unnerving. Elizabeth, watching him from the corner of her eye and knowing from Walsingham's discoveries that he was by no means as spotless in his honour as he pretended to be, turned in her saddle and observed with quiet irony, 'I perceive not *everyone* wishes me dead.'

Mendoza was summoned before the Privy Council. No one rose when he entered the room; he saw hostility on every icy, chiselled face and knew the game was up.

In passionless Italian Sir Francis Walsingham enumerated the Ambassador's crimes, with his long, yellowing fingers clasped on the table in front of him and his cold, cod-fish eyes fixed on the Spaniard's face.

'Don Bernadino de Mendoza, you have abused your diplomatic privileges. You have communicated with the Queen of Scots, encouraging her to rely on Spain and contriving for her escape. You have assisted Jesuits, corresponded with the traitor Throckmorton and made your home a rendezvous for priests. Her Majesty is no longer prepared to overlook such preposterous interference within her kingdom and it is her command that you leave the country within fifteen days.'

Mendoza's dark eyebrows shot up with outrage.

'I challenge you to *prove* these outrageous charges, sir!'

'Her Majesty feels that would be distasteful and unnecessary,' said Walsingham calmly. 'In short, sir—a waste of time!'

Mendoza lost his temper and began to shriek at the top of his voice.

'Let her look to her own actions before she questions mine! She encourages revolution among my master's subjects in the Netherlands—aye, never think we don't know it!—she protects scurvy pirates—receives stolen goods—' His voice broke on a croak of rage and he gulped a breath. 'And in any case I cannot possibly leave England without King Philip's express command,' he added irrelevantly.

He stopped and staggered back a step as the entire Council rose to its feet.

'You,' said Walsingham icily, 'are a disgrace to your King and should count yourself fortunate to be allowed to leave here alive.'

Mendoza began to sweat copiously.

'By God, sir—no one touches me without a sword in his hand!'

Walsingham made an ominous gesture and the Spaniard bolted for the door in undignified haste, muttering about the base ingratitude of women.

In the doorway he turned and looked back bitterly, his smooth olive face blotched with purple patches of colour.

'I regret, gentlemen, that I have been unable to please your Queen as a minister of peace. Pray tell her that I hope to satisfy her better in war and that I will walk barefoot over Europe to encompass it!'

The door slammed behind him on a room full of shocked, silent men, and so it was that Elizabeth's last ambassador from Spain departed from her country, vowing publicly to be revenged upon her.

CHAPTER 2

Walsingham emerged from the Queen's private apartments and walked stiffly down the length of the Long Gallery with a sheaf of papers under his arm. He was dressed as usual in cheerless black, unrelieved by bright embroidery or jewels, and his eyes were fixed and staring, seeing neither the stone and gold ceiling, nor the wainscot, whose thousand beautifully carved figurines regarded him with bleak indifference. It was bitterly cold and for once the draughty gallery was empty of its jostling, gossiping groups of courtiers. No one saw the pale Secretary pass down the quiet corridors of Whitehall Palace and enter his tiny closet with measured speed but, if they had, his narrow, sombre face would have betrayed nothing of the fierce excitement raging in his brain.

A habitual ministerial calm hung over Walsingham as he padded softly to his desk, silent in his soft kid house shoes. A medicinal draught awaited him, but he tidied his papers methodically, as was his wont, before swallowing it with a grimace. He sat and wrote stubbornly until the nagging pain became a few degrees less insistent; then he laid his pen aside and leaned his chin thoughtfully on his gaunt hands, quietly congratulating himself on what must surely be the most effective interview in all his difficult dealings with his mistress.

The Throckmorton plot against the Queen's life had been only one of the many plots he had unearthed with alarming regularity, and he had explained the only solution to Her Majesty more times than he cared to remember, without success. But today he had to admit he had surpassed himself and for once he had managed to make her listen without flying into a rage and refusing to discuss the matter further. He sat back and savoured the memory of his own skill . . .

'I respectfully submit to Your Majesty that we have enough circumstantial evidence to convict the Queen of Scots many times over.'

'Evidence of circumstance may convict a common man, Walsingham—it will not convict a queen.'

It was at this point that the Secretary's mental antennae had begun to quiver with taut anticipation. There was something in her voice to suggest she was just a little weary of playing target to every would-be assassin in Europe. Was it possible she was about to take a sane and reasonable attitude over the 'bosom serpent' at last?

He hurried to drive the slight advantage home.

'Madam, the plots grow in number and cunning, and sooner or later I fear it is inevitable that one of them will succeed. Every intrigue has been in her favour though, since she has been denied all communication with the outside world, no longer in her name. However, I am convinced if she were allowed to communicate once more—under close surveillance, of course—'

'She would suspect,' said the Queen sharply, 'she is not totally without guile, Walsingham.'

'I could contrive it without any suspicion, madam, be confident of that. You have said that evidence of circumstance is not sufficient—but what if I were to bring you proof *in her own hand* that she seeks your death?'

Elizabeth sat down in the chair of estate, pressed her fingers together tip to tip, and fixed him with an unwavering stare that made him acutely uncomfortable.

'You are aware of how I would reward forgery, aren't you, Walsingham?'

With an effort, he met her gaze steadily.

'Fully aware, Your Majesty.'

'My reputation is of value to me,' she remarked pointedly. 'I shall not use the man kindly who abuses it. Be quite certain you understand that before we proceed any further with this matter.'

'I understand, madam.' He went down on his knees before her dais. 'And this time, Your Majesty—this time you will take the final act against her?'

She stared at him, her expression calm and inscrutable.

'Bring me that proof first, Mr Secretary. Bring me the proof, written, irrefutable and positive—then we will discuss the action.'

And that was all. She had stepped down from the dais, snapped her fingers to her little spaniel, Perrico, and walked into her Privy Chamber without a word of dismissal or a backward glance, shutting the door. Walsingham left her room too absorbed to register that mark of dislike and see that it was directed at more than a personal level, or even to appreciate what lay behind her unexpected capitulation on the issue.

Elizabeth had not the slightest intention of delivering her cousin to execution; her feelings on the subject were as strong as they had ever been. But Walsingham was right; they could not rely on the careless bungling of amateur conspirators for ever. Sooner or later her enemies would employ the services of a professional and her incredible luck would run out. She had lived under the shadow of assassination for nearly eighteen years since her cousin's flight into England and the constant tension was beginning to tell on her nerves. She had begun to feel, of late that for the sake of her own sanity she must put an end to this increasing welter of intrigue. It occurred to her now that the only way to do it was completely to discredit Mary in the eyes of Europe. And to do that she would need hard evidence—evidence strong enough to elicit a full confession from Mary. When that confession had been released in Europe and circulated throughout England, it would then be safe to return her to a Scottish prison under the guardianship of her covetous son, King James. Remove the focus of discontent from England and the malcontents would scatter; there would be peace at last, and peace was beginning to wear an attractive guise to Elizabeth.

The knowledge that she could manipulate Walsingham's twisted zeal to achieve this end gave her a certain private pleasure. It would be amusing to let him stalk the bird like a hungry cat, snatching the bait away at the last moment, so that he pounced on nothing and went away with empty teeth.

She sighed. He was a good servant and she wished she could like him, for she would never find another spy half so diligent. If only he were not so bloodless and self-righteous, so convinced he had been personally singled out by God to stand as the last line of defence against Satan's forces. His attitude irritated her beyond bearing, and made her less sympathetic than she would normally have been towards his ill-health. His face was thin, the whites of his eyes faintly yellow and his forehead furrowed with furtive lines of pain. Something burned the life force slowly out of him, eating away his strength like corrosive acid—she suspected it was his consuming hatred of the Catholic Church and its figurehead. When he died, as he quite conceivably could within a short time, she would not pretend to be sorry.

Walsingham remained in his closet for the rest of the afternoon and half the night, weaving the threads of a plan which would crown his life's work. They had been over-zealous in cutting Mary's correspondence after Throckmorton's plot—now it would be necessary to contrive some means of secret communication for her. But the Secretary was not a man to let the grass grow beneath his feet—and he would not have approached Elizabeth at this point had he not already devised the apparatus for this charade.

By various ways and means—none of them too nice, but that was business—Walsingham had got his persuasive hands on John Gifford, a Catholic refugee who had been unfortunate enough to be apprehended whilst carrying a letter recommending his honesty and faith to Mary Stuart. Walsingham had had a short interview with him and discovered that those two sad little deficiencies of honesty and faith did not prevent the man from being a reasonable fellow, devoted far more to the preservation of his own life and very willing to be helpful.

Walsingham's toneless voice had settled the tiresome preliminaries very quickly and Gifford was immediately installed in the pay of the English government. He had made himself known to the French Ambassador and then travelled down to make himself a pleasant acquaintance of the Scottish Queen, hinting broadly that he would be honoured to perform any little service she might require. It had been almost criminally easy to win her confidence and now he merely awaited further instructions.

Walsingham stared down at his papers. He would contact Mary's gaoler, Paulet, and send down his own personal expert in cipher. The plan centred on the brewer at Burton who supplied Mary's household with beer. Mary was at Chartley and Gifford was confident of persuading her that the brewer was her friend, ready to smuggle her letters in and out in a watertight box concealed in a beer barrel. The brewer, paid doubly by her and by Paulet, had a vested interest in the success of the venture. He could be trusted to keep the letters dry and his own mouth shut. All correspondence would pass through Walsingham's hands en route to its destination, deciphered and resealed with a professional skill that would escape notice from the most critical and suspicious eye.

The plan was so essentially simple that Walsingham knew it could not fail. She had been months without secret correspondence, enduring Paulet's cheerless, spiteful rule. She must be desperate by now, more impulsive, more eager to leap at any chance of escape, more reckless, surely, than she had ever been in a lifetime of reckless mistakes. She would fall into his trap like a starved mouse to a crumb of cheese; he was convinced of it.

Snow had begun to tap softly against the leaden panes of his narrow little window and caught the attention of his vacant gaze. Before the snow falls next winter, he thought grimly, I shall have her tried, condemned—and executed!

Elizabeth paced the thinly frosted paths of the privy garden, wrapped in an ermine-trimmed cloak which trailed behind her with a solitary swish. Around her shoulders was a sable wrap, a New Year's gift from Leicester, its head and four gold paws studded with diamonds and rubies. Her fingers were enclosed in soft kid gloves, delicately worked with her cipher in silver-thread embroidery and edged at the wrist with pearls.

In her hand she held Perrico's jewelled leash and now and then she jerked it impatiently, whenever the little dog lingered over long about a bush, sniffing and cocking his leg. He would have preferred to go ratting in freedom along the hedgerows, but he knew better than to whine and pull. She had reduced her women to jellied silence before they got out of the palace and he knew the mood that voice indicated. The hand which caressed him so lovingly when he curled up on the bed beside her was also equally capable of administering a nasty stinging blow with shocking speed.

Perrico, like everyone else in close attendance on the Queen, had suffered from her uncertain temper since the departure of the Earl of Leicester for a vital armed mission in the Netherlands, and the women who followed her at a safe distance grumbled among themselves resentfully.

The little spaniel trundled in the wake of Elizabeth's sweeping skirts with a sort of dismal resignation. His mistress was miserable and when she was miserable she had a remarkable facility for ensuring that everyone around her should be likewise. Leicester had gone and Perrico missed that burly figure, the big gentle hands which fondled his ears and the nice, softly pillowed lap, big enough to accommodate a fat spaniel in complete comfort. There was small joy to be found on his mistress's lap, who seldom sat still for more than five minutes put together, and was so restless, even in bed, that the little dog sneaked away to his basket by the fire whenever he wanted a peaceful night's sleep.

The causes of Elizabeth's ill humour, however, were more diverse and deep-rooted than Leicester's absence alone. Alençon was dead. He had amply served her purpose in the Netherlands for a couple of years and then died unromantically, and inconsiderately, of a fever, leaving her to face the eternal dilemma of the Dutch Protestants once more. More inconsiderate still was the Dutch figurehead, William of Orange, who had got himself assassinated in his own household. She could not help reflecting angrily that it had been damned careless of him to leave the Dutch without a titular leader and herself as the head of Protestant Europe, a position she had done her best to avoid for the last twenty-five years. The Dutch had promptly offered her the sovereignty of their country, but she had flatly refused it, knowing it would be one challenge that Philip would not choose to ignore. And yet if the Dutch resistance was allowed to collapse, Philip's troops would be safely installed within easy striking distance of England. There had seemed no alternative to the course that both Burghley and Walsingham urged upon her, namely, to send over an army under Leicester, the one man with a smattering of military experience and a reputation as one of the foremost Protestant supporters in England to match it. She had done so with the gravest of misgivings and Leicester had departed on the 9th of December with a martyred air, a strictly limited authority and what he was quite convinced would prove to be insufficient men for the venture.

The royal welcome of the Dutch had put him in a better frame of mind, with bonfires and fireworks lining his route and the people cheering themselves hoarse at the sight of the man they regarded as their saviour. He had written home to tell Burghley: 'I like this matter twenty times better than I did in England.'

But since then nothing much appeared to have been accomplished. The Duke of Parma, who had replaced Don John of Austria, with a new, ruthless efficiency, bided his time and bad weather struck both sides without mercy. It had rained so hard that their clothes had rotted on their backs and Leicester's men had huddled into a church at Middleburg for shelter, hungry and cursing.

It was not an auspicious beginning and Elizabeth remained unable to shake off an uneasy premonition that the whole enterprise was going to prove a disaster. Robin wouldn't lack for personal courage on the field, but it was the first time he had undertaken any significant campaign on his own authority—the first time he had ever really undertaken anything without her at his side, constantly telling him which move to make and when to make it. She had sent a lap-dog out to war and in spite of the confidence of her advisers, she could not help but think that perhaps it had not been the height of worldly wisdom. And yet, ironically, there was no one more suitable to send in his stead. A country set for more than twenty years on peace, absorbed in trade and commercial expansion, ordered, prosperous but scarcely Spartan, had produced no real military leader. She cursed Alençon for dropping dead in such a ridiculously unheroic manner, so that now she was forced to rely on Leicester's ability, remembering uneasily how he had bungled his youthful attempt to capture Mary Tudor. Would he bungle this too?

So he was gone and in his absence she was left to face the whispered threats of invasion and the constant plotting to end her life. Burghley had been right, it was rapidly becoming a life not worth the living.

'Madam, I strongly advise against your walking unguarded, even in your private gardens—accept no gifts personally—refrain from opening letters with your own hand—inhale no perfumed articles—eat nothing, nothing at all that has not been tested—'

Christ's soul, if Burghley had his way, an armed guard would follow her to the privy! She had refused to humour his obsessive anxiety for her person and had said, with her customary flippancy, that she would sooner be dead than in custody. The London crowds lauded her courage, but courage took its toll on her, shrivelling her appetite and gnawing at her sleep, making her unreasonably irritable with her women, whose soft, silly cluckings and pretty love affairs aggravated her beyond endurance. After the disclosure of Leicester's marriage, she had been virtually unapproachable on the subject; only the death of Leicester's son had seemed to soften her.

It still hurt Elizabeth to recall her own behaviour when Leicester had come to her four years before, nervous, yet buoyed up with diplomatically suppressed excitement, the pleasure of a middle-aged man who has sired his first legitimate son. He had told her quietly of the birth and stood in front of her with his eyes filled with naked joy, silently begging for her interest and approval.

She had not even asked for the child's name. Stunned with jealous misery, she had turned away in silence, without a word of congratulation and he had gone out of her room cut to the quick by her attitude. He made no further reference to his son in her hearing; four years later she learnt from his sister-in-law, the Countess of Warwick, that the child was not expected to live long.

'Why didn't you tell me?' she cried later, as he knelt at her feet; and he looked up in his tired grief and said with brutal frankness, 'Because you never asked!'

She, who loved all children, had put her hand to her cheek as though she had been struck a physical blow. The child she had chosen to ignore brought them together by his death, as in his birth he had driven them apart. When the funeral was over there was little comfort for Leicester at Wanstead with his bitter, resentful wife. He went back to Whitehall, like a lost soul, seeking the understanding that only the Queen could give him and her response was generous. She shielded his grief from the spiteful eyes of those who rejoiced to see 'the Great Lord' brought low by any means.

But harmony crept back into their private life only to be thwarted by their public existence. The whirling vortex of crisis in the Netherlands had sucked them apart at the very moment when they had begun to know how much they needed one another. And so he had gone, leaving Lettice to entertain young Christopher Blount in his absence, leaving the Queen to fret and wait with feverish impatience for that news of his success which alone could precede his return. She chafed at the delay, but dreaded the battles which would place him at risk, no longer the young man of lightning reflexes who had won military fame on the field of St Quentin. She had warned him sternly against empty heroics, impressing upon him that the English force was purely defensive, designed to deter Philip's aggression rather than challenge it openly. She had made a public declaration to France and Spain, insisting that she sought no territorial gain in the Netherlands and she relied heavily on Leicester's common sense to ensure that relations between England and Spain were not unnecessarily inflamed by his presence there.

He knew how important that was—knew that they were not ready for war with Spain. Oh yes, he knew it all—so why then could she not relax and know the matter was safe in his hands?

Returning to the palace she found Burghley waiting for her, so grim-faced that she immediately feared the worst.

'Is there news of Leicester?'

'Aye, madam,' said Burghley stonily, 'I fear there is.'

She stiffened, holding the little spaniel against her breast in a grip which made the animal protest indignantly.

'Is he hurt?' she whispered.

'No, madam—not yet.'

She dumped the spaniel in his basket by the fire and turned on Burghley angrily.

'*Not yet!* What the devil do you mean, not yet?'

Burghley stared at her, his expression unchanged.

'I have just received news that on New Year's Day, in answer to the importunate desire of the Dutch, the Earl of Leicester accepted the title of Supreme Governor of the Netherlands.'

Elizabeth's eyes widened in disbelief.

'Is it true?'

Burghley nodded slowly.

'I'll kill him,' said the Queen briefly, and turned away.

Burghley coughed. 'With respect, madam, it will not help the Dutch resistance to see two leaders die in office in such quick succession.'

'So I'll kill him *after* he's resigned the post.'

'Madam—'

'I will not support him in this position! After all I have said to reassure the French and the Spanish—Christ's blood, I might just as well have accepted the Dutch crown myself! I shall draft a letter immediately ordering him to resign the post.'

Burghley laid his hand heavily on her sleeve.

'If you send it, madam, I shall resign mine.'

He was right, of course, and in her heart she knew it. A public humiliation of Leicester would throw the Dutch into demoralized confusion before Parma's forces.

She shrugged off Burghley's hand and marched to the door of her bed-chamber.

'Very well! A little time he may have to set this outrageous blunder to rights. But I shall still write a letter to make him smart.'

Burghley bowed stiffly. 'That, madam, is your privilege, and my pleasure. I know I can safely leave the wording in your hands.'

*   *   *

The Queen's despatch, written with icy formality in the third person, humbled Leicester into desperate attempts to salvage his mission from the ruin into which he had plunged it by that rash act. He paid his men from his own purse and worked himself into illness to draw back some vestige of standing in her eyes; and later he received a very different letter from her, one that moved him to tears as he read it in the poor candlelight at the height of his campaign.

'Rob,

I am afraid you will suppose by my wandering writings that a midsummer's moon has taken a large possession of my brain this month; but you must take things as they come into my head, though I leave order behind me . . .'

The letter accompanied him to his hard trestle bed where he lay awake trying to resolve the problems of ill-trained and half-starved soldiers, greedy officers and rank corruption, the constant bickering of niggardly Dutch allies. Oh yes, he had made a fine shambles of this and they both knew it. Yet her incredible letter, with its 'million and legion of thanks for all your cares and pains', told him simply that he had done his best and that little else mattered.

'I pray God bless you from harm and save you from all foes . . .'

A friend not won with trifles, nor lost with the like, she could love beyond desertion and treacherous disobedience. What was he doing here pretending to be a king, deserting the only significant role he had ever held in this world? He should never have come, he should never have left her, because without her he was nothing, an empty shadow with no substance. To go home now was the summit of his worldly ambitions; but home was not at Wanstead with his gay, voluptuous, shallow wife.

He could see now that it never had been.

All through the Spring of 1586, Walsingham had watched his trap with the ceaseless vigilance of a hunter. Not a word which left the pen of Mary Stuart and her correspondents escaped his eye, but for a strangely long time there was nothing significant. Harmless prattlings and dignified complaints about her treatment passed to and fro and mocked him with their innocence. He supported Leicester's wretched case in the Netherlands, but with something less than his customary snub-proof intensity, and the men who worked closely with him noted his tense preoccupation.

It was May when the first breath of conspiracy drifted into the communication channel, originating with a Jesuit priest named Ballard. Mendoza, in

Paris, informed Philip that it was the most hopeful plot of all and it followed the usual lines—the murder of Elizabeth to be followed by the accession of the Scottish Queen.

Walsingham waited on further developments and set a spy on one of Elizabeth's young Catholic courtiers, the vain, impulsive, hopelessly romantic Anthony Babington. But even Babington realized the dangers involved and for several agonizing weeks he hesitated on the brink of the plot. Just as Walsingham had begun to think he was wasting his time and money after all, Babington pushed aside his doubts and assumed the leadership of the enterprise, causing the Secretary to reflect grimly that a little patience is usually rewarded.

Once the wheels of conspiracy had begun to turn, the plot rapidly gathered momentum. Gifford approached Babington, on Walsingham's instructions, in the guise of a religious fanatic and pointed to himself as a go-between. He was well acquainted with Queen Mary and believed he had her trust; she would listen to his advice. He explained the little comedy with the beer barrels, mocking the stolid ignorance of Mary's custodian, Paulet, and saw that Babington was favourably impressed; it was easy after that.

Babington wasted no time once he had committed himself. He was very familiar with the royal household and had soon approached six gentlemen with good positions in reasonably close attendance on Elizabeth—among them a Gentleman Pensioner, the son of the Under Treasurer and the son of the Master of the Wardrobe. Attending assiduously to her public needs about the court, they awaited the quiet word from Babington to kill her.

It had all been so easy that Babington got carried away with his own importance. Posterity interested him—so much so that he actually had his portrait painted with the six conspirators, ready to be hung at Whitehall or Windsor or wherever it should please Queen Mary to hang it, for the world to see.

By the end of June the portrait was finished; and very handsome he looked too, as Gifford agreed, when invited to admire it.

Secretary Walsingham looked up from the portrait which had been placed on his tidy desk. He was not amused, but he was certainly amazed.

'You say he commissioned this for posterity?'

'Yes, sir—hard to credit isn't it? But he's been showing it off to all his close friends.'

Walsingham sucked in his breath with a long hiss, like a snake.

'I have observed some strange sights in my time, Gifford, but for shear effrontery I should be hard put to match this one.'

Gifford's ugly face was twitching with nerves and amusement. He could never look at Walsingham's pallid, passionless features without remembering the painful circumstances of their first interview and the penalty for failure on this mission.

'You never saw such a vain, empty-headed popinjay, sir, and that's God's truth.' Gifford paused and wished he had not had cause to mention God in Walsingham's presence. It conjured up memories he would have preferred to forget. 'He must be raving mad, sir,' he continued hastily. 'I wonder you take his dabbling seriously.'

'Madness,' said Walsingham coldly, 'is no deterrent to murder. Fools may handle guns and knives as well as sane men.' He sighed and stared down at the portrait once more. 'But you have done well, Gifford. This goes to the Queen without a moment's delay.'

He rose and locked his drawers automatically, frowning at the thought of Elizabeth's loud laughter. Her irreverent sense of humour appalled him and he was well enough acquainted with her nature to know that this arrogant portrait would throw her into ecstasies of amusement.

He glanced curtly at his spy.

'You will see this portrait is returned before it is missed. Babington must suspect nothing, least of all you.'

'Yes, sir.' Gifford bowed in obsequious agreement. 'I don't think we'll have to wait much longer. Babington has made all his arrangements—he should write to the lady any day now.'

Walsingham nodded and walked stiffly towards the Queen's apartments with the clumsy, linen-wrapped parcel under his arm.

Early in July Babington wrote to Mary, detailing the plot and asking for advice as to her rescue. When he had signed and sealed the letter, he handed it to Gifford, who hovered beside his desk.

'See to it she receives that without delay. And take the greatest care. It contains all our lives, you understand.'

'Anthony, you know you can trust me to be as circumspect as the case demands.'

Babington stood up and squeezed Gifford's hand with emotion.

'For Queen Mary and the True Faith, my friend.'

'For Queen Mary and the True Faith,' echoed Gifford dutifully, his face pale, serious, sincere. He went out of Babington's room without a flicker of emotion and rode hell for leather to the English court.

Next morning, Walsingham sat down to read the deciphered copy of that letter, his knees suddenly too weak with excitement and anticipation to bear his weight.

'It's what you wanted, then, sir?' Gifford watched the Secretary's face with cautious curiosity.

'Excellent.' Walsingham spread his hands in an expansive gesture. 'It couldn't be much better—exactly what I had hoped for!'

'Will you arrest them tonight, sir?'

'I think not.' Walsingham spoke without raising his eyes from the letter.

'Sir?' Gifford's head flung upwards and his mouth dropped open with astonishment. 'But the Queen—'

'The risk to the Queen is not immediate.' Walsingham's cool voice flowed on as though there had been no interruption. 'I'm certain Babington will not act until he hears from Mary. There must be no panic and no suspicion until I am ready to strike at the head of this bosom serpent. I must have her reply in writing or she will slip through our fingers again—believe me, I know Her Majesty too well to leave any loophole at this stage.' He paused and plaited his fingers together. 'Whatever it takes I must have her reply, Gifford, do you understand me—*whatever* it takes.'

Gifford stared and his high colour rapidly drained out of his cheeks.

'*Forgery?*' he whispered.

Walsingham's jaundiced eyes fixed him with an icy stare.

'Whatever it takes,' he repeated steadily and smiled, showing long, yellow teeth, remarkably akin to a rat's. He pushed Babington's re-sealed letter across the desk between them. 'You had better see that gets to Chartley as soon as possible.'

Elizabeth leaned back in her chair beside an empty hearth and handed Walsingham the deciphered copy.

'It condemns Babington and his friends,' she said quietly. 'Nothing more.'

'I admit that, madam, and for your immediate safety Babington could be arrested at once, but—'

He hesitated and his eyes flickered over her face, searching for some sign of her reaction. He was terrified of losing her support at this critical juncture and his practised mind-reading gave him no glimmer of her inward thoughts. Her face was as calm and blank as a stone wall.

'But?' she prompted coolly.

'Forgive me, madam, we would merely be striking at the branches and leaving the root untouched.'

'Yes—I *am* familiar with your obsession, Walsingham.' She glanced down to where Perrico sat with his head on Walsingham's softly slippered foot. Walsingham liked animals. She found that quite out of character, but supposed that the man must have some human failings. Privately it irked her every time she saw the little spaniel launch himself across the room to grovel on his back, white paws jerking wildly in the air in welcome. It was the sort of display she would prefer to be totally reserved for herself—and perhaps Leicester, under sufferance.

She looked up at last and said slowly, 'What is it you want?'

'Your permission, madam, to keep the trap open a little longer, until I have the positive proof you require. The bird approaches the net, but one sound may scare her off.'

'You are so sure, aren't you, Walsingham—so certain—she will agree! Have you thought what would happen if Gifford took her reply straight to Babington instead? I'm sure he has. If I were dead, all the evidence in the world would not keep her from my throne and Gifford would sit very pretty in her favour.'

'I know, madam. I also know this asks a great deal of you personally, but I have considered the matter carefully and I am convinced the risk is minimal.'

'That is a great comfort,' she remarked sarcastically. After a moment she got up and walked away to the window. He was convinced then that he had failed and in his innermost heart supposed that he could not really blame her. It was her life, after all, that he intended to juggle with and not many people could be expected to play the part of live bait with nonchalance. He was about to bow and inform her that he would make out an immediate order for Babington's arrest, when she looked at him over her shoulder and shrugged, almost carelessly.

'Well, Walsingham, if you are prepared to place my life in the hands of a renegade Catholic spy I suppose the position is very desperate.'

'Madam?'

'I will be advised by you, sir—do whatever you think best.'

He walked to the window and dropped awkwardly on one knee, kissing her hand with a sudden, unexpected wave of emotion.

'You realize, Your Majesty, that we can risk no extra guards or any measure that would give rise to suspicion?'

She laughed harshly and tapped his gaunt cheek with cynical amusement.

'I will not betray you, Walsingham, if that's what you mean. Play your little games with my life in peace.'

A tall woman in a dull grey gown, still beautiful in spite of a thickened waist, shoulders stooped with rheumatism and continual ill-health, stood by a window at Chartley. The July sun brought out the brassy glints in her chestnut wig and her long, hazel eyes were fixed on the secretary who bent over his work at the table in front of her.

At last the man laid the cipher down, shot an anxious glance at his mistress's face, and handed the letter over with considerable reluctance. Mary tapped the paper against a white hand and pinned his glance with shrewd eyes.

'What is it, Jacques?' Her voice was gentle and even after all these years still retained its French accent. 'Why that look?'

Jacques Nau swallowed nervously. 'Madam, there is sufficient in that letter to take us all to the scaffold. I implore you not to answer it.'

He saw the flame of hope leap behind her eyes then and her fingers closed convulsively around the paper.

'I will consider your advice, of course.' Mary was never imperious when she could be conciliatory and she owed much to the loyal affection of the friends who had chosen to share the hardships of captivity with her. Though she had no intention of harkening to Nau's advice, she did not wish him to think she held it in contempt. Smiling gently, she waved him from the room and watched him bow himself out.

'Wait in the next room, Jacques. I may need your services again.'

When the door had closed behind him, she took the letter to the light at the window and leaned against the casement, where Babington's words danced out from the paper, like little black imps.

'. . . myself with ten gentlemen and one hundred of our followers, will undertake the delivery of your royal person from the hands of your enemies. For the despatch of the Usurper (from the obedience of whom we are by the excommunication of her made free), there are six noble gentlemen, all my private friends, who, for the zeal they have to the Catholic cause and Your Majesty's service, will undertake that tragical execution.'

The letter slipped from Mary's hand and fell to the floor; for the moment she could read no more.

She closed her eyes and tried to think with complete dispassion what this would mean. Escape. Freedom. The crowns of Scotland and England at last. A welcome chance to settle with her dear, devoted son who ruled in her rightful place without a qualm of conscience. Not one serious move had James ever made on her behalf. He was Darnley's son, after all, rotten to the core. In all the dark story of male treachery, nothing had hurt Mary so much as the indifference of the son who had never known her. And revenge for eighteen years in an English prison, grovelling on Elizabeth's whim for petty favours like a visit to the Buxton baths, which had become the highlight of her narrowed existence. And the price? That one little phrase: *the despatch of the Usurper*.

She bit her lip and stared out of the window, seeing nothing. Never had any plot required her to commit herself in such direct terms!

Her mind framed the cousin she had never seen. Elizabeth, bastard by birth, and bitch by nature. The first, Mary had always known. The second, she had learnt slowly and painfully since that fatal day in France when she had claimed the English throne. Some people said all her troubles stemmed from that moment, others that she had been a victim of her own emotions and played false by the lusts of men. She supposed in a way they were both right, but in the end it all came down to Elizabeth. Two women fated to fight to the death. She smiled, remembering how Bothwell had once said the pair of them would not make one honest woman between them. Dearest Bothwell, never one to mince his words, even now she could still weep at the memory of his death, ten years before, chained like an animal in a Danish prison, driven violently insane by years of captivity. A fate which might yet be hers if she did not seize her chance of freedom now. All it required was her written consent to Elizabeth's murder, and she owed Elizabeth nothing at all—except her life. For nearly twenty years the English Queen had shielded that life against the Scottish lords, against the English people and Parliament and her own Council, playing the dual role of jailer and protectress.

But only a fool would think in sentimental terms of the Queen of England. Mary had done that once, lulled by false promises of friendship, and had spent eighteen years paying for the mistake. And she would go on paying for it for the rest of her miserable life unless she acted now.

This would be the last chance; Jacques's reaction had told her that very plainly. It would be the last chance and she was suddenly glad to find life or death within her reach. She had known all that life had to offer of pleasure and pain. The years of scintillating luxury and homage in France, long rides at the head of her armies across the bleak, invigorating moors of Scotland, love and hatred, passion and intrigue. Her life story read like a blood-stained legend, too extreme, too black and white, to be true. And yet it had been true. She had packed more living into her first twenty-six years than all the crowned heads of Europe put together, and all that had happened since had been in the nature of a grey, leaden shadow extending year after year with unceasing monotony. Her life had ended the day she set foot in England. For eighteen years she had existed in twilight, waiting to live again, and now she knew that if she could not live, she would rather die than go on existing in meaningless limbo.

Returning to the desk, she rang a little handbell and when Jacques Nau reappeared, she smiled and waved him to be seated.

'Trusty and well beloved . . .' she began calmly, and her expression brooked no opposition.

He took up his pen and began to write what she dictated without further argument.

The letter lay open in Walsingham's trembling, triumphant hand.

'. . . the affairs being thus prepared and forces in readiness, both within and without the realm, then shall it be time to set the six gentlemen to work, taking order upon the accomplishing of their design, I may be suddenly transported out of this place.'

'Bring me the proof, written, irrefutable and positive . . .' He had that proof now, the bosom serpent had coiled to strike for the very last time.

He had learnt more of European conspiracy over these last months than he had for a long time, for her correspondence had been truly prolific. A woman with nothing better to do, he mused with malicious amusement; soon she would have more pressing concerns on her mind!

Common sense told him to strike now, but fanaticism had taken control of his cool brain and he knew he could get more out of Babington, much more, if he let this letter go through. It needed only a little alteration and he would have the whole pack in his net.

You are aware, aren't you, Walsingham, of how I would reward forgery?

By forgery she had meant the acquiescence of Mary to the murder plot, and he had not tampered with that. The fact that he would have done if necessary conveniently slipped his mind. And, besides, she need never know. The alteration would be so small, just enough to get further information out of Babington.

Walsingham had conducted his work with masterful efficiency; he was not to know that his one error of judgement would ring down through centuries of heated controversy.

He forged a postscript, asking for names and details of procedure; but the letter was eleven days reaching Babington; and when he had read it he began for the first time to smell the faint scent of treachery.

Elizabeth had lived in daily expectation of secret death for over four months. She had gone about her duties as normal and confided her fears to no one, not even Burghley. She told herself firmly that it would soon be over, but as the weeks crawled away and still Walsingham did not act, she began to think he never would, that he would go on waiting, waiting, trying to be more and more sure, until it was too late. Could she trust him? He had little enough cause to like her, she had often been unreasonable and unkind to him. Was she in league with her own enemy?

No! It was absurd, ridiculous, she was becoming crazed with the long suspense. How could she suspect Walsingham? And yet—it was possible— anything was possible in this treacherous world where no man could be trusted.

Each night she lay staring at the bed curtains wondering whether they would shortly part to reveal the sudden gleam of an assassin's knife, while the conflicting arguments and suspicions chased through her confused brain, turning her now hot, now icy cold. She had believed she did not greatly care if death came violently, but suddenly it was so real, so close, that her nerves were stretched as taut as a piece of ragged string. She was aghast at her inward cowardice when a sudden draught moving the tapestries, or an unfamiliar creak of the floorboards sent an icy plunging through her stomach and covered her with a clammy sweat. Her public appearances were now interminable ordeals which left her trembling with exhaustion. She had begun to feel like a hunted animal, desolately alone without Leicester, who was still struggling vainly in the Netherlands and who was also the only other member of her Council who knew exactly what was happening.

Six men were at liberty in her palace, waiting for the right moment to arrange her murder, and there had been a time in Richmond Park when she had believed that moment had come. Walking with Hatton and a few of her ladies, unguarded as was her wont, she had come face to face with a man she recognized from the portrait—that incredible portrait!—which Walsingham had shown her with such fierce indignation. Barnwell was a swarthy Irishman, his eyes set a little too close together for comfort: he wore a short Spanish cloak which hid his right hand from view, and there was a nervous expression on his face.

She wanted to scream: 'Arrest this man,' but there was nobody at hand to do it, only poor bumbling Hatton, who was not even armed. To scream was just as likely to panic the man into action as drive him away and if she had been mistaken she would have destroyed the essence of Walsingham's mission. So she did the only thing she could think of and stared at him with a piercing, unwavering glance which dared him to go through with whatever he intended.

Already jumpy and uneasy, that fixed stare shattered Barnwell's nerve. He bowed, averted his eyes and began to edge away from the little group. As he did so, he heard the Queen laugh on a high, sharp note and turn to Hatton.

'I'm well guarded today, am I not, Kit, with no man near me who wears a sword at his side?'

'Your Majesty?' Interrupted curtly in mid-eulogy on her many perfections of mind and body, Hatton blinked at her in surprise. Barnwell had slipped away to the back of her attendants now and Hatton had not the faintest idea what had prompted a remark so alien to their conversation. 'I'm sorry, madam—what did you say?'

'Nothing,' she said quickly, placing her hand on his arm. 'Nothing at all. Please continue with your verses.'

Hatton frowned faintly and cleared his throat, for he had lost his thread by now and wished he had brought his notes. They walked on and after a moment the familiar, stilted voice began to pour the old honeyed hyperbole into her ears. She scarcely heard a word he said, staring abstractedly in front of her, lost in dark thought, moving with an effort on legs which seemed to have turned to jelly.

Oh Robin, if only you were with me now . . .

CHAPTER 3

The vague unease that Babington had experienced on receipt of Mary's letter grew steadily after the unexpected arrest of John Ballard, a fellow conspirator. It was true that Ballard was a known Catholic priest and that Catholic priests daily faced the possibility of arrest; but the incident alerted Babington's sense of self-preservation—better developed than his powers of political intrigue—and he began to make plans to leave the country. He applied to Walsingham for a passport to visit France and received instead an invitation to dine with Walsingham's secretary, an inquisitive man who plied him with wine and such penetrating questions that Babington hastily left the house and went straight into hiding.

Fear for the Queen's safety now panicked Walsingham into action, forcing him to abandon his devious tactics and swoop down upon the known conspirators at once. It took several weeks to track Babington down and the Secretary was weak with relief when news of the arrest was finally brought to him, knowing how close to disaster his intrigue had brought him.

The Queen of Scots was promptly removed to Tixall under the façade of a hunting expedition, and during her absence Chartley was ransacked by Walsingham's men. All her private papers, with the keys to sixty different ciphers, were seized and a mass of paper evidence was stacked high on a table before Elizabeth at Windsor.

'The proof,' said Walsingham, softly triumphant, 'written, irrefutable and positive.'

Over the neat stacks of documents her eyes met his with hatred, but he did not flinch; instead he removed a document from the Chartley papers and handed it to her.

She read through the list of English nobles who had secretly tendered their future allegiance to Mary, and dropped it wearily into the fire.

'Your Majesty!' he protested and made a move towards the hearth. But the parchment was already curling and shrivelling in the flames.

'I see but say nothing,' she said quietly. 'What else can I do?'

He was about to tell her, but she turned away abruptly and went through into her private chamber. After a moment Burghley extracted another document, exchanged a significant glance with Walsingham, and hobbled after her.

He found her sitting by the fire, staring bleakly into the leaping flames; as he entered slowly she looked up at the paper in his hand and burst out angrily, 'Christ's soul—you surely don't expect me to read that whole mountain out there!'

Burghley looked at her steadily in the candlelight.

'There is one letter, madam, which in common decency we will not produce in evidence against the Scottish Queen—nevertheless, since it is addressed to Your Majesty I feel you should be allowed to read it, in spite of,' he hesitated, 'its distasteful nature.'

She eyed him cautiously for a moment, then held out her hand for the sheets of paper. The letter was written in Mary's own hand and for sheer venomous libel it would be hard to surpass. It was a cruel and malicious catalogue of every low rumour that had ever circulated about Elizabeth's habits and morals and it contained some new and startling anecdotes, apparently related to Mary by the wife of her former custodian, the Countess of Shrewsbury. Elizabeth had bedded with Leicester and many others including Alençon and Simier, but, owing to her physical malformation, her sexual excesses could only be partially consummated. She had forced Hatton into bed against his will. She was vain to the point of open ridicule and secretly mimicked by her ladies, several of whom had suffered from her violent physical assaults. She had broken the finger of one with a candlestick and slashed another's hand with a knife. She was rotting with a foul disease inherited from her father . . .

Elizabeth glanced up at Burghley, who was watching her hopefully, and she knew quite well why he had shown her this humiliating document; he was hoping to see her wreak a quick revenge on the authoress of this filth. But, oddly enough, though shocked, she was not angry. She could imagine the mood of bitter frustration and blind hatred in which Mary had written this, obviously more for her own satisfaction in getting it all down on paper than for anything else. It had never been sent, because Mary had never found the courage to send it. She was helpless and resentful and afraid and a wealth of pity suddenly coursed through Elizabeth. How well she remembered the impotent resentment of the hopeless prisoner!

She leaned towards the fire, but this time Burghley was too quick for her and caught her hand.

'No, madam, I beg you, don't destroy it—I give you my word no one has read it except Walsingham and myself.'

She looked up at him coldly.

'It is *not* to be filed among the Chartley papers.'

'Then at least allow me to file it among my personal documents—it's a valuable piece of evidence, madam—it shows the true feelings of the Queen of Scots towards you more plainly than anything else.'

Her painted lips curled suddenly in a sardonic smile.

'You want it as a souvenir—is that it?'

Burghley smoothed the rescued document between his gnarled fingers.

'I want it for posterity, madam. Those who defend the integrity of the Scottish Queen have only to set eyes on this to see her for what she is.'

Elizabeth closed her eyes. 'It's late and I'm tired. Take your trophy and go.'

He bowed and began to shuffle backwards to the door. When he had reached it she called after him quietly.

'This makes no difference to my attitude towards her crime—no difference at all. But allow me to congratulate you, my friend. I have long suspected you would sink to anything if you felt it would further your cause and you have just confirmed that belief. I admire you a little more—and like you a little less. Do you understand me, Burghley?'

'Your Majesty.' He inclined his head in brief acknowledgement and went out to report his failure to Walsingham.

The trial of Babington and his confederates went smoothly enough, the verdict a foregone conclusion, the sentence to be hanged and quartered alive at the Queen's pleasure.

'And that,' spat Elizabeth, rounding on Burghley hysterically, 'is not enough. Devise something new and let the people see the price of treason!'

He was astonished at this sudden brutality, which seemed so dreadfully out of character.

'Madam, to alter the penalty would be illegal and, to be honest with you, quite unnecessary. If the executioner takes care to prolong their pain, I feel sure their end will be as terrible as you could ever wish.'

She turned away, grinding her fist into the palm of her hand. The first numb daze at the extent of the treachery around her had worn off in a savage reaction. She wanted them to suffer. She wanted to rend and tear all those who had lightly tossed aside her three decades of ceaseless labour, thirty years which had changed her from a handsome, high-spirited girl to a bitter, lonely old woman who had never known a moment's peace.

And so, on the 20th of September 1586, the first batch of conspirators were drawn on hurdles to St Giles-in-the-Fields to meet their tormented ends in a skilful execution which was prolonged for three hours. First hung, but cut down quickly while still alive, they were thrown to the ground and ripped open from neck to groin. The crowds pressed forward as the first animal screams of anguish tore through the air and the street became littered with burning entrails. Castration followed the removal of lesser organs. Babington was heard to cry *Jesus!* three times as his heart lay in the executioner's hands and abruptly the mood of the crowd changed. Women vomited and turned away, while the men moved forward with a low menacing growl and the executioner quailed for a moment, bloody-handed and shamefaced. The full penalty for treason was seldom exacted in this manner and no one present was prepared to believe that their beloved Queen had ordered this.

When the hideous, screaming deaths were reported in detail to Elizabeth, she was sickened by her own cruelty and gave orders that the second batch of traitors, scheduled to die the following day, were to hang until dead before the mutilation of their bodies took place. Supper was served with all its attendant ceremony, but she remained alone in her chamber and no one dared to approach her.

Her behaviour was becoming increasingly erratic and Burghley was privately disturbed. He knew that she had written a desperate letter to Mary, begging for a confession: '. . . if you will do this in your own hand as Queen to Queen, woman to woman, then you will not be tried in open court and I will find some means of leniency towards you . . .'

The answer had come in the form of a flat refusal, couched in the terms of coldly incredulous outrage, and said in effect that Mary could not confess to a crime she had not committed. Elizabeth stared at the letter in despair, franti-

cally trying to reconcile its dignified, martyred air with the evidence Walsingham had presented. For the first time she began to doubt the Secretary's
integrity. What had he done behind her back and how could she ever dare to
expose forgery at this stage? Would anyone in their right minds, knowing
their guilt, choose death when they had been offered life? Was Mary innocent of the main charge, after all?

Elizabeth was thrown into an agony of doubt and panic, for Mary's letter
was the death blow to her hope of reasonable compromise. Events were now
drawing her relentlessly towards the very act she had spent eighteen years
eluding; her advisers and her people were clamouring for Mary's punishment
with a violence that she knew she could no longer contain or deflect. To
bring Mary to trial would be the first step towards that irrevocable act of
madness, the execution of a sovereign, the one crime which she knew she
could never bring herself to accept. But Burghley and Walsingham had her in
a vice. Twist and turn as she might, there was no escape from the path she
must now tread, and with her back to the wall Elizabeth felt the first strand
snap in the threadbare fabric of sanity which she had miraculously preserved
through more than fifty years of constant uncertainty and danger. Her mind
veered like a rudderless ship, desperately seeking some loophole in the net
which had tightened around her, so that she seemed quite incapable of holding to the smallest decision for any length of time.

She flatly refused to bring Mary to the Tower, but could not seem to make
up her mind where she should go to be tried instead—Hertford was too near,
Fotheringay too far. The men who worked with her were astonished by the
treacherous, shifting bog of confused emotion which threatened to blot her
calm rationality out of existence.

It was October before Elizabeth even agreed to bring her cousin to trial,
but when Burghley, Walsingham and the rest of the commissioners arrived at
Fotheringay, the Queen of Scots refused to acknowledge their authority to
try her. She was not a subject and she was not answerable to any English
court! It was three days before Hatton convinced her that it was in her own
interests to appear, since if she refused to attend, her case would go by
default. And so at last the miserable farce began. Mary conducted her own
defence before a jury of thirty-six men who had reached their verdict weeks
before. In the Great Hall of Fotheringay, she passed the empty, throne-like
chair, symbolic of Elizabeth's presence, on her way to the prisoner's stool, set
significantly lower.

'I am a Queen by right of birth,' she said quietly, gazing up at Elizabeth's
empty throne. 'My place should be there.'

A rustle of indignation ran through the assembled men. She had condemned herself out of her own mouth. But she was not dead yet and she had many uncomfortable moments to give them before this trial was ended. The evidence against her was all produced in copies of the original documents and, as she listened to the forged postscript of her reply to Babington, she understood why.

'How can I reply to this accusation without access to the original papers?' she demanded acidly. 'I do not deny that I have earnestly wished for liberty and done my utmost to procure it for myself. In this I acted from a very natural wish; but can I be held responsible for the criminal actions of a few desperate men which they planned without my knowledge? I demand to see the original letters, my lords. It is quite possible that my ciphers have been tampered with by my enemies.' She swung round and pointed a finger at Walsingham, whose eyes were fixed on a point on the far wall. '*He* may well have composed your documents.' *For I know how he hates me and all I stand for.*

There was an uneasy stir. Walsingham got to his feet with pious indignation and looked around the court with an unblinking stare.

'My mind is free of all malice,' he lied smoothly. 'I call God to witness that as a private person I have done nothing unworthy of an honest man, nor as a public person have I done anything unworthy of my place.'

The hours dragged away, the second day set in and still she fought.

'What becomes of the majesty of princes if the oaths and attestations of their secretaries are to be taken against their solemn protestations?—I am held in chains. I have no counsel. You have deprived me of my papers and all means of preparing my defence . . .'

This had begun to go rather well. Several of the commissioners began to look shaken and ill at ease, but Burghley and Walsingham held the trial with a firm rein and swamped sympathy with raucous argument. It became a personal duel between Mary and the cold, white-bearded gentleman who had stood behind her rival for thirty years—the formidable little figure of William Cecil.

'Ah, you,' sobbed Mary at last, '*you* are my adversary!'

'That is true,' said Burghley with superb calm. 'I am the adversary of all Queen Elizabeth's adversaries—'

Fearful of the verdict that would be taken at Fotheringay, Elizabeth ordered the Commission back to London to finish their business in the Star Chamber. At the end of October, unable to influence the outcome, she received her sombre foremost councillors in silence.

'And the verdict?'

'Guilty, Your Majesty.'

Her eyes flickered a moment over their faces.

'Was the decision unanimous, gentlemen?'

'Unanimous save for one voice—Lord Zouche declared himself still unsatisfied as to the guilt of the Scottish Queen.'

Lord Zouche was a brave young man. She wished she had the courage to say she shared his doubts, but she dared not test their loyalty so far. She turned away and slowly they filed out, until only Burghley remained, hovering at her side like a bird of prey.

'Forgive me, madam—but we are all agreed that her sentencing should be handled now by Parliament.'

So they were bringing in their ultimate weapon, secure in the knowledge that she could not hold out against the demands of the Commons.

'Parliament!' she echoed dully.

Burghley lifted his hunched shoulders.

'The burden will be better shared, madam—and the world's opinion better satisfied. I strongly advise that the writs go out at once for assembly next month.'

'Hold your damned Parliament then if you must,' she spat, and walked out of the room. In the doorway she threw over her shoulder bitterly, 'But don't expect *me* to open it, will you?'

And she did not.

Along the mud-sloughed roads Leicester rode on the last stage of his journey to court, his mind full of the disasters from which his urgent recall to England had snatched him in temporary respite. A hopeless catalogue of military skirmishings designed to threaten the Duke of Parma's minor garrisons had culminated in the mad charge he had led at Zutphen. He had fought like a madman on that field and his dreams still dripped blood and the bitter memory of his brave nephew, Philip Sidney, dying of the savage wounds received that day. He wondered how he was going to face the Queen, what he was going to say to explain away the dreary cycle of failure which had hounded his every move. It had been hard to keep his mind on military action once he knew from Walsingham what was afoot in England. He had begged to be recalled immediately, but the Queen had insisted he remained at his post until the conduct of his affairs was satisfactorily arranged.

Now as he turned into the courtyard and swung down from his horse, he wondered what kind of reception he could expect. Abuse? Recriminations? Demands for an accurate account of his expenses? It was more than a year since he had seen her and there were many young men at court only too eager to step into his shoes during his absence—that virile toad Raleigh, for one, would have wasted no time, he was certain of that. And Hatton, too, would have been making hay while the sun shone. It was this uncertainty of his reception which had prompted him to bring his step-son, the young Earl of Essex, back to court with him. If she must smile on another man let it be Essex rather than Raleigh. He could control Essex for as long as the boy remained his financial dependant, but since his sojourn in the Netherlands, his fear of Raleigh had become obsessive—

By the time he had stripped and washed his muddy face and dressed again, the formal summons to the Queen's presence had arrived. He went nervously along the corridors, limping a little under the burden of increasing obesity, and the combination of speed and anxiety caused him to mop his red face with a handkerchief. He was bitterly aware that the strains of the last year had not improved his physique. What would she think when she saw him at last, a bloated old man with receding white hair, who had failed her miserably?

He had expected a formal audience, but to his surprise he was shown into her withdrawing chamber and her women, evidently on her instructions, immediately curtsied and withdrew, leaving them alone. For a brief moment, before he bowed, he looked into her ravaged face and was shocked at the change in her; like him she appeared to have aged ten years in the last twelve months.

All his carefully rehearsed excuses went out of his head, and he held out his arms to her like a schoolboy.

'Will you kiss the conquered hero?' he demanded jauntily. 'Or make him live on bread and water to pay for his miserable failures first?'

She walked up to him, keeping a tight hold of herself, and poked him ungently in the stomach.

'Bread and water wouldn't come amiss, would they—what on earth have you done to yourself out there, you bloated toad?'

He kissed her thin hand impudently. 'I've been eating for two, madam, since it's damned obvious you haven't been—you promised to eat while I was gone.'

She smiled suddenly. 'And *you* promised not to.'

He shrugged. 'Well—a lot of promises have gone under the bridge since then.' He took both her hands and put them around his neck and saw the happy tears brimming in her eyes at last.

'Oh, Robin,' she whispered against his doublet. 'Thank God you've come home safely.'

'You should have let me come before,' he said gruffly, holding her close.

'How do you think I felt all those miles away from you, knowing the danger you were in—I should have been here—'

'You're here now,' she said. 'That's all that matters.'

He grimaced slightly. 'Here to face my critics—I imagine there are quite a few of them waiting to tear my campaign to pieces.'

She looked up into his lined face and said angrily, 'If they've got anything to say they can say it to me—I'd like to see the man among them who could have done any better. Anyway, you won't be here to face them—I'm sending you straight to Buxton to take the waters.'

'Then—you don't need me at court?' There was an anxious note in his voice suddenly and she touched his face.

'It's precisely because I need you with me that I'm sending you away. It frightens me to see you looking so ill. When you come back, I shall need all the support you can give me, Robin. They found her guilty—you know that by now, I suppose—they're going to try to force my hand at last.'

He said nothing. He had come back to England for the precise purpose of joining his voice to those of his colleagues who were urging her to sign Mary's death warrant; but somehow it did not seem the appropriate moment to tell her that. She appeared to be under the impression that he was going to help her to make a stand against them all and there would be time enough for her to learn over the next few weeks that she was wrong.

Stone walls shut out the outside world, enclosing Mary in a strange serenity. The pealing bells and heartfelt psalm-singing, which had greeted the news of her trial and sentence all over London, could not penetrate Fotheringay's grim silence.

She had watched indifferently from a doorway while Paulet ripped down her cloth of estate, because in law she was a dead woman and unworthy of such trappings. Her calm smiles and idle speeches infuriated the humourless Puritan; he could sting her neither to fear nor anger, and his futility mocked him. In the bare stone patch where the cloth of estate had stood, she hung a cross and pictures of the Passion. She would not be troubled much longer by Paulet's spite; she had only a few weeks left to live and she did not wish to mar them with futile outrage.

Approaching death with the peaceful resignation of one who has knowingly taken a fatal gamble and lost, she had no regrets at her rejection of Elizabeth's promise of leniency. A proud and noble martyrdom, for the sake of her faith, was better than a shameful life lived out in prison as the object of Europe's contempt. She would leave this world with spirit and courage and hope, glad of the merciful release for, *In my end is my beginning.*

It was her motto.

She wrote a restrained and dignified letter to Elizabeth, requesting burial in France, thanking her for the priest who had been sent to comfort her last days and inquiring ironically whether Elizabeth wished her to return a diamond, which had been the pledge of friendship between them, now or later. But she finished on a note of quiet threat:

'Do not accuse me of presumption if I remind you that one day you will have to answer for your charge, and for all those whom you doom . . . I desire that my blood and my country may be remembered in that time.'

The letter was her last barb against her cousin but, in order to be permitted to send it at all, Paulet made her wipe her face with the sheets of parchment to prove that they had not been lanced with poison.

If there was peace in the winter-bound world of Fotheringay, it was not mirrored at Greenwich where revelry had ground to a halt and the corridors were hung with whispers. The Queen made few appearances in public. She was harried day and night by advisers, clamouring for her signature on the death warrant, and had taken refuge in her private apartments.

The heavy velvet curtains of her withdrawing chamber were drawn against the icy winter winds which buffeted the casements and she sat close to the fire, laced into a heavy cloth of silver gown, chewing the scarlet paint off her long nails and staring moodily at the carved and gilded ceiling.

Her supper, untouched on a silver tray beside her, caught her attention at last and made her clap her hands irritably.

'Take it away,' she said curtly.

As Elizabeth Throckmorton curtsied nervously and removed the offending tray from the room, the Countess of Warwick laid her embroidery aside with a frown and left her seat by the hearth to kneel at the Queen's feet.

'Madam—' Her voice was a stern reproach and Elizabeth looked away guiltily.

'Tomorrow,' she muttered.

The Countess sighed and gripped her hand.

'You said that yesterday, madam—and not so much as a manchet of bread has passed your lips all day. It can't go on! Another week like this and the only death warrant you will have signed is your own.'

Elizabeth freed her hand and stood up wearily.

'Burghley is waiting in the ante-room, Anne. Send him in, if you please.'

'I know where I'd *like* to send him,' said the Countess, getting with difficulty to her feet. 'It's a disgrace the way they're hounding you, madam— Robert knows my mind on the matter, Lord knows I've made it plain enough.'

The Queen smiled faintly. Leicester was Lady Warwick's brother-in-law and the Countess seldom gave him any quarter.

'Anne! You know he couldn't stand against the entire Council in this.'

The Countess sniffed.

'When did he ever stand against anyone, begging your pardon, madam?'

'I won't have him maligned in my presence,' said the Queen sharply. 'He is not well.'

Lady Warwick curtsied with unruffled calm. She was a trusted friend who knew her mistress well and was not afraid to speak her mind on any subject. She said with asperity, 'I shall tell Goodrowse to prepare you a sleeping draught,' and went to admit the old Lord Treasurer.

Burghley came into the room leaning heavily on his staff and snapped his fingers to the Queen's remaining women, signing them to leave. For a moment he awaited Elizabeth's angry reaction to his unprecedented impertinence, but she was staring into the fire as though she had not even noticed. Too exhausted to care, he thought quickly, and for once his excitement outweighed his concern. If he ever had a chance to master her will, it was now—

He surpassed himself with his own eloquence that night, and she listened, supine in her chair, like a snake mesmerized by its charmer, while his soft voice needled, reproached and cajoled in turn, undermining her determination with powerful rationality. She could not dispute the truth of a single word he spoke. It was inevitable, this execution, it was just, it was even a kindness to release the wretched woman from this cruel suspense.

'. . . and after all, madam, what have you against it save an instinct, which may be wrong?'

That broke the charm which was slowly drawing her towards submission to his will. She sat upright and glared at him.

'My instincts are never wrong,' she said acidly, and dismissed him unsatisfied once more.

When he had gone, she was aware of an aching need for sleep, an exhaustion so great she could hardly stand upright while her women disrobed her. She refused to take Lady Warwick's posset, certain that dreamless oblivion must claim her the moment she lay down, and so they blew out the lights and left her alone in the darkness.

And then it began again. A thought, like a little rat, scuttled through the rushes of her mind, and was followed instantly by another. Feverishly they chased each other, pausing here and there to nibble spitefully behind her eyes, until it seemed that her whole brain was on fire.

Her speech to the parliamentary delegation:

It is sad that I who have pardoned so many rebels, winked at so many treasons, should now be forced to proceed against such a person . . . I have had good experience of this world. I know what it is to be a subject, what to be a sovereign . . . Princes are set on stages . . . it behoves us therefore to be careful that our proceedings are just and honourable.

Just and honourable . . .

She recalled Mary's miserable son, James, her god-son, writing to tell Leicester how foolish he would be 'to prefer my mother to the title'; and, indeed, the deputation he had sent to plead Mary's life had been half-hearted and hypocritical in the extreme. James wouldn't shed a single tear if his mother died tomorrow. So much for children! Perhaps she had been fortunate never to bear any after all.

She closed her eyes and against the dark background of her lids saw the bloody carnage of Mary's last battle in Scotland. Langside! Screaming men and horses, panic-stricken, riderless, plunging hoof-deep in gore and trampling bodies where faint life still lingered. Across the night a mud-spattered girl in a torn gown rode desperately for her life, fleeing from the treacherous pursuit of her own subjects, riding against all sound advice to England and her cousin's sanctuary, deceived by the spurious promise of friendship symbolized in a glittering diamond. *I am now forced out of my kingdom and driven to such straits that, next to God, I have no hope but in your goodness, my dearest sister.*

Elizabeth got up suddenly and lit a candle, groping on the bedside table for the letter she had received from Mary a few days ago. Leicester had advised her not to answer it, and it had lain there ever since.

Do you wish me to return the jewel you sent me now or later?

She bit her lip with shame and her eyes wandered and were riveted by another line.

. . . because I fear the secret tyranny of those into whose power you have abandoned me, I beg you not to permit me to be executed without your knowledge . . .

A vision of the block paralysed Elizabeth's imagination. The roll of drums, the flash of a blade in the sunlight, a blackhaired bauble tumbling soundlessly into the bloody straw . . .

'Anne! *Anne!*'

Lady Warwick ran in from the Pallet Room, with a shawl over her night rail, and found the Queen sitting on the edge of her bed, trembling violently. She looked up as the Countess reached her side and her eyes were wild.

'Has Leicester retired yet?'

'I don't know, madam, but I expect so, it's long after midnight. Shall I send to inquire?'

'No—*yes!* Ask him to come here, Anne, if he is still awake—but they are not to disturb him if he sleeps.'

'Yes, madam.'

Oh God—let him be awake!

Ten minutes later Leicester, dressed in a velvet robe trimmed with sable, was lifting her hand to his lips and gently fending off the little spaniel who had bounded from the foot of the bed to welcome him.

'Down! There's a good boy—been keeping you awake, has she?'

'Not him,' said Elizabeth shakily, 'he's been snoring like a pig by the fire all evening. How these dogs can sleep!'

'No conscience,' said Leicester shrewdly, and sitting on the bed handed her the draught she had refused earlier, serving as taster himself. 'That will quiet yours for tonight at least—drink it to please me.'

He looked tired in the candlelight, his high colour unnatural and unhealthy. She humoured him and swallowed the draught and as she did so, his eye fell on Mary's letter, face upward on the high pillows.

He swore volubly, as he reached for the sheets of paper.

'So this is what drives you from your meat and wrecks your sleep! A pity she employed less cunning in her own kingdom, she might not now be in this pass. Oh, Elizabeth, don't let her torment you like this. The Lord knows her guilt was plain for all to see at her trial.'

Elizabeth looked away and began to play with the golden fringe of the coverlet.

'So plain that not one original document was brought in evidence against her, nor were her secretaries brought to testify! She accused Walsingham of forgery and who is to say she was not right?'

Leicester leaned forward and covered her hands with his own.

'She's guilty, my love—as guilty as Babington and the rest.'

'Then if she's guilty why won't she *confess?* God knows, it's all I need to save her life.' She stared distractedly at the letter on the bed. 'I suppose she never believed I would dare to let it go so far—perhaps a letter was too cold and impersonal. But she's had time to reflect now—don't you think perhaps if I saw her—'

'That is the very last thing you wish or dare,' he interrupted suddenly. 'If you think Burghley's spent all these years making sure the two of you never met only to give way now—' He stopped. There was a truculent expression on her face and he hastily assumed a more conciliatory tone. 'It wouldn't be wise now—would it? And in any case I'm willing to swear it would be a waste of effort. She will never confess and damn herself for ever in the eyes of the world. Believe me, I have seen her and I know her stubborn pride will take her to her death rather than dishonour. The delay is too dangerous, madam. If she would rather die a martyr than live, then for God's sake let her. She's had a dagger at your throat for nearly thirty years! The only rational act—'

'You think it rational to execute a sovereign? You think I can cut off her head without any repercussion?'

'The blow to the Catholic faith here in England will be fatal.'

She struck the coverlet irritably.

'Oh God, Robin, what a fool you are if you honestly believe that.'

'Even Burghley calls her the "Queen of the Castle",' Leicester reminded her pointedly.

'Then he, like you, ought to know that the early Christian Church was built on the bones of martyrs. Her execution will be the greatest thing for the Catholic faith since the Crucifixion—even Walsingham won't douse *that* candle. Hang every priest in England and there'll still be good Catholics in every village. And the moment she dies the path to England is clear for Philip. Do you want to see the Inquisition set up here in London? We'll have a damn good view of it, no doubt, with our heads stuck on the city gates! Why should a man go in fear of his life because his creed differs from another? God knows, I wish *I* had a faith to die for.'

He was shocked into silence, horrified by this open declaration of atheism. Talk like this, overheard by hostile ears and betrayed in public, could drag her from her throne, despised by Catholic and Protestant alike.

'Let it rest,' he said anxiously. 'You are fighting the opiate.'

She began to laugh as the drug clouded her mind and released her inhibitions.

'You,' she said wildly, 'always so afraid *He* might be listening. If you will not hear me I shall speak to Walsingham instead. I'll say "Damn all religion and damn all men!"'

She swayed across the bed towards a silver handbell, but the room was distorted to her drugged sight and in her growing confusion she could not lay her hand upon it.

It was a trivial frustration, yet suddenly the final straw, sufficient to precipitate the hysteria that had been threatening for many weeks.

'I won't do it,' she sobbed, 'I won't be forced. I shall pardon her.'

'You can't do that.' He was aghast at the suggestion. 'She's been tried and condemned before the world—and if she's indeed innocent of this crime, she's been guilty of others. Adultery—murder.'

'So was my father! I don't seem to remember anyone suggesting that he should have been executed for his crimes against humanity—God knows, there were enough. He left more corpses in his wake than a tom-cat leaves litters. Oh, he was open-handed with death was my father—but not quite so generous with coffins. She never had one, did you know that? He gave her a coronation but not a decent burial. All day she lay in a pool of blood until one of her women found an arrow chest, too short for any normal corpse—but not for her. Late May it was, a hot summer's day full of flies—odd how they always know where to find carrion—'

Frozen in his chair, he listened helplessly to her tortured laughter.

'Shall I send an arrow chest for Mary?' she demanded suddenly. 'Or the sword of a French executioner? They say the French are very good at it. They ought to be, they charge enough. £23.6s.8d.—that was the going rate in my mother's day, the best that money could buy—'

She laughed again and then began to cry, falling on her pillows and beating them savagely with clenched fists.

'It will be the end of every monarchy in Europe—you'll see that, all of you, when it's too late to do anything about it.'

That was her conscious reason against it—a good reason, he had to admit; but her unconscious reasons frightened him a great deal more at the moment. Death by the axe; he had always suspected she was not quite sane on the subject.

Leaning over the bed, he lifted her into his arms and held her in an embrace so hard it crushed the sobbing out of her.

'Listen,' he said desperately, 'be calm and listen to me. There is another way—'

He waited till the sobbing became a whimper that trembled at length into silence, and all the while he chafed her cold hands, so cold that it seemed as though the blood had ceased to run in them.

'Assassination,' he said slowly. 'Poison in her cup, a pillow while she sleeps, there's a dozen ways it could be done. It would free you of this burden and if you agree—I will arrange it with Paulet.'

She was silent. He waited a few minutes to allow her to absorb the implications of his suggestion, then added quietly, 'I was always in favour of it. Right from the beginning it has been the only course to take. You see that now—don't you?'

Silence.

He looked down and found she was asleep, dead asleep in his arms with one finger in her mouth like a child. He laid her gently on the pillows and drew the covers around her.

After tonight, he was more strongly convinced than ever that murder was the only way. He had seen and heard enough to fear that the stroke of an axe would sever far more than Mary Stuart's neck.

Well, he had done his part. He had planted the seed.

All that remained now was to water it tenderly and pray that it bore fruit.

January crawled into February on leaden feet with the death warrant still unsigned. The Council despaired and the people milled in the streets of London, clamouring for the head of the Scottish traitoress. Rumours flew like wildfire in the explosive atmosphere, rumours that Mary had escaped, that the Spaniards had landed, that London itself had been set on fire.

At last the Lord High Admiral bowed sombrely over the Queen's hand and warned her of the unrest in the city streets.

'Madam, the people will not tolerate much more of this suspense. They grow dangerous in their fear for you.'

She went to the window and stared out bleakly.

'Strike or be stricken,' she said in Latin. After a moment she glanced over her shoulder at him. 'Walsingham is ill, as you know, my lord—the warrant is in Davison's keeping. Let it be brought to me at once.'

For six weeks Davison had hung around the Queen's apartments waiting for this summons and, as he hared back through Greenwich Park, it crossed his mind that it was entirely typical of her to send this summons when he was snatching his first spell of air and exercise for many days. He had been caught napping and he had the terrified suspicion that by the time he reached her presence she would use this unforgivable delay as an excuse to send him packing. The Council would skin him alive!

'But I wasn't to know,' he argued furiously with himself. 'I wasn't to know —I'm not a mind reader, damn it!' He rushed into his closet, grabbed the warrant and a handful of other papers requiring her signature and bolted down the corridors, like a mouse in a maze.

He arrived in the Queen's room, red-faced, sweating and out of breath, expecting abuse; but to his astonishment she turned from her quiet contemplation of the gardens and welcomed him gaily.

'Good morning, William.' She smiled sunnily at his hat which he had forgotten he still wore and he flushed scarlet as he snatched it off. 'Such a lovely day—I see you have been out.'

'A short walk in the park,' he managed to gasp.

'Ah yes, exercise—' She seated herself calmly at her desk and held out her hand for the papers. 'Exercise is a cure for all ills. I believe physic to be false and unnatural to the human body.'

There was something very terrible in this easy good humour after all those weeks of tortured indecision and he entertained a fleeting suspicion that her mind was unbalanced. She began to sign the papers without looking, chattering all the time like a magpie. *And there was the warrant!* Her pen flew over the surface, adding that twirling, fantastic signature and she tossed the paper on to the floor at the side of her desk.

There was a long moment of deadly silence before she looked up at him.

'Are you aware of what has just occurred, Davison?'

He swallowed nervously, unable to take his eyes off the paper on the floor.

'Fully aware, Your Majesty.'

'And are you not heartily sorry to see it done at last?'

'I am sorry for the necessity, madam.' His voice was quaking. Why had Walsingham had to take to his bed now of all times and leave him, poor unsubtle Davison, to handle this momentous issue? 'But, of course, not to see Your Majesty take the honourable course,' he added hastily.

Again that terrifying smile flashed at him and made him shiver involuntarily. She signed the rest of the papers without a murmur and then glanced down at the warrant on the floor, frowning at it as though in an effort to recall what it was.

'Take that to the Lord Chancellor for sealing, as secretly as you can, Davison, but be sure you show it to Walsingham first—the joy of it will probably kill him outright.'

He was suddenly very anxious to get away from her dreadful levity and as he bowed and backed towards the door, he heard her begin to talk feverishly to herself.

'It's done—it's done at last—but I never desired it—all my friends know how it grieves me—yes, they all know—I would have thought by now that one of them—'

His hand touched the door handle.

'*Wait!*'

Slowly, reluctantly, he crept back to her desk, dreading what he might hear. She looked up and pinned him with a steely glance.

'I consider it a remarkable thing that those who guard her have not seen fit to ease me of this burden—'

'Madam—I beseech you—'

'Go to Walsingham.' Her voice was suddenly as cold and hard as a snap of ice. 'Together you will write to Paulet and tell him to shorten the life of this Scottish Queen in private.'

'But, madam.' He gesticulated in wild despair. 'This is neither honourable nor wise.'

'Wiser men than you have suggested it,' she snapped angrily. 'You will write to Paulet, do you understand? And from now until it is done I wish to hear no more about it.'

Paulet sat in his icy room and fingered Walsingham's letter in horrified amazement. Paulet was hard and cruel and far from clever, but he was not a fool. He had no personal regard for the Queen of Scots, but he had a very healthy regard for his own life; and he had a shrewd suspicion what the reward for obedience would be in this case. The role of scapegoat was not one that particularly appealed to him.

He took up his pen and wrote with self-righteous regret that he could under no circumstances 'make so foul a shipwreck of my conscience as to shed blood without law or warrant', neatly passing the responsibility back to his Queen.

Davison flapped out of the Queen's room and rushed to Sir Christopher Hatton's apartments in a fine twitter of nerves.

'Sir—sir, I need your advice.'

Hatton was alert immediately.

'What's amiss?'

'The Queen—the Queen, sir. I was with her just now. "Is the warrant sealed?" she asks. "Why yes, madam," I replied. "Jesus, why all this haste!" says she—I'm afraid, sir, I'm very much afraid of what she really intends—and—and of how it affects me. I recall the late Duke of Norfolk's execution and her animosity towards those who urged it upon her. My shoulders are too weak to bear such a burden alone—I beseech your assistance with the Council.'

Hatton smiled faintly and reached for his ivory cane.

'I understand, my friend. You have done well to bring this matter so far, but I think it is time the warrant was laid in Lord Burghley's hands. Come—we will go now.'

Burghley stared at the warrant on the table before him. It took him just five minutes to make the most momentous decision in his career, five minutes during which he remembered that moment when he had bowed before her and sworn that he was hers to command in all things.

Just see that you remember that, my friend. At all times.

He recalled the curious quiver of fear which he had felt as she spoke. It was almost as though she had foreseen this very moment when he would be in a position to usurp her authority in a manner both unprecedented and cavalier. But surely this was what she was waiting for him to do. And after all, it was not the first time he had staked his career on a hunch by sending a woman to her death. A great deal passed through the complex corridors of Burghley's mind during those endless minutes of hesitation, but at the end of them his decision was firm and unshakeable. He knew what had to be done now; and he sent out a secret summons to all the available members of the Privy Council.

The next morning, tense and expectant, eight men trooped into his private room and took their seats. There was a portentous silence as Burghley rose stiffly to his feet and addressed the little gathering.

'My lords, the Queen has done her part in signing the warrant, all indeed that the law requires to make the execution legal. But *despatching* it, gentlemen, as I am sure you are all aware, is a very different matter and one which could take considerable time. Time we do not have. I am sure you all understand how easily a change of mind could take place.' The cool eyes swept round all those watching faces. 'Here is the warrant.' He flourished the document from which dangled the Great Seal of England. 'For my own part, gentlemen, I see no reason to trouble Her Majesty further with details of procedure. I therefore propose that we should all take responsibility for despatching the warrant without delay.'

The response to Burghley's remarkable proposal was a unanimous agreement that no man would inform the Queen of their action until the deed was accomplished. Talking quietly among themselves, the councillors drifted out to take dinner, but Leicester lingered in Burghley's room, absently kicking a log in the hearth and sending a shower of sparks into the chimney.

Burghley watched him cautiously from the security of his armchair.

'Well,' said the Earl at last, staring bleakly into the flames, 'I only hope we've done the right thing.'

'If you had any doubts, Leicester, you should have voiced them at the appropriate time,' retorted Burghley coolly. 'I hope I don't need to remind you of your commitment to this undertaking. It would take more than thirty pieces of silver to buy your way out of this, I assure you!'

Leicester sighed; he seemed too distracted to take offence at that unkind snipe against his integrity.

'I advised secret murder, did you know?' he mused quietly. 'I hear from Davison that she took my advice, after all. Don't you think—'

Burghley frowned. 'Paulet will never agree—he knows he would shoulder the blame for it. And for precisely that same reason we'll never get an assassin of our own past his guardianship. Put it out of your mind, Leicester—it's much better the honourable way.'

'*Honourable!*' Leicester turned to look at him ironically. 'You call sending it behind her back honourable? I hardly think that will be her choice of word.'

'We're all in this together,' Burghley insisted steadily, 'and a united front will be our shield against her anger.'

Leicester shook his head sombrely.

'There's no shield in all the world that will protect you after this, my friend. I'd hazard a rough guess and say it will probably mean the end of your career.'

Burghley smiled faintly. 'Yes—you'd like that wouldn't you, Leicester? Old grievances die hard even after all these years. But whatever the outcome I shall always stand by my decision. The Queen's life must be preserved at any cost.'

Leicester turned from the fire and looked at him squarely.

'Even at the cost of her sanity?'

Burghley looked away uncomfortably.

'It won't come to that.'

'Won't it? I wish I was so sure. She worries me, Burghley, I think we've pushed her too far. Oh, Christ, man, can't you see how unstable she is? The news of this could send her right over the edge. Are you happy to face Philip with the Queen incapable of active government? Do you think we'd stand a chance without her?'

'You could be wrong,' insisted Burghley doggedly. 'Will you answer for her life if you are?'

Leicester turned away abruptly. It was an impossible choice.

'I pray that I *am* wrong,' he said dully. 'I pray for it more than anything else in this world. And if I were you, Burghley, I would start praying too, night and day, until the moment comes when she has to be told.'

In the Great Hall of Fotheringay Castle there was silence as Mary Stuart knelt before the wooden block, her eyes blindfolded and buried deep in a black cushion. She had behaved throughout the ceremony with all the tragic composure of a Druid sacrifice and her dignity had awed the hostile crowd to the point of breathless reverence. She had repented her crimes, large and small, she had forgiven her enemies and made her peace with God during that endless February night when she had knelt at her prie-dieu until dawn. She had meant to die like a saint in the eyes of man and God, but now in the all-engulfing darkness, waiting for that final act, her mind reached out not to Heaven, but to Hell.

Such a small thing really, but it had robbed her of her inward composure and made her last moment on this earth one of overwhelming hatred. In her natural pride she had taken it for granted that she would be despatched from this life, as befitted her rank, by the mercifully swift caress of a sharp sword. But in less than a second her head would be severed by the common headsman's axe which she had seen waiting, half concealed in the straw which covered the scaffold. For that and for that alone she vowed eternal vengeance on the woman she imagined had ordered it out of spite.

Dear God . . . give me grace to haunt her all the rest of her days!

The words were stifled in the black velvet of the cushion and before the last syllable had died on her trembling lips the axe had fallen. Three times it arched through the still air, hacking with all the clumsy butchery she had dreaded, before Mary's head at last rolled away from her body. The executioner grasped the head by the hair and swung it aloft, only to find himself grasping an empty chestnut wig. Grey-haired and smeared with blood, the head rolled across the scaffold like some hideous ball and a gasp of horror went up from the spectators, for the eyes were open and the lips—it was plainly seen—the lips were still moving. From beneath her red skirts Mary's little terrier crept whimpering and came to cower in the pool of blood between the head and the slumped body. For a long time no one moved and then the scene was transfigured by frantic activity. The dog was carried upstairs to be washed of his mistress's blood. The head and body were borne away for embalming and while the block and Mary's clothing were carried outside to be burned, that no martyr's relics might remain, George Talbot spurred his horse out of Fotheringay courtyard, riding through the night to bring news of the deed to Greenwich Palace.

Burghley said, 'She is not to be told yet.'

Talbot gaped at him with absolute amazement and the Lord Treasurer inclined his head with the first sign of nervousness. 'It would be better to break it cautiously to her by degrees,' he said huskily.

Talbot registered one thing with certainty from this incredible command; the great Lord Burghley was evidently a very frightened man.

In London the celebration bells rang on for twenty-four hours while the people lit bonfires and danced all night in the streets at the news. It was the bells which finally betrayed the English councillors' guilty secret when the Queen inquired the cause of their ringing from one of her ladies. What happened after that no one at the English court cared to remember. By the end of forty-eight hours, when she had stopped sobbing long enough to find her voice, Greenwich Palace was like a spiritual battleground. Davison was in the Tower, waiting to be hanged for betraying her trust; Burghley banished from court on the understanding that his face was repugnant to her sight;

Walsingham in deepest disgrace and, with Hatton, forbidden to come into her presence. Shocked and alarmed, they comforted themselves with the knowledge that she would get over it; a month later they had begun to sense the real possibility that she would not.

Burghley sat alone at Theobalds, that great country mansion which he had erected as a monument to his Queen, and brooded on the calamity which had overtaken him. Twice now in a long and very distinguished career of practised mind-reading, he had grievously misread the desires of his royal mistress—and twice a woman had died because of it. But this time he had been so sure—so *certain*—that he was doing what she really wanted; and the sudden, irrational vengeance which she had wreaked upon him had left him dumbstruck.

He was finished—all his years of devoted service thrown back in his withered face like so much trash, flung out of court like an old dog whose tricks had tired at last. She no longer had any use for him. Only his age had saved him from sharing Davison's imprisonment in the Tower.

Mildred watched from the doorway in grim silence as the crippled old figure hunched over his desk, day after day, scribbling frantic letters to his royal mistress, each one returned to him unopened, so that he must put it aside and endorse it methodically 'Not received.' At first he had said with forced cheerfulness, 'I've weathered her storms before. You'll see—she'll send for me again within a few days. She can't do without me—I know she can't.'

A week later he said, 'They say she's ill—what can be expected if she refuses to eat or sleep? But I tell you, Mildred, once she begins to feel better it will all be forgotten.'

Two weeks later he banged his fist on the table and shouted, 'I know who's behind this—it's Leicester—pouring his poison into her ears—playing on her mind when she's vulnerable—he's always done that. If only I could speak to her, if only she would send for me and give me a chance to explain—'

It was March before he got his chance to do that and Mildred thought how pathetic it was to see a white-haired old man stumbling about his room in his haste to obey the royal summons, like an elderly dog who has heard his master's whistle at last.

He was back almost before his wife had time to accept that he was gone, stumbling from his grey mule and staggering into the house, leaning heavily on the arm of his steward. Mildred found him in the library, crumpling his hat in his hands. He turned to look at her with tears running down his parchment cheeks, losing themselves in the white, wiry hairs of his beard.

'William!' She hurried across the room and helped him to a chair. 'What happened? Why are you back?'

He shook his head, unable to accept it, and his voice was broken.

'It was just the same—no—it was worse—she just stood there, leaning on Leicester's arm—she looked so different, almost old—still dressed in mourning black, a black veil over her face. She wouldn't give me her hand to kiss—she made me stand through the whole interview.'

Mildred was silent for a moment, shocked by the significance of that last detail.

'But the Queen never lets you stand,' she muttered at last. 'Once she even stopped a speech because she saw you had no chair.'

'She made me stand,' he repeated dully, almost as though it were the final cruelty which had broken his spirit. 'Her eyes were full of hatred, Mildred. I tried to speak, I tried to reason with her, but she would not hear me out. She called me false dissembler, traitor—wicked wretch—in front of Leicester and Walsingham. And even Leicester looked away at that. It's not him, Mildred, it's not him, as I thought—as I hoped. It's her—it's all her. They say the wrath of the king is death—she means to prove it in me.'

'William—you're ill—you must not distress yourself like this.'

He looked up at his wife and smiled bitterly.

'My sickness is grounded on her ingratitude—it burns deeper than a continual fever.'

Mildred knelt stiffly by his chair and laid her plain, homely face against his hands.

'William—you have the children—the grandchildren—this beautiful house and the life she never gave you time to enjoy. Take this as a God-given chance to spend your remaining years in peace and tranquillity. Forget her, my dearest—forget her! Let her go.'

He looked down at the grey head in his lap and gently touched the peak of her cap. 'When they lay me in my grave,' he said.

Once the door had closed behind Burghley's bent, defeated figure, Walsingham had bowed and crept softly out of the room, exchanging a quick, sympathetic glance with Leicester, who remained behind.

After the violent scene which had just taken place there was an uneasy silence and the Queen, in her sweeping mourning gown, began to wander aimlessly from room to room in her private apartments, driven by the morbid restlessness which plagued her day and night. Leicester followed at a distance, watching her, conducting a disjointed and fragmentary conversation which, no matter what he said, seemed disturbingly one-sided. He had begun to realize that his replies were not registering, that though she appeared to be addressing him, she was in reality talking to herself.

'I never desired her death. Never!'

'But when you signed the warrant we all assumed—'

'No one believes me. No one will ever believe me. No one!'

'*I* believe you. For pity's sake, my love, stop tormenting yourself like this.'

'I look into their eyes and tell them I never meant it to be done and their eyes look back and call me liar. *Murderess.* I've killed so many and they all lie quietly in their graves, except *her*—but then she's not buried yet. Yes, that must be it—she has nowhere grand to rest. I will give her a state funeral—all the pomp and ceremony due to a queen—whatever it costs—perhaps then she'll leave me alone.'

She walked into the bedroom and he hurried after her with an icy tingling at the base of his spine. She was staring at her tapestry frame, untouched now for many weeks, picking hopelessly at the stitches, unravelling half a rose. This time he went right up to her and took her hands in alarm.

'What do you mean—leave you alone?'

She looked up and there was fear in her eyes, the same wild, unreasoning terror that he had glimpsed occasionally when she woke from nightmares; nightmares he had never prevailed upon her to describe. He remembered the disorientation that would continue for endless minutes, until the last mists of sleep were shaken from her confused mind; his own relief when she finally sat up and laughed, while still shaking, apologized for waking him so rudely yet again, suggested that perhaps she should change his adjoining room for a more peaceful apartment.

But now there was no hope that she would wake up and laugh, however shakily; for she was wide awake.

She took his hand and pressed his fingers against her throat on the bare patch of skin between her chin and the great cartwheel ruff.

'There,' she said. 'You can feel it, can't you?'

The fine network of hairline cracks across her mind was so clear to Leicester, in that moment, that he might have been looking at some ancient Greek vase, infinitely fragile, equally precious. He knew instinctively that one false jar now would send the whole precarious structure crumbling. He was going to have to choose his words with the utmost care.

'Yes,' he said quietly, cautiously, 'I can feel it. I think—you had better tell me, how it came to be there.'

Her eyes widened on his face in an ecstasy of relief and suddenly words were tumbling from her in a great breathless torrent. Some of them went past his understanding, like the rapid pummelling of a mighty waterfall, but he caught enough of her meaning to make his own senses reel with horror. She spoke repeatedly of the chain of iron about her neck and of queens, murdered queens, *his* victim—and hers. One owned what the other now sought, a bridge back to life.

'. . . but *she* will not give me up—why should she? I was always hers. So they fight, they fight when I sleep and their conflict consumes me. I burn candles all night long in my room to prevent it—I fear sleep more than I fear death.'

As he stood and listened to her ravings, his face contorted, as though he were about to weep. She saw it and stiffened, stepped back from him with one hand at her throat.

'Am I mad?' she whispered hollowly. 'Is this what it feels like? Shall I be shut away like Philip's wretched grandmother?' She pressed her hands against her temples in gathering panic. 'I should not have told you—I should not have told anyone—'

He caught her hands and kissed them furiously.

'I swear to you,' he said, in a curiously choked voice, 'I swear to you, as God is my witness, that I will never speak of this or betray you to anyone.'

'I have been betrayed on all sides by those who are closest in my counsel,' she said dully. 'You are all that is left to me out of a pit of vipers.'

Whatever part he had played in that betrayal, she appeared to have forgotten. He alone had escaped the wrath she had visited on the rest of the Council; and now he understood why.

'Help me, Robin,' she begged him suddenly, wild with despair, 'help me to free myself while there's still time. I can't bear to be shut away again—'

It was Mary she feared, and not her mother. He had gathered enough from her rambling to deduce that, and now he thought desperately, praying for inspiration—finding it suddenly and quite unexpectedly in her own words.

'A state funeral,' he said firmly. 'She will rest when you have buried her decently, with all the ceremony due to a reigning monarch. You will be at peace when it's done, I swear it.'

Elizabeth gazed at him doubtfully. 'Westminster Abbey?'

He blinked—*Oh God, not that, not so close*—and led her cautiously away from the idea.

'Not Westminster, the London mob would never stand for it. There might be desecration of her tomb.'

The Queen shivered. 'Where then?'

'Peterborough,' he said decidedly. Peterborough was far enough away. She nodded dumbly and turned away; he saw that she was not convinced.

'Let me sit with you tonight,' he said quickly, 'and every night—until it is done.'

She smiled absently, lifting one hand to touch his cheek.

'And put you in a coffin, too? The day I do that, my love, my own must be ready.'

After all these years, it was the closest she had ever come to saying that she loved him, and he heard it with a curious sensation, as though his heart had contracted into a ball of hot, heavy lead inside his chest, a burning in the throat which made him swallow with difficulty.

Her restless wandering had taken her to her bedside table, where in a large golden casket, she kept her most precious possessions under lock and key; the casket of which he had once spoken so bitterly to Burghley. It contained his own miniature; he knew, because she had once told him—he had never been permitted to look inside for himself.

The casket was open for once and she was toying with something unseen in its depths. He came up behind her so silently that, in her taut preoccupation, she did not hear him.

And so it was that he saw it.

'Oh God,' he said hollowly. 'Dear God.'

She gasped, a frightened, guilty hiss of her breath, as he lifted out the little doll. It was nearly forty-six years since he had seen it, on that night at Hampton Court when she had first told him that she would never marry.

It was just as he remembered it; dressed in black satin; and headless.

His face was white as he turned his eyes slowly to meet hers.

'I shall burn this evil thing,' he said.

'No!' Elizabeth snatched it from him wildly. 'Oh no, not yet. *Not yet! She does not wish it!*'

She was suddenly so deeply agitated that he was afraid to pursue the matter. Reluctantly he surrendered the dreadful little object and watched her lock it back in the casket with feverish desperation. He knew then that she had been sick for a long time, far, far longer than he could ever have imagined. Much that had puzzled and frustrated him over the years was suddenly clear and strangely unimportant, for nothing mattered to him now, except the need to shield her from discovery and the fate of brain-sick monarchs. Degrading imprisonment, stealthy death—he would not allow it. There must be a way to ignite the ashes of her vanity and make her rise again like the glorious phoenix he remembered.

He could not do it; he lacked the youth and vitality. But there was one other who just might. And without pausing to consider all the possible consequences of his suggestion, he remarked casually that it was over long since she had received his stepson, the Earl of Essex.

She reacted so sharply, angrily, to his suggestion, saying she had no wish to see that rude, headstrong boy, that Leicester was immediately convinced he was on the right track; it was the first time in weeks that anything had interested her enough to make her angry.

'And why not Essex?' he remarked, artfully provoking her. 'Is it fair to damn the boy for being his mother's son—*the she-wolf's cub?*'

That stung home, the only time he had ever dared to taunt her with Lettice, to whom she never referred by name, but only by that insulting soubriquet—and never to him. Until now it had been an unspoken understanding that Lettice did not exist. When she swung round to face him, he saw he had achieved his object; for the moment, at least, she had forgotten Mary Stuart.

'I don't know what you're trying to imply,' she said sharply. 'I have been perfectly fair to all her children—I gave the girls a place at court.'

'But it's the boy who really counts—and what have you done to advance him? Nothing! The lad has no means by which to support his title and he's beginning to resent me for his dependent state—Lettice says you'll always bear a grudge against him for her sake.'

'I do *not* bear grudges,' she insisted furiously. 'How dare she measure me against her own petty emotions! By God's precious soul, I'll make her eat those words—'

'Then you'll give him a post?' Leicester considered a moment and smiled. 'Of course, you could always make him Master of the Horse.'

Elizabeth stared at him. 'That post is not vacant.'

'It could be—if I resigned—and you know I ought to. I've hung on to it for years out of sentimental attachment—the first gift you ever made me as Queen. But I've so many other offices to fulfil now and it's a young man's job. Let him have it—believe me, he could use the £1500 a year.'

At the mention of money she was immediately alert and suspicious.

'That's a great deal to pay out on an untried lad, even on your recommendation, Robin.'

'Then satisfy yourself on his suitability—see him tonight. He won't think it odd if you choose to talk and play cards till dawn. No shadow will trouble you in his company, I promise you.'

The spark of animation faded from her eyes; she pulled her hands free from his, and he knew a moment of bitter disappointment as she resumed her aimless pacing. It was no good—nothing worked! Nothing held her interest long enough to break that vicious circle of guilty despair.

He thought dully: They shall not take her to the Tower. If it comes to it, I shall keep her close at Kenilworth. And if I find reason to distrust King James, I shall take her abroad . . .

462

As he watched, she passed a wall mirror of rare Venetian glass and halted abruptly in front of it. In the mirror, he saw her frown at her reflection and pull angrily at a crumpled curl.

A moment later, she looked over her shoulder at him.

'So what shall I wear tonight to receive him? What would be suitable?'

Leicester smiled with relief as he went to take the hand she held out to him.

Whatever she wore for Essex, he would make damn certain it was not black!

CHAPTER 4

Stark and solitary amid the barren desolation in the foothills of the Guadarrama, the raw stone palace of the Escurial stood silent beneath a fierce midday sun.

Within the maze of cool corridors, hidden in his Spartan little room, the mighty ruler of half the world pored shortsightedly over the documents which lay in neat stacks on a gold inlaid table. He did not look like a mighty ruler. In his eternal black, crouched over his papers, scribbling notes in margins and writing his interminable despatches and memoranda, he more closely resembled an elderly, underfed clerk. Yet half-blind, bent double with rheumatism, Philip of Spain, at sixty-one, was still the same model of patience he had been in his lost youth. He never laughed, never lost his temper —no, not even with the exhausted secretary who had once poured ink instead of sand all over his King's newly finished letter.

'It would have been *better* to have used the sand,' Philip had remarked flatly and began to write the letter all over again. There ought to have been something endearing about such saintly equanimity, yet Philip excited little warmth either among his people or his close servants. It was like serving a living statue.

Restraint was the governing principle of life, and self-restraint was the only thing that had enabled him to wait thirty years before taking his revenge on England, that miserable little half-isle of heretics, which prospered and mocked him steadily. Thirty years *she* had held him off with an unheard-of series of shameless prevarications. She had laughed at his holy crusade against heretics:

'Can't he let his subjects go to the Devil their own way?'

She had laughed at his hostility, as though he were an imbecile child, for ever playing with model ships, never to be taken seriously:

'Good morning, Mendoza. Come to declare war again?'

And she had laughed at the chink in his armour, the one weakness she had tricked him into exposing to a tittering world:

'My enmity and his having begun with love, you must not think we could not get along together whenever I choose.'

Oh, to be avenged on her for all those cruel sallies at his expense! He had loved her once, a little—perhaps more than he would ever be prepared to admit, except on his death-bed, to his confessor. A lifetime ago it seemed now, that first brief spring when she had cut across the darkness of his accursed marriage like a knife of brilliant sunlight, an insolent, infuriating chit of twenty-one. Even now, after all his marriages and mistresses, after all his countless hours of penance, he could still catch his breath at the memory of her laugh and the elusive, come-on look in her eyes.

But of course, she would not look like that now. She was old! His foolish infatuation had long since transmuted itself into undying hatred and soon she would laugh at him no more.

The 'Enterprise of England' was a personal vendetta against the woman he now honestly believed to be the Devil incarnate. It was appropriate, when he thought about it, that the Anti-Christ should be a woman—had not a woman been responsible for Man's first fall from grace? Strange tales were afloat of her, faithfully carried to him by her arch enemy, Mendoza. How she had fainted and remained unconscious for four hours, in spite of every attempt to revive her, 'an indisposition', reported Mendoza meaningfully, 'to which she is occasionally liable'. Oh, he knew quite well what Mendoza had meant to imply. Sometimes a witch's spirit could be called forth from her body to commune in the nether world, leaving the host in a senseless state which curiously resembled Elizabeth's. From time to time she appeared to see sights invisible to the human eye. Only the previous year, on her way to chapel, she had stopped dead, staring at something unseen, so overcome with fear that she could not continue on her way to church and had to be taken back to her apartments. Where was she during those lost four hours? And what terrified her so badly that she could not enter the House of God?

Renard had warned him long ago that she was of the Devil. He had chosen to ignore it for a long time, hoping to win her for himself and his Church.

But now he knew it was true. She was a witch and she must be burnt at the stake.

He liked to imagine that burning. It was so exactly what she deserved for the way she had treated him all those years ago. No matter what she said, it was he who had put the crown of England on her head, and kept it there just long enough for her to gain the strength to hold it without his aid. What a fool he had been, gulled by a woman's wiles like any lovesick stablehand. The sense of degradation had never left him; it was a sore that festered slowly. Now he would make war on her and it was God's obvious design that his enterprise would prosper.

After years of anxiety and indecision, he was unshakeably set on action in the face of every conceivable setback. Francis Drake had delayed the expedition for more than a year by his lightning raid on Cadiz and Corunna. Done quite against her express order, Elizabeth had insisted blithely. She really must hang that damnable knave one of these days—he appeared to think he ruled the seven seas. And all that shipping destroyed—such a shame!

Oh yes, she had spread her hands with mock horror and said a lot of conciliatory things—but she had quietly welcomed Drake back and pocketed the lion's share of plunder from the *San Felipe*, Philip's personal treasure ship. That knave had captured it as a casual afterthought on his way home.

The raid had been a severe blow to Spain. Thousands of tons of shipping and vast quantities of stores had been lost in Drake's devastating onslaught. The damage had taken twelve months to repair and had fully alerted the enemy to their intentions. So-called allies had begun to snigger and backslide—even the Pope looked down his long nose to sneer:

'We are sorry to have to say it, but we have a poor opinion of this Spanish Armada and fear some disaster.'

Sometimes it was difficult to be entirely sure whose side the Pope was on. From Sixtus V, his hard paymaster, Philip received a steady stream of sarcasm, and the continual reminder that their mutual enemy was 'a great woman—were she only a Catholic she would be our beloved'.

All over Europe it was the same, from friends and enemies alike. Nothing but reverence for her name, admiration for her achievements, outright delight at her audacity; while Philip was placed with a yawn in the category of also ran. He could not compete with her glossy brilliance, her vulgar show; he was the unsung spider to her gaudy butterfly, the tortoise to her hare.

But the tortoise would triumph, the fable said so, and no calamity could cloud Philip's faith in this endeavour. Even the death of his great admiral, Santa Cruz, had not disheartened him. He refused to believe, as others did, that there was no one capable of taking Santa Cruz's place at such short notice, and devolved the responsibility on the Duke of Medina Sidonia. Certainly the Duke had begged to be excused, for he had rarely been to sea before, let alone in a fight, and insisted piteously that he was always seasick and caught cold. Assuredly, oh assuredly, he was not the man for the job!

Philip appeared not to hear. He had made the appointment and would not reconsider his decision, and in truth the man's self-effacing attitude had pleased him. He approved of humility in his subjects, and he had a fine sense of what was fitting. His enterprise would not be led by a vulgar pirate, like Drake, but by the highest-ranking nobleman at the court of Spain.

And let the Duke not fear the inadequacies of his own judgement—he would not, at any stage, be called upon to use it! A weighty dossier containing the King's personal and meticulously detailed instructions upon how to proceed at every point would accompany the Spanish Admiral. And with God at his right hand, guiding the whole enterprise, there would be nothing—*could* be nothing—but victory ahead.

With all the calm serenity of a fanatic, Philip considered the order of procedure, the plan which could not fail. One hundred and fifty armed ships would sail up the Channel, embark the Duke of Parma's army at Dunkirk and land in England. The landing was all with which Medina Sidonia need concern himself—Parma's army would do the rest. Thirty thousand of the most highly trained troops in the world would make a butcher's shop out of any battlefield the English chose to make a stand upon; England was notorious for the poverty of her military defences.

Frowning slightly, Philip took a magnifying glass to Parma's letter that lay before him on the desk.

'. . . when we talked of taking England by surprise, we never thought of less than 30,000. Now she is alert and ready for us and it is certain that we must fight by sea and land, 50,000 would be too few!'

Even Parma! Everywhere the doubting Thomases, nowhere the encouraging word for what he knew in his heart to be so unquestionably right. Was there no one in Europe who shared his faith in God's obvious design?

And yet—he dabbed absently at the watery discharge which obscured the vision of his inflamed eyes—and yet there might be something in what Parma said.

A parrot cry of peace might induce England to abandon her defensive preparations. In God's actions there was no such thing as an underhand trick.

Philip's conscience was at peace as he wrote out orders to that effect.

'These negotiations are a smoke screen to blind us,' said Leicester furiously, 'Parma doesn't want peace!'

'He doesn't want war either,' remarked Elizabeth steadily, looking up from the maps and muster sheets which crowded her table. 'Not after the wretched winter he's just spent under canvas on short rations. He's lost fifty per cent of his army through disease and desertion. Would you want war in his place?'

'No.' Leicester flushed and looked away suddenly. 'But then I'm not half the commander Parma is, nor shall I ever be. The man's a military genius.'

'Even a military genius can have his bellyful of delays and contradictory instructions. Naturally I don't trust the man's real intentions. But if I were dear brother Philip, I'd trust Parma's loyalty even less. The peace talks will continue until the last possible moment. If they fail—'

'*When* they fail!'

'Then we will fight.'

'With what may I ask, madam—an army full of raw recruits who scarcely know one end of a pike from another?'

'They'll have to land before it comes to that. I might ask you to remember that the French call me the Queen of the Sea with good reason.'

'And I might ask *you* to remember that the Queen of the Sea decommissioned her fleet last July—why, God alone knows.'

Elizabeth tapped her pen ominously on the table top, frowning a little.

'Are you suggesting that I should have kept idle seamen on full pay for over a year, waiting for a fleet which is still in harbour? Do you know what it *costs* to keep the fleet-in-being?' She made an impatient gesture as he seemed about to reply. 'No, you damn well don't! Lord knows, you can't even keep your own household solvent. Twelve thousand pounds a month those wooden sea-dragons devour—if I'd taken the advice of panic-mongers like you, we'd be bankrupt by now.'

He stood his ground doggedly; he still insisted it was a suicidal risk to take.

'A calculated risk,' she countered calmly. 'All my contacts assured me that I had a year's grace after Drake's raid. So what are you bellyaching about? Time has proved me right, has it not?'

'You're always right,' he said slowly, staring at her rather curiously, 'sometimes I almost think—'

He let the sentence trail and absently struck the enormous globe which stood near the window, sending it spinning wildly.

When it came to rest, he found he was gazing full into the English Channel.

'The fleet shouldn't stay here like a flock of sitting ducks,' he grumbled. 'I say let the captains put to sea and take the offensive.'

'The fleet stays here to defend the coast.'

She spoke without raising her eyes, intent on the document before her, but her voice was categoric.

He fell silent. After a moment she became aware of his contemplative gaze and looked up at him with a wry smile.

'And you need not look at me like that—I am in full possession of my faculties.'

'Of course,' he said hastily. 'How should it be otherwise?'

She met his gaze steadily, knowing that his memory had flown to the previous year.

'It could have been otherwise,' she admitted softly, 'but that is over, Robin —over for good. Look at me. Am I not in command of myself now?'

The contours of his weathered face, ravaged by intermittent bouts of ill-health, were suddenly softened by a gentle smile.

'In perfect command of us all, my Queen. And no difference of opinion over battle tactics will ever shake my faith in your judgement.'

She laughed outright.

'Oh, you respect my *luck*—I know that by now, Robin.'

As she turned back to her work, ignoring him once more, he found himself reflecting on the communal belief in her luck. It certainly existed. A curious blend of loyalty and optimism pervaded England, with Catholics and Protestants moving hand in hand to defend Queen and country, all informed with a dog-like faith in the ability of the woman who led them. The aldermen of London—never noted for their generosity—had roundly declared their intention of providing double the figure that had been asked of them in men and ships. All over the country it was the same, no whisper of fear or panic anywhere, just a steady pulsing vein of gay patriotism which flowed from the heart of Elizabeth's calm confidence. Mad or sane, it was her touch on the bridle which steadied and her touch alone; her unique charisma which made her people—so notoriously fickle and variable—now swear to defend her to the last man against the canting little saint in the Escurial.

In the smoky taverns, maudlin with beer, they spoke of her as Gloriana, embellishing the image of their goddess with every tale they had ever told of her brilliance, her cunning, her essential humanity. They sniggered over the long list of suitors, the crowned heads of Europe who had made fools of themselves for more than twenty years running after her.

'Chaste and well-chased, eh?'

Oh yes, they dearly loved it, the proud, insular English—a good laugh at the expense of a foreigner and no one had given it with more unfailing regularity over the years than Elizabeth Tudor. The suitors she had cozened, the pirates she condoned, the ambassadors she had deceived—one had to admire her nerve, and the astonishing manner in which she had got away with it all. They lauded her mercy and calmly ignored its few outrageous exceptions, for whatever she had done she was nothing like so hasty in revenge as her dread sire.

Thirty years of travelling among her people had taught her to understand their needs. Puritanism had raised its gaunt head in Parliament to no avail, for she had kicked out the unpopular bill to create 'the English Sunday', that bill which at one stroke would have banned cock-fighting, bear-baiting, fairs and markets—in short, everything which made a day of rest worth having to the common man. She had refused the imposition of the death penalty for adultery, blasphemy and heretical opinion, and had rescued the theatrical companies of London from suppression by creating her own company. No Puritan had yet dared to stand up in the Lower House and suggest the suppression of the Queen's men!

She still maintained a humorous indifference to the many abortive attempts to assist her to her permanent repose. It was her continued ill-guarded appearances in the streets of London which had won her the warmest response from her people, who loved spunk above all things. They said she was without fear. They were wrong. But they would never know, and that perhaps was the greatest testimony to her courage.

Leicester watched her with exasperated tenderness, the same odd, baffled, begrudging admiration which had dogged him all his life, ever since that first moment when he had scowled at her across the nursery floor. If his only claim to fame was to have been loved by the most remarkable woman of her age he would be proud of it. And for him her weakness was the only true measure of her stature. It seemed little short of a miracle to Leicester that she should be sitting still in her old place, with the reins of government firm in her hands. She had locked away the terror and the guilt which had threatened to destroy her reason, so that now once more she appeared to stand erect and unassailable on her pinnacle. Appeared—perhaps it was no more than that; but for England, for the moment, it was enough. And he was more proud of her for that than for all the long succession of political achievements which had gone before. Robert Devereux, the young Earl of Essex, had wrought the first little miracle, the initial effort of will; the threat to England had done the rest. By the end of spring 1587 she had climbed out of her dark abyss of despair sufficiently to make decisions again. And the first, the most significant, was the pardoning of her chief minister. While Drake, on her personal commission, was wreaking havoc on Philip's fleet at Cadiz, Elizabeth, with her full court, had descended on Burghley at Theobalds, at what was virtually a moment's notice.

Mildred Cecil, inwardly furious, had supervised the chaos among her staff in stiff-lipped silence, while Burghley stood all morning by the window, shaking furtively like a man with an ague, and peering down the great drive for the first glimpse of fluttering pennants which would announce the royal entourage. There was the usual chaos as the court dispersed into the Great Hall to squabble over refreshments, served by a small army of servants, while the Queen was escorted ceremonially to her old suite of rooms in uncomfortable silence.

She walked the length of the Vine Chamber and stood for a good five minutes looking over the gardens on the south side of the house, watching the marble fountain which threw up a great spray of water as high as the house.

Her silence weighed heavily on the spirits of her host and hostess, just as she had intended it should. She knew, without looking, that Mildred's face was an unflattering cherry hue, and Burghley's chalk-white with tension. Finally she peeled off her gloves and tossed them, with her cloak, into the arms of a waiting maid of honour, announcing curtly that the ladies might have her leave to withdraw.

The women withdrew in a scurry of hasty curtsies, closing the heavy double doors behind them, and Mildred went, with a sinking heart, to pour a fine, pale ale into three silver goblets waiting on a table near the hearth.

The Queen had very little use for Mildred Cecil at the best of times; now she made no pretence at civility.

'I said the ladies might leave, madam. Are you deaf—or do you believe yourself, like your husband here, to be above my authority?'

In the centre of the room, Burghley stood with his chin sunk against the base of his scrawny neck, his eyes fixed on the floor and his hands clasped around his staff for support. Over his white head, Mildred met her rival's glance with an unguarded glimmer of hostility, before she too sank into a deep curtsey, and went out of the room, leaving behind the last hope of tranquillity in the twilight of her marriage. She lingered outside the door just long enough to hear the Queen say in a vastly altered tone, 'Sit down, you old fool, before you fall'—but she did not wait to hear Burghley's reply. She was not a masochist!

Through a maze of corridors stalked the lady of the manor, frowning at all she saw on her way. The house was a mausoleum now. What had originally been conceived as a modest, private residence, destined for Burghley's second son, Robert, had grown into a sprawling palace, nothing short of a playground for the Queen's pleasure. On her first visit Elizabeth had complained about the size of her chamber. Burghley had had it enlarged to such enormous proportions that it was now big enough to sport its own fountain; and the rest of the house, year after year, had grown around it, like some monstrous, extravagant weed curled in a stranglehold around the Cecil purse. Every visit she made there cost them at least three thousand pounds.

In the privy garden, deeply sunk and surrounded by a nine-foot hedge, Mildred found the only spot which afforded her a sense of escape from Elizabeth's strident domination. There she sat for several hours, brooding among the figs and plums that grew along the walls, while the house towered above her, a pink brick façade with blue slate turrets and gilded weather vanes which seemed to mock all her austere good taste. How could Burghley have built anything so vulgar! The house *was* the Queen—unforgettable, ostentatious, overbearing—and Mildred hated it, hated to feel it sitting there self-satisfied in the sunshine, looking down on her with all its calm superiority.

No woman, thought Mildred angrily, had the right to make other women feel so colourless and drab, or to be so slim and upright at the age of fifty-four that merely to look at her was to feel as plain and stout and purely functional as a carthorse. No woman had the right to such presence! She had always been out of her depth in the company of the Queen, her dull bluestocking image overshadowed by all that effortless brilliance. But never before had Elizabeth made it quite so plain that, in the final analysis, Mildred and all the comfortable domesticity she symbolized counted for nothing. The Queen had merely to raise her little finger and Burghley, the devoted husband, the loving father and doting grandfather, would turn his back on everything he held dear to follow her shining trail.

'I am nothing,' Mildred told the smug house savagely, '*nothing*,' and great tears forced themselves between her scanty lashes to roll sombrely down her unpainted cheeks.

Shadows were falling across the garden by the time Burghley came painfully down the steps to the stone bench where she still sat.

'I thought I would find you here, my dear,' he began cordially. 'Would you care to take a turn with me in the Mulberry Walk? It will be cooler there.'

He was grey with fatigue but his faded blue eyes were alive again, alert with a joyful anticipation such as she had not seen there for many months.

She got up immediately and took his arm and they went slowly down the brick-walled walk, past the seventy-two mulberry trees that led to the Great Pond.

'So,' she said a trifle impatiently, when five minutes' silence had still produced no voluntary information from him, 'what happens now that you are forgiven?'

'I'm not forgiven,' he replied quietly. 'I never hoped for forgiveness—only for the chance to serve her again. I thank God that of her mercy she has seen fit to grant me that favour.'

Every nerve in Mildred's body screamed out in protest, but was given no voice.

'You have accepted the post,' she murmured dully, staring at the fountain ahead. 'You will return to court.'

Burghley smiled faintly. 'My dear, I could hardly refuse.'

His absent smile, his utter certainty of her acquiescence, were unbearable. For a moment she regretted all the years of patient self-restraint and wished she might throw one of Elizabeth's famous tantrums here in the grounds of his own house. But even as she thought of it, she knew she had neither the spectacular temperament nor the essential physical frailty which enabled Elizabeth to make an exhibition of her instability without looking either ugly or ridiculous.

'How long are we to be honoured by Her Majesty's presence?' was all that emerged at last in a rather dry tone from between her thin lips.

He coughed, as though realizing that this, of all things, might be the final straw.

'Perhaps a month.'

So it was not enough to break his heart and then make him jump through a hoop like a performing dog; it was necessary to bankrupt him as well!

Not trusting herself to speak, she withdrew her arm stiffly from his hand and began to march back up the Mulberry Walk.

'Mall!'

She stopped. He never called her that, except behind the privacy of the bed curtains; in the hours of daylight she was always Mildred, respectable, serviceable.

'If you want me to say no—' He hesitated, staring miserably at the gravel walk. 'I could plead my growing infirmity. If I do, I know she won't ask it again. It could be as you wish—the house—the family.'

And you would be in the grave before the Spaniards come, thought Mildred sadly. So what is the point?

'Whatever you choose to do,' she said loyally, 'I will support you, William. Don't refuse her just to humour me.'

The relief in his face made her want to weep. He squeezed her arm gratefully and they went back into the house with their marriage intact.

So Burghley returned to court to resume his post as Lord Treasurer and having drawn her chief minister back into her web, Elizabeth turned her power on every man at court, deftly weaving the separate threads of their loyalty into one strong fabric. Transfigured by her own sense of purpose she was irresistible. No one escaped the network of her charm, neither courtier nor councillor. Poets and pirates, rogues and time-servers were suddenly united in her service, as Elizabeth alone was capable of uniting them. Never before had Leicester, watching her with awed fascination, been quite so strongly reminded of a queen bee; and indeed her influence over the hive held the same sort of primitive mystery. Like workers and drones, men fell into their appointed places around her, blindly, without questioning why they placed their lives at risk in a hopeless cause.

For it *was* a hopeless cause, Leicester was certain of it. He looked at the odds against them with the cold logic of a mathematician and knew that no man in his right senses would put a single gold crown on their chances of survival. A handful of modern ships and an army of ignorant amateurs! What serious hope had they against Philip's huge vessels and Parma's savage, disciplined troops? The very thought of them bearing down steadily upon Plymouth ought to be enough to make any sane man abandon the Queen to her enemies and run for his life.

Only no one would desert her, least of all himself—that was the miracle. And when he looked into her face, he knew that in spite of the facts, in spite of the logic, they were going to win.

This self-styled mother of the people was suckling them all, from some bottomless well of strength, with an intoxicating brew that played tricks with a man's normal healthy sense of self-preservation. Each man who left her presence went out in a state of crazy euphoria, quietly convinced of his innate ability to walk through fire unscathed.

Her power was a tangible force he could no longer rationalize or dismiss; and curiosity consumed him. He simply could not help it any longer—he had to learn from whence that power came.

And what she offered in return for it!

'Elizabeth.' In his mouth his tongue felt dry and swollen, suddenly heavy with dread. What was it Burghley had once said? *A very dangerous accusation —some might say it constituted an act of treason* . . .

It could take him to the block.

Equally—it could take her to the stake.

She looked up and arched her pencil-line eyebrows in mild surprise.

'Are you still here? I thought you would have been at Tilbury by now, drilling that army of raw recruits.'

He looked down at the floor.

'Before I go—will you answer me one question?'

She sighed and turned a page over; she was really very busy.

'Ask away then, but quickly. Burghley's waiting outside.'

'Are you a witch?'

The words hung on the air for him to hear, aghast. How could he have asked it like that, without a grain of sense or subtlety, leaving neither of them any avenue for escape?

She looked at him in silence. Slowly she rose from her chair, a shadow curling upward until to his terrified sight she towered above him, all-pervading, all-knowing. It was a hot, hot summer's day and all his senses throbbed and buzzed. Instinctively he passed a hand across his eyes.

'Robin?'

He blinked, and found her standing beside him, a full head shorter than him, as she had always been, her cool hand on his sleeve.

'This heat,' he muttered and wiped his brow with her handkerchief. She smiled and patted his stout girth.

'This padding doesn't help. Now—you are not to tire yourself unduly at Tilbury, do you hear?' She frowned faintly, as the memory seemed to strike her. 'What was it you wanted to ask me?'

Was it possible that she had been paying him so little attention that she had genuinely not heard his tense mumble?

Or was she offering the only safe way out for them both?

He would never know; he would never dare to ask it again.

He laughed a little unsteadily and said it was no great matter. Then he went out to tell Burghley that he might go in.

In mid-May 1588, a vast crocodile of Spanish ships sailed under its unwilling commander into storms and torrential rain. Medina Sidonia was horrified by 'such summer seas as had never been in living memory', sudden tempests which scattered their precise formation and wreaked such havoc that they were forced to shelter at Corunna until the middle of July. By then, they had lost time and the vital element of surprise. The English fleet was rapidly mobilized, and as Medina Sidonia pored over that dossier of instructions from Philip for the conduct of the campaign, Elizabeth gave full discretion to her Admiral, Howard of Effingham, and his vice-admirals.

On the 19th of July the Spanish fleet, a stately crescent with horns seven miles apart, was sighted from the Lizard and through the summer dusk the beacon fires sprang up, blazing a trail of warning lights across England to the Scottish border.

London seethed in a fever of activity. The court moved to St. James's Palace, while the beacon signals sent a wave of mustering, training and arming throughout the south. Boys slipped away from their mothers' clutches and flocked down to Tilbury, where Leicester's army lay encamped. Huntingdon's force in East Anglia swelled daily, while Hunsdon's bodyguard sprawled to the west of London in defence of the Queen's person. The Council met in terrified debate and begged the Queen to withdraw inland to deeper security, knowing that if she were taken the main purpose of the invasion would be complete. She began to talk instead of going down to the coast and Leicester wrote in a flat panic, 'I cannot consent to that for upon your well-being consists everything—preserve that above all.'

Candles burnt all night at St James's Palace, and Leicester rode between Tilbury and London, attending conferences until three in the morning. And at last, in August, he and the rest of the Council gave way to her determination.

She would go to Tilbury to review her army in person.

The great Spanish sea serpent had rolled relentlessly towards the Cornish coast and anchored at nightfall just off Dodman Point on the 19th of July. Next day Howard's personal pinnace carried the formal English challenge to the Spanish commander and with propriety correctly observed, the battle was on.

The small, modern English ships snapped at the huge vessels and darted away. Howard's flag ship was rammed, but before the Spanish galleons could close in on their prey, small boats had towed her head around and she escaped with remarkable speed. The Armada ran a gauntlet of the English ships up the Channel, unable to get closer than three hundred yards to the swift, sharp-shooting English vessels. Medina Sidonia had discovered the first flaw in Philip's instructions. How could they grapple the enemy ships and board to settle the affray with hand-to-hand fighting and superior numbers, when they could not get close enough to site the first hook? 'Their ships are so fast and nimble they can do anything they like with them,' bewailed the Spaniard's official log-book after the first day's engagement.

The Spanish Admiral was growing desperate. He had sent frantic messages to the Duke of Parma, begging for ammunition and flyboats to outmanoeuvre the English ships, who were running circles around the clumsy galleons and 'plucking our feathers little by little.' But he had no idea at what port he could expect to find Parma's army waiting. Blindly the Spanish fleet groped its way out of the English Channel and rode anchor at Calais Roads, repairing damages, while Medina Sidonia waited anxiously for news of relief —ammunition, food and water. Their stores were almost exhausted. What was Parma doing to leave them so shamefully in the lurch like this? Was it possible he had not received Philip's command to rendezvous at sea?

A mile and a half away the English fleet watched a hundred and fifty sea monsters bobbing on the quiet waves. A council of war was held aboard the *Ark Royal* and at midnight on the 28th of July, eight English fireships filled with explosives sailed into the Spanish fleet on a rising wind. Spanish pinnaces, working under a constant barrage of English shot, had just manoeuvred two of the fireships out of line when they exploded. The pinnaces fled for cover and the remaining six fireships bore into the great Armada which lay in impeccable formation, like a flock of sitting ducks.

In the mêlée that ensued the Spanish captains panicked and cut their cables. Several galleons, caught in the grips of the current, crashed together and the careful formation disintegrated into chaos, with ships drifting as far as six miles apart, some to sink, some to be captured by the English, others to be driven ashore. Sick at heart, Medina Sidonia sailed towards the Flemish coast in search of reinforcements, but the coastline remained empty. Parma had played them false. There was nothing for it but to turn and engage the enemy alone.

For five hours Howard's ships pounded the crippled fleet, until lack of ammunition forced him to ease off. The scenes of carnage were without precedent. Priests groped their way across the splintered decks, miring their robes in blood, to minister to the dying. The Spanish troops were packed so tightly in the holds of the ships, that when one galleon keeled over blood was seen to pour from the scuppers and stain the sea around.

At noon the wind changed and, to Howard's fury, the remaining vessels were able to slip away through the mist and blinding rain into the North Sea. The fleets broke off direct contact, but no one yet knew whether the depleted Armada would return—or whether Parma would seize his advantage, now that the English fleet was virtually disarmed, to sweep across the Channel and invade in the Armada's wake.

The troops were taut with anticipation and excitement that hot afternoon when Leicester rode across Tilbury plain with his stepson at his side, to welcome the Queen and her escort of two thousand horsemen to his camp. Seeing her sitting bareheaded on her beautiful gelding, dressed in virgin white and wearing a silver breastplate in mock concession to her advisers' fears, he was suddenly starkly aware that Burghley had been right; this was madness. To let her venture out unguarded on a field of armed men—thousands of unknown, unvetted ruffians, any one of whom might easily be a fanatic or a Spanish agent, ready, waiting—And nothing could have made a more perfect target of her than that dazzling white gown. How had he ever let her talk him into this?

It was too late now; there was no way he could hustle her into his chequered and particoloured pavilion and forbid this appearance. Even if he could change her mind—a forlorn hope—he knew he could not answer for the ten thousand men assembled under his command if they were thwarted of this chance to see and hear the woman in whose defence they were prepared to die. A loss of discipline—a riot—at this stage could be disastrous. And so he took her horse's bridle with a trembling hand and led her forward, unguarded, before the dense sea of waving pikes and caps and banners. From the corner of his eye he caught sight of Essex's face, flushed, excited, admiring, his eyes on the Queen solemn with open adoration; and for the first time Leicester felt a sharp pang of envy for youth in its first handsome flush. The quick, intimate smile which had passed between Elizabeth and the young Robert Devereux was like a sudden knife thrust in his heart. Such warmth and tenderness in her eyes now when they rested on Essex's blazing red head, such a strangely familiar expression. He had seen Lettice look at the boy in that same doting way. What did the Queen see when she looked at him to make her smile like that? A son? The son she had never borne? Was that *all* it was? He, who had so deliberately thrown the two of them together, felt his first moment of real unease. There was something wrong, something just a shade unnatural in the passionate companionship which had sprung up since the previous spring, through all those long nights when they had sat together playing cards because she dared not sleep. He had thought her safe enough with such a young man, he had been glad to see Essex's boyish high spirits pull her back from the brink of a nervous breakdown; but now he had a horrible, indecent thought; was Essex her lover?

He clung to the gelding's bridle with a convulsive grip, torn between terror that he would see her assassinated before his eyes and the fierce, jealous desire to stab her in the heart himself if his dreadful fancy should be true, if she had really so debased herself as to take a man more than thirty years her junior to her bed. She couldn't, she surely wouldn't! But she was Elizabeth, a law unto herself; and she just might.

A silence had fallen over the swaying multitude as the Queen raised her white hand and now her voice was throbbing in his ears, speaking words which would live for ever in the memory of Englishmen. He had forgotten how beautifully she could speak, the strength and depth of her voice reaching out across the fields—it would breathe life into a stone. And how low and unworthy it made him feel to stand here, entertaining dark suspicions about her honour.

The sun beat down mercilessly into his eyes like white hot daggers, making his senses swim. The words began to rush past him and he tried to clutch on to them, but it was no use. The world was dark around him and he no longer knew what she was saying.

The next he knew the crowds were waving and cheering in a hysterical frenzy and it was all over. For a moment he was afraid the seething masses would surge forward, but under the control of her daunting majesty the lines held. He felt his throat close. Perhaps in every thousand years the world produced one man or woman to live in incandescence, enshrined within their span of time. What else would men call this era but *Elizabethan?*

The magnitude of his thoughts had left him dog-tired, but now he must lift her down from the white horse and watch her walk among the ragged ranks. The sun flashed fire from the silver breastplate. Men wept unashamedly as they fell to their knees and swore to die for her.

Gulls were screaming overhead, circling the rows of huts which had been hastily erected, made of poles twined with green leaves which curled and lost their sap steadily in the fierce heat. The hem of her white gown trailed in the rusty earth. He remembered thinking it was a shame—that gown would never be fit to wear again. And then the sun was lower in the sky and at last he was leading her into his tent, followed by her ladies.

He unfastened the breastplate with his own hands and saw where the sun had caught her neck, leaving red places that reminded him of another time, another place.

He bent with reverence to kiss both her hands.

'You were magnificent,' he said quietly.

But she did not seem interested. Her attention was riveted on his sweating face, scanning him with anxiety.

'You are not well.'

He laughed. 'I'm hot—as you must be. It was like Hell's valley out there. Come—let me get you something to drink.'

He held a fine banquet that night in his pavilion and while they were all still seated at the table, there was a great shout outside. A moment later the Earl of Cumberland came striding through the entrance to fall on his knees at the Queen's feet. A tense silence fell as she gave him her hand to kiss and asked for his news.

'Madam, Howard engaged the Spanish fleet a week ago at the Gravelines and dispersed its main body.'

'Dispersed?' she frowned.

'Destroyed in all but name, madam. Howard drove them through storms up the east coast of Scotland where we can safely leave the winds and rocks to finish those who have not sunk already. It was a great naval victory.'

'But—?' said the Queen, staring steadily at Cumberland's grim face, and nipping off the excited cheer around the table with a flick of her hand.

'But—' Cumberland twisted his flat cap uneasily between his huge hands, 'the rumour is now that Parma with six thousand horse and fifty thousand foot will come out on the highest tide to make a landing.'

Leicester rose in his chair and sank back again, his anxious eyes meeting the Queen's. They both knew that, if Parma came now, there would be wholesale slaughter among that inexperienced English force outside, presently yelling with delight, and lighting bonfires all over the camp to celebrate the news of victory.

She had sworn to live and die among her soldiers, and would not listen now to those who urged her to return to London and the safety of the Tower. She resumed the dinner calmly and it was very late that night before Leicester finally got her to himself for a few moments.

'They're right,' he said slowly, 'you should get away from here. It's madness for you to remain.'

She shook her head. 'If Parma comes, he'll find me waiting.'

'You know I can't defend you here. If Parma takes you—'

He stopped and she laid a hand on his arm, 'If England falls to Philip there's no place for me in this world. I would be proud to die with my soldiers.'

'You won't die in Parma's hands. When he's satisfied that you have suffered every degradation his twisted mind can devise then he'll deliver you to Philip—who will have you burnt!'

'As a *heretic?*'

Her smile mocked him, made him wonder anew whether she had heard his question the day he left court for Tilbury.

He frowned. 'Must it come to that?'

Elizabeth leaned back against the central post which supported the canvas weight of the tent.

'Walsingham's spies assured me that Parma was not equipped for such a mission, that he has only a dozen flyboats and a few flat-bottomed canal boats. I suppose it's possible we were fed false information.'

'And if that's so?'

'Then I pray he comes at once. I want this settled by the end of August at the latest.'

He stared at her blankly. 'August? Why August?'

She sighed patiently and looked out at the burning orange lights of the camp fires.

'So I can demobilize, my love, and get all those men back where they belong, at their trades and in the fields. There's a crop to be harvested if we're not to have a famine in the winter—victory is a poor substitute for food to a child with an empty belly.'

Parma's army never moved. Her original assessment of the commander's half-hearted commitment to the 'Enterprise' proved correct and the integrity of Walsingham's famous intelligence service remained unquestioned, the most efficient system in the whole of Europe.

Howard's fleet chased the surviving Spanish vessels round the east coast, without firing another shot from their empty arsenal. Behind the crippled ships floated a long trail of mules and horses, discarded by the Spanish in their haste to get away. The body of the young Prince of Ascolo, commonly reputed to be Philip's bastard son, was seen floating, face down, in doublet and breeches of fine white satin, still sporting stockings of russet silk.

What was left of the glorious Armada made for the north of Scotland through a rising storm. Winds, cruel rocks and savage inhabitants claimed many more victims, for the shipwrecked Spaniards who struggled ashore on the west coast of Ireland were slaughtered in their hundreds by ferocious clans. Of the thirty thousand men who had set out from Spain, less than ten thousand straggled back to tell their wretched tale.

Dressed in sackcloth and deepest mourning black, fearful messengers toiled through the broiling sun to bring the news to the Escurial, where Philip received the tidings with unblinking calm. Even now that monumental patience remained unshaken and he neither chastised his commander nor reproached his heavenly superior for failing him in such a manner. Instead he thanked the Lord 'it was no worse'; and no one in that dark penitential palace saw fit to point out that it could not have been much worse.

'In God's actions reputation is neither lost nor gained,' he said quietly. 'It is best not to talk of it.'

And so he did not talk, merely shut himself up in that airless, palatial tomb, to pray and plan afresh, while only his confessor dared to approach him.

Howard, who had lost only sixty men during the fight, now faced wide-spread loss from a virulent outbreak of dysentery, and turned the English fleet for home. The English seamen who had repelled the enemy lay dying for want of care in the streets of Margate, while Burghley, frantic to staunch the flow of money from a rapidly emptying Treasury, parrotted the government's defence in refusing help: *To spend in time of need is wisdom; to spend without need brings bitter repentance.* As in all epidemics, the weak would die, the strong would recover. There would be no worthwhile return on money invested merely to ease men a little more comfortably into their graves. The English sailors could consider themselves lucky to be paid for their efforts—it was more than the Spanish would be.

When Burghley's message was brought to Margate, the English commanders stared at each other in grim silence. They did not question whether the Queen knew of this decision, for it bore the familiar stamp of that rigorous and ruthless paymistress. So the English sailors received their due and nothing more, while Howard, Drake and Hawkins shrugged their shoulders and provided wine and arrowroot for the sick out of their own pockets.

When it became clear at last that there would be no attack from Parma after all, Elizabeth left Leicester to wind up the camp at Tilbury and returned to London. The city was a mad throng of pealing bells and hysterical crowds who packed so densely into the narrow streets that her progress was brought to a virtual standstill more than once. She had always been loved, but now she might have been a pagan deity, for never before had their homely affection soared to such a sacrilegious peak of worship. They thanked God for the victory, but it was to the woman who had led them through that victory that they turned the visible evidence of their gratitude, weeping and cheering and fighting to get a glimpse of her, while the open litter bore her along the streets in her moment of supreme and solitary triumph.

She drank in their homage, the unstinting love for which she had hungered since her confused and lonely childhood. But now it was so strong, so powerful, that it had begun to frighten her a little. They were calling her invincible, beginning to believe that she could go on endlessly protecting them from harm, solving all their problems. The people who milled about her in the streets saw no further than this resounding victory—the Spanish were smashed, it was the end of the war. But she knew it was only the beginning, a respite in a long series of costly hostilities which would relentlessly sap away the gains of thirty years of peace. For as long as she lived, she would never be at peace with Spain again.

As she travelled slowly through the London streets, she felt all the elation draining out of her, like wine through a hairline crack in a glass goblet. A sense of unknown dread was closing in on her quite irrationally, throwing up a silly phrase to trouble her.

What price victory?

The sun beat down upon her uncovered head, but it could not drive away the creeping chill around her heart. She found herself suddenly thinking of

God. She had gone dutifully through the motions of being a good Protestant for countless years, just as she had once presented the face of a good Catholic to the world. But she had not thought—truly thought—about God for a long time. For the past few years she had been quietly certain that He did not exist. But now, thinking of her faithlessness which He had not yet seen fit to punish, she found a fear which was very close to panic.

She would lay no claim to this victory. She would strike a medal acknowledging God's hand in this and strike it without begrudging the cost.

And when it was done, perhaps she would be free of this sense of something owing, a nameless payment as yet in shadow, casting a chill breath upon a summer's day.

She turned the medal over in her mind, feeling its weight, tracing the inscription, for already she knew what it would say.

God blew and they were scattered.

Ah—He was a jealous entity, God, as greedy of His servants' undivided worship as she was herself. But *that* ought to satisfy Him.

She lifted her hand to the crowds and acknowledged their adulation without anxiety now. When the swaying litter came to rest at length in the palace courtyard, Essex, as Master of the Horse, came to lift her down from the cushions. It had been a long and gruelling journey and he looked at her with some astonishment.

'Why, madam,' he exclaimed, 'you are *still* smiling.'

She laughed and spread her hands in a reckless gesture of triumph which seemed to embrace him and the whole palace sprawling around her.

'Let me smile,' she said defiantly, looking not at him but at some unfixed point in the sky. 'What in the world can spoil my joy?'

A heat haze shimmered over the palace and in the distance there was a faint rumble of thunder.

Essex laid her hand upon his sleeve with a familiar gesture.

'We had best go in, madam. I believe it's going to rain.'

CHAPTER 5

Night after night the bonfires flared and the people danced in the streets outside the palace, chanting the Queen's name like an incantation. The court was in a wildly festive mood, not shared by the Queen and her chief advisers. They were plagued by financial difficulties in the Armada's wake and had little heart for victory celebrations. The crown had borne the cost virtually alone, and when Elizabeth glanced at the men who shared the burden of government with her, she was alarmed to see the toll the Armada had taken. Burghley, so crippled with gout that he sometimes had to be carried into her presence in a chair; Walsingham gaunt and yellow-faced from the disease which was slowly consuming him; Hatton plagued by a liver complaint; Leicester obese and feverish. All went about their duties looking drawn and haggard, men made old before their time by the unceasing demands of high office.

The Queen, too, was nearly fifty-five, and not immune to the effects of exhaustion, but there was little time to rest. Her days were full, her evening commitments punishing, and she made only one small concession to her weariness. And that was to dine privately with the Earl of Leicester every night following his return from Tilbury, with all her servants dismissed and he alone serving as carver and taster.

One evening towards the end of August, he sat at her table and picked at the Viand Royal in moody silence. Through the glow of the candelabra between them, Elizabeth watched him steadily and thought she knew what had robbed him for once of his famous appetite.

In the warm aftermath of victory she had been filled with a sudden desire to reward those long years of loyal affection, and had had the letters patent drawn up to create him Lord Lieutenant of England. She had been on the point of signing it when Burghley and Hatton, both deeply aggrieved, had begun to harp peevishly on the dangers of raising a mere subject to such unprecedented authority. The post would give him power almost equal with her own, and it would not do, said Burghley sourly—the people would not like it! So—because the habit of considering the people had become second nature to her, she had laid down her pen and promised to give the matter further consideration before making a decision. Bitterly disappointed, Leicester had made little secret of his resentment.

Now she leaned across the table and covered his hand with her own.

'Still sulking, Robin?'

He looked at her with a tired smile and shook his head absently.

'Something amiss with the meat?' she suggested with mounting unease.

'The meat's fine.'

'Then what's wrong? Why have you eaten nothing?' She paused uncertainly. 'Are you ill?'

He looked away guiltily and fingered the silver salt cellar.

'Robin!'

'It's nothing,' he said hastily. 'Just fatigue and a touch of fever—I didn't want to worry you.'

'I *knew* it!' she exclaimed furiously. 'I knew it at Tilbury. I shall send you back to Buxton as soon as it can be arranged.'

'I don't want to leave you, madam.' His voice was oddly intense and mutinous, but she was too preoccupied to notice.

'Stupid man! Of course you must go—I command it!'

'I see.' He began to fold his napkin grimly. 'And in my absence I suppose Essex will keep you loving company.'

His tone took her so completely by surprise that she could only stare at him in bewildered silence, too amazed to be angry.

At last she said warily, 'What do you mean by that uncalled for remark?'

'I should have thought it was perfectly obvious.' He flung the napkin down and got unsteadily to his feet. 'You're replacing me, madam—do you think I don't know it?—slowly, with dignity, putting me out to grass and putting that—that arrogant little pipsqueak in my place!'

'But—it was you—'

'Oh, yes—it was I who brought Robert to your notice. For pity's sake don't remind me of it. Perhaps I thought I could trust you not to go hunting in the nursery—I should have known better! Is he your lover—*is he?*'

Her eyes on his were aghast, humiliated, hurt and suddenly full of tears.

'No, he is not my lover,' she said with tremulous dignity.

They were silent, watching each other as though their lives depended on the outcome of this encounter. Then she held out one hand to him; and wordlessly he knelt to kiss the tip of her jewelled slipper.

Court duties came first; there was no way, at this time, they could be avoided. And so it was very late that night before she dismissed all her attendants and he was able to come to her. In the big state bed they met as equals and knew that it was over at last, the long, bitter struggle for mastery between them. They met with all the passionate tenderness of a lifelong love affair, but now the final satisfaction eluded them; and Leicester, whose fault alone it was, wept and said they were accursed.

She drew him down upon her breast and no shadow of her cruel disappointment touched her voice.

'My love,' she whispered, 'it doesn't matter.'

Evidently the wrong thing to say, for he immediately stiffened in her arms and turned away from her on the pillow.

'I am impotent in your bed and you say it doesn't *matter?*'

His hair still curled thinly at the nape of his neck and was black here and there in those places where it had not turned white. She put out a hand to touch it gently.

'You're tired,' she began hesitantly. 'And unwell. It was unreasonable of me to expect—'

'A *man?*'

'You were ten men at Tilbury,' she told him stoutly.

'But not in the Netherlands.' He turned to look at her accusingly. 'I failed you there, just as I have failed you now.'

She shook her head sadly.

'No failure of yours can ever compare with the way I have failed you all these years. So let there be no more talk of blame. When you come back from Buxton you will be well again and it will be different. We could go to Ricote. Just a few attendants. Margery is so discreet—'

He smiled faintly and she was poignantly reminded of a child comforted in grief by the promise that a favourite toy could be mended. Could you mend manhood like a broken bone? She had no real idea; but she prayed it was true, knowing herself to be responsible for the breakage.

Long after he slept, she lay awake, cherishing his weight against her breast. At dawn she woke him gently and watched him dress in the cold, cruel light, furtive as any young lover creeping away to avoid discovery. The state bed was like an enormous empty cavern when he had gone; she could not imagine how she had slept alone in it for all these years. And when she met him later, in the presence of her ladies, they smiled at each other as though they shared some private joke.

Indian summer had transfigured their old stormy relationship, leaving them in a quietly happy state of perfect companionship which was evident to all. The Great Lord was in his place at Gloriana's side, and his broad shoulders cast a shadow which was suddenly long enough to envelop his stepson.

Essex felt the chill of total eclipse and found he lacked the maturity to stomach even the most fleeting exclusion from her favour.

He chewed over his resentment as he organized the victory review of the troops in the tiltyard at Whitehall, a task which would have fallen to Leicester, had he not relinquished the post of Master of the Horse. Essex decked two hundred light horsemen in orange velvet and silver and watched them take the honours of the day. As he rode beneath the window where Leicester stood with the Queen, he noted the grim set of his stepfather's jaw with satisfaction. It amused him today to excite the old man's jealousy and he left the courtyard in high good humour.

It had been Essex's day—all the court had said so, and that evening the young man waited eagerly to receive some special token of the Queen's regard. A slight gesture of her hand would single him out from the gaudy multitude and everyone else, even Leicester and Burghley, would be muted into insignificance. He believed he would never tire of the thrill it gave him to take his place at the side of the goddess, as though by right. He would dance with her and make her laugh and at length she would dismiss the court and they two would retire to her chamber, attended only by her sleepy maids of honour, to play cards until the first birds sang and dawn stole through the tall casement windows. She had not sat with him like that since Leicester returned from Tilbury.

All that evening Essex waited with growing impatience for his summons to the dais, where Leicester stood beside her chair like a sentinel. They danced very little, but they talked endlessly. Christ's soul, what could they find to talk about who had known each other all these years? At midnight the old Earl leaned forward and tapped the watch which hung on a chain at her waist. The gesture had authority and the Queen looked up and smiled and nodded. She rose and allowed Leicester to hand her down the steps of the dais; and seeing that, Essex began to elbow his way angrily through the crowd towards her.

Leicester saw him first, hastily excused himself and went to intercept the boy's determined approach. Deference was owed to his mighty patron and Essex had no choice but to bow with superficial reverence and follow his stepfather to a window embrasure.

'My lord?' His tone was hostile, his glance flicking over Leicester's ruddy face with vague contempt.

'The Queen has just agreed to retire and you will oblige me by detaining her no further tonight.'

Essex stared at him in surprise and resentment.

'Have you advised her to ignore me in this arbitrary fashion?'

'Don't be foolish,' said Leicester calmly. 'I have warned you before against imagining slights where none are intended. Do you imagine the Queen will engage you in conversation every time she holds court?'

'After my services today I should have thought some gesture of acknowledgment, however brief—'

Leicester laid his hand on the boy's sleeve, suddenly patient, indulgent—fatherly.

'Service to the Queen is in itself its own reward, Robert. Bear in mind that we are all of us here at the Queen's pleasure, and here to serve.'

'It's barely midnight,' said Essex sullenly.

'The Queen is not well.' Leicester's voice was suddenly curt. He had been forced to betray a confidence now and he was annoyed by the necessity to restrain this arrogant pup, snapping at his heels. 'It's time some of you young upstarts remembered that she's only human.'

'Like you, my lord?' Essex gave him a smile edged with insolence. 'I trust you don't mistake your own mortality for the Queen's.'

'That's enough!' snapped Leicester softly. 'It is not my intention to bandy words with a dependant. I might remind you that you are here at court through my good offices alone.'

'You *needed* me at court,' the boy retorted heatedly. 'Mother told me you would go under to Raleigh without my aid.'

Leicester smiled suddenly.

'I fear your mother's opinions on the subject are hardly unbiased. And should you choose to be disobliging now I think you will find I can quite safely dispense with your invaluable services—as indeed can the Queen herself.'

Essex flushed at the threat.

'The Queen will not thank you for parading her human frailties,' he muttered.

'That much I know, none better, but then—she won't hear of it, will she?'

The boy was defeated, inclined to be peevish and stalk out of the room; Leicester took him gently by the elbow and began to steer him towards the throne.

'Come,' he said pleasantly. 'I'm sure Her Majesty will wish to bid you goodnight.'

The Queen was surrounded by a press of people when they reached the foot of the dais, but she turned immediately and smiled as she held out her hand to Essex.

'Robert—your display in the tiltyard thrilled us all, did it not, my lords?'

There was a grudging murmur of assent from the men around her which the young man acknowledged with a haughty inclination of his head. He still held her hand and there was a shade of possessive arrogance about the gesture.

'You must come and talk to me tomorrow.' She stepped back, forcing him to free her fingers, and glanced over her shoulder as she did so. 'Kit—I believe I have lost my fan.'

When Hatton returned from the dais with the object in his hand she smiled at him too, Essex noted jealously, as though he had just done her the most noble service. But as she turned away, the smile was extinguished, like the flame of a candle, leaving her lips set in a thin line of weariness.

She seemed unmistakably relieved to lay her hand on Leicester's velvet sleeve and let him lead her from the Great Hall, past a gauntlet of courtiers and ladies who sank to their knees as she passed by.

Essex watched them go; and went to his own apartment in a chastened, subdued mood which invited no good-humoured chaffing from his friends.

Leicester left the court at the end of August, pausing briefly at Wanstead to collect his wife with the casual indifference a man shows when picking up a forgotten glove.

Lettice greeted him with a bored smile and a cool kiss and her eyes went past him to her lover, young Blount, standing unobtrusively by her horse. When they set out upon the journey Leicester found he was glad of the jingling harness and the stamping hooves, the constant hum of idle chatter among the kingly retinue which accompanied him. It seemed in part to camouflage the fact that they two alone in all this brave company had precious little left to say to each other.

Once or twice, he glanced sideways in the saddle and saw her riding slowly beside him in the quivering heat, very trim and upright on her grey mare. Occasionally a little smile touched her pouting lips, as though at a remembered pleasure for which he had not been responsible. Very handsome still, he had to admit grudgingly—it was small wonder Blount had been attracted to her, though young enough to be her son. The affair no longer outraged him. Over the last year he had been positively relieved that she had found someone to satisfy her considerable sexual appetites; he had long since lost his taste for the violent practices which gave her so much pleasure.

They were little more than strangers now, polite acquaintances who occasionally shared a bedchamber to maintain appearances. The lust which had drawn them together had been unable to sustain them through the loss of their son.

He remembered that loss now, remembered trying to comfort her with meaningless words, how she had lain on their bed stiff and unresponsive, and somehow angry, as though he were to blame for that tragedy. Then, just as he had begun to be sure his presence was doing no good, she put out her hand to touch his sleeve.

'Must you leave me?'

He had bent to brush her forehead with his lips.

'A few minutes only—just long enough to send word to the Queen of—' He hesitated, could not say it—'of what has happened.'

Lettice's hands clenched on the coverlet.

'The Queen!' she said stonily. 'The Queen, the Queen—must she intrude on everything, even our grief? Do you need her permission to stay long enough to see your son buried? I suppose I should be grateful she spared you to come at all!'

'There's no call for that, Lettice. The Queen has been deeply concerned—'

'She didn't concern herself with his birth—not so much as a christening present. So why should she care now that he's dead? Doubtless this will make your life at court considerably easier. One less cause to excite that savage jealousy of hers—isn't that so?'

He stood back from the bed, looking at her with faint disgust.

'I have no idea,' he began slowly, 'what has made you so bitter. You knew when I married you that I had other—commitments.'

She had known, but had thought she could change it. Time had proved her wrong and suddenly she could not contain her rage any longer.

'I'm tired of it, can't you see that, Robert?' She stood up and drew her wrap around herself. 'I'm sick of wearing your ring and your name and living in your house with no more status than a whore. I'm weary of trying to be grateful for the odd night when she spares me your company. Go back and weep on the Queen's shoulder, which is so much more accommodating than mine. But don't expect to find *me* sitting by the fire waiting for you when you return!'

It was soon after that that she took up with Christopher Blount, but then at least the jealous harping ceased and Leicester no longer felt obliged to excuse his feelings for the Queen.

When he showed her the draft copy of his will, she read the first lines and then handed it back to him with studied civility, not even pausing to examine the generous provision he had made for her.

First of all and above all persons, it is my duty to remember my most dear and gracious princess, whose creature under God I have been and who has been a most bountiful and princely mistress to me . . .

'I think that says it all, even for posterity,' Lettice had remarked coldly, and walked out of the room, leaving him with the document in his hand.

But slowly the bitterness had softened into mutual tolerance, until at last they had the empty, civilized relationship which characterized the majority of marriages among nobility. And life was much easier on the increasingly rare occasions when, as now, for form's sake, they must bear each other company.

They rode down into the valley of the River Thame and there ahead of them lay the great beeches of Ricote. Margery Norris, as plump and pretty as ever, ran down the steps to meet him with her arms outstretched in welcome, then stopped abruptly on seeing Lettice at his side for the first time.

'Lady Leicester—what a delightful surprise,' she said icily, dropping a perfunctory curtsey. Then she turned to take Leicester's arm and hurry him into the well-remembered house where he had spent so many hours with Elizabeth, leaving Lettice to the attentions of a steward.

'The Queen's own bedroom,' said Margery gaily, flinging the door open to reveal a large, sunny room overlooking the terrace. 'I know she would want you to have it in her absence, Robert—but of course *you*, my lady, in view of your lord's ill-health, would doubtless prefer to lodge in another room.'

Leicester caught his wife's look of murderous rage and suppressed a smile. Dear Margery, still the Queen's loyal friend! And really he would be quite glad to sleep alone in the Queen's bed, left in peace to remember the old laughing times within these walls.

At the precise moment when Lettice opened her mouth to voice her indignant protest, he laid his hand on Margery's arm and said with quiet irony, 'That is a very kind thought, madam, and I know my wife will thank you for it.'

'A kind thought indeed,' parrotted Lettice dutifully, unable now to say otherwise. She curtsied to her husband with a quick, contemptuous gesture and turned to follow her hostess out of the room.

And as she walked, she reflected with anger that there were a hundred things she would rather do than trail around the parched countryside at snail's pace in the company of a sick old man who could no longer excite her passion.

Ricote, August 29

I most humbly beseech Your Majesty to pardon your poor old servant in sending to know how my gracious lady does and what ease of her late pain she finds, being the chiefest thing in this world I pray for, for her to have good health and long life. For my own poor case I continue still your medicine and find it amends much better than any other thing that has been given to me . . . from your old lodging at Ricote, this Thursday morning, ready to take on my journey. By Your Majesty's most faithful, obedient servant, R. Leicester

The letter, written in a tremulous scrawl hardly recognizable as Leicester's bold hand, looked up at Burghley from among a pile of papers on the Queen's desk. He looked down at it with a curious hangdog expression and wondered why in God's name he had had to notice it at this precise moment.

The Queen lifted her head, smiling as she pushed a pile of signed documents across the table towards him.

'There—all done at last. You're a hard taskmaster, William Cecil, to keep me shut up in here on my birthday. May I go out to play now?'

He raised his eyes to hers uncertainly.

'Your Majesty?' he said vaguely.

'I said: Is that all for today?' She studied his gaunt face and added kindly, 'What's the matter, Cecil—is your gout bad again?'

'No,' he muttered, scarcely attending, 'thank you, madam—I am much as usual.'

She laughed and flexed her stiff fingers, straightening her rings.

'Indeed you are, with a face as long as a fiddle. For a moment I thought the Armada must be at sea again.'

She got up and went to open the window and the slight breeze from the river disturbed the papers on her desk. Leicester's note fluttered to the floor and Burghley bent with great difficulty to retrieve it, staring at it dully.

'What a lovely day,' she remarked thoughtfully. 'Had Robin been here we would have gone hunting—'

Burghley made no response. She turned in surprise to look at him and suddenly, seeing his face in the harsh sunlight, she knew.

One hand crept slowly to her throat and the other went out to him in a hopeless gesture of supplication.

'No,' she said dully. 'Not now—not after—'

She broke off abruptly to draw a shuddering breath and turned her face away from his pitying gaze.

Burghley put the letter carefully on the table and went over to her slowly, taking her trembling hand and pressing it, palm upward, to his dry lips.

'Please believe me when I say this, madam—I am truly sorry.'

Elizabeth pulled her hand away from him and rubbed it fiercely against her gown, for all the world as though he had spat upon it.

'When?' she demanded harshly.

He was hurt by her response and did not pretend otherwise.

'On the 4th of September,' he said, rather shortly. 'At Cornbury.'

She looked up and stared at him then. Even the tardiest rider could not have taken three days to cover such a distance. Lettice's ultimate revenge, as his legal wife, was to see her informed of his death like some distant business acquaintance on the seventh—her fifty-fifth birthday. Burghley saw her flinch and was ashamed of his momentary resentment.

'It was a peaceful end,' he murmured, hoping the fact would afford her some comfort. 'He died in his sleep. It is understood that the strain of the journey—'

'It was my command—the journey,' she interrupted softly, 'my command.'

All that was left of Burghley's human sensitivity curled up and cringed as though in pain. Oh God, what a blunder!

'Madam,' he began inadequately, 'I had no idea that—'

She cut him short with a curt gesture of her hand and stared out through the window, remembering the hot morning when he had come into her bedroom at Whitehall to take his leave. Dressed for travel, a short cloak swinging from his huge shoulders, a plumed cap in his hand and the red veins bulging in his temples with the heat.

She had received him alone and he had taken advantage of it, neglecting to bow or kneel or do any of those things which properly appertained to the saluting of majesty. For a moment he looked at her searchingly, turning her face gently to the cruel sunlight which flooded in from the single window overlooking the river. Then he drew a finger over her cheekbone and showed her its poppy-hued tip.

'I thought you and I were finished with deception,' he said reproachfully.

He took off his cloak and told her he would have all the horses in the courtyard returned to their stables.

'. . . with your gracious permission, of course,' he added ironically.

'Robin! It's nothing—'

'Please.' He laid a hand on her arm. 'If you knew how many times that wretched phrase of yours has put the fear of God in me you would not say it again. I have bitter experience of the utter unreliability of your judgement where your own health is concerned and I intend to remain at court until I am better satisfied.'

A week ago she might have lost her temper, but now she knew there was nothing he could say or do that would ever anger her again. She sat down at her silver-topped table and told him very calmly, very pleasantly, that he could go to Buxton of his own free will, or under an armed guard—whichever suited his mood best. After that she sat in silence, with her chin in her slender hands, watching him smack his hat angrily against his thigh and listening while he swore.

'You have to go,' she pointed out at length when he paused for breath. 'Your wife is expecting you at Wanstead.'

'My wife,' he said grimly, 'can ably fill her time with the attentions of Christopher Blount, as she has done these several years past.' He glared down at her. 'Do you think she matters now—do you think anyone *ever* mattered beside you?'

She looked at him standing there, red and fat and winded with exasperation, and thought sadly that she had never loved him better, not even in the days of his glowing, virile youth. The great white feather, which had stood so proudly in the brim of his hat, was now dangling limply, like a broken daisy stalk. He tossed the hat down on the table and she raised her eyebrows slightly at the sight of it.

'I hope you don't intend to wear that to Buxton,' she said softly.

'Forget Buxton,' he snapped. 'I never wanted to go anyway—the season's almost over. I can live with London's stench for a few weeks more, then we'll go to Ricote together—as you promised.'

She removed the broken feather and began to smooth out the crumpled velvet brim.

'You know I can't get away from London before the autumn. You'll have to come back for me.' She handed him the hat with a sigh. 'I'm afraid that's the best I can do with it. I'll buy you a new feather.'

'Your Majesty's generosity is as usual overwhelming.' He was smiling now, in spite of himself. 'I suppose you think to get your own way in the end.'

'I usually get it,' she reminded him wickedly. 'In the end.'

'Yes.' He was staring at her as though he was etching every fragile line of her face deep into his memory. 'Yes, you usually do, don't you? And what pray, am I to tell Margery Norris when I see her?'

'Tell her—November.'

'*November!*'

'At the earliest.'

He bent to kiss first her hand, then her thin cheek.

'You're a very hard woman,' he remarked without rancour, as he bowed and began to back stiffly to the door with one hand on the hilt of his sword, 'a diamond to my paltry grain of sand.'

'Robin!'

The sudden panic in her voice had made him turn sharply in the doorway to look back at her, a black silhouette against the August sunlight.

She smiled uncertainly, made a helpless gesture of confusion.

'Write to me,' she whispered, as though it was not quite what she had meant to say.

'Of course I shall write,' he said. And was gone.

Elizabeth stood very still watching that door shut over and over again in her memory, and at her side, watching her narrowly, Burghley felt cold with apprehension. Her eyes were empty, blank and cold as marble, as though there was no one behind them. If only she would move, speak, cry—do something he could accept as a normal manifestation of grief.

'Madam—' he whispered.

She moved away and began to search blindly among the papers on her desk. He stepped forward, more quickly than he had moved for many years and put Leicester's note into her frantic hand. Her fingers closed about it with relief and without a word she turned like a sleep walker and went through into her bedroom, closing the door behind her.

A moment later, he heard the key turn in the lock. It was a harsh, rasping sound, sudden, unexpected, and strangely final.

And it filled him with a curious foreboding.

For three days the Queen's door remained locked and the room beyond it shrouded in utter silence. The timid tapping of her ladies upon the heavy panels grew progressively into a frantic hammering, but there was no answer, no response—nothing.

Questions pulsed through the palace, gathering bizarre and dreadful answers, until Burghley could bear the suspense no longer. Accompanied by a few members of the Council, he gave the order to have her door broken down; and as the panels splintered he bit his lip and braced himself mentally against what he would find.

He was the first to step into the room and see her sitting at her dressing-table, staring into her mirror. As he limped to her side, she turned her head very slowly and blinked at him, almost without recognition, from glazed eyes. His glance fell to the empty spirits decanter in front of her and he suddenly understood; oddly enough, it was the one thing he had not considered.

His immediate thought was to spare her the indignity of discovery and without turning round he gestured curtly to the councillors who still hovered nervously in the broken doorway, ready to run for their lives if this unpardonable intrusion on her privacy should be greeted with a screaming tantrum. While Burghley's back shielded her from view they bowed and scuttled out beyond the ante-room, closing the outer doors behind them.

Elizabeth turned the decanter upside down over her goblet and swore softly, finding it empty. She who had always shunned drink like the devil, fearing to cloud her faculties and loosen her tongue, was now as drunk as a lord.

She said vaguely, 'I don't like wine. Tell them to bring me more of this brown stuff—aqua vitae—whatever it's called.'

Burghley leaned over and took the empty decanter from her hand.

'Madam,' he murmured gently. 'Madam, this does no good.'

'You're wrong, Burghley—why are you always *wrong* about me when it really matters? It helps to feel nothing, think nothing—be nothing.'

'For a while,' his voice was reproachful, 'a very little while. But you must see it's not the answer.'

'I see nothing,' she murmured, maudlin with spirits. 'My eyes are closed for ever and I am blind.'

Leicester! thought Burghley, suddenly savage with frustration, God damn him, God rot him, is he to be a greater threat dead than he ever was alive?

Aloud he said desperately, 'Does it count for nothing that your country is safe?'

'Oh yes—the *miracle!'* She smiled strangely. 'But we don't get miracles for nothing, Burghley and I have made full payment for mine. One gaudy hour of triumph in straight exchange for a life. The Devil drives a hard bargain.'

He was silent a moment, immeasurably shocked, groping blindly for the right words.

'Madam, it was a cruel loss—none knows better than I, I assure you. But life goes on and is ill-served by such bitterness.'

'I'm not bitter,' she said wearily, 'I'm burnt out. I'm no more use to you, Burghley, or to England. I've no cards left to play. So release me from our bondage and let me go now—while they still love me.'

While they still love me . . .

What did she see in her mirror to make her say that at the very peak of her achievement, when she stood with her power at its zenith and the people still chanted her name in the streets? What did she see in those cold crystalline depths to fill her with such utter desolation?

Never in the thirty years of their association had he ever seen her look like that—devoid of all hope, beaten. He looked past her into the mirror, frantically seeking an answer and saw the one enemy she would never defeat, the true enemy, the greatest enemy—herself.

She meant to die, he saw that now, not scandalously, or spectacularly, but by her own design all the same, setting her mind to death, as she had once set it long ago, when only fifteen. Yet suicide, however quiet and unobtrusive, was still a crime in the eyes of God and all Christian men, a crime he could not permit. There was no one to take her place but her feckless Scottish cousin, James, no child of her body to inherit. It was her duty to live and delay that inheritance for as long as possible; it was his own to make certain that she did.

He knew what to say to her now—knew what to say and how to say it.

Abruptly he reached out and struck the empty goblet off the dressing-table with the flat of his hand.

'How can you sink to this?' he snapped. 'How dare you desert your people in their hour of triumph to mope over a dead rat who was never worth a tinker's curse alive?'

She stared at him and her face wore a stunned, stricken look which hurt him infinitely. But he would not give up now. It was the right note and he struck it again, hard, in a voice which seemed rough with contempt.

'I tell you this, my considered opinion, madam: the late Earl of Leicester was a worthless, grasping knave who used you for his own ends from the day he entered your service.'

She swayed to her feet with an immense effort and steadied herself against the back of her chair.

'Liar!' she breathed. 'You white-haired snake, you lying, foul-mouthed *clerk!* Oh God, he was right about you, but I would never see it. You were behind every cruelty I ever showed him—even the Lord Lieutenancy.' She panted for breath. 'Yes—but for you and your mindless carping he would have had that and died believing in my love at last.'

Stung by her insults, Burghley shook his head grimly.

'Why deceive yourself, madam? Whatever you gave him could not alter the fact that he hated you—and given the way you treated him for thirty years what honest man could blame him for that?'

'Be silent!' She thought she had screamed it but heard it only as an anguished whimper. 'Be silent, I say.'

'Madam, I should be ashamed to stay silent. Have I served a snivelling coward all these years? Must I now stand by and watch you fret yourself into the grave for the sake of a miserable traitor who betrayed you at every turn?'

She hit him for that, a sharp stinging blow across the mouth which had uttered those unforgivable obscenities. Relief flooded through him as he staggered back a step, for he had tied her to this world with chains of rage, roused her sufficiently from that stupor of grief to know he need no longer fear for her life.

But he had gone too far, roused something worse than rage in her; he saw it suddenly in her black eyes, pulsing with indescribable venom, as though all the forces of darkness massed behind them. She held out her hand to him and gave him a smile that was soft with malice. She looked suddenly malevolent—he could find no other word for it.

'That was for him,' she said slowly, 'for him and the life you condemned him to all those years ago when you murdered his wife. *Yes!*—you wondered at the time, didn't you? You wondered if I had guessed. So now there shall be no more secrets between us, my Spirit, my twin-soul. You alone of all the men in my kingdom shall know the truth about me.'

He did not want to hear this. He tried to move away, but her cold hand fastened on his wrist with murderous strength, like the bite of steel. He tried in vain to shut out her harsh voice rasping in his ears, but it was no use; he heard.

'I lied to you all those years ago, Cecil—did you never know it?—I betrayed your precious trust. He was my lover from the very beginning. We had nothing to fear, you see—I lost the Admiral's child when I was fourteen and Dr Bill told me I could expect no more. It was safe to be stallion to a barren mare, quite safe. There is a bed behind you, Cecil, my bed, the bed of state. Look at it. Look at it and see us lying there night after night, his body swelling in mine till I wept with ecstasy. Does Mildred weep when you mount her, my friend—*does she?* No! You shall not turn away from this. You tell me I am not free to die—so be it! I will play the Virgin Queen for you a little longer. But remember this: I was always his slut and I'm glad of it.' Her smile curled deeper, knifing him like a poisoned dart. 'You have served Dudley's whore for thirty years and you will serve her to the end of your days. For just as you refuse to release me, so shall I refuse to release you. Sick, crippled, deaf or blind, you will *die* in my service, with a chain of office round your scrawny neck—I swear it!'

She dropped his hand and stepped back from him, leaving him to stare at his wrist as though her touch had defiled him. Something crumpled in his face as he turned away from her, his life's achievements like dust in his hand; a broken old man who suddenly felt he would never care for anything in this worthless world again.

The outer doors closed behind him and she was alone once more in the dreadful sunlit silence, staring at the folded note on her dressing-table which bore a single line of her own writing.

'His last letter.'

PART FIVE

The Effigy

*'She was more than a man and sometimes, in truth,
less than a woman.'*
SIR ROBERT CECIL

CHAPTER 1

Who list her hunt, I put him out of doubt,
As well as I may spend his time in vain;
And graven with diamonds in letters plain
There is written, her fair neck round about,
'Noli me tangere, for Caesar's I am,
And wild for to hold, though I seem tame.'

So, many, many years ago had the poet, Sir Thomas Wyatt, written of Anne Boleyn, whom he had loved so hopelessly and lost to King Henry. The poet's son, a bold traitor, had died to put Caesar's daughter on the throne when Queen Mary reigned. Now all were dead and only Caesar's last child lived to tell the tale—still lived in spite of the wild rumours which had flown through the palace these last three days; still lived to run in the chase.

The tall young man, lounging in a window-seat, slowly closed his book of verse and glanced obliquely round the crowded Presence Chamber. Courtiers and ladies stood in whispering groups, speculating with idle, vulgar curiosity: *what now?* More than once he had felt their hot, sidelong glances steal round upon him as he sat, apparently indifferent to their chatter, idly turning the pages of his priceless book, speaking to no one and pretending he could not hear what was being said. The doors of the Privy Chamber remained shut and no one could guess what was taking place in the room beyond it, what the faithful Lord Burghley would find to say to his Queen in the course of today's business that would persuade her to continue in her public life.

The ladies exchanged nervous glances and wondered how difficult they would find their royal mistress when they were called to dress her. They dreaded the inevitable summons to wait upon her and huddled together uneasily, mingling expressions of pity and fear.

Across the room the young men preened like peacocks, and eyed each other with hostility, angry dogs preparing to fight over a coveted bone. They knew now there was something worth fighting for. *The King is dead—long live the King!* Who would be the King of the Queen's heart now that the

Great Lord had relinquished that prize for ever? Would it be Hatton, the elegant dancer who kept his homosexuality so decorously and discreetly out of sight? Raleigh, the cultured adventurer, brilliant, dark and dangerous? Or Essex, the newest star in the firmament of the royal favour, the outspoken, wilful aristocrat who was as yet still a largely unknown quantity? No one knew, but everyone was busy guessing and laying bets on their favourite stallion, since one thing alone was certain now: the Virgin Queen could not exist without a man at her side.

And so the whispering and shifting glances went on, until the door opened at last and everyone turned to look as Lord Burghley hobbled slowly into their midst. His face was grimly shuttered as he passed through their ranks, meeting no one's eye, speaking not one word, not even to his son, the stunted little clerk, Robert Cecil, who promptly fell into step beside his father and accompanied him out of the room.

Slowly, the buzz of speculation started up once more in his wake.

The October light was failing as the red-haired man in the window-seat rose and began to pace up and down in the space which lesser minions automatically made for him. His mind was a fever of anxious anticipation and excitement.

The old man dead! What a chance, what an unparalleled opportunity— but how long did he have to make use of it before the news brought his rival, Raleigh, hurrying back from the West Country, where war action had stationed him, to claim the Queen of Hearts for himself? He loathed Raleigh, the Captain of the Guard, a low upstart who had made himself master of the gallant gesture and presumed to address his arrogant love sonnets to the Queen. A quicksilver mind to match that of his royal mistress, scholar, poet, explorer, a more polished version of Drake—he was a formidable opponent whom even Leicester had feared.

Raleigh! The boy pictured him resentfully in memory, seeing him forever standing, unchallenged, before the Queen's door, wearing a suit of silver armour; seeing him lean with familiar ease against the Queen's high-backed chair, flaunting that devilish pipe stuffed with the burning leaves he called tobacco. A pipe was a necessary accoutrement to every aspiring courtier now, but only Raleigh had dared to win a wager against his royal mistress, by solemnly swearing he could tell the weight of his own smoke. A ridiculous, extravagant claim—the whole court had gathered round to see the proud man take a fall. Raleigh had weighed the tobacco leaves, smoked his pipe, and then tapped the ashes into the scales and declared the difference in the two weights to be the weight of the smoke. The Queen had laughed and paid her forfeit with good grace, and those who had never seen her lose a wager in public before were astonished by the man's wit and daring. Oh yes—Raleigh had been dangerous even while Leicester lived. What power might not be his now that Leicester was gone?

The boy paced faster and more furiously, biting the inside of his lip and clenching his fist, betraying his tension, as he betrayed all emotion.

Whoso list to hunt, I know where is an hind . . .

It was just an hour before supper when the imperious jangle of a handbell sent the women in the room fluttering agitatedly into the antechamber. The men started and exchanged significant glances with their cronies, a rustle of taut expectation that made the boy tense with rage.

Whoso list to hunt . . .

Yes—they were all preparing to hunt now; but his would be the first arrow to pierce the heart of that elusive hind.

Like the rest of the hopeful young men, he had lingered in the Presence Chamber, hoping for a public appearance, waiting for the opportunity to stake his claim to her; and, like the rest, he eventually went away weary and disappointed. Days slid into weeks and some abandoned this regular evening vigil for the lighter pursuits of the court; but the Earl of Essex had abandoned nothing. His mental crossbow was always armed and ready, for he knew now that if he dared to shoot at all, this time it must be to kill.

The painting was finished. They had hung Mary Stuart's famous rope of black pearls around her neck, fastened the monstrous cartwheel ruff beneath her chin and drawn back discreetly while she stared at their handiwork.

In the mirror she saw a mask, skilfully executed and harshly coloured; crimson salve for a mouth that was a sad thin line, rose paste on her bloodless cheekbones, belladonna to put shine into her lifeless eyes. A snow Queen, with a splinter of ice lodged in her heart, cold and hard and unsmiling, dressed all in mourning black.

Dead but not buried, she thought suddenly, and snatched the mirror from its stand, handing it to the woman nearest to her.

'Take it away.'

'Your Majesty?' The woman stared, uncertain whether she had misheard the instruction.

'I said, take it away—take every mirror out of my sight. Do it now—throughout the palace!'

She would never look again into a mirror and see her living corpse, standing like a mighty unfallen oak, superficially magnificent still, but hollow and rotten at the core.

For almost a month she had religiously attended to state business, received

Burghley and Walsingham, conferred with her secretaries and signed all the necessary documents. But, in the evenings, she had shied away from her court, knowing what waited for her in the Long Gallery or the Great Hall. Burghley had been cool and distant when he attended her. He had made no comment, merely looked and she knew it was no use; she must begin to hold court again, walk back into that room like a hen into a cockpit, and be fought and quarrelled over by a bunch of greedy, ambitious young men, the next generation of sharp-toothed little rodents, all trying to summon the courage to take the first bite. Once it had been the game she enjoyed best of all; but now Robin was gone and she was alone with the rats.

On the threshold of the Great Hall she paused a second and stared at the vast assembly which waited for her. At her appearance, the gay talk and laughter froze into frightened silence, and her courtiers and ladies, all dressed tactfully in black for the late Earl of Leicester, sank to their knees as she passed by. Their curious eyes followed her down the room and bored into her head. She walked with an effort past the kneeling ranks, without pausing to give a smile or a word to anyone. The Chair of State at the end of the room had become her only goal, a sort of sanctuary; she had no thought beyond reaching it with dignity and decorum. Her appearance tonight was a duty, one of the many tedious rituals which stretched ahead over the barren years in front of her, empty, meaningless, void of all pleasure.

From the corner of her eye she caught a movement, a flash of silver doublet, and suddenly Essex was before her, rising from a sweeping bow, offering her his arm. For a moment he was afraid she was going to snub him and walk on, but his action had confused her single-minded purpose, so that momentarily she halted and stared at him uncertainly.

He smiled, kissed the hand she had offered from force of habit, and laid it ostentatiously on his sleeve. As he escorted her to the throne on the dais, she was conscious of a rustle of spite and envy among the courtiers behind her; and her heart sank. The first gauntlet of challenge had been flung down; it had begun; and she felt suddenly angry and resentful towards the impertinent young man who had dared to start it.

She withdrew her hand abruptly and sat down in the great chair without thanking him for his strong arm. Her eyes narrowed on the dazzling costume which made him so conspicuous among the dark multitude of her court.

'I had not expected to see you of all people dressed for a revel,' she said coldly. 'The bereaved son—'

'Stepson,' he reminded her calmly, 'and unlikely, I understand, to remain fatherless for long. Widow's weeds do not suit my mother.'

'Your mother,' snapped Elizabeth softly, 'is an infamous whore!'

For a moment their dark eyes met with hostility, like bared swords about to clash; and then some small vestige of common sense warned him to swallow the hot retort which had leapt to his reckless tongue. Only a madman would choose to quarrel with her at this moment, and he was not mad—not yet.

The Queen turned her head away, raised the company from their knees with a careless flick of her hand, and leaned back in her chair to brood.

So—Lettice would marry Christopher Blount after the shortest decent interval imaginable; but they would live no life of ease on Leicester's estates while the Queen drew breath.

I will call in every debt that Robin owed me and when that debt is settled, Christopher Blount will find he has married a pauper . . .

She turned angrily to Lettice's boy—an arrogant, insolent puppy, the she-wolf's cub—ready to vent her bitter spleen upon him; and checked, with the cruel words unspoken.

There he stood, smiling at her, cocksure, confident and red-haired, like a young reincarnation of herself. How easily he might have been taken for her son—her son, by Robin.

Suddenly, inexplicably, her anger was spent and she raised her hand to touch his cheek gently.

In the gallery above the musicians had taken their places and were waiting silently for her signal.

'The dancing begins,' she said quietly. 'Go and find yourself a partner.'

His smile deepened; he reached out and captured the hand which had touched his cheek, imprisoning it between his closed palms.

'Madam, I look now upon the only partner I shall ever desire.'

The warmth and strength of his fingers, so poignantly reminiscent of Leicester, suddenly made her want to weep. But she could not break down before this vast assembly; nor could she withdraw her hand again without arousing spiteful comment. Like a cornered cat, she shrank back a little in her chair, watchful, wary, ready to strike—but strangely unwilling to do so for as long as it could be avoided.

Her eyes on his, her lips smiling to deceive the watching court, she said in a chill whisper of command, 'Release my hand.'

'I shall never release you, madam,' he returned, equally soft, 'not until you have danced with me here before them all—and shown them how it is to be between the two of us from this moment on.'

In all her life no man had ever addressed her with such insolent mastery. It echoed through her mind like the crack of a whip, and in its darkest recess something stirred and slowly raised its head, like a snake rousing lazily from a light slumber. Behind her eyes it quivered with life and longing and its voice was a chill caress in her brain.

'This is he, my precious . . . I choose him.'

'No,' said Elizabeth, soundlessly, 'I cannot do this thing. I will not do it, not even for you. He is innocent.'

'No man is innocent. And he is arrogant . . . he deserves it.'

'Let him go. He has done no harm.'

'Give him time. Give him the opportunity. And then, when he no longer pleases you . . . give him to me.'

She opened her eyes and found Essex was still smiling at her. He did not know his danger. How should he?

'Release my hand,' she repeated, breathless against the sudden urge to scream, 'I shall dance with no man again.'

'No *other* man,' he corrected solemnly. 'But you will dance with me, madam, and you will dance tonight. Is that not so?'

'Partner me now, and I promise you will live to regret it.'

'I will take that risk,' he said steadily, 'and take it gladly.'

A moment more she fought the quivering temptation. He saw she was about to summon her maids and tightened his grip upon her hand hard enough to hurt.

'Don't do it, madam—I give you my word I will make a scene. I shall leave this hall now and make it known to everyone in it how cruelly you have wounded my pride. Dance with me once—it is all I ask.'

For now, she thought.

She rose slowly and the skirts of her diamond-studded mourning gown swirled out towards him like a wave of shimmering darkness. Beneath the watching eyes of a jealous court he lifted her hand to his lips, kissing it with masterful, mocking reverence.

She looked full into his face and gave him a smile which made his brain reel with crazy elation.

'On your own head be it,' she said; and her voice was even, steady, but ineffably sad.

He bowed low and led her to the centre of the floor, where every dancer fell back to watch, in silent wonder. Like two performers on a public stage, the Earl of Essex and the Queen wove the intricate steps of the old pavane, while the music played soft and mournful in the gallery.

And so the dice were thrown and the scene was set for the final tragedy.

They danced together and shared a strange smile—the high priestess of a heathen cult and her very willing sacrifice.

*   *   *

He was her constant companion now. The courtiers who had laid bets on Raleigh's ultimate ascendancy had long since paid up their debts with a grim frown and gone about their business. Essex found himself chained to her side by a fascination that was almost hypnotic. She had only played with him before Leicester's death, toying with vague interest, as at some cunning new dish presented to tempt her scanty appetite.

But now that she truly hungered, he was a forbidden delicacy that she must not devour. She dominated his existence from morning till night, punishing him for the desire she could not bring herself to assuage, tormenting, teasing, leading him so far, then drawing back coldly, disgusted with herself, and with him. Leicester's death had cheated her of physical fulfilment with the one man she had come to trust against her will; and now it was too late to learn to trust another. She had only to give the word and Essex would take her gladly; but she would not give it. The gulf of thirty-five years lay between them—it would be obscene! And worse, it would mean betraying Leicester's memory.

She could not enjoy his body then; but others could—and did—and she hated them for it. She had begun to hate all lovers, each and every person around her who led a natural life with a mate. The mere mention of marriage was liable to provoke an outburst of temper, and lovers avoided her glance, taking their pleasures in secret corners, in terror of discovery.

Five years slid away, almost without trace; the Queen was nearly sixty and the Earl of Essex was still at her side. Only now they were fighting. They said he was the one man left in England with the courage to do it.

He committed more breaches of etiquette than the rest of the court put together; he disobeyed her; he made love to her women without subterfuge; he withdrew from court whenever he could not have his own way in any dispute. Each time, after some brief outburst of rage, she welcomed him back and marvelled at her own weakness. And each time he returned a little more drunk on the sense of his own importance, his utter certainty that his power was growing. No woman had ever held his attention for long, except the Queen, but her subtle promise of surrender—complete and utter surrender to his will—the prospect of conquering where no man had conquered before, held him like a lodestone.

For himself, he had many assets. A real promise of military leadership, a rising influence at court, a steady, growing popularity among the people—the only one of her favourites not to be hated by the populace. The boy with the red-gold hair looked like a king when he rode through the streets to Essex

House or Wanstead and was cheered with mounting enthusiasm whenever he appeared.

But his chief asset was undoubtedly his curious hold on the Queen's affections. The sense of achievement this gave him was an intoxicating madness. She was like a tigress in his captivity, safe only for as long as he could accurately gauge the length of chain which bound her. The length of that chain varied from day to day, so that he could never be quite sure of leaping beyond reach of her paw. It was that which exhilarated his senses, bringing him back again and again to take his chance against a multi-faceted cat who beguiled and baffled, intrigued and infuriated him by turns. Her timeless magic held him fast in its steely grip and he was not troubled by its unnatural overtones, for he never even noticed them.

But she did. And once she drove her women out of her presence for some imagined fault, that she might be alone with her nameless fear. She took Leicester's miniature from her casket and addressed it with tears of despair.

'Oh, Robin—why did you ever bring him here?'

The portrait gave no answer, but she fancied it looked at her with silent reproach, and she shut it away quickly, with a horrible feeling of guilt. Oh, yes—she was playing with fire now, she knew it. But she had lived with danger all her life and she could not live without its challenge, could not fall back and watch life become quiet and safe and tiresome. She needed Essex; needed the fight which he alone seemed able to give her.

Yet there was one point on which she was obdurate, and he beat himself against it like a persistent bee hammering against a window-pane, unable to accept his inability to pass through this one petty barrier.

She would not receive his mother at court.

'Can't you see how it reflects on me?' he burst out, one hot evening when she had sent her ladies away, knowing the mood he was in. 'How can a man stay in a place where his own mother is not welcome? Well, I shall not stay. I shall depart the court, madam, and leave you to your stubbornness.'

In other circumstances, that threat had softened her, but now she looked at him steadily, her eyes dark and watchful.

'You must not make a habit of threatening me,' she said quietly. 'If it becomes too tiresome I shall be forced to cure you of it—and I fancy we will both find that cure extraordinarily painful.'

He smiled suddenly, the corners of his lips curling up in one of those sudden swings of mood which were so curiously reminiscent of her own.

'Madam! Now you sound like my mother! Will you not forgive her, for my sake?'

She turned away, the expression knocking hollowly against her heart.

'I'm *not* your mother,' she said curtly. 'Never refer to me by that term again, even in jest!'

'As you please, madam.'

Her tone had surprised him; he had expected her to laugh, as she so often did when he wheedled. When they were not at odds over one thing and another, they were always laughing—but evidently not tonight.

He sighed and went down on his knees, trotting out the humble courtier which sometimes amused her. Abrasiveness would only carry him so far and often overshot its mark. And if humility would serve, he was ready for once to be humble; he really could not bear this ill-will between his mother and the Queen to continue any longer. It genuinely distressed him.

'Madam, I beg you! Let me bring her just once to kiss your hand and I will never ask it of you again. You have no idea what these years of exile have meant to her—and surely, whatever her crime, she has paid for it by now. Your creditors stripped her of virtually every possession Leicester left her—oh, yes, I know there were debts—but *his* debts after all—'

'On his death they reverted to her,' said Elizabeth coldly. 'She was his widow.'

'She is no longer,' he reminded her tactlessly. 'She is Lady Blount now.'

The Queen's lips tightened angrily.

'Then let her new husband provide for her. I tolerate her within my realm against my will and it is enough. Within my court, within my presence—never!'

His hand clenched and unclenched on the hilt of his sword. She recognized it as a gesture of nerves, again because it was her own. Sometimes the likeness between them seemed extraordinary, almost uncanny. But then he was of her mother's kin, so perhaps some slight, family resemblance was not so remarkable after all.

'I don't understand you,' he was saying resentfully. 'You have pardoned *traitors* in your time, yet for your own flesh and blood you are without pity. If you loved me, madam, you would not deny me this one small request.'

She chewed the paint on her lower lip, aware of the tightly checked rage bubbling like molten lava beneath the surface of her mind, a treacherously dormant volcano.

'Take care,' she said, 'and humour me in this, if nothing else. I warn you now that age has not improved my temper.'

'Age,' he echoed thoughtfully, staring at her steadily, 'age has forgotten you, madam—claim no advantage of it. I will not humour you for that.'

Her eyes opened a little wider on his face.

'I am almost sixty,' her voice was thin with fear. *'Sixty!'*

'Who would know it!'

His flattery—if it was flattery—had a brutal edge to it, as though he was half-angered by his admiration. 'You are in better health now than you have been all your life. You are slim as your maids of honour and dance better than any of them. Look in your mirror, my Maiden Queen, and see what the Devil does for those he favours.'

She closed her eyes suddenly and Leicester's voice was softly fearful in her memory.

'Are you a witch?'

Oh God, she thought in terror, what price my witchery in this?

For Essex did not lie to her, she knew it. Whatever was in his mind tripped out on his tongue without a moment's thought for expediency, and in that he was truly unlike herself. He had no tact. Rude with honesty, he was the most forthright man at court and the eyes which rested on her, with such unwilling adoration, were hard and guileless. The lines concealed beneath a subtle mask of paint, white hair under an exquisite wig, teeth steadily blackening behind her clever, close-lipped smile—there was no mirror in her palace, but she knew they were there.

Only he never seemed to see it.

And he was right. Most folk were in their graves by sixty. Those who weren't were crippled wrecks like poor Burghley, toothless, hard of hearing, struggling with growing infirmity. But not since her childhood had she enjoyed such remarkable health and vitality. Her migraine attacks were increasingly infrequent. All those minor, but debilitating, symptoms which had once bolstered the ambassadors' despatches, they had disappeared since the Armada, vanished as though somehow—*they had served their purpose.*

She wondered suddenly just what part her poor health had played in staying Philip's hand for three decades, how often he had weighed the cost of invading to dethrone her against the hope of her death from natural causes.

Now, of course, it made no difference. They were still in a state of war and no such consideration would ever deter Philip again. Nor was ill-health of political advantage when coupled with encroaching age. So—was it mere coincidence that her ailments had dispersed, that no one could use the words, *old and unfit for high office,* at a time when most men should be seriously considering her successor?

Essex was momentarily forgotten as she looked back over her life, searching for explanations.

In her mind the mist was lifting a little, showing here and there a glimmer of light, an echo from the past, images and phrases jostling like pieces of some strange puzzle, never quite falling into place.

'I was suborned to this marriage by foul practices of witchcraft.'

So had her father spoken publicly of her mother, full of self-pity and self-justification for what he had done to her. But it was the common people who had first seized on the charge of witchcraft, citing in evidence Anne's two physical blemishes, both known hallmarks of the Devil—an enormous mole on her neck, always covered by a cunning jewelled collar, and a tiny sixth finger on her left hand, always concealed beneath the sweeping Boleyn sleeves designed to hide it.

The mist was still lifting. Deeper and deeper she groped into the forgotten regions of her early infancy.

Someone was fondling her fingers, counting them over and over again and laughing with a shrill, demented pleasure.

'You see, beloved, not a mark upon her skin to betray her.'

'Nan—Nan, how can you be so sure? Look at the length of her fingers—it will surely cause comment.'

'But they are perfectly formed, and they cannot fault her for beauty. Oh, George, she will be more fortunate than I. No one will ever be able to accuse her . . .'

George.

George Boleyn. Executed on a charge of incest with his sister, Anne—Queen of England . . .

Such an incredible fierce desire to eat apples . . .

The vision altered, narrowed, showed her the source of her power. Beside the state bed a golden casket, always locked; and within, a little, headless doll. Waiting!

'Let me destroy this evil thing!'

'No!—oh no, not yet—she does not wish it.'

Elizabeth opened her eyes and found Essex watching her curiously. In one hand he held an apple, appropriated, without her leave, from the bowl which stood on her bedside table. He had taken the little jewelled dagger from his belt and was about to pierce its skin.

Without warning, she reached out to strike it from his hand and the apple rolled under the state bed.

'Next time,' she said, in a strangled voice, 'ask before you take.'

'Madam?' He seemed bewildered by her sudden rage; a little colour had left his face. He stared at her like a hurt child, uncertain how it has offended, and she tried to smile.

'It had a maggot,' she said unsteadily.

'I never saw,' he began.

'No,' she said sharply, 'you never see any danger, do you?'

He smiled. 'Oh come, madam—I would hardly die of a maggot. May I have your gracious leave to take another?'

'No,' she said curtly, and turned away to sit down in the window-seat. 'If you hunger, let your *mother* feed you.'

So that was it! What a pair they were, she and Lettice, always sniping at each other; and he, like pig-in-the-middle, so painfully bound by loyalty to them both.

'I have offended you,' he said contritely.

She frowned. 'Is that not your greatest talent?'

'So it would seem—but there, I let it rest.'

She half turned to look at him with relief.

'Then—you will ask it no more?'

'For tonight. But I shall ask it again, madam, I give you my word. I shall ask it humbly, on my knees, in season and out, until I live to see you change your mind.'

'You appear to count on a remarkably long life,' she said acidly.

He laughed, honestly amused by her tart retort.

'Ah, madam, why not? I am young, I have many years left to me.'

'The two do not necessarily follow,' she said darkly. 'Those whom the gods love die young.'

'Then I am safe, for no god loves me.' He pressed her long fingers to his lips. 'Only a goddess—and she is famous for her mercy.'

Not all their disagreements ended so amicably. He had a voice in her Council now and he used it, raising it to the rafters whenever the Spanish war was under discussion. He had some of the Queen's ability to command an audience; he was convincing, plausible even when he was wrong, and gradually the younger, hotter-headed councillors began to group themselves around him, in opposition to the moderation of the Cecils. By 1591 Essex was a man to be reckoned with, possessing solid status in England and a reputation for military leadership to bolster his considerable political standing.

When Philip chose to hurl an army at the new Protestant French King in Brittany, Essex's name, already a by word in Europe, was suddenly on everyone's lips and there was a clamour in Council and among the people for an English army to be despatched to France, under his leadership. Elizabeth knew she could not stand idly by and let her ally go under, leaving Philip to occupy the Channel provinces. But when she had gathered her forces, grumbling bitterly about the cost, she did not immediately make what everyone considered the obvious choice of leader. Driven by her curious, instinctive sense, she hesitated, while a storm of protest broke out around her. The King of France had openly named his preference—Essex himself had spent two hours on his knees begging for the command—what made her hesitate?

She did not know, she could not have explained—it was just a feeling, the old intuition which so seldom played her false. But in the end, so great was the outcry, she was forced to concede to the demands of public opinion; and Essex was appointed amid general applause.

He sailed to France, there to play the gallant knight, disobeying her orders, and frittering her money away. He returned a virtual failure, but it made no difference to his standing with the people. They welcomed their handsome, high-born hero home as though he had just returned fresh from a second Agincourt, and outdid each other recounting stories of his personal bravery on the field, his perfect chivalry, his complete manhood.

Elizabeth was not amused. She was sick of his complete manhood, and his perfect chivalry, and openly contemptuous of a reckless fool bent on empty heroics. She was not interested in honourable acquittal in the field, only in concrete results that could be judged in hard, economic terms; and she received him caustically.

He told her in a pained tone that he had done his best; she told him coldly that his best was not good enough; and they parted after a heated exchange of grievances.

He took his perfect chivalry off to Wanstead, flouncing out of court rather like the temperamental woman he left behind. When he got there, he remembered all the telling remarks he ought to have made to her, the ungrateful bitch, and duly sat down in a flaming temper to pour them out on paper.

It was a grave mistake. Words spoken in the heat of the moment may be forgiven; words preserved for ever on parchment may overreach their mark once passion has abated.

'I see Your Majesty is resolved to ruin me . . . I appeal to all men that saw my parting from France or the manner of my coming hither, whether I deserved such a welcome or not.'

The letter glowed with the same extraordinary passion that marked all his love letters to the Queen, and his sentiments alarmed Elizabeth. The threat was so openly expressed, that for the first time she wondered if he was quite sane. Certainly no other man in England would have dared to write such a thing to her.

She was not angry now; she was something far more dangerous, cool, calculating, her sense of survival alerted by the one phrase which contained the whole essence of his letter.

I appeal to all men . . . Would he, one day? Would he use the people against her if she ever pushed him too far?

She folded the letter broodingly and put it away into her desk; and they were reconciled as everyone who knew them had supposed they would be. Only the Queen was aware of the significant change in their relationship. Her pleasure in the company of the man who was neither son, nor lover, was now tempered by the dark suspicion that one day he might stab her in the back.

But the prospect did not entirely displease her. She had mastered every man in her life so far with consummate ease. The mastery of Essex was still fraught with challenge; and challenge was the one temptation she had never been able to resist.

CHAPTER 2

The years which followed the Great Armada ticked away in a rapid succession of deaths. By 1595 Walsingham, Hatton and even Drake were in their graves and a new generation of ambitious men was rising at court to snap at each other's heels. Faction politics were showing signs of polarizing into two distinct camps, one led by Burghley and his stunted son, the other by the Earl of Essex; both ruled by a woman who seemed increasingly to resemble a despot.

The strange, shifting sands of Elizabeth's diplomacy continued to stalemate the affairs of Europe. Her ability to wring time out of ugly situations had become her greatest strength, but it was a fluid policy, based on underhand deals and shameless delays, which drove Essex into a frenzy of frustration. He could not abide inaction, indecision or any of the tactics which his Queen employed with such resounding success. He wanted to lay military glory at her feet, but all she wanted to know was what it would cost!

Subterfuge was an anathema to him and the Queen was like some exotic spider, spinning a fantastic web, fascinating, but repulsive to his inner code of conduct. She listened to him; she smiled; she seemed convinced; but the next day saw her frowning, arguing and dancing away to his enemies of whom frankly, there were many. *Wild for to hold* she was, just as her mother had been and how could one conquer a woman who never stood still?

Each succeeding year saw Elizabeth slip a little deeper into the graven image of a virgin goddess. Her clothes became increasingly fantastic and her behaviour correspondingly eccentric; she ceased to notice her own tyranny. She held sway over a court of headstrong, ambitious men, looking down on them from Olympian height, dwarfing them by her presence to the insignificance of dolls. They were nothing without her favour, empty vessels, petty stars in a firmament where she alone was the sun. She took them, used them, watched them crumple to their drained and dispirited deaths without pity. And was amused to find that all the men who had lived in terror of her own death were now in their graves—all save one.

Bent and withered, often too sick to attend Council meetings, Burghley still soldiered on, unable to resign either the reins of government or his spiritual bondage to the Queen. Cruel words spoken in the heat of anger had made no permanent impression on their immutable relationship. Both, in their own way, had buried their private pain deep, making the necessary mental concession to the indisputable fact that neither of them could do without the other. They two, like Alpha and Omega, seemed destined to travel side by side until the last star burnt out. Men spoke of them both as immortal—and feared them.

The shadow in Elizabeth grew darker and gained substance, making her steadily harder and more irrationally jealous of the personal happiness of others. Marrying for love had become a crime second only to treason at the English court and no courtier was immune to the dreadful penalties it carried. Even Raleigh fell foul of her on that score, when his secret union with Bess Throckmorton landed him in the Tower. It was five years before he was permitted to set foot in the Queen's presence again and he spent those five years, to his wife's intense chagrin, driving himself on mad schemes designed to attract the Queen's approval. When at last Elizabeth made the first gesture of forgiveness, Raleigh left his home and his wife without a backward glance, while Bess wept and cursed the woman no wife could hope to rival for long.

Essex, alone, was forgiven the transgression of marriage and restored to favour in a few weeks, for even the Queen, once over her initial fury, could not seriously resent his choice of wife. With the pick of her court to choose from, he had taken Sir Philip Sidney's colourless, tragic little widow to his bed, and then felt honour-bound to marry her when he got her with child. This travesty of a union was no threat to Elizabeth, and having slapped the girl soundly for her presumption, the Queen was moderately agreeable to her; she was sufficiently in contact with reality to know that it could have been worse, much worse.

Her attitude to Frances Devereux was quite without precedent and caused a whisper to pass round the court that this man was a second Leicester and could get away with anything; but if the Queen heard, she gave no sign.

I see but say nothing was still her motto.

The war with Spain drifted on in a vague, unsatisfactory fashion, because Philip, though increasingly weak and ill, would never abandon his ambitions until he was laid in his coffin. Essex pleaded for the grand open action, an all-out assault against Cadiz under his command. But the Queen preferred to hedge her bets with an offensive and defensive league with the French.

Philip had switched the war arena to France and when Calais fell to the Spanish forces, the cannon fire was clearly heard in Greenwich Palace, a deal too close for comfort, as even Elizabeth had to admit. Essex seethed at her inevitable delaying tactics, bemoaned that he was never allowed to 'do her service but against her will' and swore, with his usual extravagance, that if she thwarted his expedition at the last moment he would 'become a monk'. But in the end as usual she had her own way. She got her French treaty *and* her victory at Cadiz. The Spanish fleet assembled there was destroyed and the most flourishing city in Spain fell before the onslaught of Essex's forces.

It was a resounding victory, second only to the triumph of 1588 and Essex was loudly hailed in England as the hero of the hour. But his unaccountable delay in attacking had given the Spanish commander the opportunity to destroy Philip's West Indian treasure fleet, which had been nestling in Cadiz harbour. Medina Sidonia had the comfort of knowing that if the treasure was lost to Spain it was equally lost to England; and Essex had watched the flaming galleons with the first qualm of unease. He had promised the Queen that this expedition would pay for itself, but surely she could not be so unreasonable as always to expect victory with dividends. The inhabitants of Cadiz raised a ransom of £120,000 but no one who knew Elizabeth could expect her to overlook the fact that 12,000,000 ducats now lay useless at the bottom of the sea, along with more than forty vessels in prime condition, which would have handsomely swelled the English merchant fleet. He conferred sixty-eight knighthoods on his own officers, razed Cadiz to the ground and set sail for England on a wave of romantic public opinion. There he found that the Queen had taken advantage of his absence to make Burghley's crippled son, Robert Cecil, the new Secretary of State. His indignant protests were stopped short by Elizabeth's scathing remarks on empty-headed knaves who allowed 12,000,000 ducats to slide through their fingers. There was another quarrel, another withdrawal from court, and Essex, stung by the Queen's contempt, turned to take comfort from the blaze of public popularity which now surrounded him. If the Queen did not appreciate his achievements, there were others who did. Cheering mobs followed him in the streets and clustered around Essex House, waiting for him to appear, flocked after him to Wanstead, where he retired to sulk, drank his health in the local taverns.

The noise of his triumph spilled in through the palace windows and when she heard the chanting of his name—'Essex! Essex! *Essex!*'—Elizabeth felt blind, hot jealousy seize her by the throat. Never in almost forty years had she heard the London crowds shout for anyone but her and, with her old, uncanny instinct for survival, she sensed her danger. She had a rival at last, an enemy more potentially dangerous than ever the Queen of Scots had been.

She had flayed everyone who chose to uphold Essex's achievement as 'the greatest blow ever dealt to the power of Spain', even turned on Burghley and called him a miscreant and a coward, telling him that out of fear he had come to regard Essex more than he did herself. But now, seeing her peril, she changed her tactics abruptly and veered round upon Essex's enemies, recalled the Earl to court and made much of him, so that Essex, utterly bewildered by her change of heart, could only suppose that his presence had conquered after all. She could not do without him—his ascendancy was complete.

Once more the viols played, the Maiden Queen rose and took the hand of the knight of chivalry and beneath a blaze of candles they danced, apparently in perfect harmony. But as she rose from a deep curtsey she glanced round at the bent, old figure of the Lord Treasurer and gave him a cool little smile. Slowly, almost imperceptibly, the old man inclined his head; and though no words had passed between them, their understanding was complete.

Late that night Burghley lay abed, listening to the rantings of his stunted, hunchbacked son. Up and down the room went the twisted little figure of the new Secretary of State, gesturing wildly in his impotent rage.

'You and I, Father—we might just as well resign. He has everything—military reputation, the backing of the people, and the Queen as besotted with him as ever. She can't bear him out of her sight for two minutes put together. Mark my words, in six months he'll rule here—I see nothing likely to prevent it.'

'You are mistaken, Robert—no man has yet mastered the Queen or ever will.'

Cecil swung round, sharp with sudden irritation.

'Oh, lord, Father—how can you say that? I've seen them together and what I see *disgusts* me—she's completely under his influence.'

Burghley smiled a slow, secret smile and smoothed the white linen sheets with guarded satisfaction.

'Completely under his influence,' he murmured. 'Oh, yes—that is what he thinks now—but what he sees—and what you see, my boy—is an illusion. Her Majesty will dispel it like morning mist whenever it pleases her to do so.'

'You think so?' Cecil was patently unconvinced.

'You will allow that I know the Queen a little better than most!' Burghley's voice was touched with frost; the necessity of mentioning the fact had annoyed him. 'Lord, boy—do you really think her so devoid of purpose? The moment his back is turned she favours his opponents—only remember how you came about your present office. Secretary of State.' The old man nodded approvingly. 'It's a powerful position, Robert, mind you value it, as I did.'

'I would have valued it before now, if she had chosen to appoint me earlier, Father—God knows, I've done the job for long enough without recognition or salary. What did she think I lived on all that time—fresh air?'

Burghley waved his hand impatiently.

'You and your wife have been well provided for.'

'By you, sir. A man does not expect to look to his father for support at my age.'

'The Queen gives and the Queen takes. It is her right.'

'Oh, she most certainly takes! Mother warned me as much before I ever came to court. Doubtless, if we had a king it would be different—' Cecil looked up and caught his father's eyes fixed upon him. They were hard and black with gathering fury.

'A king,' muttered Burghley, in a thin whisper of disbelief. 'A *king?*'

'A private opinion only,' added Robert hastily.

'A traitor's opinion!' Burghley snapped, his hands clenched round the sheets, his withered cheeks whitening with the intensity of his emotion. 'By God's soul, have I sired her a viper and nurtured it in my own nest?' He caught his son by the sleeve and shook him weakly. 'Have I? God damn you, sir, answer me!'

'No,' said Robert, truly alarmed now. 'No, of course not. For God's sake, Father, don't agitate yourself like this or you'll have a seizure. Let me get you some wine.'

Burghley sank back into his pillows, breathing heavily and with difficulty.

'It's not wine I need—it's your oath of loyalty. Your sworn vow of service. You will be loyal to the Queen until she dies. You will swear it.'

Robert knelt and kissed the hand which had never before been raised against him in anger, not even in his childhood.

'I swear it, Father. I give you my word. Rest easy now, I implore you!'

Burghley closed his eyes and exhaled his breath in a long-drawn sigh of exhaustion.

'If you fail her, you fail me,' he whispered dimly. 'When I am no longer here to remind you—remember it!'

'I will remember,' said Robert dutifully. But he turned away to fetch the wine with a resentful heart.

His mother had been jealous of the Queen; he had been little more than a boy when he first began to realize it. And now he remembered the day he had gone hurrying from his father's study to his mother's private closet, as near to running in his excitement as any hunchbacked youngster could be.

'Mother—I'm to go to court with Father when my studies are complete. I've been chosen to serve the Queen.'

Mildred had looked up at him and her comfortable face was stony.

'Chosen!' she repeated stiffly, laying her embroidery aside. 'The Druids had a better word for it, I think!'

He came into the room and shut the door quickly.

'You're not pleased. Didn't Father discuss it with you first?'

'Oh yes, naturally. You know your father—the very soul of marital democracy!'

It was so unlike Mildred to speak slightingly of her husband, that Robert drew up a chair beside her and looked at her with concern.

'It's because of Thomas, isn't it?—you feel it was his right, as the eldest, to take his place at Father's side.'

Mildred's mouth set into a grim line.

'Most men,' she said harshly, 'would seek to advance their first-born son, no matter what his ability, but not your father, oh no—Thomas was always a bitter disappointment to him. Not fit for the Queen's service—not fit, his own heir! What other man would put such a consideration first? But there— Thomas might prove a liability to Her Majesty and that would never do, would it? Only the best for our Virgin Queen.' She groped angrily for her silks and needles. 'So it's to be you instead—you the child I wore myself out to rear, nursing you from one illness to the next—you who are to break your health and heart in her service. Much good it will do you!'

'Why are you so angry?' He had been hurt and indignant at last; he hated any reference to his physical frailty. 'What else am I to do if I don't go to court and win honour there?'

'Honour!' Mildred spat in the hearth without undue ceremony, 'Aye, and honour is about all you'll ever get from it. Never think to taste real power, boy. There's only one power in this land and that's the Queen—mind you never forget it.'

He was silent, sorting through her skeins of silk, as he had been wont to do as a child whenever he was troubled.

'I want this chance, Mother. I really want it.'

'Take it, then,' she said curtly. 'You're the pick of the litter—yes—your father's own words, for all it makes me little more than a brood bitch. Sometimes he makes me feel that my sole purpose on this earth was to breed a son suitable—*suitable*, mind!—for *her* service.'

'Mother,' he remonstrated uncomfortably. 'Anyone would think you hate the Queen.'

'Hate her?' Mildred lifted faded eyes, dogged with defiance. 'Every woman in this kingdom will learn to hate her in time—every woman with a husband or a son that she can take and use to serve her purpose. Granted, she gives them back when she's finished with them—gives them back old before their time, broken—*useless!*'

Now what exactly did she mean by useless? He did not like to guess and lowered his eyes, embarrassed by this unlooked-for outburst of bitterness. He tried to ease the conversation on to safer ground.

'Father says he'll need my help in the coming years to form a faction. He wants the family's influence to continue after his death, that's all. It's understandable.'

Mildred laughed shortly. 'Much he cares for the family influence when he leaves the next Lord Burghley to rot in idleness on his country estate. Don't you see, it's not the family's fortune that matters to him, it's the Queen's. *What will she do when I'm gone?* That's the way his mind runs in this matter and you're the answer to his nightmare. You're a tool, my boy, nothing more or less than another of his devices for her safety.'

'I don't believe that,' Robert had said stubbornly, 'he's always been the most devoted father—the most faithful of husbands too,' he added, in pointed reminder. 'It's not kind of you to doubt it.'

'I never said that I doubted it,' remarked Mildred drily. 'Your father is deeply fond of us all. But it's the Queen he loves!'

Robert flushed hotly and turned away.

'You're surely not trying to imply that Father of all people was ever—'

'Good God, no!' She cut him short in mid-sentence. 'Your father's never looked at another woman in that way—God knows, there've been times when I almost wished he had. I could have come to terms with his whore. I could have excused a normal transient lust, it's his utter mindless devotion to her that I can't bear. Nothing shakes his loyalty, no matter what blows she deals out to him. It's—' she paused, groping for the right word to express her resentment, 'it's *unnatural!*'

Robert was silenced, his sense of eager anticipation dulled by a vague feeling of alarm. He was suddenly no longer sure he wanted to follow his father's footsteps down such a dark and uncertain path. He did not like the sound of this woman he would be bound to serve and obey for his father's sake.

'I suppose I could always take up law,' he began diffidently.

Mildred made an impatient gesture.

'Make all the plans you like,' she said irritably. 'Do you suppose for one moment any of them will make a jot of difference? Your future is charted out for you now—the Queen will swallow up your life, just as she's swallowed your father's. I suppose I should give thanks to God for your twisted spine. She likes physical perfection in her men, so you at least will know some measure of freedom. Doubtless, your *wife* will be grateful for it.'

They had never spoken on the subject again, but it was a conversation which remained with Robert long after his mother's death. It had coloured his view of Elizabeth well before he entered her service; when at last he came, fearful and hesitant, to court, under Burghley's patronage, she chose to call him her Pygmy. And after that, it had been easy to believe that his confused emotional response to this mysterious woman was composed chiefly of cold dislike.

He sat on the edge of the bed now and watched his father slowly sipping his wine, wheezing and grunting with the multiplying discomforts of old age.

Pity touched him and he leaned over to touch Burghley's swollen hand on the coverlet.

'Father—you're a very sick man. Don't you think it's time you really did resign this post?'

'The Queen would not countenance it,' said Burghley with an air of quiet satisfaction which irked the younger man. 'I am her right hand—always have been, you know. I had my chance to leave office and retire quietly in the country after Mary Stuart's death. Your mother urged me to take it, but then the Queen came back to me—yes, she took me back, as I had hoped and prayed and thought impossible at last. Your mother wasn't pleased of course, but she held her peace. Admirable woman, your mother, Robert—admirable woman. She understood what it meant to me to regain the Queen's confidence.'

Robert was silent.

'She always trusted me,' mused Burghley softly 'trusted me beyond anyone else—even Leicester.'

'And now she has Essex,' said Robert sourly.

'Whom she does not trust at all.'

Robert stared at him in astonishment.

'She *loves* him!'

'Perhaps. That will not save him if he continues playing to the gallery in this manner. The moment he raises his hand to touch the sceptre, she'll strike him down without mercy. Believe me, my son, I know her. You may think that you have seen her angry, but you know nothing—and no more does Essex—of her capacity for vengeance. Her extraordinary talent for inflicting pain.'

Burghley's thin lips quivered for a moment and he closed his eyes on a fugitive gleam of unshed tears.

'She chose to hurt me once. I will not tell you why or how—but there was a time, I assure you, when I thought I would never care for anything again because of it.'

'Father!'

'Oh, I deserved some punishment, even expected it, but not that—I did not deserve *that!* Walsingham used to say that knowledge is never too dear, but I would have paid a king's ransom to be spared that one cruel piece. She is two people, my boy—two entirely different people. One, kind and loyal, so full of warmth and intelligence that a man would gladly give his soul to serve her. And the other—frightening! Few have seen that other side of her and those who have prefer not to dwell on the experience—the dreadful cruelty. If that side of her should ever turn its face to Essex—'

Burghley broke off and was broodingly silent. It was a long time before he looked up and, when he did, he began to speak as though his son had only that moment entered the room.

'My dear boy, it was good of you to come, but I'm too weary to discuss anything tonight. Put out the lights and leave me to my rest. We will talk tomorrow.'

Puzzled and ill at ease, the young Secretary did as he was bidden, leaving his father to nod in the rosy firelight.

Shadows bobbed on the panelled walls as the flames leapt and flickered in the stone hearth, and Burghley watched them, remembering the Queen's curious sidelong glance, and all that he believed it signified.

Oh no, she did not trust Essex; and now there was something growing in the labyrinth of her mind, something dark and secret. She was jealous of her people's affection and whenever she was jealous she was dangerous; but Essex was blind to the smouldering resentment in her black eyes. Blind and reckless and arrogant; and assuredly riding for a fall.

The knowledge gave Burghley a certain satisfaction, for it was almost like old times, a reincarnation of his lifelong battle with Leicester—his son, against the Gypsy's stepson. Very fitting, yes—supremely fitting. Intelligence and craft against charm and panache, and the Queen still where she had always been, squarely in the centre of the see-saw, holding the balance of power.

Whatever his grievances, Robert had been bred up in loyalty to the Queen, and Burghley had every confidence that he would serve her with unstinting care. He was also equally convinced that Essex would betray her.

There would be a mighty clash of titans, an earth-shattering encounter which would echo through the firmament and disturb the heavenly bodies. When it was over, the landscape at court would be irretrievably altered, scattered with flotsam and jetsam, as after some terrible shipwreck of emotion. That day might be near or far, but it would come. And when that day was over, Robert Cecil, Secretary of State, would be there to pick up the pieces quietly and unobtrusively.

'Madam, I tell you plainly, there is a new Spanish fleet bound for English waters.'

The Queen turned her head in its stiff-wired frame of lace and shrugged her monstrously padded shoulders. There was always a new Spanish fleet and it was always bound for English waters—so what was new?

'You are an alarmist, my lord, like the rest of my warmongering Council.'

Essex laughed shortly.

'Madam, Philip's hatred of you is quite maniacal. He has sworn to avenge the failure of '88 if it costs him his last candlestick. As an alarmist, I consider that to be an alarming threat. Will you sit back and allow it to be carried out?'

Elizabeth frowned. 'I've told you before, I can't afford to keep financing these offensive expeditions.'

'You can't afford *not* to!' he interrupted angrily. 'For Christ's sake, stop haggling like a—like a—'

Her finely plucked eyebrows raised in ironic challenge, dared him to say the dreadful word 'miser'. But even Essex's courage had its limits and he took refuge in kissing her hand.

'Madam—you try me too far when I seek only to serve you. Let me take the fleet to the Azores and lie in wait for them, wherever they're bound—to the south coast or Ireland. It will be Cadiz all over again.'

'It had better not be,' she said caustically. 'If I don't see a better return for my investment this time there'll be trouble.'

'This time?' He picked her up at once. 'Does that mean you consent?'

'I didn't say that.'

He half rose from his knees in exasperation, but she placed an imperious finger on his shoulder so that he sank back again.

'Madam, you're being totally unreasonable. You know I can do it.'

'I know you *say* you can do it. Just because you had a little luck at Cadiz you think you can conquer the world at my expense.'

'Luck!' he echoed in angry disbelief. *'Luck!'*

She saw the dangerous flash in his eyes and suddenly smiled and patted his shoulder.

'Now, there's no call to take that tone, I was only teasing you. You're always so quick to take offence, Robert.'

'You're always so damned ready to give it,' he said frankly, and suddenly they both smiled. She began to chew the handle of her fan thoughtfully.

'If I agreed to finance this exploit—*if*, I say—then I might be prepared to give you a joint command with Raleigh and Howard—'

He flung up his head furiously and glared at her.

'You know I won't accept that—I won't be treated like a schoolboy who can't be trusted! I'll command the whole damn thing or I'll have nothing to do with it—and you know what that will mean. The men will follow me into Hell—they won't follow Howard half as far. Is that what you want?'

She stood up suddenly and shook out the folds of her heavily panniered gown, so that the ruby aglets flashed fire in the candlelight. A mantle of white lawn trailed from her headdress and she stood twisting Mary Stuart's long rope of black pearls between her fingers.

'One day,' she said quietly, 'I will break you of that stubborn will, you wild stallion. You're as arrogant and obstinate as the Devil himself—you get it from your mother, of course—I've always said so.'

She made to turn away from him and he caught her hand and kissed it violently.

'Would you rather I cringed and whined at your heels like the rest of them?'

She was silent, watching him, and beneath her steady gaze, his own fell.

'I speak the truth as I see it.' He stole a glance at her. 'Whether it's pleasing to your ears or not. You used to say you liked that—that it was a breath of fresh air in your stifling court. Do you now mislike it in me that I will not lie like a Trojan to suit your mood?'

The Queen sighed and stroked one finger idly across his cheek.

'Some day,' she said softly, 'you will speak your mind once too often. I swear that tongue of yours will be the death of you.'

He smiled faintly. 'A duel?'

'Perhaps.' She had turned away from him, her voice curiously distant. He ran after her and flung himself on his knees at her feet, clasping both her hands aggressively between his own.

'No, madam, you shall not dance away from me again. I mean to have your answer and to have it tonight. Do I command this fleet or not?'

She freed one hand and began to twist the silver buttons which adorned his russet doublet.

'If you come back empty-handed again—'

'I won't, I swear it. You shall have your West Indian treasure fleet, madam —sufficient to pay for the expedition several times over.'

She studied the arrogant tilt of his chin, the brilliant hair, Tudor red, this young aristocrat who would pass anywhere for her son, so like herself and yet so unalike. Fear touched her for a moment, a sudden, maternal urge to protect him from himself and the creeping darkness in her own heart. If she let him go and he succeeded, he would be a greater threat than ever to her; if he failed she would never forgive him for it. Why must he strive for military glory when she could keep him at home, safe from all its attendant perils?

He touched her hand in a little, prompting gesture.

'Your answer, madam?'

She turned her head abruptly away from him and stared out at the black night beyond her window.

'My answer,' she said coldly, 'is No!'

He rose stiffly, narrowly holding himself in restraint, took her hand in a hard grip that made her wince, pressed it against his taut lips and bowed icily.

'I shall be at Wanstead until you change your mind,' he snapped; and was gone, slamming the door behind him.

The silence from Wanstead was so deep and ominous that the Council became alarmed and begged the Queen to allow Essex to lead the expedition to intercept the new Spanish fleet. She frowned, she grumbled at the cost, she baulked at the emotional and political blackmail which he had aimed against her; but, in the end, she said ungraciously that he might go if he wished.

From beginning to end the mission was an unmitigated disaster, for this time the elements were against him. A gale force wind prevented him from destroying the Spanish shipping in Ferrol harbour and, not daring to return empty-handed, he set sail for the Azores in search of the Spanish plate fleet. There a question of honour wrecked the whole expedition, when Raleigh, his subordinate officer, stole his moment of glory by taking the island of Fayal behind his back. In a blazing rage, Essex promptly attempted to outshine Raleigh by attacking the island of San Miguel. While he was occupied there, the Spanish treasure fleet, finding its route suddenly unguarded, seized the opportunity to sail safely into the impregnable harbour of Terceira and was lost to the English force for good. News was carried to Philip that while

Essex was cavorting about the Azores, the English shores were completely vulnerable to attack at last; and in a transport of holy, half-hysterical glee, the King of Spain flung his third Armada out to sea. This time—this time he could not fail!

The Spanish fleet set sail in hurried confusion, its commander not even permitted to know its destination until they reached the Bay of Biscay. Even so they were a mighty force and the news of their imminent arrival caused a panic of preparation in England. Once more the warning beacons were laid in readiness, the rusty militia was organized and the Queen cursed the men who had persuaded her to capitulate to Essex and so give the enemy both the leisure and the courage to attack. When gales and storms splattered the Spanish fleet along the coast of France, the main body of ships, leaking and battered, was forced to straggle home. Elizabeth was first limp with relief at the news and then transported with rage against the fool who was responsible for the whole situation. While Philip, half dead with disease and fatigue and despair, learned that once more his God had deserted him, Essex arrived home to discover that in his absence Robert Cecil had received the Duchy of Lancaster, and the old Lord Admiral, Howard, had been created Earl of Nottingham. As Steward of the next Parliament, Howard would now take automatic precedence over the hero of Cadiz. All his carefully rehearsed humility deserted him at that news and instead of grovelling for forgiveness, as any man of sense would have done, he promptly flew into a temper and flounced off to Wanstead, refusing to return even for the festivities of the l7th of November, the fortieth observance of the Queen's accession.

'I've had enough of this!' said Elizabeth ominously to Burghley, as Christmas approached without a gesture of conciliation from the absent Earl. 'The time has come to put an end to his nonsense.'

'Yes, madam,' said Burghley, quietly; hopefully.

'I knew it would end like this—a total disaster—nothing to show for it but expense upon expense. Doesn't he realize we could have been invaded while he played the fool in the Azores?'

Burghley said nothing, letting her mood of indignation grow slowly. She was pacing up and down like a caged tigress.

'Well, that's an end to it! I've finished with these mad exploits altogether —we seek peace from now on. The next time the fleet sails out of the Channel it will be over my dead body—do you hear me, Burghley?'

He coughed discreetly. 'Yes, madam.'

She bore down on him furiously, brandishing her fan like a dagger.

'And after all this the people *still* hail him as a hero?'

'Yes, madam,' he said grimly; there was no accounting for the people.

'They blame the bad weather—they blame Raleigh—they blame everything, in fact, except my lord of Essex.'

'My lord of Essex!' She gritted her teeth and slapped the fan viciously against the billowing folds of her gown. 'And where is he now, the conquering hero—still sulking at Wanstead because Howard takes precedence over him in a stupid procession?'

'I believe he's here in London, madam.'

'Oh?' Her glance flickered. 'Then why is he not at court?'

'Why indeed, madam!'

Burghley raised his bushy eyebrows in a significant gesture that was not wasted on her. Suddenly her eyes narrowed into a fixed stare like a cat's and her lips became a thin, grim, scarlet line in her lined face. He knew she understood how dangerous it would be to continue humiliating a man whose name was sung in all the taverns. And while he remained in London, pointedly absent from his post as Privy Councillor, he was unquestionably gathering a popular support which would make him increasingly dangerous.

'The people say that he is wronged,' she mused, staring into the fire, biting a finger as she was apt to do when she was tense and disturbed. 'He cannot be allowed to remain absent from his duties indefinitely. He must be seen to return amicably—'

Burghley's glance was steady. 'It would take some especial mark of your favour and forgiveness to bring him back this time.'

She looked round over her shoulder and smiled coolly.

'Yes—he must be made to understand that, since I am only a weak and feeble woman, I cannot do without him.'

She walked away thoughtfully, poured wine into two fine glasses and held one out to him. As he took it, their eyes locked together and they touched the rims of the glasses.

'I give you a toast, my lord,' she said quietly. 'To the Earl of Essex—the new Earl Marshal of England.'

Admiration shone out of the old man's eyes as he looked at her in the soft candlelight.

'Madam, you give him the means to hang himself!'

'Precisely!' Her smile held a gleam of icy malice. 'And I'm sure he will make a thorough job of it, as usual.'

When she had sipped the wine, she turned and hurled her glass into the fireplace. It splintered into a thousand tiny fragments and left a red stain like a pool of blood on the hearth.

CHAPTER 3

Earl Marshal of England!

Essex waited for his mother to hand back the Queen's letter in stiff-necked silence, then let out a yell of triumph.

'What did I tell you? You see now that she can deny me nothing.'

'I see an empty title,' said Lettice tartly, 'a tinsel badge of honour to pacify a sulking child. How clever she is!'

'Clever?'

'It's called playing dead. Dogs do it—and *bitches!*'

'Mother!' There was a warning note of anger in his voice suddenly. 'You will not abuse the Queen in my hearing.'

Lettice sat down at her embroidery frame, stabbing the needle in and out of the tapestry with cold rage.

'You're a fool, Robert,' she said after a moment, 'do you know that? In thrillage to an old crone of sixty-six!'

'She is not—'

'She *is!* Sixty-six! It's—it's positively indecent, the two of you.'

'Don't be ridiculous, Mother,' he said icily, 'we're not lovers.'

'Thank God!' snapped Lettice, biting off a thread with a vicious gesture. 'I really would tremble if I thought you had been so foolish. I never wanted you to go to court, but Leicester would have it that he needed you. I might have known how it would be. First my husband, now my son. Sometimes I think she singled you out simply to spite me—to pay me back for Leicester!'

Essex withdrew to the chimney-piece in frigid dignity, his pride cut to the quick.

'The Queen favours me for myself,' he insisted stubbornly. 'I won't hear you or anyone else say otherwise. Surely it's obvious from this news that she is wretched without me.'

Lettice laughed shortly and pushed her tapestry aside.

'You speak of wretchedness? Look at yourself, boy—pale as a corpse and thin as a crow. Every time she turns her back on you, you fret yourself into a shadow—it sickens me to see it!'

He shrugged off her concern impatiently and reached for his cloak.

'Nothing matters now except that I go back to court in triumph, despite the Father and the Son.'

'You don't have to go back,' said Lettice jealously. 'Not immediately. Let her wait.'

He bent to kiss his mother's cheek carelessly.

'The Queen is like the tide, Mother. She waits for no man.'

And he went out of the room with a jaunty step that made her suddenly want to weep.

The Queen was writing when the little hunchbacked Secretary was shown into her room and she did not look up as he approached her desk.

He executed a clumsy bow to the top of her jewelled head and felt the familiar sting of her indifference. By God, she would look up soon enough if Essex had entered the room, or even Burghley. Must he be constantly reminded by her cool manner that he would never have the charm of his rival or the sheer stature of his own father?

As he waited there, with a wad of papers clutched against his chest and his weak eyes dazzled by the winking diamonds in her hair, he had time to reflect on the past months of failed diplomacy in his own camp.

A brief embassy to France had disclosed the fact that the French King—supposedly England's staunch ally—was secretly negotiating a separate peace treaty with Spain. The untimely news had been received in Council like a lighted firecracker, instantly igniting the latent hostility between the rival factions. Essex had seized upon it as a vindication of his own aggressive war policies and since then a succession of violent council meetings had weighed war and peace in an atmosphere of increasing personal animosity.

'We have been played false!' Essex had insisted, shouting down Burghley's quiet pleas for moderation, 'the only way to win this war is to fight it—to spare no effort and no expense—'

'My lord,' Burghley interposed softly, 'the Treasury is not a bottomless vault in which you may dip your hands whenever you please.'

Essex turned on him with savage contempt.

'When we want the opinions of counting clerks at this table we'll ask for them—those who have lost their spirit for the fight should stay at home and sit by the fire—where they belong!'

Burghley fumbled with the Bible which lay beside him and flicked the book open at the fifty-fifth psalm. Silently he pushed it over to the young man who sat opposite him, pointing to one line with a twisted finger.

Essex looked down and read aloud: *'Bloodthirsty and deceitful men shall not live out half their days!'* He looked across at the old man and laughed suddenly. 'Is that your idea of a threat, my lord? Is it supposed to put fear and trembling into my heart? By God, sir, it's small wonder the French mock us when we follow the mealy-mouthed advice of a dotard.'

'That will do, my lord!' The Queen's voice had cut across the argument and immediately there was silence. But there had been no disguising the naked hostility which now existed between the war and peace parties. The rivalry between the Essex and Cecil factions was slowly coming to a head and the Queen was well aware of it. If she was not very careful in maintaining the balance, she might easily lose control of the game. Now, as she wrote and ignored Cecil with quiet deliberation, her mind was busy resolving the issue. At last she laid her pen down and looked up.

'Well, little man,' she said pleasantly. 'What business today?'

He laid the papers on her desk and she immediately began to glance through them. She read quickly, still possessing the power of total recall, and he knew that shortly every word on that stack would be locked in the vast storehouse of her memory. It was a gift he envied.

He cleared his throat hesitantly.

'If I might most respectfully request Your Majesty to consider the unrest in Ireland? As long as the post of Lord Deputy remains empty, Tyrone's rebel forces will continue to gain ground.'

The Queen frowned. There was always unrest in Ireland and sometimes she felt it was endemic in that savage land. As far back as she remembered a steady stream of loyal, eager men had gone out there to contain the ferocious revolts of local chieftains and had taken only heartbreak, and lost reputations, to their graves. Essex's father, Walter Devereux, had been one of them and she bit her lip angrily, recalling how that timely death had set Lettice Knollys free to cast her cap at Robert Dudley. Ireland had a lot to answer for in her book!

And yet Ireland could not be ignored. Spain fanned the treachery there, still seeking a landing point for invasion forces, and it was certainly true that the post of Lord Deputy must be filled as soon as possible, before Philip got himself a foothold in the land.

She tapped her long, painted nails on the polished table top and watched Cecil between half-closed lids.

'As you so rightly say, Sir Robert, someone must go to Ireland—Ireland or Hell—it's one and the same place I'm led to believe.' Her painted lips curled in a sarcastic smile. 'And since no Englishman makes his fortune there I suppose some unfortunate soul will have to be inveigled into accepting the post. Not a position to give a friend, eh? I take it you have a man in mind?'

The question was shot at him so suddenly that he started. He wished she would not look at him like that, as though she had already analysed every thought in his head and dismissed them as uninteresting and insignificant. It took him a moment to regain his composure and calmly parrot his prepared line.

'Madam, I can suggest no one better qualified for the post than Sir William Knollys.'

Knollys was Essex's uncle and a strong supporter in his nephew's camp. It was not difficult to see why Cecil hoped to link his rival's name with a campaign that, of its very nature, must prove at best a limited success and at worst an uninspired disaster. Cecil hoped to discredit Essex's man and thereby weaken the Earl's influence at the council table. Normally she would not take sides so openly—but now, it might be just the opportunity she was looking for to make an insidious inroad in the Earl's standing.

But she showed no active interest; that was not her way.

'The matter will be aired in Council,' she said coolly, and waved her hand in dismissal, without looking at him.

Every window made to open in the council chamber at Greenwich had been pushed wide to admit the cooler air which blew in from the river. They admitted other things too, the talk and laughter of the gaily clad courtiers who walked the lawns beneath in their stifling court costumes; and the shouts of the bargemen who sailed the river beyond. Greenwich stood close to the river, fronting the broad sweep of the Thames, so that ships sailing up to the London port could be clearly seen from the windows.

But no one in the council chamber was listening to the sounds of life which flooded in from the river on that sticky July day. The room had assumed a tense silence, the kind of silence that precedes some mighty conflagration.

It had begun quietly enough. A small group of councillors surrounded the Queen in the window embrasure where she stood, a little desperate for air, in a suffocating gown of gold and silver, which weighed like a shroud of lead on her thin frame. It was too hot for business. Cecil was sweating copiously inside his dark suit and Essex's handsome face was red and strained. No one was in a good mood, and the Queen was intent on despatching the matter in hand with the minimum of time and effort. She glanced at Cecil momentarily and then announced her intention of appointing Sir William Knollys as Lord Deputy of Ireland.

Essex stiffened, catching sight of Cecil's faintly smug expression.

'Madam,' he said with an edge to his voice, 'I beg leave to remind you that Sir William Knollys is my uncle.'

Elizabeth turned impatiently.

'And what, pray, has that to do with his appointment, my lord?'

Essex instinctively clenched his fist and took a step towards her.

'My uncle has no experience.'

'He will quickly gain it.'

'To what purpose, may I ask—merely to satisfy the whim of a hunchback? If you want the right man for the job, I suggest Sir George Carew.'

Carew was Cecil's man. Even for Essex, it was a grossly transparent move and Elizabeth laughed outright, her humour suddenly restored.

'My lord, you make yourself ridiculous. I advise you to be silent if you cannot be serious. The matter is settled.'

He caught the ruff at her wrist angrily; he was falling into the routine of a private scene with her and there was a deathly hush among the spectators.

'Madam—I will not stand by while such an appointment takes place. My advice—'

'When I want your advice, young man, I will ask for it!'

'All I ask is that you have the courtesy to hear me out before you make such an arbitrary decision.'

'I have heard all I wish to hear from you, sir.' She paused and looked around the intently listening group. 'My lords—Sir William Knollys is appointed!'

With a great oath, Essex turned his back on her, a public gesture of contempt which no man had dared to make in forty years.

With a strangled gasp of fury, she lunged forward and struck him a resounding blow across the ear and the sound of it rang in the silent room like a gunshot.

'Go to the devil and be hanged!' she spat.

He swung round upon her, white with murderous rage and to their utter disbelief they saw him reach for his sword. With a choking cry, old Howard of Nottingham rushed between them before he could strike her, clamping his hand on the Earl's arm and shaking the sword to the floor. The room was suddenly galvanized to life and Essex was seized from behind. His arms were pinned, but no one could silence his scream of rage.

'God's death, I would not have borne such an insult from your father's hand! I'll not bear a blow from you or any woman!'

There was no sound in the room, except that of Essex struggling like a wild wounded animal against his captors. With a great wrenching effort he threw off their hands and rushed to the door, slamming it open. They made to go after him, but the Queen said in a thin whisper, 'No, my lords. Let him go.'

She stood where he had left her, deathly white, motionless and ominously silent, staring after him.

She could not believe it had happened.

This time, said the court knowingly, buzzing with the news like a vast sprawling hive, this time he had gone too far. This time it would be the Tower and the block; and they waited in an agony of suspense for the guards to go marching to his apartments and make the expected arrest. An hour later Essex was seen clattering down the main staircase, with his followers at his heels. In the courtyard he vaulted into the saddle of his favourite mare and rode out through the main entrance of Greenwich, like a madman leading a force from the gates of Hell. Rumour had it he would make for Wanstead, where doubtless he would find the Queen's forces waiting for him, but by the end of that day not a single armed man had set foot outside the palace. The Queen remained alone in her private apartments and no one knew what to make of it. Why hadn't she acted? Was she paralysed with shock—or merely brooding on some terrible revenge?

The days stole away and crept into weeks. Still she did nothing. She went about her court with her pale face inscrutable beneath its flamboyant wig, apparently totally preoccupied by the news which was carried to her daily from the Lord Treasurer's house in the Strand.

And the word ran round in a shocked whisper that Lord Burghley lay on his death bed at last.

The Queen of England sat beside the canopied bed in the sunlit Strand and faithfully fed her chief minister with a spoon.

She was not very good at it, Burghley observed, with detached affection. The spoon mounted from the bowl to his sunken lips with frenetic speed, as though she felt life dripping slowly out of him and was desperate to fill him with nourishment. So might she attempt to fill a cracked vessel, working desperately against time.

He lifted his arm at length to stay her busy hand.

'Madam, let it rest.'

'But you must eat,' she insisted, a trifle wildly. 'You will never get well unless you eat.'

'My dear,' he said gently, 'you deceive yourself. Everyone in this kingdom knows that I am at my last end. Why will you not accept it?'

The spoon halted, wavered, and found its way tremulously back into the bowl. Tears welled up in her eyes and threatened to fall against her will and he saw with anxiety their sudden glisten.

'I am old and my time is done,' he murmured. 'If you will mourn my unworthy person, then I pray you, madam—let it be with moderation.'

So he thought of Leicester even now. She forced herself to smile faintly. 'Don't worry, my friend—I shall be your very merry widow.'

They were silent a moment, struggling respectively for composure. At last she said with studied lightness, 'They say King Philip, too, lies on his death-bed. You should go down to Hell together—my best friend and my best enemy. You see—I always said I would outlive you all. Sometimes I think I shall live for ever.'

She frowned; evidently the prospect displeased her. Burghley groped for her hand.

'You will live in the hearts of men as long as England endures.'

'And you,' she retorted swiftly, 'are a forward old flatterer, like the rest of them.'

But he knew she did not seriously believe that, and he was not concerned. Flattery was something to which their relationship had never sunk.

Suddenly she said with angry despair, 'You shall not die. I forbid it. What shall I do without you?'

He bit his quivering lip and looked away.

'There is my son,' he managed to say at length.

'Oh, yes, your precious son!' She glanced at him shrewdly through her tears. 'Are you quite sure Mildred never cuckolded you with that one? If I didn't know better, I'd say he was Walsingham's—cold as cod-fish! He doesn't care for me over much, does he?'

'He—' Burghley floundered for words, 'he was always—*reserved*, even as a child. Sensitive about his physical limitations. And I fear, madam, that to call him your *Pygmy*—'

'Good God,' breathed the Queen, 'did he think I referred to *that?* Then he is even more stupid than I thought.'

'Stupid!' bridled the loyal father. '*Stupid*, madam?'

'He suffers by comparison,' said the Queen smoothly. 'Beside you any man would seem a dwarf.'

Burghley coughed to hide his confused emotions. It was a full minute before he had recovered himself sufficiently to tell her his son could be trusted.

She lifted his swollen hand to her lips and kissed it gently.

'In all my life I have trusted no man save you—'

And Leicester! he added silently.

'Yes,' she continued softly, exactly as though he had spoken the thought aloud, 'and him. Must you still resent that all these years after his death?'

'You loved him!' It was an accusation.

She looked down at the coverlet.

'Then it was true,' he said brokenly. 'All those years—you and he—'

She shook her head slowly and Burghley dragged himself upright against the pillows, staring at her in breathless anticipation.

'It was said to hurt you, William, didn't you guess that? No man may strike me without receiving double the blow in return. Oh, my Spirit, do I seem like a woman who has known the joys of love?'

That small, grim touch of self-deprecation convinced him as no sworn oath could have done. When he thought how she treated young lovers, he wondered how he could ever have missed the truth. A bitter old maid—everything she said and did supported that image! And slowly tears of joy began to roll down his withered face.

It was a small enough lie to buy the happiness of a dying man, a little worthwhile perjury which she would not regret. For now, sitting here at his death-bed, as she had done day after day, adjusting his pillows and feeding him with her own hand, she found she could not do enough for him. There was so little time left in which to distil a lifetime's love and gratitude; and this was one man who must not die without knowing how much she cared.

She said kindly, 'Your son's worth is not wasted on me. I shall see him advanced as far as you could ever wish.'

'Madam,' he murmured incoherently, 'you are gracious beyond all my hopes—and loyalty will be your reward, I swear it.'

'Loyalty,' she repeated darkly. 'Oh yes, they're all very loyal, these rising young men who can't wait for me to drop dead—about as loyal as that wild beast mooning at Wanstead! And there's a pretty piece of devotion to comfort my old age.' She brushed her hand across her eyes, as though to push back the hideous memory. 'He's grown beyond me, Burghley, like a wilful, destructive child baiting its mother. Why did he have to come into my life when I'm too old to handle him? What in God's name am I to do with him?'

'The insolent lout should be flogged to death for the outrage!' muttered the old man with feeling.

She smiled bitterly and laid her hand on his shoulder.

'One does not flog heroes to death, my gentle dotard. And that is his strength if he chooses to make a stand on it. The love of the people—how well I know the power that it brings.'

'The people are ignorant fools and knaves,' began Burghley hotly.

'The people are bored,' she said shrewdly. 'Peace and prosperity are well enough for a few decades, but now they are restless for novelty, for deeds that fire the imagination and bring warmth to dull lives. War, adventure, spectacle —Essex stands for all this, and the people love him for it.'

'Madam, he is a danger to you and to all of England. Cut him down while there is still time.'

Cut him down . . .

She got up abruptly and walked away to the window, where an angry bee was beating itself stupidly against the mullioned panes. Idly, she picked up a book and began to guide the frenzied insect towards the open casement.

'This way, you stupid creature,' she muttered in mounting annoyance at its panicking perversity. 'Can't you see I'm trying to help you?'

Suddenly, without warning, the bee stung her, and in a rage at its monstrous ingratitude she flung the book at it. The heavy volume struck the window and fell to the floor, leaving the bee squashed on the narrow leaded pane, blood and guts oozing from the tail.

Her anger died as suddenly as it had flared and left her trembling as she looked at her handiwork. Unnecessary violence! It would have died of the sting anyway—died without her angry, helping hand. It might have been Essex's mangled body, splattered across the window of public imagination, blotting out the glory of her reign beneath a monstrous smear of blood. And that she did not want at any cost.

For a long time she stared out over the river, seeking a grave deep enough to swallow his shining reputation and bury it for ever. And at length she found one.

Ireland . . .

No Englishman had ever made his fortune there; no military post was more unsought than that of Lord Deputy. She would send Essex to Ireland at the first plausible opportunity, and perhaps, if God was kind to them both, he would not come back alive.

She turned, at last, to tell Burghley what she had decided and found that he had fallen asleep. She went back to the bed and looked down at the man who had been like a father to her, bent and laid her lips against his forehead, gently, so as not to disturb him. Then she collected her gloves and the lady-in-waiting who dozed in the next room, and took her barge back to the palace.

She did not see Burghley's last quavering letter to his son Robert, which lauded her to the heavens for being 'so careful a nurse' to him. Nor did she read its hammerblow of a postscript which hit the suave and sophisticated little Secretary squarely between the eyes, making him pause uneasily, as though he felt the warning presence of his father still at his side.

'Serve God by serving the Queen, for all other service is bondage to the Devil!'

Remember it . . .

CHAPTER 4

I will not do it,' said Essex belligerently. 'Not for you or any other living soul. Christ's soul, Mother, how can you ask me to abase myself in such a fashion? I tell you this, Leicester may have crept back to her, whining like a whipped cur, but I'm damned if I'll do the same. She behaved abominably, like a—like a fishwife! And if you think I'm going to accept such treatment from the hands of any woman—'

'The Queen is not *any* woman,' countered Lettice, with angry desperation. 'For God's sake, Robert, you're talking of your prince!'

'So?' He lifted his arrogant shoulders. 'Can't princes err, then? Can't subjects receive any wrong? Is her earthly power infinite?'

Lettice cast a wary glance at the door. His voice was loud and she could not vouch for the discretion of every servant in her house.

'Be silent,' she said hoarsely. 'Your thoughts are too perilous for words.'

'She *struck* me, Mother!'

'Oh, Lord, if that's all,' sighed Lettice wearily. 'And for that you draw your sword on her and put your life at risk. You stupid, stupid boy!'

Suddenly he put out one arm and pulled her roughly to the shelter of his doublet.

'Mother—don't weep. You know I can't bear to see you weep.'

'Then don't give me such cause!' she sobbed.

'You puff this out of all proportion,' he said reasonably. 'If she was going to send me to the Tower, she'd have done it by now.'

He paused and stared ahead fixedly, at some new grievance of thought, suddenly come to light.

'You don't think—you don't suppose for one moment that she can have *forgotten* about me?'

Lettice wiped her eyes and sat down by the hearth.

'They say she is so crushed by Burghley's death that she cares for little else but mourning at the moment. That's all I know—make what you will of it.'

'She *has* forgotten me!' Essex clenched his fist convulsively. 'Am I of so little account to her that a dead man can oust me from her mind? Am I to compete with a doddering ghost for her attention?'

'Be glad of it,' said Lettice shrewdly, 'grief is the only thing that makes her vulnerable—you'll never have a better opportunity to make your peace with her. Robert, I'm asking—no—I'm *begging* you to lower your insane pride for once. Admit your fault humbly on your knees and I swear she'll welcome you back with open arms. Swallow your arrogance, or, I warn you—the next blow she gives you will be a mortal one.'

He turned away abruptly, riven with internal conflict.

'If I go back now and grovel,' he began slowly, 'it will appear I do so for profit—purely for what I can get out of her. And it's not like that. It's never been like that.' He made an impatient gesture. 'You can't begin to understand what I feel for her.'

A dark, resentful look crossed Lettice's face.

'You think not?' Her voice was suddenly ugly with emotion. 'You think I was ten years wed to Leicester without learning anything of what makes that woman function? The Queen destroys every man she sets her eyes upon. If you love me, Robert—if there's an ounce of pity in your soul—don't break my heart by letting her do to you what she did to Leicester.'

'I won't be compared with Leicester,' he said contemptuously. 'I am the only man in the country who has ever dared to stand up to her. If you only knew how she respects me for that—how she despises the spineless creep-mice who surround her. *Little men!*—how many times have I heard her say that? Don't you see? I can be the only master she has ever had! All I have to do is hold out a little longer and she'll give in.'

'What is it about her?' demanded Lettice darkly. 'What is it that drives men to this madness?'

'I admire her,' he said steadily, 'I freely admit that I admire her beyond any other creature alive. Oh, Christ—I worship her, if you must hear it. But I will not serve her as a villein or a slave. I will not grovel, nor will I crawl, because if I do—I know she will hate me for it.'

Lettice lifted her face and looked at him squarely.

'You honestly suppose she does not hate you now?' She got up and went slowly to the door like an old woman. There she paused and looked back at him for a moment.

'You fool,' she said softly, 'you poor fool. I truly believe you are beyond my aid at last.'

They were silent, staring at each other helplessly across the room.

'I shall pray for you,' she said after a moment; and closed the door with quiet despair.

So, no apology came from Wanstead and the rift between the Queen and the young Earl widened, a quarrel that might have continued indefinitely, but for a sudden military disaster in Ireland, where the post of Lord Deputy still remained vacant.

The English army, seeking to relieve their garrison at the Blackwater, had been outflanked by the Earl of Tyrone's rebel forces and ambushed at the Yellow Ford. By the end of that day, 2,000 English soldiers, together with the Marshal of the army and thirty of his officers, lay dead in the marshes. Within days, every local chieftain had given his allegiance to Tyrone. The whole of Ulster lay open now to the rebels, and a wave of burning and pillaging swept across the countryside to Dublin. It was said that Tyrone awaited only the arrival of Spanish troops to drive the English out of Ireland for good.

It was such a serious reversal for England that Essex, as Earl Marshal, knew himself honour bound to return to court. He found the Queen cool and distant, but very ready to reopen the question of appointing a Lord Deputy.

A short list of names had been put forward in Council and she sat back in her chair at the head of the table, taking no part in the heated discussion that followed. Essex waxed critical and, finding his criticism unchecked, had something scathing to say about each candidate.

A little silence fell when at length it seemed he had had his say. He looked up and saw the Queen's eyes upon him, her lips curled in a smile which filled him suddenly with curious foreboding.

'You seem remarkably well appraised of what this post demands, my lord—I begin to think that perhaps you are the only man fitted for the job.'

He stared at her aghast. Appalled.

'Madam, you overwhelm me. I swear I did not anticipate such an honour—'

'I'm sure you did not—we are all well acquainted with your modesty, my lord.'

Someone sniggered at the foot of the table and quickly stifled it. The Queen smiled at Essex again, a little look of mockery which held a gleam of malice. Across the table his eyes met hers in frantic mute appeal and found them suddenly hard, inflexible as stone. He could not believe she meant to do this to him. Ireland—the graveyard of Englishmen's reputations, the most hopeless military task in existence. She had baited the trap and he had walked right into it, shackled by the bonds of his own reputation.

The Earl of Southampton was lounging on a cushioned banker and looked up with a lazy smile when Essex entered the room.

The smile froze on his lips as he saw his friend's face.

'Christ's soul, what ails you, Rob? Did the Queen turn on you after all?'

Essex sank down on the hearth stool and stared into the fire. After a moment he smiled bleakly over his shoulder, and held out his hand.

'On your knees, Harry, and pay your respects to the new Lord Deputy of Ireland.'

Southampton paled and said, 'Oh, God!'

'Precisely my sentiments, my friend!'

'But *Ireland*—what possesses her?'

'The Devil,' said Essex shortly. 'I looked into her eyes today and saw him as plainly as I see you now.'

'And I thought she loved you.'

Essex's mouth tightened to an angry, embittered line.

'No one is safe with her—my dear, departed stepfather told me that, before I ever went to court. I did not believe him then.' He frowned. 'But I do now. By God, I do.'

Southampton spread his hands helplessly.

'But surely you can get out of it.'

Essex shook his head. 'I have my pride.'

'Damn your pride, Robin—think of your *life!* It was Ireland killed your father—for God's sake go to her—tell her the task is beyond you.'

Essex got up and turned to go.

'I will die first,' he said.

Ireland was his destiny; and his downfall. Time, money and men slipped relentlessly through his fingers as he battled against savage chieftains and hostile weather. From Kilkenny to Clonmel to Limerick he marched, burning and pillaging, while his men dropped dead in the fens from dysentery and malaria. His own health, never robust, began to give way and his hold on the campaign slowly loosened, as though the stinking bog-mists had rotted the roots of his brain.

When the creation of fifty-nine knighthoods (in direct disobedience to her express command) and the capture of one minor castle seemed to be the sum total of his achievements to date, Elizabeth inquired, with biting sarcasm whether she gave him £1,000 a day to go on progress! Action against Tyrone was what she wanted now, and action she would have or know the reason why. She wrote caustically to her Lord Deputy, commanding him to engage Tyrone's forces immediately; he was not to dare to leave Ireland until he had done so.

In a dark Dublin hostelry, Essex's discontented young friends clustered round the fire and clinked tankards morosely. A low grumbling rose steadily among the acrid smoke of several pipes and a seedy, spitting fire of damp sea-wood.

'So it's true, then—we march to Ulster tomorrow with five hundred men lost already. It's madness!'

'It's suicide.'

'Aye—and who sends us out to it? That little Crookback Cecil, who couldn't lift a sword, let alone wield it. It's his poisoned pen the Queen writes with to my lord. There'll be no joy for us from England while Cecil lives.'

'And the Queen?'

Silence! A deathly hush broken only by the quiet shifting of a wooden stump on the fire.

'My lord would never agree to that.'

'Would he not? Let him once get back to England—and then we shall see.'

The mugs clinked and there was a fugitive burst of laughter.

Essex met the rebel leader, Tyrone, on horseback in the centre of the River Lagan, to parley. From the high ground above the ford at Bellaclynthe, the English officers looked down fearfully, knowing that behind the northern hill the entire Irish army lay encamped.

For nearly an hour the two men talked, each with his horse up to its belly in icy water; then at last they saluted each other curtly and separated, Essex spurring his mount up the steep incline at the far side of the bank.

Southampton was the first to reach him.

'A truce,' said Essex breathlessly, forestalling the inevitable question. 'An honourable truce.'

He saw Southampton's face.

'I know,' he continued peevishly, 'I know it's not what I was sent to do, but will you tell me, in God's name what alternative I have? They have enough men to wipe us out in a single encounter.'

'Then why do they choose to treat?'

Essex was silent. The reason was obvious. At this juncture delay suited Tyrone, who was still awaiting Spanish troops. Once they had arrived no

English force, however enlarged, could hope to contain them; and Ireland would be free of the English scourge for good.

They rode back to Dublin Castle, nervous and ill at ease, to find another letter from the Queen awaiting him. It was a caustic letter, dismissing all Essex's futile activities to date, castigating his 'impertinent arguments' and once more demanding immediate military action.

'You had your asking, you had your choice of times, you had power and authority more ample than ever any had, or shall have . . .'

Essex let the letter fall from his hand and slumped into a chair, burying his face in his hands. Southampton picked up the paper, read it in silence, and handed it around their small company.

No one spoke. There was no need to stress the fact that after that there was no hope of Elizabeth accepting the terms of his shady truce.

Essex sat up wild-eyed and hurled his goblet across the room.

'This is Cecil's doing, God damn him. She is surrounded by men who speak against me. I must go back to her now.'

'But not alone,' warned Southampton anxiously. 'Pick a thousand men and we'll march on London.'

'We'd be hard put to find ten fit to go,' remarked Essex's young stepfather, Christopher Blount. 'My lord,' he turned to Essex, once more hunched in his chair, 'will you desert your post in defiance of the Queen's command?'

Essex closed his eyes and pushed the wet strands of hair back from his burning forehead. He felt drained and weak from the bouts of dysentery which had plagued him since he entered this wretched land and ate its tainted food, drank of its foul water. Surely Elizabeth would be moved by the sight of him now, stricken with sickness got in her service. He had feigned illness before and it had always brought her running, sending her personal physician and trusted potions. Suddenly, he ached to be with her again, safe and sheltered beneath the mantle of her old affection. All this filthy failure would be behind him when he knelt once more at her feet and kissed her hand—she had forgiven Leicester worse in the Netherlands.

And, once he was back, he would show her he had learnt his lesson well, that he knew his place at last. No more telling her what to do, trying to snatch the reins of government from her old hands. She knew what she was doing, she had known all along; and now, at last, he saw it.

He must get to her quickly with his news, before his enemies could make capital out of it.

He would go home—and be humble; he would go at once.

*   *   *

Across the Vale of Evesham, through the northern Cotswolds and down into the Vale of the White Horse they rode without pausing for food or drink. Reaching Lambeth, they discovered the court was at Nonsuch Palace, ten miles south of London; but their horses were done and swayed where they stood. There was a frantic search among the back streets, until sufficient stolen mounts were found to carry them on the final stage of that desperate journey, a small party riding as though all the forces of Hell were on their tail. The countryside heaved and merged before Essex's starved gaze and blood drummed in his ears, competing with the thunder of horses' hooves. He became dimly aware of a shouting voice and turned his head vaguely in its direction.

'My lord, my lord, they have news of your arrival. Lord Grey rides ahead even now to warn Cecil.'

Someone plucked at Essex's sleeve, causing him to sway violently in the saddle and curse.

'Let me ride ahead, my lord. I'll kill Grey and Cecil before they reach the Queen, by your leave.'

A red, sweating face swam into Essex's blurred sight. God's light, who *was* this man? Then he remembered. St Lawrence of course, who else? Always a hothead—but a loyal knave—a good friend; he had so many good friends. And yet—

'Bide your time,' he snapped, snubbing the man for no accountable reason. 'We're not here to do murder.' *Not yet. Not unless she won't listen to reason and there's no other way. Oh Elizabeth, my Queen, my goddess—let it not come to that.*

The horses plunged on madly, trampling a carpet of red-gold leaves into the soft mud, until at last the fantastic towers crowned with onion-shaped domes were clearly glimpsed between the leafless branches of the surrounding trees. Ahead lay Nonsuch Palace, gleaming in the early morning sunshine, its walls curiously patterned, like a sugar cake, unique, eccentric, whimsical—as strange and fascinating as the woman within who ruled it.

Essex tumbled from his horse in the courtyard and dragged his mud-splattered sleeve across his sweating face. There was no sign of Lord Grey or his horse as he burst into the outer precincts of the palace.

Grey stood in Cecil's narrow panelled closet and wiped his own face with a fine lace handkerchief.

'You are sure he comes alone?' inquired the Secretary quietly. 'No army at his back?'

'Alone as far as I could tell.' Grey was breathing quick and shallow. 'But riding like the devil and half out of his mind by all accounts. He's making for the Queen, I tell you. For the love of God, rouse the guard before it's too late.'

'I think not,' said Cecil smoothly, studying his short nails with great interest.

'But she's defenceless—and God only knows what he intends in such a mood!'

'Oh, I don't imagine he intends violence.' Cecil glanced at his clock and smiled unpleasantly. It was ten o'clock in the morning. 'It was after dawn again when she retired last night—she might just be awake at this hour. I believe she finds she's too old now to manage on two or three hours' rest. I expect she's with her women—dressing—painting on the mask of majesty. It seems rather a shame to spoil her surprise—don't you agree, my friend?'

Grey stared at him in amazed silence.

Essex had fought his way through the token guard and the fluttering women who clustered around the royal apartments. On through the Presence Chamber, the Privy Chamber, the ante-room to the Bedchamber he strode, with one hand on his sword hilt, leaving behind a trail of confusion and chaos. The sound of his own boots clanking on the wooden floors beat her name in his mind. *Elizabeth! Elizabeth! Elizabeth!* No one else mattered, no one else existed. He would have fought his way through Hell itself to throw his weary body at her feet.

The door of the bedchamber was shut. Without pausing to knock, he flung it violently open and rushed in like a madman. Then he stopped, like one turned to stone at the sight of Medusa's head, the breath he had drawn to cry her name dying to a gasp of shock in his dry throat.

Elizabeth!

Even the face of Medusa could not have dealt him a more deadly shock than that of the astounded, wrinkled, white-haired creature who sat at the dressing-table in a plain, shapeless robe and turned her ravaged features towards his horrified gaze. The brilliant jewelled wig, the carefully painted mask, the fantastic gown and monstrous ruff were gone; and with them the woman he knew and acknowledged as his Queen. In their place he saw an old woman, who might have been anyone's grandmother—withered, frail, almost —*insignificant!* Never in his wildest, most treacherous outrage had he ever guessed how much she owed to clever artifice. He was shocked, dismayed— disgusted! It was as though a false mirror had suddenly smashed in his mind, and his hand tightened on his sword as he restrained the sudden, instinctive urge to vomit at a sight so repugnant to his inner imagination. Once, not much more than a decade before, he had hoped to conquer her in bed, as well as in the council chamber; but now his flesh crawled with revulsion at the thought. He had loved her! How could she—how *dared* she be this shrivelled hag?

Elizabeth sat stock still, one hand in a convulsive grip around a vial of perfume. Somewhere at the back of her mind that part of her which was vain and eternally eighteen screamed and wept with humiliated rage against the wicked injustice of this dreadful moment. To be seen thus, by the one person in this world who must never see, was unendurable. The old, fugitive desire to crawl away into a dark place for all eternity had never been stronger in her; yet she gave no glimpse of the mental turmoil she experienced.

Her eyes went to his hand clenched on the hilt of his sword. Had he come to kill her at last? Certainly he looked wild enough to do it, his eyes deep, burning sockets in a pallid face. She had no way of knowing if his Irish army surrounded the palace at this very moment. She knew only one thing—if he meant to run her through with his sword, her women would be powerless to stop him.

She held out her hand in a gesture of easy regality and smiled at him.

'Why are you here, Robin?' she inquired, as casually as if he had returned unexpectedly from a hunting expedition.

One flicker of weakness, the smallest gesture suggesting fear or panic on her part, was all it would have taken in that moment for him to kill her where she sat. But that inherent gallantry conquered him, showed him again a timeless image of the woman he had worshipped on the fields of Tilbury, wiped out the last of his outraged disappointment. A woman who could look death squarely in the face and smile was beyond the plane of physical ruin. His love for her, stripped, as by an acid bath, of all its layers of greed and ambition, flared suddenly incandescent. He fell on his knees at her feet and wept as he pressed her hand savagely against his lips.

A babble of words tumbled from him incoherently—indignation, recrimination—remorse.

'—you wrote so coldly—I had to see you, to make you understand—I knew how it would be behind my back—everyone speaking against me.'

'You believe the worst of me too easily, Robin,' she said softly and released one hand long enough to touch his mud-splashed cheek. 'You are chilled, my dear—soaked to the skin—you must change into dry clothes or you will be ill —and I—' she shrugged her shoulders, half humorously, 'well—I hardly look my best to receive you, do I?'

He looked up wonderingly into her merry eyes. How could he ever have doubted her, and she so kind, so understanding, in spite of being caught at such a wounding disadvantage? For him she had conquered her petulant vanity; together, they might still conquer the world. He felt safe, sheltered, as he had not felt since he was a very small boy at his mother's knee; and suddenly, overwhelmed with emotion, he buried his face in her hands, kissing them over and over again.

'I have suffered trouble and storms abroad,' he whispered. 'Madam—dearest madam—I thank God I find such sweet calm at home.'

For a moment her hand rested on his wildly dishevelled red head and he felt it trembling violently against his skull.

'Go now, Robin.' Her voice was hoarse and suddenly shaken, as though tears were massing in her throat. 'Go now—and rest. I will receive you later and hear all your news.'

He stumbled out of her room, weak with triumph, and began to boast of her kindness to anyone who would listen. He had been right to come—by God's precious soul, how right he had been to put his faith in her love!

Summoned to her presence later, he went jauntily, full of self-confidence, to find her sitting in a high-backed chair, attired with even more than her customary splendour in cloth of gold—transformed almost miraculously by the exquisite wig, dressed with diamonds, which seemed to snatch away at least twenty years from the raddled creature he had seen this morning. She looked magnificent sitting there with her glittering skirts spilling over the carved arms of her chair. And though her smile was a shade less warm as she gave him her hand and waved him to be seated, he still had no fear of her—no glimmer of suspicion. She offered him wine and inquired graciously after his health; he thanked her for her kind interest and assured her that he felt greatly improved simply for setting foot on English soil once more; and for the sight of her incomparable face.

At that her expression flickered momentarily and seemed about to change into something else; but then she smiled and filled his goblet again. Warming beneath her calm and pleasant demeanour, he began to relax and drink freely, pouring out his troubles.

'—and your army,' she murmured at length, casually, as though it was a matter of minor significance, 'where is the main body now?'

He looked mildly surprised at the question. 'Why, in Ireland, madam—most of them laid low with fever or dysentery—it's worse than the plague over there, I went down with both myself, more than once.'

She nodded sympathetically. 'I suggest arrowroot and the lightest of diets—but tell me, with so many sick, who then was fit to come with you?'

'Oh, Southampton—St Lawrence—just a handful of close friends. We had to travel quickly, you see, to reach you in time.'

'In time for what?' she inquired, deceptively quiet.

He looked up at her, startled, and then laughed.

'Why—in time to explain, that's all—you surely did not imagine—'

She filled his goblet once more.

'I did not know what to think then, my dearest. But I know now.'

He reached out and grasped her hand gratefully.

'Then—you understand my position?'

'Oh, yes,' she said, ominously calm, 'I think you could say that I understand it perfectly at last.'

She had discovered all that she needed to know. The palace was not surrounded, his men were not swaggering in London. At ten o'clock that evening, he was under guard in his own lodging, awaiting his punishment for desertion and disobedience.

CHAPTER 5

The next day, disgraced, disillusioned and despairing, he was removed to the custody of the Lord Keeper at York House in the Strand, forbidden to see the Queen, or his mother, or his wife. Even his body turned traitor on him as vicious bouts of dysentery and fever wracked him, each attack leaving him a little weaker than the last, until he was barely able to crawl from his bed to the close-stool. Each day he waited for some sign of the Queen's forgiveness, but none came; and he collapsed into apathy, eating nothing, caring for nothing. Exactly one month from the day he had stormed her bedchamber at Nonsuch, Elizabeth received the news that his death was expected at any hour.

She sat with her hands clenched in her lap in the withdrawing chamber and glanced up at Leicester's little ruby clock which stood on the chimney-piece, carelessly ticking away the last minutes of Essex's life. He had cried wolf so many times before, subjected her to so much emotional blackmail—how did she know it was not just another of his clever devices, a trick to win her sympathy? She dared not give in to him again. This time she must make her final stand and show him that there was in this land but one mistress and no master. He must be shorn of his insane ambitions, stripped of his influence—broken and cast out of her court for ever.

I will not go to him. I will not!

But what if he died surrounded only by servants and guards, alone and in agony, because she had refused him the company of his wife or his mother? Never to look upon his face one last time—never to forgive! She began to pace stiffly up and down her room, leaning heavily on the stick she used when she believed herself to be unobserved. It was almost four o'clock on a cold November afternoon and the day was dying steadily beyond her window— like him.

Suddenly she stopped abruptly in her pacing, snatched up a handbell and rang it vigorously. The Countess of Warwick appeared from the bedchamber and curtsied in the doorway.

'Is the barge still waiting at the privy landing stairs?'

'Yes, Your Majesty.'

'Then fetch my cloak—I shall take the boat for York House and see for myself what condition he is in. I want you to come with me, Anne.'

It was pitch black when the royal barge moored before the gardens which ran down to the river at York House, and Lord Worcester, with a torch in one hand, lit her path to the silent house. She went alone into the Earl's bedchamber and his body servants, awed at the sight of her, bowed themselves out at an imperious wave of her hand.

'Robin,' she said quietly.

He moaned and stirred at the sound of his name, but made no reply and she went silently across the room. He lay hunched at the extreme edge of the curtained bed, his great body shaking with ague and the red hair clinging to his forehead in damp tendrils. He looked up at her blankly, without recognition and she felt her eyes fill with tears because he looked so ill and vulnerable, with death on his face. The room stank of sweat and worse, but though her fastidious senses recoiled, she sat on the bed beside him and pushed the hair back out of his eyes. Whimpering, he pushed her hand away and rolled on his side, his arms and legs jerking convulsively in spasms, sobbing and cursing in the ravings of delirium. She sat frozen with horror, listening to her own name, spoken now as a curse, now as a caress, a horrible, twisted mingling of love and hate.

The enormity of what she had done appalled her, revealing to her clearly, for the first time, the extent of her blame for his crimes. At length he quietened and sank into the deeper sleep of unconsciousness, leaving her to look down on him hopelessly with tears streaming down her face.

She knew instinctively that she was looking at him for the last time; he could not last long like this, no one could. And though her heart was squeezed, as though in a vice, by that realization, there was a measure of relief in the thought. It was inconceivably better for him to die of natural causes in his bed, rather than by her command. And he had no choice but to die, for there was nothing left for him to live for, no way that she could ever hope to take him back after all he had done.

She stood a moment more by the bed, her quivering hand suspended just above his hair, aching to touch him; and then drew back. One caress, however brief, would crumble her composure and her resolve; it was better to hold aloof.

She turned and left the house and made her way back through the darkness to the waiting barge. Beneath the windswept canopy she sat like a graven image, so still and silent that Anne Warwick never dared to attempt conversation.

But, as the barge drew into the water steps of the palace, the Queen turned her head and found Lady Warwick's eyes upon her.

'I shall send his wife to him,' she said dully.

Lady Warwick looked at her steadily.

'Only his wife, madam? What of his mother?'

The Queen clenched her fingers, so that the rings bit into her flesh.

'Only his wife!' she said and looked away.

The barge bumped gently against the landing steps and the barge-men drew up their oars, but the Queen still sat in the darkness and the water lapped around her.

Essex was dying and she was to be spared the tragedy she feared—the tragedy she deserved. His death would not stain her hands, for God would take him in His infinite mercy—that innocent soul corrupted in its bright youth by the Devil's Daughter.

Who had called her that—Feria? It hardly seemed to matter. Over the years it had been said many times, by many different people. *A spirit full of incantation* had been granted to her and paid for in Hell's debased currency; but now she had nothing left with which to make payment. Now at last the price was too high.

When he was gone, she would look on no man with love again.

She swore it.

They gave Essex the last Communion, but he did not die—sheer perversity, opined his enemies. The physical crisis passed and he slowly recovered to face the unbearable knowledge that his fallen star would never shine again. He suffered over a year's quasi-imprisonment, while his misdemeanours were published for the edification of the people; and the year dragged for him in steadily mounting resentment against the woman whose affection he had misread so drastically.

In August of 1600 he was summoned to see Cecil and informed coldly that the Queen intended to release him to a life of retirement. He might have his liberty on condition that he faded unobtrusively from public life and came no more to court. In the depths of the countryside his name would be forgotten and would cease to be the parrot cry on the lips of malcontents. There was no communication from the Queen. She had made it perfectly clear that they had nothing more to say to each other and she would not see him again. She dared not, fearing her own weakness, the deadly, brooding sense of isolation and loneliness that had driven her to soften towards him again and again against her better judgement.

He sat at Essex House, surveying his mountain of debts, stewing in a cauldron of indignation and fear. His one lucrative source of income, a monopoly of the farm of sweet wines, was nearing the end of its tenure and his whole future depended on its renewal. He wrote frantic, begging letters, he prayed, he hoped against hope and finally he received word from court; the Queen refused to renew his licence.

It was the final blow and it snapped the perilously thin thread of his sanity. He went berserk, raging about his house like a madman, cursing Cecil—cursing the Queen herself, screaming out that 'her mind is as crooked as her carcase'. When he had calmed sufficiently to take stock of his position, he realized she had left him no choice. He put out tentative feelers to King James in Scotland and gathered a growing knot of discontented friends around him in London.

By January of 1601 Essex House was a rival court, unashamedly harbouring the seeds of revolution.

Saturday, the 7th of February, was a cold, drizzling night, and the flickering lights of Essex House shimmered eerily behind the misty windows.

Secretary Herbert, hunching his cloak around his shoulders, stormed down the steps into the courtyard, leapt on his wretched, shivering horse and rode back to inform the Queen and the Council that the Earl of Essex refused to answer their summons to present himself at court and explain his dubious activities in person. He left the steaming room behind him in a hubbub of confusion, wreathed with the blue-grey smoke of tobacco.

A clamour of contradictory advice was showered on the angry young aristocrat at the centre of the dispute.

'Now the Council are warned of our intentions we daren't delay, Robin. You must strike at once.'

'Or fly, my lord,' suggested Sir Charles Danvers, a small stocky man with nervous eyes that rolled doubtingly over his patron's face. 'Take a hundred men into Wales and secure some ports.'

Essex tapped his spent pipe angrily into the hearth and spat. Smoking was a filthy habit—he wished it had never become so fashionable. All Raleigh's fault of course—

'I have no intention of fleeing like a knave,' he observed flatly, lounging against the chimney-piece and pulling fractiously at the silver fringe that adorned his doublet. 'I have been wronged—grossly wronged by the Queen and I mean to have my grievances redressed. The people will support my cause—'

'But, my lord, you have three hundred men armed and waiting—sufficient to attack the court tonight and seize the Queen.'

'The Queen is not enough alone. We need Cecil and Raleigh and the rest of the pack—they could be scattered anywhere.' Essex strode from the hearth and snapped his fingers to his secretary. 'Temple—find out how matters stand for us in the city.'

Within an hour Temple was back, sweating with his haste, to tell them that a thousand London militia could be roused to fight for the Earl's cause.

'Tomorrow, my lord—tomorrow.'

And so by dawn messengers were striding through the narrow streets of the capital, summoning his supporters for the final encounter between Essex and his Queen.

At ten o'clock on that frozen February morning the Privy Council's delegation arrived and made a futile attempt to push their way through the milling crowds assembled outside the main gates of Essex House. They were kicked and bruised and at length admitted through a side entrance, there to be jostled through crowds even louder and thicker in the courtyard. A servant bore the Great Seal of England, symbolic of their authority in this mob, and he clutched it to his chest to protect it from the mocking hands which grabbed at it. They were four in number and they were lost among a press of three hundred men who were saddling horses and distributing arms.

Oblivious to their danger, they shoved and elbowed their way to where Essex stood, surrounded by a knot of cronies.

'My lord!' yelled the Lord Keeper, Egerton, above the hoots and jeers of the crowd. 'My lord, what is the meaning of this unlawful assembly?'

'My life was sought, sir,' said Essex haughtily, for this was the line he had opted to take with the people. 'I was to have been murdered in my bed.'

Egerton blanched at the blatant lie, but continued courteously, determined to avoid a confrontation if it could be avoided. 'My lord, the law exists to protect subjects from such dangers. If you would have recourse to the legitimate channels—'

He was interrupted by Southampton, who spat and informed the crowd loudly that he himself had been murderously set upon by Lord Grey, who was Cecil's man, only a month before. So much for justice!

'Grey was punished for his assault,' insisted the Lord Chief Justice bravely, as the crowd began to stamp. 'My lord, may we talk privately? I give you my word I will be most happy to carry any legitimate grievance of yours to the Queen and see it redressed.'

At this the crowd shifted forward in an angry, ugly mood and began to roar abuse and advice.

'Away, my lord, you lose time!'

'They abuse you, my lord—they betray you.'

Girding his courage to the hilt, the Lord Keeper replaced his hat with dignity and turned to address the chanting crowd.

'I command you all, on your allegiance, to lay down your weapons and depart,' he roared.

Shrugging his shoulders, Essex turned his back and strode into the house. As the crowd surged forward, brandishing weapons and screaming, 'Kill them —throw the Great Seal out of the window!' the Privy Councillors made a narrow escape in his wake and bolted the great door.

Essex was waiting for them by the main staircase with a gracious smile.

'If you will be pleased to accompany me, gentlemen, I shall show you to a room where we can talk with more privacy.'

The Lord Keeper inclined his head, closing his lips on a sigh of relief, and the little party swarmed up the stairs at the Earl's heels. He escorted them to his study, and then, with his famed courtesy, stood back to let them enter first. One by one the councillors smiled nervously as they walked past him into the disordered chamber.

When the last was safely in, still beaming effusively, Essex slammed the door shut on them, locked it, and called for a guard of musketeers to be placed outside.

Shocked silence was followed by a volley of indignant cries from the other side of the door and Essex began to laugh hysterically.

'My lords—my lords, be patient a while. I promise faithfully not to keep you waiting. I go now to take London, but I give you my word on this: I'll be back in half an hour at most.'

As the uncanny echo of his laughter died away down the corridor, Egerton moved away from the door and slumped down on a stool.

'He was never stable, my lords—I fear his brain is utterly overset. Her Majesty is in the hands of a madman.' He bowed his head and continued quietly, 'There is nothing more we can do now, but to pray for her deliverance.'

Essex's boots thundered on the bare wooden staircase as he ran down the steps two at a time and burst into the courtyard, waving his hat in mad triumph.

The mob stamped and clapped a welcome.

'To the court!' they yelled. 'To the court!'

At court, less than twenty minutes distance away, the Queen was defenceless but for her personal guard. He had only to march west, surrounding the palace, cutting her off from outside aid, and she would be entirely in his power.

He paused at the gates of Essex House for a moment, and then with deliberate determination, turned his horse towards the capital city.

'To the court!' screamed the mob in desperation. 'To the *court!*'

But they screamed in vain.

Essex, stubborn and opinionated to the last, rode east to take London from his Queen.

They told all this to Elizabeth who sat very calm at dinner in Whitehall Palace and they saw the faint, knowing smile which hovered for a brief moment on the thin line of her lips.

He had had her at his mercy in that one moment, but now her sure instinct warned her he had thrown that chance away. He had turned to win London—London, the city she had held in the palm of her hand for nearly fifty years. Oh, what a fool he was, a blind, misguided child; her heart ached with the bitter knowledge of how this all must end. She had tried to avert it —God alone knew how she had tried! But there was no time to spare now for heart-searching and regret, there was room only for action, bold decision and calm, unquestioned authority. Suddenly, without conscious effort, she found herself possessed by all three qualities. Confidence was what was needed to rally her supporters and stabilize her position; and confidence was what she would give them.

'God who placed me on this throne will preserve me on it,' she said calmly, smiling at Cecil. 'I shall not sleep tonight until I hear that they are all under lock and key.'

She picked up a chicken wing and began to issue a series of crisp and businesslike instructions for the defence of the city.

London had not seen a rebellion for nearly half a century and the few laggard citizens straggling home to dinner from the Sunday service at St Paul's, regarded the rebel cavalcade with polite bewilderment. A few cheered half-heartedly; some waved, for there was no treason in a wave after all; and then they passed quietly on to their homes and their food. Excitement was all very well in its place, but London had its priorities. Little boys, eyeing the armed body with awe and envy, were swept in off the streets by angry, irritated mothers who were tired of calling them. Soon the position was horribly clear, as Essex rode up the filthy streets in despair, soaked with sweat and calling for a fresh shirt. What the devil was amiss with this lethargic, chicken-hearted multitude that had once roared itself hoarse in support of him?

While they rested in Fenchurch Street, a royal herald roamed the twisting roads, promising the Queen's pardon to all followers who deserted the Earl's cause.

'A herald will proclaim anything for a few shillings,' jeered Essex loudly, but behind his back his men were already creeping away down side streets, seeing the way the cat had jumped.

It was useless. Even Essex could see that, as he struggled with his dwindling force back to Lud Gate. The Council had been busy on the Queen's orders and now a small band of pikemen barred their way, repulsing all their frantic efforts to break the line and pass. The Queen's men were moving in to trap the little band of traitors, like rats in a maze.

Back up Lud Gate Hill they fled from the pikes, desperate for some means of escape from this dreadful fiasco; but Friday Street had been barred with chains against them. At length a few citizens came out of their houses and quietly raised the chains to let the shattered band creep away down to the Thames. They scrambled with undignified haste into the little boats which were moored there and struggled back to Essex House through the falling dusk.

'We're not lost yet,' muttered Essex grimly. 'We have the Privy Councillors as hostages—we can bargain.'

But when they got back, it was to find that the birds had flown the coop, freed behind their backs. He had no more cards to play and the Queen's forces were already surrounding Essex House and demanding his surrender. He flew to his room and began feverishly burning all his incriminating correspondence, among it a letter from King James, that alone would be sufficient to claim his head.

At the end of a brief siege, the rebels left the house one by one, fell on their knees and surrendered their swords to the Lord High Admiral, who waited grimly in the light of the flickering torches.

At three in the morning Essex and Southampton were removed from Lambeth Palace to the Tower; and at Whitehall Raleigh bowed before the Queen and informed her that the day's business was at an end.

'A senseless ingrate has at last revealed what has been long in his mind,' she said bitterly to the French Ambassador.

An hour later the candles in her bedchamber were finally extinguished; snuffed out like tiny traitors in the dark.

The trial was over and a silence descended on Westminster Hall, as the new Lord Treasurer declared sentence on the Earls of Essex and Southampton.

'You shall both be led from hence to the place whence you came and there remain during Her Majesty's pleasure; from thence to be drawn upon a hurdle through the midst of the city and so to the place of execution, there to be hanged by the neck and taken down alive—your bodies to be quartered and your heads and quarters to be disposed of at Her Majesty's pleasure.' The Lord Treasurer paused and added with grim irony, 'And so God have mercy on your souls.'

Southampton was visibly trembling, his face gaunt and deathly white, but Essex walked out of the crowded hall like a man in a trance.

He could not believe she had let it go so far; he had hoped to be spared the indignity of public trial. But *execution*—she could not do it, surely she could not do it. Why, all these years he had only to pout and pester and at length she gave in, for peace and quiet, as a weary mother does to spare herself the tantrums of a spoilt child. He saw himself clearly in his own mind for the first time then—saw what she had made of him; it was all that his mother had feared, and worse. He had not lost his manhood in the Queen's service—he had simply never attained it; she had warped and stunted his natural growth. So much that he had missed in her was clear to him now, above all that dark look in her eyes as far back as that evening after Leicester's death when he had first claimed her against her spoken wish. He could not deny that she had tried to warn him.

Partner me now and I promise you will live to regret it.

He had never given those words a moment's serious thought, but now he dwelt on them with morbid fascination and saw how relentlessly she had danced him to his death.

He had admitted publicly during his trial that the Queen would never be safe while he lived. He had no idea what insane impulse had prompted him to stand there and sign his own death warrant, when he longed so passionately for life. Something had compelled him to speak, and as soon as he had spoken he had known he was a dead man.

'I have nothing left,' he said hopelessly after the trial, 'but that which I must pay the Queen.'

She sat alone with the death warrant before her on the desk, her chin propped in her hands as she stared, unseeing, into the fire.

The room was deathly silent except for the occasional crackle of the flaming logs in the hearth—she had always hated coal. The windows were patterned with white frost and beyond them the February morning lay bleak and indifferent to all that would be decided within this room today. She could hear the wind rattling the casements and her own restless, shallow breathing, the echo of her rapid heartbeat thudding dully in her head. In spite of her furs and the blazing fire, she was shivering and her hands were blue with cold. She felt frozen inside, a block of ice which no fire could ever hope to penetrate.

Elizabeth, by the Grace of God, Queen of England . . .

She could get no further than the first line of the warrant, but she knew what it said. He was to enjoy the privilege of his rank and die by the axe; no hanging, no quartering—they should not butcher that beautiful body.

He was to die virtually alone, for she had shown mercy to most of the captured rebels. Of the eighty-five arrested, thirty-two had been released without penalty and in all only six were to go to the scaffold. Southampton, that miserable, timid, lily-livered youth, she had spared to life imprisonment, moved unbearably by the sight of his mother, debasing herself at her feet and begging for his life.

Lettice too had knelt, and wept and begged. She ought to have enjoyed that, savoured the sweet revenge of seeing the She-wolf on her knees, a pitiful supplicant, grovelling without shame before her. Yet strangely there was no triumph, only a tired, sick sense of pity that compelled her to raise the weeping woman to her feet and try to speak kindly.

Lettice clung to her hand and made it wet with tears, till she was aware of a scalding dampness seeping beneath her rings.

'Madam, I beg you—pardon him. You have shown mercy to others, why not to him?'

'I will not pardon him,' said the Queen unsteadily, 'because I cannot.'

Lettice's eyes, huge in a white face and mad with grief, centred on her with one mute question: *Why?*

Why? Because his death was inevitable, unavoidable, written in the stars a lifetime ago and sealed by another death. *A life for a life.* They all expected her to pardon him because, after all, his rebellion had been so pathetic, so futile, that it seemed a gross exaggeration to even term it treason. There had been times when she was sorely tempted to do it, to shy away from this dreadful act and hope that he had learnt his lesson. But he would not learn—he was not free to do so. Like her, he was caught up and controlled by a dreadful whirlpool from the past—the chosen sacrifice which would expiate her father's crime in murdering her mother. He had no choice but to work against her; and now she had no choice but to kill him for it.

All her life with slow and fatalistic tread had led her to this moment. The time had come for her to cut off the head of the one she loved and to do it almost without hesitation, cold-bloodedly, self-righteously atoning for Anne's death, as Anne's spirit relentlessly demanded. Leicester had narrowly escaped the satisfaction of this morbid vendetta against manhood. Leicester she had loved too much, while Essex she loved just too little to spare him from his allotted fate.

Those whom the gods wish to destroy they first make mad . . .

She took up her pen and paused, looked back to that night after Leicester's death when he had sealed his doom with that irresistible arrogance, remembering how her heart had leapt in recognition of that which she had sought throughout her restless life. The man who would make a crazy bid to master her; the man she could kill for it. She had taken him—young, high-bred, unstable—and sent him reeling into an abyss of insanity. Utter madness, men had castigated his last rash act of rebellion—she alone knew how true the charge was and how great the weight of guilt was on her tortured soul.

And yet she could not help herself. She seemed to stand apart from that other self, grimly fascinated, and watch a black-haired, black-eyed woman scrawl the flamboyant signature of Elizabeth of England in letters two inches high at the head of the warrant.

> *My care is like my shadow in the sun,*
> *Follows me flying, flies when I pursue it,*
> *Stands and lies by me, does what I have done*

Does what I have done . . .

She laid the pen down. For a moment she sat very still, staring at nothing, then she got up and went blindly through into her bedchamber.

It was empty; she had already sent all her women away. Beside her bed the casket still stood, silent, glittering, magnificent as a miniature tomb. She unlocked it and searched beneath her most precious possessions for the little headless doll.

The black satin skirts had faded to silver grey with age and were creased with long confinement. She shook them out and smoothed the creases, stood for an endless moment staring at the doll, before she turned and flung it into the hearth where a great log fire burned.

The flames leapt up in a sudden flare as the material caught, shrivelled and disintegrated around a charred stick.

To be burned or beheaded . . . at the King's pleasure . . .

She stood and watched until there was nothing left to see. And somewhere in an unplumbed depth of darkness, her shadow laughed and said:

'Well done!'

CHAPTER 6

February 25th was a bitterly cold morning and the palace was strangely silent, but for the steady twang of the virginals which echoed from the Privy Chamber.

When the messenger from the Tower arrived, he fell on his knees before the Queen, who sat dressed from head to foot in black on a cushioned stool at the instrument.

She stopped playing and looked down on his bare head, a chill, silent glance that made him stammer with nerves as he said his piece.

'If—if it please Your Majesty—just sentence upon the Earl of Essex was carried out this morning. Today a traitor died.'

There was a moment of absolute silence in the tense room before, without a word, she turned her back on the company and began to play once more. The men who were watching her closely exchanged looks of gaping astonishment and it was a full five minutes before mumbled conversation returned slowly to her staggered attendants.

But she would not weep; not in public. Her fingers played on by instinct alone; she could no longer see the music and when at last the inward trembling forced her to stop, before her clumsy touch betrayed her, she looked up and found Raleigh looking down at her. Beneath his glowing sea-tan, his clever, handsome face was pale. As Captain of the Guard, it had been his duty to stand and watch while Essex's blood was spilt on the scaffold. Essex had been his enemy, but Raleigh had a heart beneath his cold mask of pride and he, more than any other, guessed what the Queen must feel. He looked at her with silent sympathy, white-faced beneath a red wig which seemed harsh and garish in comparison. He had never seen her look so old, nor her dark eyes so desolate; he wondered how much longer she would be able to maintain that rigorous self-control.

When she rose stiffly, he offered his arm and she laid her hand on the white ruffle at his wrist with a look that might mean gratitude. They moved apart to the fireplace, where he threw some more logs into the fire; her hand on his had been chill as ice.

'Shall I send for wine, madam—aqua vitae?' he said, very low, but she shook her head slowly. She was staring at him, with haunted eyes.

'You saw him die?' she asked at last, still quiet and controlled, betraying nothing.

'Yes, madam—he met his death with calm and courage, repenting his error and his treatment of you.'

'Was it—' there was tremor in her voice now, 'was it clean and quick?'

He hesitated. It was useless to lie. She would only find out later and be enraged that he had deceived her.

He shook his head faintly. 'Three blows of the axe, madam.'

Three blows! Three blows to kill the Scottish Queen and the Admiral, a man of much wit and very little judgement. Like Essex!

She said, very low, for his ears only, 'It should have been a sword.'

'Madam—' He laid a hand on her arm in concern. She had the grey, glazed look of shock, a look he remembered seeing before now on the faces of men who had lost a limb in battle and only afterwards begun to register the pain.

'My thoughts are not for sharing,' she said dully. 'You may leave me to them.'

He bowed reluctantly, leaving her sitting alone by the hearth, staring into the fire with fixed eyes.

The flames were leaping and dancing on the spitting logs, making a strange shifting landscape of light and dark.

She felt as though she was staring into the deepest pit in Hell.

In his dull little study Sir Robert Cecil sat and dealt with the vast correspondence on his cluttered desk. When the door opened to admit the Captain of the Guard, he unobtrusively slid a letter into the darkest recess of an open drawer and pushed it closed. He had no desire for Raleigh to catch a glimpse of his secret correspondence with the King of Scotland, England's obvious, but unnamed, heir presumptive. It was littered with one or two darkly subtle hints that the notorious Sir Walter Raleigh, wit, poet and adventurer *par excellence*, was unlikely to prove King James's loyalest subject in the future. Cecil had no intention of sharing power in the next reign with the flamboyant adventurer who had once been his best friend. He was obsessed with the future and his own part in it; and the future, as Cecil saw it, was King James. With Elizabeth he was merely marking time, waiting with carefully concealed impatience for the moment when that remarkable old bitch would drop dead.

He looked up now and smiled as Raleigh lowered himself stiffly into a chair, easing the old wound in his thigh which was his personal legacy of Essex's exploits at Cadiz. Cecil's physical disabilities had ruled out any possibility of vigorous military activity when he was no more than a boy, dreaming of conquering the world by himself. Now he saw Raleigh bite his lip at a stab of pain and felt a faint throb of malicious pleasure to see this magnificently-built man at the mercy of a physical weakness which would cause him to limp for the rest of his life—however long that life should be. He had not rid himself of Essex simply to put a more dangerous and able man in his place and, sooner or later, Cecil mused quietly, cold-bloodedly, it might be necessary to dispose of Raleigh too. King James had a most unhealthy preference for strong, virile men and Raleigh would always bear watching. Certainly he stood high in favour with Elizabeth once more, his marriage forgotten if not forgiven, the last of the men who remembered her with passionate friendship from the autumn days when she had still been a handsome woman.

'To what do I owe this unexpected pleasure?' Cecil inquired at last, turning to cast an eye over his papers in a desultory fashion. 'I thought this hour would have seen you with the Queen.'

Raleigh frowned and began to peel the feathers of a freshly cut quill from the neatly tied stack which stood in a pewter holder on the Secretary's desk. 'Lady Warwick tells me she has shut herself up in a darkened room where she weeps alone and calls on Essex's name.'

'Oh?' Cecil glanced at the ivory clock on his chimney-piece and compressed his lips in a tight, humourless little smile. 'Now, let me see—' he studied his papers thoughtfully and patted the stack in front of him, 'if that runs true to form we can expect her to emerge from her room some time this afternoon, reduce her women to tears and then settle to state affairs shortly before dusk. I don't suppose I'll see my bed before dawn in that case—thank heaven there's nothing here that can't wait till this evening. It would be so much more convenient if she confined these morbid frenzies to the hours of darkness.' He saw Raleigh raise his dark eyebrows and he shrugged his hunched shoulders indifferently. 'There's a great deal that requires her attention—the show must go on, you know, even if the principal actor is no longer up to the role. Have you noticed how violent her moods are growing? I can tell you I don't much care for the way she keeps that sword beside her all the time, as though she expects an assassin behind every curtain. She gave me a nasty fright the other day, leaping out of her chair and plunging it into the arras, then coming back to the table and taking up our conversation just where it had left off. I scarcely knew where to put myself. Not the first time it's happened either, I understand. If she keeps on like this, there'll be no tapestries left in the Privy Chamber. It will cost the devil to replace them—'

Raleigh looked at him steadily, with a flicker of dislike and disgust.

'It doesn't trouble you at all does it, Cecil—witnessing the slow disintegration of the finest mind in Europe? For my own part I find it remarkably painful to watch.'

'Her Majesty's mind has always been beyond a mere mortal like myself,' said Cecil calmly. 'I have never presumed to understand her. As long as she remains capable of transacting state business that is all that concerns me. I'm surprised it concerns you so much—I never marked you as a sentimental man for all your poetry. And you've felt her injustice more than once—look at your marriage.'

Raleigh lifted his elegant shoulders.

'I knew the price, I chose to pay it, that's all. I could never complain she didn't make the risks quite clear.

'Fain would I climb but that I fear to fall . . .'

Cecil sighed. Everyone knew how Raleigh had once scratched that on a window with a diamond ring to test the Queen's affection. And how the Queen had written below it:

'If thy heart fail thee, then climb not at all.'

He considered it vain and ostentatious of Raleigh to draw attention to the occasion and now said coldly, 'I see you did not take her advice. You climbed and you fell. Was it truly worth the effort to climb again?'

Raleigh smiled absently into the fire.

'My wife's question—almost, my wife's tone. You are surprisingly like her and half the wives in England—jealous of the Queen.'

'Jealous—*I,* jealous?'

Raleigh turned in his chair to look at Cecil shrewdly.

'You hold no place in her heart. Do you suppose no one has ever guessed what eats you from within, Robert?'

Cecil's hand clenched on the desk in front of him. Raleigh would never know it, but in that quiet, unguarded moment, he had uttered words which would lead him relentlessly to the block in the next reign.

'She cared for *you*,' Cecil said at last, controlling his cold outrage. 'And little enough you have to show for it, apart from Sherbourne and a justly bitter wife.'

Raleigh shrugged, twirled the quill between his fine fingers.

' "*She gave, she took, she wounded, she appeased,*" ' he quoted softly.

'Aye,' snapped Cecil. 'To all her lovers.'

'England was her lover,' murmured Raleigh, suddenly lost in thought. 'The rest of us were shadows—mirror images—even Leicester! She spurned us like spaniels and made us all fawn upon her. And then Essex broke the mirror, shattered her world. To see her mourn, one would think she had killed her own child—'

He fell silent, his dark face etched with lines of grief which goaded Cecil into real rage. That a man as hard and intelligent as Raleigh should still sit there immortalizing his cruel goddess in verse was beyond bearing.

She is old, he wanted to shout, old, *old!* Can't you see it?

But Cecil had never been admitted to the magic circle of her intimacy and the knowledge was a poisonous awareness of inferiority in his galled heart. He was forever on the outside looking in, of insufficient personal stature to gain entry to her heart. *Little man*, she called him—and now he would never know, never understand the secret of her charm, so envied by all, so fatal to some.

'What was she to you?' he burst out unexpectedly in a tone of bitter frustration that made Raleigh glance at him with quick surprise. There was a moment's uneasy silence while Raleigh chewed the feathers of the quill, considering the question.

'She was my friend,' he said at last, softly, looking inward, 'the only woman who has ever been that to me. She struck sparks from my mind. Even my wife, dear as she is to me—and dearly bought—even she could never do that. A whole era dies with her, my friend—an era, the like of which will not be seen in England again.'

'So,' a light lit suddenly in Cecil's eyes, 'you also think the end is near.'

Raleigh sighed.

'She puts me in mind of a candle flickering in a draught. She may go out at any moment or burn on indefinitely.'

'God forbid,' muttered Cecil to that last, and hastily covered it with a cough. He picked up the ragged quill that Raleigh had carelessly dropped on his desk, disposed of it methodically in the paper-basket at his side. He could not bear things out of place.

'I only hope your candle can produce one more flare,' he continued with a wry smile. 'The writs for Parliament go out next week and given the present mood in London I'd say it's likely to be the most mutinous session she's ever been driven to hold. She'll need to play an ace this time and no mistake. I pray she can rouse herself sufficiently to do it.'

Raleigh was silent and his worldly eyes were sad; like Cecil, he had very little hope of seeing such a miracle take place.

She had killed his body, but the martyred memory of Essex lingered on, almost more powerful in death than it had been in life. The wind in the streets whispered his name with sad and reverent sighs, while in the taverns new songs sprang up to mourn him in the maudlin clink of tankards and the acrid haze of tobacco smoke.

'Sweet England's pride is gone . . .' sang the men who had not troubled to join his rebellion, yet viciously condemned those who had brought him down: Cecil, Raleigh—and the Queen. The death of Essex had cast a shadow over the crown and a slow, moody questioning of the sovereign's rights had begun to gather momentum.

Elizabeth was acutely aware of it and the knowledge weighed heavy on her heart at a time when there was much to cause her anxiety. Tyrone had received his Spanish troops and she was in desperate straits to finance Mountjoy, her new Lord Deputy in Ireland. She had sold land and jewels and forced loans from niggardly allies in France and the Netherlands. But it was not enough. She was forced to turn reluctantly to the one source of income she had instinctively sought to avoid throughout her reign.

And so it was that in October, Parliament gathered to consider her request for the extraordinary measure of taxation.

She thought of this Parliament as Pandora's box; she did not want to open it for fear of what she would release. But autocracy would not serve her now, nor would age and increasing infirmity excuse her the ordeal of a public appearance, a slow, jolting journey past sullen crowds, an endless walk down rows of grim-faced parliamentarians, whose traditional, deafening roar, 'God save Your Majesty' had shrunk to a few isolated cries.

She had faced some cruel moments in her varied life, but this was the worst, this was the one thing she had believed inviolate—the love of the people, that had been hers so long it seemed no man could take it from her. Yet one man had. Hundreds of hostile eyes were on her now and saw not the Virago of Tilbury, but the murderess of a national hero. And the bitter irony of it was that no one grieved for that death more than she who had set her hand to it.

The great hall was airless, the robes of state too heavy for her shrunken frame and at the foot of the throne she suddenly knew she was going to faint.

Not now, she thought with anguished panic, not here—But the ringing in her ears, the darkening of her vision were unmistakably familiar. She was suddenly dimly aware of men's urgent hands on her arms and the indignity was like a crutch against the threatening veil of darkness. How *dared* they touch her! How dared they show that they had noticed a momentary weakness she could have conquered without their aid?

Rage upheld her through the weary hours of ceremony and at length it was over and the shrill voice of a gentleman usher cried out, 'Make way for the Queen to pass.'

But no one moved in all that press of bodies that barred her path to the door; and someone shouted in a rude, raucous voice that they'd be hanged if they would make more room.

England is a fickle shrew who may one day break even your stony heart . . .

She drew a shuddering breath. The voice was so clear in her memory that it seemed impossible more than fifty years had passed since the Duke of Somerset had spoken those very words. She felt as though she had run upon the point of a sword; she wanted to crumple up with a pain beyond bearing. But she did not move, or show by a flicker of an eyelash what she felt. She stood alone and outfaced their silent hostility until, one by one, their eyes fell from hers and dropped shamefaced to the floor. Slowly the Lower House began to jostle and shuffle and fall back, so that a pathway opened before her, cut out of petty defiance by the strength of her unwavering stare. No man among them was man enough to stand his ground beneath her bitter scorn, and the drum farthingale of her gown was unimpeded as she swept down their ranks.

There was new vigour in her movements now, new purpose in her resolute stride, for there was something left for her to do after all, one last, impossible challenge to face.

She had lost the love of a people notorious for their fickle hearts; but she would win it back. She would make them love her again in spite of all the odds against it; and when that love was hers once more, she would be free to die of the wound she had received at their hands.

*   *   *

The houses sat taut and tense, like a pile of tinder-dry wood waiting for a spark. When one angry member rose in a passionate denunciation of the royal monopolies tax, it was like the sudden flare of a torch. Seconds later the whole of the Lower House was in uproar, as lists of articles subject to this tax were read out.

'Is *bread* there?'

'If order's not taken it *will* be before next Parliament!'

The nebulous, simmering, sulky resentment had suddenly become a raging conflagration, a flaming attack on the privileges of the royal prerogative which couched the first real attack on the security of the throne in England.

'I never saw the house in such confusion,' sighed Cecil in alarm as councillors and courtiers alike struggled to make themselves heard above the stamping and jeering of open brawls. The noise of it spilled out into the streets and soon they too were filled with jostling crowds, roaring their support for their Parliament.

Elizabeth sensed the wave of revolutionary discontent which threatened to break against her shores, sweeping the reins of government from her hands, like driftwood after a shipwreck. Whatever else had decayed within her, her political instinct remained true and unerring; she had ridden too many storms to sink now for want of bending to the prevailing wind. Her reign was crumbling round her like some brittle sugar ornament left over from an age-old banquet, but for her there would be one last flowering before the field of loyalty was laid waste in a barren future.

With that sure touch of grace which had never yet failed her in her dealings with England, she laid a soothing hand on the heart of discontent. Monopolies tax was abuse on public liberty and therefore all abuses of that system should be set right at once. She sent Cecil to convey her artful capitulation to the house, yielding the one iota sufficient to win her the day, a first, small concession to what monarchy must now become in England if it was to survive at all.

Even Cecil, cool and hardened statesman that he was, could not remain unmoved at the tumultuous reception the Queen's message received. Suddenly all the moody carping and bubbling resentment were swept away by a mighty wave of gratitude and someone cried out emotionally that her message was fit to be written in gold.

The memory of Essex was buried beneath a mound of fierce affection, as they recalled once more what they all owed to this frail old lady. She still understood their needs, as she had always understood them, Gloriana—their Faerie Queen. For a moment it was as though the spirit of the coronation and the glowing memory of the Armada had joined forces in a monstrous snowball of emotion and Cecil, watching it all, remembered his father, smiling knowingly behind a grey beard and murmuring, 'She is the wisest woman that ever was.' He had thought it fatuous—the distorted, exaggerated, sentimental memory of a very old man; but now at last he understood what Burghley had meant. She knew how to stoop to conquer, how to turn defeat into resounding victory.

For she had conquered the Lower House. Their only quarrel now was over who should go to thank her, and the walls of Parliament shuddered behind the thunderous demand.

'All, all, all!'

She smiled and said she would be glad to receive them all, or at any rate as many as her council chamber would hold without bursting. So it was that at three o'clock on a cold, dank November afternoon, with the candles already flickering in their sconces and the torches blazing on the walls, one hundred and forty gentlemen knelt before her canopied throne to offer the love and loyalty of the Lower House. And when she spoke in return, it was to thank them for the lifetime of affection she had known, '. . . though God has raised me high, yet this I count the glory of my crown, that I have reigned with your loves.'

Across the years their love unfolded in her memory like a reel of silver satin, far, far back to that journey into disgrace at Woodstock when they had first taken her into their hearts and claimed her for their own, almost half a century before. Their love had cost her dear in personal happiness, but their love transcended everything, so that she knew she would rather die than live without it. And so she told them, '. . . it is not my desire to live nor to reign longer than my life and reign shall be for your good. Though you have had, and may have many princes more mighty and wise sitting in this seat, yet you never had, nor shall have, any that will love you better.'

The emotion in the room swelled towards her like a physical force and lifted her to the peak of her attainment, a triumph snatched from cold ashes where none had believed such a spark could linger still. They felt as though they were hearing her speak for the last time and when she asked that they might all be brought to kiss her hand before they departed, they knew then that that was exactly what she wanted to convey.

One hundred and forty gentlemen knelt reverently, one after another, and lifted that pale, withered hand to their lips in a final gesture of farewell and left her room immeasurably moved.

It was as though a swan had sung.

*   *   *

She had set her affairs in good order. There was a lull in the succession of crises which had marked the last years of her life, a peaceful pause which allowed her, without guilt, to attend to a piece of unfinished business. Burghley had been wrong. It would have been better after the Armada and this time she did not mean to be gainsaid.

That winter she had the coronation ring sawn from the finger in which it had become embedded and everyone guessed that she meant the act to symbolize the end of her marriage to the state. Ignoring the anxious protests of her women, she dressed in summer silks through the harshest winter in living memory and began to refuse food. By March she was shrivelled to skin and bone, running a low, continual fever, ignoring all the advice of doctors and refusing to go to bed, even at night. Instead she lay on cushions on the floor and when they asked her why she said sadly, 'If you were in the habit of seeing such things in your beds as I see when in mine, you would not ask me to go there.'

So they stopped asking. For hours at a time she lay silent, sucking her finger, wretched with some untold grief that kept her from sleep and made her sigh and seem at times about to weep. Once she began to talk wildly of a chain of iron about her neck and they thought her wits had wandered. Cecil asked her outright if she had seen any spirits and she recovered her senses sufficiently to snap that she would not answer such an impertinent question. He backed off like a whipped cur at that, surprised that she still had the strength to retaliate. She knew then that she must guard her rambling tongue more carefully than she had done even in her prison days under Mary. She had not named a successor; it would suit Cecil's plans to have her declared insane. And once that was done, he would not wait for her to die in peace . . .

She sank deeper into the labyrinth of her own mind, wandering alone and frightened down a maze of endless corridors, fleeing from the darkness that pursued her, seeking the sanctuary of a voice that had been silent now for fifteen years.

Help me, Robin . . . help me to free myself while there is still time.

But she could not find Leicester. The chain grew tighter and dragged her down in the darkness and behind her that other shadow grew close, close enough now to be heard at last.

One day you will have to answer for your charge . . . I pray that my blood and my country may be remembered in that time.

The time had come. The hour of death was upon her, but the chain on her spirit was still unbroken. And if she died now she would be ensnared in dark torment for all eternity . . .

'No!' Her sudden cry rang out in the silent room, galvanizing her weary attendants into action. Women knelt beside her and asked what was wrong.

'I must stand,' she sobbed, 'help me.'

'But, Your Majesty—'

'I must stand! I must!'

They looked at each other in astonishment, for surely no creature so frail and wasted could get to its feet again. But her command was so urgent, so anguished, that it could not be ignored as a mad fancy.

They lifted her to her feet and stood around her with hands outstretched, expecting her to fall. But she did not fall. For fifteen hours she remained on her feet, a living skeleton in a golden dress weighted with pearls, staring at a fixed point in front of her, as though at an adversary.

Beyond the window the bare branches of the trees were blasted by the wind which raged through Richmond Park. For those who stood and watched the night was endless. Several of her young women fainted with the strain of standing so long and the word 'unnatural' began to be spoken again in awed whispers. They said she must be fighting Death itself; but it was not death she fought, only a phantom in her own mind; her own guilt.

It was just before dawn when they saw her lift one hand to her throat and smile a little, as though in triumph. They caught her as she swayed at last and laid her back on the cushions. And there she remained, because after that no one dared to touch her or move her against her will, until at last the old Earl of Nottingham, braver than most, picked her up as easily as if she were a large doll and carried her to the state bed.

Cecil received the news in his study and immediately began to tidy his papers with reedy fingers, knowing that if she had allowed that snapping of her earthly authority at last, then the end must be in sight. He felt relieved and at the same time faintly aggrieved that an old man should have succeeded where he had failed; for he, too, had tried to make her go to bed, because it offended his sense of order and dignity to see her lying on the floor like a sick animal. He had told her she must 'to content the people', and she had smiled up at him, in that manner which made him feel so damned insignificant and told him that 'must' was not a word to use to princes.

'Little man, your father, if he were alive, would not have dared to use that word to me.'

Little man! By God, he would see to it that the next reign was that of little men, with himself the foremost among them. James was weak and malleable, open to influence, and Cecil knew he had already made an excellent job of ingratiating himself. The masterly secret correspondence would surely bear fruit once the old harridan was dead, but she must not die without giving her consent. It was the last thing he wanted from her, the one word which would make everything so easy for him. There was no way his plan could possibly fail unless, at the last moment, she should name another heir for spite or jealousy or whatever twisted emotion still flowed in her shrivelled veins. Her last whim, and his whole future could depend upon it. The thought made him sweat with nervousness as he gave the order for the Council to assemble.

The corridors of Richmond Palace were crowded, but a deathly hush oppressed the atmosphere and as Cecil strode past the silent groups, the mingled grief and fear infuriated him. He wanted to shout, 'What's the matter with you, you fools? It's not the end of the world.'

But for most of the court, who had never known another monarch, that was exactly what it was. There was no excitement, no joyful anticipation, just a bleak and fearful depression which clouded even Cecil's ambitious spirit. He shrugged it off impatiently and marched past the grim-faced guards into the bedchamber, with the Council at his heels.

Rain was teeming down the tall windows and candles were flickering in their sconces. The light was failing, and an irritable wind rattled the shutters, as though something unseen was growing impatient to claim what was owed to it. Involuntarily Cecil shivered and the councillors hung back, nervous and ill at ease, as he approached the great bed silhouetted in the red firelight.

He knelt to take the hand which lay nearest to him on the coverlet. It felt stiff and icy cold in his grasp and for a dreadful moment he thought he had come too late.

Come back, he begged her silently, come back, God damn you!

As he lifted his head and stared full into her black eyes, he saw the gleam of hostility in their shadowed pits and knew she had heard his thought. He swallowed his sudden terror and forced himself to speak.

'Your Majesty—the succession. Is it to be the King of Scotland?'

Nothing!

He got to his feet frantically and leaned over the bed, shielding her from view.

'Madam—if speech tires you, a sign will do. Is it to be Scotland?'

But there was no movement from the bed, only those dark, dreadfully knowing eyes staring up into his in their last moment of challenge.

James! Yes—she could well imagine the clumsy, uncouth lout pacing his northern castle, waiting for news and cursing her for the delay, as heartily as this little man who was so eager to plant his foot in the future. Cecil would make his king, set him high and keep him there, and nothing she could say or do now would alter it. And so she would not say it, would not humour Cecil's conscience by giving her consent to what would happen as naturally as day following night. Let him go away and stew, he and the master to whom he had already transferred his allegiance; let them wait till she was ready.

She closed her eyes. For one anguished moment he stared down at her, hardly able to believe that this living corpse had defeated him; then he bowed, gestured to the Council, and followed them out of the room.

Outside, as the heavy double doors swung shut behind them, the little group of grave-faced gentlemen turned to look at the Secretary with appraising eyes. He was very pale and a nerve was jumping in his cheek, his slight stoop more pronounced than ever, as though a great weight rested on his crooked shoulders.

'Well, Sir Robert?'

He was staring at the panelled wall ahead of him, seeing nothing but the memory of her mocking glance; but at last he realized the absolute necessity of brazening it out.

He fixed them with a haughty stare, as though daring any man among them to deny it and said, in a tone he tried desperately hard to make casual and convincing.

'By the Queen's own wish, my lords—who but her cousin of Scotland?'

EPILOGUE

'We are such stuff as dreams are made on and our
little life is rounded with a sleep.'
SHAKESPEARE: The Tempest

Within the labyrinth she walked slowly down this corridor, knowing it to be the longest and the last. She had conquered and no fear informed her stately progress now, only idle curiosity to see what waited at the end of this journey inwards. When she found the door she was not unduly surprised; and since she had nothing better to do, and there was no one here to do it for her

—as there had been for as far back as she remembered—she chose to open that door herself.

The door gave out on to an unfathomable expanse of darkness; cold, empty, remarkably uninviting, it made her hesitate and look back down the endless passage, a narrow tunnel that ended in a bright pin-prick of light— the world she was about to leave.

'It *will* go on without you, you know.'

She whirled round, wild with hope. *'Robin!'*

'You were expecting perhaps the Devil in person?'

His voice was exactly as she remembered it, amused, cynical, slightly peevish.

She laughed a little shakily and took an uncertain step towards the darkness.

'I don't know what I was expecting. What place is this?'

'Oh, this is no-where. The boundary between our two worlds.'

'Then—then I'm not dead.'

'No, you're not dead.' The voice paused, sighed, seemed to consider. 'You may return even now if you wish. Or you may come with me. But if you go back now, I shall not wait for you again.'

She took another step towards the engulfing abyss and stretched out desperate hands.

'But I can't see you!' she cried. 'How do I know this isn't a dream, or some trick of the Devil's? How do I know you are really there?'

'You don't know,' he said quietly. 'That is the final test of your love, you see—to take me on trust in death, as you never did in life.'

For a moment she was silent.

'What must I do to reach you?' she asked at last.

'You must step off the edge,' he said.

Instinctively she recoiled from the prospect and drew back from the emptiness.

'Will you not do that for me, even now?' he asked sadly. 'Are you still afraid to fall?'

She smiled and flung up her head with pride.

'I'm not afraid of anything—in this world or the next.'

'I don't believe you,' he said with soft challenge. 'Prove it to me.'

She walked alone into the void.

The corridor was gone and the light at the end of it; the darkness around her was absolute. She mastered a scream and held out one hand.

'*Robin?*'

'*I am here.*'

Joyfully, triumphantly, he took her hand and pulled her forward into infinity.

BIBLIOGRAPHY

Beckingsale, B. W. *Elizabeth I*
Chamberlin, F. *The Private Character of Queen Elizabeth*
Dunlop, I. *Palaces and Progresses of Queen Elizabeth*
Ericson, C. *The First Elizabeth*
Fraser, A. *Mary, Queen of Scots*
Harrison, G. B. *Letters of Queen Elizabeth*
Hurstfield, J. *Elizabeth I and the Unity of England*
Irwin, M. *That Great Lucifer*
Jenkins, E. *Elizabeth the Great*
    Elizabeth and Leicester
Lacey, R. *Robert, Earl of Essex: An Elizabethan Icarus*
Luke, M. *A Crown for Elizabeth*
    Gloriana: The Years of Elizabeth I
MacNalty, Sir A. S. *Elizabeth Tudor—The Lonely Queen*
Neale, Sir J. *Queen Elizabeth I*
Plowden, A. *The Young Elizabeth*
Read, C. *Mr Secretary Cecil and Queen Elizabeth*
    Lord Burghley and Queen Elizabeth
Rowse, A. L. *The England of Elizabeth*
Scarisbrick, J. J. *Henry VIII*
Sitwell, E. *The Queens and the Hive*
Smith, Lacey Baldwin *A Tudor Tragedy*
    Elizabeth Tudor: Portrait of a Queen
Strachey, Lytton *Elizabeth and Essex*
Waldman, M. *Elizabeth and Leicester*
Williams, N. *All the Queen's Men, Elizabeth I and Her Courtiers*
    Elizabeth I: Queen of England
    The Life and Times of Elizabeth I